To Janie my former neighbor, classmate, sister in Christ, and always my dear, dear friend. Here's to a special place and a special tree. 'Hope you enjoy! Thanks TG

Shades of Sugar Tree

D1475721

By
TG Griffith

International Standard Book Number 0-87012-722-5
Library of Congress Control Number 2004111562
Printed in the United States of America
Copyright © 2004 by T.G. Griffith
Dille, WV
All Rights Reserved
2004

Camera-ready material provided.

McClain Printing Company
Parsons, West Virginia 26287
www.mcclainprinting.com
2004

ACKNOWLEDGEMENT

This book is dedicated to my family. To Mom and Dad who taught me that happiness will come to those who can appreciate, enjoy, and be satisfied with the life they live, no matter what may come. And for their foresight and presence of mind to rear our family in the environment and spirit of these wonderful mountains of West Virginia. To my brothers who still keep the spirit alive and well after so many of these years have come and gone. I have tried to portray as much of that spirit as I cound in this book and in some way share it with others.

I also want to personally thank all of those friends, neighbors, aunts, uncles, and cousins who were so much a part of my upbringing. It was a time when the whole community was involved in the care and raising of its own.

I certainly thank our good Lord above, only by whose divine mercy and grace, was any of this allowed to happen just where it did and when it did.

I found that encouragement from my Dad was always a chief motivation to keep me going when the prompt for writing seemed to become drudgery and lethargic. He'd just say, "Aw, write about what you know and just keep it simple. That's all there is to it." Sadly, my Dad passed away before ever getting to read any of that which he so greatly inspired.

All individuals and events mentioned in this book are a compliation of the characteristics and personalities of many different people and events, and no one person or event should be inferred from these writings. Most of the places depicted in this book are also ficticious, but there are a few actual towns and cities mentioned to help lend some authenticity to the story line.

HOME

It was a damp and chilly November afternoon; Sunday afternoon, as Chip Gates trudged the last few yards to the top of the hill behind his grandfather's farm and stood quietly catching his breath. A crisp breeze danced across the open field in front of him. He turned around with his back to the breeze and pulled the collar of his cotton jacket up around his neck. The ground was mushy and soft even up on top of the hill. The broom sage stood in proud clumps all around the meadow stubbornly standing to bear up against the winter harshness that was sure to come, and soon. The breeze would gust now and then bending the sage and tumbling the dead leaves ahead of him. He knew the old folks would say you could feel winter in that wind. He remembered part of a poem he had read somewhere about November. Only part of it came to his mind. The part went something like; no sky, no ground, no blue, no green.....November.

He loved it here. He came up here every chance he got. He loved these hills. Right now he wouldn't care to spend the rest of his life here. Afraid that if he left, he'd miss something. He just couldn't get enough of their beauty, their mystic, haunting solitude and peacefulness. He came here when he was troubled, to be apart from the rest of the world, and the solitude provided an opportunity to focus on his problems and sort out answers. He came here when his heart was light and joyful to share his elation with this close friend who had given him so much inspiration over the years.

He reverenced this place. Each time he walked here it was different. Different smells, different colors, different moods. He felt closer to God here than at any other time or place he could ever be without dying. It seemed that the spectacular sunsets, crisp autumn colors, awesome and fascinating electrical storms, and peaceful snowfalls were performed by the Master solely for his experience. It was as though they were created at this minute, in this place, just for him, and he was saddened because there was just no way he could share this experience with anyone who wasn't here to experience it first hand. This is where he wished to be buried and to thus become a part of this exquisite grandeur.

He had watched summer thunder storms roll up from the west, turning a brilliant blue sky into a churning, black cauldron of ugly clouds in a matter of minutes. Sometimes in the fall, the foliage was so bright and diverse it would hurt your eyes. Other times the colors were so mixed, you couldn't discern a particular color. They just faded to a purple haze in the distance.

Many times he'd lie on his back and look up into the sky and imagine the sky a great lake. The horizons all around became the shoreline. The jets and planes that passed overhead were ships and boats in the lake that left their wake as they sailed across. From this prone position he could watch the night sky for hours, looking for strange, and always hoped for, scary movements of the unknown among the stars. Some nights the meadow would be bathed in moonlight that was almost as bright as day. Other nights the stars were so bold and numerous, it seemed he could reach right up and grab a handful.

He'd stood here knee deep in the soft snow when it was so quiet, he could actually hear the snowflakes drifting by and landing.

Chip's love and fascination for these hills were, no doubt, something he inherited from his dad and grandfather. They brought him up here when he was so young, he had to be carried and all he could do was sit. Together they would watch the hawks soaring beneath the puffy white clouds and watch the sky turn from red to purple as the sun went down.

He sensed that both his grandfather and father had known the joy of these experiences and they knew the only way to share them was to bring him here and let him become lost, as they had, in the rapture and reverence of this place.

Even after Pawpaw Gates got too weak to make the climb anymore, Chip and his dad would still come, and as the years passed, even his dad could only come occasionally, but he was like Chip, they just couldn't stay away for a very long time.

There was only one girl Chip ever brought up here. She was Judy Brown, his high school sweetheart. Sometimes Judy would pack a small picnic lunch and on a lazy Sunday afternoon, they'd trek on the hill. They'd spread a blanket on the ground and spend the evening lying in each other's arms, watching the clouds drift overhead. Later in the evening, the sunset would turn the clouds

2

from flame, to gold, to purple, and when the evening breeze began to stir the sage brush around them, they would know it was time leave. Six years later, on a bright, new spring day in late April, beneath the dogwood blossom and the wild cherry bloom, Chip would ask Judy to marry him.

He sat down on the only rock in the meadow, stuffed his hands into the warmth of his jacket pocket, and surveyed the area about him. Off to his right, the steep, corrugated foothills of the Appalachian Mountains of central West Virginia, rolled away to the distant horizon. Off in the distance, an old logging road, barely discernible, zig zagged its way up the side of one of the mountains.

To his left, adjoining the meadow, there was another small pasture laying over the ridge like a greenish-tan doily draped over the arm of an overstuffed chair. It was surrounded by the woods on all sides and connected to the larger meadow by an old wagon road that broke through the woods.

Turning almost due south and looking directly in front of him, Chip commanded a view of the entire valley. The pasture he had just traversed fell off down the steep hill to the valley below. The valley ran east to west before him. Now and then a glimmer from Lick Run would define which way was "up" the valley and which was "down". It meandered left to right, through the little valley. Parallel with the creek, ran a one lane, paved country road. Chip's view of the valley, the creek, and the road covered a distance of a little more than a quarter of a mile.

At the widest spot in this little valley, his home, and his grandparents' home snuggled together. The only flat land in this part of central West Virginia was found either on the floor of the narrow valleys or on top of the ridges that capped the rolling hills.

Clint Gates, Chip's grandfather, had bought this land in the late '20's and had lived here, raising some cows, pigs, chickens, a little garden, and some fruit trees while working as a tipple foreman at Red Dog, a nearby mining town. Most of the farm work was kept up by Maw Maw Della Jane and her crew of three girls and three boys while Paw Paw was at work.

Chip's dad was the youngest of the six children. Theodore had gone into the service at the beginning of WWII and then returned to the farm after the war to build a house beside his parents. Ted

3

was the restless Gates, the independent one, the intellectual and the creative, artistic one. He had traveled and experienced the world, earned a college degree, and had gathered a wealth of worldly experience. Yet, when all but one of his brothers and one sister married, they moved away. Theodore had apparently realized there was nothing "out there" that was compelling enough to draw him away. Chip didn't understand that part of his dad's life choice then, but in the years to come he would realize that much of what influenced his dad, also had an impact on him.

Chip's mother was college educated also. In fact, Edna Gates had earned a Masters degree from West Virginia University. She had come here to central WV in the late '30's to teach English at the high school in Red Dog. That's where she met Chip's dad, who at that time was an electrician in the mines at Red Dog. After a short courtship, they w ere m arried a nd l ived w ith Gr andma a nd Grandpa Gates for a short time before Theodore went off to the service.

Edna moved back to her old home place in Pennsylvania until the war was over. After the war, Theodore and Edna tried to make a go of it in a little retail business at the behest and cooperation of some relatives in Elkins, but it was not what they had envisioned their lives would be. The simple, unhaggered life they had left in the Lick Run valley of Seneca County kept intruding upon their lifestyle. S o a fter a bout s ix m onths, t hey p acked up a nd moved back to the old home place. They built a little house beside Grandpa's and raised three boys. Chip was the oldest. Three years behind him was Riley and three years behind Riley came C lint. Clint was born the same year Grandpa Clint died, and was so named after him.

Edna Gates was rehired to teach at the Red Dog High School and Theodore went back to work in the mines as an electrician. Even though he had a college education, there was no work in this area that would pay as much as the mines at Red Dog paid and besides that, Chip's dad loved the challenge this kind of work provided to stimulate his creative thinking and manual skills.

Years later, Chip drove his mom to a University reunion and during the mingling part of the reunion he overheard a comment made by one of his mother's old acquaintances. The comment related to where Mrs. Gates had been living these many years past. In the course of that conversation, intimations were made regarding the lack of, and depravation of, culture and the social amenities found in more "proper" and "enlightened" societies. Chip also remembered how his mom quietly, and soundly put them away by saying something he never forgot. All she said was, "It is the greatest place in the world for a child to grow up".

One of Edna Gates' most prominent personality characteristics was her annoying penchant to challenge other people's opinions. It didn't matter if the subject was as general as religion or politics, or as personal as community, neighborhood, or family matters, if a statement of opinion was tossed out in conversation, Mrs. Gates always took an opposing view. If facts were in evidence to substantiate a point of view, she could leave well enough alone or might even agree with an opinion, but personal opinions and off-hand remarks were fair game. Chip used to think she did that just to see if she could get a rise out of someone but as he grew older and more mature, he began to realize she did that not to frustrate anyone, but to get them to think and delve deeper into the subject before making shallow and repetitive remarks. She felt that a good thinking process should always be behind one's opinion and if they didn't have any, she could quickly shred it to meaningless drivel.

Theodore was in his late twenties when he completed his military service in WWII and returned home. Chip was born a year later. By the time Chip was in his teens, his dad was too far past his prime to be able to participate in many physical activities with his oldest son and was even more constrained by the time Riley and Clint were born. Still Theodore liked to toss the baseball around in the back yard once in a while. Chip wasn't too keen on playing catch with his dad because his dad threw too hard and could put some funny moves on the ball. They did like to go fishing and hunting together and even today, the three sons and their dad manage to get away at least twice a year and spend a weekend camping and fishing in the wilds of the WV mountains. Theodore also taught Chip and Clint to play golf and though neither of them developed their golf skills to the level of their dad, they still enjoyed playing a round together every so often.

Both of Chip's parents were accomplished musicians. Chip's dad was a self taught jazz pianist. When Theodore was ten or eleven, Grandpa Clint had traded for a player piano. Theodore liked watching the roll run through the piano and liked the sounds of the piano but the Gates' only had three different rolls to play on the piano and Theodore soon got tired of hearing the same old songs, so he removed all of the player mechanisms from the piano (the mechanisms are still stored in the attic of the cellar) and learned to play the piano himself. When he was twenty, he formed his own quartet which included two black guys, and called the band "The Dominoes". After WW II, he formed the house band at a dance club near home called the "15+ Club". The band played at various functions in the Seneca County area for almost twenty years. They once joined forces with "Bill Blacks' Combo" to play for a spring formal at Virginia Tech in Blacksburg, Virginia.

Edna Gates had taken formal piano lessons when she was very young and her piano talent was steeped in the classics. The Gates brothers thus were indoctrinated with a love and appreciation of music that ran the gamut from Mozart, through Hank Williams, to Chuck Berry and everything in between. Chip learned piano and guitar from his dad. Clint was taught piano by Edna and bass by Theodore, and Riley learned piano and singing from Edna.

Chip thought of his grandparents' life here. Paw Paw passed away when Chip was only nine but he remembered those decent qualities of life Grandfather and Grandmother tried to instill in him; the love of family, the blessings of the Father, and the respect and appreciation of this land. They were both simple, but beautiful Christian people and though they put the Lord first in their lives, they did not at any time, ever throw the Gospel in anyone's face. They lived their lives as best they could and let their happiness and joy in the Lord make others envious and thirsty for what they had. Their life was their testimony and their witness. Paw Paw died when he was sixty-nine. Maw Maw lived thirty more years before she passed away. As far as Chip knew, both of them had spent their entire lives here, never venturing more that 100 miles from this little valley.

After Grandpa Clint passed away Grandma Della Jane eventually got rid of the cow and the pigs. As Della Jane grew older and less able to handle the chores by herself, she began to enlist Chip to help her feed the chickens and gather the eggs and before he knew it, he had inherited the job all by himself. It was also his job to chase down a chicken so Grandma could chop its head off, pluck its feathers, and fry it up for Sunday dinner. By the time Chip was in high school, all of the chickens had been killed and eaten and that part of his chores was over.

The general area where Chip now sat was referred to as "on the hill". It could be a mile away from this very spot, but your location would be defined as "on the hill".

"Mom, we're goin' on the hill", meant that whoever "we" were, we would be somewhere in the vicinity of the farm only up on the ridge instead of down in the valley. Other phrases would be; "Goin huntin' on the hill". "Goin camping on the hill".

"Where's Dad?" "Oh, he took your brothers on the hill to pick berries."

"Someone's got to go on the hill and check the TV line. The picture's no good." Chip remembered that the Gates' had one of the first TVs in the community. Without an antenna situated on the highest point around, no signal could find its way to the set. Fortunately, there were only two TV stations with signals strong enough to be picked up in this remote area and because both were located towards the southwest, both of them could be picked up on one antenna by positioning it in that direction. The problem was, they had to put the antenna "on the hill". Mr. Gates' reasoning was; why cut and put up poles through the meadow to hang the TV line on, when the good Lord had already provided an abundance of trees already in place for them to use.

So they ran the TV line along the woods that skirted the pasture. Instead of a straight line through the meadow to the top of the hill, the TV line followed a circumference route around the edge of the field which used not only about twice as much TV line, but traversed some pretty steep ravines. There were a few brier patches thrown in just for amusement. Because the line ran in and around the woods, it was susceptible to falling branches, limbs, and trees. They also had to hang the line low enough so you could work on it

7

without having to carry a ladder with you, or having to climb every tree, so occasionally a deer would run through the line and not only break the line, but usually managed to tear it off of two or three hangers.

Though most catastrophes of the TV line could be explained, like the time Chip blew the line in to with a 16 gauge shotgun while firing at a pheasant that flew up in front of him, (Boy, was his dad mad that time. He was home watching the seventh game of the Yankees/Pirate world series) others remained a mystery.

It was a beautiful looking system when it was new; brand new shiny copper ladder wire with white plastic insulators. The line was hung with new screw-in metal and plastic hangers spaced at fairly even intervals through the woods. A shiny new six foot aluminum antenna was mounted on a piece of one inch iron pipe, sunk into the ground, and strapped to a little red oak tree about six inches in diameter.

To "set" the antenna one turned it to the best position to get a fair signal from both stations. They could get a really good signal by pointing it directly at one of the stations but the signal from the other would not be very good. So they set it sort of in between. Setting the antenna was a delicate, complex, and highly coordinated effort involving the whole family. Dad manned the antenna. Chip was positioned first, about a 100 yards down the hill. In second position was brother Riley, about halfway down the hill. At the bottom of the hill was little brother Clint, about one hundred feet from the house. Edna watched the TV. Mr. Gates would have to start at an antenna position based on his guess as to the general direction in which the TV station lay, a hundred to a hundred fifty miles away. Actually, by using a WV state highway map and a compass, Dad's first position was pretty accurate and usually produced a good signal. Now however, came the task of fine tuning the signal.

Once Theodore was finished with his first setting, Edna became the directional finder. From where the TV was in the front room, she could stand in the side door on the porch and still see the picture. Her messages were relayed to Clint, about 100 feet away standing at the edge of the garden. There were two reasons why Clint was so close to the house. One, he was only six years old and ᴜᴄ couldn't make it up the hill very far and second, his voice was not strong enough to carry very far.

Mrs. Gates would yell to Clint, "TURN IT A LITTLE TO THE LEFT". Clint would yell as best he could to Riley who would yell on up the hill to Chip. Chip would holler to his dad, "LITTLE TO THE LEFT". Mr. Gates would turn the antenna a little to the left.

Edna watching the TV would yell to Clint, "TOO FAR".

Clint to Riley, "TOO FAR."

Riley to Chip, "TOO FAR."

Chip to his Dad, "TOO FAR."

His dad would turn it back to the right.

Sometimes the message would get garbled "A LITTLE MORE TO THE RIGHT."

"MORE RIGHT"

"IT'S ALL RIGHT"

"IT'S OK!"

" Ok?" Theodore didn't turn it. Mrs. Gates waited at the house but the picture didn't change.

"WELL DO SOMETHING!, she'd yell, "WE GOT NOTHING HERE."

"DO SOMETHING!"

"DO SOMETHING"

"MOM SAYS CHANGE IT"

"Well, what the heck does that mean?"

And so it would go. They didn't change the antenna position very often. About five or six years later, Chip's dad bought another antenna and put it up right under the first one. He borrowed a field meter from a tv repairman friend of his and set both antennas with the meter. They could now get five channels. They even strung a line over to Maw Maw's so she could watch TV too..

Chip's grandparents never had a TV while Paw Paw was living. Guess they just had no need for one. Grandma bought one about three or four years after Grandpa passed away. Interestingly though, for about a year before Grandpa got sick, his regular Saturday night routine would be to come over to Chip's and sit on the couch and watch a local, live wrestling show for two hours. From 9:00 until ll:00, Paw Paw sat on the couch and never said a word. Just watched wrestling, then got up, and went home. Paw

Paw never would check ahead of time. The Gates' Saturday night schedule was built around Paw Paw. Company didn't bother him nor did company mind him.

Sometimes Chip's mom would bake cookies or fix popcorn for Saturday Night Wrestling. Chip and Riley began to look forward to Paw Paw's visit. They would sit on the couch for awhile watching or get down in the floor and mimic the action on the TV. It was the latest the two boys were ever allowed to stay up.

To Chip's knowledge, that was the only tv Paw Paw ever watched in his life and without a doubt, it was the latest he ever stayed up at night.

Riley Gates loved tv westerns. He was so enthralled by them that every time the Gates' had beans and cornbread for supper, Mrs. Gates would serve Riley's to him in a tin pie pan with a couple of pieces of fried bacon. Riley would then be allowed to excuse himself from the supper table. He carried his pan of beans and bacon into the bathroom, shut the door, turned off all the lights, and sat down in front of the open gas heater to eat. He was a cowboy and he was sittin' by the campfire out on the range eatin' his beans and bacon.

Because Chip was the oldest, the job of maintaining the TV line was passed on to him by Mr. Gates. After two or three hands on lessons from his dad, Chip became adept at spotting broken spaces in the line, twisted or crossed wires, and of course, torn down line.

In time, when supplies of real hangers, insulators, and ladder wire ran out, Chip learned to improvise. He could cut and fashion insulators out of green twigs. He learned to hang the line by repairing old torn up hangers, using electrical tape, or cutting a tree limb back to just the right angle and length. His splicing technique was quick and so good that when limbs crashed down on the line, it never broke at one of his splices. He could "walk the line" from the house to the antenna and be back in about an hour if the repairs were not too extensive. His TV line tools were kept in a cloth sack in the woodshed ready to go. They included a roll of single strand copper TV wire, a hammer, nails, sandpaper, wire pliers, and wire cutters. Also handy was a machete for cutting undergrowth, briers, and overgrown brush, as well as protection from wild animals from which he never was confronted. He also had a pocket knife which he carried with him all the time.

There was no doubt that "walking the TV line" so many times contributed to Chip's stamina and leg strength. That would become an asset in his athletic endeavors, but still he dreaded those words, "Well, somebody better go check the TV line. We don't have a picture".

Why did they always say somebody? There was only one somebody in that house to do it. Chip! He didn't mind doing it most of the time. But there were times when it wasn't much fun. Take a dark rainy night when he had to carry a dim lit light of some kind to alternate between searching for broken TV line or looking for a path to walk with no underbrush, briers, or snakes. And if he did find a break, he had to hold the light with one hand and do the repairs with the other and repair jobs normally took both hands to do even in daylight. Windy times were scary too, day or night. With the wind bending and swaying the tops of the big trees and all the while dislodging small debris all around, he kept one eye on the TV line and one on the canopy of tree branches overhead. On these windy days, he made his fastest repairs.

Snow was a different challenge. Not only did it make the climb up and down the hill treacherous, but where it lay on the line, he had to clean off every inch to inspect the line and relieve the weight on it. With the snow, usually came the cold. Cold or wet feet were a distraction as well as the cold hands that tried to perform intricate work that could only be accomplished with gloves off.

But of course, the only time the TV went off, was during these aforementioned conditions. Never during a nice bright, sunny day. If the TV lost signal after 9:00 PM, they usually just turned it off and went to bed. Repairs would be done the following day and if that were a weekday, it couldn't be done until after 5:00 because nobody would be home till then. If it was Friday or Saturday night, then repairs would be made the next morning.

The only time Chip would not "walk the TV line" was during thunder or lightning storms. Day or night, didn't matter. He stayed at the house. The antenna was grounded somewhat by the iron pipe that was set in the ground, but lightning runoff still made it's way down the line to the house. The first time it burned up the switch on the TV. After that, at the first hint of thunder or lightning, the TV line was unsnapped from the TV and tossed out the window into the yard until the storm was over.

Over the years, the Gates' TV system became pretty dilapidated though it remained functional. The location of the antennas was never changed nor were the original antennas ever replaced despite their broken, bent and twisted arms. Those five channels were broadcast to the Gates' home via this system for twenty-six years. The entire length of the TV line was probably replaced a little section at a time over that time span and Chip would "walk the TV line" well into his forties before the miracle of "cable" would be available to the Gates' home.

The Gates brothers grew up with three memorable pets. Two of those pets were the family dogs, Major and Specks. Major was a red bone hound and Specks was a kind of shrunken collie. Specks was long haired with a white coat that had black speckles all through it. Hence the name Specks. Chip's dad found the two dogs one night coming home from a 15+ Club performance. It was around 2:00 in the morning when he topped over a little hill in the road and had to swerve to miss a cardboard box lying in the road. He stopped the car and went back to move the box and found it was full of puppies. He couldn't take all the pups, so he picked out two males and put them in the car and brought them home.

The two pups grew, as did the brothers, and they became inseparable companions. The two dogs followed the boys everywhere they walked or bicycled. Neither Specks nor Major ever got to ride in a motor driven vehicle other than that first trip home as puppies.

The dogs got so used to "going on the hill" that every time someone went out into the yard, they would run up by the barn and stop to wait and see who was going on the hill. The dogs wanted it known that they would be in the lead. The boys couldn't slip out and go on the hill without the dogs knowing about it.

During squirrel season, they had to lock the dogs in the wash house so they could go hunting without the nuisance and disturbance the dogs would create in the woods. It didn't matter. As soon as someone turned the dogs out, t hey he aded r ight f or t he woods where the hunters were. No matter where the hunters were, the dogs would eventually find them.

Major was a laid back, take it easy, don't get excited kind of dog. Once he was lying in a pile of sand sleeping when some of the neighbor dogs began barking at something in the valley. Major never even raised up. He just started barking lying there in the sand. His first two barks blew sand all over his face so he quit and went back to sleep.

Specks was the hyper one. He would run and run and run until his spring ran down then he'd just flop over and go into what amounted to a kind of coma for awhile. The problem with Specks was, he had real short legs and on more than one occasion, after spending the day running and playing with the boys on the hill, someone would have to carry him back to the house.

Speck's claim to fame was his snake killing ability. He would circle around a coiled up snake and dart and bob and weave in and out like a mongoose. When an opening came, he would strike quickly. Grabbing the snake in his mouth, he would shake his head so violently and rapidly that the snake would absolutely fly apart. The head usually was whipped off first, then the rest of the snake flew apart. Specks wouldn't quit until there was only a stub hanging out of his mouth. The brothers knew as soon as Specks made his strike, they better get the heck out of there or be pelted with the blood and guts of flying snake.

One time a huge black snake crawled in an open window in Clint's bedroom. It knocked something off of the dresser and when it fell to the floor, Mrs. Gates went in the bedroom to see what the noise was. She saw the snake just as it slithered under the bed. She carefully closed the window, shut the door and went outside to call for Specks.

When Specks came he must have thought he was going to get something to eat. Why else would he be escorted into the house. The dogs were never allowed in the house unless it was thundering. Then you had to let them in so they could go hide under the bed or they would make their own way in right through the screen door.

Anyway, Mrs. Gates got Specks to the bedroom door and then he sensed the snake. She closed the door and Specks finished off the snake in two or three minutes. The Gates' had to take down all of the bedroom curtains, take up all the bed clothes and the rugs and wash them twice to get all the snake debris out of them. The walls and the ceiling had to be painted and the wood fixtures and floor had to be cleaned with Murphy's Soap. There was no need to worry if they ran upon a snake in the woods if Specks was with them.

Specks and Major were faithful and loyal to the Gates brothers and their love for the brothers was only surmounted by the brothers' love for them. The dogs fondness for each other however, was another story. They more or less just tolerated each other. They never played together like other dogs, even as sibling puppies. When they weren't with the boys, they led their own separate lives.

Their dislike of each other usually only manifested itself in a growl or a snap at one another but on a few occasions, it would rise to a snap and a nip on a hind leg or an ear. They never really went at each other with any viciousness.

Their food dish was the door off of an old burnside coal stove. Turned upside down, it made a perfect dinner dish because it was big enough so you put Major's food on one side and Speck's on the other. It was the same food, mind you but they wouldn't eat it if it was all piled up together. Each had to have his own pile and even then at times, it was still too close. The two dogs would stand side by side over their food and growl at each other. Growling would grow to raising the lips and showing the teeth. Chip had seen their food actually freeze solid in the dish, while they stood growling at each other. What the boys liked to do when the dogs got to growling at each other over their dinner was sneak up behind one of them and punch him with a stick. He'd think the other dog did it and he'd start snipping and snapping.

Thinking back on it now, Chip considered the idea that maybe the two dogs weren't growling at each other, they were really growling at the food they had to eat. Maybe it tasted better frozen. The Gates' dogs mostly ate what the Gates' had left over. Mrs. Gates tried to fool the dogs by mixing in just a little dry dog food for flavor but it couldn't have changed very much the taste of green beans, mashed potatoes, oatmeal, spinach, peas, pancakes, cold cereal, tapioca pudding, beans and cornbread, cooked cabbage, and burned popcorn, Delicacies like a piece of bacon or some chicken bones or a half eaten hot dog or hamburger were rare. The dogs always ate good on Sunday but the best eating all year for them, like the Gates, came at Thanksgiving, Christmas, and Easter.

The third, and most screwed up, of this pet menagerie was Peep, the duck. Mr. and Mrs. Gates had got the duckling for the boys one Christmas. They brought him home two days before Christmas and kept him kept him hidden in a box on top of the China closet to be presented to the boys on Christmas morning. Every so often when one of the boys would pass through the dining room, the duckling would start peeping. They'd look around in the room for a moment trying to locate the source but either the duckling would stop or the

15

boys would hurry on to some other endeavor and the incident would be forgotten.

The mystery of the peeping all came to light on Christmas morning when the boys invaded the front room to open Christmas presents at five o'clock in the morning, as was their custom. The boys spent Christmas eve over at Grandmaw's because they knew they wouldn't sleep much that night and of course Santa Claus wouldn't come unless you were asleep, so they decided if they stayed over a Grandpa's that night, it wouldn't matter to Santa Claus if they were awake or not. If they weren't home, he could deliver his stuff at anytime that night. Whichever of the three was awake at five o'clock would wake whoever might be asleep and they would make their way quietly over to the house.

After letting the duckling out of the box to let him run around in the front room and poop all over the place, they fixed up one of their Christmas boxes with newspapers and put Peep in there along with a dish of water and one of cracked corn. "Peep" was the most appropriate name they could give him.

Among Riley's Christmas presents that year was a plastic, six-shot revolver that he could actually load and shoot plastic bullets. The first thing Mom and Dad told him was "DO NOT SHOOT AT PEOPLE. If we hear of you shooting at one person, namely one of your brothers, we'll take the gun away from you and give it to a poor kid. You understand?" Oh yeah, Riley understood.

Well after awhile, Riley got tired of shooting at teddy bears and toy, plastic barnyard animals so Clint suggested they move on to something more challenging. The cardboard flaps on top of the box that Peep was in were closed but there was a small crack in the middle of the box where the flaps didn't come all the way together. The crack was just big enough for Peep to stick his head out and he did often. Riley and Clint set the box in the middle of the front room and hid behind the couch. When Peep stuck his head up through the crack in the top of the box, whoever had the gun would get off as many shots as they could at Peep before he ducked back down inside the box. Mr. & Mrs. Wilson never did catch on to the shooting gallery and fortunately for Peep, the plastic bullets were soft enough not to injure him but that experience began to toughen him up.

16

By the time spring came that year, Peep was a full grown duck and had been moved out of doors. The Gates fixed up a nesting place for him in the creek by the chicken house but he pretty much had the run of the farm. Major didn't pay much attention to Peep but Specks tried right away to test him out. Peep immediately became the aggressor. After Peep pecked out two or three clumps of hair and wing-beat Specks clear up into the orchard, Specks decided he could live with a duck on the farm.

Peep became very protective of the Gates brothers. Once a neighborhood bully tried to intimidate Riley and Clint by coming into the yard and mocking the boys. Peep heard the racket and came on the run around the house and headed straight for the bully. At first the bully didn't know what to make of Peep and by the time he realized what was up, Peep had lit into him. Peep chased the bully right up the middle of the road, pecking the backside of the guys' legs.

Peep also liked to chase after a ball which made playing any game involving a ball a little difficult because no one was about to try and chase that duck off.

Peep made one mistake. One time while Major and Specks were standing over their food growling at each other, Peep slipped in between them and started eating. It was too much for Major so he snapped at Peep and bit a hole through the top of his bill. After that, every time Peep quacked, he kind of whistled through the hole in his beak and there was always feathers and grass and stuff sticking out of it.

Peep was a tough old duck. He liked to peck at the reflection of himself in the hubcap on the Mercury. Often times the Gates had to smear some mud or dirt on the hubcap or throw an old rag over the wheel so Peep couldn't see his reflection or he'd stay out there all day pecking at the hubcap.

One evening Mr. Gates wheeled the Merc into the driveway and Peep went right after his reflection. Unfortunately, Peep didn't wait for Mr. Gates to park the Merc and Mr. Gates drove right over his leg and broke it. Luckily, Peep wasn't killed, but he flopped around on the ground for a couple of minutes before Mr. Gates and the boys could subdue him.

Theodore made some wooden splints out of some orange crate slabs and while the boys held Peep, he straightened out Peep's leg until it "looked right", then lashed the splints to the leg with electrical tape.

The splinted leg didn't slow Peep down much. He hobbled around on it in the yard and he tended to swim around in a circle when he was on the water, but after three or four weeks passed, the splint was removed and Peep seemed to be as good as new.

Like all the kids in the neighborhood, the Gates brothers spent a good deal of their time playing in the creeks and streams in the area. There was no such thing as the EPA in those days and the water in those creeks and streams wasn't what one would call, pure. To be on the safe side, many of the parents made their kids get typhoid shots. Typhoid shots hurt, and the first time they were given to a child, there was a series of five of them. After that initial series, you only had to have one shot a year unless you missed a year, then you had to take five more again to get started. Well, Theodore Gates wasn't going to worry about his boys getting typhoid, or drowning by accident in some water hole, or getting their foot sliced open on a broken piece of glass, he was going to build a swimming pool in the front yard.

There wasn't much of a yard in front of Chip's home. Even though the grassy part was about sixty feet long, it was only forty feet wide. The rest of the front portion of the property, between the yard and the road was overgrown in elderberry bushes, bull rushes, hedge, and sand briers. The boys called it "the swamp". It was a neat place to play. The boys had rabbit like trails that ran in and around and under the heavy foliage. They had even built a little secluded shelter out of creek rocks and pine boughs, and a used shower curtain. The real drawback to the swamp was that the ground stayed wet and soggy most of the year. Between November and April the ground was so swampy, no one played in there. Since that part of the front yard wasn't good for much, Theodore decided to locate the swimming pool there.

He hired a guy with a bulldozer to come in and doze out the hole where the swimming pool was to be. The dozer made three passes through the swamp before it got buried up in the mud. The dozer had a winch on the rear so they stretched the cable out and wrapped it around a big hemlock tree in the front yard and winched the dozer out of the mud. The guy said he couldn't do anything in there because it was too swampy, so he left. A year later the hemlock died from injuries inflicted by the dozer winch and it had to be cut down. Edna Gates was distraught to say the least. Her most favorite place to sit and read and lounge around was in the shade of that grand old hemlock. It was weeks before she would even talk to Theodore.

Somehow Mr. Gates talked one of the men he worked with in the mines to drive the mine company's end loader all the way over to the house on a Saturday to scoop out a hole for the swimming hole. The rubber tired end loader didn't even make one pass through the swamp before she got stuck. The Gates' worked all the rest of that Saturday carrying Papa's locust fence posts from the barn down to the swamp and laying them crosswise to the loaders tires. Eventually they got the loader up on the cross ties and were able to back it out of there onto solid ground. The guy drove the loader back to the mines.

Another year went by while Chip's dad tried to figure out how to get his swimming hole dug. One Sunday on a drive through the country, he spotted a 1941, navy surplus, four wheel drive, three quarter ton weapon carrier sitting in a pasture on the side of a hill. After stopping and bargaining with the farmer who owned the weapon carrier, Theodore was able to purchase the truck for one hundred dollars. The frame and running gears were in good shape and the front cab was intact, however the engine had thrown a rod and cracked the block so it wouldn't run. Theodore and his brother, Roy towed the truck with a log chain, thirty-five miles back home. The boys named it "The Bomb Truck" because they were told it carried the bombs around to be loaded in the planes during the war. In the meantime, Mr. Gates had borrowed a horse drawn dirt scoop from a neighbor with the intentions of hooking it to the weapon carrier and scooping out his swimming pool. But first they had to replace the blown engine, with a good one, then they could use the scoop to dig out the swimming pool. Thus began a cycle destined to haunt the Gates' for generation after generation. Chip's dad coined the expression that would come to sum up all of their frustrations while attempting to complete some seemingly simple and well thought out plan, "YOU'VE GOT TO DO SOMETHING, BEFORE YOU CAN DO SOMETHING, BEFORE YOU CAN DO SOMETHING!" It would become the story line of their lives.

Another year went by. They finally got the truck running and by hooking the dirt scoop up to the truck with a long cable, they were able to keep the truck on s olid g round w here it c ould g et g ood traction and pull the dirt scoop through the mud. Sometimes they would run the cable through a pulley lashed to a tree and change the direction of the scoop. The three boys and their dad took turns driving the truck or operating the scoop, Even though Clint was the youngest, he did a lot of the driving because he was too small to handle the dirt scoop. Their dad always warned them about handling the scoop, "Now boys", he'd say, watch what you're doin' or you'll ruin yourself." The boys didn't know what that meant but it sounded serious.

They always scooped with the truck backing up. That way the driver could keep watch on the scoop operator and stop or keep going whichever the need might be. Once when Riley was driving the truck, Chip was scooping along fine until the scoop hit a big rock buried in the mud and before Riley could stop the truck or Chip could let loose of the handle, the scoop tipped up and catapulted Chip ten feet right over the scoop and into the mud, face first.

By changing directions, they were able to deposit the mud into heaps all around the hole they were scooping out. Little by little the hole got deeper and the mud turned to clay which was easier to scoop. Once in a while a neighbor would pull his vehicle off the side of the road in front of the Gates home and watch the excavation. Some stopped often as if they were keeping track of the development.

The water table in the swamp turned out to be only four feet from the top of the ground, and if it were a rainy season, the water table would rise right to the top of the ground. To dig any deeper, Theodore had to figure a way to keep the water out of the hole. The first thing he did was set up an old electric, shallow well pump in the bottom of the hole and let it pump the water over to the creek by way of some garden hoses hooked together. It worked fine for awhile but water kept getting in the pump motor and shorting it out and for one reason or another, the electric cord kept coming unplugged. Fortunately, Chip's dad decided to find a better method of pumping out the pond before anybody got electrocuted.

Another year went by but at least there was a hole of water in the front yard. It made good ice skating that winter. When spring came, Theodore had bought a gasoline powered Marlow water pump. With the intake line on the bottom of the water hole, the pump up on dry land, and the discharge line running to the creek, they could easily keep the water pumped out while they scooped deeper and deeper. Theodore designed the pool with a slanted bottom and they reached his desired depth by late summer. Before school started that fall they had completed the form for the floor and had the local cement company bring over three or four truck loads to run the floor. The ground was too soft around the water hole to chance bringing a cement truck too close, so they laid a wooden runway from the truck to the pool using one by six inch planks and all of the Gates males, with some help from some other neighborhood boys, trucked the cement from the truck to the pool in wheelbarrows. They got the floor laid and kept the water pumped out long enough for the cement to set up. The pool would be ten feet deep on one end and four feet deep on the other. The floor measured twenty-five feet by forty feet. The water hole with the cement floor sat idle, except for ice skating, until the following spring.

That following summer the Marlow was put to work and once the hole was pumped dry, Mr. Gates hired a local carpenter to lay the first three or four rows of the cement block walls. It was important to get a correct, plumb and level start on the walls. After that, Chip's dad was able to lay the rest of the blocks himself. The boys mixed the mortar, and carried the blocks.

Chip was about fourteen years old then and Theodore taught him how to lay block. Chip wasn't much on block laying. He was fast but the blocks ran up and down, some with wide mortar joints and some with small. Riley was better at laying blocks than Chip, and his blocks were perfect. Only thing was, it took him forever to get a block just right. He might lay one block while Chip and their dad could lay four or five. They finished more than half the wall that summer.

Next summer they finished the pool. Mr. Gates talked the local mining company he worked for into letting him have some one inch steel cable that had been discarded The Gates' snaked the cable down through the open topped cement blocks to reinforce the walls. They cut the cable so that it stuck up two or three feet above the top of the block wall. Their intention was to bend the cable over and lay a cement walk all around the pool which would further reinforce the walls. They poured cement down through the blocks to secure the cables and help strengthen the wall.

The pool wasn't water tight because there was just no way to keep the water completely pumped out while they were building the walls. There were small little cracks and leaks where the water had seeped through the cement joints before they could set up.

The Gates' men built a small dam in the creek that ran out of the hollow behind their house and used four inch vent pipe to run water from the creek over to the pool to fill it up. The pool could be filled up to within a foot or two of the top of the walls, as it was designed to do, but unless water was kept constantly flowing into the pool, the water in the pool dropped to its original water table level. They found that by letting the water stay at its original level, the deep end of the pool would be five feet deep and the shallow end would stay about two feet deep. The pool was easier to maintain at that level too. If the boys had company come over to swim, and if there was enough water running in the creek, they'd rig up the vent pipe and fill the pool clear up. The last two weeks of the summer was spent swimming and frolicking in the pool. They built a make shift diving board on the deep end of the pool. Neighborhood kids all came by at one time or another for a swim. Peep liked to swim around in it with the kids and would playfully peck them on the backs of their necks if he got the chance.

Summer had been particularly dry that year and the little creek that fed the pool just hadn't had enough water in it to fill the pool. Late in August, a good rain storm had raise the little creek enough so that water could be diverted to the pool. While in the process of filling the pool, an unexpected and torrential downpour occurred and the water quickly filled the pool to overflowing. The pool hadn't yet been completed and the walls were almost free standing because the earth had not been filled in around them yet. The pressure of the water on the walls from the interior of the pool was too much for the still green cement to withstand and with no back fill against the walls, the pressure pushed the highest wall, the one on the deep end, to the outside. The wall was anchored to the far outside wall by the steel cable. When the end wall fell out, it pulled the wall on the farthest side to the inside and the entire length of that wall crashed into the pool. One end and one side of the pool still stood but the other end had fallen out and the side wall had fallen in. The Gates' were stunned. More than five years work was gone in seconds. It was devastating. All that work and they had only got to use the pool for a couple of days.

They couldn't use the pool as it was for fear the other walls might fall. The Gates more or less abandoned the pool for that year. They needed the time to reevaluate the situation and decide what to do.

In the meantime, Peep made the dilapidated pool his domain. The duck could sense when it was time for the school bus to stop at the Gates home in the evening to discharge the boys and before the bus arrived, he would climb out of the pool and waddle out to the end of the diving board. The bus would stop, let the boys off, and continue on down the road. Peep would wait until the bus was passing directly by the pool then he would launch himself off the end of the diving board and with wings flapping, make a graceful landing in the pool. It wasn't a fluke either because it got to the point where he did it every single evening. The kids on the bus would pile over to the windows to watch and the driver started slowing down so they wouldn't miss the show. Peep was a showboat.

The partially collapsed pool was a puzzlement to those who passed by the Gates'. They would slow down and stare perplexed at the jumble of blocks, dirt, and steel cable with water bounding all about. One time some men working on the road stopped and leaning on their shovels, began to discuss the mystifying site before them.

"Looks like it was a garage or somethin'", one man said.

"Naw", the other said, "looks more like it was a basement for a house or somethin'".

Chip thought it looked like some kind of ancient ruin that over the centuries had slowly sunk into the swamp and just a little part of it was left sticking up.

The pool sat in disrepair and disuse for fifteen years. The Gates' lived and played and worked around it, but just couldn't find the incentive or motivation to do anything more with it. .

If the Gates brothers suffered any regrets about their childhood experiences, the one that would linger with them throughout their lives had to do with Paw Paw Gates' barn.

In 1939, Paw Paw Gates built a small log barn on the hill in which to store the winter hay. He had made a deal with Bob Howell, a neighbor who lived about a mile on out the ridge from the barn. Bob mowed, raked, and put up hay with a team of horses. If Bob would cut Grandpa's hay and put it up in the barn, he could have whatever hay was left in the field for himself. The barn held enough hay to help feed the cow over the winter and it was convenient to store it close to where it was cut. The Gates' could then transfer the hay to the barn down in the valley as it was needed.

By the time Chip, Riley, and Clint were big enough to help put up hay, they had learned that the barn was a great place to play. Their job was to tromp the hay down when it was tossed in through the loft window. By tromping the hay, it would settle and pack down better to allow them to store as much hay as they could. Their dad would fill the barn until the space between the hay and roof was so small the boys could no longer stand up and tromp the hay. It was more like play than work. The boys liked tromping hay in the barn.

The barn only had one storage area but the bottom and upper sections were separated by logs that were spaced two to three feet apart and ran the entire breadth of the barn. The logs helped to strengthen the structure. The boys never went on the hill without spending time playing in the barn and it became a favorite recreation place where the boys took visiting friends and relatives to play. Unlike Chip, Riley and Clint's only purpose for going on the hill was to play in the barn.

24

The barn was a great place to play when it was cold or raining or snowing. Hide and seek around the barn was a favorite, but not as popular as the free style wresting matches that took place in the hay filled arena.

One hay tromping session, Riley talked Chip and Clint into tromping the hay in the lower section until it got to within two or three feet of the logs that separated the upper and lower lofts. When the hay got that deep in the bottom, they'd scatter what came in after that but not tromp it until it was three or four feet deep, that way there would be a crawl space between the upper and lower section. It would make for an even better place to play.

When the barn got full, Theodore and Bob Howell came around and climbed up in the upper loft. They looked around a little bit and scratched their heads. "I never noticed", their dad commented, "but I reckon it must have been a better growing year than I thought. We've never had that much hay left over." The boys looked out the window or down at their feet; anywhere but at their dad. He shook his head again and climbed back down the ladder. The boys could still hear him muttering to Bob, but couldn't make out what he was saying. They had pulled it off.

The level of the hay in the barn fell as it was hauled to the barn in the valley and fed to the cow. When the hay level fell below the upper section was when the barn was best for a variety of games and one of the innovative games that Riley and Clint came up with was called "Rescue 8" after the television show of the same name.

Whatever the number of participants in Rescue 8, one member would make up a predicament to place himself in and the others would be part of the rescue team that had to save him. Maybe the hayloft would become a quicksand bog or a pool of acid; one slip or fall and the participants would be horribly killed. The rescue might be stranded on the side of the barn wall with a pretend broken leg or left dangling from a log above and it was up to the rescue team to save him. The boys could get quite creative when it came to rescue predicaments and that's where the trouble started.

Riley had gone out to burn the trash late one evening at home and after he'd got the fire started, he stuck the box of matches used to light the fire, in his jacket pocket and forgot about them. The box of matches were from the 15+ Club. Mr. Gates always picked up a box or two when they played there. Taking the trash out to the incinerator to burn every other day wasn't one of Riley's chores. It was Chip's duty. The reason Riley wasn't assigned to burn the trash is because it would take him an hour or more to burn the trash. He'd empty all the trash into the incinerator and then take the discarded refuse and set it around like little buildings and houses and would create a little town in the incinerator. Then he'd turn his back on the incinerator, light a match, and toss if over his shoulder into the incinerator. That gesture represented a careless fire that started and began to spread through the little town. Sometimes Riley would have to toss four or five matches into the incinerator before a fire flared up. Other times he'd give up and deliberately set the fire. Sometimes he'd have water handy to represent the fire department and would extinguish the fire before it did too much damage. He could restart the fire later. Trash that contained any kind of boxes took longer than usual to burn because Riley would use his pocketknife to cut doors and windows in the boxes. Clint often came out and helped Riley burn the trash. It didn't take so long with two guys erecting a town to burn down. Chip usually just went out, set the trash on fire, and came back in.

Riley, Clint, and their friend Elihu Samples, were playing Rescue 8 in the barn when Riley discovered the box of matches still in his jacket pocket. He decided to make this a real test of rescue ability. He climbed up on the side of the barn wall and had Clint to start a small fire in the middle of the hay. The fire smoked a little at first but at the sight of the first orange flame, Riley jumped off the side of the wall onto the flame, extinguishing it with his body; pretty heroic. Clint and Elihu each followed Riley's lead and each one took a turn diving on the fire. When it came Riley's turn again he decided to make it even more real, so he let the flame grow just a little bigger than usual. Clint and Elihu kept pleading Riley to jump, but Riley ignored them. He knew about fire and he knew he wouldn't let the fire get too big. Finally, he jumped into the fire. Instead of putting the fire out, the blow from his landing scattered embers and flaming pieces of straw everywhere, setting three or four fires in different parts of the loft.

The three boys tried gallantly, in a real rescue effort, to put the flames out, but the smoke was becoming so thick they couldn't breathe and they couldn't see where all the fire was. When the smoke and heat became too unbearable and they realized it was a lost cause, they bailed out of the upper loft door with thick gray smoke trailing after them.

They stood watching the barn until the flames began to lick out from under the roof, then they turned and ran around the ridge and into the woods. They figured the farther they were away from the scene, the better off they would be.

They worked their way along the ridge for a quarter of a mile or more before slipping down off the hill, all the while, undercover of the woods. They crossed the valley a half mile above the Gates' farm. All three laid down in the creek with all of their clothes on in an attempt to rid themselves of the smell of smoke.

Meanwhile, back home, Edna Gates was hanging up clothes in the back yard when she first saw the smoke. It was barely discernible. Because of the light gray, cloudy day and the distance between her and the smoke and the fact that she couldn't see the source of the smoke she didn't think much of it at first, but the white-gray column kept growing larger and getting darker in color and she realized it was coming from a place where it didn't have any business being.

She yelled for Theodore. Both he and Chip were over at Grandma's fixing a light socket. On the second yell, they came outside and joined Edna at the clothesline. Chip's dad knew immediately when he saw the smoke that the barn was on fire. He and Chip grabbed a couple of garden rakes out of the woodshed and headed on the hill.

Ten or fifteen minutes after Chip and his dad left the house, Riley, Clint, and Elihu showed up. They found Mrs. Gates still out back hanging up clothes.

"Where's Dad and Chip?", Riley asked.

"They went on the hill to see where all the smoke was coming from."

"What smoke?", the three answered in unison.

"That smoke!", Edna stated, pointing her finger toward the top of the mountain.

"Wonder what that could be?", Riley asked.

"Your father thinks it might be the barn."

"The barn? I thought the barn was on over that way."

"Well, why don't you boys go on up and see. Maybe you can help."

"Gee, I'd like to Mrs. Gates", Elihu said, "but I'd better be gittin' back home. I'm already late". He was backing up all the time he was talking.

"We're too tired, mom", said Clint. "We walked all the way from over at Levi's." Levi's home was exactly in the opposite direction from where the barn was located. "We'll just go in and fix us some peanut butter and jelly sandwiches." They went in the house.

When Chip and his dad got to the barn it wasn't much more than a pile of black, smoldering ashes. Bob Howell was off to the side of the fire scene leaning on a rake.

"You see what happened, Bob?", Theodore asked.

"Well, I just happened to be coming back home and saw the smoke. I figured I'd better come over and see what was goin' on just in case. I seen three kids headin' for the woods on the dead run and they were followed by a red bone hound and some kind of little white dog."

Now Mr. Gates knew that Bob knew whose dogs those were because he'd seen them together a hundred times. He respected Bob's blameless and disassociated truthfulness. "Oh, and I found these laying over yonder by the barn", he added, handing Mr. Gates a box of matches from the 15+ Club."

By the time Theodore and Chip got back, the two brothers had decided they had better fess up and take whatever punishment was meted out. So before Mr. Gates had a chance to confront the boys, they threw themselves into a complete and remorseful confession.

Their dad was understanding and no doubt their volunteered confession went a long way in softening their punishment. The fact that it was an accident and that the boys were young and had never been involved in any kind of malicious conduct before certainly could be a cause for leniency. The boys were sentenced to spend two weeks in their room. They were allowed out only to attend school and church, to do their chores when granted permission, and when summoned to help their mom or dad. They were allowed no visitors during their grounding. Their dad also removed all radios, took the needle out of their record players, and moved all of their model car stuff to the hall closet. The boys could read and do homework during their incarceration.

If their punishment seemed harsh, the boys accepted it with thankfulness; it was certainly better than being sent off to Pruntytown. Pruntytown was the Industrial Home of Wayward Boys in WV. The boys knew all about Pruntytown because they had to pass by it when they went to visit their grandparents. They had seen the bars on the windows and the boys out working on the grounds supervised by armed guards. It was known that boys who too often pooped their pants were sent there. Burning down a barn probably would get them a life sentence to Pruntytown.

II

The Lick Run Elementary School was located just off Rt.11 about three fourths of a mile east of the Gates' farm. The school was a one room building with about thirty-five students attending first through eighth grades.

There were no buses for these students and some of them walked three or four miles to attend. During hunting season, there were always two or three students who would carry a shotgun or rifle to school in the morning and leave it hidden in some special place like a hollow tree. When they went home after school in the evening, they got their gun and would hunt through the woods on their way back home.

Lick Run had the old fashioned student desks that were fastened to the floor. The seat and back of one student's desk was connected to the front of the desk behind. Any movement on the part of one student would wreck havoc with the stability of the writing and paper work of the student sitting behind. The desks were in eight rows of six or seven desks. The smallest desks were in the first row for the first grade. The biggest desks were in the eighth row for the eighth graders.

There were windows along only one side of the school but they reached from the ceiling down to within four feet of the floor. By design, the windows had a southern exposure so the sunlight streamed in, though sometimes weakly, during the school year. There were four gigantic (gigantic to an eight year old) globes that hung down four feet from the ceiling with one hundred fifty watt light bulbs in them. If it rained very hard, the roof would leak and water would run down the electrical cords to the lights and fill the globes with water. The teacher would have to turn off the lights, wait until it stopped raining, get the ladder, and take the globes off and empty the water out of them.

The school had a King-O-Heat coal stove right in the back of the room that kept the room warm and toasty on mildly cold, winter days. On frigid, blustery winter days, there was just no way that little stove could warm the whole building, not with a twelve or thirteen foot ceiling that was uninsulated and eight or nine foot tall, single pane windows.

The walls were uninsulated and in some places had cracks big enough to see clear through to the outside. On those mid-winter days the kids sat in the floor or scooted some chairs and a bench right up to the stove along side the teacher. They spent the day reading and indulging in educational activities.

If the weather was too bad, only nine or ten of the older kids would show up. A day at school with friends sled riding, building snow forts, having snowball fights, and socializing was certainly better than staying home carrying wood and coal, feeding the cows and chickens, cleaning up the house, or doing other chores.

A little room was built off to one side of the building which contained a well pump for furnishing water for the school. It was called the well house. The well house had one little window up high on the wall for lighting purposes and had two doors; one led outside to the playground and the other opened into the classroom. A wooden rack on the wall behind the pump was used to store the various drinking vessels the students brought to school. The rack had sequential numbers painted on the shelves to identify a particular students' storage space. If number 9 on the shelve was vacant, a student would bring a cup or glass to school with the number 9 painted on the side (nail polish was best for painting numbers) and keep it in the number 9 space. It was always prudent, especially in the early fall and late spring, to thoroughly check your glass or cup for little critters like salamanders, crawdads, snails, and night crawlers before using it. How they got in there, no one seemed to know. They could have crawled in there by themselves. They seemed especially fond of glasses and cups belonging to girls. Must have been the scent that attracted them.

The water in the well was the sweetest, coldest water in three counties. Chip was in the third grade before he had enough weight on his bones to pull the pump handle down by himself. Before that, to pump water he always had to get one of his classmates to swing on the handle with him. The seventh and eighth grade boys would pump water for each other but would never be caught pumping water for anyone under the seventh grade.

The older girls, however, loved pumping water for anyone. It was there in the dim coolness of the well house on a hot, muggy, May afternoon during recess, that Chip, then in the fifth grade, with a red face and great drops of sweat plowing little rivulets through the playground dirt on his face, stopped in for a quick head splashing of cool water. Instead, he did, at that very instant, for the very first time in his life, become smitten with that strange and mysterious attraction to the opposite sex. It was more of a smash in the head with a two-by-four that it was smitten. The smiter was 8th grader, Sheila Windon. There she was jacking that pump with a long, slow, motion and with such a light, feathery touch, she hardly seemed moving. Despite the heat, Sheila's blue print dress remained as crisp and clean as the moment she had put it on that morning. Wisps of hair over her forehead stayed as shiny and light as angel hair and her big blue eyes never broke away from Chip. He was done for. He just stayed in there the rest of the recess oblivious to anything going on anywhere else and allowed Sheila to continue to pump water over his head. It was not only the safest response Chip could muster to this fascinating encounter, it was the only one his befuddled brain could come up with.

Chip's great aunt, Ruby, was the only cook Lick Run School ever had. The school didn't serve hot lunch until a little kitchen was built adjoining the well house in 1950. Before that, the kids carried their lunch to school.

The US Government supplied the school with "commodities" and they were delivered once a month by a Seneca County Board of Education truck. Lick Run was supplied with its allotment of food for its thirty-five/forty students to last for one month. There were the same food stocks that families on welfare received once a month. Instead of giving needy families foot stamps, the government distributed food supplies to certain areas of the country and the people went there and could pick up their food supply for the month, based on the size of their family. Folks just referred to the food supply as commodities.

Commodities inc luded f lour, m eal, beans, peanut butter, cheese, canned pork, canned beef, salt, syrup, canned fruits like peaches, pears, and prunes, butter, powdered milk, powdered eggs, and sugar, and on special occasions a turkey or a ham was included.

The Seneca Board of Education also purchased and distributed to their schools food items such as; potatoes, eggs, pudding & pie fillings, chicken, ham, canned green beans, spinach, kale, canned soup, milk, and ground beef. It seemed every other day Lick Run's lunch included something made with ground beef.

Aunt Ruby loved to cook and she was very good at it. Lick Run students ate like kings for three weeks but then, that last week before commodities arrived, they ate some strange concoctions. Stuff like jello mixed with tapioca pudding, scrambled eggs and peanut butter sandwiches, tomato soup and fried potato cakes would show up on the menu. It was still good, too.

At the beginning of each school year, a note was sent home asking the family to send at least one dinner plate to school for each of their children who planned to eat a hot lunch. Plates would be returned at the end of the year, if possible. The school had an extra supply of plates on hand from those that were never retrieved at the end of the school year. The extras were used to replace cracked, chipped, or broken plates, for students who never brought their own plate, and for guests. Silverware was furnished by the school. Water for cooking and washing was pumped from the well.

It cost ten cents a meal to eat at school and everyone who ate, paid. There were no free lunches. Some of the kids would bring their lunch to school and if they had perishable items in their lunch, Aunt Ruby would store them in the milk cooler. In lieu of paying for lunches, some families would donate potatoes and other vegetables and fruits to the school so their kids could eat a hot lunch.

Outdoor toilets served as rest rooms. The boy's toilet was built on the farthest end of the playground in front of the school and the girls' was built at the farthest end of the playground in back of the school. Residential outdoor facilities were called outhouses or johns but the same facility at school was referred to as a toilet.

There were no doors on the toilets at school but the doorway faced away from the school building and there was a wooden alcove that wrapped around the side of the toilet which shielded the front opening and offered privacy from the outside world. By climbing up in one of the big maple trees in the back of the school, the older boys could peer over the alcove into the girls' toilet. After the first day of school each year, the old "no climbing trees" rule was reinstated.

33

The toilets were two holers. They were freezing cold in the winter and stifling hot and stinking during the warm seasons. When you had to go, you didn't spend much time in there. Mild days and rainy days often found both toilets crowded. The girls' was crowded because it was their refuge when the boys were chasing them for whatever reason and the crowd in the boys' could be recognized from the puffs of white cigarette smoke that drifted out from under the top.

At least once a week, usually on Friday, a couple of eighth grade girls would take a bucket of bleach water and some brooms and thoroughly scrub the girls' toilet. A couple of eighth grade boys would do the same for theirs. It was done more frequently if the weather would happen to run a hot spell.

The play ground in front of the school was about ninety feet long and thirty feet wide. The first sixty feet extending from the school building w as a n o pen a rea. I t p rovided e nough r oom f or playground games but even then, the ground sloped downhill to border L ick Run. The last thirty feet of the playground's length extended into the woods which provided some shade and shelter and natural creations that were utilized as playground equipment.

The play area in the rear of the school was the only real flat parcel of playground. It was fifty feet by fifty feet square but was broken up by three big maple trees and a couple of huge flat rocks scattered about. The trees and rocks also served as playground equipment.

The school had two swings; one in each maple tree in the rear playground. There were no other manmade pieces of playground equipment. The rocks and trees and the natural lay of the land were used to devise different forms of recreation.

Sedate playground games included run sheep run, hide and go seek, kic k t he c an, various forms of tag, and a variation of the national pastime called "round town."

Round town was played just like baseball or softball with the same rules applying. All stick ball games were played with a rubber or sponge ball whose size was a little bigger than a baseball and a little smaller than a softball. The school kept a couple of sponge balls on hand and sometimes some kids would bring their own.

Another stickball game, called "long town" was the game of choice. There were only three bases in long town; home base, first base and second base. It was only fifteen feet from home to first base. Second base was located on a straight line from home, out to the center of the outfield, fifty feet away. A base runner went directly home from second base.

When a batter hit the ball they ran to first base. When the next batter hits the ball, the runner on first can run to second if they want to, but they don't have to. You could have eight people on first base. A batter can go to second after touching first whether any of the other runners already on first go to second or not. You might have eight people on first and eight people on second. Base runners can carry other base runners with them from base to base if they wish.

If all of the batters on a team are on base and there is no one to bat, the team in the field has to toss the ball around to each other until someone on base makes a daring attempt to steal home.

The team that is batting gets only one out. There are only three ways a batter can be called out. Two of the three are by standard outs. A batted ball that is hit in the air and caught by a fielder is an out and a swinging strike or foul ball that is caught by the catcher in the air or on one bounce is an out. On a standard out, the teams switch positions and the batting order is reestablished as best as can be determined.

The non-traditional out is where things can get convoluted. The non-traditional out occurs when a fielder retrieves a batted ball and throws it at one of the base runners. If the runner is hit by a thrown ball but is still on base or has made it home, then it is not an out and the next batter is up.

If a runner is not on a base and is hit by a thrown ball, then it is an out. But, once a runner is hit, they or anyone else on their team, can get the ball and try to hit someone on the opposing team before any of them can get to a base. Any base is safe. If all the team members make it to a base safely without being hit, then whoever on that team made it home safely can bat. Runners stay where they are and advance at their own choice.

If the hit base runner can retrieve the ball and hit an opposing player before they get to a base, then his teammates have to get to a base to be safe. Sometimes ten minutes would go by with players throwing at each other and chasing each other all over the playground. There were no out-of-bounds in long town except for foul balls.

The bigger kids like to burn opposing players with the ball, especially girls and little kids. A good trick would be to let the ball soak in the creek for a minute or two so it weighed about two pounds. It would leave a really good red mark when a player got smacked on the side of the head or in the back. Long town later was renamed "burn out".

"Antne over" (pronounced ant knee) was a good game. The game was started with equally numbered teams. The teams stood on opposite sides of the school house. One team had a ball and they would yell "antne", which means they were ready to throw the ball over the schoolhouse to the other team. The team on the other side of the schoolhouse yelled "over" if they were ready to receive the ball. The antne team couldn't throw the ball until the other team acknowledged they were ready by answering "over".

Once the antne team threw the ball over the schoolhouse, the over team had to retrieve the ball. Sometimes somebody would catch the ball in the air as it bounced off the school house roof. Sometimes the ball would get by them and they'd have to chase it down. Once they had the ball in their possession, they could chase the other team around the schoolhouse and capture the opposing players by tagging them or hitting them with the ball. Once you were captured, you became a member of that team and would help try to capture members of your former team. If members of the antne team could make it all the way around to the opposite side of the schoolhouse, they were safe and it would become their turn to receive the thrown ball.

There was a lot of strategy involved in antne over. The throwing team would try to toss the ball over the school house where it would be hard for the receiving team to get it.

They would put all of their team members on one corner of the schoolhouse and toss the ball over on the other end. Sometimes the tosser would throw the ball so that it would roll up one side of the roof and down the other. By the time the receiving team got the ball, the whole antne team could be safe. A good tosser could also throw the ball clear over the roof and put enough distance on it that by the time the over team chased it down, the antne team would be safe.

The receiving team on the other hand tried to anticipate the throwers move. They would put their best catchers and their fastest runners in strategic positions. Catchers often relayed their catches to designated throwers on the team so they could make the hit. Receiving teams sometimes didn't chase right away either, they'd sneak around the corner or send a spy on a recon mission before deploying chasers and hitters. Teams could run either direction around the schoolhouse.

Needless to say, from time to time, there were some horrendous collisions at the corners of the building which often resulted in gashes, lost teeth, broken glasses, and assorted bruises. The water logged sponge ball often came into play here as well.

The trouble with games that involved a rubber ball was, the ball never lasted more than a day or two. Balls were always getting knocked into the creek, across the road, or into the woods and were lost. The balls that didn't get lost were so used and abused that the rubber became cracked and brittle and as pieces flew off here and there the ball eventually was reduced to the size of a plumb. And the older boys were always doing things like deliberately throwing the ball into the chimney during "antne over" or hitting it through a schoolhouse window. Once, eighth grader James Caldwell hit a foul ball that carried over the creek and landed in the back of a cattle truck that happen to be passing by. James claimed he planned it that way and became an instant hero to the younger set. Weeks might go by before someone brought a new ball to school or the teacher had a chance to go to town and buy a couple at the five and dime.

As sedate as "long town" and "antne over" were, there were some more violent games like red rover, crack the whip, dare, and sliding down the hill on a solid ice that had been nurtured and cultivated with snow and water and finely packed by hand until it was as smooth and slick as any ice rink.

At the beginning of every month, Mrs. Martin, the teacher at Lick Run, would select a responsible, hard working eighth grader to be the janitor for that month. The term of employment was from month to month. Not all of the eighth graders wanted the job and some eighth graders were never asked, so the duties were distributed throughout the year to two or three capable young boys. The pay was about ten dollars a month. The janitor had to come in about a half hour early in the mornings and empty the ashes out of the coal stove and fire her up. Generally, he was to check around to make sure everything was ready for school. In the evening he had to sweep the building, empty and burn the trash, set out the garbage for whoever picked it up to feed their hogs, turn out the lights, and padlock the doors.

Freddie Martin, no relation to Mrs. Martin, got the call to be janitor one January. That January was particularly bad and Freddie had to walk two miles through the woods in the deep snow so he ran late a couple of mornings. Mrs. Martin was late too because she had to drive eight miles over a Rt.11 that hadn't been plowed or treated for two weeks. The ten or fifteen kids who did show up those mornings wound up standing around in the cold and snow waiting to get inside a cold building. Some of them had already walked thirty or forty minutes through the snow.

On the second day of the delay, Marvin Johnson decided he'd take charge. Marvin was the kind of guy who, when the water was low in the creek, liked to get to school early enough to hide under the bridge that crossed Lick Run and would look up through the cracks between the wooden planks so he could see up the girls' dresses as they walked over the bridge to school. Marvin was a good sized eighth grader and with the help from some of his freezing schoolmates, he managed to climb up the side of the schoolhouse to the well house window. The window was only a foot and a half wide and about a foot tall but somehow, he managed to jimmy the window pane out of the sill. He squiggled and squirmed his way through the window. On the inside of the well house the window was a good five feet above the floor. Marvin had to slither down the wall and drop head first on to the floor.

He couldn't open the school house doors because they were padlocked on the outside so he opened the lower section of one of the big windows and with the help of those outside, pulled everyone in through the window. They lit a fire in the stove and by the time Mrs. Martin arrived, everything was hunky dory inside.

Mrs. Martin was anything but appreciative. She verbally lit into all the kids, covering everything from liabilities to catastrophes that could occur. She did not exercise any corporal punishment probably because she did understand their predicament, but she made it explicitly clear that they were never to do this again. She made Marvin put the window back in. Freddie showed up about twenty minutes later.

One morning a week later, Marvin and the kids found themselves in the same predicament only this time everyone was even later arriving. Marvin waited as long as he could and then went ahead and climbed up and removed the well house window. He got stuck half in and half out of the window.

Mrs. Martin showed up about that time. She drove her car right past Marvin and up to the door of the schoolhouse. She got out, unlocked the door, and let the kids in. Marvin was still struggling to free himself from the window but wasn't about to bring attention to himself. Mrs. Martin lit a fire in the stove and went into the coatroom. She took out the stepladder and picked her paddle up from off her desk and carried them both outside. She set up the stepladder right beside Marvin, climbed up to the window, and proceeded to pound his rear end until she beat him the rest of the way through the window. Freddie showed up twenty minutes later.

Two weeks later another blizzard stranded the kids outside the school. Marvin waited an extra long time for somebody to show up and open the school. Finally, he gathered everybody up, walked them the half mile down the road to his house for pancakes and syrup. Mrs. Martin and Freddie arrived an hour and a half late to find an empty school house.

Twice a year the board of education sent a couple of men to the school to oil the floors. They coated the floor with some kind of oil, perhaps for termite control or maybe to help preserve the wood. They always oiled the floors on a Friday evening after school so the oil had two days to soak into the wood and wouldn't cause any problems. It was the responsibility of the janitor for that month to inform his close friends the minute he found out what Friday they were coming. He would work a little later that evening, waiting for the men to leave. Once the men were gone, the janitor would signal a couple of his friends who had been hiding in the woods nearby that the coast was clear. They would spend the next hour or so skating around on the oiled floors in the school house.

Skating on the oil was harder than roller skating but they could use the desks to hold on to. They did everything they could to keep from falling in the oil and getting their clothes soiled but their shoes and pants' legs would become soaked with the oil. If it ever ruined Chip's clothes, his mom never mentioned it. When they were finished skating, they wiped the excess oil off their shoes and it not only made the shoes shine, it water proofed them too.

There was one kid who infrequently attended Lick Run School named Buddy Smith. Buddy only went to school when the truant officer threatened to send him to Pruntytown or put him in foster care, so he attended school for a week or so about three times a year.

Chip remembered Buddy because he was sixteen years old and still in the second grade. Not even the eighth grade desks were big enough for Buddy. Buddy didn't think Mrs. Martin was big enough to handle him either but she was. She was determined to discipline Buddy the same as all of her students. She wound up devoting most of her day keeping after Buddy. The rest of her pupils were neglected to some degree but Mrs. Martin knew what she was doing. She stayed on Buddy for two or three days until he realized he was not going to get his way and then he'd just up and walk out of school. Mrs. Martin could then go back to teaching. Buddy would return in three or four months for another round.

When the polio vaccine was developed, doctors came to the school to give polio vaccinations to all the kids who had signed permission forms. The kids learned quickly that those first series of shots were painful and made your arm sore for what seemed like a week. The older boys at Lick Run turned those polio vaccinations into a kind of ritual of manhood. The first part of the ritual subjected the younger kids to teasing and taunting in order to weed out the cry babies and namby pambies.

40

The second part of the ritual began the day after the shot had been administered when the arm was sore and lifeless. Then the test was who could do the most pull ups, first with both arms and then with just the sore arm. The last part of the passage into manhood was completed that same day; trading punches to that beat up, strained, bruised, and battered arm. Chip never made it to the final stage but did make it as far as doing the pull ups. His arm hurt so bad for the next two days he couldn't sleep. He never let on though.Chip attended Lick Run for the first five years and Riley was able to go until the third grade. When Clint was old enough to start school, their mom and dad moved all three of them to the school in Red Dog. That way the whole family could ride together to same school.

It was while attending Lick Run School that Chip developed a friendship with Maynard Samples. That friendship continues to exist to this very day. Chip cannot recall the time when Maynard and he first befriended each other. It seemed to Chip that they had always been best friends. Maynard was a year older than Chip. Give Maynard a cold RC and he would slug it down and belch, in alphabetical order, the first nine counties of WV. Pretty darn impressive for a fifth grader.

Maynard lived a half a mile from Chip. The Samples family was big. There were two brothers, Maynard and Elihu and eleven sisters. Maynard's dad was Ezra Samples. He worked in the mines at Red Dog and was a lay Baptist preacher. The Samples' kept up a small farm with some chickens, cows, a hog or two, two work horses, and a nice size garden. The food produced on the farm helped supplement the store bought food necessary to feed fifteen mouths. Louise Samples and her girls tended the garden and the housekeeping chores while Ezra, Maynard, and Elihu worked the farm. Elihu was the same age as Riley Gates. Chip liked to help out on the Samples' farm whenever he got the chance. He loved the honest, hard work of the land where he could be outside in the fresh air and sunshine and Mr. Samples appreciated the volunteer labor. He rewarded the boys by letting them ride the horses down to the creek to water them after a good day's work in the field.

41

There were other benefits Chip enjoyed while visiting the Samples'. The family always served full course meals at breakfast, lunch, and supper. Breakfast itself was a feast with eggs, bacon, ham, fried potatoes, oatmeal, biscuits, home churned butter, hot blackberry jam, and fresh milk. Lunch and supper were always hot cooked food which would include meat and vegetables, all from their own farm. Even wintertime meals consisted of farm food that had been canned, dried, or frozen from the fall harvest and every kind of homemade side dishes. The Samples' weren't much into snacking between meals. They did grow their own popcorn and that usually was their Saturday night treat. It was funny, though, when Maynard came to Chip's house to stay, all he ever wanted to eat for breakfast was toast and butter. He could eat a whole loaf of sliced bread and a half pound of butter for breakfast and be the happiest guy in the world.

Because Maynard had eleven sisters, just through the process of osmosis, Maynard learned to be very proficient at things like washing and ironing clothes and cooking. Over the years, he passed on these skills to Chip as the need arose. As it turned out, those skills would become invaluable to Chip when he went off to college.

Maynard's sisters also taught the boys how to dance. Chip's Saturday night stay overs at the Samples' meant plugging up the record player on the back porch and dancing a couple of hours with the five or six sisters who didn't have dates for the night. When Chip went off to Jr. High School at Red Dog, he became the dancing king of that set. Even the high school girls kept his dance card filled for those dance party nights and sock hops. During their high school years, dancing would become their ticket to those prep activities that otherwise, they may never have experienced.

Maynard and Chip were separated as schoolmates for four years Chip was in school at Red Dog for three years while Maynard attended Lick Run, then Maynard went on to Elk River High School as a freshman. Chip began his high school career at Elk River as a freshman the following year when Maynard was in the tenth grade and they were reunited again as schoolmates. Those four years of school separation didn't in the least bit affect the two boys' friendship. They still spent much of their free time together, and attended boy scouts and church together.

One thing about it, if you stayed overnight with the Samples' on Saturday night, you were expected to attend church with them on Sunday morning. In fact, that was a prerequisite to being allowed to stay overnight on Saturday, you had to be prepared to attend church with the family on Sunday. Somehow Ezra was able to pack fifteen or sixteen folks into the Pontiac station wagon and haul them off to church on Sunday morning.

Ezra didn't preach at the Sugar Tree Baptist Church but he was a deacon there and did teach a Sunday School class. Ezra was an evangelist. He filled in for other pastors and preachers when they couldn't meet their appointments for whatever reason and was called on frequently to hold revivals at other churches in the tri-county area. It didn't matter to Ezra whether it was a Baptist, Methodist, Nazarene, Church of God, or Independent church, church doctrine wasn't a consideration. He preached "salvation through Jesus Christ", nothing added, nothing subtracted. He also held funeral services and conducted marriage ceremonies.

Although his devotion to the calling of the ministry was stern and strict, outside of the pulpit Ezra was a rather easy going, down-to-earth, witty guy who liked practical jokes and sometimes acted like a person half his age. He was a fun and happy person to be around and was able to be that person without ever comprising his Christian ideals.

One of the strongest, binding characteristics of Maynard's and Chip's friendship had to be the shared experience of coming to the altar together to accept Jesus Christ as their person savior and later, they were baptized together in Sugar Tree Run. Although they were young boys at that time and although they drifted far from the Lord's graces as their young adult lives moved in other directions, eventually they were drawn back to reestablish that relationship once again. Ezra's influence on the boys had a more profound effect on their lives than they would realize until years later.

Back on the hill, Chip could see a solitary car gliding slowly along the one lane road down in the valley below but its noise never reached him. That little one lane road was County Rt.11. Rt.11's existence began eight miles east of the Gates' farm where it branched off of US Rt.19 at the little village of Hob. Hob's population wavered between three hundred, and three hundred fifty.

US Rt.19 was THE main north-south route through West Virginia, and for the half mile that it ran through Hob proper, it was main street. A number of establishments were built along both sides of Rt.19 in Hob. Most notable of the establishments were the three general stores, four service stations, three beer joints, and three churches.

Twenty-five miles south of Hob, on US 19, lay the town of Seneca, the county seat of Seneca County. Seneca was the metropolis of central WV boasting a population of two thousand people. Seneca also boasted a hospital and a number of retail businesses. Elk River High school was located in Seneca.

County Rt.11 left Hob, twisted its way up on top of Renzee White Hill, and ran along the ridge before zigzagging back down into the Lick Run Valley and the Gates' place.

The car disappeared out of sight around the bend off to Chip's right. If you were traveling in that car, you would continue following Rt.11 as it skirted around the bottom of Blue Knob, the mountain that lay south of the Gates' farm, and made its way up the valley on the other side of Blue Knob. One mile from the Gates' home around Blue Knob Mountain on Rt.11 and you would come upon a cluster of little houses in a wide spot in the valley pretending to be a quaint little village. The little village was called Sugar Tree.

Sugar Tree was so named because of the groves of sugar maple trees that grew in the head of the hollows around there. It was said that in the spring, the creeks ran full of maple sap instead of water. At just the right time of spring, the distinct aroma of maple sap whiffed down out of the hollows and hung heavy in the air around Sugar Tree.

Sugar Tree had a post office and those who got their mail there, lived in Sugar Tree but anyone who lived within two or three miles of Sugar Tree were considered residents of Sugar Tree also. Chip lived a mile from Sugar Tree but he was from Sugar Tree. There were about two hundred people living in and around Sugar Tree proper.

Those who lived in the same vicinity of the Gates' home referred t o t he t rip t o S ugar T ree a s " Goin around the road". It meant the same as "goin' on the hill".

"Goin around the road to church.'

"Goin around the road to the store, need anything?"

"Goin around the road to play ball. Be back after while."

Or sometimes just "Goin around the road."

Everyone knew where you were going and where you would be. If you were going someplace other than Sugar Tree, you'd be more specific.

Right in the middle of Sugar Tree, the road formed a Y. Rt.11 came in at the bottom of the Y, branched off to the right, and continued up another narrow valley for seven tenths of a mile. This was called the "Sugar Tree Straight". There were about ten houses stuck to the hillside along the right hand side of the Sugar Tree Straight. That side of the valley was sloped enough to allow for houses to be built there and they were the typical hillside dwellings so common to this part of West Virginia. The front porch was twenty feet off the ground and at the rear of the house, one could step from the ground right over onto the roof.

This steep, narrow valley stayed ten to fifteen degrees cooler, year around, than the surrounding countryside because the sun was never able to peek over the hills and into the valley for more than an ho ur o r t wo a da y. S ugar T ree R un w as t he l ittle c reek that gurgled its way down the valley paralleling Rt.11.

At the far end of the Sugar Tree straight, heading out of Sugar Tree, Rt.11 climbed up Sugar Tree Hill. It was just a little over a mile to the top of Sugar Tree Hill. Another mile along the ridge and County Rt.11 ended at an intersection called the Red Dog Turnoff. The road continued on straight through the intersection but it crossed over the Seneca County line into Rose County and became Rose County Rt.1. County Rt. 1 wound its way through the woods for twenty-five miles to the county seat of Rose County; the incorporated town of Mill's Bottom. There weren't ten houses along the road from the Red Dog turnoff to Mill's Bottom. The road was so crooked the old folks used to joke that the State engineers laid it out by following a black snake through the woods.

The Red Dog turnoff was so named because by turning left at the intersection, you immediately dropped straight down the hill, referred to as Red Dog Hill, on a unpaved, private road at a 15% to 20% grade. The road finally flattened out a half mile down the hill into the sprawling, dingy, mining town of Red Dog. There was no other road in or out of Red Dog.

The left fork of the Y in Sugar Tree was County Rt. 9. It was known as Painter's Fork. because it followed Painter's Creek one mile up the valley to the foot of Panther Mountain where the road and creek parted company. Painter's Creek headed on up a narrow and steep ravine to the ridge top on Panther Mountain while the road would angle its way on around the side of the mountain before it reached the summit at three thousand feet elevation. Panther Mountain was the highest mountain in the central section of WV.

Painter's Creek's source was in the head of one of Panther Mountain's many wilderness hollows so it should have been called Panther Creek, after the mountain of its source. But it seemed that the dialect of the early Appalachian settlers in the area spoke the word "Panther" as "Painter". Now as to why the mountain and the creek were pronounced differently, no one knew or much cared.

The Painter's Fork valley was a little wider than the valley of Sugar Tree Run and its mountain sides were not as steep. Painter's Fork was able to accommodate thirty houses scattered along both sides of the valley. The Baptist Church was located about halfway up the valley. A little further up was a whopping two acres of flat, bottom land where the Sugar Tree Grade School was situated. The grade school's first through eighth grade enrollment varied slightly each year from between one hundred and one hundred twenty students. There were no buses serving Sugar Tree Grade School either. The main attraction at the grade school was the totally flat, expansive playground. It was as big as a football field. Any flat piece of land in this part of the country was coveted and it was

46

constantly in use. Autumn weekend touch and tackle football games wore the grass down to mulch and then pounded it into the dirt. Spring and summer found the town folks and the kids keeping the playground well manicured for late evening and Sunday afternoon softball games.

Painter Creek was a fair size stream even before it was absorbed into Sugar Tree Run at the fork of the Y in Sugar Tree. At the Y, the stream grew to the size of a small river and continued down the main stem of the Y paralleling Rt. 11. A half mile from Sugar Tree, the creek and Rt.11 parted company. The creek turned north and funneled down a narrow valley to empty into the Elk River some three and half miles away. This valley was called "the holler".

The beginning of the "holler" marked the midway point between Chip's home and Sugar Tree. An old county road followed along beside Sugar Tree Run as it meandered down the holler. The road crossed the creek at least six times and in some parts, the road actually went down the creek bed for a ways. The road didn't follow the creek all the way to Elk River. It ended right in the middle of the creek a half mile from the river. The lower end of the holler was so narrow and the terrain so rugged, there just wasn't room enough for the road and the creek so, eventually the two merged. The road disappeared somewhere under the flow of Sugar Tree Run while the creek continued a rocky and wild ride to the river. There were three good swimming holes down the holler; the Red Fin Hole, the Big Rock, and the Pino Butcher Hole. The Gates' brothers and their friends would spend many a day in recreation activities "down the holler".

The holler was very isolated and rugged near its mouth. No one ventured that far down very often. Chip remembered seeing some strange looking fish down in there. Some had weird lumps and growths and things hanging off them. Some had smoke gray eyes that seemed lifeless. Others were colored strange shades of orange and blue. Chip wondered if maybe those were mistakes that God had made in creating them and he put them down in the bowels of the holler so no one would see them.

The biggest building in Sugar Tree was the WYGARB Company Store. It was erected right in the forks of the Y.

WYGARB was the name of the coal company that owned the coal town of Red Dog, along with approximately 100,000 acres of property surrounding it. WYGARB owned none of the surface land in Sugar Tree but its property reached the hill top ridges surrounding the southern quadrant of the little village and WYGARB's mineral rights allowed them to mine under all the hills surrounding Sugar Tree. WYGARB was the company name formed by the first initials of those six men who owned the company. They were all from Pennsylvania.

The WYGARB Company Store in Sugar Tree w as C ompany Store #4 because it was the fourth one built. Store #3 was built in the center of Red Dog. #2 was built at WYGARB's lumber mill and mill town called Bumtown. The mill town was named Bumtown because unlike the mine operation in Red Dog which ran twenty-four hours a day, the lumber mill only operated during the day. Since the residents of the mill town seemingly did no appreciable work during the night, they were said to just "bum around". Bumtown was halfway between Red Dog and Mill's Bottom on WYGARB's private railroad.

Store #1 was located near Mill's Bottom and had been built first when WYGARB began operations there in the early 1900's. Over the years, as the operation expanded and the central offices were moved to Red Dog, WYGARB abandoned its store near Mill's Bottom but because it was the railroad terminal with the B&O railroad, WYGARB kept its company houses and the railroad shops there.

Store No. #4 was simply called the Company Store. It was a massive, two story, wooden structure. Inside, on the first floor, was located the post office, a grocery store, clothing store, and the first telephone in Sugar Tree. Upstairs you could find hardware, farm tools, including farm tack, toys, and furniture. Outside, around back, was a feed and grain building. In front of the store were two gasoline pumps, a kerosene pump, and a mobile rack of assorted lubricants for your automobile. A huge portico covered the front of the building and extended out over the gas pumps and service island. The steps of the company store was a good place to hang out in Sugar Tree after store hours. A huge hand painted sign stretched across the front of the building between the first and second floors which read, "WYGARB STORE #4, Sugar Tree, WVa".

A hundred yards from the company store along the base of the Y was located a little country grocery store owned by the Keener family. Wyatt and Sarah Keener had built a store in Sugar Tree in 1926, and had the post office located in the store as well. Their first store was built where the company store now stood. In 1948, WYGARB bought the store from the Keener's, had it torn down, and built their majestic mercantile on the spot. Instead of living off his new found wealth, which was no small sum, Wyatt used the money to build a new store on property he already owned. He also built a small building adjacent to the store wherein the Sugar Tree post office would be relocated.

Wyatt was heard to say he couldn't abandon his folks to unscrupulous, money crazed, coal barons. Besides, Wyatt knew he still stood to make a good living in the store business.

One thing could be said about the Keeners, they were always fair in their dealings and anyone who did business with them came to know a special, personal touch. Wyatt had been a deacon and Sunday school superintendent in the Baptist Church for 40 years and his character and reputation were beyond reproach. Sarah was also very active in the church being a Sunday school teacher, youth fellowship leader, member of the choir, and president of the Ladies Association Committee.

The Keeners extended credit to those who couldn't pay right away, never asking the reason why, and they always seemed to come out ok. They were known to have traded necessary commodities to families living around there for livestock, hand crafted articles from knives to quilts, for bales of hay, for a good day's work chopping wood or mowing a field or cleaning the store or house. If it were truly known, they were probably the ones who left that box of groceries or that sack of medicine on the porch in the middle of the night when someone was down on their luck or hurtin'. No one knew for sure except maybe Wyatt and Sarah. Those who wouldn't or made no attempt to ease their debt to the Keeners would find dealings and relationships with other town folks going sour. In such a tight knit little community, word got around quickly as to who was and wasn't abusing their privileges as residents of Sugar Tree.

Two of the Keeners' sons, Bucky and Lewis, came home after serving in the Korean War and went to work for their dad. After Wyatt died, the boys built and operated a service station garage right beside the store.

Wyatt was never intimidated by the grandeur of The Company Store even though he was almost under its shadow. You see, he was there before they were and he was one of Sugar Tree's own. After his passing, as far as the people of Sugar Tree were concerned, Sarah and the boys were just Wyatt's own spirit continued in a different form. Underneath all of this, Wyatt was a businessman with a vision, a keen insight and a shrewd mind.

Wyatt began planning ahead as soon as the Company approached him about selling his first store. He knew the Company Store would accept "scrip" at full value for merchandise purchased there and he also knew that the only store in Red Dog was Company Store #3. Somehow, Wyatt made a deal with the Company which many thought was part of the original sale of the old store, though it was never divulged by either side. The deal was this; one, Wyatt would accept WYGARB scrip for his merchandise at face value. The Bank of Red Dog would redeem the scrip for US currency at .09 cents on the dime. That was the going rate for scrip exchange for everyone. There were no other privately owned businesses anywhere that would accept WYGARB scrip. Two, Wyatt got exclusive right to solicit his store business in Red Dog. The only other private businesses that had sales in Red Dog were a few local farmers who got permission from the Company to peddle their home grown produce up and down the streets.

"Scrip" was money the Company made. Actually made. It was like monopoly money only it could be redeemed at face value, same as real US currency, but only if it was spent at, for, or in Company owned businesses or services. Scrip was all minted in metal coins, no paper. It had the WYGARB name and company logo along with the coin's denomination which was embossed on both sides of the coin. Coins came in denominations of one cent, five cents, ten cents, quarter, half dollar, one dollar, and five dollars and each was the approximate size of its US companion. There was also a five pointed star cut through each coin a little off-center. That's so you could tell a real dime from a ten cent scrip in the dark or if you had some coins in your pocket, you could distinguish them apart without taking them all out.

The Company paid its employees by check every two weeks. Most took their check to the Red Dog Bank and deposited it in an account. Others would cash their check at the Red Dog Bank for US currency (at ninety cents on the dollar), and then deposit it in another bank. The bank at Mill's Bottom was the only bank outside of Red Dog that would honor WYGARB checks.

There was no advantage in using scrip outside of Red Dog. The Company honored their scrip at full value. You could buy ten dollars worth of groceries at the Company store for ten dollars worth of scrip. Ride the rail bus to Bumtown or Mill's Bottom for fifty or seventy-five cents, scrip. Scrip could get you into the Company owned movie theater for fifty cents. Get your hair done. Go bowling. Buy a cheeseburger and a coke all at facilities provided by the Company.

Being paid every two weeks was not often enough sometimes, so if you needed some cash money to carry you over till pay day, you could go to the Company Office and get scrip which would be charged to your scrip card. The Company only paid cash in scrip, never in US money. When pay day finally rolled around, the scrip you had borrowed that month would be deducted from your paycheck. Also deducted from your paycheck would be any services or products furnished by the Company to you. These might included; rent for the Company house you were living in, house coal, electricity from the Company powerhouse, and Company store accounts. Granted, the rates and prices were much lower than you found living outside the Company town, but it was a seductive and enticing web of dependency the Company wove around its town and people. Sure, the company also accepted good old US green for barter, but nowhere else outside of Red Dog was WYGARB script any good. Except at Wyatt Keener's store.

Every Tuesday, Wyatt or Sarah or one of the boys would drive over to Red Dog and take grocery orders from the town folks. If you wanted to place an order you would put a little red painted can on the banister of the front porch or on the front steps, or on the sill of a front window. When one of the Keeners would spot the can as they drove through town, they would stop and go up to the house and take the order. If you wanted to leave an order on Tuesday, but would not be home, you could leave your list in the can or give it to a neighbor who was ordering that day. The Keeners took the orders on Tuesday and delivered them on Thursday.

They boxed everything up in the morning, packed it in the back of an old one ton Chevy truck with a canvas cover over the back, and spent half the day delivering groceries to the houses in Red Dog.

Some folks paid on delivery and some had a credit account that they would pay monthly. Some would come by in a day or two and pay for their delivery. Some paid in real money and some paid in scrip. Wyatt found it was much easier to charge everyone the same for his merchandise even if they paid in scrip. He figured the increase in the volume of business he did was money he otherwise would not have coming in anyway.

As the Keener's business blossomed, they were able to hire Dimple Young as a clerk to work in the store.

Bucky & Lewis Keener's Esso service station was the first business, heck, the first anything in that part of the country, to have a paved lot out front. It really wasn't paved. It was concrete. The concrete ran the entire width of the station front clear out to the hard road. There was even a little concrete island that the two gas pumps sat on. Crowded between the pumps was a rack of oil cans, an old bent up watering can, and the pole that held two globes with lights in them suspended over the island. The outside lighting was another first in Sugar Tree.

The station itself had a corner room which served as an office/lobby. There were two floor-to-ceiling plate glass windows that came together at the right front corner of the station. From behind the L shaped, wooden counter inside, not only did one have a clear view of the entire area in front of the station but could also view any traffic coming into Sugar Tree from the west on Rt.11. The little station lobby was stocked with a snack rack of chips and crackers. There were two pop coolers in the office. You didn't have to put money in them to get a bottle of pop. Just raise up the doors on top, reach into that icy cold water and get what kind of pop you wanted; orange, grape, lemon lime, chocolate, or cherry. Ginger ale, Pepsi, RC, Upper Ten, little cokes, and little 7-ups were also available.

Behind the counter were shelves full of candy bars, gum, cigarettes, chewing tobacco, snuff, cigars, peanuts, and snack pies and cakes. In the stock room at the back of the office, one could find some staple items such as bread, soup, can goods, salt, flour, and sugar. There was also one refrigerator full of milk, eggs, cheese, and lunch meat and one freezer with some frozen steaks, fish, and hamburger. The store room was so small that only one person at a time could be in there and open any doors, so generally you told one of the boys what you needed and if he had it, he'd go get it.

One reason the station stocked snacks and staple food items even though there was a more plentiful variety and quantity at both the company store and at Keener's grocery, was for the customer's convenience while having their car serviced at the station. Also, the Esso station was the only business outside of Red Dog that stayed open after six o'clock. Sometimes, Bucky or Lewis wouldn't close until 9:00 or 9:30 depending on who was there and what was going on. The station was also open on Sunday from 1:00 until 5:00. It was the only thing you could find open on Sunday in this country except for churches and beer joints.

The station had two service bays. The middle bay contained a full size lift rack to raise cars and pickup trucks. It was operated by compressed air. There was also a work bench, tool rack, and assorted oil and grease guns located against the back wall. The shelves lining both sides of the grease bay stocked various common auto parts, lubricants, auto lamps, of various sizes and uses, tires, tubes, and patching material, fuses, hoses, fluids, and cleaning supplies. If you needed a particular part not in stock, the boys could get it for you and have it there in a day or two.

The third bay was a wash bay, tire shop, and general repair bay. Used as such when the weather was too nasty to work outside.

A little walkway ran from the office/lobby door around the front of the station and down along the side of the building to the women's rest room. The walk then continued around the corner to the back of the station to the m en's r est r oom. B oth r est r ooms were no bigger than a closet but contained a commode, a sink, and a little open gas heater to keep the rooms warm in winter and to keep the fixtures from freezing. There was a little s ign o n e ach door that read, "Rest rooms are locked. Please see attendant for key." At one time there had been a key. It was the same key for both rest rooms. However, it was lost soon after the station was built. You could use a screwdriver, a knife, a dime, a popcicle stick, anything that would fit into the key slot and turn the cylinder would open the door.

Chip would become very familiar with the operation of the Esso station. After he went off to Marshall College to pursue a degree, he returned home each summer and worked at the station. In fact, after his first summer working there, Chip learned enough about the day-to-day business of the station that Bucky and Lewis would leave the operation solely in his hands for up to a week at a time while they went on vacation.

Directly across the road and across Sugar Tree Run from the Keener's store was Jobe Frame's furniture and hardware store. Jobe and his wife and their three daughters lived beside the store. There were two accesses to Jobe's store. If you were walking or riding in something that weighed less than 3 tons, you could cross a bridge over Sugar T ree R un t o t he s tore. T he b ridge w as l ocated r ight beside the Company Store. If your load was heavier than 3 tons or wider than the little one lane wooden bridge, you just took the lower route which went down the creek bank, through the creek at a shallow gravel bed, and up the other side to the store.

Jobe's store had the usual household furnishings and appliances, used and new, for sale or trade. And he had an amazing supply of hard to find, essential, tools, power equipment, and every kind of household supply from electrical to plumbing needs. He had house jacks, floor sanders of every description, pipe dies, paints for every use, g lass and glass cutters, roofing and tar, sewer tile, lumber, nails, and plumbing supplies. If it was something to work on the house with, Jobe had it!

Jobe also owned two large moving vans and at least a couple of times a month would be seen moving a family in or out of the area. Generally, one moving truck would be big enough to hold a family's belongings. The other truck would be ready if needed but Jobe could only drive one truck at a time and he was very particular about who drove his truck when it was full of someone else's personal belongings. He always could find a couple of young men to help with the moving and driving and he had a couple of favorites who he could trust and who had helped move and pack before. They were always willing to help 'cause it was a chance to get out of Sugar Tree and see some far off wonders like Cleveland and Lodi, Ohio, Lexington, Va, Dunbar, WV, etc.

One time a colored man from Red Dog came to Jobe and asked if he would move him and his family to the Detroit area. At the time, he didn't have any money to pay Jobe but he was moving because he had found a good job out there and would be able to pay after he went to work. They agreed on a price and Jobe loaded them all up and headed out to Detroit. It was after they had unpacked everything, said their farewells, and were about three hours out of Detroit heading home, when Jobe realized not only did he forget to give the family a bill, he forgot to get their address as well. About a year later, the Sugar Tree postmistress handed Jobe a letter addressed, "To The Man Who Moved Me--Sugar Tree, WV". In the letter was the full payment for the price agreed upon.

Chip recalled another time when one of the elders of the church had passed away whose name was Rad Adkins. Everybody knew him as "Preacher Adkins". Anyway, Preacher Adkins' widow had to have all of her household possessions appraised for estate tax purposes. Now Jobe was always available to help with appraisals of this nature since it was his livelihood. This time he asked Chip along with Frank Woods, if they would help with the appraisal. The trio worked their way through the house following Jobe's lead and coming to a consensus on the estimated value of each item. Mrs. Adkins led the way pointing out each article and explaining its history. Eventually they came to a fine looking wicker rocking chair on the front porch.

"About ten dollars" announced Jobe, writing in his notebook.

55

Mrs. Adkins was taken aback. "I'll have you know that rocker cost fifty dollars!"

Jobe never blinked, just kept on writing. "Well, you might have paid fifty dollars for that rocker new, but it's cheaply made and someone obviously cheated you on that deal. It ain't worth nearly that much now."

Mrs. Adkins just stood there with hands on hips for a moment, staring down Jobe Frame. "Why you miserly, old coot", she grunted, "I bought that rocker in your store two years ago this coming June!".

The most outstanding feature of Jobe's store was the big, neon lit clock that sat in the front display window. It was round, about three feet in diameter with a white face lit from behind by a soft light from a couple of appliance bulbs. That made the large black numerals and the black hour, minute, and second hands easily readable from across the road or from the steps of the company store. But around the clock face itself was a scrolled, glass neon tubing that read, "Frame's Furniture". It was lit up in a soft pink and violet color that blended beautifully with the soft white of the face itself. It was a work of art. The clock ran all the time and was always within a minute or two of the correct time. It was lit all the time and its glow provided just enough light at night for the teenagers to hang out on the bridge or on the steps of the company store. The closest thing to a street light or a dusk-to-dawn light was the clock.

Chip's first cousin, Benjamin Lewis, and his family lived in Sugar Tree. Their house was up Painter's Fork just a few hundred yards above the Company Store. Frank Lewis had married Theodore's older sister, Bess. Benji was a year younger than Chip. He went to grade school in Sugar Tree until he was in the fifth grade, then when Chip's mom transferred her three boys to Red Dog with her, Uncle Frank and Aunt Bess asked if Edna would mind taking Benji to Red Dog also. They picked Benji up at the Company Store every morning and dropped him off there in the evening.

Benji had three sisters but they were all much older than Benji and no longer lived in Sugar Tree. One was married and lived in Seneca and one was married and lived in Ohio. The third sister wasn't married but she was a professor of English literature at Colorado University. Thus Benji was kind of an only child and he and Chip became more like brothers than cousins. Although they didn't attend the same elementary school, much of their carefree, summer youth was spent living for weeks at a time at each other's homes and participating in the family life and activities. Whether at Chips' or at Benji's, they were treated as one of the family. On at least two memorable occasions, the Gates and the Lewis's spent a week of summer vacation together at the beach in North Carolina.

At Red Dog, the two cousins became involved in the same school functions like band and basketball and later, their high school years would be spent together at Elk River High School.

From the time he was in the fourth grade, Benji could urinate his entire first and last name on the hardroad, in script, in one continuous motion, without moving from his spot.

The appearance of four deer prancing out of the woods into the meadow interrupted Chip's recollections momentarily. The deer stared at Chip curiously and then turned away and ambled along the edge of the meadow, stopping now and again to nibble lazily at the grass. Chip looked at his watch. It was 3:00 pm. Would've been time for the shift change whistle over at Red Dog, only there was no shift to change these past forty years.

Red Dog was a mining town, not a coal camp. It was a town that rivaled any town in the four county area with a population of twenty-eight hundred. The name "Red Dog" came from what the local folks called the final stage of coal waste. When the shiny, black bituminous coal was mined, there was a lot of slate, slag, rocks and other unrelated debris mixed in with the coal when it came out of the mines. The whole contents of the mine car was dumped onto a conveyer belt that carried the whole mess to the coal tipple. There the coal was washed, sized, and separated from the unusable waste. This waste product at Red Dog was called "gob". Gob was then loaded onto side dump railroad cars and carried a short distance away where it was dumped onto the ground and spread out by locomotives with huge steel side spreaders attached to each side. They were called gob spreaders. After forty years of coal mining at Red Dog, the gob piles grew into mountains as high as those natural ones surrounding the town.

There were two mountainous gob piles at Red Dog. The smallest one was located just outside the upper end of the town and the other, larger one, was located about a mile and a half below town.

Because the process of cleaning the coal then was not real efficient, some coal was mixed in with the gob and dumped in these piles. After twenty or so years passed, spontaneous combustion would ignite the coal under the gob piles. These fires would smolder for years and years. Once in awhile a smolder would break out into a full fledged fire but there was never enough fuel to keep it burning. Mostly the gob piles just moldered, producing quite a bit of heat and a very acrid, sulfur smelling smoke. The ash left from these smoldering gob piles had a reddish, orange color and was called "red dog" by the locals. Thus was born the name of the mining town, Red Dog.

As long as the mining continued, the dumping would provided fuel for the gob pile fires. In fact, the gob piles at Red Dog burned for over fifteen years after the mining operations there had been shut down, and would probably be burning to this day if they had not been reclaimed and contoured by order of the Dept. of Natural Resources and the Dept. of Environmental Protection in the late '70's.

The ash called red dog was a valuable and much sought after commodity in the area for road building purposes. Red dog in its ash state, formed small flat cinders ranging from the size of bread crumbs to pieces as big as a man's hand. Pieces bigger than that usually were in large lumps and not as usable for road building material. Mixed in with the red dog would be some small rocks and gravel and pieces of slate that wouldn't burn.

The County Department of Highways would bring an endloader to Red Dog two to three times a year, mostly in the summer, and dig the red dog out of the side of one of the gob piles. They had a couple of places quarried out in each of the two gob piles. The DOH would load the red dog into trucks and haul the stuff all over the county. Most of the roads in Seneca and Rose County were hard surfaced roads which at one time had dirt or gravel berms. Now the berms were red dog.

Red dog was easy to dig, didn't weigh as much as gravel or dirt, and was easier to spread. It packed down easily to form a smooth, hard surface. Most of the unpaved roads in the area, and there were a lot of them, were surfaced with red dog.

WYGARB did not charge the DOH for the red dog. It was glad to get rid of it and the DOH found an abundant supply of free road building material. Private citizens also used red dog on their driveways and farm roads. They could load it themselves, as much as they wanted and whenever they wanted but first had to get the ok from WYGARB officials. The easiest way for the public to get red dog was to wait until the DOH came to load it because they would squeeze you in between their own loading and fill up your pick up, dump truck, or trailer for free.

One good feature of red dog was the fact that no dust was kicked up when vehicles traveled over it no matter how hot and dry it was or how fast the vehicle was traveling. In the winter, the DOH would also dump small piles of red dog along the side of the road on steep hills to be used like cinders or sand when the road became snow covered. Chip remembered that during the winter, most of the folks carried a small shovel in the trunk of the car or in the back of the pickup for just such an emergency. He remembered a few times in a heavy snow storm when drivers or passengers, his dad included, would get out of the car and use that shovel to scatter red dog on the road then the car or cars could slowly inch their way from pile to pile up the hill till they got to the top.

Red dog did have its drawbacks however. Because it was such a light material, heavy rains and quick downpours would easily wash gullies and ruts through it, especially on hills and small grades. When the freezing-thawing cycle began in the winter, red dog had a tendency to hove up and become very soft. If the depth of the red dog was less than six inches on the surface, ruts and ridges would quickly develop as vehicles plowed their way over it. When the cycle was over in the spring, the red dog could easily be scraped back to its original smooth surface if none of it had washed away.

A few years before the Dept. of Environment Protection and the Dept. of Natural Resources had the gob piles reclaimed, those two agencies had red dog banned from private and public use of any kind. It seemed that ground water runoff associated with red dog was not only very acidic but was carrying other pollutants into nearby streams and creeks.

Though the gob piles grew to loom ominously over the town, they too were put to use. As the gob was dumped and spread out and leveled, it filled the little hollows up to create a wide, expansive level surface on top. The smaller gob pile at the upper end of the town was almost a mile long and about two hundred yards wide. In the late '40's the Company had bought and hauled into Red Dog on railroad cars, the finest Georgia dirt to build a baseball field. The company leveled a nice piece of land in a little shaded cove at the upper end of the town, dumped their Georgia dirt there and manicured it into one fine baseball field. On the hillsides surrounding the ball field the Company built benches and dugouts so spectators would have a place to sit. Red Dog played baseball against other mining towns in the central part of the state in a sort of industrial league. The players were young men in their mid to late twenties and the competition was always tough and serious and the games were played on a semi-professional level. Chip can remember his dad taking him over to a Sunday afternoon game and sittin' with a couple of hundred fans in the shade on the hillside. The best part about attending those games was going down to the concession stand and buying an orange Crush. After paying a dime for your drink, you got to reach down into a tub of ice water so cold you had to grab your Crush quickly before your arm lost all feeling. That was the coldest, best tasting soda a young boy could ever dream of.

Red Dog also formed a Little League baseball franchise of its own for the kids that lived in town and they played their games at the ball diamond too. The high school at Red Dog played their home baseball games there as well and there were always pick up games going on there when nobody special was playing.

The company protected and sheltered this little ball diamond over the years but outside, at the mouth of that little cove, the gob pile continued to grow. By the late '50's, when Chip was old enough to play in pick up games on weekends at Red Dog, the gob pile was at least one hundred feet high all the way around the edge of the outfield. In fact, any ball hit to the outfield in fair territory that landed on the side of the gob pile in the air was counted as a home run. If an outfielder ran up the side of the gob pile and caught the ball, it was an out.

The ball diamond and the upper gob became Red Dog's "lover's lane". That's where the high schoolers and young singles went to park. First, it got you out of the lights and noise of the town and out under the stars and moon without having to drive very far at all. Second, you didn't have to worry about getting stuck up and if your car broke down or it wouldn't start, you could walk the short distance back to town or get one of your friends parked up there to give you a jump start or a ride back to town. That brings up the third reason. It was a very secluded spot. You could park fifty up there and none would be within shouting distance of each other if you picked your spots with privacy in mind.

The upper gob also provided enough room for a few of the local men to use it as a driving range for hitting golf balls. The men could always round up two or three young boys to take with them to chase and retrieve golf balls at two cents a ball.

The finale of the 4th of July celebration at Red Dog was the fireworks display. People from all over the county along with most of the people in Red Dog, would drive up to the upper gob and park and watch the fireworks that were put off from the big rock across the hollow. It was quite an impressive show; paid for and produced by the Company for its employees and patrons.

The upper gob was finally fashioned into a landing strip for some of the Company officials who had airplanes. They were flown in and out quite regularly and some were even kept there. Chip remembered at least one occasion when a plane on a different route had used the air strip at Red Dog for an emergency landing. During the 4th of July celebrations, other planes would come into to Red Dog and rides were made available during the day at $5.00 per passenger.

During the summer the Company brought in an under-the-big-top circus for a two day show and they would set up on the upper gob pile. The best part of the circus was when they had to unload the circus animals from off the trucks at the top of Red Dog Hill and walk them down the hill. They always had the traditional parade through town to the big top and everyone would come out to watch the parade but Red Dog Hill was too steep and dangerous for the large trucks and trailers to try to descend with their valuable cargo on board. When Chip and others found out when the circus was coming, they would get to the top of Red Dog Hill and walk down the hill with the circus animals, up close and personal.

The lower gob pile was the bigger of the two. On top, it stretched for three quarters of a mile down one valley, cut between two small hills, then spread right and left in the adjoining valley for a distance totaling a mile and a half on that side. In some places on top, it was almost a half mile wide. It rose to a level height of three hundred feet above the valley floor. The lower gob pile was not utilized by the town as much as the upper one was, probably because it was a mile and a half below town and it was a much more difficult drive to get up to the top. Still, there was another ball diamond tucked back in a shady cove but there was no hillside seating fashioned under the trees. Spectators had to make their own seating arrangements.

The Boy Scouts had built a shelter in the woods at the top of a mountain just next to the lower gob and many of their outdoor activities were carried on around and on the gob.

The lower gob was a good place to learn and to practice driving in preparation for that big driver's license test. When Chip first got his learner's permit, he could see his dad taking him driving all around the neighborhood and all of his buddies could see him driving by. Instead, his dad took him driving not only around on the gob piles, but on little, out of the way, crooked, dirt roads where they encountered every kind of road hazard, road obstacle, road surface, and weather condition imaginable. Chip would have to stop and start on a steep incline. Turn around in a confined area. Drive short distances in reverse. His dad would say, "Son, if you can learn to drive well on these roads, you can drive anywhere else in the whole US with no problems." Over these same roads Chip took his three girls when they were learning to drive.

No one much ventured onto the gob piles anytime the temperature during the day went above eighty-five degrees. The surface temperature of a gob pile on a hot summer day probably reached one hundred and twenty degrees or more. The heat coming back up into your face was hotter than the heat from the sun pouring down from above. Ball games were played in the evening or on cool cloudy days, in the afternoon. And if it didn't rain, the coal dust lay an inch thick, stirred up by the slightest movement of animal, man, machine, or breeze. After a few hours of activity on a dry gob pile, you couldn't tell the white kids from the black kids.

II

The town of Red Dog was unique, not only because of its size, but for a number of other peculiarities. Red Dog was a private town. Built on private property with only two accesses in and out, the privately owned railroad and a privately built and maintained road. Red Dog was the eastern terminus of WYGARB's railroad and was located just about in the center of the almost 100,000 acres of land that WYGARB owned.

WYGARB's board of directors bought this land from a Pennsylvania State Senator who was related to three of the board members. The Senator had received this land by heirship from one of his ancestors who had been given the land as a gift by King George of England, or so the story goes. WYGARB began their operations near Mill's Bottom because their property bordered the Baltimore and Ohio Railroad there. Once WYGARB had established its company headquarters at Mill's Bottom, it began to expand operations eastward following Mossy Creek, upstream. Branching off from the B & O railroad, WYGARB built its own rail line and purchased its own railroad equipment. The short line was called the Mossy Creek and Elk Railroad.

The MC & E followed Mossy Creek east into the mountains of Seneca and Rose County. Its eastern terminus was to be the town of Red Dog which had not one building erected on site yet. Engineers, surveyors, and geologists had already determined that the most lucrative, practical, profitable, prudent, and lasting site for WYGARB's main operations would be at this unnamed, undeveloped spot in the middle of the forest.

WYGARB's first big operation was nine miles upstream from Mill's Bottom. There, in the midst of a rich, virgin, hardwood forest, WYGARB set up a good size lumber mill. The mill was steam operated and the coal came from a couple of little punch mines at Mill's Bottom that WYGARB had originally dug to supply coal for the MC & E. Water for the mill and for the steam engines was pumped from Mossy Creek. WYGARB purchased a couple of logging engines to work the lumber mill as the MC & E pressed onward up the Mossy Creek valley. At that time, most of the lumber milled there was used on the MC & E railroad but some was used for building houses and Company buildings around the mill. Later, all the lumber used for building the town of Red Dog would come from this mill. After Red Dog was built, the mill continued to produce beautiful hardwood lumber that was sold commercially all over the US. The mill town grew to a sizeable community as the lumber operation expanded. It became known as Bumtown.

By 1911, the MC & E had reached the end of its line, seventeen miles along Mossy Creek from Mill's Bottom and the B & O. By 1915, WYGARB was deeply involved in the coal mining business and by 1920, the town of Red Dog was almost completed.

Red Dog was a dirty town. Dirty because of the soot, coal dust, and smoke. Hundreds of houses burned coal for heat. Coal was burned as fuel in the steam house and the power house, and all of the locomotives that chugged up and down the MC & E through the middle of town burned coal. Coal dust was everywhere. Whipped up by natural breezes, or by traffic, or by machinery, it moved from the tipple, from the gob piles, from the railroad tracks, from the playground, from the parking areas, and from the streets, to settle elsewhere in town. Because Red Dog was nestled in a deep valley and sheltered from any strong winds, the coal smoke and dust and ash just settled on and in everything.

There were only two conditions under which Chip could remember the town being anything close to picturesque. One was a few hours after a heavy snow. For awhile, everything was covered with a beautiful blanket of white snow. Once it quit snowing, the snow quickly turned black and the streets would turn to mud. The other was in the summertime when all the foliage was abundant and a good strong thunderstorm would not only blow all the smoke and soot out of the valley but would wash the dust and soot off everything and settle the dust all around.

The town of Red Dog that Chip grew up with was in its heyday. The coal business was booming and the Company had established its empire. Red Dog had become the largest nonunion mining town in the US. Nonunion being the crucial phrase here. The United Mine Workers of America had tried three times to organize and unionize the coal operations at Red Dog. Workers for WYGARB had formed their own union and it had all the offices, bargaining power, grievance procedures, and representation that the UMWA could offer. What it didn't offer that the UMWA could, was much higher union dues and retirement benefits.

The first labor strike at Red Dog was in the late '30's and it was more or less, a token strike. Most of the local union's body voted not to go union. However, there were still enough workers at Red Dog who felt they could do better with the UMWA so with the help of a few UMWA organizers, they went out on strike. The problem was, WYGARB's property was so expansive that the only place a picket line could be set up was where WYGARB's property bordered public property. There were only two accesses to Red Dog, the main road into town and the railroad. The railroad's junction to public property was twenty five miles away by car so the UMWA decided to set up their picket line at the top of Red Dog Hill where the only road into town met County Rt. 11. The presence of the strikers at the top of the hill kept the workers who lived outside of Red Dog from crossing the picket line to go to work and they did keep a few supplies and materials from traveling down into Red Dog. But the town and operation were self-sufficient. Ninety percent of WYGARB's workers lived in town and the railroad was still the main source of supplies and materials for the Company. The drift mines at Red Dog had also expanded under the hills in the surrounding areas and there were five or six places where a main line track would come out of a portal on one side of a hill, cross a narrow valley on public land or land owned by someone other than WYGARB, and enter into another portal under another hill. Mine workers who lived outside of Red Dog could catch a main line motor as it passed from one hill into another at these various spots. They would ride the buggies through the mines to the head house in Red Dog, punch their time card, and go to work. They went home from a shift of work the same way. The motor operators always slowed down between openings at these spots to either pick up a new shift or to let the last shift off. The UMWA strikers were just too few in numbers to cover all these access so the strike didn't have much impact and after four or five weeks, it was called off.

Chip's dad and mom always like to tell about their dating scheme during this first strike, like it was a covert operation against a military regime. Chip's mom was living in Red Dog and teaching there and his dad was living on the farm at Sugar Tree but working in the mines at Red Dog. Theodore would wait around at the drift mouth up Dry Fork and catch the main line motor when it came through heading for the head house and ride it to work. He couldn't ride the motor into Red Dog just to go on a date. How would he dress? What would he tell the foreman at the head house? How could he catch a motor heading out of Red Dog? If he tried to drive over to Red Dog he'd be stopped or harassed by the picket line at the top of Red Dog Hill. Most of the strikers knew him and they might confuse his going on a date as going to work. To remain covert, Theodore and Edna came up with four operational plans that they could mix and match in part or whole, at their discretion. Plan 1: Dad would walk up the mountain south of Sugar Tree, walk out the ridge through the woods for a half a mile, and drop down the other side of the hill coming out near the upper gob pile. Edna would drive through town and meet him there at a prearranged time. Later, she would drive him back so he could walk back through the woods to Sugar Tree.

Plan 2: Dad would take a flashlight, enter the mines at the fan house at the bottom of Sugar Tree Hill, and walk through the mines to Red Dog. Because he worked in the mines at Red Dog, Chip's dad knew his way around in there and by taking the right couple of spurs, he would come out one of the portals away from town. Chip's mom would drive out there and meet him at a prearranged time. She could later drive him back to the mine opening if that was the plan for that night. The only real danger in walking the mile and a half through the mines was meeting a motor pulling a string of coal buggies. There was not much room to get out of the way and of course, the motor operator would not be concerned at all about anyone being where he was not authorized to be. Still, Chip's dad knew pretty much when it was safe to pass through and where there were recesses and enclaves for safe havens.

Plan 3: Theodore would take an extra set of clean clothes with him when he went to work and after his shift, he would stay with his brother Roy and his family at Red Dog. He could either shower and clean up at the wash house or at Uncle Roy's. He might stay one or two nights in Red Dog or he might go home that night by the other two aforementioned routes.

Plan 4: Edna would get in her car and drive over to Sugar Tree and either they could court there on the farm or drive somewhere for an evening out. The strikers knew Chip's mom and because she was a teacher and being a woman, they let her pass in and out of Red Dog as she pleased. Chip thought that plan 5 could have been for dad to hide in mom's car when she went in and out of Red Dog but maybe that would have been pushing their subterfuge a little too far.

After WW II, Red Dog's mining operation grew so prosperous that it got the attention of John L. Lewis. This time the UMWA went all out to unionize. They had enough strikers to picket the main road into Red Dog and to set up strike lines at all of Red Dog's mine entrances that were not on their own property. They also set up a picket line at the B&O junction near Mill's Bottom. Though a large faction of WYGARB's workers became union sympathizers during this strike, WYGARB was able to use enough of its employees who lived in town, to keep the mines operating and to keep the town functioning.

This became a bitter and violent strike. WYGARB employees who sided with the UMWA were fired and if they lived in or on WYGARB property, they were evicted and in some instances, their belongings would be confiscated by the Company for bills or debts they might still have. In some instances, families would be split into two factions; one, union, the other nonunion. Brothers sided against each other. Father and son rivaled each other. Lifelong friendships were severed. Sadly, in some cases, the bitterness of this strike kept those ties from ever being bound up again.

The UMWA became persistent in disrupting WYGARB'S empire. The picket line at the top of Red Dog Hill, began to harass and taunt anyone who tried to go in or out. Often times at night, gunshots could be heard cracking away at the top of the hill. WYGARB c laimed it w as t he U MWA. T he UMWA claimed it was WYGARB shooting at them. Two railroad bridges on the MC & E were blown up with dynamite to keep the rail line closed. MC

& E workers attempting to repair the line were shot at from the wooded hills surrounding them.

WYGARB became as militant as the UMWA to see that its mine operation and its town life were not disrupted. W YGARB hired armed guards to ride the trains. They built guardhouses on their property near the picket line at the top of Red Dog Hill. Strikers and WYGARB guards liked firing off their weapons once in a while to let the other know they were still around.

The violence and tension of the strike began to spread over to Sugar Tree and to Hob and to Mill's Bottom. There were WYGARB employees who lived outside of Red Dog who were not union supporters. They couldn't go to work so they just stayed at the house or on the farm and tried to wait the strike out. There were WYGARB employees living outside of Red Dog who were union supporters. They not only joined the strikers on the picket line but in the Sugar Tree area alone, two garages and a barn belonging to WYGARB workers were burned and two houses had been shot at in the dead of night.

Anytime representatives of these two warring factions would happenchance to meet, say at Wyatt Keener's store, arguments, shouts, and fist fights were likely to erupt. Once during the strike, Chip was riding back from Seneca, which was the county seat of Seneca County, with his dad and when they got to Hob, his dad stopped at Walker's General Store to get something he needed at home. Of course the first words out of dad's mouth when he stopped was the same old order, "Stay in the car. I'll be right back."

In the years since the phrase, "stay in the car" had been uttered by t heir da d, C hip a nd his b rothers b egan to deduce their dad's motives behind the phrase. More than once they had thought they smelled Hersey's Chocolate on his breath or a little whiff of Planter's Peanuts. There were also tattletale stains of what appeared to be Nehi Cherry or Grape Soda on his lips. Once, outside o f t he C ompany S tore in S ugar T ree, R iley m anaged to climb out the car window and stand on the top of the car where he could actually see inside the store through a first floor window. Though his view was obstructed somewhat by the glare of the sun and dirt on the window, he swears to this day that he saw his dad eating a banana popcicle.

69

To either cover up the real reason for keeping them in the car, or to make amends when he felt the boys had discovered his real motives, their dad began to bring them Doublemint chewing gum. He would always tear the sticks in half. There were always half sticks of gum for everyone, even himself. The boys would go searching through their dad's overcoats, jackets, golf bag, and tool box for gum and they would always find some but only Doublemint and only in half sticks. Chip didn't know Doublemint came in whole sticks until he was old enough to buy gum with his own money.

Chip waited fifteen minutes in the car outside Walker's. He rifled around in the glove compartment and found a half stick of doublemint. Fifteen minutes turned into thirty. There were only three or four cars parked out front so Chip could not figure out what was taking his dad so long. After about forty five minuets or so, a Seneca County sheriff's deputy pulled up in front of the store, got o ut, and went inside. Chip didn't think much about that. In another fifteen minutes, his dad came out, got into the car, and started home. He had no package, no item of food, nothing to suggest he'd bought anything. He said not a word as they made the journey home but that was nothing unusual. Chip's dad was a man of few words but when he did have something to say, it definitely would be significant and poignant.

Chip broke the ice, "Dad, you were in there all that time and didn't buy anything!"

"Aw balls! I forgot what I went in there for", was all he said.

Chip learned from his mom a few days later that when he went into Walker's, he walked right into a rather heated shouting match between Ovis Tinney and Bill Cook and Bill's brother Jack. There was only the four of them in the store and poor old Mrs. Walker behind the counter was beside herself, not knowing what to do or what was going to come of the situation. Ovis had grabbed an ax handle out of the tool barrel and was emphasizing his argument by shaking the ax handle at Bill and Jack with every word. Bill and Jack had maneuvered themselves to an attack position front and back. Ovis could only get one of the brothers before the other one would pounce. Whatever they were about to come to blows over, it was strike related.

Chip's dad knew both parties very well. He worked in the mines with all three of them. Ovis was something like a third or fourth cousin and Bill and Jack played golf with Chip's dad since whenever. His dad just innocently wedged his way among them and began talking to them as if nothing out of the ordinary was going on. In the meantime, an unobserved motion to Mrs. Walker had sent her back to the office to call the sheriff. Things cooled off, but Theodore had decided to hang around, not wanting to leave Mrs. Walker alone with them again and by the time the deputy arrived, Bill and Jack had already paid for their purchases and left.

There were a few more strike related incidents that came to Chip's mind. Chip's dad would not cross the picket line to go to work, so while he was off, the Rose County Board of Education offered him a teaching position at a three room school located about half way between Sugar Tree and Mill's Bottom. That was the end of his dad's career as a coal miner. He would retire having served the education community as a teacher, both elementary and secondary, an elementary principal, and a high school band director.

Driving by the picket line at the top of Red Dog Hill, especially at night, left an indelible image on Chip's mind. His dad no longer worked in the mines and his mom was still teaching in the high school at Red Dog and though they were allowed to pass in and out of town as needs be, they were detained long enough for a quick identification and a quick flashlight search of the interior of the car every time. They were always checked twice, once by the strikers at the picket line and once by Company guards at their road check at the bottom of the hill, just before entering town. Though both his parents made frequent trips to Red Dog, Chip rarely went with them. You never knew what might happen. It was just too risky to expose children to any danger. Chip does remember the firelight flickering from half a dozen burn barrels scattered around, illuminating the grizzled faces of the strikers, some with guns or clubs in their arms, as they peered in the closed car window at his family as they passed through the picket line.

Once, when Chip's mom was going to school in the morning, she passed through the strikers road block and started down Red

Dog Hill in the old Mercury. Because the hill was a fifteen percent grade, everyone stopped about halfway down and shifted their car into low gear to help keep the brakes from becoming hot and inoperable. Just as his mom started ahead in low gear, the car slipped out of gear and quickly began picking up speed. Going too fast to even shift into second gear, his mom shifted into high and let the car go. She did ride the brakes just a little but the car was going too fast on the loose gravel hill and she was afraid it would start sliding and she would have no control over it. So she let the car go and steered the best she could. Company guards stationed at the foot of the hill, looked up to see this sedan, dust and gravel flying from behind, barreling toward them at break neck speed in an apparent attempt to run their road block. Every guard trained his weapon at the front windshield or the tires and clicked off the safety. Fortunately, a couple of the guards were former students of Mrs. Gates and they recognized her and the car in time to put a "hold your fire" to the pending disaster. Mrs. Gates waved daintily, if not cautiously, to the men as she sped on by into town.

Interestingly, there were no pickets at the Company Store in Sugar Tree. Chip figured that the store was on WYGARB property and it bordered the county road so there was no middle ground for the strikers to set up a picket line.

The strike began in early September. By the middle of December, it had turned violent with neither side backing off. Three days before Christmas, at 12:30 in the morning, a car carrying four WYGARB employees returning to Red Dog from a night on the town, was stopped by strikers at the top of the hill. Being a little drunk and resenting the intrusion and resenting an unnecessary, prolonged interrogation in an already agitated situation, one of the employees pulled a .38 pistol from under his seat and shot a striker in the face, killing him. Before the the car could speed off, the strikers opened fire with everything they had and in the hail of gunfire, two employees were killed and one was critically wounded.

The next day, more than twenty-five WV State Police rolled into Sugar Tree. They headquartered at Wyatt Keener's Store and kept half of the troopers deployed at all times wherever there were strikers set up on public property. Executive order from the

72

Governor gave the State Police authority to have free reins on WYGARB property. WYGARB did not oppose the order and in fact, gave their full cooperation to the State Police in all strike related matters.

The strike had reached a stalemate. The UMWA had spent hundreds of thousands of dollars during their campaign there and had made no inroads into unionization and it didn't look like another month or year of picketing was going to make any difference. WYGARB's mining operation was down to forty percent of full production. They were losing money having to replace and rebuild damaged property caused by the UMWA and their payroll of private armed guards was beginning to grow beyond their capacity to support them. Operating another month or another year under this kind of situation would be devastating to the Company, its town, and its people. The UMWA withdrew from the picket lines, the State Police went back to their respective detachments, and Red Dog went back to mining coal.

III

The town of Red Dog was a fascinating place during its nonunion days. Right in the center of town was WYGARB's business operation. A four-story coal preparation plant, or tipple, was the mainstay. On the hillside north of the tipple was a head house. All of the coal mined in the hills north of town came out of the mines at a central location called the head house. The mine cars were dumped into a loading bin that fed the coal via conveyor belt, down the hill to the tipple. South of the tipple and directly across the valley opposite the north head house was a second head house that fed the tipple with all of the coal mined in those sections south of town. When the tipple was running the noise was so deafening you couldn't carry on a normal conversation even with someone standing right beside you until you got at least fifty yards away from the tipple.

WYGARB's Red Dog operation worked in three shifts five days a week. The first shift ran from 7:00 am until 3:00 pm. That was called the day or daylight shift. The second shift worked 3:00 pm until 11:00 pm. It was called the evening shift or matinee shift. The third shift ran from 11:00 pm until 7:00 the next morning and was called the night shift, hoot owl, graveyard, cat eye, or midnight shift. Chip's dad worked on the evening shift as long as he was at Red Dog.

The shift change whistle at Red Dog was located on top of the steam house. It blew at 7:00, 3:00, and 11:00 sharp every day of the work week. The whistle was also used as an emergency signal when it was blown in short blasts for three or four minutes. Most emergency signals involved an accident at the mining operation or a house fire. Whatever the emergency, it summoned emergency personnel to the medical building and fire house. It was like the town just froze in motion when the emergency blasts went off. Chip remembers the hush that would descend upon the school when the emergency blasts went off during school hours. It was a very anxious time because you knew there was a serious situation developing and you also knew it involved someone you would know.

The shift whistle at Red Dog could be heard very distinctly clear over to Sugar Tree and beyond. Chip could remember roaming the hills around Sugar Tree and never venturing far enough in one day to be out of hearing range of the whistle. In fact any instructions given by Sugar Tree parents regarding their children's afternoon outdoor rompings would include a specific time to be back home for supper; 4:00 or 5:00 for example. As a kid, no matter what you were doing, as long as you were within two or three miles of Sugar Tree you could hear that 3:00 whistle and you knew exactly what time it was. There were no excuses for being late unless it was on Saturday or Sunday.

The railroad came into town from the east end and skirted along the back edge of town until it branched into four different tracks that ran under the tipple. The railroad tracks then continued west of the tipple for about half a mile around the hillside above town on a gentle grade. Empty coal cars were pushed up this back track by the steam locomotives and then were cut loose one or two at a time by the yard workers and allowed to drift into their respective stalls under the tipple where they would be loaded with coal. Chip spent many a summer evening sitting on the porch at home with the family listening to the sounds drifting in over the hills of the steam engines jostling the empties around on the back track.

The MC & E short line railroad ended at the back track yard. In the early days of Red Dog it was the only transportation in and out of town. However, from Red Dog, one could ride the MC & E to the junction of the B&O at Mill's Bottom and from there, travel to any railroad city in the US. In those early days, WYGARB provided daily passenger service on the MC & E to and from Mill's Bottom. After WWII, WYGARB suspended its passenger train service but did run a rail bus for passengers, light freight, and the mail twice a day from Red Dog, through Bumtown, to Mill's Bottom.

Included in this mid town complex was the wash house where miners could shower and store their work clothes and everyday clothes. It also included a miner's supply room and battery charging station. Also included in this mid town complex were the railroad repair shop, a row of freight warehouses, a medical center where two doctors and three nurses were on duty during the day and always available in emergencies, anytime.

WYGARB's main office buildings, which housed the paymaster's office where all payroll checks were issued, engineering offices, map rooms, personnel offices, offices of the general superintendent, and offices for all of those subdivisions like the railroad, the lumber mill, the mines, the tipple, housing, commodities, and recreation were located there.

The Bank of Red Dog was there along with the volunteer fire department. There was a building that boarded females only and one that boarded males only. Boarding fees for both sexes included three meals a day at a WYGARB run establishment called "The Annex". The Annex also catered special dinners and functions for the local civic groups active in Red Dog like the Rotary Club, the Kiwanis Club, and a Sportsman Club. Various other organizations held meetings there as well; PTA, Little League Committee, Boy Scouts, etc.

The biggest building in the business/industrial district was Company Store #2. It was three stories above the underground basement and was one hundred feet long and sixty feet wide.

The second largest building was the Town Hall. The Hall was a two story building. On the first floor you could find a pool hall (had to be sixteen to enter), a barber shop, a beauty shop, a lobby with a public telephone and a couple of pinball machines, and "The Grill". In The Grill you could order up ice cream, hot dogs, hamburgers, fries, barb-b-ques, cold cut sandwiches, coffee, hot chocolate, freshly popped popcorn, candy bars, snacks, chips, fountain sodas, and milkshakes and sit and eat at the counter or at a booth while listening to the latest hits on the jukebox. The Grill was the hangout for the young adult set. There was also a five lane bowling alley on the first floor.

Upstairs in The Hall was a two hundred seat auditorium. The Hall ran first-run movies on Friday, Saturday, and Sunday nights all year round. The movie screen was located at the back of a performing stage and was covered with a stage curtain when not in use. The stage was used for high school and community plays. Well recognized performers appeared on stage including Tex Ritter, Flatt & Scruggs, Helen Keller, and the Air Force Jazz Band. The high school band concerts were held there as well as recitals and performances by local talent. The high school graduation was held there. There was a good size room off the auditorium with a small stage where small gatherings like dances and parties were held quite frequently. The high school prom was always held there.

The first honest to goodness movie Chip ever saw was at The Hall. Mr. Gates took Chip and Riley over to see the animated "Alice in Wonderland".

Built right next to the tipple was the steam house. The steam house contained a humongous boiler that supplied steam heat and hot water to all of the buildings in this district. The steam was transferred from the steam house in a six inch pipe to the various buildings where it would branch off into a two inch line to supply the steam to the steam radiators located in each room of the particular building. The farthest the steam traveled from the steam house was two hundred yards to the school building complex. In a few spots, the main steam line ran along the banks of Mossy Creek or crossed the creek and in those spots where the line was exposed to the elements, it was wrapped in layers of asbestos for insulation. For the most part, the line was buried about two feet deep. During cold winter days steam would rise up out of the ground anywhere there would be a leak in the line or a faulty connection and unless it was a major break or occurred in the middle of the street or walkway, no one bothered to repair it.

Except for the school complex, only those buildings in the center part of town were heated from the steam house. It was not a very efficient method to heat those buildings but it was economical because WYGARB used water from a small dam it built on Mossy Creek and heated the water with its own coal. The superintendent's mansion, located on an oak tree shaded green knoll, was included in this central part of town and was heated by the steam house. There were a few of the larger homes scattered about mid town that were occupied by foremen at the mine, the bank president, and the head engineers. Their houses were heated from the steam house but no other houses or dwellings in town were afforded such luxury. This was central heating on a very large scale.

The school house complex was located two hundred yards up the street from the tipple away from the deafening noise and the dusty, dirty conditions. The main building contained the high school, seventh through twelfth grade. Third through sixth grade was also in the main building but in a separate wing. The first and second grade classes were in a separate building on the campus. There were three other smaller buildings on the campus that housed a home economics department, a band and music department, and a small physical education building. Enrollment in the high school averaged between one hundred and one hundred twenty.

The school did have an open area that served as a playground for the elementary school with swings, monkey bars, maypoles, seesaws, and the like and was used by the high school PE classes for softball, flag football, volleyball, etc. At one time the playground probably was dirt and had some grass on it but it was located between the tipple and the school. Being as close to the tipple as it was and over the many years of its existence, the dirt and grass had long ago been covered up with fine pieces of coal, gob, and coal dust. Showering after PE classes on the playground was a necessity.

For the elementary kids, recesses were short with extended bathroom time given when they came in. Teachers and parents prayed for rain or snow for it not only settled the dust, but kept those white blouses and tee shirts inside the school.

In his very first year at Red Dog High School, the new band director raised enough money to buy new uniforms for the marching band. His shoes of choice? White bucks! White bucks in Red Dog? The last and only time they were white was when they were taken out of the box. Even then they had black finger smudges on them. The next year and after, the shoes were black. Those who already had semi-white bucks used black shoe polish to change them over.

WYGARB was the single largest financial resource of the Rose County Board of Education. It was the largest employer in the county and the revenue it provided in terms of Business and Occupation taxes, land, timber, and mineral taxes far exceeded whoever was in second place. In gratitude, the Rose County Board of Education allowed the Company some sayso in who was placed in Red Dog's schools, pending certification. The Company also paid those teachers at Red Dog a stipend beyond what the Board paid in an effort to get the best teachers available. Chip knew this to be a fact because Mrs. Gates' first teaching position was at Red Dog and she had been there since 1938.

WYGARB had used its materials and laborers to build one of the finest gymnasiums in the tri-county area. The basketball court was laid out to college specifications. The interior was finished in yellow poplar cut from WYGARB property and finely milled at Bumtown. There were permanent bleachers along one side of the gym only, but at each end of the bleachers there was a small stage where temporary seating could be arranged with folding chairs if the need arose. The stages provided an area for the high school pep band to play during ball games. DJ's, small bands, and other performers used the stages for sock hops, dances, and talent shows. There was a concessions stand at the one end of the bleachers that provided all the usual snacks found in concession stands everywhere. The locker rooms and showers were located downstairs underneath the gym. WYGARB had also furnished an electric scoreboard that was situated on the wall directly across from the bleachers. The gym was built with large windows spaced completely around the upper reaches of the high walls which helped with the lighting in the daytime. At night, the ceiling lights, along with the light shaded poplar interior, made the lighting excellent.

The backboards were fan shaped and made of metal. The gym was the only building in Red Dog heated with natural gas. Two gas fired heaters with thermostat controlled fans were suspended from the lofty rafters, one over each end of the playing floor. It was a beautiful facility. The high school and junior high school played all of their home games there. Red Dog also had a men's and women's industrial league team that played there.

There were two garages in Red Dog. One was a filling station and garage, the other was just a garage. WYGARB must have had an exclusive contract with the Gulf Oil Corporation because the one filling station in Red Dog sold only Gulf products and besides that, all of the lubricants, oils, and grease used by WYGARB in its vast operations were solely of the Gulf brand.

There were three churches in Red Dog, a Baptist Church for those of the Christian faith, a Catholic Church for those of Italian, Hungarian, and non Bible Belt descent, and a Baptist Church for the Black population. The Black race was referred to as "Colored" in Chip's time. The churches were not segregated and in almost all services, the congregation would be found to be mixed. However, there were those who chose to exclusively worship their faith in their own church and that was ok. At times there were other special services that were reserved for only members of a particular church.

The streets in Red Dog were all named after the counties in the area; Seneca, Rose, Franklin, Pocahontas, Jefferson, Clay, and, Greenbrier. The streets were not paved though they were kept scraped and maintained regularly. They received a new layer of red dog at least once a year. In the winter they were muddy and sloppy when not frozen, though the Company did keep the snow plowed off. The streets were oiled every other day in the   summer during dry spells to keep the dust down. They were sprayed with used oil from the garages and the mining operation by a truck much like a water truck that is used to wash down streets in the city. Under a hot baking sun and the pounding of town traffic, the street surface would become as hard as concrete until a summer rain or thunderstorm came along.

The walkways that ran along each side of the street were formed by laying railroad ties end to end, three feet parallel and filling the space between the ties with red dog until it was even with the top of the ties. Thus the walkways were a little wider than three feet and they suffered the same weather effects as the streets did except they were not cleared of snow nor were they oiled. The walks ran along both sides of every street in town and separated the houses from the street. Some houses were separated from the walkways by a board fence. Others had hedges or shrubs as boundaries. Other houses had nothing at all.

There was no parking on any of the streets in Red Dog, there just wasn't any room. Residents who owned cars could park them in the alley that ran behind the rows of houses or could fashion a drive way between their house and the next. Red dog was good material for a driveway base. If you wanted to stop and visit someone and park on the street in front of their house, you had to leave your motor running and lights on or leave someone in the car so the local constable would know you weren't staying long.

There were a number of parking areas in the town provided for employees and patrons. Anyone could park in these areas for as long as they wanted without charge. There was one at The Hall, a large one at the medical building and wash house, one at the tipple, one at the Baptist Church, another large one between the bank and the Company Store, one at the high school, one at the annex, and one at the boarding house.

There were approximately five hundred houses in Red Dog and they were of only two different styles. One was a single story, five room dwelling. These were all built with rough lumber from the Bumtown mill. They were double walled structures with no insulation either in the outside walls, the attic, or under the floor. They all had a double fireplace that opened to the front room and the opposite side opened to the master bedroom. None had running water when they were first built and all had an outhouse built in the back. These houses were absolutely identical in style and built side by side and except for a few instances, were separated from each other by no more than ten to twelve feet.

The only other style house found in Red Dog were two story dwellings that were double occupancy. One family lived on one side of the house with their own entry in the front and back and another family lived on the other side with their own entries. The house was divided inside by one double walled partition that reached up through the second floor to the roof. Families shared a common front porch but had their own separate outhouse in the back. These two story dwellings were exactly alike and built in the same manner as the single houses. They had double fireplaces on the first floor and the second floor. These houses could be found in only two areas of town; on both sides of Clay Street, which was a short street at the north end of town, and along one side of Franklin Street.

Over the years, many of the families who lived in these houses did manage to individualize their homes on their own by painting them or enclosing the porch as a room. Many added shrubs or flowers to the little front yard. Some painted or renovated the board fence around their yard. Others tried to grow grass and tend it in their front yard. The Women's Club of Red Dog even sponsored a monthly "Yard of the Month" award. And naturally, just by living in Red Dog over the years, you could find your way to the right door, in the right house, just by instinct, but there were always incidents of individuals mistakenly wandering into the wrong house, especially at night, and especially when they had had too much to drink. On more than a few occasions late at night, individuals were known to have made it clear into a bedroom and disrobed before being chased, driven, threatened, shot at, or whipped out of the house clothed and unclothed.

The most feared and frightening threat to the town of Red Dog was fire. It was even more dreaded than a mining accident for two reasons. Red Dog had experienced more fires than mining accidents and a fire was no respecter of person. The houses were dried wood, tinder boxes permeated with fine coal dust. Almost all of them were heated with coal burning fireplaces or coal stoves and in an effort to keep warm during a winter cold spell, fires were stoked up a little more than usual and sometimes left unattended. House fires burned hot and fast and spread rapidly from house to house because they were crammed so close together. The only way to contain a fire to one or two houses was to dynamite one or two good houses on each side of the fire. Not only did the families who were burned out lose everything, so would those families living on either side of the fire.

Another unique characteristic of Red Dog was the location of Jefferson Street. All of the colored families lived on Jefferson street. Typically, all the mining towns of that turn of the century era, located the colored section of town at the farthest, back section, away from the main traffic area of town. When Red Dog was first laid out, Jefferson Street was situated as the last street on the north end of town, away from everything. In the first few years of Red Dog's existence, the only way in and out of town was by the MC & E which came into the south end of town where the hub of all the town's activities were located. Later, WYGARB decided to build their own private road into town. To make it accessible and practical, they wanted to link it up with State Rt. 11. After exhaustive planning and numerous engineering proposals, all inhibited by the terrain, WYGARB came to the conclusion that the easiest, shortest, least expensive plan would be to bring their road off of State Rt.11, straight down the hill, and hook it on to the end of Jefferson St. So that's what they did. It shifted the colored section of town from the isolated back section, to the very first part of town. It was the first street that a traveler encountered when they came in on the new road. It became the primary avenue in and out of Red Dog.

The new road down the hill into Red Dog was steep. So steep, that in the early 1930's, there were townspeople who bought new automobiles that could not pull Red Dog Hill with more than two people in them unless they went up in reverse. As late as 1959, Red Dog's volunteer fire department, which consisted of two trucks and a jeep, were no good to anybody outside of Red Dog, because one truck could not pull Red Dog Hill at all when loaded and the other one had to pull the hill in mule gear, which at that speed, would take at least ten minutes to make the half mile to the top of the hill.

Red Dog Hill was graded to slant to the bank on the upper side of the road. If your car had a tendency to slide, it would slide towards the ditch against the hill, unless you were going down the hill too fast. In which case you could just as easily slide across the road and go over the hillside into the woods for a couple of hundred feet. There were no guard rails or posts or cables along the road up Red Dog Hill. A few times on a cold, snowy, wintry morning, Chip, Riley, and Clint would have to get out of the car as Mrs. Gates eased the Merc down the hill, and walk along the ditch line on the upper side of the road to hold the front end of the car up in the road to keep it from sliding into the ditch. There were other mornings when it was just too bad for Mrs. Gates to negotiate either Sugar Tree Hill or Red Dog Hill, so she would leave the Merc at the Pennzoil station in Sugar Tree and have Bucky drive them all over to school in his jeep. He would come back and get them at 3:30 that afternoon.

Jefferson Street was called "colored hollow", "colored street", or "colored town". Colored town had its own elementary school with two colored teachers, a church, and recreation building called the "colored Y". The colored Y was first built as a YMCA building. It had a small eatery, a couple of pool tables, and a room in the back for serious, high roller card and checker players. But the biggest draw at the colored Y was the Saturday night dance. The early hours were reserved for the teenage crowd and after 10:00 the adults took over. Occasionally, a local band or a local musician would provide the music but there was always hot stuff playing Saturday night at the colored Y even if by juke box, and there was always a lively crowd struttin' their stuff. The young white teens in Red Dog like to hang around the colored Y on Saturday nights and soak up the rhythm and blues and soul music pouring out of the open doors and windows. The colored Y closed in the late '50's.

Except for the fact that all the colored folks lived on Jefferson Stet, nothing else was segregated in Red Dog. There were even some white families who lived on Jefferson St. on the end nearest town. Colored folks had equal access to all of the same facilities as the white folks. The whole left hand section of the theater in the Hall was always referred to as the colored section but everyone, both black and white, sat wherever they wanted and nothing was ever said.

The colored grade school just went up to the sixth grade. When the kids reached the seventh grade, they attended Red Dog High School. The high school was integrated long before government ordered desegregation came to be. In the early '50's, there were only a few all colored high schools in West Virginia. Red Dog High had always accepted their colored population as part of the student body without a second thought. Out of the enrollment of one hundred, more or less, at Red Dog High, the colored enrollment averaged between fifteen and twenty students. They all were active in the school's activities; playing in the band, members of the athletic teams, honor society members, drama club participants, and class officers.

In fact, many of the colored families in Red Dog took in high school aged children from relatives and friends living in other parts of the state just so those kids could go to high school in Red Dog. Colored parents knew their kids would get a quality education without any hassle.

Red Dog was a dry town. Dry in the sense that there were no retail businesses in town that sold beer and there were no liquor stores. However, there were two places on Jefferson St. where one could purchase from a private supply of assorted liquors at reasonable prices. One would be at Melvin Washington's. Melvin kept his stock of bootleg on his enclosed back porch and that's where you went to make a buy. One never stopped on the street in front of Melvin's and never went up on the front porch if you were there to buy. Melvin was about six feet three and weighed close to three hundred pounds. If you went around back to buy, Melvin was the most congenial and easy going person you could ever find, but if you didn't know any better and went to see Melvin about his stuff around front, you might find yourself in a confrontation with an outraged giant wielding a baseball bat while launching a barrage of threats to your life and limb. If you just went to visit Melvin and his family you went in the front. Everybody knew Melvin was the local supplier of liquor but he was never hassled by the law or Company officials. Truth be known, some of Melvin's stock could be found in the homes of some of those company officials.

Only a handful of folks knew where Melvin got his supply but everyone knew when he made his supply run. It was the only time Melvin ever drove out of Red Dog without any of his family in the Chevy station wagon. Chip and his friends never went to Melvin's except when they were with one of Melvin's boys, Little Melvin or Timothy.

Momma Haywood's was the other place on Jefferson St. where you could find some spirits. Momma sold wine. Homemade wine. Very good homemade wine. Though she didn't have much variety, only red grape, she always had an ample supply. She must have made the stuff year around. It was different at Momma's than at Melvin's. Momma didn't care why, how, or when you came. She was always hospitable and more times than not, even if you didn't come to buy wine, she'd offer you a glass while you were there.

Momma had two daughters and they were certainly fine looking sisters. Momma liked to show them off so she always had them going around doing little domestic chores when anyone was visiting. Chip didn't mind.

85

You didn't always have to pay money to obtain some of Momma's wine. You could barter. Momma liked wild game, so some of the boys would bring her a rabbit or two or some squirrels. That would be good for a pint. Entertaining Momma and the family for half an hour by playing a musical instrument like the guitar, accordion, harmonica, banjo, or fiddle was good for a pint. Just singing wouldn't help you any unless you could accompany yourself with an instrument.

The whites and coloreds in Red Dog worked and played and lived together without giving their racial differences much thought. However, there was no serious courting or romancing between them, at least none that the general public was aware of and it would be awfully hard to keep it a secret in such a close knit community. White kids and colored kids did date and did accompany one another to various social functions about town but those relationships never ventured beyond the social nuance of the town of Red Dog.

In the beginning, there was no community water system for Red Dog. WYGARB had drilled or dug wells every two hundred feet or so along the walkways beside all of the streets and installed hand pumps to pump the water. Residents filled whatever containers they could with water from the pumps and carried it back to the house.

Later, the Company built a small open reservoir in one of the hollows above town and that water was pumped to a water storage tank on a hill above town. That system however, only provided water for the business/industrial part of town which included the superintendent's residence, the homes of the top executives and engineers, the medical building, the town hall, the annex, the boarding house, and the school. No residential domicile of the laborer was included. The water from the pumps and the reservoir contained sulfur gas because it always had the smell of rotten eggs about it. When the drinking water was chilled it was hard to believe that it could taste so good. That's what made the Red Dog Grille's fountain sodas the best fountain sodas Chip had ever had.

Not only was the well water contaminated with sulfur, it had iron in it and when left standing uncovered it would turn a rusty red color. It turned even quicker when the water was heated. Needless to say all of the sinks, wash basins, cookery, and light colored clothes had a red-to-pink tinge about them. By the mid '50's, most of the residential families had private wells dug or drilled on their small lot and had their own independent water supply. The water came from the same source and was of the same composition as the street pumps and town reservoir, but now homes could have the luxury of running water and inside bathrooms. Some homes kept their outhouses, some installed septic tanks, some installed cesspools, and some diverted their sewage straight into Mossy Creek.

Two miles out of Red Dog, up the valley of Mossy Creek, away from the dust and dirt and noise of town, and in a wide area of the valley floor in the middle of the woods, the Company built a recreation complex on its property. It was called The Sportsman Club Park. Though it was built for employees of WYGARB, it was open to the public in general.

There was a one-acre fishing pond, as well as trout fishing in Mossy Creek. There was a tennis court that could be lit at night, and there was a small concession stand that was open during the summer season. There was a playground full of swings and other equipment for the young and the young at heart and a picnic area with tables and stone built grills for cooking out.

For the younger set, the main attraction of the area was the Olympic size swimming pool. It was from four feet deep on the shallow end to twelve feet deep on the deep end. There was a low diving board and a high diving board. There was also a wading pool built right beside the big pool. The water in the pool was not chlorinated and it was not filtered by recycling. A small dam had been built on Mossy Creek just above the recreation area and that water was fed through a six inch water line by gravity to a tank filled with sand. The water then passed out of that filter by gravity and ran into the pool. There were two outlets from the pool, one on the bottom and the overflow near the top. The overflow was kept open all the time so there was always fresh water running into the pool and it kept the pool level constant. The bottom drain was opened from time to time to allow the bottom water to be refreshed and to drain the pool at the close of the season.   The big problem with the pool was that Mossy Creek was a cold, mountain stream. It came out of the mountain side not too far away and tumbled along through the deep woods until it got to the dam just above the pool. It never saw the sun and had no time for its water to warm before being dumped in the pool. You couldn't stay in that cold water for more than ten minutes and then you had to lay down on the concrete walk around the pool in hopes that the sun and the heated concrete would warm you up. Now the wading pool water was only changed every other day so usually the water in the wading pool would warm up very nicely. On cloudy or overcast days, you might find fifteen or twenty teenagers lying in the wading pool trying to warm up while the toddlers played around and over them.

The main attraction of the Sportman's Park for the adults was the Sportsman Lodge Hall. Built near the entrance to the recreation area, it was a one story structure built of cinder block but beautifully finished inside with yellow poplar like the gym. The front entrance opened to a ball room that had tall windows spaced neatly around three sides of the room and it was furnished with small tables and chairs situated around the perimeter of the dance floor.   Directly across the room from the main entrance was a raised stone fireplace with a stone hearth and exposed chimney that ran from the fireplace through the ceiling. The fireplace was six feet wide and six feet tall. To the right of the fireplace was a stage for the musicians. A dining area that could seat one hundred and fifty people was off to the left wing of the ballroom and a well equipped kitchen occupied the remainder of the rear of The Lodge.

The Lodge was reserved for only the most lavish, extravagant, and special occasions. The Company's Christmas dance and party was always an annual dress-up affair. The Woman's Club always sponsored a spring formal. Recognition and testimonial dinners were held there. The Governor of the State was honored in person there on two different occasions.   The Company was always throwing a dinner and dance for their business partner's executives and representatives and their wives.

The recreation area was kept open as long as the weather permitted. Even after the pool was closed, which was usually right after Labor Day, there were still picnics and fishing and tennis and camping to enjoy. When the weather made the little dirt road from Red Dog too difficult to traverse in the family car, the Company would close and lock the gates at the entrance to the park. There were four creek crossing you had to make if you drove all the way to the park so high water in Mossy Creek meant the gates to the park would be closed and locked as well. Of course high water could come at any time of the year but the public used common sense as the guide to when the road might be closed then. If one were to make their way up to the park, even if the gates were closed, they could still walk in. There were paths around the creek crossings. The Company always made sure the road was passable when the lodge was to be occupied no matter what the weather might be barring high water. Eventually, the Company installed large metal tubes as culverts so the road could pass over two of the crossings and they bulldozed a new section of road that went around Mossy Creek at the last two crossings making the road passable year around.

Mossy Creek went through quite a metamorphosis on its journey from the mountain to the Elk River some twenty-four miles away.

It began as a hillside spring that tumbled fresh, clear, and cold, down the mountainside to the valley. Once to the valley floor, very little sunshine was ever able to break through the thick forest canopy of trees to warm the stream as it splashed over small rocks and drifted along small eddies. The creek ran year around and the water flow never seemed to abate more than a few inches but it did swell out of its banks once in a while when heavy rains came.

It grew in size as it picked up the flow from small branches and little brooks along the way. It was two miles from where Mossy Creek entered the valley until it encountered its first human diversion at the dam built for supplying the swimming pool at the Sportsman Park. The creek supported native brown and brook trout in those two miles and was only accessible by walking along a hiking trail the local boy scout troop had cut into the wilderness. The creek pretty much kept its ideal mountain stream identity as it passed through the park but once it got below the park, the next two miles into Red Dog began to alter its makeup.

Hardly any fish except suckers and minnows were found in the creek below the park because the traffic kept the dirt and mud stirred up in the creek crossings. There was no white water in the creek there, only slow flowing eddies with heavy silt bottoms from the runoff on both sides of the valley; valley hillsides whose third growth of timber was just now beginning.

Just before the creek entered the town of Red Dog, it had to pass around the edge of the upper gob pile for a quarter of a mile. The gob pile had grown so big that its base had actually spread into the creek and caused the creek to change its course. At one time the company had built a wooden dam in the creek there above town to use as a water source and for recreation but the gob pile had covered over three fourths of the dam's face and had squeezed the creek to change its course by fifty to seventy-five feet to skirt around the gob.

Mossy Creek swayed back and forth for a mile and a half as it snaked its way through the town of Red Dog. At the lower end of town the creek was still only about twenty-five feet wide but as it exited the town, it looked like a thin ribbon of roofing tar oozing along. In the mile and a half through Red Dog, Mossy took on the pollution and runoff from a gob pile, hundreds of raw sewage outlets, industrial waste from the shops, and the wash house. All of the ground water runoff in Red Dog traveled through inches of coal dust and slag, not to mention the oil and red dog applied to the streets. It was probably a good thing the creek was so black running through town. At least the people couldn't see what was really in the water. The creek looked like it was flowing along at a pretty good clip and indeed the top one foot layer of water was moving along, but the bottom two foot of water was the one with all the sediment in it and it didn't ooze very fast. Residents of the town were grateful when the high water came so it could flush the creek out.

The sludge washed from cleaning the coal at the tipple was pumped by pipeline up one of the hollows at Red Dog into a settling or sediment pond. When the sludge had settled, the water layer on top was pumped by pipeline around on the other side of the hill and then gravity fed through more pipeline, back off the hill and into Mossy Creek just below town.

The creek then had to skirt around the biggest of the two gob piles, the one below Red Dog, where it collected all the ground water runoff that washed huge, jagged gullies into the side of the gob pile, before continuing its trek toward Bumtown.

From the lower gob to Bumtown, Mossy Creek was diluted a little in those nine miles by a number of small branches and streams and two or three large creeks that emptied into it, but the damage had already been done. There was not a living creature nor plant that could be found in or around this semi-liquid solution still known as Mossy Creek.

WYGARB dammed the creek up at Bumtown so the town would have a water supply to run the lumber mill, wash down the timber to be milled, provide heat to the Company offices, stores, and the school, and fill the water tanks for the steam locomotives on the MC & E. The creek then actually swung around the town of Bumtown, giving it a wide berth. Mossy was now a slate gray color but there was still no aquatic life to be found in its environs.

Eight miles below Bumtown, Mossy Creek vomited her contents into the clear blue waters of the Elk River where it would mix in swirls and whirlpools and stain the rocks, the river bed, and the river bank for years and years. Anyone could tell exactly where the mouth of Mossy Creek was located on the Elk River.

WYGARB had hired a police chief for the town of Red Dog but he was referred to as a constable. For the last ten years of WYGARB's ownership of the town of Red Dog, the constable had been Argil Woods.

Argil was a short chunky man with a blond crew-cut. His face was so red that you could see little blood vessels almost popping out of the surface of his skin. In his younger days Argil had been a heavy drinker and a hell raiser. Muscular for his size, he was able to make up for lack of stature by being tenacious. Argil had a few scars and a couple of broken fingers as a testament to his rowdiness. He had gone to work for WYGARB at the tipple right out of high school. For ten years Argil dropped the empty coal cars down the back track and under the tipple for loading.

91

One freezing cold February night, Argil cut two empties loose from the string on the back track and rode the hind one in under the tipple and set the brakes just under the loading chute. Unknown to Argil was a third empty car whose brakes weren't set and whose coupling had been opened by the day shift yard worker. The third car didn't break loose right away but drifted out and quietly followed the first two down the track. Because of all the noise around the tipple, Argil didn't hear the empty bearing down on him from behind until he had set the brake wheel and stepped down onto the rear car's coupling. By then the onrushing empty was upon him.

He tried to jump off the side of the coupling but his feet slipped on the thin sheet of ice on top and his left leg slipped down into the open coupling and he fell hard onto the coupling just as the runaway and the stopped car hit together. Argil's leg was crushed by the coupling and the force of the impact tore his body completely away from his crushed leg.

After a long and painful recovery, Argil was fitted with a wooden leg and as compensation for his accident, WYGARB kept him on the payroll and eventually appointed him as constable of Red Dog. He was referred to by the younger crowd as "Chester" after deputy Chester Goode on Gunsmoke.

Crime was almost nonexistent in Red Dog. Not solely because the townspeople were so neighborly and congenial, though that was true, it was mostly the result of WYGARB's own judicial system. The whole town was private property. The people lived in homes not their own. They worked for a private business concern and they were dependent on that concern for their basic day to day necessities of life. Argil's job was more of a reporter than an enforcer. He handled the minor infractions and domestic cases at his own discretion, yet still had the authority of the Company behind him. Actually, Chester, er uh, Argil, developed into a fair and reasonable litigator between the town and the Company.

Argil's first duty would be to investigate the incident. If it were between residents, he would try to settle or rectify the situation without involving the Company. If the incident involved the Company in any way or it could not be settled between the parties involved, then Argil's second duty would be to report it to the general superintendent of WYGARB's empire, Mr. Bradley Krantz. Reports to Mr. Krantz would be of two findings: one, the perpetrator or perpetrators pleaded guilty and would pay or accept whatever Mr. Krantz deemed would be fair restitution. Two, the perpetrator or perpetrators had committed serious crimes or were habitually involved in violating Company statutes and would have to appear personally before Mr. Krantz.

Mr. Krantz had the full authority to act on behalf of the Company so in the latter case, he had the authority and power to threaten the accused with termination of employment, eviction from home, garnishing of wages, suspension of pay, or bringing actual criminal charges to bear. Mr. Krantz disliked bringing criminal charges because it involved powers outside the jurisdiction of the Company and Mr. Krantz would lose all of his judicial authority and control. Then he never knew what might happen.

Argil did his best to keep cases from coming before Mr. Krantz because he did not want to see his friends and neighbors any more at the mercy of the Company than they already were. All in all, this justice system worked well in Red Dog because the townspeople knew of the precarious position they could find themselves in if they got out of line with Company policies and proper social conduct. Company justice, to a lesser degree, extended to those living outside of Red Dog but still worked for the company. Argil's jurisdiction extended to any incidents occurring on Company property.

Problems in the system arose when crimes against the Company or against the townspeople were committed by outsiders. Outsiders were those who had no affiliation with the Company in any way. In these cases, and there were few, Argil's duty was to report to Mr. Krantz and let him decide whether or not to notify the local law enforcement agencies.

Needless to say, the Red Dog school system had no major discipline problems either. Fathers of unruly and rowdy students who could not seem to be corrected after more than three visits to the principal's office, often found themselves facing Company justice dispensed by Mr. Krantz. His words of justice were short and to the point. "You better talk to your boy/girl!".

The Independence Day celebration in Red Dog was the most festive day of the year in the tri-county area. It began at 9:00 am with a parade that started on Pocahontas Street at the lower end of town, wound its way through the middle of town, turned right on Greenbrier Street, and ended up on top of the upper gob pile.

There were numerous parade units entered; decorated floats by various civic organizations or marching units that included Kiwanis Club, Rotary Club, Boy Scouts, Woman's Club, 4-H, Little League, woman's and men's industrial league basketball and baseball teams, and local church and school representation.

The local American Legion Chapter led the parade and always presented a rousing flag raising ceremony to open the festivities. There was also a jeep parade. Locals washed and shined up their jeeps and decorated them in imaginative ways to parade through town. There was always a number of various breeds of horses as well as riders and horse drawn contraptions in the parade. Every convertible in the tri-county area was rounded up to haul the beauty queen entrants through town. There were a few antique cars in the parade, one of which always carried the parade marshall, Mr. Bradley Krantz. The Red Dog High School Marching Band, in their almost white-bucks, was always the second parade unit right behind the American Legion. The Company always invited a local marching band from one of the other high schools in the area like Mill's Bottom or Elk River.

The 15+ Club band set up in the back of a two ton flat bed truck and jazzed their way along as part of the parade. There were times when Chip just wanted to walk along beside the truck and listened to the band play through town, but he was usually stuck somewhere in the parade himself. He'd heard his dad play piano at home all the time, but he never did get to hear the whole band play together because they played and practiced where he wasn't allowed. After the fireworks display, the 15+ Club Band would play for the dance at The Sportsman Lodge until the wee hours of the morning.

After the parade, opening ceremonies were held on the upper gob. Other activities going on up on the gob pile included; a talent show, a horse show, a couple of high school band concerts, a watermelon seed spitting contest, a pie baking contest, a hot dog eating contest, a greased pig event, and a number of vendors who were set up to sell you anything to eat related to a 4th of July celebration.

You could find something going on almost anywhere in town that day. Up at the Sportsman park there was family picnicking available for as long as you wanted to stay. There was a swimsuit beauty contest with no less than thirty entrants each year. Minimum age of eighteen to enter. Individual swimming races and diving events were held at the pool when the beauty contest was over and the pool would remain open all day for the public after those events. There was a horseshoe pitching tournament and a tennis tournament. There was a shooting match, shotguns only, and a fishing contest for folks under twelve years old. At two o'clock in the afternoon, the road from the recreation park to Red Dog was closed so a bicycle race could be staged. It started at the park and ending at the upper end of Greenbrier St. The road was opened again after the race.

Airplane rides were available all day for $5.00 a person. Planes took off and landed on the upper gob pile. There were baseball games all afternoon both at the upper and lower fields. Some were little league games but there was always a men's game between Red Dog and some other town who had been invited.

The finale was a fireworks display at the upper gob pile at dusk. During the 4th celebration in Red Dog, a thief could have loaded Sugar Tree onto a truck and carried it off without a bit of trouble. The only people left in Sugar Tree were Wyatt and Sarah Keener and the boys running their businesses, which needless to say, did a heck of a good business that day. Even the Company Store was closed and after 5:00 that evening, the Keeners all closed up and went over to Red Dog too.

Though the town and people of Red Dog were an independent and close knit lot, outsiders, those living outside of Red Dog, always felt welcomed and accepted, and were never viewed as an outsider to town. In truth, ten percent of the WYGARB's work force lived outside of Red Dog but were as much a part of the Red Dog family as those who lived there. Those families not only shared the same employer but were involved in the same activities and organizations and enjoyed the same privileges offered by the Company. Interestingly, though outsiders flocked in and out of Red Dog with regularity, you very seldom would run into a Red Dog resident in any of the surrounding towns. It was rare to see a Red Dog resident even passing through Sugar Tree as close as it was. You never saw them at other community festivals or events. Never saw them in Seneca or Hob or Mill's Bottom shopping. Chip guessed they had no reason to go anywhere else for anything so were quite content to stay home.

If there was one small exception to the aforementioned peculiarities regarding outsiders, it came from the Jr. High and High School group. New student enrollees to those grades were generally accepted by their peers without incident, especially if the family had just moved into town. New student enrollees from out of town found acceptance a little longer in coming. Problems usually arose when a new student, male or female, thought they had to establish their "not going to be not intimidated" role when they really didn't have to. Some Red Dog students just couldn't pass up such a bold invitation. There were as many fights between Red Dog students as there were between residents and outsiders.

Chip was accepted quickly by his Jr. High School peers partly because his mom had taught school there for so long. His only fight at Red Dog was in the sixth grade that first year and it was with Otto Murphy, another kid who lived outside of Red Dog. Wasn't much to it really. Chip couldn't even remember what it was about but he could remember Mr. Gibson breaking them up on the playground and marching them to the principal's office. Fighting in school usually brought a paddling and two weeks in noon detention or the combatants were allowed to go to the P.E. gym at noon and put on the gloves and go at each other till one quit. Chip and Otto decided on the way to the principal's office that they really didn't want to fight anymore so they would throw themselves on the mercy of Mr. Truman, the principal.

Mr. Truman was stern and strict and addressed the boys in that authoritative dialog designed to make Jr. High students tremble in their penny loafers. Chip kept looking around the office trying to spy the infamous Truman Paddle but never did spot it. Must have kept it in a desk drawer. In their defense, Chip claimed they were only horsing around and not really mad or really fighting. Mr. Truman's demeanor changed somewhat. If the boys promised not to fight anymore, he'd let them off with just detention. The two boys solemnly swore to such and shook hands. As they left the office Chip wondered in the back of his mind if Mr. Truman had let them off because he was Mrs. Gates' son. At any rate, he and Otto decided they would have to tell everyone that they were paddled. After that, Chip and Otto became close friends.

The only other time trouble brewed with outsiders was when small groups from other towns or schools would show up uninvited to a school function. It was ok for non Red Dog students to attend school dances and the like if they were invited by a Red Dog student. No outsider with any brains at all would be foolish enough to attend a Red Dog school activity in Red Dog alone and uninvited. Red Dog students were very protective of their own and if a group of three or more outsiders showed up at a school function, they would politely be asked to leave. If they chose otherwise, they would have to contend with an element five times more in number and determination. These confrontations always ended with the outsiders piling into a car or jumping in the back of a pick-up and tearing out of town with fifteen to twenty young people, boys and girls alike, chasing them up Jefferson Street on foot.

Even when small groups of outsiders attended public events in Red Dog or ventured up to the pool, there was always a small contingent of Red Dog's young who, although kept a distance from them, kept a distrustful watch on them at the same time.

The town's athletic events never drew in very many visiting fans but nary did very many Red Dog fans follow their team when it left town to play somewhere else.

You knew if you were accepted by the folks, both old and young, in Red Dog if you were given a nickname. Nicknames are not out of the ordinary in small communities but in Red Dog, it was developed to a new level. From young kids to old folks, including some girls and women, almost all had a nickname, and it was so prevalent that it actually became a person's surname.

Some were named because of their appearance or some obvious physical characteristic. Birdlegs, Cowhead, String, Too Tall, Whiskers, Shnoz, Bad Eye, Greasy, Red, Hoot, (looked like a hoot owl), Mule, Dimple, Rabbit, Skinny, Fat Man, Mouthy, Wool (which was short for Woolhead), Troll, and Shorty were some. There were two Shortys. One was named Shorty because he was very short in stature and the other was called Shorty because he was a very tall individual. It was a reverse nomenclature. There were a lot of those.

"Speed" was the name given to a boy who always wanted a pair of ice skates. One Christmas he finally got them and it had snowed some but there was no ice anywhere. Didn't matter, he put on his skates Christmas morning and skated all the way up the middle of Rose St. to The Hall and back in the mud. Thus the name "Speed".

"Tommy Gun" was a guy who t a l k e d v e r y s l o w l y.

Some names came from famous people: Bugs, after Bugs Bunny because he was always munching on a carrot stick he carried around. Yogi, after Yogi Berra because he was a catcher on the Red Dog baseball team. Didn't matter that he was colored. Chester, of course after Chester Goode on Gunsmoke. Beaver, after Beaver Cleaver on TV because he resembled Beaver when he was small. Casey's name was really Keith but his last name was Jones so everybody called him Casey, after Casey Jones.

Other names came from a person's peculiarities: Ham, because he always had ham in his lunch bucket. Wiener and Peanuts also from what a person liked to eat. Danny Bologna came not from what he liked to eat but what people always said he was full of. Jeep, because all his life all he ever drove was a jeep. Truck, not because he drove a truck but because when he was a little kid his crying sounded like a truck shifting gears. Potslinger was given his name because one day he went out to empty his grandmother's bed chamber pot and some kids across the street started teasing him about something so he just took a big swing and heaved the pot clear across the street at them. The pot didn't hit anyone but it scattered the contents all over the place. Mudflaps was named because one day he took a pair of mudflaps out and put them on his dad's car. Problem was he nailed the mudflaps directly onto each rear tire with roofing tacks. His name was later shortened to just Flaps.

Doc was named because when he was a kid he wanted to be a doctor and got a doctor's kit for Christmas every year. He never became a doctor. There were two or three guys named "Preacher" because they were ordained ministers who were pastors of local churches or were evangelists. Cappy wore a ball cap all of the time, even to bed at night.

Some names were shortened versions of a real name. Woodsy from Woods, Butch from Butcher, Murf from Murphy, Nobe from Nobel, Rosey from Roosevelt. Mac came from McMillion but Mac's son was called Muck.

There was a girl called Hawtee. Her real name was Helen but her little brother couldn't pronounce Helen. The closest he could come was Hawtee so all of Helen's girl friends just started calling her Hawtee.

It seemed every person born in the area whose name was Ronald Lee, was always nicknamed Jake. Probably the first Ronald Lee was nicknamed "Jake" and so tradition must have laid that title on to every Ronald Lee born thereafter in the area.

Many times the offspring got the nickname from their father so not to be confusing, you had Big Mouthy & Little Mouthy, Big Knute & Little Knute, Big Wiener & Little Wiener, Big Mule & Little Mule.

Chip's nickname was Face. Actually it was #%*! Face but you couldn't say that in public so it was shortened to Face. When he was eleven or twelve years old, he had a very bad case of acne. It was so bad he had to go to Charleston every month one summer to be treated by an dermatologist. One day someone asked how come his face was so #%*! up and there you are! In spite of the acne, the girls thought he was called Face because he was so good looking.

Some names Chip knew not from whether the nickname came. Knute, Tay Boy, Cracker, Ji Bo, Moe, Pecker, Goose, Cab, Squirrely, Horse, Corky, Fats, Dog, (Dog's brother, Pup), Pudge, Fritz, Kraut, Popcorn, Steamshovel, Pickles, and Pistol were just a few. One person, whose real last name was Smith, was called Keener. Everybody said he looked like a Keener so they called him Keener. Chip couldn't remember his first name.

Charles was nicknamed Chazzy. Someone found out that Chaz was a nickname the upper crust society used for Charles. Our Charles was anything but upper crust and debonair so he was renamed Chazzy, a name he hated just as well.

Philip was nicknamed Phyllis. This came about one day when a gang of boys where outside Philip's house trying to get him to come out and play ball with them. Philip was busy inside trying to finish lunch and finish watching an episode of "Sky King" on TV.

"Hey, Phyllis," it was Philip's best friend, Frankie, "Ask your mom if you can finish ironing the clothes after the ball game."

Now all the rest of the guys took up the taunting too. "Yeah come on, Phyllis it's gonna be too hot to play afterwhile."

Finally Phillip had had enough. He stomped out on the porch and shook his finger at the gang around the porch. "Listen, you little punk jamisons , the next one of you pukes call me Phyllis, I'll beat to a pulp. You got that?"

Everything got deathly quiet. Frankie, looking forelorn and ashamed, stepped up on to the porch step and looked at Phillip in a sideways glance. It was he who spoke first, "Ok, Ok", he pleaded. "Geez, no need to get so ticked off at everyone.......PHYLLIS!" The place broke out in raucous laughter. Phyllis became the name that could have died on Phillip's porch that day if he'd just left it alone.

Rarely was anyone referred to by their last name unless they shared the same nickname. You would have to make it clear if you were talking about Preacher Adkins, instead of Preacher Frame or Preacher Griffith. Same for Shorty Jones or Shorty Morris or for Jake Woods or Jake Conner.

One girl was nicknamed Doody because her greeting to everyone she met was always, "Howdy".

Your nickname stayed with you your whole life, even if you moved away. An eighty year old man was still called Sunshine by those who were still close to him. A ninety year old woman was still known as "Chatty". Nicknames were even included in obituaries so the public would know exactly who had died: Milton "Big Tator" Brown of Canton, Ohio, formerly of Red Dog, WV, died at home Sunday, May 12. He was 83. Survivors include his wife "Dimple", two sons "Professor" of Canton and "Cat Gut" of

Red Dog, one daughter "Gypsy" Demoss of Charleston, WV and two brothers "Little Tator" of Red Dog and "Bad Eye" of Lodi, Ohio.

In the summer of 1963, Mr. Gates took Chip, Riley, and Clint to Washington DC, to see the sights. While they were still in the area before returning home, Mr. Gates remembered a close friend whom he had worked with in the mines at Red Dog and who had moved to Alexandria, VA. Chip's dad figured he'd stop by and visit Steamshovel Johnson while they were in the vicinity. When they got to Alexandria, Mr. Gates stopped at a service station where there was a public phone and an Alexandria phone book. Try as he might, Chip's dad couldn't recall Steamshovel's real first name. He wracked his brain over and over but couldn't come up with it. He looked in the book for Steamshovel Johnson, knowing it would not be there. Then he thought if he looked at all the first names of all the Johnsons listed in the book, it would come to him. There was only about a thousand Johnsons listed in the Alexandria area. Mr. Gates just got back in the car and headed home.

Chip watched the four deer as they finally sauntered back into the woods and then he turned his attention back to the valley that lay before him.

The little country road that led in and out of the Sugar Tree Valley held a fascination for Chip that was hard to explain. It was almost like it had a magical quality about it that attracted the adventurous side of him. This began when Chip was but a young lad. The more he thought about it, the more he realized that most of his adolescent and teenage experiences revolved in some way around that little ribbon of asphalt.

County Rt.11 was just a little one lane, paved road, but to Chip it was much more. To him it was his first real connection with the world outside Sugar Tree. Sure, there was radio and TV and the telephone, but all of those, except for the telephone (of which Chip didn't have access), were a link to places and people he knew only as names. They were places he had never visited and they were people he would never meet. This little road however, led to real places and the people that traveled it were real people; people that Chip knew and who knew Chip. Even when an occasional stranger passed by, Chip knew it was a real live person going to or coming from a real live place. Throughout his young life this little road would beckon him to explore its destinations and to partake of the experiences it had to offer. Before there was natural gas in Sugar Tree, before electricity, and before the telephone, the first modern convenience of Sugar Tree's civilization was Rt. 11.

The paved part of the road was only eight feet wide. The berm that skirted along both sides of the road consisted of gravel, dirt, or red dog or a combination of the three. The berm of the road, or the shoulder as it is called in some circles, was four feet wide in some places and some places where the creek had washed the road bank away or mud and rocks had slid off the side of the hill, the berm could be any where from four feet down to nothing. When two vehicles met they had to yield one half of the road to their counterpart. There were only a few places where that might be a problem. One of them was the aforementioned no berm to drive off on to and the other one was where there might be a one or two foot drop off to the berm due to a wash out or where some type of excavation had occurred and the berm was never filled back in.

The folks who lived in and around Sugar Tree and traveled the road frequently knew where those hazards were located and if they met another vehicle there, one or the other would pull off before the hazard and wait so the opposing vehicle could pass and not have to get off of the road until there was room for both to pass.

Of course sometimes drivers just didn't have the luxury or the time to pull off where they would like. Your choice would be to hit the other car head on or get off on the berm and take your chances. If a driver went off on the berm at one of these bad places and didn't go over the hillside or hit the road bank, they might have to drive a hundred or two hundred feet on the berm before they could find a safe and smooth place to get back on the road.

This designed configuration of the road kept most drivers at a safe speed of between thirty and thirty-five miles per hour during day light hours. At night speeds increased considerably because drivers were somewhat forewarned of oncoming vehicles by the flash and reflection of their headlights. There were always a few hot rodders and those who seemed to always drive with reckless abandon no matter what time of day.

Because Rt.11 was the only paved road in the Sugar Tree area, it was referred to as "the hardroad". All of the other roads that branched off of Rt. 11/1 were dirt or gravel roads.

Traveling directions to strangers always included "the hardroad". "Well, you go down here to where the hardroad crosses a little wooden bridge, then turn left at the first mailbox." "Go down this road until you come to the hardroad then turn right and go two miles. You can't miss it."

The hardroad was also a reference point for local conversations. "Kelly Rhodes wrecked his motorsickle last night."

"Where was he?"

"You know where the hardroad's got that big dip in it at the bottom of Renzee White Hill. He met a truck there and when he went off on the berm, his sickle slid in the gravel and went into the culvert. He didn't get hurt none but tore up the sickle pretty bad."

103

In the fifties, the hardroad was a tar and chip mixture. In the summer, when the temperature rose above ninety degrees, the tar would melt and separate from the gravel and form little pools on the road surface. Passing cars and trucks would run through the tar and sling it all over the bottom of the vehicle. It was hard work for Chip to clean the tar off of the bottom of the Gates' Mercury in the summer, but it also meant that the tar was ready for other amusements. When the tar was hot enough, Chip would twirl a stick around in it long enough to get a good size glob on the end. He would take it to the creek and hold it in the water to cool it off or just leave it in the shade for awhile. Once it was cool, he could mold it into a ball and use it to play home run derby at the Lick Run school playground. As long as it stayed cool, the tar ball worked pretty well. He never used it with a ball glove of any kind. Pools of tar on the hardroad were also good to stick objects in so they would stand up in the middle of the road. Drivers often times rounding a curve or topping over a hill might find a large stick or a small tree branch sticking up in the middle of the road. Beer cans and pop bottles turned upside down would also appear from time to time, just standing up in the middle of the road.

From the time the hardroad first became a fixture in Chip's life, he envisioned the day when it would evolve into a real honest-to-goodness, viable, and crucial thoroughfare. In the Gates brothers' minds that could never happen until Rt.11 was paved into a two lane road. Never mind that the road didn't lead to or from anywhere important. Never mind that only fifty or sixty vehicles passed over it in a day. Never mind that it was just a county road. The most important factor in the boys' minds was that this road could never achieve any status until it became a two lane road like US Rt. 19.

US Rt. 19 had double yellow lines, dotted lines, and combinations of single/dotted lines. It even had a little white line painted along both edges of the road to show drivers where the berm was. You didn't even need to use the berm on 19 because it was so wide. Chip figured it was a least twenty-four feet wide from shoulder to shoulder. Tractor trailer trucks could pass each other with plenty of room to spare. Rt.19 had guard posts with little "cat eye" reflectors in them along its roadside. The guard posts had two stands of cable running through them to catch and hold vehicles and keep them from going over the hillside. The state highways were just as good as the US highways. In fact you generally couldn't tell one from the other when traveling on them. Rt.11 had none of these amenities.

The Gates brothers made it a point to check on the progress of upgrading Rt. 11 anytime they saw or heard anything or anybody connected with the State Road Commission.

Guys would come over to put up the school zone signs in the fall and the Gates brothers would make it a point to check with them. "Hey, mister. Going to put in a two lane?"

Maybe a work force of high school boys would come along cutting the brush and picking up trash along the road. The Gates' would look for the guy wearing the white hard hat. "Hey, mister. Puttin' in a two lane?"

Any type of work on Rt.11 brought the boys out for the inevitable question. State road workers who would be but passing by their home were interrogated. Cleaning the ditch line, patching holes, putting up or taking down road signs, grading and filling in the berm, all might be preparations for a two lane paving operation.

This time really could be the time. They didn't want to miss it and they wanted to be the first ones who found out so they could go around and tell all of those who were waiting so anxiously for the momentous event.

As if to placate the Gates' for their concern and diligence of Rt.11's fortunes, the State Road always asked for and received permission to park their equipment in the wide place beside the Gates' garage across the road from their house.

Now those guys had to know that curious and inquisitive young boys would eventually find their play time culminating around these machines but they didn't waver in their decision. "Hey boys. Run over and ask your mom and dad if it would be ok to park our equipment over here tonight."

The Gates' always consented and so after many years, neither Chip or Riley actually went to the house and asked their mom or dad permission. They just pretended to. Then they would come back and tell the State Road guys, "Yeah, they said you could park your stuff there as long as you needed to. We would be glad to keep an eye on things for you. Don't worry. Nothin' or nobody will bother your stuff."

Theodore Gates would come home from work, "Why in the world does the State Road always have to park that stuff across the road? Don't they have anywhere else to put it?"

As the brothers got older, their play around the State Road equipment grew bolder and developed from just climbing on and around the equipment, to eventually climbing up into the cab of the grader or the control seat of the roller and pushing and pulling levers. They could grade and roll Rt.11 from Sugar Tree to Hob in about twenty minutes and never leave the parking spot across the road. Other times the roller became a great ship that sailed the broad Ohio River with Chip at the helm. The grader was transformed into a rocket ship that carried the boys on explorations to distant planets.

When that play got old, they began to invite other neighborhood kids to come and join in the fun. They were so assured that the State Road would make its usual stopover on the Gates' property that they would invite kids to come on over as soon as they spotted any equipment work in that area of Sugar Tree.

Now the Gates brothers had been around that equipment for many years and had watched the State Road men come in the mornings to start up their machines and warm them up before going out to work. It seemed like it took them ten or fifteen minutes of concentrated effort before they finally got those intricate pieces of machinery running.

One late evening, Junior Dodrill showed up with the rest of the neighborhood kids to scramble around on the equipment. Junior was a couple of years older than Chip and though he was still in grade school, he could drive a car and handle any type of firearm as well as an adult.

Junior was the "Eddie Haskell" of Sugar Tree, only Junior was about three times as nasty and despicable as Eddie was. He was no respecter of social class or age. He aggravated everybody the same. It was very difficult to get back at Junior because of his older sister, Jeannie. Junior aggravated Jeannie just as much as anyone else, so it was very surprising that she always took up for him. Chip figured it must have been the same malicious Dodrill gene in

106

her too, and by taking up for Junior, it allowed her to let that mean streak come out.

Jeannie was three years older than Chip.. She was five feet eleven inches tall and weighed about one hundred and eighty-pounds and she was fearless. She was quick to attack anybody, boy or girl, anytime they messed with Junior. Nobody ever messed much with Junior except when trying to get back at him for some wrong doing. But everybody learned quickly that retaliation and revenge could only be exacted when Jeannie wasn't around. Junior knew this too, so when he would pull one of his "stunts" on someone, he'd hightail it to whereever Jeannie happened to be, and stay close to her until he figured the urge to avenge the wrong had passed to a lesser degree.

Chip learned that lesson early on. Junior had borrowed Chip's brand new sponge ball at school to play "antne-over" and the first thing he did was throw the new ball down the school house chimney. Chip was mad but decided to slip up the road when school let out that evening, and confront Junior on his way home.

It was a good plan and when Junior got a good distance from the school, Chip stepped out from behind a rock beside the road and met Junior face to face.

Chip never had a chance. Jeannie never said a word, never waited for an explanation nor a "let's talk this thing over". She stepped in front of Chip and landed a right hand hook to Chip's jaw that sent him reeling off into the brush at the side of the road. Before he could gain his footing, Jeannie began peppering him with rocks. He managed to get to his feet and continue running in the direction Jeannie had sent him flying, but even the ever widening gulf between Jeannie and him didn't seem to lessen the sting and knocks that the whizzing sand rocks had on the back of his head.

Junior usually didn't hang around much with a bunch of little "snot noses" as he called the younger bunch, but on this particular evening, the lure of heavy equipment was too much for him. He and Chip climbed up into the cab of the road grader and closed the big glass side door.

107

Junior looked around at all the gauges and knobs and levers and gear shifts and pedals then reached down to the instrument panel and pushed one of the black buttons. The grader gave a little jerk, the engine coughed and chugged and roared to life, spewing black diesel smoke from it's front exhaust stack. All the kids scattered like a bunch of chickens running for their lives. Chip and Junior bailed out of the cab of the grader and headed for home. Clint ran on into the house and into his bedroom and hid under the bed. Chip was able to chase Riley down and grab hold of him before he got in the house. Chip managed to calm him down enough to get him to walk with him back out to the end of the driveway. They looked across the road. The place was deserted of humans. Everybody had headed home at break neck speed. When Chip looked up the road he caught the last glimpse of Junior going out of sight around the curve at the upper end of the straight. The road grader sat there all by itself still idling away.

Chip didn't know what to do. He couldn't let the thing run all night. Mama or Mom or Dad would surely notice it. Maybe he could just let it run and it would run out of fuel in a little while. Then again if it didn't, the men would come to work tomorrow and it would still be running and Chip knew they would never, ever park their stuff there again. If he went over there and tried to turn it off he might cause it start moving or grading or something and then what would he do? He could go get Junior and make him turn the thing off but Chip realized Junior didn't know anymore about the thing than he did.

"Come on Riley", Chip urged, "let's just go over and look around in it a little. Maybe we can figure out how to turn it off."

Riley grabbed Chip by the arm and hung on to it. "Noooo", he began to wail, "don't go over there. You'll be killed!" There was terror in his eyes and in his voice. "Please. I'll tell Dad and he'll fix it."

Chip was getting bolder now. "Don't be stupid. If you tell Dad, first he'll beat our hind ends off with the belt and then he'll tell the State Road and they'll never, park their stuff here again. Now turn me loose. I'm going over there." He jerked loose from Riley.

Riley fell to his knees. Big tears rolled down his cheeks. "Oh don't go Chip. For God sakes, don't go over there. Just don't do it." He covered his eyes with his hands so he couldn't see.

Riley's pleas began to fade as Chip drew closer to the grader. He just stood there awhile looking up at the cab. Just go slow, he told himself. Don't make any sudden moves. Don't touch anything that looks like it's not for holding on to.

He eased himself up the ladder and stood on it while looking into the cab. His eyes were about level with the cab floor. He scanned everything in a slow, deliberate fashion but from where he stood he could see nothing that offered a solution to the problem. He eased himself up into the cab and slipped in behind the huge steering wheel. He stood up behind it just like he had seen the men do when they ran the grader. From here he could look completely over the instrument panel.

On the far right of the panel he spied a toggle switch that was larger than the other toggle switches and it was in the "on" position. He figured that whatever this switch controlled, it would do nothing if it were turned "off". "Off " means it doesn't work. Whether it turned the engine off or not Chip wasn't sure but "off "was still better than "on" no matter what it was. Maybe someone had bumped it on without knowing it while they were playing around up there.

With his heart pounding he reached through the spokes of the steering wheel, touched the switch, closed his eyes and flipped it down. The grader kept on running.

He looked for another "on" switch. Any "on" switch. He found four more smaller switches in the "on" position. He didn't hesitate this time. He quickly flipped each one to the "off " side and the engine died.

He looked across the road for Riley but Riley wasn't there. Instead he saw his mom standing on the porch. Her arms were crossed and there was a wooden stirring spoon sticking up out of one hand. She had her apron on and was glaring across the road at the kid in the road grader. Chip didn't move and in a moment his mom turned and went back into the house.

Chip's mom never mentioned the road grader incident to anyone as far as he knew and that was perfectly alright by him because he never mentioned it to anyone either.

There was one piece of State Road Commission equipment that struck such horror in the Gates boys' hearts, that Clint was tormented by nightmares every night it was parked across the road. When this monstrosity was parked alongside the rest of the equipment, the boys would not even venture to cross the road. It was frightening enough just to stand in the front yard, behind the hedge, and stare at it from a distance in daylight. After dark they wouldn't even go out into the yard. It was the "TAR MACHINE", a hideously mutant piece of machinery.

The tar machine had no lively color at all in its make up. It was black, a dirty black and yet shiny in some way. It was so dark black that it was hard to discern its edges and compartments and boundaries, especially from such a safe distance away. It had no symmetry to its shape. Wheels were located where they couldn't be of any practical use and whatever form of motivation the tar machine used to move around was hidden deep beneath the low slung creature.

It had a huge gaping mouth that traversed its entire front. The tar machine should have smelled of tar but instead it had an odor that could be best described as human sweat mixed in with some week-old horse manure. But the most disturbing characteristic of the tar machine was the great black, oozy, drops of tar that hung from every rail, edge, and surface of the monster. In Clint's nightmares, they were real drops of blood. Blood from other little boys that had wandered too close to the tar machine and had been devoured. Blood that still dripped from it's hideous, clanking mouth as it chased after Clint across the familiar hillsides of home. In the daylight it appeared as if something or someone had dumped a cauldron of blood over the thing and even in its apparently dormant state, it crouched low in the tall grass across the road waiting to snatch the first unsuspecting kid that passed too close. Clint's nightmares were like an omen to the brothers and although neither Chip nor Riley ever experienced such dreams as Clint, the foreboding thoughts of the tar machine's character were stored in a little corner of their minds for reference.

110

If the tar machine was Clint's scar in his psychological makeup, Bucky and Lewis Keener's hot rods were Riley's.

While they were running the Esso station in Sugar Tree, the Keener brothers each built their own hot rod. Both of the hot rods were '38 Ford coupes. The doors had been welded shut, the glass had all been removed except for the windshield, and the fenders had been removed. The front grill had been removed and the engine compartment was open on both sides with the hood still intact covering the engine, which was a flat head V8. The hot rods ran stock, straight tread tires on the front and back. The Keener boys had built a roll cage inside and even added a seat belt. The hot rods both were ready to run on any dirt track in the state. One of the hot rods was painted baby blue with a yellow "1" on the side. The other hot rod was yellow and had a "2" painted in baby blue on the side. None of the Gates knew which one belong to which brother.

The first time the two hot rods blasted past the Gates' farm it scared Riley so badly he never got over it. The boys were playing out in the yard that afternoon when they heard a muffled rumble coming from around the bend down the road. As was the custom, the boys dropped whatever it was they were doing and hurried on out to the front yard to catch a glimpse of whatever it was coming up the road.

Suddenly, these two hot rods burst around the bend in the road and thundered up the straight past the Gates' place. The two cars were running single file, one behind the other and the noise level was so deafening it seemed to make the ground tremble beneath their feet. There was orange and blue flame and sparks flying out of the large megaphone exhaust header on the side of each hot rod. With rocks and dirt scattering like leaves after the wind, the Keener brothers ran wide open up the little straight. They had come around the bend and upon the Gates boys so fast they really didn't have time to see everything they wanted to see, except for Riley and he saw and heard too much. He covered his ears with his hands and ran screaming back towards the house. He ran right past the house and on up through the orchard and kept on going, all the while his hands over his ears and screaming like a child possessed.

111

Chip and Clint stood looking up the road trying to take in as much of the race as they could before the two land rockets disappeared around the bend. Then they decided to go look for Riley. While they were up in the orchard looking for Riley, the hot rods came roaring back down the road heading for home. That was the first and only time Chip and Clint missed the return trip. Wherever the hot rods were headed, their origin was the Esso station in Sugar Tree and that's where they would have to return. The boys never knew when the hot rods would be racing by; morning, evening, Sunday or Thursday, but after that first experience they could tell when they were coming from the first distant rumble of engines.

Riley developed a sixth sense when it came to the hot rods. He was like Radar O'Riley on M*A*S*H. He could tell when the hot rods were coming long before their sound gave them away. He would start screaming and running. "They're coming! They're coming! Oh my God, they're coming!" Sometimes he'd just run around in ever widening circles. Other times he'd run for the orchard.

Chip and Clint ran too but they ran out to the road to get a good close look, hear, and smell of the hot rods. Sometimes it was really dangerous because on a couple of occasions Lewis and Bucky would be running side by side on the little one lane road and the dirt and rocks would be flying helter-skelter. Because neither would give up the road, both had to run with one set of wheels on the road and one set on the berm.

As fascinating and as set up as they were, Bucky and Lewis never raced their hot rods on a dirt track or a drag strip anywhere, only on Rt. 11. Another strange thing Chip remembered about the hot rods was the fact that of all the hundreds of times he had been in and around the Esso station, he never ever saw the hot rods there. If fact, he never saw them anywhere else except when they sped by his house.

Some said that first hot rod experience was so traumatic to Riley that it just screwed him up for life. Clint and Chip knew better. They knew there were two other things that had screwed with Riley's mind before the hot rods. One was the Whippoorwill that came every spring and sat on the barn roof and

Whippoorwilled all through the night. The haunting call of the Whippoorwill on those quiet, spring nights filled the Lick Run valley and was disturbing enough by itself, but one night Riley's dad took him outside to show him the bird. They quietly sneaked up to the barn and Theodore shined the flashlight on the bird. There it was; a big ball of feathers with a huge red eye blinking at them. From then until he was eight years old, nights of the Whippoorwill were spent sleeping with Mom and Dad.

The other bit of mind altering material was a record album cover that Mr. Gates had bought. It was a Les Paul album entitled "The New Sound" and on the cover there was a picture of Les Paul with eight arms and he was playing four guitars. Riley never got over that picture. The hot rods just added to the growing anxiety in the young fellow's life.

II

As a youngster, Chip was warned numerous times to stay in the yard and away from the road, but anytime there was noise that gave the slightest hint that a large truck was coming along the road, Chip dropped whatever he was doing and ran out to the front yard to catch a glimpse of the vehicle. He was as interested in where it was from as what kind it was.

Usually it was just local; someone to wave at or holler to. Sometimes though, it would have its place of origin painted on the side; produce from Seneca, Clendenin, Mills Bottom, Charleston, Clarksburg, Gauley Bridge, & Richwood. Furniture and household appliances from Sutton, Webster Springs, Weston, Jillpoke, Parkersburg, and Fairmont. Logs from Cowen, Little Elk, Hico, & Lookout. Mining equipment from Beckley, Prince, Gassaway, Morgantown, and Spencer. Exotic places all. Chip made it one of his lifetime goals to one day travel down old Rt.11 to each and every one of those places and get to know them firsthand.

He loved sitting on the front porch of Grandma's house and watching the vehicles passing by on Rt.11. His Aunt Eleanor could tell whose car or truck was coming even before it came into view just by the sound of it. She was right about ninety percent of the time. Aunt Eleanor spent a lot of time on the porch watching the traffic.

Sunday afternoon was the best time for sitting on the porch and watching traffic. After Sunday dinner, the whole family moved out on the porch. Sunday traffic was slow and casual around Sugar Tree and the reason was practical. Sunday afternoon was a time for visiting. If a family was driving by a house slowly and the folks that lived there were outside on the porch or in the yard, then the driver would slow to a stop and a visitation would commence. Sometimes the conversation would be from the car in the road to the porch at the house. If it was more than a casual visit, the folks on the porch would all mosey out to the car. Some would be leaning on the car at every window conversing with someone inside while others just might be standing by the edge of the road talking. Visitation would last until another slow moving car came upon the group and the first driver would have to move on. Maybe the second car would stop for a short visit since there was a group already out at the road or maybe it would just move on.

Sometimes a car would deliberately pull off the road in front of the house to see if anyone was out on the porch. If there were, maybe the folks in the car would get out, maybe they wouldn't.

There was another reason why Sunday traffic was slow and casual. Suppose a family got in their car and decided to make it a point to go visit a specific neighbor. You couldn't be sure that the neighbor would be home. They might be out visiting too and there could be the possibility that you might pass each other on the road. If you drove slow enough, you would be able to recognize the occupants in the oncoming car with enough warning to flag them down. Then both families could visit whilst setting side by side in the middle of the road. This practice was very common on Sunday around the Sugar Tree area.

There was an unwritten law that residents of Sugar Tree seemed to abide by on Sundays. If you were a driver of a vehicle that came upon two cars setting side by side in road visiting, you stopped at such a distance from the two that you couldn't eavesdrop on their conversation, and far enough away so as not to seem to crowd them or hurry them along. You just sat patiently waiting, not blowing the horn or slowly creeping closer to them but respecting their privacy for the moment. If you were the driver of one of the vehicles stopped in the middle of the road talking and another vehicle approached you slowly, you would finish as quickly as possible whatever conversation needed to be concluded. You never cut anyone off short but neither did you ramble on at the expense of the waiting vehicle. Sometimes if the visitation was important enough, the two cars would separate enough to let the other vehicle pass through. Everyone exchanged pleasantries then they would pull back together on the road again to complete their visit. This was but another reason that traffic moved slowly along on Sunday. You just never knew when you might run upon some folks visiting in the middle of the road. Whether they were in their cars or standing around in a group by the edge of the road, you surely didn't want to run over them.

As Chip and his brothers got older, restrictions concerning the road laid down by their   parents began to disappear. As their restrictions fell by the way, their fear and caution began to wane as well and the road became their avenue to entertainment and a social life.

Chip remembered when the first rural delivery of the mail came to the Lick Run Valley. Before, the Gates' always had to pick up their mail at the Sugar Tree Post Office. But now it was delivered right to the front gate by Wilburt Sattler. Wib, as he was called, began the mail route driving a 1946 Chevy, half ton pickup. If Wib happen to see any of the boys out in the yard or close by when he delivered or picked up the mail, he'd blow the horn and wave them on over to the truck. They would hop on the running board and ride up or down the road to the next mail box on the route, depending on which way Wib was headed. That went on for three or four years until Wib bought a '55 Ford pickup. It had no running boards. By that time the boys were too old to be hanging on the side anyway. Wib delivered the mail on that route for forty-six years before retiring.

Another treat the boys looked forward to in their early days of road entertainment came twice a month from the NuWay Laundry truck. The NuWay Cleaners were located in Weston but they sent a Laundry truck along the Sugar Tree route every other Wednesday. The people around Sugar Tree had a big NuWay Laundry sign that they would stick up in a front window or on the side of the house so the laundry driver could see the sign from the road. If the sign was up, he was suppose to stop and pick up some laundry. Of course if he had clean clothes to deliver he'd stop anyway.

The NuWay Laundry driver always threw a handful of Double Bubble bubble gum to the kids he'd spy along the route. The more kids he saw, the more bubble gum he'd throw. Chip and his brothers didn't get to see the NuWay truck in the winter. He ran on Wednesday afternoons when the guys were in school. During the summer it seemed too much work to try and keep track of which Wednesday he was coming and besides there was always something else to do. However, if someone in the community put a sign out early in the morning or happened to mention that it was laundry day, then the kids in the neighborhood got the word out.

A little after 1:00 in the afternoon, the Gates boys, Maynard and Elihu, and Junior and his sister, would all walk up the road about a

116

quarter of a mile above Junior's house to his next door neighbor. They would hang out there until the Laundry truck would come by. He'd throw out two or three handfuls of bubble gum. Two of the urchins would stay behind to pick up the bubble gum while the rest of the crew would run down the road to Junior's house and set up. This worked best if the driver threw the gum out first and then stopped at the house to pick up or deliver the laundry. That would give the whole gang time enough to run on ahead to the next house and get ready. They could only work this scam within two or three houses. After that, the distances became too far and the kids became too tired. Besides it would be time to hand over "the bubble gum con" to the next crew down the road. They could really make a bubble gum killing if the driver had to stop at more than two houses in a row. After the driver had passed on down the road, the gang would divide up the bubble gum among the participants. Chip wondered if the driver of the NuWay Laundry truck thought there were hundreds of little kids living in those few houses on his route.

III

The first mode of travel around and about Sugar Tree was by foot. Hitch-hiking or thumbing (short for thumbing-a-ride) was forbidden in those early years by Chip's parents and to tell the truth, it never entered Chip's mind as an option for getting around until a little later in his teen years. Besides, a nine year old might miss something adventurous if he was traveling in a car with no way to stop and explore.

By the time he was eleven, Chip and the gang were walking everywhere. The composite number and make up of the gang changed from time to time. Sometimes Riley went with the guys and sometimes Maynard's brother Elihu tagged along. A few times even Junior Dodrill hung out with the guys, but mostly it consisted of four close friends; Chip, Maynard, Benji, and Lincoln Parks.

Lincoln Parks lived around at Sugar Tree and was the same age as Benji. Link was an only child. Link's family was not from Sugar Tree. They had moved in about two years earlier from Elkins when Link's dad, who was a mining engineer, was hired on as an engineer for WYGARB at the Red Dog mine operations. They bought a ten year old house that sat on a little piece of property on Painter's Fork in Sugar Tree. That house had gone up for sale because the family that used to live there had to move back to their parent's old farm when the father was injured in a mining accident at Red Dog and was no longer able to work in the mines.

Link's mother was a teacher and went right to work teaching at the elementary school in Red Dog. In the income standards of Sugar Tree, the Parks were rich folks. Link's parents were always dressing up and going out to high class affairs in Charleston and to their old haunts in Elkins on the weekends. They held patio parties and cocktail parties at their home for strange guests that came from parts unknown. They hired Icie Given, a fifty-five year old widowed saint who lived next door to them, as a housemaid to clean and do the laundry and serve as a maid for the Park's dinner parties and gatherings. Icie kept the house and grounds immaculate.

Benji and Lincoln met because they were in the same grade at Sugar Tree Elementary and since they both lived in "uptown"

Sugar Tree, they just gravitated together. Chip and Maynard met Link through Benji and eventually they became the gang.

Even though Link was not a Sugar Tree native he was a West Virginian, so it made his acceptance into the gang a little easier. Actually, Link was an easy person to get to know and easy to get along with. Maybe because he had no siblings to share and fight and buddy with, he was eager to make friends and to fit in. He couldn't play basketball. Didn't like football. He had little interest in sports in general but would play a little softball once in awhile. He could listen to rock and roll but it didn't do anything for him. He had no interest in cars whether it be the real thing, magazines, or models. He would go hunting and fishing with the guys but wasn't very good at either. He said he just liked to go so he could get out in nature. So all the things that motivated this adolescent gang, were of no real significance to Lincoln Parks.

He did have two vices and one obsession. One of his vices was reading. Lincoln had his nose stuck in a book every free minute of the day and night. His weakness here was MAD Magazine and he was so versed in that crazy world that he could recite story after story, panel after panel, month after month, word for word. He would entertain the rest of the guys hours on end, spinning those tales. Anytime the gang was at his house, they always had to find a good MAD Magazine story to act out or even better, record the story on Link's portable tape recorder with each guy playing the different parts, using different voices.

Link's other vice was the attraction to the opposite gender, and as Link grew older, this vice became the chink in his armor. The bounce of a long blond curl or the coo of the female voice could pull Link out of the most intense endeavor the gang might be involved in. He would just kind of slip away and before you knew it, he would be puttin' the moves on some girl who happened along. Link never had a steady girl until he was a senior in high school and he wound up married to her, but he must have dated every girl in the tri county area. He was smooth no doubt, but it was his obsession that actually went a long way in making Link the ladies' man that he was. He never hit on girls who had a steady boyfriend or who were dating someone routinely. However he was always ever ready to console a brokenhearted damsel before she had time to repine her lost romance.

Lincoln Parks obsession; neatness. He was meticulous. Everything about him had to be perfect. His hair was perfect. When it went from a DA, to a flattop, to the Steve McQueen look it was perfect.

Because his folks were well off and he was their only child, Link always had the best in shirts, slacks, jeans, shoes, underwear, and socks. He had a pair of wing tip dress shoes, five sports jackets and two hand tailored suits. His clothes always matched perfectly and were always immaculately kept. The toughest job Ms Icie Given had at the Parks' residence was to keep Lincoln's clothes always perfect.

Everything he owned was perfect. His bike was always clean and shiny. His dog, Domino, was always clean and shiny and smelled better than Maynard. Link had the best of everything money could buy and that turned out to be a godsend for the gang. When they decided to go camping for instance, after scraping together whatever they might need, they could always count on Mr. Parks contributing beyond what might otherwise be necessary. The gang never asked for anything extra and never expected to always get extras. They expected Link to contribute his fair share same as everyone else, whatever the mission or the undertaking was.

At opportune times the rest of the guys used Link's meticulousness to try to get his goat. Sometimes it worked beautifully and other times Link acted like he was too cool to be riled up.

Take the time Link left his bicycle overnight at Benji's. The three had all decided to stay at Benji's house overnight and Link had ridden his bike down to Benji's. The next morning Link's parents came by to pick him up because he had a dentist appointment. When he got back to Benji's from the dentist that afternoon, he found his bicycle in the basement. The guys had completely dismantled the bike and laid out every piece very neatly side by side in order of assembly on the basement floor. Link went berserk. The guys figured it had something to do with the medication he might have been given at the dentist. Link ran around the basement like a madman hurling obscenities and death threats and taking swings at whichever one he could get the closest to. The guys were able to keep out of range of Link's wild swings by running and dodging around in the basement but their laughter kept him spurred on. Finally, when Link began to run out of steam, the other three piled on top of him and held him down until things calmed down. Then they helped him put the bike back together.

Link was the only one of the guys who never carried a handkerchief, (commonly referred to as a "snot rag"), or a bandanna. Link could blow his nose by laying a finger on one side of his nose and press that nostril closed. He'd lean his head over to the side of the open nostril, and casually give it a quick, hard snort, and blow it clear. Then he'd close off that nostril, lean over the other way, and clear the remaining nostril. No fuss, no muss, no bother. The rest of the guys tried it the first time they saw Link do it but not having the years of practice that Link had, it turned out to be pretty disgusting.

About this same time, one of the top hits on the radio was "True Love Story" by the Jive Five. The guys thought the name of the artists was really cool and they wanted to adopt it as the name for their unofficial gang. The problem was there were only four of them. So they called themselves the Jive Five Minus One.

Looking back on it now, Chip had come to the realization that there were actually five members of the gang because in many of their escapades, the good Lord himself or one of his angels had to have been with them, watching over them. They were truly the Jive Five.

By the time Chip was twelve, destination had become more important than the adventure, and catching a ride had become paramount. No one in the group as yet had begun to hitchhike because it was still forbidden. When walking the road, one always walked on the right hand with the traffic so if a driver did stop and offer a ride the walker would be on the side of the road that would make it easier for driver and walker to make a connection. The hope was always there that a driver would stop and pick up the walker. Here, a couple of dilemmas occurred. On the one hand, walking with a group of three or four meant it would be more likely that a driver passing by would know or recognize at least one of the group so they wouldn't be hesitant about picking up a stranger. On the other hand, not every one who passed by had the room to pick up three or four riders.

Walkers had another decision to make. Some walking distances could be cut in half if they took a short cut over a hill or through the woods. If they went by the short cut they knew they would have to walk all the way but the distance would not be as long and walking was easier in the shade and over soft ground. If they went by the road the distance would be twice as long but there was a chance somebody would come along and pick them up. If nobody stopped and gave them a lift, they would have to walk twice as far and it would be hotter, dustier, and more dangerous than taking the short cut.

Early walking experience for Chip and Maynard came when they joined the Boy Scout troop at Red Dog. Every Monday night for three years Chip hoofed it the four miles to Red Dog and then back. Maynard lived a half mile closer to Red Dog than Chip. Scout meetings were held every Monday night at 6:00 at the American Legion Hall from September until June. The Scouts didn't meet during the summer.

Sometimes the Scouts went on cookouts or attended campfires on Monday night instead of meeting at the Legion Hall in Red Dog. That meant that Chip and Maynard had to make the four miles over to Red Dog and then sometimes do another mile or so to wherever the cookout/campfire was being held. It was never held outside of WYGARB property.

Chip would leave home between 4:30 and 5:00 when it was still daylight and walk the half mile around to Maynard's to pick him up. Usually someone would stop and pick up the two walkers. Some rides took them just around the road to Sugar Tree. Some rides would take them to the top of Red Dog Hill and occasionally someone would take them all the way into Red Dog but more than a few times, they wound up walking all the way to Red Dog. Getting to Red Dog was never the real problem but getting home was.

Scout meetings were dismissed around 8:00. If the Scouts were out at a campfire, it might be as late as 9:00 before they were even back to Red Dog. With not much traffic moving that late in the evening, the boys almost always had to walk up the hill out of Red Dog and then walk the three and a half miles down off the ridge to Sugar Tree and around the road to home. Sometimes the parent of another Scout or the Scoutmaster would take the boys to the top of Red Dog Hill and let them out but that was not very often.

Benji joined the Scouts two years after Chip and Maynard did but he only lasted two months. Lincoln Parks was never much interested in Boy Scout stuff although the Girl Scouts seemed to pick his interest.

Because Chip was an accepted outsider in Red Dog and because Maynard was Chip's friend, he was accepted into the Red Dog Scout troop with little confrontation and eventually was allowed to mingle freely with the Red Dog teens with little harassment. The two boys felt at ease then passing through the streets of Red Dog at night except for going up "colored holler" on their way out of town.

At first, the boys passed by with no problem probably because they were never noticed. Then one warm, autumn evening as they walked up the sidewalk in front of the row of twenty or so two story houses in the colored section, a couple of dogs started barking at them. When the owners of the dogs came out to investigate the noise, they were probably surprised to see two or three white boys walking up their street at that particular hour. White teens from Red Dog were never seen in colored town after dark unless they were up to something, so one or two residents thereof began yelling at the boys and questioning their motives. Before they knew it, black people from every house were coming out on the porch or yelling out the windows and every dog in the neighborhood was barking at them. That night they quickly hastened their departure from colored street and the town of Red Dog.

Every Monday night from then on the boys had to decide how best to get through colored holler and get on out of town. First thing, they would walk up to Grill and see if there were any cars parked out in the parking lot that belonged to anybody they knew from out of town. If there was, they might wait outside until the owner showed up and then ask him if they could catch a ride out of town. If there was no car in the parking lot that they readily recognized, they would just go inside The Grill and look around for somebody they might know from out of town. In either case if there was somebody they could ride out of town with, they might get to leave right away or they might have to wait an hour or so before the driver was ready to leave. If they had to wait more than an hour for a ride, they'd decided to just go ahead and take a chance on walking through town. If there was nobody there to catch a ride with they would go ahead and start walking up colored street.

Secondly, if they had to walk up colored street, they now walked up the middle of the street instead of on the sidewalk. There was less chance of being spotted and more of a chance to catch a ride if someone happened along. Sometimes the boys made it out of town quietly and sometimes they were verbally harassed all the way from one end of colored town to the other. They had already agreed that once they started up colored holler, no matter what happened they would not turn around and go back into town.

After a month or two of enduring this predicament, Chip began to realize that there was no maliciousness in the verbal harassment from the residents of colored town and that no threatening atmosphere existed except in the boys' imaginations. In fact it seemed almost to Chip that this once dreaded confrontation had become a form of entertainment for the black community. It was like they knew every Monday night, Chip and Maynard would be walking up their street unless they had caught a ride. There was always some laughter, snickering, and guffaws that followed the yelling and hollering from inside the houses. Then one night was heard, "Hey Gates, you better be gettin' your skinny little self on out of here." Chip recognized the voice as that of one of his classmates at Red Dog Jr. High, Tony Nash. Chip never mentioned the incident to Tony but after that, the boys had no qualms about walking through colored town no matter how late it was. They did however stay to the middle of the street instead of the sidewalk and never, though often tempted, hurl any comments back in response.

The boys always scraped up a little change before they headed off for Scout meetings and after Scout meeting, they always tried to stop off at The Grill to buy some pop, or gum or candy or something to eat or drink while they walked towards home.

One night Chip talked Maynard into buying cigars instead of something to eat. He said a cigar would last longer than food and it would afford them some entertainment on their walk home. Because they were Scouts and were always prepared. They had some matches with them and were lighting up before they were out of The Grill.

By the time they had walked halfway up colored holler, they were really starting to enjoy their smokes and were feeling pretty cocky when a car came along heading out of town. It stopped to pick the boys up. It was two door sedan so the front seat passenger had to lean forward and pull the rear part of the seat forward so the boys could slip in the back. They had just got their cigars going good and didn't want to throw them away and since they didn't want to take the time to put them out, they scrambled in the back still smoking them.

Chip didn't recognize the driver but did recognize the front seat passenger. It was Maynard's dad. He jabbed Maynard in the ribs with his elbow to get his attention but Maynard didn't pay any attention and it was obvious he didn't know his dad was in the car with them. He took a big drag off his cigar and as he exhaled the smoke he commented to the two up front, "Boy, sure am glad you stopped to pick us up. I'm tellin' you it's colder than a well digger's ass out there tonight, colder than a witch's tit, it is!"

Chip almost swallowed his cigar, and after regaining some composure, managed to slip his cigar out the rear side window while Ezra Samples was struggling to get the seat pulled up and the door shut. There was no need to get Maynard's attention anymore because as he settled back into the seat, Chip could see even in the dim passing light from the Red Dog street lights, the color drain from Maynard's face as the recognition of the front seat passenger began to sink in.

The driver was oblivious to the whole thing so he struck up a conversation to pass the time. "What you boys doin' out here this late at night?"

"We're just going home from Boy Scout meeting", answered Chip. The driver went on mumbling about when he was in Boy

Scouts but Chip just heard a word here and there. He was watching Maynard trying to get rid of his cigar. He quietly put it out in the rear seat ash tray. Mr. Samples never said a word the rest of the way home and neither did Maynard. Chip was sure Mr. Samples knew it was his son in the back seat cussin' and smokin' but he never let on like he did. Chip and the driver carried on a continuous conversation. If they kept on talking, then Maynard and his dad might not have to confront one another.

The driver was heading home, all the way to Hob so they came to Maynard's house first. Mr. Samples got out thanked the driver, Gilley, for the ride and said he'd see him tomorrow. Maynard never moved. He was now squenched as far back in the rear seat as possible. Mr. Samples closed the door and the driver pulled back onto the road.

Chip told Gilley where he lived just as they rounded the curve below the farm. Maynard got out with Chip and they both thanked Gilley for the ride. Gilley pulled out and headed on up the road to Hob, leaving Maynard and Chip standing in the middle of the road on this frosty, December night.

"See you tomorrow maybe", said Maynard as he started walking back down the road to his house. He took three steps, stopped, and started fishing around in his coat pocket. "Hey you got any more matches?", he asked, as he stuck his cigar stub in his mouth.

"Got one left", answered Chip. He dug it out of his shirt pocket, struck it on the back side of his pants leg, cupped his hands around it, and lit Maynard's cigar. "See yuh", he said. Maynard turned again and started back towards home.

As Chip left the road and started up the driveway to the house his mind kept trying to figure out what Maynard's actions could accomplish. Mr. Samples knew that his son went to Scout meetings on Monday night with Chip. He had also heard Chip tell everybody in the car that they had been to a Scout Meeting. When Maynard got home where was he going to tell his dad he had been? Not at Chip's house that's for sure. If he told his dad he was at the Scout meeting in Red Dog and was just getting home, who did he expect his dad to think that other person was in the back of Gilley's car? I don't know, thought Chip, maybe this was just Maynard's way of postponing the inevitable. Anyway that was Maynard's problem.

Junior Dodrill went with Maynard and Chip to Scouts only one time, and even then he had no intention of joining the scouts, he just wanted to go somewhere. That particular night happened to be a Monday in January, right after a weekend snow storm that left six to eight inches of soft snow on the ground. This was during Benji's two month tour of duty as a scout, so he was with them as well.

After Scouts that evening Maynard and Chip made their customary stop off at The Grill to get cigars and candy. Benji and Junior waited outside in the parking lot. Benji gave Chip some money to buy him a coke but Junior said he didn't want anything. He was saving his money to buy a '41 Ford or something.

Junior took advantage of the wait outside and of the perfect snow, to make a snowball. He instructed Benji to do the same. As soon as they were finished, Junior positioned himself behind a parked car directly across the lot from the front door of the grill.

"Come on over here Benji", he said. "As soon as Maynard or Chip opens that door we'll let him have it. They won't be able to see who it was that blasted them and we'll cut in back of the cars to where they left us. They'll never think it was us."

"Aw come on, Junior", answered Benji half-heartedly, "let it go. Let's just get our stuff and get on out of here".

"No, man. If you don't want to do nothin'. Then just stand over there and keep your mouth shut." He hunkered down behind a car.

Fifteen seconds later the front door swung open and two boys emerged from the yellow glow of The Grill's inside lighting. Junior stood up and fired and without waiting to see where the snowball landed, ran to the corner of the parking lot.

The snowball whacked the boy in front on the right side of his forehead just above the eye. The kid went reeling backwards into the guy behind him and they both fell in a heap in the doorway; right in front of Maynard and Chip as they were coming out.

The kid who was hit lay on the cold ground holding his head and moaning. The other one was already back on his feet and scraping snow off the hood of a parked truck and screaming at the two boys standing in a corner of the parking lot out by the street. "You little punks. I'll bury your butts for this," and he headed on a dead run right for them.

Junior's plan was doomed from the beginning. No matter what he and Benji did or where they hid, a blind person could tell they were the culprits because they were the only two people out there in that whole parking lot. Junior wasn't backing down. He was ready for a fight. He was looking for it. He ducked behind a car and in one motion, rapidly scraped together some snow into a snowball and began firing at the guy coming at him. Benji didn't know what to do. He wanted to run but he was afraid he'd miss Maynard and Chip. If he stayed where he was, he was gonna have to stand and fight. He jumped in behind Junior and started throwin' snowballs.

Under heavy fire from Junior and Benji, the lone Red Dog foe had to duck in behind a row of cars opposite Junior.

Two more from inside the grill pushed past Maynard and Chip and took up positions on either side of their buddy and began firing snowballs at Junior and Benji. They were high school students from Red Dog.

"What we gonna do?" whispered Maynard, poking his head out the door.

"Well, we can't leave them two out there alone to take on these guys, besides this might be fun. Come on", urged Chip, and they piled out the door and made a wide flanking circle to the left. They cut in behind a row of cars on the far side of the parking lot along the creek bank and finally joined Junior and Benji.

"Well, it looks like Sugar Tree against Red Dog", remarked Junior in between tosses.

"How did this get started?" demanded Chip.

"How else do you think?" replied Benji sarcastically.

"No matter now", interjected Maynard. "We got these boys on the defense."

Just then four more older guys came running out the door of The Grill and fanned out to up the advantage of the Red Dog crew.

Snowballs were flying like autumn leaves falling. Benji caught one blindsided right on the side of his head, knocking his toboggan off and filling his ear with snow and ice. That one had come from off to his left somewhere. Chip heard Benji's yell from the impact of the snowball and when he looked to his left, he saw at least six Red Dog guys across the street up on the MC & E backtrack making a flank attack. The Sugar Tree bunch had to move around in between cars which left them open from straight ahead. Red Dog recruits were coming out of The Grill like stirred up yellow jackets and taking their places on the firing line. The Red Dog assault now began to close in.

Junior crept back to the edge of the parking lot and dropped down along the creek bank in an effort to escape. The three remaining Sugar Tree combatants didn't see him leave. They were huddled together between two cars just trying to protect themselves from the onslaught. Suddenly they heard somebody yell, "Come on Sugar Tree. I'll help you."

Chip raised his head up to the window level of the car beside him and through the frosty windows he could see a flat bed truck sitting in the middle of the street. The truck was between them and the Red Dog guys coming down off the bank from the railroad tracks. The driver's window on the truck was open and he was frantically motioning for them to run to the truck.

As soon as Chip realized what was happening he dropped back down to the huddle. "Come on guys. This is our only hope. Let's get out of here". They bolted from out between the cars. They ran bent over as close to the ground as they could. It was but ten quick strides to the truck and it was already starting to move up the street, out of town. They swung up onto the back of the truck. "Go, baby, Go", yelled Maynard as he pounded the truck cab with his fist. "Hey, where's Junior?" They looked around frantically.

"There he is", pointed Benji, as the truck bumped across the bridge over Mossy Creek. The last glimpse the three had of Junior as they bounced on up the street out of town, he was wading for his life right down the middle of the creek while a barrage of snowballs and ice balls rained down on him as the Red Dog posse began closing in.

"Serves him right", mumbled Benji under his breath.

Maynard grew tired of stumbling around in the dark on the road between Red Dog and Sugar Tree so one night he carried a flashlight to Scout meeting. It would have been a good idea except at the Scout meeting that night it was decided to study Morris Code by turning all the lights out in the Legion Hall and sending messages from one end of the room to the other using Maynard's flashlight.

It turned out to be one of those evenings when the boys couldn't catch a ride and had to walk home. They didn't need the flashlight walking through Red Dog because there was some street lighting. Walking up the first half of Red Dog Hill wasn't too bad either because the night glow from Red Dog helped somewhat, but after they made the turn about half way up, it got dark. Really dark.

It was a cloudy and windy evening in late March. No moon or stars were visible in the night sky. The closer to the top of Red Dog Hill they got, the warmer the air became and the windier it got as well. There were no houses, no dwellings of any kind between the last house on colored street and the first house in Sugar Tree, a distance of three miles.

Chip and Maynard had no trouble walking in the dark until they got to the top of Red Dog Hill and started out the ridge. They hadn't gone but a couple hundred yards when they heard a rustling sound just up ahead. The rustling sounded like it was coming from a spot in the middle of the road. They weren't close enough to really see anything yet so being as quiet as they could, they crept a little closer. Maynard whipped out his flashlight and turned it on. The glow from one of the boys' cigar would have been brighter. All that Morris Coding had depleted the batteries.

Chip grabbed the flashlight from Maynard, unscrewed the bottom cap, dumped the batteries into his hand, licked the tip of each one, then put them back into the case and turned on the light again. Nothing.

The rustling stopped for a moment. Neither boy moved a muscle. Then the rustling started. "What we gonna do?", whispered Chip.

"Let's get closer", answered Maynard. He reached in his pocket and pulled out his pocket knife. "Got your knife?" he asked. Chip was already ahead of him. He was armed with his open Scout knife at the ready.

They inched closer, their knives held before them. A couple of steps closer and they could barely make out the large black form sitting in the road no more than twenty feet away. The form was

130

moving its head around like it was gnawing on something. The rustling sound came from that area.

Chip's hair stood up on the back of his neck. He tried to speak but nothing came out. "Oh Jesus". Maynard was almost crying. "It's a bear."

On shaky legs the two boys started to back up. Just then a car popped around a curve ahead of them. Its headlights swung around and caught the form in the road in a blinding glare. The car then swerved off unto the berm to miss the object in the road and the two boys standing there frozen in fear. With rocks and gravel flying, the car swung back onto the road behind them and sped away into the night, car horn blaring.

The bear turned out to be a very large cardboard box about the size a floor model TV set or a clothes dryer would fit in. When the wind blew, it would flop the top part of the open box back and forth and produce the rustling sound. Who would have figured a big old cardboard box to be sittin' in the middle of the road?

Once the situation was defused, Chip and Maynard were able to laugh and joke about it. They smashed the box flat, threw it off to the side of the road, then resumed their trek on to Sugar Tree.

Dead Man's Curve marked the halfway point down Sugar Tree Hill. Every mountain in WV probably has a dead man's curve. This curve had been called that as long as Chip could remember. He couldn't remember anyone ever telling how the curve got its name, but that was obvious. Before Chip finished high school, there would be two separate wrecks in dead man's curve that would take the life of two Red Dog high school students.

At Dead Man's Curve there is a rock cliff about twenty feet high that borders the road on the upper side of the hill. The boys were talking and joking as they passed by this area. As dark as it was that night, it seemed that the further down the hill they walked, the darker it got. All at once there came the sound of rocks and dirt falling off the top of the cliff and at almost the same instant, a small dark form whizzed across in front of Maynard's face, he was walking on the inside next to the cliff. It let out a short but high piercing scream just as it hit the road in front of the boys. Maynard matched the critter's scream with one of his own but his was much longer, louder, and more frightful. Chip made a long, round house swing with his right hand and hit Maynard flush on the side of the head and knocked him to the pavement. Chip didn't hit Maynard to bring him to his senses, though that would have sounded reasonable. He hit Maynard because when he screamed, he screamed right in Chip's ear, putting him deaf for the moment.

Whatever the critter was, it must have been scared off by Mayard's scream. The boys could hear the patter of its pads as it ran down the road ahead of them and then turned off the road, down over the hill, crashing through the brush and leaves.

Maynard was ok. "What'd you do that for?" he whined.

"Cause you 'bout put me deaf you jack ass."

"That's ok. Doesn't mean nothin' that I probably saved our lives."

"Yeah it would have been if that's what you were doing instead of peein' yourself. You sounded like some little scared girl."

"Easy for you to say. That thing didn't attack you."

Chip helped Maynard up and they continued on down the hill. It had been a little too much for one night. They never could agree on what it was that jumped off the hillside at them but they did narrow it down to either a bobcat or a wildcat. When their tale was retold the cardboard bear had become real, and there was no mention of Maynard's momentary display of fear.

One of the havens for Maynard and Chip on their walk to Red Dog and back was the men's rest room in the back of the Esso station. The key was broken off in the lock of the door to the men's rest room and could be opened with a knife, or a screwdriver, or a nail file, or any kind of narrow, flat piece of metal. The rest room was only the size of a small closet. It was about five feet by five feet and contained a sink, a commode, and a small, open faced gas heater. The heater was kept turned on low in the winter to keep the water from freezing in the pipes and the commode and for customers' convenience.

On cold winter nights, walkers could always go into the rest room at the station, turn on the light, turn up the heater, if necessary, and warm up. They could also use the facilities, dry out whatever apparel was wet, or sit down and smoke a little before going back out into the dark night. No one ever vandalized or otherwise misused the rest room.

Chip and the guys always stopped off there on their return trip from scout meeting to warm up and finish their cigars.

IV

Walking, thus became a part of Chip's life. The more he walked, the easier it became and the less he had to think about it. He learned the little idiosyncrasies of Rt.11 in and about Sugar Tree and thus made foot travel easier and less dangerous.

When walking in the darkest of nights, Chip learned by watching the tree line above the road, he could see the path of the road outlined against the night sky. Another trick to help him find his way on the road in these conditions was to walk with one leg on the road and the other one on the berm. He could kind of feel his way along in the dark.

One portion of the road from Chip's to Sugar Tree passed by an area known as "the cut". When Rt.11 was first being built, the construction crew had to skirt around the bottom of Blue Knob Hill. They cut into the hillside on the inside of the curve to save a little distance and in the process used the dirt from the excavation to fill in along Sugar Tree Run where the road was designed to go. It left a high wall of dirt about sixty feet high on the inside of the curve. Directly across the road from the excavated side was a deep ravine that ran perpendicular to the road. Both sides of the ravine were very steep and very high. The bottom V of the ravine was just wide enough for the little stream that tumbled down from back on the mountain. Undergrowth and laurel thickets grew so dense along the sides of the ravine that a person could not fight his way up along the stream bed to follow the narrow hollow. The ravine was so deep and so heavy in undergrowth that even in the daytime it was as dark as a coal mine back in there. There were no houses within a quarter mile on either side of the cut and it was always deathly silent in there. It was scary enough to walk through there in the daytime but after dark you hurried by as quickly as you could.

One night as Chip was just about halfway through the cut, a wildcat's scream cut through the still night. It came from somewhere on top of the mountain behind the ravine. The hair on his neck rose in pitch with the scream and he froze momentarily in his steps. Then he covered the half mile to his front porch in what seemed like five or six strides.

Clint always claimed that one day as he was walking through the cut, he could just barely make out a Falls City beer bottle wearing a straw hat and carrying a cane, dancing in the deep shadows of the ravine. That was in the daytime. Clint still sticks to that story to this very day.

Through all the phases of transportation Chip would experience; bicycling, hitch-hiking, and driving, walking would still be the mainstay until the time came that he owned his own car.

By the time he was in high school he might be found walking to Sugar Tree ten or eleven times a week. In the evenings after school he'd walk around to the Community Building to play basketball or walk up to the grade school to play football, or softball depending on the season. Judy lived in Sugar Tree and while she and Chip were dating off and on, he would walk around to her house on Friday night, Saturday night, and maybe Sunday afternoon. Sunday morning, he'd walk around to church at Sugar Tree, walk back home. Walk around to Sugar Tree Sunday afternoon to play ball, and walk back home. Walk around to Sugar Tree Sunday evening to BYF or to visit Judy a little, then walk back home.

The teenage, female population around Sugar Tree must have felt it their duty to host a party of some kind at least once a month at one of the homes in the neighborhood. This obligation must have been either genetic or attributed to some microorganism in the water and air around Sugar Tree. Holidays were always a justification for a party. So at least once a month Chip usually wound up walking a mile or two to some gal's party. Sometimes he'd catch a ride with someone and most times he would find a ride home, but not always, and no matter what the weather was like, he would rather walk to a party than have one of his parents take him in the car. If Chip couldn't find a ride to or from a party, he could always find somebody in the same position he was, so at least he'd have somebody to walk with.

The first official date Judy and Chip had came about as a result of a party at the home of one of Judy's best friends. Chip really didn't know who Judy was at the party, but was captured by what he saw. After mentioning her to Maynard, it turned out Maynard knew all about her because she was a distant cousin of his. Chip used that fact to strike up a conversation with her. After a dance or two together, they shared a coke and a bowl of potato chips and seemed to hit it right off. They were very much at ease with each other, just like it was a natural thing. It was around 9:00 that the party began to get serious when numbers were drawn for a hot game of "Post Office."

"Do you want to play?" asked Judy.

Chip didn't know how to answer. "Well, I don't know. Do you?"

"I don't really care whether I do. I'd just as soon go home. You could walk me home unless you'd rather stay. It's not very far."

Well, that answered that question thought Chip. "Sure, I'd like to do that."

So they walked the quarter mile up the road to Judy's house. They walked along slowly, talking about school and this and that. A few times they would brush sideways against each other with their shoulders or arms touching. The time went too quickly and then they were at Judy's house. She invited Chip to come and sit on the front porch swing while she went in the house to get some lemonade for them.

They sat out on the front porch for an hour or more just talking and swinging. Finally, Chip decided he'd better get on home. Judy walked with him out to the gate at the end of the lane and there under a crescent moon she thanked him for a fun evening and said goodnight. He said goodnight too, and in the little hesitation she made afterward, Chip bent down and kissed her lightly. They said their goodnights over again like it was the first time. Chip didn't remember walking home that night. To this very day when he hears the Danlears sing their hit "One Summer Night", a wistful, yearning feeling knots up in his stomach.

Judy and Chip spent a lot of their dating snuggled up on the front porch swing, weather permitting, listening to Harvey & the Moonglows, The Mellowkings, and Shep & the Limelights on Chip's transistor radio.

Anytime Chip walked around the road to Judy's house to court her, he always tried to leave her house by 11:30. If he could leave by then, he could walk down to the Company Store and always catch a ride with one of the miners going home from the evening shift at Red Dog. If the big clock in Jobe's store window hadn't reached 11:45 yet, he knew he was in luck.

One Saturday night in late spring, Judy and he sat all snuggled up on the front porch swing covered up with Judy's favorite quilt her grandmother had made and they dozed off to sleep. They must have slept there until the wee hours of the morning because what woke them up was the sound of Judy's mom pounding on the wall of their bedroom which was right behind the front porch swing. They both woke up with a start.

"Chip. Chip. You've got to go," Judy pleaded. She was already folding up the quilt and pushing Chip down the front porch steps.

"Sorry, Judy. Hope I didn't get you into trouble."

"Don't worry about. It'll be alright. I'll see you at church tomorrow." She gave him a quick kiss, said goodnight, and went into the house.

As Chip walked down the lane to the road he turned back toward the house just getting a final glimpse of Judy as she locked the front door and turned the front room light out. He sauntered on down the road towards the Company Store and home. He knew this night would be a longer walk than usual.

When he got to the Company Store he looked across the creek at the clock in Jobe's store window. He just stood there staring, trying to figure out what in the heck was going on. The clock read 9:13.

9:13, he thought. Here it's Saturday night and I'm through. Wonder why Judy's mom ran me off so early and what the heck am I gonna do for the rest of the evening? One thing's for sure. I can't go back to Judy's. Maybe ever.

He walked over to Benji's to see what he was doing but Benji had gone to a party over at Red Dog. Aunt Bess and Uncle Frank were home. They were just getting ready to pop some popcorn, fix a coke, and watch a movie on TV so they invited Chip to stay with them and watch the movie. They got two more channels on their TV than Chip's did.

Chip stayed until 11:00 then walked over to the Company Store and caught a ride home with an evening shift miner.

The next morning when Chip got to church, Judy and her family were already there. Usually he sat with Judy, but was afraid to that morning, so he sat way in the back with all of the other teenage boys who were in church because their parents made them come.

137

When it came time for dismissal to Sunday School classes, Judy waited on Chip at the door to their Sunday school class and took him by the hand when they went in to class.

"It's alright," she said, "It's kind of funny. I'll tell you about it after church."

A ton of troublesome thoughts lifted from Chip's shoulders.

It turned out that after Judy and Chip went to sleep, somehow they kept on swinging and the swing kept banging against the back wall of the porch. Judy's mom was pounding on the wall so they would quit swinging against it. She didn't know that Judy and Chip had gone to sleep. She promised to make it up to Chip by inviting him for Sunday dinner that afternoon but she also told him since pounding on the wall worked so good at getting him to leave, that from then on, anytime he heard it, he was to leave immediately.

As Judy and Chip's dating became more serious, Chip began to sacrifice the opportunity to catch the 11:30 evening shift ride home for more precious time to be with Judy.

Before Judy, there was Eva Carte. Chip dated her some when he was a sophomore in high school. Eva was a freshman that year. Eva lived about six miles from Chip on a farm out on Devil's Backbone. Devil's Backbone was a twisting, turning, up and down, ridge that ran about sixteen miles before eventually trailing off to the Back Fork River. The Devil's Backbone turnoff was halfway between Sugar Tree and Hob.

Six miles was too far for Chip to walk and there just wasn't enough traffic on the little dirt road out Devil's Backbone to rely on catching a ride with someone. Chip found out that Paul Boggs was dating a girl who lived three or four miles past the Carte farm on out the ridge and Paul had a car. Before Chip could ask Eva if he could come out on a Saturday night, he had to find out if Paul would be going out to see his girl that night as well. If he was, then Chip would see Eva on the bus and ask her for a date that Saturday.

Chip always dressed his sharpest when going out to see Eva; khaki slacks, sweater, and pointed toed, black loafers with red quilted insides, worn over white socks. A good soaking of Jade East cologne helped him get ready for action. He topped things off by slapping on a good palmful of Brilliantine Hair Oil. Brilliantine cost something like twenty-nine cents a gallon. It was also perfumed, so a guy could not only slick down his DA, he could smell good at the same time. Brilliantine looked an awful lot like automatic transmission fluid. Come to think of it, its masculine aroma suspiciously smelled a little like transmission fluid. All of this preparation was good for attending any event, anywhere, except for going to Eva's.

Paul would pick Chip up at the house and then drop him off out on the ridge above the Carte's home place. The Carte farm was actually located down in a valley off of Devil's Backbone. The farm road that led to the house wound its way around the meadow on the side of the hill, passing through two or three gates before emptying out in the front yard. It was a long walk down the road to the house but there was a footpath that led from the mailbox along the side of the road at the top of the ridge, straight down through the meadow to the house and it was a much shorter and quicker trip. Paul would drop Chip off at the mailbox.

Chip usually got out at the mailbox between 6:30 and 7:00 in the evening and it would already be dark. He had to feel his way along the path down through the meadow and it would be hard to find the path if the night was very dark. He also had to be careful not to bump into any of the cows or horses wandering around grazing in the pasture and of course there were the inevitable scatterings of cow pies and horse dung that couldn't be seen in the dark. The path also had a tendency to become slick if there was a heavy dew or if it had been rained on, and if it snowed, the path became treacherous.

By the time Chip arrived at Eva's front porch his khaki slacks would be mud covered or have grass stains on them. His fine leather soled loafers would be soaking wet with mud and dirt ground in between the uppers and the sole, and they smelled of cow pies and horse dung. His white socks would be spotted in mud with other slop mixed in. Try as he might and as careful as he could be, Chip always fell at least twice while walking the path down to Eva's.

The first time Eva opened the door for him she couldn't help but burst out laughing, nor the second, nor the third, nor anytime after that. It seemed to be a treat for her to open the door and not know in what condition she would find Chip. She always helped Chip clean up as best they could and he left his shoes outside on the porch with the other farm boots and shoes.

Eva had three older sisters who were all married and gone from home. Eva's parents were simple farm folks who seemed kind of old to Chip to have a daughter only fifteen years old. They always stayed up to greet Chip and spent a little time visiting in the living room. Then they would excuse themselves and retire to bed usually before 8:00. The Carte's had no TV but did have a console radio/record player. Eva and Chip couldn't play records because it would be too loud, so they turned the radio on low and sat on the couch and made out until 11:00 or 11:30. Sometimes they would pop some corn or work a jigsaw puzzle or play a board game but mostly they just made out. After the first hour and a half of kissing, Chip would have to excuse himself to the bathroom so he could wipe off the Brilliantine that had begun to trickle down his forehead and seep down the nape of his neck. The last hour and a half of kissing would cause their lips to crinkle up.

Around 11:00 their attention would be diverted somewhat because they had to listen intently for the faint sound of Paul's car horn up on the ridge at the mailbox signaling the arrival of Chip's ride home. Eva would turn on the porch light which Paul could see from up on the road to acknowledge they knew he was there and let him know Chip was on his way. There was no reason to linger and make their good-bye kisses, they were kissed out anyway, so after saying their goodnights, Chip made a hasty retreat.

It was ten times harder trying to get back up the hill than it was going down. Chip fell twice as many times going back up than he did going down. He fell backwards going down the hill and he fell frontwards going up the hill assuring that all areas of his clothes would suffer some mess up. It also took twice as long to scramble up the path than it did to slip and slide down.

When Chip finally made it to the road and the security of Paul's car he would be out of breath from the climb up the hill, his clothes and hair would be in disarray, some of the fault here could be attributed to Eva, and he would be soaked and grime covered. The first time Chip opened the door to get into the car after his first date with Eva, Paul couldn't help but burst out laughing, and the second time, and the third time, and every time after that. Chip went calling on Eva for most of that winter but eventually they both found other interests and drifted apart as steadies, but remained best of friends.

For most of the guys in Sugar Tree, the dating ritual involved walking or catching a ride to their girl's house. No high school aged guy in Sugar Tree had his own car except Lincoln Parks. It was even hard to borrow the family car for a real date except for a special event like the prom or other formal affair, so everybody tried to date someone who lived within walking distance.

On Friday and Saturday nights Rt.11 would be full of guys walking to and from their date's house. One night Chip and Robbie Conner ran smack into each other walking home in the dark from their respective dates. Another dark night Chip was walking home from Judy's and was just coming out of the curve at the cut when up ahead a glowing red object appeared as if floating in mid air. Chip stopped and stood still. The red glow seemed to be undulating in intensity and bobbing up and down. It could have been a mile away or a few feet away. It was just so dark that he couldn't seem to focus in on the distance or the size but it was definitely coming closer. Chip remained frozen and as silent as a statue. The glowing object floated closer. He finally bent down along the berm and felt around until he found a good size rock. Just as he started to stand up the red glowing object passed right by above him and he could hear the soft footsteps of the passerby not more than two feet away from him. It was an unidentified walker coming along in the dark smoking a cigarette. Chip waited a good three minutes before he stood up and continued his journey home. If the passerby knew Chip was there he never let on like he did.

There were two walkers who could never be mistaken or collided with in the middle of the night. One was Billy Reed. Billy had dropped out of high school when he was a sophomore and was now eighteen years old. He was the poster boy for rock-a-billy cool. He had the greasy DA, black or white tee shirt worn under cotton jacket with the collar turned up in the back or a black leather jacket with fifteen zippers on it. He had tight pegged blue jeans with just a little half inch cuff turned up at the bottom. A little white belt, a quarter inch in width, ran through the belt loops just for appearance. The white socks would flash in and out of sight when he walked. He smoked Camel cigarettes, one of which he always kept tucked over his ear, and the pack of which he kept rolled up in the sleeve of his tee shirt. Billy's dress shoes were a made like a normal pair of lace ups but instead of laces there was a big tab that flipped down to loosen the shoe and flipped up and snapped shut to close the shoe. Billy also had a pair of engineer boots and a pair of motorcycle boots. But what set Billy off was the heel and toe taps he had on all of his shoes. No matter where you were or what you were doing you knew when Billy Reed was around because you could hear him clicking along.

Billy was a roller skating fool. He was king of the skating rink in Hob. Every Friday and Saturday night Billy was the first one on the floor and last one off. Every skater under the age of ten had been taught by Billy, and the females used to stand in line to get to skate with him. He could skate for three hours solid and never get a hair out of place or get one little wrinkle in his clothes.

The other identified walker was Harley Rogers. Harley was the first guy in Sugar Tree to have a pocket sized transistor radio. It was a Westinghouse radio about the size of a cigarette pack. It even came with a little ear plug. When Harley was walking at night he would always turn the radio up loud and stick it in his pocket to keep him company. So not only did Harley have a companion while walking, it also served as a sonar device for others walking the road in the dead of night.

Whether it was jealousy or typical adolescent teasing, everyone made fun of Harley accusing him of just being afraid of the dark otherwise he'd carry his radio in his shirt pocket even in the daytime. Harley dismissed the taunts however. He said his radio couldn't pick up anything in the daytime. He was right about that.

V

The next step up in the evolution of transportation for Chip was the bicycle. The Gates boys each got a brand new bicycle for Christmas when they reached the age of nine or ten. They learned to ride in the yard and around the house and soon were bicycling all over the farm. They were allowed to ride anywhere around on the farm and did. They even pushed the bikes up on the hill and rode the paths through the woods and around in the meadows. It would be at least a year from first learning to ride until they would be allowed to ride on the road. Until such time was granted, they had to keep their bicycling on the farm. The learning experience on the farm developed excellent skills in balance, maneuvering ability, pedaling strength, and endurance. It was just like learning to drive a car on those old country roads. If you could bicycle around on the farm without incident, you could bicycle anywhere.

The greatest day in Chip's bicycling evolution came quite unexpectedly. He was helping his dad do some type of home repair, plumbing, electrical work, carpentry, he couldn't remember exactly. What he did remember was, that of all the hardware supplies the Gates always kept on hand in the workshop on the upper side of the barn to complete various home repairs, they didn't have in stock exactly what they needed that particular day.

After looking through everything in the shop, Mr. Gates finally turned to Chip and said, "Take your bike and go around the road to Jobe's and get a (whatever it was they couldn't find)."

Chip just stood there like he didn't hear.

"Did you hear what I said. I need a (??????) and I need it now." Then shaking his head in frustration he walked out of the workshop. As he walked away, Chip could hear his dad mumbling, "You've got to do something before you can do something, before you can do something."

Theodore Gates never threw anything away and everybody knew that. If there was something that could be salvaged from a broken object, he would keep the whole thing. He said you never knew when you might need just that very piece so might as well have it on hand, right there on the farm. When a neighbor came to borrow a tool or needed a particular piece of hardware, the Gates' always had on hand, the exact item the neighbor needed but when the

143

Gates' needed a tool or a particular piece of hardware for themselves, it couldn't be found on the farm. None of their neighbors would have what they needed so they would have to go to Jobe's or drive to Hob, Seneca, Red Dog, or Mills Bottom and buy a brand new thing.

Anyway, Chip didn't have to be asked again to go to Jobe's that day. He jumped on his bike, coasted down to the end of the driveway, looked up and down the road, turned out on the hardroad, and headed to Sugar Tree. He quickly pedaled those first few hundred yards, until he was out of sight of the house. He wanted to be out of hearing distance from the house just in case his dad came to his senses and ordered Chip back to the house. Once out of range, he slowed up. He wanted to take his time to enjoy this ride and to make sure as many of his buddies as possible had a chance to see him.

He stopped a Maynard's but Maynard was back on the hill putting up hay. He did linger long enough for Mrs. Samples to ask him where he was going.

"Got to run around to Jobe's and get some stuff for dad," he said seriously. "Tell Maynard I stopped by. See yuh." He pedaled off.

At every house along the way where he had friends, he would slow down or stop. He used every kind of excuse to help prolong the journey. "Is Nancy home?

"Do you know what time it is Mrs. Johnson?"

When he got to Sugar Tree, he pulled in out front of the wash bay at the station and parked the bike. He went in just to see who was there. Nobody was there except Lewis and Bucky and not much was going on so after a couple of cars drove in, got gas and left, Chip went back out, got on the bike and went on up the road.

He rode right past Jobe's and turned up Painter's Fork. He had already decided he was going to ride clear through Sugar Tree before he went to Jobe's. When he went past the Company Store he saw Benji sitting on the front steps drinking an orange Nehi. He just waved nonchalantly as he went by, pretending this was no big deal, hoping all the while to arouse Benji's envy a little.

He rode clear up to the bottom of Panther Mountain and back, then cruised up Sugar Tree Run straight to the bottom of Red Dog Hill and back to the middle of Sugar Tree. Riding deliberately and casually, he wanted as many people to see him as possible. He thought that everyone who saw him wondered what in the world he was doing riding his bike so far from home. He finally went over to Jobe's and got whatever it was that his dad sent him around the road to get and then started for home.

When he got back home, Mr. Gates was furious. Chip had been gone for ninety minutes. "My god, boy, I could have walked around the road and back twice in the time you been gone. I been sittin' here waitin' on you. Suppose you tell me why it took you all day?"

Chip had no idea that he had been gone so long. He had to think of something quickly.

"Jobe wasn't there, Dad", was his response. "Mrs. Frame said he had to take some stuff up to Offie Caldwell's and that he would be back pretty soon. She couldn't help me look for what you needed cause she didn't know where it might be, so we just had to wait on him. Guess it took longer than he figured it would."

"That sounds like a lotta bunk", he said, " I'm gonna check with Jobe next time I see him and find out what really went on." Chip was concerned now, though he still didn't break. His dad would have to confront him with more than just mere words before he'd confess. If Mr. Gates ever did ask Jobe, he never mentioned it again to Chip and Chip felt more relieved as each day went by.

That day opened another door to the world of "the road". For the first few months after that historic trip to Sugar Tree, Chip had to ask permission to ride his bike to various places up and down Rt.11. He was usually allowed to go, but he was told to leave the bike at home. After those first few rejections, he never asked specifically if he could take his bike. He just asked if he could go to Maynard's for example. If his parents said yes, he'd go get his bike and ride it to Maynards'. If his parents didn't tell him to leave the bike home, he figured the choice was more or less, left up to him.

The biggest drawback to bicycling around the Sugar Tree area was the terrain. A bicycle rider couldn't ride more than a quarter of a mile any direction before he would have negotiate a hill. Riding around in Sugar Tree proper was no problem, there were only a couple of small inclines and a few little humps one would have to pedal over, but you couldn't get out of Sugar Tree without going up a long, steep hill. The only consolation found in going up hills was in the anticipation of eventually getting to coast back down. That's why Junior Dodrill never owned a bicycle. He said it was stupid to pump your legs off for ten minutes just so you could give your rear end a thirty second ride.

Chip's bike was your average Western Flyer, just two wheels a frame and two fenders. It held up well under heavy usage and constant maintenance kept it in running order. It had no horn, no rear carrying rack, no handlebar streamers, and no saddle bags. For Christmas one year his dad did buy a Western Auto siren and attach it to the bike. The siren was engaged by pulling a chain that was attached to the siren and ran up to the handle bars. When the chain was pulled tight, a wheel on the siren contacted the side of the front wheel and spun the siren. The faster he went, the louder the siren screamed. To get real friction between the siren and the wheel, Chip rigged the chain so he could push the chain tight with his foot. Problem with that was he couldn't pedal and push the chain with his foot at the same time.

If he pedaled hard and pulled the chain with his hand the siren would work but it would just produce a low droning sound. If he could coast downhill, he could push the chain with his foot and make the siren run better but then the tension from the siren against the front wheel made the bike run slower so he just got that low droning whine again. Chip wound some friction tape around the metal wheel on the siren to give it better traction. It made the wheel a little bigger in diameter and did help bolster the rpm's but there were only two places around Sugar Tree where the optimum, true scream of that siren could be attained.

One place was Sugar Tree Hill. There, he didn't need to go the whole mile clear to the top. He could gain sufficient speed to make the siren scream by coasting down from Dead Man's Curve, but there was nobody around to hear the siren except Chip and anyone else who might have been stupid enough to go all the way up to Dead Man's Curve just to hear a bike siren the way it was meant to sound.

The other place was Renzee White Hill. Chip could push his bike up to the first hairpin turn on the hill and could coast a half mile down the hill and then continue coasting right back to the house. Rt.11 down Renzee White Hill had two hairpin turns on it which meant if Chip went clear to the top and started down, he'd have to slow down so much to make both of the curves that by the time he made it around the bottom curve, his speed would have been about the same as if he had started there in the first place, so there was no advantage gained by going clear to the top.

It was embarrassing to Chip to be seen pushing a bicycle anywhere. So over the years Chip built the strength and endurance to conquer every hump, hill, and incline around Sugar Tree but so could almost everybody else. So he worked even harder until he could pedal up to the first turn on Renzee White Hill and he could pedal up to Dead Man's Curve on Sugar Tree Hill. As far as he knew, nobody else in Sugar Tree could top that feat and nobody but a world champion cyclist with a ten speed racing bike could pedal clear to the top of either one of those hills.

He finally took the siren off and passed it down to Riley to let him wrestle with it for a while.

Maynard's bike had seen better days. He had traded a fishing pole and a harmonica to one of his cousins for two bicycle frames and a box full of bicycle parts. Maynard used the parts to build a runable bicycle. It ran very well but had no fenders, no chain guard and no coaster brakes. To slow down or stop, Maynard stuck his foot in between the front forks and the tire and applied as much pressure as needed. The coolest thing about Maynard's bike was the steering wheel. It was a steering wheel from a '47 Dodge pickup truck. Maynard's dad had taken the bike over to the mine shop at Red Dog and had welded the steering wheel right to the steering stem where the handle bars would normally have been. It worked like a dream. The steering wheel was wide enough to easily help with the balance of the bike and it made steering very easy once you got used it. Nobody had ever seen a bike so equipped anywhere at anytime.

Benji's bike looked like something from a circus. It was loaded. It was a Shelby with a full tank accessory built in between the cross bars. That was where the horn and horn button were located. It had two bullet like head lights about the size of a flashlight, built in right below the handlebars. The head lights worked off of a little generator attached to the rear frame. The generator could be switched on by flipping it into a locked position so that a little wheel spun against the rear tire, much like Chip's siren worked. The bike also had a rear carrier. Benji had accumulated a number of accessories over the years; handlebar streamers, a speedometer, little leather bracelets with a rhinestone fastener that hung over each wheel axle to keep it shiny, and a pair of saddle bags that hung over the rear carrier.

Maynard and Chip had fashioned a set of fender skirts out of corrugated tin barn roofing. They attached the skirts to the rear fender braces of Benji's bike so that the ridges in the tin were horizontal, emulating the effect of bubble skirts as was a customizing trend in those days. They mixed enough black and red enamel paint together to paint the skirts and came pretty close to matching the original dark red color of the bike. Maynard and Link painted white sidewalls on both tires. They painted the whitewalls with Kem-tone interior wall paint. Every time Benji ran through water or washed his bike, the paint washed off and they would have to paint it again because the half painted tires made the rest of the bike look shoddy.

Benji's bike was set up for showing off while cruising around Sugar Tree. When the guys headed out on long excursions Benji would remove most of the accessories to strip the bike down to a lighter and more manageable vehicle.

Link had an English racing bike. It was the first one seen in the Sugar Tree or Red Dog. It had real thin tires and just the smallest of fenders. It had no coaster brake but had front and rear hand brakes. It had a three-speed shifter located on the handle bar. Link said first gear was for going up hills, second gear was for cruising on the level, and third gear was for speed. The bike came with a little leather tool pouch that hung just behind the stream lined, narrow racing seat. There was also a long, thin tire pump attached to the frame rail and the handle bars were narrowed in towards the body.

It took some riding around on the racer to become proficient at handling it. Especially hard to adjust to was the correct use of the hand brakes; knowing which was front and which was rear and how and when to apply pressure to each, lest one pitch over the handlebars on too quick of a stop was important. The other tough adjustment was trying to sit on that little hard pedestal of a seat.

Of course Link was the expert and had no trouble cruising around with the rest of the guys but even Link couldn't do much with the racer when excursions headed out on dirt roads or into the woods. That bike was built for speed and smooth pavement but on off road jaunts, it was pretty much useless. Poor Link would absolutely wear himself out on those trips. He was constantly fighting to keep the bike upright when those little thin tires were kicking left and right over the smallest of gravels and he had to do his best to keep moving so those tires wouldn't sink into the soft ground, clay, or dirt they might be passing over.

Maynard & Chip tried bicycling to Boy Scout meetings a couple of times but riding bikes to Red Dog and back was too cumbersome. Maynard's bike had no fenders so even if it was just a little damp, Maynard would have a strip of mud as wide as his tire up the front of his shirt and down the back. That didn't bother him if he was just ridin' around Sugar Tree, but if he had to wear his uniform to the Scout meeting, then it bothered him.

The first time Maynard rode his bike to the Scout meeting, he wore a pair of engineer boots that had just been half soled about a week earlier. Trying to keep his bike under control going down Red Dog Hill into town was futile. He did fine the first few hundred yards but by the time he'd started down the steep part, both of his boots were getting hot from the friction he was applying in an effort to brake. Though he switched from left foot to right foot, the front wheel was not only making the soles of his feet hot, it was wearing a groove right through the leather of those brand new half soles. Finally, a hundred yards from the bottom of the hill Maynard had to let the bike go and concentrate on keeping from sliding and wrecking on the loose, red dog covered hill. The soles of his feet were burning up and there was actually smoke coming from the bottom of his boots.

Chip was coming down the hill behind him on his bike and he could see the whiffs of smoke and smell the odor of burning rubber. Chip was having enough trouble of his own because he could smell the hot metal from his own coaster brake and was now having to stand up and put all of his weight on the pedal to curtail his speed even a little bit. It was getting pretty hairy for both.

Up ahead Maynard was fighting to stay upright. The front wheel was bouncing and wobbling as it skipped along the loose red dog. The rear end fish tailed right and left as it seemed to hit the ground only every few seconds. Chip knew Maynard was in trouble. He was absolutely flying. Chip closed his eyes and said a little prayer. If Maynard wrecked at this speed and spilled onto the gravel and red dog, all they would find of him would just be little pieces and his hot engineer boots.

Chip didn't have time to worry about that, his own speed had reached a critical level. Chip's bike was heavier than Maynard's so it wasn't bouncing around as much as Maynard's and he was able to handle it fairly well. If it didn't slide in the loose road material he might be able to ride it out.

Through sheer strength, remarkable agility, and a lot of luck, Maynard made it to the bottom of the hill and as the road leveled out through Colored Town, his bike slowed down enough for him to regain control. Half way through Colored Town, Maynard laid his bike down in a controlled skid and slid to a stop facing back up the street. Chip was able to hang on to his runaway cycle but his brakes were too hot to work at all and he wasn't about to lay his bike down on that hard, dirt street. He shot past Maynard and coasted through Colored Town, past the Town Hall, went under the tipple, turned up the mine road that led up to the main shop, and stopped.

He waited there for his brakes to cool off and in a few minutes Maynard caught up with him. They both laid their bikes off to the side of the road and laid down beside them under an old poplar tree, right there on the hard gob that was scattered along the side of the road. Maynard was still trembling from his close encounter with disaster and both of his feet were blistered. The brand new half soles on his boots had a groove burned clear through to the inside. Chip had calmed down enough so that his breathing had returned to normal. Now that it was over they both thought, man oh man what a ride!

When Maynard got home his mom whipped him with his dad's mine belt for ruining his good pair of boots. She made him stuff an old piece of inner tube into his boots and he wore them like that all that winter.

After that, bicycle rides to Red Dog involved walking the bikes at least three quarters of the way down Red Dog Hill before swinging unto the seat. Going from Sugar Tree to Red Dog meant pushing the bikes up Sugar Tree Hill, riding out the ridge to the top of Red Dog Hill, then walking the bikes more than half way down that Hill. Coming back home meant pushing the bikes all the way back up Red Dog Hill, and even though they could ride all the way out the ridge and coast all the way down the hill into Sugar Tree, it wasn't worth the effort. And there was no way they could catch a ride home as long as they had that bicycle with them. Bicycle trips to Red Dog were few and far between.

In the summer of Chip's thirteenth year the Esso station became a kind of community gathering spot for local teens on Friday nights for some reason, and as far as Chip could remember, it was just that one summer. It may have been because Bucky and Lewis kept the station open later in the evening that summer or it may have been because it was the only place in Sugar Tree proper open on Friday nights where the kids could find snacks and cold drinks and just hang out. It could have been because it was the thing to do but for that one summer, it was fun.

There didn't seem to be much to do at the station at first. One could get a pop and a snack and sit outside on a pop crate leaned up against the front of the station. It was a good place to just sit and cuss and spit, if you had a mind to. It didn't get dark until around 9:00 and then the Keener brothers would turn on the outside lights above the pump island and soon after, the bugs would start congregating. Before long, the bats would start flittering around devouring insects for their evening meal.

There was a Bally-Hole pinball machine in the main lobby of the station. It was the kind with no flippers. It had about twenty-four holes in the playing surface guarded by a bumper post or two right above it. A player got to play five balls for a nickel. The object of the game was to direct the balls into the holes so they would light up the corresponding numbers on the pinball's display board. If you got three numbers in a row lit up, you won five extra

151

games. Four in a row would give you twenty extra games. Five numbers lit up in a row was about twenty five extra games.

You could use up the extra games by trying to earn extra balls to play, trying to increase the payoff odds on the number of games in a row, or by trying to maneuver the lighted numbers around to make them line up three, four or five in a row.

Bucky and Lewis paid a player five cents for every extra game they won if they wanted to cash the games in. You had to score at least twenty extra games before you could cash them in. The younger kids played it mostly for fun because they didn't have enough money to put into the game to make it profitable, however the older, high roller crowd would sometimes feed anywhere from two to ten dollars worth of nickels in the machine trying to hit for big money.

One night, somebody brought to the station, a box that had one of those flipper style basketball games in it. A ping pong ball rolled around on a simulated basketball floor until it landed in a hole with a flipper underneath. The player would use a little lever located on the outside of the box to flip the ball into a little basket. There was a basket on each end of the playing floor with a two digit scoreboard located right above it. Score was kept on the scoreboard by turning the two wheels that posted a number in the two windows--one for the ones digit and one for the tens digit.

Some of the flippers were made to shoot toward one basket and some of the flippers shot toward the opposing basket. There was an equal number of holes and flippers for each basket.

There were three flippers on each side of the box and all of the flippers on one side shot towards the same basket. Conceivably you could have three players on each team, each one manning a different flipper. Most of the games just involved one against one.

The first team to reach twenty-five points signaled half-time. Players would switch sides and baskets and then the first team to reach fifty points won. The winner had to win by two or more points. Players started arriving early on Friday evenings to sign up for their turn to play. The winner stayed up.

The game was set up on the main counter in the station lobby and it developed into quite an intense competition. Someone even brought an old Big Ben Westclock alarm clock so the games were played in five minute halves to make them move along faster so more people would have a chance to play.

The high roller crowd even came to wager on the games and in those cases where a bundle of money might be riding on the outcome, Bucky and Lewis officiated and handled all appeals. Since it was their station, their decisions were final and binding.

Link even brought his portable tape recorder down to the station a couple of times and recorded his own play-by-play of the action. It was easy where there was a team of three playing, but when there was only one against one, he had to make up names for at least two flippers on each side. Since Link wasn't much of a sports fan, Chip tried to help him name the players after the ones he was familiar with, like Jerry West, Willie Acres, Bill McGill, Cotton Nash, Jerry Lucas, Oscar Robertson, Bob Cousy, Bob Pettit, Wilt Chamberlin, and Hal Greer to name a few. But it was Link's tape recorder so he named the players after players he knew like Marty Willis, the Nash brothers, Lanty White and Paul Boggs. They were local high school players.

Kick-the-can turned out to be a popular game played at the station. A bunch of kids turned out for kick-the-can and the game would last an hour or two in and out of the lights at the station.

Then for about a month that summer, the big Friday night attraction at the station turned to bicycle drag racing. It just got started one evening when somebody challenged somebody else to a bicycle race. They raced from the corner of the Company Store at the Y, to the portable sign resting out by the roadside in front of the station. The sign advertised the price of gas that summer; $0.28 per gallon for regular, $0.34 for high test.

The starting point at the company store was on a little hump so one could get a little extra help from a dead start but it was fair to both racers. There were never more than two at a time racing because the single lane road was too narrow to be safe for any more than that. The total length of the race was two hundred and thirty feet.

After that first Friday night of racing the word got around and by the next Friday night, a large number of Sugar Tree boys showed up to race. By the third Friday night, there were racers from Red Dog and some said there were even a couple of guys from Hob who had brought their bikes over in a pick up truck. The wagers of the high roller crowd began to grow as did the crowd standing under the lights at the finish line in front of the station. Benji had some white liquid shoe polish for his white bucks so he brought it over and painted a start and finish line on the hardroad. He had to paint it over every Friday night because it wore off or was washed off during the week.

The drag racing fad just faded away after those first three or four Friday nights but the consensual king of bike drag racing in Sugar Tree was Chip. Nobody could remember ever beating him and truthfully, he couldn't remember anyone ever beating him but he never boasted about his exploits. He took on every challenger with grace and never belittled his opponent, unless the opponent was one of the Jive Five. And after their first few races against Chip, they wouldn't race him anymore.

Chip never gave anyone a head start. Races were always side-by-side starts but Chip never beat anyone by more than a bicycle length. Bobby and Tony Nash even came over from Red Dog one evening to race and though they both beat everybody else they raced, neither could take Chip. Years later when Chip was running track for Elk River High School, he faced off against Bobby Nash, who was running for Mill's Bottom High School then, in the hundred yard dash event at the New River Conference Track and Field Championships. Chip beat Bobby in that race and Bobby always said that Chip was the only white guy who every outran him.

Some said it was the set up on Chip's bike that gave him an advantage, but his bicycle was just the same old Western Flyer he'd got for Christmas. In fact, on a couple of occasions, Chip rode his own bike to victory against an opponent, traded bikes, and beat him again. It was probably Chip's leg strength that vaulted him to drag racing prominence in Sugar Tree. All of those treks up the mountain to fix the TV line and the numberless miles he had walked to and from Sugar Tree had all contributed to the development of his leg power.

Although Chip never bragged about his drag racing record, there was one incident that he still likes to allude to even to this very day. That would be the "Cotton Triplett Event".

Cotton Triplett was about twenty-three years old when his encounter with Chip took place. Cotton had graduated from Red Dog High and had gone to Ohio to work in an auto plant out there. Soon after going to work he bought a '59 Buick convertible. Every weekend Cotton headed back to WV and on this one particular Friday night, he happen to tool into Sugar Tree with the top down, during a bike racing lull.

He whipped the Buick into the parking area beside the station, strolled inside and got a cold coke from the cooler. He shuffled back outside, parked himself on a pop crate, and began to strike up conversation with whoever was closest. It didn't take long for the conversation to turn to the topic of bike racing. The more Cotton listened, the more interested he became. When there was a prolonged silence in the conversation, he spoke up. "Hey, anybody here want to race my Buick?". Silence. "Surely somebody would like to. Just for fun, huh? I'll even give them a head start."

"Yeah. Come on Chip. You can beat that pile of junk", volunteered Benji.

"Yeah, come on Chip", prodded Cotton, "you can beat that pile of junk. What have you got to lose? I'm the one on the line here. What if I get beat by some punk jamison? How would that look?"

Cotton was trying to goad Chip into racing but Chip couldn't figure out why. Cotton was right. What did he have to gain by beating a bicycle? Chip was still reluctant.

"Hey Chip." It was Bucky Keener calling from inside the station. "Come here and help me with this register a minute, will yuh?"

Chip went in the station and walked around behind the counter to the cash register where Bucky was waiting. Bucky was pretending to be fiddling with cash register drawer. "You want to race Cotton?", he asked.

"I don't know", answered Chip, "I don't care."

"Well listen, if you do, you can beat him in the short distance you've got marked off out there. Don't race any further than that. And don't race him more than once. You can get him off the line

155

the first time because he won't know whether to romp on it or pull off smoothly but he'll figure it out if you race him more than once. Don't give him a chance to adjust or he'll beat you."

Chip listened to Bucky and took it all in. He walked outside where Cotton was still pleading for a race. A number of kids had gathered around Cotton's shiny red Buick and were admiring its innovative styling design and wondering about the horsepower nestled under the hood.

"No one's ever outrun a car on a bicycle", someone stated. "You could be the first ever, Chip!"

"No he won't", someone interjected, "'cause he can't beat the Buick and that's a fact!"

"Come on Chip. You can't let this opportunity pass by. It'll never happen again, anywhere."

"Ok", answered Chip. "Let's do it-----but listen, now. We're only gonna race the same race the bikes race."

"Yeah. Yeah. Sure. Whatever you say", responded Cotton as he got up off his pop crate and chugged down the rest of his coke. When he put the bottle back in the empty's rack, he patted his billfold in the back pocket of his jeans. "Anybody got any money to put on this baby?" he asked.

"Yeah. Here's twenty says you can't beat the boy." It was Bucky.

"Oh I'll see your twenty and raise you ten if you ain't chicken", bragged Cotton.

"All I got is a buck thirty-eight", whined Maynard, looking at the pitiful amount of change in his palm.

"Well, which way you gonna bet boy?" asked Cotton, dumping the change into his own hand.

"No way I'm bettin' against Chip", Maynard announced.

The money began to pile up so Cotton asked Lewis to handle it and keep it straight.

"Now before we do anything else, we need somebody to start the race and somebody to judge the finish," said Cotton.

"I'll start the race", volunteered Link, "if that's ok with everybody."

"Fine with me", said Cotton.

"Me too", agreed Chip.

"Now I want somebody with no investment in this race to call the finish and I don't want some punk kid neither", demanded Cotton.

"You trust me with your money, don't cha?" asked Lewis. "Got any problem with me callin' the race?".

Cotton thought about it for a minute as he looked around at who else was available. "Well, I reckon you'll have to do."

Chip settled down on the bike seat and slowly peddled his way up to the Company Store where Link was already waiting.

Cotton slipped under the wheel of the Buick and started her up. He backed out on the hardroad and jerked the automatic into low as he was still drifting backwards. He stomped the accelerator to the floor and buried the Buick in a cloud of gray smoke and squalling tires. He finally let off and cruised the convertible up to the Company Store and turned around.

He positioned the Buick at the starting line on the right side of the road where the normal traffic flow in that direction should be. Chip pulled up beside him on the driver's side and set his front wheel on the starting line. Link motioned Cotton forward until his front bumper was over the starting line. It was kind of comical seeing those two vehicles resting at the starting line. Chip was almost two bicycle lengths ahead of where Cotton sat in the front seat of the Buick. Link stepped over to the side of the road beside the Buick.

As Chip sat waiting for the race to begin, he looked down the road to the station where Lewis and a whole crowd of folks were standing along both sides of the road. Then a chill ran up his spine.

"Ready?", yelled Link, as he raised the red bandanna starting flag in the air.

"No. No. Hold it. Hold it. Go get Lewis. Now!"

"What's a matter? Come on let's go, baby", demanded Cotton.

Chip wheeled his bike off the starting line and pulled around behind the Buick to wait on Lewis.

The starting line was located right in the forks of the Y, slightly on the left hand fork. Where the two forks came together it was wide and the pavement covered a wide area. However, the bottom stem of the Y where they were going to race, narrowed down into a single lane road. It was barely wide enough for the Buick. How could both of them fit side by side on that narrow, one lane road?

Lewis came trotting up the road behind Link. "Come on boys", he said, "I got places to go and women to see."

"How we gonna race on that road?" Chip pointed out. "It's not wide enough for both of us."

"Well, let Cotton run on half the road and you run on the other side."

Cotton got out of the Buick and left it setting in the middle of the road. "Like hell I will", he confronted Lewis. "I ain't runnin' on the berm while this punk gets to run on the road. That ain't right."

"Well, let's just forget the whole thing", suggested Chip.

"Yeah, we'll forget it-----if you want to forfeit all bets to me. I'll go along with that."

"You can't do that," Lewis said.

"Look. This punk agreed to race me. He set up the rules for the race and I agreed with everything. Now he wants to back out. That's ok by me but no matter how you call it, it's a forfeit and he loses. The only way I lose is if he beats me racing---that's that!"

The crowd down at the station was getting restless. They could hear a raised voice from time to time drifting down to them from the Company Store but they couldn't tell what was happening.

Lewis drew Chip aside. "Whatcha gonna do?" he asked. "He's got a point. We'll have to give him all the money if you don't race. I don't like him and I don't like this setup but, I certainly don't want you gettin' hurt neither."

"Let me think about it a minute", said Chip. He wandered over and sat down on the steps of the Company Store. Cotton leaned back on the front fender of his Buick and lit up a cigarette. A car came down Painter's Fork and slowed down when he got to the Buick. Cotton waved him on around and the car pulled around and crept on down the road toward the station. When it got to the crowd at the station its brake lights came on and it slowed even more. The crowd waved it on through.

Chip was worried about being run off the road by the Buick. What if it kicked sideways when they started? If the Buick hit him anywhere during that race, he'd go flyin' off onto the berm and who knows what could happen? There was a chance he could even get run over. A bicycle wasn't very wide at first glance if you didn't take into account the handle bars. Was there enough room for that big Buick and a bicycle side by side on the narrow road? Cotton knew exactly what he was doing. He was going to come out the winner in this deal no matter what happens, unless I can beat him, thought Chip.

Lewis interrupted his thoughts. "Listen, Chip. There's one chance you've got. If you can get ahead of Cotton right off the start and stay ahead of him till you get to the parking lot in front of the station, then you won't have to worry about having enough room. You're either gonna have to try that or we'll give the bum his money back. It's up to you. If you don't want think you can stay ahead of him, don't try it. It ain't worth it."

Chip thought back to what Bucky told him. Bucky knows his stuff when it comes to cars and racin'. He's seen me race. If he didn't think I could win, he would never have brought it up. As long as I don't get right directly in front of Cotton, there's not much chance of gettin' run over. I don't think he'd deliberately try to run me over just for a few bucks. If I can't stay ahead of him or if it gets too close for comfort, I'll just back off and get off the road and take my chances.

He got off the steps and walked back to his bicycle. He pushed it up beside Cotton and Lewis. "Let's race", he said.

Lewis looked Cotton right in the eye. "If you do anything to put that boy in danger, you'll never get back to Ohio in one piece. You hear me?"

Cotton flipped his cigarette in a high arch across the hood of the Buick, "I ain't gonna do nothin' to your precious boy here, 'cept beat the pants offin' him. I'll race him fair and square. I'll keep to my side of the road but I ain't goin' off the road neither, so he better watch his own way."

"Remember what I said", Lewis finished as he started back down the road toward the station.

Cotton yelled after him, "Yeah. And you remember what I said!" He climbed back into the Buick and started her up. "You ready kid?"

What had started out as a nice, friendly evening of fun and games had suddenly turned serious and nasty.

Chip pulled up along side the front fender of the Buick. He said nothing. He raised the rear wheel of the bike and turned the pedals around with his foot so that the left pedal was in the ten o'clock position. . He didn't know why he liked the first push to be with his left leg, his right leg was actually stronger. The left gave him confidence though, and he'd always been successful doing it that way. No reason to change now.

Link stepped back off to the side of the road. There was not enough room between the bike and the Buick to stand. He got out the red bandanna and waved it up and down so Cotton and Chip could see it. He pointed to Chip and Chip nodded his head. A point to Cotton and a similar affirmation from him showed they were both ready. Link raised the bandanna high in the air. Cotton revved the Buick's engine. Link held the bandanna overhead a moment and then brought it down in one swoop of his arm.

Chip stood on the left pedal and pulled on the handlebars, transferring all of his leg and arm strength down on the pedal. He leaned over the handlebars and as the right pedal came up he swung all of his strength and momentum to that side. He could hear the Buick's deep gulp of gas and air through the wide open four barrel, followed by the squall of rubber on the pavement as the rear tires tried to gain some traction. The Buick was heavy and it squatted down low in the rear enhancing the rear tire's grip on the road. Traction came quicker and better than even Bucky had figured.

As the bike picked up speed, the power to the pedals came easier and smoother. Chip looked to the side but couldn't see the Buick. The image of that ominous hulk coming up behind him made the hair on his neck stand up, but either the fear of the moment or the sheer exhilaration of the confrontation released enough adrenaline into Chip's system to enable him to surpass any of his past racing performances. It was almost too easy. Chip shot past the finish line amid a cheering crowd and beat the Buick by the length of a bicycle.

Chip slowed down and turned back to the station. Cotton took a little longer to stop but he threw the Buick into reverse and backed back up to the station and parked where he had been before. "Come on kid, let's do it again. I bet you couldn't do that again in ten years."

Chip was feeling cocky. He didn't have to think about this one. He answered almost too quickly, "I'm ready, let's go."

The money began to flow around again. The last pot totaled close to one hundred dollars but this one was nowhere near that amount. For one thing, Bucky wasn't going to bet on this one. All that money and none of it went to Chip. He didn't care. He was racing for pride. From inside the station Chip could see Bucky shaking his head and mouthing the words, "STUPID."

At the starting line Cotton got out and went back to the rear Buick where he proceeded to let some air out of the rear tires. When he thought they were just right, he got back in.

Chip rolled up to the start line and spun the pedals around for his own start. Link got out his bandanna and raised it in the air. Cotton gunned the Buick a couple of times then backed off the accelerator. He pulled the shift lever down into low and with one foot solid on the power brake, he pressed the accelerator down with the other one until the Buick seemed to raise up on its haunches. It groaned and creaked and strained ahead, ready to pounce off the starting line.

Link looked at Chip and then back to Cotton and dropped the bandanna. Chip jerked the bike hard forward and came off the line quicker then he had ever done before. The Buick emitted a little bark and sprung off the line. The first twenty feet passed quickly and the pedals became a blurr as Chip built momentum as quickly as he could without getting out of rhythm. He bent over the handlebars, straining to put every ounce of energy into his driving legs. Out of the corner of his eye he caught the wide, red, front fender of the Buick creeping up on him.

Chip tried to keep his focus on the finish line ahead and tried to maintain a straight line while under control. He was as close to the edge of the road as he could get without losing the flat surface. The Buick's front fender was now even with Chip. It wasn't coming any closer but it wasn't losing any ground either. If he could just hold for thirty more feet, he'd be home free. He poured what was left of his determination into action and the bike flashed across the finish line. The crowd cheered even though no one was real certain who had won.

Chip honestly felt that he had beaten the Buick by the radius of a bicycle wheel. Cotton must have thought Chip won too because he just kept on cranking the Buick down the road and around the bend out of sight. Everybody waited a few minutes for him to come back but he didn't. So they began pounding Chip on the back and congratulating him. Even Bucky came out of the station and offered his hand in congratulations. When Chip stretched out his own hand to accept, Bucky jerked his up and smacked Chip a playful, if none to gently, slap on the side of his face. He smiled a might and said, "Well, I guess you lucked that one out, but that was pretty stupid to take a chance like that. Ole Cotton, he don't usually take losin' too gracefully."

Chip was feelin' good about his wins and he didn't want to spoil it by thinking about what could have happened if he had dropped off the edge of the road or if Cotton's Buick had just nudged him a little. He had beaten a car, not some pile of junk but a fine set of wheels----and not once but twice.

The days passed quickly by that summer and the race with the Buick was forgotten by everyone but Chip and the Jive Five. Putting any cautious and negative thoughts out of their minds and spurred on by Chip's urging, the boys adopted a new bike riding code: When meeting any motorized vehicle while riding a bicycle on the hardroad, the biker shall steer his bike as far to the right hand side of the road as deemed safe but shall not ride off the road onto the berm to accommodate said motorized vehicle. They decided not to give up their fair share of the road to any oncoming traffic. After all, they figured that while riding on the hardroad they were, in a way, a legal vehicle as much as anything else was, even if they weren't motorized. Motorcycles and motorbikes didn't go off the road to give up the entire road to anyone. And why should they? It was dangerous dropping off the hardroad unto a berm that could be as low as eight or ten inches. If you survived the drop off, you still had to fight to keep control of your two-wheeler for now you were speeding over ruts and holes, and ridges or through sand or gravel or red dog or a combination of all the above.

162

Keeping a bicycle on the road was a very scary and potentially fatal decision to make, especially the first few times it was tried but the boys were determined. At first they would slow the bike almost to a stop when they met a vehicle and just barely moving, they would keep right to the edge of the road. At that speed and that close to the edge of the road, all they had to do was lean over a little out of the way to keep from being hit. Surprisingly, the first cars they met swung off onto the berm to afford the bike riders the whole other half of the road. The boys began to ride with more confidence and swagger after that. They were being treated as equals on the hardroad---shown the same respect that any other vehicle sharing the road was given.

Somehow the word must have gotten around in Sugar Tree that bicyclists were to be given a share of the road. The source didn't come from any of the Jive Five but they were nonetheless, grateful. They never flaunted their new found freedom but over time, just took it be the way things are. The boys now rode more toward the center of the road. Once in a while they'd meet a disgruntled driver or a young "too hip" driver who begrudged having to run off on their side of the road and they'd yell obscenities and blow their horns and shake their fists, but they always got over.

One Sunday evening, about a month after the Buick race, the Jive Five were returning to Sugar Tree from a leisurely ride out the ridge towards Mill's Bottom and were coasting down Sugar Tree Hill, single file, at a speedy little clip. Chip was in the lead as they coasted through Dead Man's Curve and entered the little straight stretch that led to the bottom of the hill. Suddenly, a '59 red Buick convertible swung around the curve at the bottom of the hill and headed up the straight right at the Jive Five. The hair on Chip's neck stood up, the color drained from his face, and he found it hard to breathe.

The Buick had just been cruising along when it rounded the curve but when the driver saw the line of bicycles heading down the hill toward him, he actually sped up. Upon his recognition of the lead rider, his eyes grew to the size of a fifty cent piece and he mashed the gas feed down a little harder.

The distance between the Buick and Chip was closing quickly. The three guys behind Chip had already abandoned their principles and had pulled off on the berm as far as they could and stopped. Chip kept on speeding down the hill. He knew Cotton wasn't going to get off the road and he had already decided that he wasn't gettin' off either. The two unrelinquishing spirits bore down on one another.

As they got closer, Chip could see Cotton laughing but he also noticed that Cotton was steering the Buick over as close to the edge of his side of the road as he could without dropping off. Chip took the movement as a sign of capitulation and cruised his bike over to the very edge of the road on his side. Now only one question remained: was there enough room for the wide fins on the Buick and the handlebars of Chip's bike to pass without hitting?

The two met in the middle of the straight. Chip closed his eyes at the last second. It wasn't the fins on the Buick that Chip needed to be so concerned about. The front fin slipped by easily, but the door handles located on the outside curve of the Buick's swooping body, stuck out at least four inches farther than the fins. Either the wind slipping between the car and the bike, or the actual door handle itself brushed the hair on Chip's knuckles. That's how close they were when they passed.

Cotton waved his hand in the air above the windshield and blew the horn and kept right on gettin' it up the hill.

Chip slowed to a stop still somewhat shaken and waited for the rest of the guys to catch up. He looked at the knuckles on his left hand. Everything looked ok. No bleeding or anything, but there was a kind of itching, tickling sensation in them. Kind of like when a hand or foot goes to sleep.

After that little confrontation, the boys decided that maybe getting off the road, out of people's way, might not be as disastrous as some other results could be.

VI

As the years passed by, Chip's bicycling jaunts expanded beyond the confines of the Sugar Tree Valley. Ironically, as much as Chip depended on biking to get around in those early years, the older he got, the less he used it. By the time he was fourteen or fifteen, bicycling was reserved only for long, serious excursions.

One of the Jive Five's most frequent and favorite trips was out to the Horse Ridge Fire Tower. The Horse Ridge Fire Tower was located, of course, on Horse Ridge. The road out to the fire tower left the hardroad at the top of Red Dog Hill and wound its way through the woods, casually gaining altitude as it went. At the end of two miles the road circled around a little raised knoll and ended abruptly in a little clearing at the top of the knoll where the fire tower sat.

The CCC had build the fire tower in 1939. It was constructed of a maze of angle iron steel sections bolted together. It was one hundred eight feet high and tapered down in size as it went up. An open wooden stairway zig-zagged its way up the inside of the steel skeleton. The steps grew smaller and smaller as they neared the top. At the top of the tower perched a little eight foot by eight foot observation enclosure. The bottom four feet of the walls of the little room were made of steel plates, bolted together at the corners. It gave a person a small sense of security. The top three feet of the little room was made of glass set inside steel frames. The steel framed windows could be swung out from the bottom and propped open a little if the weather so inclined one to do so. A metal roof capped the top of the little observation room.

One got inside the fire tower by climbing all the way to the top of the stairs which led right to the bottom of the observation room. Then pushing up the trap door in the bottom of the floor you could climb on up into the room. Once everyone was inside the fire tower, the trap door was dropped shut and became a part of the floor.

Horse Ridge wasn't the highest peak in the area but the one hundred eight foot tower made it the highest observation point in a twenty air mile radius. The tower stuck up twenty or thirty feet above the trees. No matter how many times Chip climbed the fire tower, it was still scary. It was scarier up in the top of the tower than it was outside on the stairway. At least outside he had a handrail to grab a hold of, but up in the tower there was nothing to hang on to. He was helplessly trapped inside this little cubicle that was surrounded by emptiness for as far as he could see and there was no visible support to keep this tower from falling over, except the four little bolts that were anchored into a concrete base at each corner of the tower down at the bottom, one hundred eight feet below. Chip tried not to think about it too much. If the other guys were scared, they never let on like they were and neither did Chip.

No matter how calm it was down on the ground, there was a perpetual wind that buffeted the little observation room atop the tower. Some days it rattled the metal sides and shook the windows so bad you couldn't hear yourself think. Unfortunately those windy days were the worst for forest fires and those were days the observer had to maintain a constant vigil over the mountains.

In the middle of the floor of the observation room was a pedestal, four and a half feet high which had upon its surface a large, detailed, topographical, circular map of the surrounding countryside. There was a sighting device that was anchored in the middle of the map and could be swiveled three hundred and sixty degrees around the map. If a person spotted a fire or some other interesting phenomena out there, they could swing the sighter in the direction of the spectacle and then sight it in precisely by looking along the sighting rod like one would sight a rifle. Once the object was sighted, the sighter could be locked in place so it wouldn't move. Then the observer could follow the sighter's path along the map below until he reached the recognized area on the map where the object was located. There was a mileage indicator built right into the sighter which would give one the approximate location of the object in air miles from the tower. There was also a compass laid out in the map's legend so with a little practice, the observer could pinpoint the area where a fire was located by referring it to a well recognizable landmark on the map.

There was also a short wave radio and a telephone in the fire tower.

Fire spotting was done by using binoculars to look for smoke. There were different kinds of smoke both in color and in appearance. If a forest or brush fire was spotted, the observer would then radio two other fire towers in the direction of the smoke. There were at least four other fire towers within a distance of thirty air miles of each other and their observation areas overlapped. The observer would provide his direction and mileage to the other towers and they would in turn triangulate the exact location of the fire. Once that was accomplished, the location could be radioed or telephoned to the Forest Service.

In 1939, no one was better at spotting and reporting fires than Luther Goff. No one was better in 1949 than Luther. By 1959 though, the years had begun to take their toll on Luther. He was probably in his late sixties when the Jive Five first began riding out to the fire tower, but he looked like someone eighty years old.

Luther had been the only caretaker the Horse Ridge Tower had ever known. Luther had gone to work for the Department of Natural Resources in 1939, when he was already a middle aged man. He was never married.

The CCC had built a little, one room cabin beside the tower so the observer could stay close to the tower twenty-four hours a day. The cabin was built over top of a rock walled root cellar where some canned goods, potatoes, etc. could be stored. Upstairs, the cabin contained a gas stove, a bed, a refrigerator, and a sink. Water was pumped to the sink by a hand pitcher pump attached to the sink. Luther had a radio, which by the way, had excellent reception out there on the ridge. The cabin was also equipped with a telephone extension and another short wave radio. The outdoor privy was located just at the edge of the woods, about twenty yards away, down over the knoll.

Luther was expected to be on duty in the tower all during daylight hours for the duration of fire season. Fall fire season in West Virginia began the first day of September and ended the last day of December. Spring Fire Season began the first day of March and ended the last day of May. Actually, fires were not a real danger until middle of October in the fall, but could become a danger as early as middle of March in the spring.

The reason fires became such a danger in middle October was because squirrel hunting season opened then and some desperate hunters liked to start a fire at the bottom of a hollow tree to smoke all the squirrels out that might be dwelling there. Most of the time when the hunter had smoked out all the squirrels in the tree, he put the fire out and went on his way and nothing happened. Sometimes though, if the tree was dead, the insides of the tree would be ignited from the hunter's fire and it might be hours before the wood inside would flare up. Once some of those old dead trees caught fire, fire could spread quickly if the woods were dry. Also at that time of year the leaves had begun to turn and fall, covering the ground with easily burning fuel.

The only days Luther got out of fire spotting duty were days when it rained or snowed. Neither did he have to work as long as there was at least a two inch cover of snow on the ground. On those days Luther would hop into his '53 Willys sedan, drive over to Sugar Tree, and buy a few necessities to replenish his lonely outpost. Also on those days, he would usually stop off at his sister's family home in Sugar Tree and take a good hot bath, shave, and clean up a might.

As the years of the lonely, tedious duty on Horse Ridge dragged on, Luther made less and less trips to his sister's to clean up. He still made his trips into Sugar Tree for supplies but weeks of bathing in a warmed-up water basin didn't do much for Luther's personal hygiene. Luther also began to make little side trips over to Momma Haywood's in Red Dog, for a little homemade wine to keep the long hours going by a little faster, but the boys had never found Luther drunk or even drinking on the job. His disheveled appearance however, to the unfamiliar, projected the image of a street corner wino.

Two other important features of Luther's physical condition had also begun to fail. One was his hearing. Years of working in that little metal and glass cubicle at the top of the fire tower while constantly being assaulted from every side by gusting and gale force wind had seriously damaged his hearing. The boys noticed it when they talked to Luther. Up in fire tower they had to repeat everything twice to be understood but everybody had to do that to be heard over the top of the rattling and banging that went on. But talking to Luther down in the cabin in the evening, they still had to repeat everything twice.

Luther's eyesight had also begun to fade. It was probably just the natural degeneration that comes with age but it was also helped along by the hours and hours of blazing sun, bright blue skies, and the constant strain of searching hundreds and hundreds of miles of hazy, undulating landscape for minute, indistinguishable objects that at about forty miles out, all began to blend together into one undefined mass.

None of the boys could remember the first time they went out to the fire tower. It was probably when their dad took them and it was probably at a young age. Young enough so they were too stupid to be scared or cautious.

After they turned off onto the fire tower road, they would pedal a mile or so up the road until they came to the top of a little swag in the road then they would stop. From the top of that little swag they could see the fire tower out on the end of the ridge and from there they could tell whether or not Luther was up in the tower. It didn't really make much difference if he was in the tower or not, that wouldn't have any bearing on whether the boys would continue on the last mile to the tower. They went whether there was anybody up in the tower or not. Sometimes the tower would be open and Luther might be down on the ground fixing dinner or attending to some other chore. Other times the tower would be closed and there would be nobody out there. The boys never could remember when fire season was in or wasn't in, but it was always a lot more enjoyable when Luther was up in the tower.

If Luther was up in the tower when the guys pulled in at the base, he'd always yell down to them out of one of the windows. "Come on up boys. See if you can give me some help."

If Luther was on the ground he'd meet the boys at the bottom of the tower. "Go on up", he'd say, "I'll be up shortly." Luther was always glad to have company.

There was an ominous sign bolted to the bottom of the fire tower. Written in very large letters and visible from any approach to the tower, it read "WARNING-CLIMB TOWER AT YOUR OWN RISK." That haunting message always remained imprinted in Chip's mind all the while he was at the tower.

If nobody was around, the boys would climb up to the last steps which ended just under the trap door in the floor of the observation room. Benji never went up the steps like everybody else. He always climbed up the outside structure of the tower until he got to the top steps. Maynard and Lincoln always kept egging him on but Chip wouldn't even watch. It was scary enough just getting himself to the top. He refused to even watch Benji. He didn't want to be witness to that horrifying, fatal fall. Benji always climbed up the outside of the tower but when he went down, he always used the stairs. Maybe he didn't want to push his luck too far.

If Luther was in the top, he always had the trap door open when the boys got there. They'd scramble up inside and move around the room so Luther could close the door. There wasn't a whole lot of room to maneuver around up there. The map stand took up about half of the room right out of the middle. There was just enough room for one person to walk around the map so with five people up there, they just kind of rotated around the room in single file. Two people could squeeze by if need be but it was a tight fit.

The first thing Chip did was look for the home place. He had been there enough to pick it out right away and he always had to announce where it was to everyone, like they had never been up there with him before. "Hey guys, see that third ridge of hills over there," he would point. "Now, follow that ridge a little to the left and you'll see the top of the meadow that falls away to the other side of the ridge. That's right above my home." He might as well have been up there by himself 'cause nobody was listening to him. For one thing it was too noisy and for another, everybody else was busy doing their own reconnoitering.

"Hey, there's the upper gob pile at Red Dog." A very common and easily identifiable landmark seen a hundred times and without binoculars. Nothing new there.

"Look! Right there you can just see a little patch of the hardroad right at the top of the hill where it turns down to Sugar Tree." No reaction there.

"Hey, that looks like one of Jobe Frame's trucks passing by there." Mild interest as a few heads turn to see if they could see it.

Maynard was scanning the northern horizon with Luther's binoculars. He could spot George Barnett's house and farm out on Devil's Backbone. He focused in on the house. "Maybe Loretta is out behind the house sunbathing naked," he announced hopefully.

Loretta was George's oldest and the most well endowed of his three daughters.

"Lemme look", demanded Benji trying to grab the binoculars from Maynard.

"Get your own or wait until I'm done", snapped Maynard.

Link was leaning on the sill of an open window scanning the southeast horizon. "Hey, that looks like smoke over there." Nobody paid any attention. "I swear that looks like a fire or something. What do you think, Luther?"

Luther didn't hear Link. He was sitting on a little stool in the corner by the radio, eating a sandwich and drinking some coffee out of his thermos.

"Hey Chip, come over here and look at this," Link motioned without taking his eyes off the terrain.

Chip reluctantly sidled around the map to the other side of the tower and followed Link's finger pointing out towards the horizon. He suddenly perked up with interest. "Hey Luther, what do you make of this?", he questioned. Luther still didn't respond. He kept on munching and looking out towards the north.

"Come 'er Maynard and bring the binoculars," Chip said. Link went around to the opposite side of the map and began to use the site rod to locate the area where the smoke continued to rise. Maynard brought the binoculars over to the open window but didn't give them up to Chip. He used them himself to scan the territory. "By God," he declared, "it looks like there's a forest fire over there."

"Of course there's a fire over there, you dork head. Now give me the binoculars." Chip jerked them away from Maynard and zeroed in on the location.

They all had seen the smoke with their naked eyes. All except Luther. When Chip looked at the fire through the binoculars it was evident by the size of the fire that it had probably been burning for a little while. He figured either Luther had already called it in or surely somebody else had. Luther was now watching the boys congregate to the same side of the tower and he even looked out the window in that direction but he never acknowledged that he was aware of any fire.

'You guys move out of my line of sight so I can pinpoint that son-of-a bitch", commanded Link and he sighted in on the position of the fire. He locked the sight rod in place He then oriented the visible landmarks close to the fire location with the landmarks on the map. Finally, he used the compass on the map's legend and the piece of string attached to the map and calculated direction and distance to the fire's location. It impressed the heck out of the other three guys.

Link, who was the closest to Luther stepped over and very slowly and deliberately shouted right in his face, "LUTHER, COME OVER HERE AND SEE IF THIS IS A FIRE".

Luther stared at him for a second or two then he put down his sandwich and coffee, moved over behind the map where Link was, and looked out the windows to the southeast.

Chip handed the binoculars over the map to him. Luther looked through the binoculars for half a minute or so and then said almost to himself, "By God, that looks like a damn forest fire over there".

Link stepped back, leaned against the window, and folded his arm across his chest. He was playing the part of the hero and eating it up.

Luther hunkered over and peeped down the sight rod. He stood up and placed his finger on the map where the approximate location of fire was.

Link interjected slowly and loudly again, "LOOKS TO ME LIKE IT'S ON THE SOUTH SIDE OF LITTLE BIRCH MOUNTAIN."

Luther grabbed the hand held radio mike out of it's cradle just above him. The coiled lead cable slid out behind and hung in an arc above the map. He clicked on the mike. There was an urgency in his voice as he spoke into the mike. "Horse Ridge tower to Point Mountain. Come in Point Mountain." There was ten to fifteen seconds of static before the radio answered back.

"Point Mountain. Go ahead Horse Ridge. Over."

"Eddie, this is Luther. Give me a fix on Little Birch Mountain and see if you can confirm a code red. Over"

"Roger, Luther. Stand by, I'll get back to you. Over."

This was by far the most exciting thing that had ever happened out at the fire tower. They waited as the minutes dragged by. Even

172

though they were expecting a return call, when the radio finally crackled to life again, it gave everybody a start. "Point Mountain to Horse Ridge. Over."

Luther was quick to hit the mike button, "Horse Ridge. Go ahead. Over."

"Looks like you were right, Luther. Got a big fire out down there. It's barely visible for us even through the glasses. Would never have spotted it until it got much bigger. It's definitely on Little Birch though. Good job. It's your spot so go ahead and call it in. We'll be on standby here. Point Mountain out."

Luther picked up the telephone and called whoever he was suppose to at the Department of Natural Resources to report a fire. After a short conversation with whoever on the other end, he hung up the phone and looked at the boys. He looked like he was about to cry. "Boys, you done good", he choked. "You saved old Luther's hind end on this one. I would have never spotted that fire until it had grown too big. They probably would have fired me. Then what would I do?" He hung his head down and just stared at the floor. He pulled his bandanna out of his back pocket and blew into it. The boys didn't know if he was really crying or just had to blow his nose. Anyway it was getting kind of uncomfortable and embarrassing in there.

Link finally broke the uneasiness. "Listen Luther, anytime you need some good help, some good company, or some excitement, you just call on us. There is nobody around here who could bring you all that at the same time and that's a fact." The rest of the guys answered in agreement and gradually everybody loosened up and before long, things were back to normal.

Link never let the guys forget that if it hadn't been for his expertise and quick action that day, half of southern West Virginia would have been burned to a crisp.

No one ever seemed to know where Luther Goff went during mid-winter or where he spent his summers. He didn't live anywhere near Sugar Tree or he surely would have been spotted once in a while. Some said he just drove all around the country in his Willys, visiting relatives and seeing the sights. Others said he had a little apartment in Canton, Ohio, and that's where he headed during his off season. If someone really wanted to know about

Luther, all they had to do was go and ask Luther's sister who lived in Sugar Tree, but it was more intriguing to speculate.

On the boys' first trip to the fire tower the following spring, they were surprised to find a new DNR jeep wagon parked beside the cabin and a new spotter working the tower. He was a young fellow who looked to be about twenty-five or so. He wore the khaki uniform like the game wardens wore, with green DNR insignia patches on the shoulders.

As the boys started their ascent of the tower the first thing the new guy did was yell out of the window down to Benji, "Hey, boy! Get off that tower---now. I catch you climbing around on that thing again I'll fine you and your old man a hundred dollars."

Benji just stood there in mid grip, staring up at the new face, then he started mumbling to himself . Instead of climbing back down, he worked his way from the outside over towards the middle until he finally swung over to the stairs.

When they got to the trapdoor to go inside, the new guy would only let two of them up into the top at a time. "Against regulations to have more than three people in the tower at any one time", he stated.

There was no way Benji was going to go inside and none of the others cared whether they went inside or not but they did want to find out what happened to Luther. Chip and Maynard decided to go inside. As soon as the new guy shut the trap door Chip asked him straight out, "Where's Luther?"

The new guy picked up the binoculars and started sweeping the terrain, "He's been sick all winter," he said, "got pneumonia or something but it's not life threatening. He's just not able to work the tower right now. Maybe he'll be back next fall. Excuse me." He worked his way around Chip and started looking in the opposite direction.

After five more minutes of silence, Chip and Maynard pulled up the trap door and climbed down the stairs to Benji and Link. Before they could ask the other two if they wanted to go up, the new guy closed the trap door.

"To heck with this", announced Maynard, "I'm going down and I ain't coming back till this clown has vacated the premises!" With that he started climbing over Benji and Link. The rest of the guys started following him down the stairs.

"You reckon he was tellin' the truth about old Luther?", asked Chip.

"What'd he say?", asked Link.

"He said something about Luther bein' sick and not able to work."

"I think he's full of bologna", retorted Maynard. "This just ain't right. They shoulda told us something."

"Well, I'll tell you one thing," said Benji, "I'm with Maynard. If old Luther ain't gonna be here, I'm not coming back neither. I'm not gonna have some snot nose college punk ordering me around. I been here longer than he has."

Luther never returned to the fire tower and the boys never found out what happened to him. As the years passed by, Luther kind of slipped into the recesses of the boys' mind. Every once in a while someone would bring up his name and they all asked, "Wonder what ever happened to him?"

The boys continued to visit the fire tower but they only went when there was nobody staying out there and they still found a number of ways to entertain themselves. They always climbed to the top of the tower just to check to see if the trap door leading to the observation room was padlocked. It always was, but they would sit on the steps under the room and survey the the vast terrain and heavens spread out before them. Other diversions included carrying objects to the top of the tower and dropping them off. Rocks, pieces of wood, sticks, broken branches, other types of debris were good for bombing selected targets on the ground. Spitting tobacco juice was also a favorite pastime but it was only successful from about halfway up the tower due to the wind factor and sometimes even then it tended to be too messy. Peeing from the top of the fire tower was forbidden at any time, under any conditions. Even Benji, who claimed he could pee over an eight foot fence was not allowed to pee off the fire tower. No matter how far one could pee or in which direction he peed, it would drift back into the tower and sooner or later, they would have to climb back down and pass through it. Benji also returned to his life-restoring escapade of climbing up the tower on the outside.

One sunny, Sunday afternoon in early March, the boys decided to make a round trip excursion from Sugar Tree, up across the Panther Mountain shortcut to US Rt.19, down Rt. 19 into Hob, and continue on back to Sugar Tree on good old Rt.11.

The Panther Mountain shortcut began where the hardroad up Painter's Fork ended, right at the foot of Panther Mountain. The shortcut was a dirt road that wound over a mile and a half up the mountain to the top. Once on top, the road followed along the ridge for another three miles before dumping out onto US Rt. 19 right at the crown of Panther Mountain. It was called the shortcut because it was only four and a half miles from US 19 to Sugar Tree along the dirt road. If you stayed on US 19, drove off the mountain into Hob, turned onto Rt.11 and drove into Sugar Tree, it would be approximately 13 miles. There were no houses, no dwellings, no human contact on the shortcut road. Because the State Road never cleared the little dirt road during the winter, it was almost impassable except for jeeps and other four wheel drive vehicles.

The four boys left around noon on Sunday, right after church. The first leg of the trip meant riding their bikes up Painter's Fork in Sugar Tree until they came to the bottom of Panther Mountain. Then they had to push their bikes the mile and a half up the Sugar Tree side of the mountain. The air that day was warm for early March with the temperature at noon around fifty degrees. The road climbed up the north side of the mountain so the sun didn't do much to warm it up. The ground and the dirt road were still frozen from the cold, hard winter. Pushing their way up the mountain wasn't too difficult on the hard, firm dirt surface.

The second leg of the trip would take them three miles out the ridge on top of Panther Mountain to the turnoff on Rt. 19. The day had begun to warm up and the air was warmer up on the ridge. The sun was also able to radiate what little heat it had this time of year directly on to the top of the ridge. The boys thought it to be a blessing at first and after a short rest to catch their breath and soak up a little of the sun's heat at the top of the mountain, they swung on their bikes and peddled off. They only peddled for a couple of hundred yards before they discovered what the warm temperatures and sun had done to the dirt road.

The road had become an impassable quagmire of clay mud. It wasn't the oozy, sloppy kind of mud, although there was plenty of that in the many holes and ruts that lay in the road, this was the heavy, thick, globby, sticky, slick kind. It stuck to the bicycle tires, and as the wheels turned it picked up more and more clay mud and before long, the wheels wouldn't roll anymore because the mud was caked between the wheels and the fenders and the frame. Not only wouldn't the bike roll, it weighed fifteen pounds heavier than it should. Even Maynard's bike with no fenders wouldn't roll because the mud had encased the wheels against the front and rear forks.

Pushing the bikes so they would slide over the mud became a chore because as the boys tromped along in the mud, the build up on their shoes kept them from gaining any traction with the muddy ground. As the mud built up on their shoes, they became heavier and heavier. It was more work to break their heavy feet out the mud glue than it was trying to push the overweight and immobilized bicycle along.

They tried pushing the bikes. They tried pulling the bikes. They tried carrying the bikes but it was all weary work. In one hour they had managed to struggle only a quarter of a mile along the ridge. The only reason they went that far was to get around a bend in the road so they could see if the road condition got any better. It didn't. Before them stretched at least two and a half miles of rutted, water filled, deep, clay mud. "You couldn't whip a billy goat through there", remarked Benji.

There was no other way to move ahead except in the road. Bordering the left side of the road rose a steep bank. The bank was only eight or ten feet high but it was straight up and was compiled of the same clay mud that the road was made of. On the right side of the road, the mountain dropped straight down for hundreds of feet.

After another hour and another quarter of a mile had passed, the boys found a little wide spot on the right hand side of the road under a big red oak tree and collapsed there from exhaustion. Chip left his bike standing up in the middle of the road, held there by the adhesion of the mud. "I'll bet you couldn't even kick that bike over", he breathed through clenched teeth. They rested there under the tree contemplating their options.

"I don't care", announced Maynard, "I don't know about the rest of you but I'm not gonna fight that mud back the way we came. I don't care if it takes the rest of the week, if I'm going to bust my balls, it's gonna be gaining new ground. Not for somethin' I've already done once."

Maynard's statement not only made sense, it rejuvenated everybody's spirit. "Hey! Hey! I'll tell you something else", perked up Chip, "if we make it to the gas line we can get off this road."

"Yeah, that's right", added Benji, "not only can we cut off a mile or so, we can probably ride the bikes through there some."

With renewed determination the boys set about the task before them. First they dragged their bikes out of the road and over to the wide place. They used sticks to poke and scrape away as much mud as they could from their bikes.

Link's English racer was a light bike so he was able to carry it over the mud on ahead. Because Maynard's bike had no fenders, it was relatively easy to carry too, once the mud was removed. Even with most of the accessories removed, Benji's bike was still too heavy and cumbersome to carry. Chip's bike, being just a basic bike, was also too heavy and cumbersome to carry. Link and Maynard would carry their bikes up ahead a hundred feet or so then go back and help Benji and Chip push and slide their bikes through the mud. Sometimes Chip and Benji would help Link and Maynard carry their bikes and they would all go back and work the other two bikes through the mud. By working in tandem this way the boys progressed a little easier along the road until they finally came to the gas line.

Hope Gas Company had laid a gas transmission line across Panther Mountain in the early 1930's. The gas line right-of-way was about thirty feet wide and was always kept cleared of brush. The right-of-way ran in a straight line across Panther Mountain whereas the road tended to curve and turn and twist its way along. The road crisscrossed the gas line three times along the top of the ridge.

Once they got to the first gas line crossing, they had to again clean the mud from Benji's and Chip's bike before they could head off. The right-of-way was sown in grass which was now dormant and a cover of dead leaves helped firm up the ground but more important, there was no mud. They could now ride their bikes and make up some time.

The right-of-way ran in a straight line but that meant it also ran straight up and down the ravines and knolls. Fortunately, up here on top of the mountain, the gas line only dipped down into a few small swales and the boys were able to coast down one side and peddle most of the way up the other side. Some of the dips were too steep to ride down safely or to peddle up but walking the bikes up or down from time to time wasn't hard.

Warmed by the sun after being blanketed by the winter snow for four months, the musty smell of rotting leaves and rich forest loam drifted up from the floor of the woods on either side of the boys. It was an encouraging sign that spring wasn't that far away.

The second road crossing came after a half a mile of gas line riding but it ate up almost a mile of dirt road. The boys paired off and helped each other carry their bikes across the road, then they set off again. They couldn't believe their luck. This was working out better than they figured. It was too good to be true. They knew for sure something was going to happen to gum up the works.

They made it to the last road crossing with no incidents. Here, the gas line dropped straight down over the mountain and the road turned away to the left. The second gas line route had taken another mile off the road. There was now less than a quarter of a mile of muddy road left between the boys and US 19. There was nothing else to do but to push onward.

From where they were, the road had a slight downhill grade and the mud didn't seem as thick and gooey as it had been back on the other end. Maybe the sun hadn't warmed this end up as much as the other. Link found the going even easier along the very edge of the upper side of the road, so they all fell in single file and followed him. After fifteen or twenty minutes of travel they could hear cars and trucks pulling Panther Mountain on US 19.

The closer they got to the highway, the more urgent their work became. The last hundred feet of the short cut dropped off straight

179

down to the highway and the road base was stone covered and solid as could be. Chip thought how the appearance of the beginning of the short cut could really fool somebody into taking that road, thinking that it would be just like this all the way to Sugar Tree. Man, would they be surprised. If they got their vehicle stuck out there on the ridge, it might be May before they could get out.

The four waited at the edge of Rt. 19 listening for cars to come over the top from both directions before attempting to cross. When they thought it was clear, one of them would push his bike across the two lane to the wide place on the other side of the road. They pushed their bikes across one at time for two reasons. First, it was better if only one person was run over rather than all four of them. Second, if a car did come when you were in the middle of the road, you had a better chance getting out of the way if you were on your feet instead of sitting on a bicycle. They all made it across without incident. It was 4:00 in the afternoon. It had taken them four hours to travel four and a half miles from Sugar Tree.

Now they had to come up with a strategy for traveling the next three miles down Panther Mountain on Rt.19. They did this while they cleaned and scraped the mud out of their bikes. There were a couple of small water puddles in the wide place and they were able to run their tires through the water to help clean the mud off.

It was decided that Link would go first since he had the fastest coaster. Maynard would go second since he had no brakes except for his worn out engineer boots. Benji would go third since he had the speedometer. That way he could judge their speed from the fastest to the slowest. Chip would go last just by the process of elimination.

It was agreed that whoever coasted the farthest on the level after they reach the bottom of the hill, would stop and wait for everyone else to catch up. It was also agreed, without any debate, that no one would use their brakes going down the hill unless it was an emergency and emergencies included only those incidents where an animal or a car would be obstructing the right of way. If someone braked going down the hill, he would no longer be a part of the group and would thereafter be known as a chicken livered, no balls, pussy faced coward, and that was that. Maynard had no objection at all to the no brake rule.

They made last minute adjustments and double checked all nuts, bolts, sprockets, chains, cables, wheels, and tires. It would not be very productive to have an axle come loose at sixty miles an hour. They buttoned up, zipped up, buckled up, and tied up every loose piece of clothing. Link pulled a pair of light, leather gloves out of his tool bag and put them on. Maynard pulled the ear flaps down on his woolen cap and buckled the strap under his chin. The sun was still high in the southwest but the boys were headed down the east side of the mountain, away from the setting sun.

They lined up the bikes one behind the other along the edge of the road and then waited until they could hear no vehicles coming up either side of the mountain. When all was quiet, Link pushed off, pedaled twice and hunkered down over the handlebars. Maynard and Benji both hit the road at the same time one behind the other. Chip watched them disappear into the dark shadows below the top of the mountain as he too, peddled out of the gravel and unto the highway.

The first thing Chip noticed as his speed began to pick up was the unbelievable smoothness of the road. There were no humps, bumps, holes, gravel or paved over edges to worry about. His bike stayed steady and smooth. The second thing he noticed was that he had a very wide avenue in which to maneuver his bike. His lane down the mountain was twelve to fourteen feet wide. Plenty of room to take a turn at high speed and drift to the outside or the inside if needed. He would know for sure in another thirty seconds because he was coming to the two sharpest curves on the Hob side of Panther Mountain.

The steepest part of Panther Mountain was the first quarter of a mile down from the top. At the end of that steep part the road made a sharp bend to the right heading out away from the mountain side and then turned back in to it again. Chip's bike picked up speed quickly and he knew in just that little distance from the top, he was already going faster than he had ever gone on a bicycle in his life. The road was smooth and his speed was deceptive but he knew he was flying. He could see the curves coming up ahead. He glanced over his shoulder. The road behind him was still clear of traffic.

He headed the bike as close to the inside of the first turn as he could without getting in loose gravel and dust on the edge and without going off unto the berm which would have been disastrous. The cabled guard posts swished by only twelve inches away. The bike took the inside route and stayed right where Chip steered it. He just held it to a straight line and she crossed over the lane and sailed through the inside of the second turn slick as could be.

The road straightened out a little and Chip could see he was closing the gap on Benji. He figured he was doing about sixty. He wasn't worried about passing Benji because Benji had rear view mirrors on his bike and he figured Benji would see him coming and move over. Benji moved over a little and as Chip went around, he glanced over at Benji. Benji flashed four fingers and then five fingers. Forty-five thought Chip. When Chip turned his head back around frontwards, the wind caught the bill of his frazzled, faded, beloved Cincinnati Redlegs baseball cap and jerked it right off of his head. He tried to snatch it with his left hand but it was already gone. He looked back over his shoulder in hopes that Benji could grab it but Benji was laughing so hard he had to keep both hands on the handlebars to keep from wrecking. He could see the cap laying in the middle of the road. "Son-of-a bitch", mumbled Chip. No way he could stop and retrieve the cap and he was too far from the bottom of the mountain to walk all the way back up there and look for it. The more he thought about losing that ball cap, the madder he got.

Two cars coming up the hill whizzed past. The frustration of losing his ball cap was slowly replaced by the exhilaration of the adventure. This is so cool, he thought, I bet we took them by surprise. He glanced back over his shoulder again and all he saw was Benji back there slowly fading behind.

After a couple of gentle turns in the road, Maynard came into view up ahead and Chip began to catch up to him. Maynard was going faster then Benji was, so it took a minute or two before Chip could catch up to him. Maynard had his feet propped up on the top part of the front forks and was holding the steering wheel straight and firm with his knees. He was steering right down the middle of the road. As Chip kept getting closer, he watched for Maynard to look behind him so he would know Chip was passing him. Chip kept getting closer.

To pass Maynard on the outside would be too dangerous. He could go off on the berm and wreck into the guard posts or go over the mountainside. He could slow down but that meant he would have to use his brakes and he would never get back up to this speed again. Maynard still hadn't turned around. Chip caught up to Maynard coming out of a little curve to the left and with nothing coming up the hill in the little straight stretch ahead of them, Chip crossed over the double white line and slipped by Maynard. Maynard looked over and gave Chip the finger.

There was no doubt that Maynard wasn't using his brakes but Chip wondered about the others. It would be very easy to use the coaster brakes on the bikes and no one would ever know. He couldn't worry about that now. All he knew for sure was he hadn't used his, yet.

A blast of cold air struck Chip in the face. He could tell the temperature was dropping as he descended the mountain. He was now more than halfway down into the valley and there was snow still laying along the edge of the road and on the moutain side above him to his left. He looked off to his right across the valley and caught a glimpse of the fading, orange rays of the setting sun as they splashed against the very tips of the tallest peaks of the opposite mountains. He wasn't prepared for the biting cold air that lay heavy in the valley below. Without his ball cap to deflect the wind, his eyes began to water and his cheeks began to burn. His hands began to turn red from the cold wind assaulting them. He couldn't bow his head down to keep his face out of the wind because he had to keep his eyes on the road ahead.

He whipped by a trailer truck crawling its way up the mountain and behind the truck were four cars snuggled in one behind the other. Waitin' for a place to pass, thought Chip. As that thought lingered a moment in his brain, it jolted him clear into his heart. My God, he gulped, if a car pulled out in our lane to pass, we wouldn't have a chance. We'd be dead meat! Killed! These thoughts rolled over in his mind. We're too small to be seen coming down the mountain and we're going too fast to be able to stop. There is no where to go to get out of the way. He frantically began looking up ahead, along the side of the road next to the guard posts and cables to calculate if there would be enough room between them and a car for a bicycle to shoot through if they met headon. He glanced back over his shoulder for what seemed like the tenth time. The road was clear behind him. Lord Jesus, he prayed, please watch over us till we get to the bottom of this mountain. Please, please, don't let a car or truck try to pass. Please. I'll come to church every Sunday. I'll quit cussin' so much. Please God.

It seemed as if his speed was beginning to drop off some as he approached the last turns before the bottom of the mountain. He glanced over his shoulder--still nothing coming up from behind. The highway made a slow, gradual turn to the left and then another gentle swing to the right and then he was at the bottom. A straight stretch of highway ran two or three hundred yards up ahead of him but there was no sight nor trace of Link anywhere up there. Chip's bike began slowing down dramatically as he coasted down the straight. He began to breathe a prayer of thanks. Thank you Lord. Thank you Jesus.

He drifted into a little wide place by the side of the road. He got off the bike, kicked the kick stand down, leaned the bike over, and stood watching for Benji and Maynard. A car passed by heading for the mountain. "Just go slow", he whispered after it, "and watch out for the bicycles."

In a couple of minutes Chip spied Maynard emerging around the bottom turn and drifting as silently as a shadow. All of a sudden he let out a loud "Yeeeeee Haw" as he drew near Chip. Thank you Lord, whispered Chip to himself.

Maynard was almost breathless. "Man, oh man, what a ride! I'm ready to walk back up and do it again." He swung off the bike right beside Chip as it was still moving and let it coast over into a pile of brush at the back of the wide place.

Chip was trembling. "What's the matter with you?" asked Maynard as he looked at Chip.

"Just cold", answered Chip, which wasn't completely untrue.

Just then Benji popped around the bottom curve. He was peddling as hard and as fast as he could. He was getting all the speed he could with whatever downgrade was left.

Apparently though, it wasn't speedy enough for the drunks in the pickup truck right behind him. The truck was just inches from his rear fender and the driver was honking the horn and flipping his lights at Benji. Hanging out the passenger side window of the truck were two unshaven, red faced loudmouths yelling and taunting Benji. Benji just kept on peddling.

As soon as Benji and the truck hit the straight, the driver shoved her up into second gear, stomped the gas, and shot around Benji. A beer bottle flew out the passenger window and sailed over Benji's head. As the truck whizzed by Chip and Maynard they could hear the drunken laughter drifting out of the open cab window.

Benji was still peddling as hard as he could. It looked like he was trying to catch the truck. He was shaking his fist at it and yelling at the top of his lungs, "Come on back here you bastards. I'll kick your butts all over the road. Bunch of dumbass punks." He screeched to a stop in front of the Chip and Maynard.

"Them jackasses came up behind me about halfway down the mountain and started foolin' with me then. I thought they were going to run over me a couple of times. Bunch of sorry ass bastards!" Benji was shaking--could have been from anger--could have been from fear, could have been from the cold.

Chip was still praying silently. He looked at his watch. The whole ride had taken less than seven minutes. In those seven minutes Chip had experienced the full spectrum of emotions-- from anxiety to anger, to exhilaration, to frustration, to fear, to thankfulness---and he was spent.

Benji sat straddling his bike. It took a few minutes for him to calm down.

"Where the heck is Link?" Maynard asked. "Anybody seen him? You Chip? You were the first one down behind him."

"No. I never seen hide nor hair of him."

"Must be on up ahead then", Maynard concluded.

"Well, I'll tell you this", said a calmer Benji, "the fastest my speedometer read coming down the mountain was forty-nine. Now that's the truth and I was doin' that up there below those two "s" turns. Now Chip you'd be goin' a little faster than that. Maybe fifty-two or so. But it seemed like my bike wouldn't go any faster. I thought about peddling but I probably couldn't have peddled faster than my bike was going anyway. After about halfway down, my speed dropped off to between forty and forty-five and stayed right there until AJ Fartface and his buddies started messin' with me. There at the bottom I had to peddle my rear end off to keep my speed above thirty."

"Link must have been going sixty then", said Chip, "cause I never did see him."

"You don't reckon he wrecked somewhere back there and went over the mountain", pondered Maynard.

"Naw. We'd have seen somethin' of him," stated Benji. "I say we move on down the road like we planned. He's probably waitin' on up ahead a ways. Besides it's gonna get dark before we get home if we don't get movin." So with that said, the boys headed off towards Hob, still almost two miles away.

It was easy riding now. They put Benji in the back so he could see traffic coming up behind in his rear view mirrors. If he saw anything coming he'd yell, "Car!" as loudly as he could and the boys would drift over along the edge of the road in single file so the traffic could scoot on around them.

A mile went by and no Link to be spotted. They were becoming a might worried now.

Another mile passed and still no Link. As they coasted into Hob their concern for Link was lifted when they all three spied his bike parked in front of the Gulf station across from the Sugar Tree turnoff.

"Now you know that sucker didn't coast this far. Couldn't wait on us back there I guess", grumbled Maynard.

"Yeah, like it would worry us what might have happened to him," Benji chuckled.

"Well, let's not give him any satisfaction in being here first and if he throws any of his smart ass talk at us, we'll just get back on the bikes and leave him here without saying a word."

They coasted off the highway and onto the parking lot beside the station. Benji and Chip snapped down their kick stands and leaned the bikes over on them. Maynard laid his bike down on the concrete---he didn't have a kick stand.

They strolled into the service station like cowhands who had just rode into town. There was Link leaning up against the counter taking a long slug from a bottle of RC. He kept drinking till the other three were standing in front of him then he lowered the bottle and nodded to them. "Help yourself gentlemen", he said and nodded again to his left. There stood three cold cokes opened and beside each bottle, ready for consumption, a bag of Planter's peanuts---all taken care of by Mr. Snooty himself.

The boys dug in. Their once planned word assault on Link now forgotten. All expressed their thanks to their benefactor either verbally or by punches on the shoulder or slaps to the head.

The cozy warmth of the little station thawed more than their physical bodies. After pouring his peanuts into his coke, Chip asked Link how far he coasted from the bottom of the mountain.

"Not as far as I thought I would", he answered. "I seemed to lose some of my momentum near the bottom of the mountain. I coasted clear through the straight stretch at the bottom but had to peddle up that little incline just before you hit that right hand turn. I figured instead of waitin' on you guys I'd just go ahead and ride into Hob and get us something to refresh us. Say, you guys didn't have any kind of a run-in with some guys in a green pickup truck did you?"

"Damn right", spoke up Benji, jumping down off the pop cooler he was sitting on. He swaggered over to Link playing the tough guy. "Them jerkheads try anything with you?"

"Kinda. They tried to run me off the road but I saw them coming up behind me and just coasted off the road. They hollered some stuff at me but I couldn't tell much about what they were sayin'. I was just wondering. I saw their truck parked down at the Night & Gale."

"There you go, Benji," prodded Maynard, giving Chip a jab on the arm and winking at him. "Now's your chance to get those idiots."

"Are you crazy?" replied Benji, "I'm not going down there. All their drunkin' buddies are down there. I'm not old enough to go in there anyway."

"It don't matter how old you are, you dote. As long as you don't try to buy any beer. Anybody can go in there, besides you don't have to go in there. Just call them outside there in the parkin' lot."

"Yeah. Right. Then I'd have to fight fifteen of them. Any of you guys going with me?"

"I don't think so", said Link as a matter of fact. He put his empty RC bottle in the wooden rack on the wall. "I don't know about the rest of you guys but I'm headin' for Sugar Tree. Like to get there before it gets dark. You know what I mean?"

"I'm right behind you baby", declared Chip.

They said their good-byes to Gaylord Hall, the station owner, and piled out of the door. Benji was still talking the good fight. "If those guys come over to Sugar Tree and try to start something, I'll clean their clock." Nobody else said anything but they kept their heads turned away from Benji so he couldn't see or hear their muffled chuckles and grins.

The eight miles to Sugar Tree proved uneventful. They made it home in an hour and a half even after having to push their bikes up Renzee White Hill.

On the school bus the next morning heading for school, the Jive Five became the center of attention. The ride up Panther Mountain went way too fast that morning. They fell over each other relating their experience of conquering the mountain while trying to point out every detail of the trip as the bus passed by each landmark, no matter how insignificant it might have been. It was like one of those historical bus tours where the tour guide explains and describes each marker they pass by. "Here is where Chip's cap blew off." Everybody looked but no cap could be seen. The other males on the bus didn't pay much attention but the girls were interested and seemed somewhat impressed. That was all that counted anyway.

VII

The Jive Five's most memorable and enjoyable bicycle trips were those expeditions down to the swing on the Back Fork River. They tried to make that trip at least once a year and sometimes they got to go twice. They usually planned their trips for early or late summer when there would be less chance of a crowd being there. Mid summer was not the time to go if you wanted to spend a night or two because there was too much going on. During miner's vacation whole families set up camp at the swing and stayed for a week or more. The boys found out about the swing on Back Fork when Maynard's dad took them and about fifteen other kids from Sugar Tree, down there in the back of his pickup for a Baptist Youth Fellowship picnic one Sunday afternoon.

The road down to the river went all the way out Devil's Backbone and then circled its way down off the ridge to the river valley. It was sixteen miles from Sugar Tree to the river---too far to ride bicycles there, enjoy the river, and return in one day, so they always planned to stay at least one night and sometimes they stayed for a couple of nights.

It took them a couple of hours to round up everything they thought they might need; bread, Vienna Sausage, some cans of potted meat, jar of peanut butter, a handful of potatoes, matches, a cooker or pan, a skillet, two or three flashlights, and some packages of kool-aid. These could all be found at home, and their parents were always very helpful in the endeavor. They were about as happy to get rid of them as the boys were to go.

Benji had a 10x10 ft. tarp they always used to make a lean-to to sleep under. Each guy had a sleeping bag except for Maynard and he just brought a couple of quilts rolled up together. Link carried his CO2 pellet pistol. Fishing line, hooks, and favorite lures were stashed away in a carrying pouch somewhere. Because fishing poles were too cumbersome to carry for a long distance on a bicycle, only Link took one because his could be broken down and carried in a little round metal case that he lashed to the side of his bike. The others were adept at fashioning a fishing pole from a stick and Link let everyone share the real fishing pole. Anyway, fishing wasn't their main objective.

Chip's boy scout hatchet hung from his belt, secure in its leather case. Chip never went anywhere into the wilderness without his trusty hatchet. Benji said the thing was so dull he could ride on it down to the river and back.

They pooled their resources before setting off to make sure they would have enough money to buy other provisions once they got to the river. That way they wouldn't have to worry about packing so much stuff or worry about it spoiling. There was a little country store within an easy bike ride of their usual campsite.

Benji and Chip could carry their necessities lashed to the fenders or the carriers on their bikes. Link had to tie his to the frame because the fenders on his bike were so small. Maynard didn't have any fenders so he carried his stuff in a backpack he'd made from a feed sack. It worked very well. In fact it worked so well that Maynard usually wound up toting the bulk of supplies.

Link and Benji hooked up around at Sugar Tree and rode around to Maynard's. Then the three of them stopped off at Chip's to rearrange the gear as best they could so no one was overburdened. After a last minute check of everything, they peddled off, heading for the river. As usual, they only peddled about a quarter of a mile before they had to get off and push their bikes the mile or so up Renzee White Hill.

Once they got up on top of the ridge it was pretty easy going. There were a few dips and low gaps but nothing that took much more than ten minutes to push up to the top, especially if they could get up a little head of steam up cruising down the opposite side.

They turned off Rt.11 onto Devil's Backbone and made the speed adjustment from hardroad to dirt road. They learned long ago that there was a difference between riding on the hardroad and riding on a red dog/gravel road. It was three miles from Chip's to the Devil's Backbone turn off and then ten more miles out the ridge before they started their descent off Devil's Backbone. The road dropped sharply away at the end of the ridge and only used up one mile to reach the bottom. There were no hairpin turns to maneuver through but there were a number of sharp turns around the side of the mountain they had to traverse.

Benji started off the mountain first, then came Maynard and Chip. Link came last because he had to ease the English racer down the hill as it was prone to sliding in the red dog and gravel if he went too fast.

Benji had spent the whole morning at home arranging his gear on his bike so that it was just right. It was so perfectly neat and well placed that you would have thought Link did it. Well, he had. Chip and Maynard came around a turn about half way down the mountain and there before them sitting on his bike in the middle of the road was Benji. He was looking down at something in the pasture over the hillside. Chip and Maynard slid past Benji, one on each side, trying to get stopped in the gravels. It was as they slid by that they noticed all of Benji's gear that had been so diligently packed on the back carrier of his bike was now missing. It was scattered down over the hillside. It seems that every time Benji hit a bump in the road, the cord that lashed down his gear on the rear carrier would rub against the rear tire. Eventually it wore through the cord and just at the moment Benji took a sharp turn, it broke. His momentum going around the turn pulled him to the outside of the curve and slung all his rearward gear down over the hillside.

By the time Link arrived on the scene, Maynard and Chip were in stitches and Benji was having to scramble down over the hill to retrieve his gear. "There's cow crap and stuff all over my sleeping bag", he whined. "And look at my good jacket." He held it up for the rest to see. "It's got cow piss and grass stains all over it. What am I gonna do?"

"Quit crying around," said Maynard, trying to be serious. "Get your hind end on up here so we can fix you up and get on down the road. All that stuff is on the outside anyway. It won't hurt you. Besides you can wash it off in the river if we ever get there. Come on you big baby."

They finally got all of Benji's stuff packed back and lashed down on the bike although it didn't look quiet as pretty as it did when they started and it smelled so bad they made Benji go last--to heck with safety.

It was another half mile down the mountain, then another two miles of slight downward incline to the river. The boys made it easily.

At the river, the dirt road crossed over on a three hundred foot long, one lane, wooden bridge to the other side where it intersected with River Road. River Road was a single lane hardroad much like County Rt.11 in Sugar Tree. It ran the length of Back Fork River on the opposite side---thus the name River Road.

The boys deserted the road at the approach to the bridge and made their way upstream about three hundred yards. On that side of the river, the Baltimore and Ohio Railroad paralleled the river along the hillside, keeping forty to fifty feet above the river's surface. The boys followed the old county road that crossed the railroad tracks and dipped down to the river. Before the bridge was built in the late '40's, the only way to cross the river here was by ferryboat. Though the river was only about a hundred feet wide, it was between eight and ten feet deep.

At this spot on the river where the ferry landing used to be, a small peninsula of sand and gravel jutted twenty feet out into the river. The river flowing down into the peninsula cut a deep cove back into the river bank where the water settled, quiet and deep.

Nobody knew when "The Swing" had been established. It had always been there during the boys' lifetime. "The Swing" was made of one inch metal cable. It was attached to the broad limb of a huge sycamore tree that grew at the bottom of the steep river bank at the river's edge. The swing cable had been there so long that the upper part of the sycamore's limb had grown over the cable. It was buried at least an inch deep which indicates it had been there a long time. The bottom end of the cable passed through a metal pipe and was fastened together with cable clamps above the pipe thus forming a triangle in which the pipe was the handhold as the bottom part of the triangle. The swing was forty feet long.

One could swing off from a spot on the old county road up on the river bank, out over the water above the little cove to a height of twenty feet above the water. At that height, one dropped into the water where it was between ten and thirteen feet deep.

Sometimes folks would pull a car or truck up on the old road right at the edge of the riverbank and swing off from on top of the car roof. It would add another five feet to the apex of the swing.

Seasoned veterans would wait just till the swing hit the peak of its upward swing before letting go with a dive into the water. Those divers would do swan dives, jackknives, somersaults, and layouts. Most others just grabbed ahold and swung out as far as they could, let go at the highest peak, and tried not to drop into the water at too crazy an angle so as to hurt themselves. Maynard and Chip could do a straight dive off the swing but they always released and dove before the swing got more than eight to ten feet off the water.

They set up camp quickly on the old road just a little upriver from the swing. Chip and Link set up the lean-to, stored what little food they had in the rear part of the make shift tent, and gathered up some river stones for a campfire site. Maynard and Benji went looking along the shallows and the river's edge below the swing gathering up firewood. When that was done all the guys climbed up the bank to the railroad track and scavenged around for coal. There was lots of it. It had tumbled and spilled off of the overloaded coal cars that rumbled up the track. They piled the coal up in the campfire before turning in for the night. It would burn all night and then there would be enough live embers in the fire in the morning to get a cook fire going quickly.

They had enough stuff to fix sandwiches and soup for supper that evening and even found some snacks for later on in the evening. In the morning a couple of them would ride across the bridge and up to "Pistol" Dawson's Riverside Grocery and Bait Shop, a mile or so, to buy some bacon, eggs, light bread and other essentials for the next day.

With supper over and daylight beginning to fade, they settled back and talked and watched the stars come out. There was a small trace of the new moon. The early summer night was warm and lazy and the music from Benji's little transistor radio seemed distant and far away. Every hour or so a car would rumble across the wooden bridge or one would glide along River Road. The boys watched the car's headlight beams bounce around in the dark and stayed focused on the car until its red tail ights faded away in the distance.

They kept the campfire just glowing enough to provide some light for the campsite. Because you could see a big campfire from the bridge as you crossed it, or from the road on the other side of the river, they didn't want to attract any undesirable company or any company for that matter, wandering down to their camp to see what was going on.

Around ten o'clock the ominous sound an approaching car roused the boys attention and they sat up searching for the headlights across the river or on the bridge. Instead they saw lights flickering through the trees as a car rattled and banged up the old road towards them. From the sound of the car, the muffler must have been hanging down and dragging along the ground behind it. It inched its way agonizingly toward them, then about fifty feet from them it just quit, its one dim headlight spotlighting the four boys.

"My Lord", choked Benji, "what are we gonna' do?"

Link took control. "Just sit still and don't provoke anyone. We don't know who it is yet. Just check around as easily as you can and get hold of a knife, a rock, a stick, a can opener, anything. It might be just a couple of fishermen or anything. Besides, I got my baby right here." He patted his sleeping bag where his pellet pistol was nestled just inside.

The headlight, though growing dimmer by the minute, was still shining right in their face. No one raised their voice to ask politely to turn the thing off. It went out quickly and except for the glow of the campfire, the darkness closed around them again.

They could hear the muffled sound of voices coming from the car but it was still too far away for them to make out what was being said.

"Sounds like at least two of them", whispered Chip.

The driver side door opened and from the dim dome light inside the car, they saw a woman sit up and begin to rearrange her hair. Seconds later from out of the darkness and into the glow of the firelight, stepped a brute of a man. His shirt was ripped down the side and his bulging muscles glistened with sweat. In one hand he carried a Mason jar half full of moonshine. He staggered towards the four boys, stepped one foot into the hot coals of the campfire, and fell face first into the dust.

Chip watched dumbfounded for a second then jumped up and dragged the man's leg out of the fire. He beat out the fire that had spread up his pants leg then stepped back and the other three boys closed in by his side ready for what might come. It was more than they had expected. From across the fire, in the spot of the first great entry, came two more even bigger men.

The two reached down and helped their buddy to his feet then they stood weaving and a might unsteady in the classic drunkard's stance. The man in the middle who had just fallen into the fire dropped to his knees and stirred the dust with his excited hands. "Oh. No. Come on boys help me find it. I dropped the damn bottle and that's all we got."

The other two men searched frantically in the dark for the bottle, falling and stumbling over each other. The boys watched mesmerized until one of the men came up with the dirty jar.

After regaining their feet once again the tension eased somewhat when one man stepped towards them and spoke in slurred, choppy sentences. "Watch youall boys doin' down yhur? Some feeshin'?"

Benji spoke first and with a little squeak in his voice. "Yeah. We're just campin' out for the night."

"Well listen you boys, we gots us a woman down yonder in the car and we still got a little shine left and ifin you want, yurr a welcome to both of 'em."

Benji spoke again, "That's alright. We don't drink on account of the training we have to do as high school athletes and besides that, Maynard here has a bum ticker. Doc says if he drinks any, it could kill him, but you guys can hang around if you want." The line about Maynard's heart always worked to get them out of trouble with drunks. The other boys looked at Benji with an incredible eye. Benji just shrugged his shoulders. What else was he gonna say?

"We be a thankin' yuh but shore you don't want no drink?" spoke up one of the other men and he reached the jar out towards the boys and waved it in the air.

"No thanks anyway", laughed Chip, waving the bottle away.

"Well, ok, if you say so," shrugged the man. "This here's Duke", he said nodding his head half-heartedly towards the man on his left. "Dukes a been messed up in the head ever since he wrecked

195

his car three years ago this coming winter." Duke sat down on the ground and stared into the fire. The man continued. "Yeah you boys 'member all them fires people been settin' out in the woods around here? That was Duke. Give him a match and he'll fix up the purtiest fire you ever seen. States a been after him for four years and ain't caught him yet. Ain't that right Duke."

Duke lifted his head enough to look at the boys. "Right", he said, after a momentary pause.

"And this here is Pudge", he went on. "Don't say much but meanerinhell when he gits riled up."

Pudge pointed to a huge black, ugly, oozing, boil on his arm. "See that", he said, "that's cancer. Doc told me I only had six months to live and that was two years ago. Them doctor's only after yur money."

"My name is Eli", he said, extending a burly hand and shaking each boys' in turn. He unscrewed the lid on the jar, took a short sip, screwed the lid back on, and passed it over to Pudge. "Hey, Duke", he nudged Duke with the toe of his shoe, "go on down to the car and get Georgie and bring her up."

The boys watched Duke get up, swearing under his breath, and stagger off into the dark. They heard him fall once or twice but the other two men weren't paying any attention. If it didn't bother them, it didn't bother the boys.

When Duke came stumbling back into the firelight, he was dragging a straggly looking woman by her skinny arm. She looked to be forty or fifty years old but she could have been nineteen or she could have been ninety. She might have had a couple of teeth left but it was hard to tell in the dark. She was skinny as a bone. Her hair was knotted and stringy. She was as drunk as her escorts. As soon as Duke released her from his iron grip she ran to Eli and threw her arms around him. She was shaking like a leaf and pleaded desperately, "Eli, honey, please take me home 'fore all these here boys screw me."

Eli looked helplessly towards Pudge, "Here, you brought her. You take care of her", and he pushed her towards Pudge. Pudge pulled her away from Eli and dragged her around behind the lean-to. Chip and Benji sneaked around the side of the lean-to to watch but it was too dark back there to see anything. By the time their eyes became accustomed to the dark, Pudge was finished and came around the other side of the lean-to.

Eli looked disgustedly at his buddy and said, "What in the world did you take her back there for? It's probably filthy dirty. Hard to tell what's back there."

Pudge grabbed the jar of moonshine from Eli, unscrewed the lid and took a short slug. "Thas awright. Don't bother me none. She's on the bottom anyway".

Georgie stumbled back around the lean-to and ran to Eli again and threw her arms around him and whimpered in between sobs, "Eli, he tore my panties clear offin me and I can't find them nowhere."

Eli roared with laughter, "Woman you ain't even had none on since we left your place." He pushed her away again and this time she walked to the edge of the firelight. She stopped and looked pitifully first to Eli, then to each person in turn. Then she turned and began sobbing again in short little gasps and walked off in the darkness towards the car.

While all of this had been going on, Duke slipped off down over the river bank to take a leak and from the darkness below them came the joyous yell of an important discovery.

Eli and Pudge sauntered over to the edge of the road on the river bank. Eli had to grab Pudge at the last moment before he toppled over the bank and fell into the river.

Eli yelled down into the darkness below, "Hey Duke. You awright there boy?"

The boys looked at each other afraid to reassure themselves of Duke's discovery. Finally, Link said it, "My God. He's found the swing."

Just then Duke appeared out of the dark at the top of the bank. He was out of breath and covered with dirt and mud from the treacherous assent. Behind him, in his hand, he had managed to drag the swing up to the top of the bank with him.

Eli grabbed the swing and stood at the edge of the road. He thrust his chest out manly, took a long swig of moonshine, reached the jar back to Pudge, raised his feet off the ground and swung out into the dark night. Every muscle and every ear back on the road strained out towards the dark and waited anxiously for the yell or the splash or both. Everything seemed to stop. Not a sound could be heard. The tension was heavy. It seemed like an eternity passed, then-------. Then out of the darkness into the firelight swung Eli. His eyes were wide open and his feet and legs braced for the crash into the bank. At the last moment, he pulled his legs up and landed on the edge of the bank as gracefully as a bird.

He let go of the swing and before anybody could congratulate him on his daring feat, he swayed back and forward a might, hung in mid-air for a moment, and then with arms revolving wildly, toppled down the riverbank and into the mud and cold water at the edge of the river. From somewhere down below came only two angry words uttered in disgust and embarrassment, "Well, hell!"

While Eli tried to scramble back up the bank, Duke retrieved the empty, still swinging cable. He made several false starts before building up his courage to really go. "If Eli kin make it, then by God I can." With those parting words he leaped off the bank and swung out over the river. His departure was more magnificent than his return. He did manage to somehow turn around to face the bank coming back in but he failed raise his legs up on the approach and the top of the bank struck him just below knee level and he went sprawling into the dirt, just missing the campfire.

Once the first trip had been made, their fear disappeared and both Eli and Duke took turns swinging. They tried to see who could swing out the farthest or do the fancier trick. Once they even went out together but on that trip their momentum failed to carry them back all the way to the bank. They swung back and forth helplessly in shorter and shorter strokes until they could no longer hold on to the pipe. Finally, they both had to drop reluctantly into the water.

All this time Pudge just stood at the top of the bank and watched. He never volunteered to show his skill on the swing, in fact, he never ventured any closer to the edge of the riverbank than where he sat, near the campfire. Each time Eli or Duke had gone out, he took a nip from the jar, cradled the jar in his arms, and closed his eyes.

Eli and Duke, now soaking wet from their late night dunking, managed to get the swing back to the top of the bank. Eli held it out to Pudge. "Come on you chicken son-of-a-bitch", he teased,

"It's jus lack you was a big bird." Pudge squeezed the jar of moonshine so tightly the boys thought it would shatter.

"You know I can't go messin' 'round on somethin' lack 'at. 'member the doc said I had cancer!"

Eli let go of the swing and went over to Pudge and put his arm around his shoulders. "I'm sorry, old buddy. I guess we sorta over done it tonight. We'd better be gittin' you and Georgie home."

With Eli and Duke supporting Pudge between them, they slopped off into the dark. Every once in a while they heard the men give a big horse laugh. In a few moments the dim light inside the old car came on. Georgie could not be seen. If she was there, she must have been in the back seat because all three men piled into the front seat. The car fired right up and backed down the road from where it first appeared some two hours ago. They got the car turned around and banged and rattled out of sight across the bridge and down the river.

The boys moved back to the camp in silence and uncovered the knives, and hatchet, and can opener that had been hidden but still at easy reach in case trouble would have developed. Nonetheless, the boys breathed a little easier when the taillights of the car disappeared into the darkness down the river road. Link drew out his pistol. "Good thing they didn't start anything", he said, turning the pistol over and letting it gleam in the firelight.

"Right", broke in Maynard, "we coulda' killed 'em with all this stuff."

Now that everyone was assured that they could handle any trouble that came their way, the tension eased off.

They decided to sleep outside the lean-to since it was warm and the night sky was clear with no sign of rain. They spread their sleeping bags and blankets side by side half in and half out of the lean-to. Link was on the outside next to the road bank below the railroad tracks. Benji and Maynard slept in the middle and Chip wound up being on the outside next to the river.

"Hey listen Benji, said Chip, "I'll flip yuh to see who sleeps on the outside."

"What's a matter you scared somethin' gonna get you?" laughed Link.

"Ok man. I'll sleep on the outside, it don't matter to me. I jus' thought maybe Benji might want to, that's all."

They sat or reclined on their sleeping gear talking about Eli and the men until the fire had died down to a soft red glow.

"Guess we better fix the fire and hit the sack", said Maynard, getting up and piling on some wood. "I'll check to see if anything's left scattered around out here". He went off in the dark with a flashlight. The fire sprang to new life again bathing the campsite in its flickering light. Maynard returned empty handed. Benji turned up the transistor radio to find out what time it was. After joining in on a rousing "Duke of Earl" with Benji singing lead and the rest doing the background doo-wop with a little Imperial's choreography thrown in, they found out it was 10:30 in Chicago, according to WLS, which meant it was 11:30 back on the river. Benji turned down the radio but it played on, destined to play for the entire thirty-six hours or so they would spend on the river this trip.

Chip crawled into his sleeping bag and lay quietly on his back looking up through the sparsely mangled tree branches at the starry sky. It wasn't the fact that he was on the outside that bothered him, he thought. He had been the outside man plenty of times. The thing was, that this time he was the outside man facing the river. The river bank was only about twenty feet away and anything could crawl up out of the river------Crawl! Crawl! Why did he think of a crawling thing? For that matter, why did he think of anything like that at all? He reached behind him and turned the transistor up a little. Of course if anything did crawl up out of the river, he'd be the first to get.......what is all this stupid thinking about anyway? He turned over on his side with his back to the river. He was facing Maynard.

"Maynard. Maynard", he whispered.

Maynard stirred a bit then opened his eyes and looked at Chip.

"Listen Maynard", he went on, "you a light sleeper?"

"Sure man", he said, "You might say I sleep with one eye open. Any little noise or movement or anything like that, man I'm on my toes."

"Ok. Ok. I just wanted to make sure."

"Listen son, you got nothing to worry about. My grandpa once said......"

"I said ok", interrupted Chip, "I believe you. Say, you wouldn't want to sleep over here would you?"

"No, but I'll sleep out there tomorrow night. Don't worry now. I told you I was on my toes", with that he turned over on his back and drifted off to sleep.

Chip turned back over on his back and laid there very quietly for a long time. You know, he thought, the heat from a person's body does attract animals but that's when it's cold out. It's not cold tonight. His hand slid up the handle of his scout hatchet lying beside him and he drew it under the sleeping bag close to him and before he knew it, he was asleep.

He awoke with a start. It was still dark. Something must have awakened him. He lay quietly, still on his back. The fire was out now and the little sliver of the new moon had long since dipped behind the horizon. The place was drowned in darkness. He could still see the stars and the sky overhead. It was awfully quiet. Even the usual din of river racket had ceased. Then he realized that's what woke him up. It wasn't a noise. It was the eerie absence of noise.

He slowly rolled his head to face toward the river and there it was, standing only a few feet from him-----towering over him----- outlined against the starlit sky. It was a dog, a huge dog. Oh God! It's not moving. Why's it not moving? Oh lord, don't move, it'll get me. "Maynard", he whispered without taking his eyes off the dog. "Maynard. Oh God, Maynard, wake up". He kicked at Maynard under the blanket. He kicked hard. He was almost crying but he still kept his eyes on the shadow of the dog. I gotta move fast or he'll get me. "For God's sake Maynard wake up!" He was surprised at how loud he was now yelling.

Something surged through his whole body. He couldn't stand it any longer. He wasn't going to die without a fight. It was probably pure fright and adrenaline that hit him but he grabbed the hatchet and in one motion seemed to jump out of his sleeping bag and on to his feet. At the same time, he let out a yell that woke up everything on the river within a mile in both directions and hurled the hatchet with all his strength at the dog. The dog was gone but

Chip could hear it crashing through the brush heading on up the river.

With that yell, everyone scrambled to their feet, weapon at the ready, and stood prepared for action. Every one but Maynard who just sat up and looked about in a stupor.

"What's goin' on?" demanded Link.

"It was dog. A big dog!", stammered Chip, "right on top of me he was". He was still shaking a little. "I threw the hatchet at him but I missed. I swear I thought he was going to get us all."

"He probably was just lookin' for somethin' to eat", said Benji.

"Yeah, man. Us", replied Chip

"Hey, what's goin' on?" mumbled Maynard, still half asleep.

"Nothin' ", answered Chip disgustedly, "nothin' at all. Jus' go on back to sleep. You's jus' havin' a bad dream-------you jerk head."

With those words, Maynard pulled the blanket up over his head and laid back down to sleep, mumbling to himself as he dozed off.

For the second time that night, everybody settled down and tried to get some sleep. Chip was so tired he laid down on top of his sleeping bag. He was still the outside man but without another thought, quickly fell asleep.

The sun came up fast over the river valley and the early summer day's heat began early. The fog lifted off the river and things began stirring all around the sleeping boys. The trees were filled with chatter and clatter of birds and sounds carried from all over, up and down the river. Traffic began to clatter across the wooden bridge and left clouds of dust that hung in the lifeless air above the dirt road. A small boat drifted down the middle of the river carrying two fishermen to their favorite early morning spot. Across the river a farmer began his day's work in the garden beside his house.

The night had been a long one and an exciting one and the boys, as exhausted as they were, slept on. It was cool in the shade where the boys slept but as the sun moved its way up the hazy sky behind the camp, the dark shade began to retreat up the bank away from the river. Before long the boys were lying half in the shade and half in the hot sun. When the sun began to soak into the hot blankets and sleeping bags and the heat became unbearable, the boys would scoot and wriggle their way back into the comfort of the shade.

By the time nine o'clock rolled around, the boys found themselves squeezed together against the upper bank of the old road. There was no more level ground for here, the bank rose straight up ten or fifteen feet to the railroad tracks. In the course of a couple of hours the boys had managed to move almost fifteen feet from the lean-to. Now the sun had them backed up against the bank and was beating down on them unmercifully. They kicked the blankets and sleeping bags off and lay only in their underwear under the summer sun.

Chip was the first to hear the whistle but he was still half asleep and it seemed more like the whistle was part of a dream he was having. Benji heard it too. He blinked his eyes to clear the fuzziness from them then turned over on his stomach and dozed off again.

Slowly the river valley was being filled with the churning and grinding and pounding of the two huge diesel engines as they strained their way up the valley pulling a string of loaded coal cars. The whine and scream of the engines had completely enveloped the river valley, echoing back and forth between the steep hillsides, but not until the ground began to rumble beneath the sleeping four did they take any notice.

Benji sat up with a start and tried to shake the grogginess from his head in an attempt to grasp what was happening. The ground began shaking even more violently and sparks from the engines showered down on the boys. The wind swirled the dust and dirt into the air and as it settled down on the boys it watered their eyes and choked their breath. Small rocks and ballast jarred loose from the rumbling train, tumbled down the bank, hitting the boys like hail from a thunderstorm. Small chunks of coal and coal dust from the overloaded coal cars rained down on top of them. Chip and Link jumped to their feet yelling and pointing at the train as it lumbered on by but the noise was so loud they couldn't even hear each other. As the cars rumbled by, Maynard buried his head in his blankets and started to pray, for surely the end of the world had come. Chip and Link helped Maynard and Benji to their feet and they backed away from the close proximity of the coal drag, out past the campsite to the edge of the riverbank. There they stood under the warm summer sun in just their underwear and watched the train pass by.

When the dingy caboose finally clamored by, Chip turned around and looked across the river. Evidently the farmer across the way had summoned his wife and all the kids to join him in the garden where they had a front row view of the preceding developments of the scantily clad participants. Chip nudged Link with his elbow and he too turned to gaze across the river.

The farmer and his wife were now pointing towards the boys but they were too far away and the noise of the train was still too loud for Link or Chip to hear what they might be saying. The audience across the river then waved to the boys and went back to their regular chores. The wife and kids headed back to the house and the farmer bent over his hoe and went to work. The campers acknowledged their admirers by returning a quick, half hearted wave and then pretended to be tending the fire and the campsite as they reorganized the mobile sleeping set up and put their clothes back on. Chip's first duty that morning would be to go off into the bush and hunt for his scout hatchet.

Benji and Link pushed their bikes up to the dirt road, rode across the bridge, turned right up River Road, and headed for the Riverside Grocery. They returned in an hour with a few eggs, some bacon, a loaf of bread, some Beanie Weenies, and an onion sack full of softdrinks which they promptly sunk in the shady cove of the river to keep cool.

Chip cooked up breakfast and by 11:00, they were feasting on scrambled eggs, bacon, fried potatoes, toast & butter, and coffee.

By the time breakfast was devoured and the camp cleaned up, it was after 12:00 noon. Not being the best time of day to fish, they went swimming and took turns diving and jumping from the swing. They walked over to the middle of the bridge and spent an hour or so there spitting and pitching rocks off into the river. The afternoon passed lazily along.

A little after 6:00 that evening, Link and Maynard waded down along the river bank to fish the shoals under the bridge where it was shady. Since Link and Maynard were close enough to the camp to keep an eye on everything, Benji and Chip decided to go up to Dawson's and buy something for snacking on later that night and they decided to walk instead of bike just for the heck of it.

They walked across the bridge and had just turned up River Road when a car going in their direction pulled up beside them. It was a '49 Lincoln coupe painted purple. Chip noticed the very small but neatly stenciled lettering on the rear passenger side fender that read "Honest Abe". The Lincoln was anything but honest. If the color of the car couldn't convince one that this was not the original, the vibrations from the deep rumble of the dual exhausts and the full moon hubcaps certainly would. The windows were all rolled down so the driver leaned over toward the passenger side while holding on to the steering wheel with his left arm and spoke with a raised voice to be heard over the rumble, "You guys need a lift?"

Well certainly they needed a lift. Especially in a fine ride like this one. They opened the door and slid across the front seat. "Nice set of wheels", remarked Benji as he pulled the door closed beside him.

"Well, I just got this baby done a few days ago," answered the driver, as he let the car roar through first gear. He was a young man in his early twenties, well groomed and slicked down. He had on crisp clean clothes and shined shoes, probably heading out on a date for tonight. Chip sat in the middle of the bench seat with his legs off to the right side of the hump to get them away from the four-speed floor shift that sat in the middle of the hump.

As soon as the Lincoln began straining for relief from first gear, the driver stomped the accelerator flat to the floor and yanked the gear shift to second. Benji and Chip were pinned back against the plush rolled and pleated Naugahyde seat. The first thought that flashed into Chip's mind was of all those clichés designed to spur a driver on to exhibitions of daring speed: "Now pour the carbide to her", "Stomp on it", "Pour the sand to her", "Turn 'em over", "Jump on it", "Scratch a patch", "Rip one off", "Stand on it", "Smoke 'em" "Pour the coal to her" "Shower down on her". No need for that now as Old Abe screamed from second to third.

Chip looked at the speedometer. It was just passing fifty when the driver jerked her into high gear and it kept on climbing---past sixty--past seventy. Benji and Chip were now holding on for dear life as the Lincoln seemed to be just floating along above the little one lane hardroad. Oh God, thought Chip, please don't let us meet any cars and please don't let us run off the road. Even though the road was a narrow one lane affair, it was level as it followed the river and had no sharp turns in it, at least on this side of Dawson's.

As the speedometer passed eighty, two boys came into view standing by the road one hundred yards up ahead of them. The driver saw them too and let off the gas and began braking and downshifting. The Lincoln was bucking and sliding and squealing and whining as the driver did his best to get stopped. He finally managed to slide to a stop sideways in the road, fifty feet past the two boys. They ran to catch up with the car. When they got along side the passenger door, Benji, still shaking a bit and still a little pale in color, opened the door, and leaned up to fold the back part of the seat down enough so the two boys could jump in the back.

The first kid to reach the open door stopped and looked in at the three on the front seat. When he saw the driver, his eyebrows jumped up and his eyes widened in disbelief. "Buzzy French! Oh, hell no. We ain't ridin' with you." And with that, he slammed the door shut almost catching Benji's knee. Chip and Benji just looked at each other.

Buzzy didn't say a word, he just revved the engine a couple of times, jammed her into first, and followed all of the aforementioned clichés.

No more than twenty seconds had passed, though it seemed like an eternity, before a small camp on the river side of the road came into view. Benji took the opportunity as a blessing from heaven and used it to their advantage. "We'll be gettin' off right up here at my uncle's camp." He didn't sound too convincing to Chip but he must have to Buzzy because Buzzy started going through the whole routine of trying to stop. This time he got stopped only twenty five feet past the camp. Benji and Chip gratefully got out and thanked Buzzy for the ride. "Take care of this baby", cautioned Chip, "you've got a cool rod there."

Buzzy waved and took off at a decent and reserved clip this time.

Benji and Chip waited until Buzzy drove out of sight, then they started walking up the road to Dawson's. It didn't appear there was anybody home at the camp.

When they got within sight of Dawson's, they could see Buzzy's Lincoln parked out front. They slipped down over the roadside next to the river and watched and waited from there for Buzzy to leave. When he finally pulled out, he headed back down River Road and roared past the two hidden in the tall grass below the road. After a minute or two they scrambled back up the road bank and walked the rest of the way up to Dawson's.

All the way back to camp they kept one ear attuned to the oncoming traffic in case Buzzy might be buzzing back their way. Not a single vehicle passed by in either direction.

Link and Maynard caught three little bass under the bridge but each one was too small to keep so they would toss them back in. After Link caught the third one, Maynard figured out it was the same fish they had caught all three times.

Supper consisted of peanut butter and fried Treet sandwiches, pork & beans and fried potatoes. They washed it down with the last of the soft drinks. The river didn't keep the soft drinks as cold as the boys hoped it would. Benji said the pop tasted flatter than piss on a plate.

Chip had bought four Blue Ribbon cigars at Dawson's that evening so they all lit up after supper. The cigars went well with a cup of hot, black coffee. They would only smoke half of the cigar now and save the other half for later on that night.

The setting sun had reddened the horizon by the time camp supper had been cleaned up and put away, but the summer evening was still warm and humid and there was about an hour of daylight left. A farm tractor clattered into hearing range from across the tracks behind the camp and in a couple of minutes, it wheeled up the old road into camp.

It was piloted by a young man probably in his late teens or early twenties. The side cutter bar on the tractor was locked in the upright position and both the young man and the tractor were covered with hay seed and straw. He wore a white tee shirt that was soaked from his sweat, a pair of jeans, and a pair of leather work boots. He was brown from the sun and dirty from the dust of the hayfield. "You guys mind if I hit the river for a little bit", he asked.

"Well first off", chided Maynard, "it ain't our river to say. And second, it's big enough for all of us if you don't mind sharin'. My name's Maynard."

Maynard reached his hand up and shook the boy's as he swung down from the tractor. "Hi. My name's Jink. Jink Adkins. Been cutting and stackin' hay all day. I'm about done in and I don't mind sharin' the water a bit but I'm so dirty I'll probably leave a ring around the river bank." He laughed a hearty laugh and the others chuckled along with him.

Jink was not hesitant. He unlaced and pulled of his boots and then ran straight down the bank under the swing and dove out into the river with all of his clothes on. Chip figured that way he could wash everything at the same time.

The Jive Five joined in and they swam and splashed around and dove off the swing until it began to get dark. Benji and Link built the campfire up and they all settled in around it as the moon, a little bigger than last night, suddenly appeared almost directly overhead. Jink stood over the fire drying his clothes. "You from around here?", asked Link.

"Yeah, I live down in a holler off of Devil's Backbone", Jink answered.

"Hey, you don't know a guy named Buzzy French, do you?"

"Oh yeah!", laughed Jink. "Crazy Buzzy."

"What's his story?" Link continued.

"Why? You guys have a run in with Buzzy or somethin'?".

"No. Not exactly. We caught a ride with him up to Dawson's this evening. Thas all", broke in Benji.

Jink shook his head. "Ooooo! Bad timing", he said. "Buzz's a great guy. Do anything for you. A kind old soul. Works in a plant down in Huntington that makes railroad cars. Makes real good money. Lives by himself in a little apartment down there but comes back home every weekend. Likes to drink a little beer but never gets drunk. Spends all of his extra money on cars and women."

Jink stepped away from the fire and shuffled over to the tractor. It wasn't completely dark yet but the boys couldn't see what he was doing. They heard him rummaging around in the wooden tool box right behind the driver's seat. When he was finished, he walked back to the campfire with a bottle of Falls City beer in his hand.

He stood across the fire in front of the boys so he could dry the front of his clothes as he talked. He took a sip of beer and continued. "You see Buzzy spends all of his money on cars because he's the worst driver that ever lived. He's about the most non-drivin' son-of-a-gun you'd ever meet. I swear my dog's a better driver than Buzzy and he's blind in one eye."

"Buzzy has to get a new car every two months 'cause he tears them all to hell. I'm not lyin'. He don't buy junk neither. Always a nice, clean set of wheels. Lets see---I know he's had a '54 Plymouth convertible. Had a '47 Chevy coup. Had a '40 Ford tudor and I think he had a '51 Hudson. Oh yeah and a '46 Crosley pickup. Wrecked every one of them. I don't know how he's not killed hisself. Had one really bad wreck over here on the river about two years ago. Was in the hospital for three weeks. Doctors thought he'd never walk again. Why, in no time at all he was back runnin' up and down the road in a another rod. You know, I guess he thinks he's Fireball Roberts or somethin', and since Fireball's been known to wreck a few, then it must be alright, if he does too."

Jink took another drink of beer then stepped back across the fire to finish drying the back of his clothes. " When Buzzy first got his license nobody was afraid to ride with him. He was cautious and mild mannered, but the longer he drove, the worse he got. It got like that with his cars too. When he'd get a new set of wheels of some kind, he'd drive reasonable for two or three weeks then it was like somethin' snapped in him and he'd start rippin' up and down the road till he smashed up somewhere. People soon learned that it was safe to ride with Buzzy the first two weeks or so after he got a new car. After that, nobody who knew him would ride with him and he'd have to drive around alone until he'd wreck again. Funny thing too, Buzzy was never in a wreck that involved any other car."

"You know how long it's been since Buzzy's last wreck?" asked Chip.

"No. Don't have any idea. I don't have time to keep up with Buzzy. Besides it don't matter to me. I ain't ridin' with him anytime---unless I'm already dead. Say boys, it's gettin' late and I gotta get outa here. Thanks for sharin' the fire."

"Wait a minute", Link interjected, "how about givin' us a beer before you leave?"

"Only got one left", answered Jink as he walked back over to the tractor, "and I ain't gonna give it to yuh. I will sell it to yuh though." That perked Link's interest even more.

"How much", he said.

Jink thought about it for a second or two before he answered. "Fifty cents."

Chip thought that was kind of steep for a warm bottle of beer but he was quickly overruled by Link's quick response. "Done", he said.

Jink fished the Falls City out of the wooden box while the boys pooled together some change to pay him. With the deal done, Jink climbed up on the tractor and fired her up.

He turned on the two cockeyed head lamps on the front of the tractor. One shone almost straight down into the ground and the other shone straight up into the trees. Jink got off and twisted them around until he got them about where they seemed to do the most good. Then he climbed back on, backed down the old road, turned around, and clattered back across the railroad tracks and out of sight, heading towards Devil's Backbone and home.

The boys reclined around the campfire late into the night, savoring every minute of the experience. They passed around the bottle of beer, each taking a little sip. It made them a little giddy. Chip broke out the peanuts and potato chips they had procured at Dawson's earlier that evening. WLS was coming in exceptionally fine that night and they sang along with every hit, using whatever they could find to substitute for a microphone; stick, beer bottle, flashlight.

They finished smoking the cigars, laid back, and languished in the freedom and serenity of the moment. In an attempt to divert attention from the inevitable time to turn in, Link uttered the words that became the overused trade mark phrase that would echo down through the annals of the Jive Five. "Hey guys. Let's do everything one more time!"

Unfortunately, they were out of everything and dead on their feet. Maynard had already dozed off and was lying on top of his blankets, snoring away. All the rest decided to call it a night as well.

The next morning, after a breakfast of peanut butter and potted meat sandwiches washed down with coffee, they cleaned up the campsite, packed up their meager equipment, and headed back to Sugar Tree. They took their time and enjoyed the day traveling back home.

In early October of that year, they made one more trip back to the swing. Since school was in session, there was no way they could leave on Friday and stay the whole weekend, so they decided to go Saturday morning and just stay one night and come back on Sunday.

Saturday turned out to be a beautiful autumn day. The sun was warm but there was no humidity so the air was dry and crisp. They packed their swimming trunks along just in case it would be warm enough to swim.

They took one pen light with them in case they would need some light, but Benji assured them that the moon would be almost full and they could use the generator light on his bicycle for lighting around the camp. All they had to do was turn the bicycle over, let it rest on the handlebars and seat, and crank the pedals around so the rear wheel would spin the generator and make light. The light on the front of the bike could be adjusted to shine wherever they needed it.

It seemed like a good idea at the time, but it wasn't. First off, somebody had to hand crank the pedals fast enough to get more than a dim glow from the bike's head lamp. To make any worthwhile light at all, the crank had to be spun at a speed that was just too fast and too hard to be continued for more than twenty seconds. A slow leisurely pace just wouldn't produce much more than an orange glow. Second off, as soon as the cranking stopped, the light went out. There was just no way they were going to keep that light working for very long intervals, it was too much work. They soon abandon the generator theory as a source of light.

Benji was right about one thing, the moon that night wasn't quiet full, but it still bathed the whole river valley in a soft gray

211

light and it, along with the campfire glow, provided all the light they needed. They banked up a good campfire that night because after the sun went down, the temperature of the autumn air dropped significantly. Because the river was a little warmer than the air, a little fog began to rise and hover in wisps above the water. It was kind of eerie in the pale moonlight.

Maynard spent most of the evening staring across the river. A couple of times he got up and left the campsite to walk down to the river and stare across from down there. Around 10:30 he revealed the intent of his staring. "You guys know what would really be good to eat tonight?"

"Yeah", snickered Link, "a big ole T-bone steak with fries, hot rolls, and a salad."

"Well since we got no steaks, or fries, or rolls, or salad", asserted Maynard with a scowl, "how about some hot, fresh roastin' ears."

"Yeah", Benji interjected, "they would go great with the steaks and fries and rolls and salads that we don't have either."

"No we don't", said Maynard very calmly, "but farmer John over yonder does."

Everyone rose and looked across the river where Maynard had been staring.

"Looks like the whole lower half of his garden is corn. All we got to do is slip over there and take an ear or two for ourselves and we can roast them right in their husks, right in the fire."

"How we gonna get over there and back?" asked Benji.

Link answered that question by grabbing Benji by the shoulders and twisting him so he was facing down stream then he shook him as he spoke, "See that big bridge down there, you mule brain? That's what they built it for, so we could cross over the river and steal some corn." He turned Benji loose with a disdainful push.

Benji whirled back on Link as soon as he regained his balance, "Well how about if I just knock your ass across the river, that way you can save some time." He came right at Link but Link backed away from him.

"Oh I'm sorry I hurt your feelings, mule brains. Please don't hurt me," pleaded Link.

"Now hold on a minute. Let's cool off ", said Chip as he stepped in. "You can knock his ass across the river after while, mule brains. Right now let's figure this thing out."

Maynard went on. "Thank you boys and girls". He paused for a moment. "I been watchin' Farmer John's. I think they all went to bed. See. There's only one dim light in the whole house and I'll bet that's in the bathroom. See what a little window that is. I haven't seen anybody movin' around for about an hour. No light flickerin' from the TV. Nothin'."

"We need to leave two people here and have them move around a bit and make like everyone's here in case one of 'em happens to look back across at us. It'd be easier and safer to just wade across the river down at the shoals and then slip up the other side. The garden is right beside the river. It would be easier, but I think the river's too cold and we really can't see that well, so maybe it would be better to cross the bridge and then slip down over the road bank into the garden. The garden is far enough away from the house that I don't think they could hear us. Who's goin' with me and who's stayin'?"

"Aw, me and Benji'll stay here if he'll promise not to knock my ass across the river," feigned Link.

"Can't guarantee it", chided Benji.

Maynard and Chip pulled on their jackets and walked off into the night, down the old road, across the railroad tracks, and over across the bridge. Benji and Link stayed back in camp and tried to catch a glimpse of the other two as they crossed the bridge in the moonlight.

It didn't take long for Maynard and Chip's eyes to become accustomed to the light from the overhead moon. By the time they reached the end of the bridge on the River Road side, they could see almost as good as if it were daylight. Farmer John's house and garden lay down over the steep bank beneath River Road, a hundred yards away from the garden. Maynard and Chip just stood silently at the end of the bridge waiting and listening to see if any cars were about or if anything at all was stirring on that side of the river. They must have stood there for ten or fifteen minutes before Maynard decided to move out.

213

They walked along the edge of the road looking down over the bank trying to find a good place to slip down to the garden without getting too close to the house. Behind them, seemingly out of nowhere, the rumble of a car crossing the bridge shattered the stillness of the night and sent the two boys scurrying down over the road bank into the weeds. They waited there, breathing in little gasps with their hearts pounding. They weren't scared, only startled, and a bit unnerved by the sudden disturbance of the silent night. The car turned up River Road and sped past the two boys. The driver had the headlights turned off and was driving by moonlight.

When the noise of the car had faded away, the boys turned their attention back to the task at hand. From where they were on the road bank, they were only fifty feet or so from the garden and the corn. Maynard let himself slide and slip the rest of the way down the bank using small shrubs and bushes as handholds. Chip followed close behind.

As soon as they reached the lower edge of the garden, a dog started barking at them from up at the house. They couldn't tell exactly where the barking was coming from because it seemed to move around some. Maybe the dog wasn't tied up and would be sneaking around behind them. Maybe it was the same dog Chip saw this summer in camp. Maybe it was a German Shepherd police dog--an attack dog. Whatever kind of dog it was, it didn't seem to be getting any closer. The boys hunkered down in the weeds beside the garden in case Farmer John came out on the porch with a light to check what the dog was barking at. They waited another five minutes---no Farmer John. In another three minutes, the dog stopped barking.

The two boys stood up and tip-toed into the corn patch. It was deathly quiet. When Maynard reached up to pull off an ear of corn, the crunching and tearing and ripping was so loud that he knew it could be heard clear across the river at the camp and certainly loud enough to wake up Farmer John. The dog started barking again.

"This is no good", whispered Maynard. "It makes too much noise."

"Wait", answered Chip, "we can't spend anymore time in here. We're gonna get caught. Listen, just pull up two whole shocks of

214

corn out of the ground. That won't make half as much noise. We'll have two or three ears of corn on each shock then we can carry the whole thing out of here without too much noise."

"Right", whispered Maynard, shaking his head in the affirmative.

The boys each grabbed two stalks of corn and easily and quietly pulled them out of the ground. The battle was only half over. They had to get back up the bank. There was no way they could climb back up that steep bank and carry the corn too. They could sneak back up towards the house and the dog where there was a nice gentle, wide driveway that lead right past the house up to the road. They could see the campsite across the river. The reflection from the red glow of the campfire wriggled and squirmed in the black water of the river. So near, yet so far.

Maynard turned and started wading through the weeds and brush down river away from the garden and the house. Chip followed behind, stopping to look back every once in a while to see if there were any new lights on in the house. They maneuvered through the brush another twenty feet before Chip looked back at the house. That's when he saw the porch light flick on and he could he see Farmer John leaning on the porch banister directly under the naked bulb. The porch light wasn't directed in a beam nor was it bright enough to reach the boys at that distance. Farmer John went back into the house but left the porch light on. Chip wondered if he was coming back with a gun or a spotlight or both.

He turned back to Maynard but Maynard had kept on plotting ahead and was now a good thirty feet away. He tried to get Maynard's attention by yelling to him in his loudest whisper. "Maynard------Maynard. Wait a minute will yuh. I can't tell how you got through there."

Maynard answered in his own loud whisper from somewhere up ahead, "No, I ain't waitin'. Come on. We ain't doin' no good down here. It gets worse. I don't know how we're gonna get out of here."

"If you'll just wait a minute we'll figure something out". Chip's words came out in a frustrated tone, which was how he felt. Maynard stopped and waited until Chip caught up.

While there was a lull in the getaway, the two boys made a quick reconnaissance of their situation. Chip looked back at the house and didn't see Farmer John standing on the porch with a gun or a light. What he did see was Farmer John's lantern light bobbing up and down as he carried it through the yard, straight towards the garden.

"He's comin' after us", whispered Chip, trying not to sound panicky.

They looked around for a place to hide. They were almost directly under the bridge now. Maynard quietly slipped down to the river with the thought of wading along the edge of the riverbank until he found a place to hunker down below the top of the bank and be hidden in the dark shadows. Unfortunately, when he stepped down into the river it was at a spot where the river was about four feet deep. Maynard went in up above his waist. The cold water soaked through his clothes and in no time he was shivering. He had to hold on to the brush along the bank with one hand to keep from being swept downstream, and with his other arm, he cradled the two precious corn stalks to his chest.

In the meantime Chip had managed to climb up into the dark shadows under the end of the bridge. He kept possession of his two corn stalks also. After a few moments passed, he peeked out from his hiding place to locate Farmer John.

Farmer John had walked down to the upper edge of the garden, shined his light around in a few spots, then turned it off. He stood there motionless in the moonlight as if his hearing and vision were radar, penetrating the very places where Chip and Maynard were hiding. Wonder if he let the dog loose, thought Chip. After three or four minutes, Farmer John turned and walked back through the yard to his house. He never did turn the lantern back on. He walked across the porch, entered the house, and turned the porch light off.

Chip waited another fifteen minutes to be sure Farmer John wasn't trying to trick them into coming out. When everything seemed to quite down, he slid down the bank and went in search of Maynard.

Maynard wasn't where Chip had last left him. He went to the river bank and looked up and down the river but couldn't see him. He gave a low, sharp whistle. There was no answer. He knew Maynard wouldn't have gone back up river toward the farm house so he started feeling his way downstream along the bank.

and Chip will go down to the river, get some driftwood, and build a big fire down there. Chip, get Link's bike and take it down there. We'll hang Maynard's clothes on it to dry." Benji was on a roll now.

Link went to work on the corn. "Wait a minute", he whined, "this isn't sweet corn. It's field corn---hard, no tastin', field corn. What we gonna do now?" Disappointment was evident in his voice.

"I don't care if it's Indian corn", barked Chip, "we risked our lives for that corn and by God you're gonna roast it, and we're gonna eat."

Benji and Chip found some drift wood and built a nice big fire down by the river. The fire and clothes would be easy to watch from the campsite. They set up Link's bicycle beside the fire and hung Maynard's soakin' wet clothes over it. In no time at all the steam began to rise from the clothes.

Maynard was drying out and warming up in the sleeping bag and the corn was roasting in the fire. When Maynard unrolled his blankets he found his swimming trunks stashed away in them so he put them on while he was in the sleeping bag. By the time Benji had tended the drying fire and rearranged Maynard's clothes a couple of times, the corn was done and the boys were putting together a midnight snack of fried Treet sandwiches, roastin' ears and hot coffee. The corn was tough and tasteless but covered with butter and salt, it wasn't bad. Forbidden fruit is always delightful, especially when eaten in the wilds as it was done centuries ago. After stuffing themselves, Chip produced the cigars he'd secretly stowed away for this very moment, and those, along with the hot coffee, topped the evening off perfectly. Maynard was so content and warm and dry that he fell asleep in Benji's sleeping bag. Benji went back down to the river and built the fire up and shuffled Maynard's clothes around for the umpteenth time. They were almost dry.

A lull set in at the camp and soon the only noise emanating from there was Maynard's snoring, the fading static on the transistor, and the crackle of the drying fire.

An unusually bright reflection caught Chip's attention in his half-awake, half-asleep mode. It took him a second before he

After passing under the bridge and following the river's bend to the right, Chip spotted him fifty yards ahead standing on dry land by the riverbank. He hurried along as best he could through the brush until they met up again. Maynard was soaked from head to foot. "Son-of-a-bitch I'm freezin", he said. There was no reason to whisper now they were out of sight of the farmhouse and the muffled roar of the shoals covered their voices. In fact they had to talk a little louder than normal just to be heard. Chip took his jacket off and put it over Maynard's clammy one.

"Come on", he said, "I think we can get back up to the hardroad over there". He nodded towards what looked like in the moonlight, an old overgrown footpath that angled up the bank to the road.

The dry ground they were on now was mostly devoid of bushes and they found the going easier through clumps of dead tiger grass and sage brush. "I couldn't hold on no more", shivered Maynard, "when I let go, the river carried me down to the shoals. I finally was able to get my feet under me and get out of the water---but looky here, baby!" Maynard held up his two corn stalks dripping wet but with ears of corn still intact.

"That ain't nothin' ", remarked Chip, "looky here!" He held up two battered and tattered corn stalks with ears still attached.

The boys climbed up the footpath to the hardroad, then paused for a second to listen for any cars. There were none. Maynard sloshed up the road leaving a trail of wet Red Ball Jets tennis shoe prints behind. They made the bridge and crossed over safely, meeting not man nor vehicle on the way.

"Where the hell you been," demanded Benji when Chip trudged into camp, but when he saw Maynard, his tone changed. "Geez, we thought Farmer John got yuh for sure. Look at you, man. We gotta get you out of those wet clothes and warm you up."

Maynard was standing by the fire but he was still shivering. He spoke through chattering teeth. "These are the only clothes I got."

"Don't worry man. Take all of your clothes off, wrap yourself up in your blankets, and get in my sleepin bag. We'll build up a fire and dry your clothes in no time", directed Benji. "Link, you go ahead and pull the ears off the stalks but leave it in the husks. We'll roast them in this fire since we've got some good coals. Me realized what was happening and to sound the alarm. "Benji----Benji", he yelled, "Maynard's clothes are on fire!"

Link, who was half alseep himself, stared at the fire a moment, blinked a couple of times, and then jumped up and ran down the riverbank to the fire. He was yelling as he ran, "My bicycle! My bicycle! Got to save my bicycle." Link reached the burning clothes and grabbed the safe end of a burning piece of driftwood that was sticking out of the fire. He held one arm bent up over his face to shield off the heat and with the other arm, lifted the whole tangle of flaming clothing off the bicycle and slung stick and all out into the river. The clothes fizzled and hissed and sent a cloud of steam into the night air and then floated away down the dark, lazy river. The only articles of clothing left were a pair of steaming tennis shoes on the ground by the fire and a pair of dry socks hanging on the bicycle. Link grabbed the bike and wheeled it away from the fire, then he began examining it carefully by the light of the drying fire. It had come through the disaster unscathed.

Maynard awoke to all the hubbub and was horrified to see his clothes on fire. He was even more horrified when Link threw them into the river. "You stupid jackass," he yelled "what'd you do that for? Now I got nothin' to wear."

"Shut up moron," Link yelled back. "What'd you want me to do? Let my bicycle and your stuff all burn up.

"No", remarked Maynard, very calm and deliberate, "Your bicycle was in no danger. I would have expected you to carry the clothes over to the river and dip them under, to put out the fire. And then I would have something to wear even if they were burned here and there."

Link stared back at Maynard as if he were having a credulous moment. "Well, next time you can use your own bicycle and save your own clothes". That was all he could come up with and he trudged back up the bank to the camp.

The ride back to Sugar Tree the next day was uneventful. The sky was a deep autumn blue and the sun beat down on the boys all day. The air was crisp and dry and in the shadows, the air had a chill to it. Maynard rode home wearing only his swimming trunks and shoes and socks. Swimming trunks that Benji said were so thin you could read a newspaper through them. Maynard was still fuming over the demise of his clothes and had refused offers from the others to wear bits of clothing they were willing to donate to him.

By the time they got back to Sugar Tree that evening, Maynard's skin was red as a tomato. Mr. Tomato Head---that's what the guys called him. His exposure to the sun and the wind on the ride back home had turned Maynard's skin to the color of a bright red tomato.

That was the last great escapade the Jive Five ever made on bicycles. By the time the following spring rolled around, bicycles and bicycling ceased to be a factor in the exploits of the Jive Five. Chip could not remember whatever happened to his Western Flyer Bicycle.

VIII

Chip knew the Gates' prohibition against hitchhiking was still enforce when he made his first serious attempt at it. It was not a planned out deal of any kind, it just kind of came by accident. Chip did give some thought to his parents' caution at first but the more he thought about it, the more he reasoned that no actual, verbal warning about hitchhiking had even been mentioned in two or three years. It was easier to ask forgiveness than ask for permission.

It happened during second semester exams at Elk River High School when Chip was a freshman. A student could be exempt from taking semester tests if they had an A average in the class and hadn't missed more than three days of school during the semester or they could be exempt if they had a B average and had not missed any days of school. During the week of testing, students took two semester tests a day, one in the morning and one in the afternoon.

As things turned out, Chip had to take a Civics test one morning but was exempted from his science class to Mr. Collins that afternoon. When he finished his Civics test that morning he headed down to the cafeteria for lunch. He was thinking about going over to the gym that afternoon and playing some basketball to kill the rest of the day, then catch the bus home. Judy was exempted from all of her classes so she wasn't there with him at all that week. He happened to run into Steven Browning in the cafeteria and they sat down to lunch together. Steven, it seems, was exempted from the science test that day as well.

"You wanna go over and play some basketball after lunch?" Chip asked.

"No, man. I don't wanna play no basketball."

"Well, we don't have to. I just thought........"

"Hey, lets hitchhike home", Steven interrupted.

"Say what?"

"Yeah, man. Let's cut out of this place and hitchhike home. I don't want to waste my whole afternoon hanging around here. I spend enough time here the way it is. Come on now whata yuh say?"

Chip was hesitant. "I don't know. I'm not suppose to hitchhike."

"Aw don't worry about it. We can be home before anyone's the wiser. We'll just go on around to the station when we get there and wait for the bus to go through and you can tell your folks you just rode the bus around to Sugar Tree for some reason or other. You got all afternoon to think up an excuse."

Chip began to feel a sense of adventure taking over so he hesitantly agreed.

They finished lunch, walked up to the main office to sign themselves out of school, and walked down School Hill into town. It was an absolutely gorgeous, late spring day.

They hot footed it on through town and didn't start hitchhiking until they were on the outskirts of town along Rt.19. Traffic was less congested here and not only was a hitchhiker more visible, his intentions for catching a ride were unmistakable.

It wasn't necessary for both boys to stick out their thumb so Chip let Steven do the thumbing. Though it is sometimes more difficult for two to catch a ride than it is for one, it wasn't very long before a car pulled over and picked the boys up. Their luck was even better than they had hoped for because the driver was a mine equipment salesman heading for Elkins so the guys got a ride clear into Hob.

They got out at the Sugar Tree turnoff , thanked the guy for the ride, and starting walking next to Sugar Tree. Steven figured they would just walk along for a little while and enjoy the day. They were way ahead of schedule and this way they wouldn't really be hitchhiking. They would just be walking along and if somebody picked them up, so be it. No harm done. The first two or three miles of walking was enough for Steven so they decided to start hitchin' again. They walked another mile and three cars passed going in their direction but didn't stop. Then their luck changed again.

Just as they were starting up the Hob side of Renzee White Hill, a brown Pontiac station wagon slowed down and stopped. Chip got to the front passenger side first and looked in the window as he opened the door. The driver was Uncle Roy from Red Dog.

Steven had already opened the back door and gotten in. Chip just stood there on the edge of the road with the door open. The

Gates' rule against hitchhiking was beginning to raise its ugly head. What would Uncle Roy have to say?

"Get in the car, Chip", Uncle Roy said. Chip slid into the front seat and shut the door. Uncle Roy pulled back on the road and headed for Sugar Tree. No one said anything for a couple of minutes. Uncle Roy looked over at Chip. "What are you boys doin'?" he asked in a stern voice.

"Well,..........we're going home", answered Chip half heartedly. He explained the whole thing about test exemptions and getting out of school early. That didn't seem to cut much of an impression with Uncle Roy.

"No. I mean, what exactly are you doin' out here on the road?"

"Hitchhiking home", stated Steven from the back seat.

"Hitchhiking!", Uncle Roy exclaimed. "That right, Chip?" Chip nodded in the affirmative. Uncle Roy paused a moment. "Now I'm gonna tell you boys somethin' and you better listen. First of all, you guys are on the wrong side of the road to be hitchhiking. You got to be on the right of the road so if a car stops he can pull over out of the way and you don't have to cross the road or the traffic to get in. Second, I had no idea what you were doing. You've got to get that thumb stuck out there early and hold it high so a driver will know exactly what your intentions are." He held out his arm and stuck out his thumb to demonstrate. "I can tell you guys haven't been doin' this very much so just remember those two things and you'll be alright."

Uncle Roy dropped the boys off at the station in Sugar Tree at Chip's request. "Don't want your mom or dad to know you been hitchin' huh. I understand. Listen boys, you be careful now, hear." They thanked Uncle Roy and he drove off. If Chip's parents ever knew of his first hitchhiking episode, they never mentioned it.

There never was much of a reason to actually hitchhike in and around Sugar Tree. If you were just walking along the road, sooner or later someone would recognize you and stop and offer a ride. Usually you were so close to your destination anyway you would just wave the driver on and more often than not, the driver would wave back in understanding.

In Chip's life, there were only two events where foot travel outside of Sugar Tree required hitchhiking as a necessity. One was the three years he spent trying to get home from after school practice at Elk River High School and the other was trying to get to and from Marshall University during his freshman and sophomore years there. In all of those instances Uncle Roy's hitchhiking advice became a standard for Chip as he entered the world of the serious hitchhiker.

Hitchhiking was simple in those days. You got out on the road and stuck out your thumb and sooner or later somebody would stop and pick you up. You didn't worry about being kidnapped or molested. You were more worried about being dropped off in the middle of nowhere. But that was a chance you had to take. You never passed up a ride going in your direction no matter how far it was going. You would still be closer to your destination.

Drivers didn't worry about being robbed or carjacked or mugged. If they saw someone hitchhiking and they had room for them, they would pick them up. Most drivers would even indicate to the hitchhiker why he didn't stop and offer a ride. If there was not enough room for the hitchhiker, the driver would slow down, hold his arms out with the palms up and shake his head in a negative fashion which meant, "I don't have any room for you." If a driver didn't pick up a hitchhiker because he was just going up the road a short distance, he'd slow down and point in an exaggerated fashion in the same direction he was going while at the same time mouth something like, "Just going right up here." That always bothered Chip some because he was going that way too. Of course there were always the trucks and vans and company vehicles that had a big "No Riders" placard stuck up in the window somewhere. Chip never gave them the satisfaction of gettin' off that easy. If he spotted one in time, he'd look as pitiful and forlorn as possible and exaggerate his thumbing technique to show how desperate he was. It never worked. If a driver was going to pick him up, he'd stop and pick him up regardless of what he did or didn't do.

Chip did pick up quickly on the fact that any hitchhiker in a service uniform was ten times more likely to get picked up than some civilian schmuck standing along the road. While he was in high school, the closest thing Chip could come to a uniform of any kind would be his varsity letterman jacket. He couldn't get one as a freshman even though he lettered in track, because freshman couldn't be inducted into the varsity club until next year. Anyway, he didn't have to hitchhike home from practice that year since practice was held during the last two hours of school. Donning that varsity jacket next year before he set out hitchhiking on the road, not only gave Chip confidence, but in his own mind it was an open statement to the public that here was a trustworthy Elk River High School athlete doing his best to contribute to his school and needing some help in getting back to his home and family. Thusly, he would be more likely to catch a ride wearing the jacket than he would by wearing anything else.

Getting to and from Marshall College in Huntington, WV was an adventure in hitchhiking. It was just too far from Sugar Tree to Huntington to make the trip home too often, but Chip tried to go at least once a month. There were two other guys and three other girls from Elk River High who were also attending Marshall and a couple of times he was able to scrounge up a ride clear to Seneca with the parents of one, but most of the time he was out on the road alone.

He had no varsity jacket for a uniform because for one thing, varsity jackets just weren't the cool thing to wear in college except on the coldest, snowiest days and for another thing, three years of heavy use in high school had pretty much worn out the beloved old jacket. So Chip adopted a new uniform for hitchhiking. He wore a sport coat and tie when thumbin' a ride and he carried a cardboard sign on which was written one word, "HOME". Sometimes he taped the sign on the side of his small suitcase and would set it out in front beside the road in easy view and other times he held the sign up with his left hand while he stuck out the thumb on his right hand. It usually worked very well. In fact, it worked so well that Chip used the same sign when he headed back to Marshall.

Catching a ride out of Huntington wasn't too difficult because he usually left on Friday afternoon, a peak time for homeward bound travelers. He'd first try to get somebody at school to take him out of town to Rt. 60 where the traffic flow was less congested than downtown. If he couldn't get a lift out of town, he'd start hitchhiking right there beside the college on 5th Avenue which was a straight shot out of town to Rt. 60 east. Rt. 60 east led straight

225

into Charleston. Chip never had to wait long on Rt. 60 for a ride. If the ride didn't take him clear to Charleston, it always dropped him off along the way where he would quickly pick up another ride. The question invariably asked when he got into a car was, "Where is home?" That usually led to a good conversation about who knew what about the areas around each other's respective homes and communities.

Once Chip reached Charleston a real dilemma was posed. If he stayed on Rt. 60 through Charleston it would continue on east to Rt.19 which headed north through Seneca and on to Hob. It was a circuitous route that swung way east and then circled back around to the north. It was almost a hundred miles from Charleston to Sugar Tree via that route. The other route ran directly north out of Charleston just bypassing Mill's Bottom by a couple of miles. It was about sixty miles from Charleston to Sugar Tree via Mill's Bottom. The shortest route was the less traveled of the two and the last twenty-four miles of that trip, from Mill's Bottom to Sugar Tree on county Rt.1, ran entirely through the woods with no more than ten farmhouses along the way. The trip from Rt. 60 to Rt. 19 and to Seneca probably had three times the volume of traffic that the northern route did, but still, even on Friday night, there just wasn't much moving between Seneca and Hob and once you made it to Hob you still had eight miles of old, lonesome, one lane County Rt.11 to hitch down.

Chip solved his dilemma by making up his mind early about what he was going to do. If a hitched ride took him through Charleston, he'd go whichever direction the ride took him and work from that premise. If a ride dropped him off in Charleston, he'd head for Rt. 60 and Seneca without hesitation. If it was late when he got to Seneca he could always stay at Bill and Marilyn Cook's house. Marilyn was Chip's first cousin. She was ten years older than Chip and had three small children of her own. Her husband Bill worked the day shift as a yard master for the B & O Railroad at at local coal yard. He dreaded catching a ride north out of Charleston for he didn't know how or if he could make that twenty-four mile jaunt through the woods from Mill's Bottom to Sugar Tree. He didn't know anybody who lived in Mill's Bottom. They did have a hotel there where he could stay overnight if things didn't work out or he could even call Uncle Frank in Sugar Tree from the hotel and have someone drive down and pick him up.

Looking back on it, Chip realized that his dread of the northern route seemed justified at the time, but after all these years, it seems now to have been quite unfounded. He always made it to Mill's Bottom without too much trouble. Every ride he caught out of Mill's Bottom came along within a tolerable amount of waiting and every ride took him clear to Sugar Tree or to the top of Red Dog Hill. He guessed there was no where else a body could be driving out of Mill's Bottom on Rt.1 unless they were going to Red Dog or Sugar Tree.

There were only a couple of incidents of any significance during Chip's hitchhiking exploits from Marshall, home. The first one occurred when Chip caught a ride with the Charleston City Police while hitchhiking along Rt.60 between South Charleston and Charleston. At first he counted it as a piece of good luck on his part until the officers informed him that there was a city ordinance against hitchhiking within the city limits, punishable by fine or jail time. Chip had no idea such a law even existed. His first thought was wondering how he was going to pay his debt to society. Right behind that was his embarrassment at breaking the law, and lastly was his pitiful attempt to plead ignorance and throw himself upon the mercy of the officers. They drove on in silence through the streets of Charleston until they pulled off the side of the road on the outskirts of the city.

They informed Chip that they were now out of the city's jurisdiction and there was no law as yet against hitchhiking on Rt.60 out here. They let him out with a stiff warning against hitchhiking within the city limits of the state's capital city. Chip took the warning to heart, thanked the officers for their help and advice, and never hitchhiked in Charleston again.

A second incident also took place in Charleston when Chip was picked up by a guy in a '57 Cadillac convertible. Another good piece of luck, he thought, gettin' to ride in this fine machine. As soon as Chip got in the car he knew he was in trouble. The guy was nippin' from a bottle of Old Man McCreedy's Paint Thinner or something acquainted to it. The pint bottle, now only one quarter full, was nestled between his legs. He pulled back out into the traffic amid the screech of tires and the blaring of horns and paid them no mind whatsoever. "Where you headin' boy?" he slurred, too loud.

"I'm just goin right up here to Court Street", Chip answered. He wasn't exactly sure where Court Street was but he'd heard about it and saying something exact like that might make it sound more convincing. He wasn't too keen on traveling very far with this guy.

"Court Street huh. You lookin' to find a little snatch over there are you? Well, son, I'm tellin' you right now, this your lucky day. This here pussy wagon draws the honeys like flies--er, draws flies like honey---aw, you know what I mean." He slapped Chip on the leg and the Cadillac drifted over into the left lane. Fortunately, there was no one over there.

They weaved their way on into town but the driver wasn't sure of where he was going and because he had to focus on his incessant talking, he couldn't concentrate on driving to Court Street. Finally, he pulled over by the curb on Virginia Street. "Hey listen buddy, I got to take a whiz bad. I'm gonna run over there to that fillin' station and use the facilities. I don't want to drive in town no more so why don't you get over here and drive us over to Court Street and I'll rustle us up some chicks."

With those words he swung his door open, right in front of a car cruising down the street. The driver of the car slammed on his brakes and slid to a stop not only to avoid ripping off the door of the Cadillac but to keep from running over the drunken driver who had fallen out into the street. The driver got up, brushed himself off as he exchanged obscenities with the irate driver in the passing car, and staggered across the street amid the downtown traffic to the service station. If he hadn't been drunk he probably would have been hit by three or four vehicles and killed. Instead, he miraculously stumbled in and out, and in between the whizzing automobiles and made it safely to the other side. Chip closed his eyes. He couldn't watch. He waited for the sound of screeching tires and the dull thud of body being hit. When he didn't hear any noise of that nature, he opened his eyes and saw the Cadillac driver entering the service station.

Chip slid over the pint bottle of bourbon on the seat and under the wheel of the Caddy. He quickly familiarized himself with the essentials---brake, gear shift, ignition switch, etc. He reached down to slide the seat forward and found it to be electric powered. He figured the driver would never be lucky enough to make it back across the street without being killed so he started the Caddy and waited for the traffic behind him to get caught at the nearest red light. As soon as there was a big enough break in the traffic flow, Chip swung the Caddy out away from the curb and sailed smoothly across the street to the service station. He pulled up beside the outside rest room and waited for the driver to come out. He turned on the radio and tuned it to 580 AM, WCHS. This was too cool. Cruising the capital city in a Cadillac convertible while Chuck Berry was cranking out "Sweet Little Sixteen".

The driver came out of the rest room, opened the door on the passenger side, and got in just as if this was where Chip was suppose to have driven the Cadillac. He retrieved his pint from the seat and after a quick sip, motioned Chip to move on out. "Come on boy, lets go get us some poontang. You drive and I'll tell you when to stop."

Chip pulled out into traffic and headed up Virginia Street like he knew where he was going. Well, actually he knew where he wasn't going. He wasn't going to Court Street. He figured he'd just cruise on through town in a round about way until he got out on Rt. 60 and then he'd figure out something.

The former drunken driver now turned drunken passenger leaned over the side of the Caddy as they sped along. "Hey boy, pull over close to the curb there. I want to see if I can pick that chick up. I'd sure like to buzz butter her buns!"

"I can't. There's too much traffic", Chip pretended.

"Well hell boy, that don't make no difference. Now look. We already passed her. She was good lookin' too." He was looking back along the street. "Come on now. If you want to drive my baby, you'd better be doin' some drivin' or I'll take her back myself".

Chip finally eased over alongside the curb. "Hey, see that chick up yonder?", his passenger slurred. "Pull right over against the curb and slow down and I'll slap her right on her ass. And what a fine one it is at that". Chip didn't know what to do. If his passenger slapped the woman at their current speed he'd most likely break his arm and send the woman crashing to the pavement, inflicting serious injury. If he slowed down, the guy was just liable to do what he promised. Chip slowed down to a crawl but let the Cadillac drift out away from the curb just enough so that his passenger couldn't reach the woman. His depth perception impaired by drink, he made a big roundhouse swing at the woman but missed. He swore something unintelligible but stayed focused on the street ahead.

Chip swung right at Brooks St. and headed for the Boulevard that ran along the outskirts of town along the Kanawha River, hoping his passenger wouldn't notice he was heading away from downtown. Once he got on the Boulevard, he knew there would not be any female pedestrians to harass and they could move along at a much greater clip.

As luck would have it, two blocks from the Boulevard, Chip caught a red light. He drew up right beside a crowd of pedestrians waiting for the traffic to clear so they could cross the street. Among the crowd and standing right next to the Cadillac was a stunningly attractive woman dressed in very expensive executive attire. Chip could tell she was all class. Of course the first thing his lecherous passenger did was put the move on her.

He leaned out of the car as far as he could. "Hey baby, what say you come on in here and take a ride with me and my buddy here. We'll shore show you a good time. Hell, we'll do anything you want---go anywhere you say. What say? You are one fine looking babe, you know that."

To Chip's surprise the woman bent down and whispered in a most sexy tone right in the old cuss's face. "Listen you smelly old slob. First of all you couldn't afford me and second of all, I don't usually even give jerks like you the time of day. Now if you don't get out of here and leave me alone, I'm either going to call a cop or I'm going to take this .38 pistol out of my bag and shoot your balls off right here!" She started fumbling around with the catch on her leather shoulder bag.

The light hadn't changed but Chip flipped on the right blinker, gunned the Cadillac in a right-turn-on-red maneuver, just missed a couple of folks crossing the street, and sped away from that corner. Cruising through town wasn't turning out to be as cool as Chip first thought. He began to worry about police reports coming in relating to two intoxicated men in a Cadillac convertible harassing women and causing general mayhem. If they were stopped, he'd be arrested for being an accomplice.

At the next street Chip turned left and drove out to the Boulevard. Once on the Boulevard, he steered the Cadillac east and kept right on moving despite the protests from the owner of the car who was now upset with Chip because he wouldn't drive around in town. Chip didn't care. He just wanted to get out of town and out of that car. He kept glancing in the rear view mirror, afraid of spying the flashing red lights of a police car.

A mile out of town and now on Rt. 60, Chip pulled the Caddy off in a wide spot beside the road. He opened the door, got out, and pulled his suitcase from the back seat. "Thanks for the ride", he said and started walking up the road.

The old guy didn't say anything but Chip could tell he was mad. He heard him slide across the seat and slam the driver's side door. He heard the Cadillac start up and churn the gravels as it started to move. He thought he better turn around to make sure the Caddy wasn't going to run over him. As he looked back, the Cadillac made a big U-turn and headed back down Rt.60 towards Charleston and away from Chip.

One other Friday, Chip had made it from Huntingon to Seneca in so many little hops and jaunts that it was nine o'clock at night before he arrived in Seneca. It took him twenty minutes to walk through town on Rt.19 before he could even start hitchhiking. Traffic was sparse that night for some reason and Chip had to wait another forty minutes before a car slowed down and pulled over for him.

Chip trotted up to the car carrying his suitcase and opened the door. He started to slide his suitcase in behind the front seat of the two door sedan but the driver stopped him. "Just put your suitcase up here on the front seat. Don't want you to wake up my other passenger", he whispered. He jerked his thumb a couple of times towards the back seat where a sailor in uniform sat up asleep in the back seat. "I picked him up an hour or so ago out of Beckley."

231

Chip put his suitcase on the seat between the driver and him, got in and shut the door. Instead of driving on, the driver just sat there. He looked over at Chip. "Can you drive?" he asked.

"Yeah. Sure.", Chip answered.

"Well listen," the driver went on, "I been drivin' since 7:00 this morning and I can't stay awake any longer. I just need a ten or fifteen minute nap and I'll be ok. I've got to be in Morgantown in the morning. Can you drive ten or fifteen minutes for me before you have to get out?"

"Sure", said Chip.

"Come on then. Take over."

The driver and Chip switched places. The driver watched Chip for the first couple of minutes to make sure he was capable and he must have felt comfortable with Chip's driving because in another minute he was sound asleep, sitting up with his head resting on the side window. The car was easy to drive. By the time fifteen minutes were up they were barely into Raven Valley so Chip just kept driving. He drove all the way through the valley, over Panther Mountain and into Hob.

In Hob, he eased the car off the road to the side of the Texaco station, now closed for the night. He stopped under one of the station's outside night lights right beside the only telephone booth in the country. As quiet as possible he opened the door, slid his suitcase out, closed the door with a gentle nudge, and started walking down Rt.11 towards Sugar Tree, leaving his two passengers sleeping on soundly.

It was easier getting from Marshall to Sugar Tree than it was trying to get back to Marshall. Chip's best bet was to find another Marshall student from the tri-county county area who would be going back to Huntington on Sunday. He'd always start inquiring about rides back to Huntington while at school and he would begin searching the first of the week prior to the weekend he was going home. Most of the time he was successful in finding someone accommodating. Then all he had to figure out was a way to get to his ride on Sunday. Most rides left for Huntington early in the afternoon. Ordinarily Chip's dad would drive him to his ride and a

232

few times, Link did. Usually they would have to go to Seneca to meet the ride but once or twice they drove to Mill's Bottom.

Link was the only Jive Fiver to have his own car while still in high school. He liked to volunteer to drive Chip to his ride. He would rather drive Chip all the way to Huntington. He just liked to drive. When he turned sixteen, Link's parents bought him a brand new '62 Ford Falcon. It was nothing fancy, just you're basic mode of transportation. It had a rubber floor covering, a four cylinder engine and a column shift, three speed transmission. It did have an excellent AM radio.

One Sunday afternoon during a heavy, wet snowstorm, Link and Chip spent almost two hours trying to get the Falcon over Panther Mountain so Chip could catch his ride in Seneca. The Falcon just didn't have enough weight to get any traction in the heavy snow. They were able to get a good level run at the bottom of the mountain but at the first sharp turn less than a quarter of a mile up, Link had to let off to keep the car from sliding through the turn and into the ditch. He successfully negotiated the turn but when he tried to pick up speed again, the rear wheels lost traction and spun the car sideways off onto the shoulder on the upper side of the road and into the ditch.

Link tried to rock the Falcon out of the ditch but it wouldn't budge. Chip got out and tried to push it backward down the hill while Link kept her revved up in reverse---nothing. Chip decided to try and use the bumper jack to jack up that rear corner that was in the ditch. When they got it up high enough, maybe they could push the car sideways a little in the snow to eventually get the rear end up out of the ditch. It was slow, hard, and sloppy work but little by little they were able to scoot the Falcon over onto the berm and out of the ditch. All the while they were working on the stuck car, not more than three cars came down the mountain. They all had snow chains on. Not one vehicle passed them going up the mountain and while this was all going on, it snowed another two inches.

Link didn't have any chains but he did have some brand new sawdust, winter tread tires on the rear. Chip got in the back seat for a little added traction. Link found out that by running with the outside set of wheels on the berm and one on the road the Falcon could make some steady headway and he was able to control the steering to a much better degree. That maneuver worked fine for another half mile up the mountain until they came upon another car stuck in the ditch on their side of the road. They couldn't go around the stuck car without having to swing out into the middle of the road. Two things could happen then, and neither was good. One, they could lose what little traction they had and get stuck in the middle of the road or slide clear across the road and into the guard posts on the lower side the road. Two, a car coming down the mountain might not be able to stop and slam into them. They decided their best bet was to see if they could help the other car get out of the ditch and thus, out of their way.

Link stopped a short distance from the stuck car in a little wide place that allowed the Falcon to be completely out of the road. The stuck car was a big Pontiac. Link and Chip helped the driver push her back down the hill while the driver's wife steered and used reverse very gently. She did a good job and they had the Pontiac out of the ditch on the first try. The driver then set the emergency brake and while the wife turned the power steering, he and the boys pushed the front end of the Pontiac around until it was headed back down the mountain. He thanked the boys, got in the car, and drove off down the road, very cautiously. It snowed another inch.

The two piled back in the Falcon but the snow depth was now becoming a hazard. The little Ford would barely move forward at all. Link had to back up three times to get a free running start. She was starting to push snow with the front bumper.

Chip tried to talk Link into just turning around and going back home. Even if they made it to Seneca now his ride would be long gone. It didn't matter to Link. He wasn't turning back now. It had become a challenge he couldn't pass up.

Once the Falcon gained a little momentum, Link was able to keep her steadily moving up the mountain. The speedometer would surge up to sixty miles per hour but the Ford was still only going at a snails pace. The rear driver's side wheel, the one on the snow covered pavement, was doing all the work. The spinning wheel had heated up and was slowly melting the snow and ice under it as it went.

A '52 Chevy came up behind them, swung over a little to the middle of the road, and passed them right up. The car had no chains and the tires, front and back, looked pretty much devoid of any tread. He must have been doing thirty-five or forty. He waved at the two boys as he swirled around them and kept on truckin'. Chip recognized the driver. It was "Preacher" Gill from Hob. The Lord's surely with him, thought Chip.

They finally made it to the top of the mountain and Link pulled over in the wide place. They both got out and looked at the driver's side tire. All of the tread and sawdust had been burned off. Now Link was ready to turn around and go back to Sugar Tree much to Chip's relief . The snow was still coming down hard when out of the drifting veil emerged a lumbering snowplow. Behind it, following closely, like ducks in a row, were ten or fifteen vehicles. Link spun the Falcon through the snow bank and took his place in the line winding its way down the mountain and back to Hob.

They made it back to Sugar Tree safely but Chip still had to find a way to Marshall. There was no way he was going to find one that day. He rode around the road with Link to see if there was anybody at the Esso station. Nobody was there except Lewis and Bucky. Chip and Link told about their experience on Panther Mountain and Chip explained his dilemma. Lewis thought he might have a solution.

It seems that Monday is the day the Betsy Ross bread man comes to Sugar Tree. His route starts out of Charleston but he comes all the way to Sugar Tree first and then makes all his deliveries working back to Charleston. "I have to call in my order to him this evening", explained Lewis. "I'll just ask him if you can ride back to Charleston with him tomorrow. I'm sure he would let you as a favor to me. You can get from Charleston to Huntington, no sweat. Only one thing", he went on, "Billy is here by 6:00 in the morning so if you're going with him, you'd better be here".

It was still snowing and Chip knew he'd never get out of Sugar Tree tomorrow by any other means. "What if it's still bad tomorrow and he doesn't come?" he asked.

"We've been in business here for over ten years and Billy has never, ever missed a delivery because of weather. He'll be here. Just you be here."

Chip showed up at the station the next morning at 5:45. His dad drove him around the road in the Mercury. He had put chains on the evening before. It had quit snowing sometime during the night and turned bitterly cold. The snow was fifteen inches deep and there were only two wheel tracks to indicate where the road might be. Mr. Gates plowed his way down the driveway out to the road and then let the Merc settle into the tracks. It practically steered itself around the road to the station.

Instead of just dropping Chip off at the station, his dad insisted on waiting for Bucky, or Lewis or Billy, who ever showed up first. He kept the engine running and the heater on and Chip was grateful. He was still a little skeptical about this sure fire ride to Charleston but he maintained a positive attitude mostly for his dad's benefit. He didn't think his dad was all that confident in this good fortune either.

In less than five minutes Lewis showed up in his jeep. He unlocked the front door of the station, went in, and turned on the lights. Chip told his dad he'd go on inside and wait. He thanked him for the ride and told him he'd try to get back home in a couple of weeks.

Lewis and Chip waited inside the station for Billy. The Keener boys never opened up before 7:00 but one of them had to come in early on Mondays to let the bread boy in. 6:00, no Billy. 6:15 came and went, no Billy. By 6:30 the daylight shift workers at Red Dog had begun to push their way through the snow past the station in an assortment of trucks and jeeps. It was a little before 7:00 when Billy eased the bread truck to a stop right in front of the station where the Mercury had sat two hours earlier. The entire front of the stub nosed truck was covered with ice and snow. The massive two piece windshield had a little space cleared about the size and shape of a porthole on the driver's side. Evidently Billy was able to see out of it well enough to navigate his way there from Charleston.

Billy told Chip to throw his suitcase in the truck and help him carry some stock into the station and they'd be able to get going soon enough.

They left Sugar Tree heading for Charleston by way of Mill's Bottom. Billy had dual wheel chains on the rear of the truck and had no problem negotiating Rt.1 in the heavy snow. It would be weeks before the State Road plowed through there. The truck had a good heater in it but no windshield defroster. Billy had to keep rubbing his little view through the porthole with his gloved hand to keep it clear. The only door in the front of the truck was a sliding one on the passenger side. They used it for most of the deliveries they made that day. There was no seat on that side of the truck so Chip had to stand up all the time.

They pulled into the Betsy Ross bakery in Charleston at 4:00 that evening. Chip had no idea there were that many stores, beer joints, and markets between Sugar Tree and Charleston.

Now he'd lost the whole day, missed all of his classes, and still wasn't in Huntington. He didn't hesitate. He grabbed his suitcase and walked four blocks uptown to the Greyhound Bus station. There he bought a one way ticket to Huntington on the 5:00 bus. This was not the first time Chip had used the bus to get from Charleston to Huntington. It seemed they ran about every two hours or so. The bus stopped about as many times between Charleston and Huntington as the bread truck did between Sugar Tree and Charleston but at least Chip was sitting back in a nice comfortable seat and was able to take a good long nap.

He got into Huntington around 7:00 that evening but then he had to walk and carry his suitcase through the snow and wind, five long city blocks from the bus station to his dorm. It was almost 8:00 when he finally made it into his room. A normal weekend trip back to Marshall from Sugar Tree could take as long as five hours. This one turned out to be thirty one hours.

The hitchhiking phase of Chip's life would come to an end when he left Marshall after his sophomore year there. There were a number of factors that rendered hitchhiking a nonessential and though being able to drive was certainly one of them, owning his own car was not. Driving however, was interspersed throughout the hitchhiking phase, especially during the latter years.

IX

Maynard earned his driver's license first. He was a year older than Chip and two years older than Link and Benji. Maynard bought a '40 Ford Tudor when he was still a sophomore in high school; more than a year before he would get his license. He had traded a twelve gauge, double barrel, shotgun for the Ford. It was a solid looking vehicle. The interior was all original mohair stuff and in good condition except where the headliner drooped down in the back above the split rear window. It didn't have a motor. Maynard had got his uncle to pull it around behind the house and left it parked out next to the barn. He and Chip used to go out by the barn and just sit in the car. Sometimes they took the six volt battery out of Maynard's dad tractor and hooked it up to the terminals in the Ford so they could listen to the radio. It had an outstanding radio. Instead of a normal tone knob , which was usually located behind the station select knob, the Ford had a tone control knob that when you turned it, the fidelity changed on the radio and in a little window below the dial face and between the Conalrad Signals, it showed what phase the tone was switched to; bass, hi fi, classic, and talk. From old discarded radios and phonographs lying about they were able to salvage three or four good speakers which they hooked up to the radio and placed in strategic spots inside the car. A couple of nights they even slept all night in the car with the radio crackling out the sounds of WKBW in Buffalo until it began to fade out along with the early dawn.

Maynard eventually traded the Ford for a 1952, belt driven, Indian motorbike. The Indian was a good little motorbike except it didn't have a drive belt, which worked out fine too, because it didn't have a motor either.

The Indian would simply fly downhill and would coast forever on the level. It had a big roomy saddle seat on which two could ride with comfort, but wherever it couldn't coast on its own, it had to be pushed. For a while Maynard insisted on taking the motorbike wherever the Jive Five rode their bikes. It was best for him if he could get someone to buddy up with him to help push. As the novelty of the motorbike wore off , it became increasingly more difficult for Maynard to get anyone to ride with him. Finally, he too, saw the futility in working that hard just to get a few moments rush, so he traded the motorbike for a Remmington Model 12, sixteen gauge, pump shotgun.

Even though Maynard had his license before the rest of the Jive Five, he rarely got to use the family car. The family car was a '57 Chevy station wagon. Mr. Samples' everyday driver was a '60 Corvair. Chip remembered Maynard taking the Chevy to the prom a couple of times and keeping it out all night at his high school graduation.

Maynard was allowed to have the Corvair occasionally on the weekends. He always loaded Benji, Link and Chip up in the Corvair and usually they'd just drive around for four or five hours. They'd put a hundred miles on the Corvair just driving around Sugar Tree. They made a couple of trips over to Seneca to go to a dance or party, but most of their driving time was spent cruising the road between Hob on one end, and Red Dog on the other.

Gas was thirty cents a gallon, regular, and with two dollars worth of gas in the Corvair, they could have driven around for days but Mr. Samples did put three restrictions on Maynard's use of the little Chevy. One, Maynard had to have it back and parked by 12:00 midnight. Two, he had to leave it parked with approximately the same amount of gas in the tank as there was in it when he got it. Third, he couldn't put more than seventy miles on the speedometer. As long as Maynard complied with those three stipulations, his dad would never ask where he had been, what he had been doing, or who he had been with him.

There was nothing Maynard could do about the first directive. When it was 12:00, it was 12:00 and nobody could do anything about that. If Maynard wasn't parked at the house by 12:00 he was dead---there were no excuses, no emergencies, no compromises. Heck, Maynard couldn't get around that one even on the Saturday night when they changed daylight savings time back to eastern standard time. True, you got to turn the clock back an hour, but you weren't suppose to do that until 1:00 AM, Sunday, an hour past the time when the Corvair was suppose to be parked.

The second and third restrictions could be fudged upon a bit. In the former case, the Jive Five always had some money to pool together to buy gas. In the latter years, it became an unwritten Jive

239

Five rule that whoever did the driving didn't have to buy the gas. So the first thing the guys did when they got the Corvair was drive around the road to Keener's or over to Hob and fill the tank. Then they'd just keep a close watch on the gauge so as to time things for 12:00 midnight and finish up, leaving the gauge about where it was when they first took off. A couple of times they had to come in early because they would be short on the gas gauge. Maynard was sure his dad checked both the gas gauge and the speedometer before the Corvair was let out on those nights.

Then, as if he were making an attempt to thwart whatever devious plans Maynard had for the Corvair, his dad began leaving it with a full tank of gas for Maynard. It was obvious why Mr. Samples engineered this plan and it was a very clever ploy. When Maynard drove off in the Corvair, it had a full tank of gas. When he returned that night, it had to have a full tank of gas. The guys couldn't put any gas in it when they started the evening because it was already full. They had to drive around for a couple of hours to use any gas at all. There were no service stations anywhere around that were open after 9:00 PM, so they had to get the tank filled before then. That meant if they drove around very much after 9:00 they couldn't return the Corvair with a full tank of gas. The first few nights under that handicap they filled it up in Hob then just drove out to the Horse Ridge fire tower and fooled around out there till 11:00, 11:30. One other time they drove around to the Company Store and hung out for a couple of hours.

Those evenings didn't seem to be too adventurous so together, they devised their own countermeasure. When they drove off in the Corvair, the first place they headed was around to the station. There they bought ten gallons of gas and had Bucky or Lewis put it in two five gallon cans. They hid the cans out back of the station, with the Keener brothers' help. Then they could drive wherever they wanted. Just before they had to turn the Corvair in, they drove around to the station, got the gas hidden in the cans out back, and filled her back up.

The mileage problem of course, was solved by the age old trick of unhooking the speedometer when it got close to showing seventy miles, then hooking it back up again just before they turned her in for the night. They made only a couple of night cruises that were noteworthy. Once they drove three hours through a snow storm to Elkins to watch Mill's Bottom play in a regional championship basketball game. They got to the game with two minutes left in the fourth quarter. Mill's Bottom was down by seventeen and wound up losing the game, but they didn't have to pay to see the last few minutes.

On the return trip to Sugar Tree that night, they stopped a couple of miles outside of Huttonsville where the WV State Minimum Security Prison was located, and spent thirty minutes trying to wrestle an eight foot tall road sign out of the ground that read "Beware. Do Not Pick Up Hitchhikers". They finally got the sign out of the ground but the only way to transport it home was to roll down both backdoor windows and stick the sign through one side and let it poke out through the other. They stuck the post end of the sign all the way through from the passenger side and left the end with sign on it hanging out on that side away from traffic. Link and Chip rode in the back and kept the sign as equally balanced as they could. When Maynard spotted an approaching car, Link and Chip would slide the sign over to the right as far as possible so that the post end of the sign wouldn't hit the approaching vehicle as it passed. Problem was Maynard would almost have to stop the Corvair because now the longest end of the sign was sticking out of the passenger side of the car which put it dangerously close to other road signs, bridges, mailboxes, telephone poles, parked vehicles, trees, and other roadside obstacles.

After traveling less than two miles from the scene of the sign abduction, the plan for getting the road sign home was abandoned. Link and Chip were freezing cold. There was an inch of snow in the back seat and two close calls with the sign, one with a passing snowplow and the other with a concrete bridge railing, impressed upon the kidnappers the realization of how much destruction and injury would be inflicted upon them and the Corvair if a collision between the sign and any outside obstacle should occur. They left the sign leaning up against an old oak tree right beside a "No Dumping" sign at a wide place off the side of the road. They wiped the sign and post clean of any fingerprints. Then they had to hightail it back to Sugar Tree as fast as the weather and road

241

conditions would allow in order to refill the gas tank and park the Corvair by the midnight deadline. They just did make it.

The second adventure Chip called to remembrance, came about on a late October weekend when Mr. Samples loaded his family up in the station wagon and drove out to Lodi, Ohio to visit Mrs. Samples' brother's family. Even Maynard's brother Elihu went along. They left on Friday evening after work and miraculously, Mr. Samples left the key for the Corvair hanging on the nail in the kitchen where it was always kept. This was too good to be true. Maynard figured it was either a test or a trap. The only instructions Mr. Samples left for Maynard was that he had to go up on the hill and check the TV antenna. The Jive Five had already gotten permission from their parents to spend the weekend at Maynard's, but of course there had been no mention of the Corvair in the scheme of things.

Trap or no trap, the first thing Maynard did was unhook the speedometer on the Corvair and Friday night, he and Benji cruised around in Red Dog and Sugar Tree. Chip had already promised to take Judy to a BYF party at Marianne Dancy's house. He would come by Maynard's later. Link was at Marianne's party too, so he and Chip made plans to meet later at Maynard's. Chip took Judy home around 10:30 but he stayed at her house till almost 12:00. On his walk around to Maynard's, he found Link sitting on the steps at the Company Store waiting for him and they walked together around to Maynard's.

It was too late that night to do any running around, so they stayed up as late as they could, eating, playing records, and horsing around.

By the time they all were up the next morning and fixed and ate breakfast, it was close to high noon. Maynard wanted to get his task of fixing the TV antenna out of the way first so they would have the rest of the weekend to run around. It normally took between forty-five and sixty minutes to climb up the TV line to the antenna, check and repair anything, and return, but since all the guys were together, and since he had free use of the Corvair, Maynard decided to drive up to the Morris Cemetery, which was only a half a mile out the ridge from the Samples' TV antenna.

There was an old logging road that continued on past the cemetery and passed right by the antenna.

The road to the cemetery was rough and a little muddy but it was kept in passable condition most of the year. Most of the dead in Sugar Tree, Red Dog, and surrounding areas were buried in the Morris Cemetery. The logging road was a bit more rugged and as soon as it left the cemetery, it disappeared into the woods. For the first two hundred yards the briers and brush hung over on both sides of the road and the heavy foliage kept the sun out. The road was level from the cemetery on out, but the roadbed itself was slick, red clay. They eased their way, spinning and sliding a little, through the woods until they emerged into what once had been somebody's fine open meadow, but now was grown up in sagebrush, greenbriers, and the abominable multifloral rose. It had taken them only twenty minutes to drive up to the antenna.

They parked the car and got out and waded their way the last fifty yards up through the knee high brush and grass to the top of the hill and the antenna. Chip was the resident TV line and antenna expert so he inspected the setup and found where one of the lead-in wires had broken apart right at the antenna connection. He quickly used his trusty scout knife to unscrew both connectors, cut and strip the wires, and reconnect the line to the antenna. They were done and back in the car in ten minutes. They were ahead of schedule.

Maynard tried to turn around right there where they had stopped by jostling back and forth with little jerks and turns of the wheel. When he got the car halfway turned around and crossways in the road, it slipped on the red clay and slid off the road backwards into a rut on the upper side. The rear bumper and frame caught the opposite side of the rut and hung the car up with the rear wheels suspended in the air, two feet over the rut.

The Corvair was not a very heavy car but a combination of the slick clay and the position of the car made it too difficult for the four boys to manhandle it out of their predicament. The only tools they had to work with were the bumper jack and tire tool. They jacked the rear of the car up and filled the ruts with rocks, stones, and fence rails. Stones and rocks were hard to come by up in the old field where they were, so they all scattered out and searched for rocks and stones big enough to do the job. Once found, the stones had to be carried or rolled back to the car. The fence rails were scattered here and there, relics of a once common boundary marker. They too had to be carried back to the car and used to fill in the ruts in the road. Once they got the Corvair straightened up and headed back out the road to the cemetery, Maynard was able to guide her through the woods without getting stuck. It took over an hour and a half to get the car back on the road and out to the cemetery.

It was 2:30 in the afternoon when they got back to Maynard's. A job that would have taken forty-five minutes to complete by walking, took two and a half hours by doing it the easy way. The Corvair was covered in red clay mud and had mud inside on the floor and seats where the boys had carried it in. They too were smeared in mud and dirt from wallowing around in the clay and carrying rocks and fence rails.

Maynard said he'd wash the Corvair off and sweep out the dried mud inside but Link argued him out of that. If they were going back out cruising later that night, what would be the use of cleaning the car up now? They could clean it up on Sunday and only have to do it once. All agreed and they went inside. After taking turns showering and cleaning up, they all found a place in the living room to sack out for a couple of hours.

Around 6:00 they cooked up a supper of eggs and bacon and toast and then sat around watching TV until after the news went off at 11:30. Chip popped some popcorn and put it in brown paper bags to take with them to snack on and Benji made a gallon of cherry Koolaid and put it in an Aladdin thermos to go along with the popcorn. At 12:00 midnight they piled in the Corvair and headed out for adventure.

Maynard was doing the driving, so he had already decided where they were going. Chip remembered they drove over to Hob, turned north on US 19, drove about twenty minutes, and then turned off Rt. 19 onto a dirt road that seemed to go, for the most part, in a westerly direction.

Where they were wasn't really important. They had an almost full tank of gas, they had some munchies, and WHK from Cleveland was blastin' in just fine. In fact, they stopped once right in the middle of the road and got out and danced in the headlights to "Sherry", by the Four Seasons. Benji almost popped a vessel trying to sing like Frankie Valli.

They drove on for a couple of hours along the ridges and down in the valleys along those dirt roads. When they came to an intersection, Maynard took the road that seemed to have carried the most traffic, lest they drove up someone's driveway or just ran out of passable road and had to turn around and drive back out. In fact, on one wrong turn, they did drive right up into some farmer's back yard. It sounded like a hundred dogs started barking and by the time the back porch light flipped on, Maynard had the Corvair turned around and headed back out of there.

The night was pitch black and much of the time the road was crowded in on both sides with woods or brush. All they could see was the hundred feet or so ahead of them that was illuminated by the Corvair's headlights. A few times they topped out on little knolls along the top of a ridge where there would be meadows on both sides of the road. Maynard would stop the car and they would all get out and after allowing their eyes to adjust to the darkness, they searched the horizon and far valleys for landmarks or lights or anything that might indicate where some form of organized civilization might be located. There was nothing. It was now obvious that not even Maynard knew where they were. They just drove on and on into the night and seemingly deeper and deeper into the wilderness.

At 2:45 AM Maynard swung around a steep turn in the road and slammed on the brakes. The Corvair wasn't making much speed but it slid sideways on the dirt road and threw the unsuspecting passengers frontwards out of their seats. "Whatcha doin' stupid? Trying to kill us?" demanded Benji as he picked himself up out of the floor and settled back on the seat.

"No, look. There's a guy standing in the road", answered Maynard excitedly, pointing up ahead.

Everyone looked out the windshield and sure enough, a man was walking towards the car in the glare of the headlights. Maynard hadn't jammed on the brakes to keep from hitting the guy, he was still thirty feet or so from the car, he was just startled to see someone out here in the middle of nowhere at 2:45 in the morning.

The eerie specter of a human being materializing in the middle of nowhere, out of nowhere, momentarily froze everyone else too.

The man was swinging a flashlight and he walked right up to Maynard's side of the car. He wore what looked like some kind of uniform. When he got up beside Maynard, the boys could see he was a Department of Natural Resource Fire Warden. Maynard rolled down the window.

The man bent down and spoke through the window, "Boy, I sure am glad you guys came along. Listen, I need some help. There's a fire out just up the road there and I'm by myself and I need you guys to help me get it under control." He smelled of smoke. The boys all looked up the road but they didn't see anything. "Well, what you say? I can't do this by myself and right now it's mostly a ground fire and it would be easy to contain but if it boils up and gets into the trees, it'll be bad. Come on, my truck's just up the road there and I've got everything we'll need." He started trotting back up the road. Maynard eased the Corvair along behind him, lighting the road ahead. The guys discuss their situation as they drove along.

"You know he has the authority to commandeer us to fight fire", Link spoke up. "He's playin' it smart though. Notice how he asked us to help and then didn't even wait for us to give him answer. They can do that though if they want. Heck they can set up road blocks and stop motorists and make them get out and fight fire."

"They can't do that. Can they?" asked Maynard.

"Sure they can", Link went on, "and they can even put you in jail if you refuse to go."

They were at the forest service truck now and Maynard pulled off the road behind it. The boys got out and walked up to the back of the truck where the warden was pulling shovels and rakes out of the back. The boys could see the fire line now. It was about a hundred yards down over the hill below the road in a small thicket of dead chestnut trees. The blackened ground where the fire had already burned came to a point just ahead of the forest service truck right by the road. It was obvious the fire had originated from a spot right beside the road.

The warden divided the boys into pairs and directed them to where he wanted them to go. Each one grabbed a fire fighting implement out of the truck. Benji and Chip were paired and they worked their way down the hill to the left side of the fire line. The warden had told them the fire wasn't big enough to set up any kind of backfire or fire break. Since it was burning down the hill, if they would carefully pull and drag the fire back up the hill into the area it had already burned, it would burn itself out. Maynard and Link worked the right hand side and the warden worked back and forth helping each pair as needed.

The fire fighters had the ground fire dead and out in thirty minutes but the real problem now was the five or six dead chestnut trees that were burning and smoldering inside. The native chestnut trees in West Virginia had been killed by a blight in the late 1930's. The trees had lost their branches and were mere dead, hollow trees but they were still standing and some of them were thirty or forty feet tall. The ground fire had set the trees on fire. A couple of them were burning on the outside but the others were burning up on the inside . When they burned enough to lose their structural strength, they fell. As the trees fell, the sudden rush of oxygen supply to the fire sent it into a roaring blaze. The boys could actually hear the fire roar to life as the tree fell. When the old hollow tree hit the ground, it burst apart, throwing flame and fire in all directions. It was fascinating to watch. It was as if someone had dropped a barrel of gasoline and it smashed open right in the middle of a fire. The ground fire hadn't bothered the live trees in the area.

The danger now was from these trees falling and spreading the fire again. Most of the trees still burning were in the part of the woods that had already been burned so there was no new tender to catch fire. There were two trees along the edge of the fire line that if they fell down the hill, they would fall onto unburned territory and thus start another fire. The fire fighters' job now was to stand vigil over these burning structures. So they sat around on the black and burned ground and watched for places where the fire might spread. There was enough light from the burning trees to chase away some of the darkness.

After thirty or forty minutes had passed, the warden came around and gathered up his helpers. "I think if we can take care of those two lower trees that are still burning, you fellows won't have to wait around here for too much longer. I can watch what's left. I'd like to see if we can push those two trees over and put out their ground fire. You fellows ready?" The boys nodded in agreement. They wanted to get back on the road as soon as possible.

The job wasn't that hard. The five of them working together were able to use their fire fighting tools to shove against the dead stands and the fire had done its job of weakening the base so the two trees toppled over fairly easily. The danger was not to be in the vicinity where the tree fell. The workers pushed the trees from the upper side and that's where they made their escape when it started falling. They had to wait a few minutes for the embers and flames to die down enough for them to beat or scatter the fire till it was out.

The warden led them back up the hill to his truck and they put the tools in the back. He went up to the cab and turned on the cab lights. "I need to get your names and addresses", he said, "so I can send you some money for helping to fight fire". He got out a pad and a pencil and handed it to Chip who was standing the closest.

"Aw, you don't have to do that", Link interjected, "we were glad to help. We don't want any money. We're just thankful we were able to do our little part to help save our precious resources." The rest of the boys stopped and looked at Link for a moment. They felt pride and admiration for their friend and took his inspiring words to heart. Then they went back to completing their addresses on the pad. Hey, if Link didn't want paid, fine and dandy, but the rest wanted some compensation for their hard and dirty work. Eventually, Link sauntered over to the open cab door and filled out his name and address too.

"I want to thank you fellows again.", the warden said when they were finished, "This could have turned into a serious forest fire without your help. I'll be able to watch it now until the danger's passed. They'll be a little somethin' in the mail for you in a couple of weeks. So thank again." He shook each boys hand as they turned to leave.

They got halfway back to the Corvair when Maynard stopped and turned back to the warden. "Hey", he yelled to get the warden's attention. "Do you know where in the heck we are?"

"Well, I'll tell you as best I can." the warden answered as he walked back towards the boys. "You're on a ridge just between Webster and Randolph Counties."

"So how's the best way to get to a main highway?" Maynard asked.

"You'd probably be better off to keep on going ahead on this road", he pointed. "About six miles you'll come to an old iron bridge. There's an intersection just on the other side of the bridge. You need to turn right at the end of the bridge. You can't see the turn off to the right unless you're looking for it. It looks like the main road goes straight ahead but you don't want to go that way. Turn right and go another three miles. You have to drive through the creek a couple of times but the water level is low and you shouldn't have any trouble". He looked at the Corvair in a skeptical way before continuing. "At the next intersection, take a right. Stay on that road for about five miles and you'll come to the hardroad. Once you get to the hard road, if you go left, that'll take you over next to Monterville. If you go right, you'll come out over around French Creek. Got all that?"

"Sure. Sure", answered Maynard a little too quickly. "We sure do thank you sir."

"Glad to help and thanks again", he said as he turned back towards his truck.

The boys got in the Corvair and Maynard pulled out and eased around the DNR truck and started the homeward journey. It was ten minutes after four.

"Listen you dumb asses", Link started, "Don't you know if they get your name and address, they put it on file with the State Department and anytime there is a forest fire around home anywhere, they can come and get you and make you go fight it. They just tell you that stuff about paying so they can get your name and where you live." Nobody said anything for a moment.

"Hey, wait a minute. You signed that paper too", said Benji.

"Yeah, that's right. Only I didn't want the guy to know that I knew what he didn't want us to know, so I made up a name and made up an address in Clarksburg. They'll never get me."

It was an uneventful return trip home that took almost two hours. They all had to stay awake to keep Maynard awake. They were worn out and done in when they finally stumbled half asleep into the living room at Maynard's. They left the Corvair parked in the driveway. There was nothing they could do with it now. They would have plenty of time to clean it up, refill the tank, and park it by the barn before the Samples got home from Ohio.

The boys left their shoes outside on the front porch but they were too tired to even clean themselves up, though they did wash their hands and faces. They smelled like smoke and their clothes were smeared with black dirt and ashes. They took off all of their clothes except their underwear, and piled them outside the door beside their shoes. Maynard dragged out some of his camping quilts and blankets and spread them out on the linoleum floor in the front room and the boys, clad only in their underwear, laid down on them and were all asleep in less than ten minutes.

The plan had been to sleep for a couple of hours, clean themselves up, eat some breakfast, and then clean up the Corvair. That plan was dashed to bits when the Samples came home around 1:00 in the afternoon and found four boys sprawled around on the living room floor in their underwear and the Corvair parked in the driveway covered inside and out with red clay mud and black soot.

Upon the discovery of the boys, Mrs. Samples gently woke each one and steered them down the hall to Maynard's room.. She broke out the bath towels and let each one in turn go to the bathroom and shower. They could put on some of Maynard's clean clothes until theirs could be washed and dried. She sent two of Maynard's sisters out to fetch the boys' discarded clothes on the front porch and she dumped them in the washer along with their underwear.

Mr. Samples never made it in the house. He couldn't get past the Corvair. In a mostly incredulous stupor, he inspected every facet of the car.

After the boys each had a hot shower and had dressed in some of Maynard's clothes, and Mrs. Samples had cooked a bite to eat, they all met at the kitchen table. While waiting for their clothes to dry on the clothesline, Maynard had the others to rehearse the story he would have to tell Mr. Samples about how the Corvair got into the condition it was in. He would tell the truth about the forest fire but only move it a little closer to home. He would leave out the part about going out past the cemetery. Maynard even told the guys

250

they didn't have to stay if they didn't want to. He could talk the old man right into believing they had been performing a community service and could do it so convincingly, he probably would have the old man out helping him clean up the car. Well, the rest of the guys just couldn't pass up an opportunity to see if Maynard was as brash as his talk,so they decided to stick around and see.

At the table, of course the first thing Mr. Samples wanted to know was how could his car get in such deplorable condition? He listened intently as Maynard spun his yarn; how he and the boys had gone over to the Grannie's Creek Drive-Inn last night and watched the Saturday night double feature. On their way home, they decided to take the short cut over Panther Mountain. About half way out the ridge, they came upon two DNR trucks parked by the side of the road. When they asked the DNR guys what was going on, they found out there was a fire down over in the Mud Lick hollow. They knew it would be dangerous work but there was nobody else around except those two DNR men and they couldn't just let the woods burn up so they stayed and helped fight fire for three or four hours until they got it out. "We didn't get back here to the house until about 7:00 this morning and we were just beat. We intended to clean the car up but as you see, we didn't make it that far. We'll go do that right now, if it's ok."

The boys sat around listening to Maynard and then watched Mr. Samples for his reaction. Pretty fair story, thought Chip, I might believe it myself had I not been there.

Mr. Samples didn't say anything right off. He just sat there for a second or two. It was very quiet in the kitchen. Even Mrs. Samples paused in her dish washing to eavesdrop.

"You're absolutely right", Mr. Samples finally said, "you need to get the car cleaned up this evening. If Chip, and Benji, and Lincoln want to help, it shouldn't take you too long. I'll get some cleaner for the inside and run the extension cord out there so you can sweep the inside too."

The boys started to get up but were stopped in mid-rise by Mr. Samples.

"Just one thing though", he went on, "that mud on the car. I never knew that kind of red clay mud could be found on Panther Mountain. The only place I know where that kind of mud is common is up around the Morris Cemetery and I know you weren't stupid enough to be drivin' my Corvair out in there." The boys made it to a standing position.

Mr. Samples continued, "And another peculiar thing. There's hardly any gas left in the tank. I always fill it up when I park it. Funny you would use a whole tank of gas just driving over to Grannie's Creek and back."

Maynard looked at the guys across the table, then looked up at the ceiling. Things were beginning to turn sour. They took one step toward the door, but were halted again by Mr. Samples' words.

"Oh yeah. One more thing". He rose out of his chair and addressed Maynard in a calm voice. "I think you forgot to hook the speedometer back up. Make sure you do that before you're done and don't forget to park it over by the barn where it belongs. I've no doubt there is some truth in that cock-and-bull story you just wove for us all. It's evident you have been fighting fire somewhere but I wouldn't be surprised if you guys weren't somehow responsible for it in the first place."

"But Dad......", Maynard began to counter, but he was cut off by Mr. Samples' raised hand.

"Don't want to hear it," he said. "You've got work to do so get at it," and he left the room.

The boys went outside and helped Maynard clean the car up. All the while Maynard kept mumbling to himself. "Aw don't worry about it", he said. "The old man will forget about it in a couple of weeks and we'll be back cruisin' in no time."

Truth was, Maynard never got the Corvair again just for cruising around. The boys never asked about the Corvair and Maynard never prompted any discussion of it. Four weeks later Maynard, Benji, and Chip each received a letter from the WV Dept. of Natural Resources. Each letter had a check in it made out to the bearer for the total sum of $1.00 for services rendered in fire fighting. Maybe there was some guy in Clarksburg wondering why the heck the DNR would be sending him money.

X

Maynard's discontinued use of the Corvair put a small kink in the Jive Five's cruisin' agenda but it only lasted a little while because two months after the Corvair incident, Benji bought a car of his own. It was a '53 Chevy four door sedan. The car ran very well and the body was solid and clean. The previous owner had intended to paint the car but only got as far as painting on the dull red primer before he sold it to Benji and truthfully, the primer job looked good. One flaw in the Chevy was that there was no back seat; not even the back part of the back seat. The floor behind the front seat stretched all the way back to the trunk lid. There were some metal cross members that ran from the rear deck below the rear window to the floor but one could still gain access to the trunk from the rear seat area. That was ok with Benji because he could get his tools and other necessities out of the trunk without getting out of the car. What was not ok, was the exhaust fumes, gasoline smell, and road noise that filled the interior of the car. After paying $150.00 cash for the car, Benji just didn't have enough money left over at the time to buy another back seat and install it. Until that time, he would just have to tolerate the problem as best as he could. The tires were fair except for the right front. Benji said it was so bald that when he drove over a dime he could tell if it was heads or tails.

The car's heater worked very well to keep the front seat area warm and under normal conditions probably kept the whole car warm, but it just wasn't designed to overcome the cold December air that seeped through from the trunk into the rear seat area. In most cases, four people could ride fairly comfortably on the expansive front seat but for convenience sake, Benji did invert two five gallon feed buckets and set them in the back for others to sit on if need be.

Chip found out about Benji's new car on the Saturday it had been purchased. He had a Saturday night date with Judy at her house but he didn't have to be there until 7:30. He started walking around the road about 6:30 because he wanted to stop off at the station and goof off there for awhile. He hadn't walked but five minutes when Benji pulled up in the Chevy and offered a ride.

Chip didn't know it was Benji until he got in. He was quite impressed and Benji answered all of his questions as they cruised around to the station. That's where Benji was going also. He said he had to gas up the Chevy and Chip figured that was true but he figured Benji wanted to show off the car to whoever was around and that was understandable too.

While Benji was gassing up the Chevy, Chip got out and went in the station. There was a surprising number of guys hanging around inside. Besides Bucky, there was Rocky Miller, Paul Boggs, Melvin Hall, and even Link was there. When Chip told them about Benji's new wheels, all but Bucky went outside to check it out. After a few minutes of inspection, inside and out, the group came tramping back in. They milled around awhile talking about this and that, and then one by one, each departed into the cold and damp December evening. Only, Bucky, Benji, Link, and Chip were left.

"Hey, you guys want to go for a cruise?" Benji asked nodding towards the Chevy still sitting outside by the pumps.

"Well, I don't care", Chip said, "but we can't go very far. I've got to be at Judy's by 7:30."

"What about it Link?" prodded Benji. He noticed that Link was all spiffed up.

"Sure. Why not. But listen, I'm taking Kate Strickland to a dance over in Seneca later this evening so I got to be back here in a little while. You're not going very far, are you?"

"Naw. I was just goin' over to Red Dog. Check things out. But you guys don't have to go. I see you got more important things to do." There was disappointment and hurt in his voice. Link and Chip looked at each other. Not wanting to seem callous or unconcerned, Chip tried to smooth things over.

"Yeah sure, Benji, we'll take a ride with yuh. Only we didn't know you had your new car and we already made plans for tonight or we could do some cruisin'. Maybe we can get together later tonight?"

"No, that's too much trouble for yuh. Just forget it."

"Well, let's figure on doin' somethin' next weekend", broke in Link.

"Maybe. Maybe", said Benji, "only I'm going to Red Dog now. If you guys want to come along, you're welcome. If not, I'll see you later". He started for the door.

"Well, now wait a minute", Link said. "Don't go off in some kind of a huff. We'd like to ride in your new wheels only I told you, I have to be back here shortly and Chip's got a date too. Now if you want us to go we'll go, but don't get your bowels in an uproar. You want us to go or not?"

Benji paused for a moment before answering. "Yeah, come on", he grinned, "I was just foolin' with yuh." The boys climbed in the Chevy and headed for Red Dog.

When he got to Red Dog, Benji pulled into the parking area in front of the Grill. The packed down snow crunched under the tires of the Chevy as he eased her up close to a pile of dirty, soot covered snow. "Hey", Chip protested, "thought you were just going to drive around a little."

"Don't get excited", answered Benji. "I'm just goin' to run in here and get a milkshake. Be right back." He got out of the Chevy and went into the Grill. Link and Chip stayed in the car.

"What's with him?" Link ask Chip, after Benji had gone inside.

"I don't know", answered Chip, "you know how he gets sometimes."

They waited at least five minutes for Benji but he never came back out. It started getting cold in the car. "Come on, let's go see what he's doin'", Link said.

They got out of the car and went into the Grill. As soon as they stepped inside the door, the warmth of the place and the smell of onions and cheeseburgers hit them smack in the face. It was all so good they just stood there for a minute taking it all in while they scanned the room for Benji.

There was a booth full of girls sipping fountain cokes at one table and a boy and girl hugged up together feeding each other french fries. The rest of the booths were empty, but it was still early. By eight o'clock the place would be full. Brenda King was over at the jukebox trying to decide on what number to play, so Link went over to help her. Chip spotted Benji at the pinball machine in the corner. He was intensely involved in the game. His milkshake was sitting in front of him on the glass top of the pinball machine. Chip went over to him. "I thought you were just gonna get a milkshake and be right back." he said.

"No, I just said I was gonna get a milkshake. Didn't say nothin' about coming back out." His focus never seemed to leave the pinball game.

"Well, then when are we leaving?"

"I don't know when you're leaving but I'm gonna finish these two games and my milkshake before I leave."

"Come on Benji. Link and I got to get back to Sugar Tree."

"Well, maybe you can start hitchin' a ride and if you don't catch one, I'll come along in a little while and pick you up."

Chip was mad now. He stomped over to the jukebox where Link and Brenda were. "Listen", he said, "Benji's in one of his poutin' moods. He's just jerkin' us around. He's not going to go until he's made us sweat a little. I bet we can catch a ride outa here and beat him back to Sugar Tree. Anyway, that's about all we can do now unless you want to just hang around over here with him until he decides to go back home."

"No. I ain't givin' him the satisfaction," Link stated. "Let's get outa here and let him stew a little."

The two boys walked out of the warmth of the Grill into the now frigid night. The temperature must have dropped fifteen degrees. Chip was pretty much prepared for the cold because he knew he would have to walk back home from Judy's that night so he was ok, but Link only had on a sweater and a light cotton jacket. He zipped up the jacket to the neck and turned the collar up. They started crunching up the street through Red Dog hoping to catch a nice warm ride to Sugar Tree before long.

They walked for ten minutes but no one came by. Just as they reached the mouth of colored holler, a car slowed down and stopped beside them. It was Benji.

He reached across the front seat and opened the door. "Come on in guys", he beckoned. "I's just foolin' with yuh. I'll get you to Sugar Tree. Whatcha say?"

Link and Chip looked at each other for a second then shrugged and got in the car. There was no use standing out there in the cold and besides they might have to walk clear back to Sugar Tree and here was a sure fire ride, at least they thought it was. When they got to the top of Red Dog Hill, however, Benji turned the Chevy left towards Mill's Bottom instead of right towards Sugar Tree. It was Link who was mad now. "Where the hell are you going now? You know we got to get back to Sugar Tree."

"We'll get back to Sugar Tree. Don't worry. I've just got to run down the ridge a little way to check on something. Besides you got in my car remember. I never said I was going to Sugar Tree right away." Benji was still playing his game of aggravation.

Link looked at his watch. It was 7:25. "I'm not going through any more of your stupid crap. Stop the car. We'll get out here."

"Oh I couldn't do that", Benji feigned concern. "If something would happened to you out there in the cold wilderness, I'd feel responsible. I think it would be better for you to stay in the car with me for now." He drove on.

Chip was riding shotgun. He looked over at Link then he looked over in the backseat. He climbed over the seat and sat down on one of the buckets back there. He picked up a tire pump. "If you don't turn this car around or let us out right now", he said, "I'm going to throw this tire pump out the window."

"I don't care", shrugged Benji, "I ain't stoppin' ".

Chip rolled down the backseat window and the cold air blasted into the car. "I ain't kiddin', Benji."

"I told you, it don't matter to me what you do with that thing." Chip gave it a little toss right out the window.

Link was dumbfounded. Benji drove on. Chip searched around for something else. "How about this bumper jack? You need it?"

"Don't reckon so."

Chip heaved it out the open window and grabbed a small tool box.

"Probably won't be needin' this either", and he tossed it out the window too.

Link was now bent over with his head in his hands. He was shaking his head in disbelief.

"No", responded Benji, "besides that was the old man's tool box. Mine's back there in the trunk somewhere. I'm just going down here to the rock quarry to turn around, but if you think you have to throw anything else out the window, go ahead."

Chip found a box of tire chains. It was awfully heavy so he thought he'd wait and see if Benji turned around at the rock quarry. He might not have to dump them out the window.

Benji swung the Chevy off the road in a wide arc at the rock quarry and jammed her into second gear to plow his way back out onto the hardroad. They were headed back towards Sugar Tree but there was no guarantee that's where they'd end up. Benji rolled the window back up and sat in silence on the feed bucket in the backseat. Nobody said anything on the ride back to Sugar Tree. Benji pulled in at the station, let Link and Chip out, and headed out towards Hob. It was 7:40.

One Friday night during Christmas break a few weeks later, Benji talked Maynard and Chip into cruisin' around Sugar Tree with him in the Chevy. During the evening's drive, Chip happen to notice that there was a tire pump and a bumper jack lying in the floor in the back seat area but he never spotted a tool box. He felt it better not to mention anything about them. They drove over to Red Dog that evening and stopped off at the pool room in back of the Town Hall and shot a couple of games of cutthroat. When they went back outside to leave, the Chevy wouldn't start. The starter made a whirring noise but it wouldn't turn the motor over. The battery was good because the lights and everything else worked.

"Must be a bad solenoid", suggested Maynard. "I'll see if I can jump it. Got a screwdriver?" Benji got a screwdriver out of the trunk and gave it Maynard. Maynard went around and opened the hood. "When I tell you, turn the key on." He checked a couple of wires and said, "OK turn her on." He crossed the screwdriver over two connections on the side of the engine and the starter kicked in but it just whirred like before. "That's funny", Maynard said, "there's nothing wrong with the solenoid and it doesn't sound like there's anything wrong with the starter. Well, tell you what. Let's push this baby back out in the parking lot and Benji can pop the clutch in reverse and start it."

The Chevy was fairly easy to push with Maynard and Chip at the front. Benji had the door open and was pushing against the door post. When they got her rolling good, Benji jumped in, turned the key on, shifted into reverse, and let the clutch out. The Chevy lurched once and started right up.

A couple of days later Benji took the Chevy to the station and Lewis put it up on the rack and with the help of three or four shade tree mechanics who were lounging around the station that day, they found out that the flywheel had two teeth broken off side by side. Lewis said that he could tell the teeth had been broken off some time ago. Definitely before Benji bought the car. It didn't happen often but the flywheel was like a roulette wheel; every once in a while it would stop just in the position where the two teeth were missing and the starter gear would not engage the flywheel and in turn, it would not turn the engine over so it could start. Lewis said to change the flywheel, they would have to pull the motor out and then find another flywheel of the same model at the junk yard. Either that or play flywheel roulette.

Benji didn't want to pull the engine and fix the flywheel here in the dead of winter. Maynard said he'd do it himself but there was nowhere to put the car in out of the weather so they could work on it. If they had a good flywheel ready, they could probably change it in a day. Couldn't use the station's extra bay because Bucky had a car in there now that was getting a new clutch installed.

Benji decided to wait till spring to fix the flywheel but in the meantime, he parked the Chevy behind his house, backed up on a little incline so he could jump start it in gear if the starter wouldn't work. When he went anywhere else and wouldn't be out of the car for a very long time, he would just leave the motor running. If he had to leave the car parked for a while, he always parked it in a place where he could coast it to start it, or if there were some other guys with him, he'd park it where they would push it easily if the starter wouldn't start it. Sometimes it meant parking the Chevy a ways off from where he was going but he didn't want to take any chances, especially if he had a girl with him.

Parking in the Chevy with a girl was not the most ideal situation either. Since he parked on a downhill incline, there was a propensity to roll forward off the seat. He thought of parking facing uphill, that way he could coast backwards to start the car but the car had no backup lights so he couldn't see where he was going and that was too scary. He couldn't leave the motor running when he

259

went parking either because the exhaust fumes that came up through the open trunk and rear seat area would have driven anyone out of the car long before it could kill them.

Chip had no vehicle of his own until he was a junior in college. He did have the use of the family's '50 Mercury when he needed a vehicle, if it wasn't being used for some other domestic chore at the time.

His first solo driving experiences came by just driving around in Sugar Tree and Red Dog. These were essential trips however, like going to the Company Store or to Jobe's to pick up various articles for the family. If his dad or mom had to go Seneca or Mill's Bottom for something and Chip was around, he'd volunteer to drive them wherever they needed to go. The only time he remembered ever getting the Merc just to drive around to the station or to cruise around to Sugar Tree was an occasional Sunday afternoon.

The first time Chip ever got to take the Merc out of Sugar Tree by himself was in the spring of his junior year at Seneca. The New River Conference Championship track meet was always held on the second Friday in April, a school day, but because of heavy rains and thunderstorms that Friday, the meet was postponed until Saturday. Chip would have to be at the high school at 8:00 Saturday morning to catch the team bus to the meet and he wouldn't get back to Seneca until 5:00 or 6:00 that evening. Mr. Gates figured there was no reason to make four trips to Seneca and back that day, so he let Chip take the Merc to Seneca and leave it at the high school and drive it back home that evening. Benji was also on the track team so Chip got to take him along as well. Possibly because there were no incidents or catastrophes with the car and everyone arrived home safe and sound, after that day, Chip pretty much inherited the Merc. He still could only use it by permission, but permission seemed to come a little easier.

Chip was hitchhiking home from basketball practice at Elk River High School every evening and stayed over at Seneca after late night ball games, but on a few occasions there would be practice or a game scheduled on a day when school wasn't in session and Chip was granted permission to take the Mercury. During Christmas break of Chip's senior year, practice was scheduled for the three days after Christmas at 9:00 in the morning so he drove the Merc over to Seneca and back those three days. The weather those first two days was uneventful but on the third day it snowed. A few lonely flakes were falling when Chip got to Seneca that morning but by the time practice was over, around noon, it had already snowed four or five inches and was still coming down hard.

Of course several of Mr. Gates's driving lessons for Chip had involved driving in snow and ice conditions and though Chip had actually done the driving then, this was the first test he would face alone.

The Mercury was a big, heavy car and not easily swayed from her intended course if the driver handled her just right. Chip eased his way off the hill at the high school using first and second gear and staying off the brakes just like his dad had taught. It was hard at first because his natural instinct was to use that brake to slow down but after he realized that the brake was only needed to stop, the more confident he became in his control of the car.

He slipped through town without any trouble. Out on Rt.19 the traffic seemed heavier than normal and it was all moving along about half as fast as normal because the road had not been plowed or treated yet. Chip's entire being was now focused on keeping the Merc in the road and keeping his momentum moving forward while keeping a safe distance from the car ahead of him in case they had to stop. The snow was still coming down hard and the vacuum windshield wipers were losing the battle of keeping the windshield clear. The snow began piling up where the wipers ended their direction and was cutting their path shorter and shorter. After a while there was only a little one foot window Chip could see out of. Because of the slow speed he had to travel, whenever he did speed the engine up, the vacuum wipers would almost come to a dead stop. If he let off the gas, the wipers would pick up to their normal speed and knock some of the snow aside only he couldn't slow down very much or too often or he'd lose traction.

By the time he was halfway through Raven Valley, the snow had completely covered the rear window and the side window so that Chip had no idea who or what was behind him. The closer he got to Panther Mountain the more heightened his anxiety became.

He was already starting to worry about how he was going to get up the mountain and down the other side.

About a half a mile from the Moonlite Tavern, Chip slowed down a hair to let the wipers clear the snow off the windshield. In the blink of an eye, the Mercury did a perfect three-hundred-sixty-degree spin around right in the middle of the road. Chip didn't have time to do anything. The spin seemed like it took forever and in that fraction of a second that the Merc was turned around facing back towards Seneca, Chip got a look at the traffic following him. He thought there must have been twenty or thirty cars following along behind him but there was no time to consider their dilemma because the Merc had completed the spin and was once again heading the direction it was suppose to be going.

Chip slowed down even more and steadied his hand on the wheel. It happened too fast for him to even get scared. He was getting close to Panther Mountain and by slowing down he let the vehicles in front of him pull away. He wanted to speed up and get a clear run at the mountain but he was afraid if he went too fast he wouldn't make it around the sharp curve at the bottom of the hill. He eased the Merc up to forty-five then just as he entered the turn, he let off the gas, stayed off the brake, and steered the Merc through the turn without any trouble at all. He shifted into second and slowly built up some speed as he began to climb the mountain. He left the Merc in second gear so he wouldn't have to shift. He held her at a good steady speed and she just kept digging through the snow right on up the mountain.

He was going into the last turn, one hundred yards from the top of the mountain, when he ran upon a pickup truck inching its way along. The truck had chains on the rear tires and why it was going so slow, Chip didn't know. He did know if he didn't let off the gas, the Merc'd run right into the back of the truck. He let off, avoided the rear end collision, and stayed in second gear but that was the end of the line for the Merc. She had lost all of her momentum and the traction had let go as well. The speedometer read thirty-five but she wasn't moving at all now.

Chip kept the Merc spinning in the middle of the road while he was trying to figure out what to do. There was nowhere to get off the road out of the way and he couldn't go forward anyway. He couldn't drift back down the hill because he couldn't see out the back and he didn't know if there was anyone behind him or not. Just as he had decided he would stop the car right there in the middle of the road, get out, and hope for some help, he felt a jolt from the rear of the car. The impact was hard enough to jerk his head back a might but amazingly the Merc started moving on up the mountain. Chip didn't know if he was helping her along or not but he left her in second gear and kept a steady foot on the gas.

At the top of the mountain he swung the Merc off the road at the wide spot. Three or four other cars had already pulled off there as well. Chip rolled down the window just in time to see Gaylord Hall clatter by in his jeep. Gaylord used the jeep at his station to push vehicles around and he had installed a big wooden bumper on the front. To help out the jeep's the four wheel drive on this occasion, he had put tire chains on the front. Chip waved a big thank you to Gaylord as he drove on past and Gaylord acknowledged the thank you by beeping the horn. It seemed like there were twenty cars behind Gaylord's jeep. Chip figured that Gaylord knew that none of those people could have gotten over the mountain if he was still stuck there in the middle of the road, so he kept everything moving by shoving Chip right on up the hill.

Chip got out and put chains on the Merc. It was another lesson learned from Dad. Chip was so confident in the Merc and in himself when she had chains on that he wasn't afraid to take her anywhere. With the chains in place, the Merc dug her way back to Sugar Tree without a hitch.

Chip became very adept at putting on, taking off , and repairing tire chains and could do it almost as fast as a pit stop at the Indy 500. He might have to put on chains to get out of Sugar Tree because sometimes it would a week before the State Road would come over to plow County Rt. 11. But if he was going to Seneca, he'd have to take the chains off at Hob because Rt. 19 might be cleared. If he didn't take the chains off, he would beat the chains and the Merc to pieces on the bare road. You just couldn't drive very fast with snow chains on anyway. On the return trip home he'd have to stop in Hob and put the chains back on so he could traverse Rt.11. There would be times when a set of chains stayed on the

Merc for two consecutive weeks because she never left Sugar Tree other than to go over to Red Dog.

One time on a trip over to Seneca for a Saturday night basketball game that had been postponed from an earlier date, Chip left the chains on the Merc when he got to Hob because it was still snowing and the State Road had not plowed Rt.19 over that way yet. There wasn't much traffic that evening and many of the vehicles he saw on the road also had chains on. Driving through Seneca on the way home after the ballgame, Chip was contemplating whether or not he should take the chains off the Merc. He hated to take them off now because he knew he'd have to put them back on to get from Hob to Sugar Tree. It hadn't snowed much during the game and he was sure the State Road had had time to clear Rt.19 into Hob. It was late and he was tired and it was cold outside so he pressed on towards Hob.

The road had been plowed but, for the most part, there were only two tracks of bare asphalt. The traffic was light and he didn't have to drive very fast so most of the time he was able to keep the Merc out of the tracks. Sometimes he had to drive down the middle of Rt. 19 to keep the chains in the snow and sometimes he had to drive with one set of wheels on the berm. And there were a few places where he just had to clatter and bang and rumble his way through the bare spots. He had to stop once and reconnect a broken cross chain with a monkey link but he made it to Hob ok. Once there, found out that his decision not to take the chains off was a good one because they had not plowed the road to Sugar Tree and he would need chains to get up and down Renzee White Hill.

The first time Chip asked Judy to go on a car date with him, it didn't turn out exactly like he'd planned. Judy had consented to go to the Grannie's Creek Drive-In with him if her mom and dad would let her. Chip was to come around to the house at his regular Saturday night time and ask if it would be ok to take Judy to the drive-in.

Chip was surprised when Mr. Brown not only gave his permission, but didn't even pause to consider before consenting. Not only that, but he offered to let Chip take the family station wagon and to top things off, gave him a two dollar bill to buy some gas for the wagon. Then came the biggest surprise of all, Judy's dad gave him some extra money not only to pay for his and Judy's way to the drive-in, but to also pay for Judy's two other sisters and two other brothers who would be going along with them. Judy wasn't too thrilled with the arrangement but Chip didn't care. He got to go to the drive-in free, drive somebody else's car, and still get to be with his girl on a real date, sort of.

By Chip's senior year, the Merc had become an indispensable factor in Chip and Judy's dating. They often went to the Grannie's Creek Drive-Inn where they met up with other couples and friends from high school. They usually drove up and down the isles first looking for Link's Falcon. Most of the time he was there, and it seemed each time he was in the company of a different girl than before. A couple of times Chip and Judy double dated to the drive-in with Link and his date and a couple of times with Benji and his date.

Judy and Chip's favorite place to park was up on the hill across the road by the Morris Cemetery. There was a wide spot in the road where funeral processions parked and the next of kin then walked up to the cemetery which was right on top of the hill. The parking spot looked over the mountains and valleys for miles to the south and east. It was a beautiful and quiet place. No other couples in Sugar Tree ever came up there and Judy and Chip never divulged their secret parking place for fear it would be overrun and spoiled. One of the reasons nobody came up there was probably because even in good weather, the road up to the cemetery wasn't in the best of condition and unless someone knew the road well, they could seriously damage their car or get hung up. Chip knew the road. Another reason was because there were other, more convenient places where couples could park. The gob pile over at Red Dog was a popular spot. So was around behind the Sugar Tree Grade School, behind the Eureka Baptist Church, the Coulter Low Gap, and the Horse Ridge Fire Tower before the "Fire Ball" incident.

The Horse Ridge Fire Ball came upon the scene quite suddenly. Chip and Benji were the first to hear about it and they heard it within a half an hour, directly from the three guys who first

265

encountered it; Gary Butler, Onas Johnson, and Onas' cousin Murl from over around Dog Run. They were all in their early twenties.

Benji and Chip were sitting on the steps of the Company Store in Sugar Tree listening to WLW from New Orleans on Benji's transistor around 10:00 that evening, when Onas came tearin' down the Sugar Tree Straight in his Ford pickup. When he went by the Company Store, he must have seen Benji and Chip sitting there cause he locked the pickup up and went sliding into the intersection. The truck slid right through the intersection but stop just short of Jobe's bridge. Onas threw her into reverse and backed up to the Company Store. Murl rolled down the passenger side window. "Boys! Boys!" he yelled. "You've got to come with us out to the fire tower. Somethin' awful's happenin'."

"IT'S THE END OF THE WORLD", came the remark yelled from inside the cab.

Murl turned back to the inside of the cab and addressed one of his buddies. "Would you shut the hell up! You say that one more time and it will be the end of the world.........for you, you stupid jerk."

By now the boys' interest had been pricked and they turned off the radio and sauntered over to the pickup still idling in the middle of the road.

"What's goin' on Gary?" Benji asked.

"That you, Benji? Listen man, I'm tellin' you there's some strange doin's out at the fire tower. Some kind of big, flamin' fire ball or somethin' just shot up outa the woods and flew right over the truck. It scared the hell outa me."

Benji was cool. "You guys been drinkin'?" he asked. Benji knew they had been. They always were.

"Yeah, but we only got through one bottle of whiskey. We ain't drunk. That THING scared me about half sober anyhow."

"I seen it." said Murl. He was visibly shaken by the incident. "We ain't lyin'. It was this big red thing. Burnin' like. And it just shot out of the ground."

"Where did it go?" Chip asked.

"Don't know. It just shot up into the air over the pickup. We couldn't see it no more. We tried to look up, out of the windows

266

but couldn't find it. I tried to get Murl to get out and look for it but he was too chicken livered."

"Yeah, well why didn't you get out and look yourself?"

"Cause. Ballbaby Onas was scared so bad I's afraid he'd piss his pants. He was yellin' and screamin' about the devil comin' after him or somethin'. We got the hell outa there."

"You guys need to go out there and find out what's goin' on."

"Where you guys goin'? asked Benji.

"We got to get cry baby Onas home before he croaks. I'm gonna run back to the house and get my 12 guage. We'll meet you guys out there in a little bit, if you ain't too chicken, too." With that said, Gary smoked the tires on the Ford and headed up Painter's Fork.

"Reckon there's anything to that?" Chip asked.

"You know them guys. Probably drunk. Probably saw the reflection from their cigarette in the window or somethin' and scared the beejeebees out of 'em." Benji paused for a moment. "Still. We got nothin' else to do. What say we go up to the house and get the Chevy and cruise on out there just for the heck of it."

Chip felt the hair on the back of his neck begin to rise. "Sure", he said, trying to sound like an enthused participant.

The boys rode in the Chevy all the way out to the top of Red Dog Hill in silence. When Benji turned off onto the fire tower road, he cut the lights off. The Chevy eased on out the ridge in the dark. The boys were hoping to sneak up on whatever it was out there. The night was warm and quiet but the skies were partly cloudy and the winds aloft must have been strong because the clouds were racing across the sky. It was early summer and no one was manning the fire tower.

Chip wasn't scared, but he was anxious. Benji didn't't let on like he was scared either but Chip could tell he wasn't much at ease. The boys rolled down the windows and stuck their heads out to get a better view. Benji was still just crawling along in first gear with one hand on the steering wheel and his head stuck out the window.

Chip took a quick glance up into the night sky and his heart almost stopped. His breath got caught in his throat. In an opening between the clouds, Chip saw a formation of about six bright shiny objects racing across the sky. They were only visible for a second or two before they disappeared behind some more clouds.

After the initial shock of seeing the UFO's wore off, Chip was able to speak. "Stop. Stop the car", he half whispered to Benji. Benji stopped.

"What is it?" he asked.

"I saw something. Up there". Chip pointed in the direction of the UFO's.

Benji followed Chip's point and stare. "I don't see nothin".

"Wait. They're behind some clouds."

Both boys stayed in the car. They kept searching the heavens for a glimpse of the UFO's. "There they are", exclaimed Chip. The formation came into view again. It was in the same spot as before and in the same formation. Chip realized too late what he'd seen.

"You dufus", said Benji. "Those ain't UFO's. Those are stars. It just looks like their movin' 'cause the clouds are passing by so fast. Come on, Chip. Get a grip on yourself will yuh."

Chip slinked back inside the car window and Benji drove on. The false sighting did seem to bolster the electric atmosphere in the car.

Benji crept closer to the fire tower, but they saw nothing. Even at the fire tower, after Benji had turned the Chevy around and parked downhill so he could shut the engine off, they saw nothing. Heard nothing.

Minutes crept by. Benji finally got out of the car. After another minute, Chip followed suit. It was quiet and just a little breeze stirring. There was no moon but it wasn't completely dark. The boys stood in silence by the car waiting for something to happen and knowing if it did, they would poop their pants.

Minutes dragged on. Nothing. Finally Benji spoke up. "Let's get the heck outa here. There ain't nothin' up here and them guys didn't see nothin. Can't believe I wasted my time drivin' all the way out here." He got back in the car. He didn't have to ask Chip twice.

The Chevy fired right up. Benji turned on the lights, turned on the radio and left the scene as if he were in a great hurry. Chip watched out the window for any signs of the fire ball but didn't see any. Gary, Onas, and Murl never showed up.

It wasn't a week later that Junior Dodrill was down at the Esso station tellin' everybody how he and his girlfriend Darlene were parked out at the fire tower the night before when this big, glowing ball of fire whizzed right over his car. He said it was about as big as a hubcap and that there was flame and fire coming out of it. Even worse, when he and Darlene left, the fireball came at them from behind when they got out to the end of the fire tower road at the top of Red Dog Hill. Junior didn't say what happened to the thing. He didn't care he just wanted to get out of there. Benji and Chip dismissed the story as one of Junior's stunts.

Two days passed before another "fire ball" report filtered in to Sugar Tree. Edgar Davis was coming home after working the evening shift at Red Dog when he saw a flaming ball of some kind, streak across the sky. Edgar was just topping the Red Dog Hill when he saw the oject. Said he couldn't really tell how big it was 'cause it was a good distance from him off towards the Horse Ridge Fire Tower. Said it looked like someone had shot off a giant roman candle. Edgar would have no reason to make up the story. He was just a guy coming home from work one night.

Benji's and Chip's interest was renewed. They checked with Link. He was interested too. His explanation was a phenomenon called "swamp gas."

The next report of the fireball was all Benji, Chip, and Link needed to move to action. It didn't matter that this report came from another, less-than-reputable source who was also a heavy drinker, the boys were going to get to the bottom the matter, one way or the other.

The following evening, around midnight, Benji picked up Chip in the Chevy and the two drove back around to Link's and got him. Benji had his CO_2 pistol lying on the seat beside him just in case.

The moon was almost full that night so when Benji switched the headlights off once they hit the fire tower road, they could easily see the road ahead. As before, Benji crept along the fire tower road in first gear. Both front side windows were down. Benji was looking out his side and Link was looking out the passenger side. Chip was in the middle watching the road ahead.

Just before they got to the swag in the road, Benji shut the engine off and let the Chevy drift to a stop. The boys listened and watched intently but didn't ' see or hear anything.

"Maybe the fire ball doesn't know we're here," Chip offered. "The last time we came looking for it, we slipped in. Everybody else who saw it was just going on their merry way. They weren't expecting anything. Maybe it gets mad if people come around its territory."

"Might have something there," agreed Link. "What say, Benji."

"Might as well," Benji answered.

Benji fired up the Chevy, turned on the headlights, cranked up the radio, and rolled on toward the fire tower.

He turned the Chevy around at the fire tower and got her pointed back down the hill. He turned the engine off, tuned the radio to WBZ, Boston, and the three sat back with the windows open and waited for the fire ball.

They didn't talk but kept scanning the horizon and the heavens for signs of the fireball. The moon was high overhead and there was plenty of light. Fifteen minutes passed and nothing happened. After another five minutes of nothing, Benji opened his door, grabbed his pistol and stepped outside. He closed the door and leaned against the car.

Ten minutes later Link got out and held the door open for Chip. They all stood around the car, scanning the area in three different directions but nothing seemed out of the ordinary.

"Enough of this," Benji whispered. "Come on. We'll find that bastard." He started for the fire tower.

"Whata you doin?" Chip pleaded.

"I'm goin' up the tower and see what's what. If that son-of-a-bitch fireball is here, I'll make him come out."

"Wait for me," said Link.

Chip strained back to look up towards the top of the tower. He couldn't see it from where he was standing near the base of the tower. "I'll just stay here and watch," he said.

The late night hour had grown even quieter than the last time they had come out here. There was but a gentle, warm breeze whiffing through every few minutes. From time to time Chip could hear the clatter of the boys steps as they ascended the tower. The tower itself would rattle and moan every so often, protesting the assault on it at such a late time of night.

Finally, the two boys reached the last steps just below the observation room and then there was only silence. Chip reached inside the car and turned the radio off.

The minutes passed slowly and no fireball appeared. Just when Chip was about to give up on the whole deal and crawl into the car and lay down, he heard Benji screaming from the top of the tower. His voice, shrill and loud, cut through the nighttime silence like razor sharp dagger. Chip was jolted to his senses. He was sure they could hear Benji as far away as Seneca.

"COME ON OUT YOU LOUSY, STINKIN', CHICKEN FIREBALL! COME ON. WE'RE WAITIN'' FOR YOU, YOU SON-OF-A-BITCH. COME ON NOW!" Benji was either hysterical or fed up. Chip stepped back away from the tower until he could see the top. Benji was leaning way out over the steel work and waving his arms like a mad man.

"WHERE ARE YOU....YOU......YOU.....CHICKEN PUSSY. COME ON OUT. SHOW YOURSELF. BY GOD I DARE YOU. NOTHIN' HUH? YOU AIN'T EVEN GOT THE BALLS TO SHOW YOURSELF. COME ON OUT, CHICKEN FIREBALL." Nothing........ "I AIN'T NEVER COMIN' BACK UP HERE NO MORE TO LOOK FOR YOU, YOU SORRY ASS BASTARD."

Benji went on for a couple of more minutes but the fireball wouldn't come out. Chip knew Benji was quittin' when he heard him and Link coming back down the steps. They were making as much noise as they could. Every once in a while Benji would stop and hurl another barrage of challenges into the night, but only his echo would answer.

When they got to the car, both Benji and Link were in a good humor. They were laughing and joking around with each other. Everybody got back in the car and Benji hit the starter. The starter motor just whirred. Benji let off the parking brake, shifted her up into second gear, let her start rollin' down the hill, and popped the clutch. The Chevy roared to life. Benji laid on the horn all the way back out the fire tower road.

The fire tower was now dead as a place to park. Couples found other secluded spots for sharing their passions. There were never any more reports of the fireball.

Parking at the cemetery was Judy and Chip's secret and special place. They never went there with anyone else, they never double dated there, and they coveted their time together there after social

271

affairs elsewhere; dances, parties, ball games, drive-in movies, etc. It is the place they went after the junior-senior prom and after their high school graduations.

In the soft glow of the dash lights or under the watchful eye of Mr. Moon, those nights were filled with passion, playfulness, quiet talks, or just sleeping. Cuddled together in the dark listening to the rain pattering on the roof, or rolling down the windows to let the sweet, warm breezes of summer drift through the car, they made love, talked about their future together, or just quietly reflected on the moment. Sometimes neither spoke for long intervals. A few times they climbed up on the hood of the Merc and lay back on the windshield and watched the heavens. They spent two hours one evening watching the lightning dancing and playing in the clouds of a thunderstorm that was going on some two or three miles to the southeast of them. All the while the radio, tuned to Richmond's WRVA Gaslight program, and turned down low, supplied them with the proper background atmosphere.

In March of 1963, Ruby and the Romantics came out with a smooth hit titled "Our Day Will Come". That became Chip and Judy's song. Judy was still a senior in high school when Chip went off to Marshall College and their time together parking at the cemetery became more precious than ever. When Judy graduated from high school she went to work for the FBI in Washington, DC. Chip was still at Marshall but did come home in the summer to work at the station. Nonetheless, for a period of three years, the two saw each other only nine or ten times a year. When they were reunited on those occasions, they both confessed that the thoughts and anticipation of coming to this place and the inspiration of their song helped to sustain them over those times of separation.

When Chip was a junior at Marshall he had saved up enough money working at the station in the summer and working as a car hop at Wiggin's Restaurant in Huntington during the school year, to buy a four door '55 Plymouth Plaza. The car had belonged to an elderly lady who lived in Sugar Tree. Her husband had died about five years before and she felt she was not able to drive herself anymore. She could use the money from the sale of the car and the money she would save on insurance and upkeep of the car to pay someone to take her to places she really needed to go. It was a good deal for Chip as well. The car was in good condition and the selling price was fair to both parties.

The first and most important advice Chip's dad had ever given him when he first began to drive was that with regular maintenance and a watchful eye, there was no reason why a vehicle wouldn't run forever. Chip learned that valuable lesson when he began to have more control of the Mercury and it was natural that he carried that learned behavior over to the Plymouth. His dad said maintaining a vehicle in good running condition was like a doctor who not only practiced preventative medicine, but knew that the earlier an illness was detected, the chance for a cure would be better and easier.

As a driving intern then, and as a former Boy Scout who was always prepared, Chip learned from his dad, the steps to becoming a safe and carefree car owner.

(1). Never travel anywhere without your tool box. The tool box should contain at least one of every size wrench, open end and box end, a pair of pliers, a set of vise grips, a phillips and a flathead screwdriver, some electrical tape and a crescent wrench. That was the bases for a minimal set of tools. As the years passed, in an effort to be prudent, Chip slowly added other essentials to the tool box this included assorted nuts, bolts, screws, sandpaper, feeler gauge, socket set, a metal file or two, more electrical tape, a small piece of a mirror, screwdrivers of different lengths and sizes, a pipe wrench, a cold chisel or two, different lengths and sizes of electrical wires, and assorted bulbs (brake lamps, park lamps, interior lamps, etc.) Every year or so Chip would have to find a bigger size tool box. Your tools were like your umbrella, if you had it with you, it would never rain. If you had your tools with you, you would never break down.

(2) Get another box to put other necessary tools and articles in. The other box would contain things like a couple of rocks or a brick or two, a ball-peen hammer or a claw hammer, if that's all you had, some bailing wire, a set of jumper cables, a tow rope or a set of tire chains which could also serve as a towing device, a small hydraulic or screw jack, containers of water, anti-freeze, motor oil, brake fluid, transmission oil and/or gear grease, a siphon hose, a canvas ground cloth, and some old rags. In that box he also put old

car parts that had been replaced but would still be usable in emergencies. These included things like hoses, belts, muffler clamps, odd gaskets, rubber bushings, used spark plugs and a one gallon can of gas. Sometimes there wouldn't be room in the trunk for luggage, but there was always room for that in the back seat. At least he wouldn't get caught broke down for long, out on the road.

(3) The more time you spent with your vehicle, the more attuned you became to its nature. Listening to and feeling subtle changes in the normal operation of the car could help with early diagnosis and repair. Keeping a watchful eye on the temperature gauge, oil pressure, and amp meter while driving was also crucial.

When Chip first got the Plymouth, it was in pretty fair running condition. During that early life of the car, mechanical problems weren't such a deep concern. If an unusual noise started coming from the car while he was coming home from Marshall for the weekend, he would turn the radio up louder so he couldn't hear the noise and then attend to the problem after he got to the station in Sugar Tree. The longer he kept the Plymouth though, the more diligent he became in watching and listening for problems.

The Plymouth served Chip well for those last two years of college. He and Judy were married in August of the year Chip graduated from Marshall. They kept the car because they couldn't afford a newer vehicle at that particular time but it was beginning to show the wear and tear of thirteen years and one hundred twenty-five thousand miles.

The first crucial part that failed was the tuning knob on the radio. The knob didn't break but the tuning string that turned the frequency wheel broke. Chip removed the back from the radio and by laying on the floor of the car he could see well enough to stick the eraser end of a pencil up under the dash, through the back of the radio, and turn the tuning wheel by hand. In the day time he kept the radio tuned to 580 WCHS, Charleston, because it came in the best no matter where you might be in the local area. If they were out at night, Chip would set the radio to WRVA because they knew it would come in no matter where they might be traveling within the state.

By this stage of the Plymouth's life, Chip was replacing something at least once a month; a water pump here, generator brushes there. Fuel pump, voltage regulator, battery, starter bendix, tires, brake shoes, wheel cylinder kits, wheel bearings, mufflers, tailpipes, shock absorbers, fuses, and universal joints were regular maintenance jobs. The real mechanic work came when things like throw out bearings, clutch plate, rings, carburetor, ball joints, valves, camshafts, main seals, and head gaskets had to be replaced. Chip figured that sooner or later the car would actually recycle itself into a new vehicle but it never happened.

Sunday drives in the country then became a real challenge for Chip. He was now alternating time between gauge watching and scouting along the road ahead looking for wide places where he could pull off if he had to work on the car. Judy would see a beautiful pastoral scene unfold before her or gaze at a golden sunset and she might remark, "Oh, my look at that!" Which would send Chip into a panic and he would quickly start scanning the gauges.

"What? What is it? We runnin' hot? Oil pressure drop? She not chargin'? What?"

Judy would just stare at him for a moment and shake her head. "Never mind," she'd say, "it wasn't anything."

They finally did have to buy a new car but not because the Plymouth died on its own. It was killed. They had driven the car around to Judy's parent's house one Saturday night for a family gathering and since the driveway and front yard were already full of cars, Chip had to park the Plymouth out beside the road. A drunken sailor, home on leave, ran off the road just at that particular place and plowed into the back of the Plymouth, totaling it. The insurance paid Chip all $100.00 for the car and let him keep it.

Because Rt.11 was such a prominent factor in the ever evolving life of the Sugar Tree community, it was only natural that the road became the focal point of some of Chip's recreational activities. Those activities were sidelights beyond the bicycling, hitchhiking, and cruising aspects of the road.

Some of the games Chip could recall were "Help Help, Somebody's Hurt!", "The Pocketbook Trick", "The Phantom Tire", "Smoke Screen" and the "The Hubcap Trick". These were simple games that were designed to dupe the public, provide fun and laughter at the public's expense, and required very little ingenuity. They would do all that, if not overused. By playing the games infrequently on a rotating basis, the public usually could be duped for a short time. Looking back now, Chip could not understand the point of these games nor could he see what they provided in the way of entertainment. He figured it was because he had forgotten just what motivated the mind and psyche of a twelve or thirteen year old.

"Help Help Somebody's Hurt" was a harmless game that Chip and Riley invented, but its short life was destined to be but one summer. The game involved at least two kids. One kid would lay down close to the road and lay a bicycle on top of him, while the other kid stood along the side of the road and tried to get people to stop by pointing and yelling in his most convincing voice, "Help! Help! Somebody's hurt!" Both boys would wait until the duped victim would stop and get out of their vehicle, then the two would jump up and run off.

They learned that the game worked better if they could put the faked injured kid away from the road. Down over the road bank was good. Down over the road bank in a creek like Lick Run was better. That way when the injured one got up to run away, there would be less chance of the duped party chasing after them. It was also harder for the driver of the stopped vehicle to tell from that distance what injuries the bike rider had sustained. In that momentary pause while the driver was trying to figure out what to do, the boy by the road side would slip off and run away from the scene. He always had a predetermined route that led away from the road and through terrain that would be challenging enough to deter most anyone else of an older age from chasing after. At the same time, the injured kid would jump up, leave the bicycle, and run off into a safe haven as well. The distance from the accident scene to the road pretty much assured that the bicycle would not be snatched away for retaliation. The object of the game was to get the "mark" to stop. They were cautious enough to play the game on a straight stretch of road and near a place where the drivers could pull off the road out of the way, or at least get partly out of the road so oncoming traffic would have time to stop or to go around. Sometimes the driver just stopped and got out and left his vehicle sitting in the middle of the road.

Riley always played the part of the kid who was hurt and Chip played the part of the roadside help. The reason for fitting those roles as such was because Chip could readily identify the approaching potential victim. The game was reserved for strangers, those whom Chip didn't recognize. There would be no reason to stop someone who knew them and their family. Even if they did run away, they would be recognized and no doubt their shenanigans would be quickly reported to Mom or Dad or Grandma. Riley was always located in a place that couldn't be seen from a driver or passenger's perspective. If the vehicle was someone Chip knew or thought he knew, he wouldn't do anything other than maybe just wave at the driver as they sped on past. All they saw was Chip standing by the road. Chip would only flag down vehicles he didn't recognize. It didn't matter if Major and Specks tagged along. This wasn't a trick where the identity of the culprits needed to be hidden. Riley was best at just lying there unconscious. To add more realism to the scam, they would sometimes smear some ketchup on his head.

The first couple of times they played the game it worked beautifully. The unsuspecting victims stopped and were prepared to do their good Samaritan deed for the day until they realized too late, they had been had. As Chip and Riley ran for cover, those early victims all tried to impress upon them the error of their deeds.

"Young fellow," one yelled at Chip, "we pray that your attempts at fooling good hearted people don't put your soul or personal being in real danger." From somewhere there in the underbrush by the road, Chip snickered.

Other admonitions weren't quiet as subtle. "You little snots. I'll beat your sorry asses to a pulp when I catch you, and make no mistake, I will catch you. Maybe not today, maybe not tomorrow but I know who you are and I'll get you, little pricks." Riley started to cry. Chip just snickered. Some victims didn't say anything. They just stood there for a moment, got back in their car, and drove off.

The first time things went sour was when Riley took it upon himself to make his injuries look even more realistic. He wanted it to be a surprise so he didn't check with Chip. That morning Chip flagged down the perfect "mark". It was a car with two middle aged women in it. The driver got out with much concern and Chip took off but when she looked over the bank at Riley, she started laughing so hard that Chip stopped when he heard her. He watched from the bushes as the woman got back in the car still laughing. She paused for a moment, apparently explaining something to her passenger, and then drove off. Both were heard laughing loudly.

Chip waited a little bit then he came out of the woods, walked across the road, and looked down to where the bicycle was. Riley was just emerging from the his hiding place under a laurel thicket. Chip immediately knew what the woman had found so funny. In an attempt to make his injuries more real, Riley had not only applied the ketchup generally, he had wrapped a bandage around his head, stuck about twenty band aids here and there on his face and arms, and put his arm in a sling. Chip guessed the woman saw through the charade immediately. Either Riley's injuries had already been attended to and whoever worked on him just left him lying there under his bicycle or he had been injured in another accident somewhere and had just had another one. Evidently the lady didn't buy either scenario.

The next faux pas occurred when Chip and Riley swapped roles. Chip didn't go to the extent of playing injured that Riley did. He just laid down in the creek with bicycle on top of him. Riley didn't know about Chip's identification process so he stopped the first car that came along. It was a State Policeman.

When the state trooper got out and Riley saw who it was, it scared him so badly he just stood there. He was frozen in fear. He couldn't run. He couldn't talk. He couldn't do anything.

Meanwhile Chip was lying down in the creek. He couldn't see what was going on up on the road but he would follow the same instructions he always gave Riley; just lay there till you see someone look over the bank at you, then you push the bike off you, jump up, and run. Just then the state trooper appeared at the top of the bank. Chip didn't run either. He just laid there.

"You all right, son?" the trooper called down to him.

"Yeah. I'm ok," Chip yelled back weakly. He pushed the bike off him and slowly got up. He was trying to formulate a way out of this predicament. Fear kept him from looking up the bank at the trooper so he stared at the bike when he spoke. "I don't know what happened", he said loudly. "I guess I just got too close to the road bank and it gave way." There was no reason for Chip to talk loudly because the trooper had scrambled down the bank and was tiptoeing his way across the creek to reach Chip.

Chip stood and watched as the trooper approached. "I don't know what happened," he repeated. "I guess I just got too close to the road bank and it gave way."

The trooper gave Chip a quick once-over to see if he could spot any blood, bruises, or bones sticking out, then he felt Chip's arms and shoulders and neck, checking for same. It seemed to Chip like the trooper was eight feet tall. His uniform had just the faintest smell of wet wool and leather. "You're very fortunate," he said, "you could have been seriously injured." He looked the bike over and he looked around at the accident scene. "Doesn't look like your bike is hurt either. Well, come on. Let's see if we can get you back up on the road." He picked the bike up and cradled it to his body with one arm and with the other arm he gently steered and pushed Chip ahead over the creek and up the road bank.

With some effort they reached the top of the bank and there stood Riley. He hadn't moved an inch since the trooper stopped. Riley's philosophy must have been; When in doubt or fear; do nothing.

"Listen boys," the trooper said, putting down the bike, "I better run you over to the hospital and have you checked out by a doctor.

You could have internal injuries and you could bleed to death and not know it. We can call your parents from there and let them know what happened."

Riley seemed to snap out of it, "Hey, yeah. Will you turn the siren on?"

"Uh, that's ok," stammered Chip, "I really feel fine."

"That's one of the first symptoms," continued the trooper. "You feel just fine. In fact, you even feel better than you've ever felt. Then it hits, and you're dead. Maybe I'd better take you to your home, that way your parents will know what happened and they can make any arrangements they feel will be necessary. We can put your bike in the trunk."

"Hey, yeah!" Will you turn the siren on?" Riley piped up again.

The trooper's offer was enticing . Getting to ride in a state police cruiser with the lights and siren on would be something Chip envisioned........but a dark cloud drifted in and squashed the scene. If they pulled in the driveway in a police car with lights and siren on, Mom and Grandma would both have a heart attack. Worse than that, Chip would have to explain to them what happened, no doubt with the state trooper in attendance and it was hard to tell what Riley might say about everything if asked.

"Honestly sir," Chip went on, "I'm ok. We just live right around the bend there". He pointed back from where the trooper had just come and away from where they really lived. The trooper would be less likely to stop at their house if he had to turn around and go back than if it was just up ahead in the direction he was already headed.

Riley started to correct Chip but Chip cut him off. "We'll go straight home though and let our mom know what happened".

The trooper contemplated the matter a little before he answered. "Ok boys, but you go straight home now and tell your parents exactly just what happened. I'll check back in a day or two to see how everything is. You boys go on now and try to be more careful with those bikes, ok."

The trooper got back in his car and Riley and Chip started back up the road towards their fabricated home. The trooper drove off and disappeared up around the bend in the road. Riley and Chip then stopped by the side of the road. Chip was mauling over the whole incident in his mind. Did the trooper believe him or did he suspicion the real truth? Was he just passing by or did somebody report the boys' shenanigans? Was he really being concerned about Chip's condition or was he just trying to scare them? And say, how could he check with their parents? He didn't know their names or where they lived. Of course he could probably find out just by stopping by the station or the company store and asking around. Still, they'd be better off not saying anything about this to anybody and wait and see what happens.

The boys suffered under a cloud of guilt for about a week anxiously awaiting the arrival of the state police to follow up on his promise but as the days passed slowly by, no family meetings were ever called. After another week went by, their guilt and anxiety slowly faded away altogether. Now you'd think that the run-in with the State Police would have folded up the "Help. Help. Somebody's hurt" game but not so. With a little coaxing from Maynard, Chip was ready to give it another go, albeit reluctantly.

This time Maynard wanted to play the part of the injured kid so Chip became the lookout. They moved the accident scene from Lick Run around the road to Sugar Tree Run which put it a little closer to Sugar Tree. Maynard smeared a little ketchup here and there to make things interesting.

Chip stopped the first car that came along because he hadn't seen it before. The driver got out and walked over to the edge of the berm and looked over the bank. Chip took off but he could hear the driver in a near panic voice. "Oh my Lord, it's Maynard!" He turned to his passenger still in the car. "Martha, it's Maynard," he exclaimed. He turned back to the road bank and yelled down to Maynard. "Don't worry boy. You hang in there. We'll go get some help". He jumped back in the car and speed off.

Chip slipped out of the woods and crossed the road. He got to the edge of the bank just as Maynard reached the top. "What was that all about?" Chip asked.

"You jerk off. That was my Uncle Verl and Aunt Ida. They're probably already at the house and got everybody stirred up. Uncle Verl, he's a strange agent now. Wouldn't surprise me none if an ambulance and the police showed up here."

"Well I didn't know who it was," argued Chip. "How was I to know it was your uncle? I don't know him from apple butter and I surely don't know his car."

"Well Mom knows how he is. She'll get him calmed down but we better think up something 'cause they'll be back here no doubt."

No sooner had the words left Maynard's mouth when Uncle Verl came flying back around the road and slid to a stop right beside the boys. He got out and so did Aunt Ida, Maynard's mom, and Elihu. Elihu was smiling but Mrs. Samples found the situation less than humorous. "Maynard get in the car. I don't know what you boys been up to but I 'spect it better be done with right now," she said. "Chip, you best be gettin' on home now. You boys need a little time off from one another."

"Yes ma'am," answered Chip.

The Samples clan got back into Uncle Verl's car. He turned around right there in the road and they sped off back to Maynard's. Chip went back down to the creek and got his bike. Instead of trying to climb up the steep bank with his bike at that spot, he pushed it downstream through the creek to a place where the road bank wasn't as high or as steep and made it up to the road with little effort.

Chip found out that Maynard's dad had whipped him and then confined him to the inside of their yard for one week, except for going to church. Chip figured that Maynard's punishment was more for what he'd done to Uncle Verl than for playing the road game, but he also figured that Maynard had it coming to him for talking Chip into playing the stupid game again anyway.

If Chip's parents knew about "Help. Help. Somebody's hurt." they never confronted him about it and it was never mentioned again in the Gates household.

The "pocket book trick" was an old ploy handed down from juvenile generations before. They took a woman's purse or a man's wallet, tied some fishing line to it, and laid it in the middle of the road. Then they'd hide over the road bank and wait for someone to stop to get the pocketbook. When a person stopped, they'd retrieve the bait back by the fishing line and run off down into the woods, bait in hand.

Oddly enough, even though the pocketbook trick was old hat, it always seemed to work like a charm. That was probably due to the fact that it was only played every other year or so, and because it preyed on mankind's two most endearing qualities; greed and good neighborliness. If a driver didn't stop, Chip guessed it was because they weren't paying attention to their driving and either didn't see the pocketbook or didn't recognize it.

To play the game, they first needed a pocketbook or a billfold. Maybe that's why the trick wasn't played much. It was hard to find a discarded pocketbook. Next, they needed some string. Any kind of string would do but it had to be strong enough not to break when the pocketbook was jerked out of road and small enough to be inconspicuous to the traveling public. Fishing line met all of those criteria.

Next, they needed a place where they could not only hide off the side of the road, but it had to be a place where they could make a hasty retreat. It was even better if this place could help hide their identity and discourage any of the "marks" from chasing after them. There were two ideal places. One was just below the bottom hairpin turn on Renzee White Hill and the other one was just below Dead Man's Curve on Sugar Tree Hill. Both places provided a hiding place just below the edge of the road and in both places the hillside below was very steep and led down into the deep woods. They were perfect.

No more than two boys ever played the trick at one time. Actually one boy could easily play the trick by himself but it wouldn't be nearly as much fun. The getaway was made more cumbersome with two or more players. The more perpetrators there were, the more likely one of them might be recognized by the "mark". Chip either played the pocketbook trick with Riley or with Maynard. He never played it alone.

The Gates brothers had to fasten up Major and Specks and keep them penned up until they retired the pocketbook trick for the day. The dogs would be a dead giveaway to the identity of the perpetrators and even if Chip and his brothers could slip away from the dogs, as soon as the dogs discovered them gone, they would track them down no matter where they went walking. Everybody in Sugar Tree knew who those dogs belonged to.

Because both the Renzee White and Sugar Tree Hill locations were slightly removed from the immediate vicinity of the little community, a little planning was required to pull off a successful and rewarding run of the trick. When the particular day was decided upon, Chip and whoever his accomplice was, would work both sides of Rt.11 for a couple of miles picking up pop bottles. They'd load the bottles in Clint's wagon and take them to the station. The Keeners paid two cents a bottle if they were in good condition. They paid five cents for a quart size pop bottle. If the bottles were chipped or cracked or were of a brand not sold by the Keeners, they couldn't be redeemed there. With the money from the bottles, the boys would buy a stock of provisions at the station like pop, candy, chips, peanuts etc. depending on how much money they had. They carried their provisions, including string and pocketbook, to one of their two favorite locations and set up shop. They usually planned to spend two or three hours playing the trick or until their supplies ran out.

Chip even went as far as to stick a couple of play money bills from one of Clint's board games into the pocketbook. He left just enough of the bills sticking out so the driver could see it was the right color but couldn't tell it was play money.

They didn't retrieve the bait until the driver got out of his vehicle. If they yanked the bait back too soon, the driver would just drive off. If they waited too long, the driver could get close enough to see the line or the play money. Retrieval at just the right time not only fully duped the "mark" but in those cases where the "mark" decided to go on and chase after the pranksters, since he was already out of his vehicle, a perfectly timed retrieval gave the boys plenty of time to disappear over the hillside into the woods. By the time the "mark" got to the edge of the roadbank, the deceivers were nowhere to be seen.

Trouble with the pocketbook trick was rare. One time the line on the pocketbook broke during the retrieval process. The old guy who had stopped just walked up to the pocketbook, picked it up from the middle of the road, stuck the play money in his pocket, rummaged through the empty compartments, and then tossed it over the hill where the boys had been hiding. He got back in his truck and drove off.

Another time Flavy Knight stopped his car right on top of the line, opened the door, reached down and snatched the pocketbook up, shut the door, and drove off. Evidently he had been duped at least one time before.

One time a car traveling at a high rate of speed ran over the pocketbook. The driver lammed on the brakes and slid to a stop a few yards passed the boys. Chip didn't like the sound of the squealing tire stop so he quickly reeled in the pocketbook from the middle of the road and without waiting for the driver to get out, tucked the pocketbook under his arm and he and Maynard ran down through the woods for cover.

They settled into the dark shade of their hiding place under a rhododendron thicket and waited. The boys couldn't see the driver from where they were but they heard him get out of his car. A few seconds passed before they heard the driver. He was standing at the edge of the road and yelling down into the ravine. "Junior Dodrill. You little snot. I know you're down there. If I wasn't in a hurry I'd come down there and kick your little butt all over this hill, you little fart, so I'm gonna stop and tell your dad what you're doin' and he'll blister the hide ofen yuh. I catch you out on the road, I'll beat the tar outa you. You hear me, you little bastard."

Chip and Maynard were afraid their giggling might give them away.

There were two times when playing the pocketbook trick was not fun. The first time was when Maynard and Chip wanted to play the trick but couldn't find a discarded purse or wallet, so while Grandma Gates was out hoeing in the garden, Chip slipped in and borrowed one of her less often used purses from the little closet under the second floor stairs. He made sure he got one that didn't have anything in it. Chip was so worried about something happening to the purse that he prayed all the while he and Maynard were walking up Renzee White Hill. They only played the trick twice before Chip's conscience got the best of him and they packed everything up and went home. Chip put the purse back where it belonged and confessed to Grandma that he had borrowed it. He was just thankful the good Lord hadn't punished him for his misdeed.

The other time that no fun was derived from the pocketbook trick turned out to be the last time Chip could remember playing it. Riley and Chip had scrounged up enough pop bottles to by a quart bottle of Par-T-Pac gingerale, a couple of bags of Planter's Peanuts, and one each of a Hollywood, Zero, Zag Nut, and Clark candy bar. They headed off to Renzee White Hill figuring to spend the whole afternoon playing the trick. They stashed their cache in a hollowed out base of an old beech tree on the hillside between their hiding place under the road bank and the woods where their escape route lay. Now and then they'd take a break from the trick and sit by the old tree and partake of their bounty.

Junior Dodrill and Mickey King happen to be walking down Renzee White Hill about the same time the boys were playing the pocketbook trick and when they discovered what the boys were doing, they decided to hide in the brush up the hill a ways off and watch them play the game. It wasn't long before they also discovered the boys' stash of treats and where it was hidden.

On the ensuing trick, Riley and Chip slipped the pocketbook out of the road and made their successful escape down the hillside and into the woods. As soon as the frustrated driver drove off, Junior and Mickey jumped out from their hiding place and ran down to the trick site. While Mickey waited up on the roadside, Junior slipped down over the hillside, took all of the stuff out of the beech tree, and climbed back up to the road. When Riley and Chip came up out of the woods to see what was going on, Mickey drove them back into cover by pelting them with rocks from his vantage point up on the road. He kept Riley and Chip pinned down long enough for Junior to split up the booty and then the two raiders skedaddled on down the road, off the hill.

Chip was incensed. He scrambled up the hill to the road. He looked up and down the road for Junior and Mickey but they were nowhere to be seen. "I'll get you for this, Junior," he yelled. "You better be watchin' 'cause I swear I'll get back at you one of these days, you punk jamison." Chip didn't know if Junior heard him or not. Riley finally made it up to the road. He was bawling his eyeballs out. "Did you get hit with a rock or somethin'?" Chip asked.

"No!" stammered Riley.

"Well then SHUT UP, you cry baby. Let's get this stuff and get outa here. If I see either one of the chicken punks, I swear I'll beat the livin' crap out of 'em."

For weeks Chip harbored revenge against Junior and Mickey. He laid awake at night hatching schemes of retribution in his mind and playing out each scenario with a justified punishment being administered by him. In the case of Junior, those schemes would have to be played out in the absence of Junior's sister, Jeannie.

The weeks passed by and Chip never came in contract with either one of the two perps, so eventually the incident, and Chip's plan for revenge were tucked away somewhere in the recesses of his mind; never to be brought to mind again until now. That was the last time Chip could remember playing the pocketbook trick.

II

The short lived "Tire Trick" came about by accident and an indirect result of Clint's fascination with cars and trucks. One day while he was playing around in the creek near home, he found an old car tire. He dragged the tire out of the creek, emptied the water and sand out of it, and rolled it back down the road to the house. After that, everywhere Clint went he rolled that tire along with him. A week later he found a better tire so he rolled that first tire around behind the barn and parked it there like it was his first car.

Clint was always on the lookout for a better tire and once every two weeks or so he'd venture around to the station to see if there were any new, old tires he could trade for. He had a winter tread tire for snow and ice, a straight tread tire for summer, and two favorites.

One favorite was a 7.00-20 truck tire. He like it because it was almost as tall as he was and it was easy to roll, except when he had to go uphill.

His very favorite one though, was a wide, low profile, white sidewall tire. He only brought that baby out on fair weather days. The rest of the time he kept it in the barn out of the weather, where he would rub it down with brake fluid to make it shine and scrub the whitewall clean with a Brillo soap pad.

One day Clint and Chip were playing in the creek up near the head of the little straight stretch that ran by the Gates' house. Clint had left his latest, everyday tire parked, standing up, on the berm across the road from where the boys were, down in the creek. When they climbed back up to the road, the tire wasn't where Clint had parked it. They searched the area around where the tire was last seen, figuring it had fallen over, but they couldn't find it. Nobody had come along while they were in the creek so they were sure no one would have stolen it. What would anybody want with an old tire like that anyway?

Perplexed, they started walking back down the straight towards home. Halfway down the straight they spotted the tire laying on its side in the ditch by the road. It had somehow become unparked from where Clint had left it and starting on its own, had rolled halfway home. Clint was happy finding his lost tire but he and Chip were contemplating the successful trip the tire had made all on its own. They wondered how the tire would do if it were given a little help?

While Chip stayed where they found the tire, Clint rolled it back up to the head of the straight. He waited a moment for things to quiet down so he could hear if a car was coming or not, and when all seemed quiet, he aimed the tire down the middle of the road and gave it a good rolling start. The tire stayed upright and true, right down the middle of the road. When it got to Chip, he stepped out and grabbed it to stop its course.

Clint, who had been chasing the tire down the road, ran up to Chip huffing and puffing. They looked at each other, then turned and looked on down the road. From where they were standing, there was still more than half of the straight left. As brothers are apt to do sometimes, they both had the same thought at the same time. There wasn't even any need for dialogue. With Clint rolling the tire along, they turned and walked back up to the upper end of the straight.

They carefully and meticulously selected a hiding place down over the creek bank at the head of the straight. From there, they could start the tire on its journey down the road and jump out of sight over the creek bank. It was also from a spot where they could peer over the creek bank, through the tall grass at the road's edge, and watch the entire sequence of events as the tire made its trip down the road. The two boys would remain completely out of sight of passersby.

Clint made the initial roll. He stood up on the road with the tire ready, listening for the noise of an approaching vehicle. Chip hid over the creek bank. Clint finally detected something heading their way and he waited until the vehicle was almost around the lower turn of the straight before he gave the tire its sendoff. Then he jumped down over the creekbank and joined Chip. They watched through the grass as the tire picked up speed heading down the middle of the road.

The car rounded the turn at the bottom of the straight and began to accelerate when the driver saw a lonely tire, seemingly on its way to Sugar Tree, coming down the road. He slowed the car but when he realized the tire was heading straight for him, he stomped on the gas and jerked the car off to the right hand side of the road.

The tire sped on by going who knows where. The boys could see the driver raise up in his seat and try to get a glimpse of the tire through his rear view mirror. He sat there a little bit and then pulled out and headed on up the straight past the boys. Now this is cool, the boys thought.

Chip's turn to roll the tire came next. He waited a little longer than Clint would have, but he gave the tire a stronger start and it ran a little truer down the middle of the road. The approaching car got almost halfway up the straight before the driver realized his dilemma. He pulled the car over on the berm as the tire whizzed by. He opened the car door, got out, and watched the tire roll straight on through the lower turn, off the road, and into the creek. Then he turned around slowly and yelled in all directions at once, "Junior Dodrill, you little hellion. I know you can hear me. I'm gonna stop and tell your dad what you're doin' and I hope he beats the livin' tar outa you. You just better hope I don't catch you, you little prick. I'll cut your ears off!" He got back in the car and tore out, spinning rocks and gravel and reddog all over the place. Clint and Chip could see the driver talking to himself as he sped on by them.

All afternoon Clint and Chip took turns playing out the tire trick and there were all kinds of mixed reactions from surprised drivers. Some pulled over as the tire went by and then continued on their way as if the tire was just another vehicle passing by. A couple of times the tire drifted over to the left side of the road and in both cases the approaching car swung to the opposite side of the road to avoid the tire. A few times the tire ran clear off the road before encountering a vehicle and those drivers passed on by, never getting to experience a truly notable event.

One vehicle, a big Turnpike Mercury, made no effort to get off the road at all and hit the tire dead center, sending it sailing, twenty feet into the air. The tire came down just beside Grandma Gates' garden and fortunately didn't do any crop damage. The Mercury just kept cruising on up the road. Chip noted the elderly woman driver commanding the Mercury. She had both hands on the wheel and both eyes locked on the road ahead. Part of her mink stole was fluttering in the breeze of her open window.

It seemed only appropriate that Clint would be the last Gates to perform the tire trick. He was waiting for the sound of an approaching vehicle before setting the tire off down the road but he must have gotten confused about the direction the vehicle was coming from. He started the tire rolling at just the right moment and slipped over the creek bank to watch the action. Both boys were quite startled when a pickup truck swung out of the curve BEHIND them and into the straight. As it glided by they both recognized the truck as belonging to Elliott Browning from Hob. Clint's heart sank. He watched Elliott slow the truck down as he pulled up closer behind the rolling tire and followed it down the road. The tire finally rolled off the right hand side of the road down near the end of the straight and came to a stop, resting over on its side in the ditch. Elliott stopped the truck, got out, retrieved the tire out of the ditch, and tossed it in the back. He got back in the truck and drove off, disappearing around the bend in the road.

Now Clint was both angry and disheartened. He was disheartened because Elliott had taken one of his good tires, and was mad at himself for not using one of his expendable tires. He was also mad because he had mistaken the direction from which Elliott was coming.

Chip tried to soothe his ruffled nature. "Ah don't worry," he said, putting his arm around Clint. "We'll get us a new tire tomorrow and start all over."

Clint jerked free. His eyes were getting misty. "Maybe you will," he replied, "but I ain't never doin' this again. If you want to, you find your own tire." And he shuffled off towards home.

III

The life span of the "smoke screen" was even shorter than the "phantom tire". Junior Dodrill's dad had brought some dynamite home from the Red Dog mines to blast through some bedrock he had encountered while digging his water well a little deeper. He had stored the dynamite in a box out in the barn. It didn't take Junior long before he discovered the explosive and decided to experiment with it. The first thing he did was to steal a stick of it and get it away from the barn.....not the best place to be fooling around with black powder and matches. So his dad wouldn't catch him playing with dynamite, Junior carried his paraphernalia down to the oak tree where he could experiment in peace.

The oak tree marked a pull off spot along the straight stretch that ran by the Gates' farm. The wide spot was created when Rt.11 was only a wagon trail through the valley. Early settlers found it to be a quiet spot where they could pull their wagons off to the side of the road and let their horses water in Lick Run. On the bank across the creek at the oak tree, someone discovered a cold water spring and painstakingly chiseled out a catch basin in a solid rock ledge just below the spring. Travelers found the spring water not only refreshing the whole year round. Even after Rt.11 was paved, travelers still stopped at the spring often to fill their thermoses and various water containers with the cool water or just to grab a long drink. It was referred to as "The Oak Tree" because a large white oak tree grew right beside the road and it was an easy identifiable landmark. The tree was as old as the spring.

The second thing Junior did with the stick of dynamite was to cut the end out it and pour all the powder out into a can. About this same time, Chip and Maynard happened to come along. They had been out collecting pop bottles to take around to the station and sell for the deposit money when they passed by the oak tree. Normally Chip and Maynard didn't have much to do with Junior but their curiosity and sense of adventure overcame whatever social obstacles seemed to hinder their relationship.

Junior poured out a little pile of powder on the ground and stuck a lit match to it. The powder flashed and left a heavy gray cloud of smoke hanging in the air. That was cool but there were other things they could do. The three boys spent the afternoon playing with the black powder. They poured it out in long streaks and lit one end to watch the red flash run along the ground. They put powder in holes in the ground and covered the holes with dirt or rocks to see if the powder would exploded. It didn't. They poured powder in a pop bottle, laid it down on the ground, and lit it like a rocket to see if it would blast into the air. It didn't, but it gave them another idea for experimenting. They figured if they could put the powder in something lighter than a pop bottle it might fly.

They used a piece of iron pipe and a piece of plastic pipe but no matter how much powder was stuffed into them, they were just too heavy to fly.

After a couple of hours of experimenting, Maynard and Chip realized it was past supper time and too late in the evening to go around to the station, so they told Junior they had to be heading home. Junior didn't ask them to stay any longer, but he did mention that he'd be back down to the oak tree that night if Maynard and Chip wanted to come back up for some more experimenting. The two boys couldn't pass up an opportunity like that, so they all agreed to meet back at the oak tree just after dark.

There was still some light left when Maynard and Chip returned to the oak tree that night. Junior was already there and it appeared he had been there for some time. He had a fresh supply of black powder in a Maxwell House coffee can, there were little black burned areas all over the ground. He had an empty Old Export beer can stuck in his jacket pocket, a flashlight was sticking out of his back pocket, and he held a handful of soda straws. There was one soda straw lying on the ground. "Hey guys. Watch this," he said. He struck a match and stuck it to one end of the soda straw. Instantly the straw whizzed out into the night trailing a spectacular shower of sparks and flame.

He pulled out another straw. "Here Chip, hold the flashlight. See, whatcha do is tape one end of the straw shut like this". He pulled out a roll of black friction tape, doubled over one end of the straw, and ran a piece of tape around it to seal it. He then poured out a little rivulet of powder on the ground and used the open end of the straw to scoop up the powder, filling the straw as best as he could. There was powder on everything. He laid the straw down in the middle of the road this time and aimed it up the road away from the boys.

Chip held the flashlight on the straw so Junior could see to light it. He lit another match and touched the end of the straw. The straw shot straight ahead for ten feet, rising three or four feet off the ground, then it twisted and turned and assumed about the same flight line as a balloon does when you let the air out of it. It was a fiery spectacle.

Encouraged with the success of the previous fireworks, they continued on. However the next launch shot five or six feet straight out, made an instantaneous one hundred eighty degree turn, and whipped its ragged flight right back at the three boys standing in the middle of the road. Other than the widening of their eyes and the stopping of their hearts, they had no time to react. The straw shot head high, right through their midst before sputtering out in the darkness. Miraculously, the only injuries were a few little pricks of pinpoint burns where the sparks from the passing rocket had fallen on their arms and neck. They rubbed at the burns like it was a small itch. "Well, ok, " said Junior, "let's let that one rest for a little bit. I got something even better." He pulled out the Old Export beer can.

Old Export beer came in a can but the can was made in the shape of a short, fat beer bottle. "Ok, Chip, give me some light over here", he instructed. Chip beamed the flashlight towards Junior. Junior turned the can upside down and screwed the top into the ground so that it was upside down. The bottom of the can was concave and Junior proceeded to pour the bottom full of black powder. He lit another match, turned his face away from the beer can, and keeping as far away from the powder as he could, he stretched his right arm, with lit match in hand, over to ignite the powder. With a muffled thump, the powder went off in a brilliant flash. A heavy, thick gray smoke cloud hung in the air over the beer can. Chip shined the flashlight into the cloud but the smoke was so thick the beam didn't penetrate but a few inches.

"Cool, huh," said Junior. Chip nodded in agreement but Maynard wasn't impressed.

"So what," he retorted.

Junior went on like he didn't hear Maynard. "Now we wait till we hear a car coming, then set off the powder by the side of the road. We can slip over yonder and hide in the grass and watch what happens." That seemed to prick Maynard's interest enough.

"Come on and help me fix this thing up."

The boys went to work. Chip held the flashlight so the other two could see what they were doing. Maynard picked out a soft spot in the berm by the road and firmly set the beer can in the sand and gravel. Junior filled the beer can bottom full of powder from out of his supply. They selected their escape route and hiding place. Maynard laid down behind a small mound of dirt and tall grass over by the creek. It was about thirty feet from the hardroad. Chip would hold the flashlight for Junior so he could see to light the powder and then shine it so Junior could see the way over to his hiding place behind the oak tree. Chip would then use the light to find his own way over to where Maynard was hiding. While they were setting up and planning all of this, a car and a truck had already gone by.

They had to wait another fifteen minutes before their first victim was heard approaching. The vehicle was coming up the straight so Junior waited until the car was almost around the bottom turn before he lit the powder. With another brilliant flash, the heavy gray cloud rolled in slowly over the hardroad. Junior made four or five quick steps to the backside of the oak tree and Chip, with winged feet, glided over and laid down beside Maynard.

Maynard and Chip raised up enough to see over the dirt mound and through the sage brush. They could see the outline of the oak tree taking shape as the car got closer but they never did see Junior. The car slowed down perceptibly as it approached the smoke bank and finally stopped right in front of it. The headlights threw weird shadows into the smoke but even their brightness couldn't shine through. It was deathly quiet. The only noise was the gentle riffling of the creek and the muzzled clatter of the car engine running at idle speed.

A spotlight came on. For a moment its beam whipped all over the place like the driver was trying to figure out how it worked, then it settled down to make a horizontal stab into the smoke bank. Still nothing came through the back side. Maynard and Chip were stifling their chuckles as best they could. The spotlight made a slow turn away from the smoke and began to sweep the woods on the opposite side of the road.

Junior must have taken that opportunity to slip away from the oak tree and make a run out to the creek. Maynard and Chip heard him tiptoeing through the shallow water of the creek just behind them. By the time the spotlight had finished its search along the other side of the road, Junior had progressed a couple of hundred feet up the creek away from them and the car.

Maynard and Chip ducked down behind the mound and flattened themselves as close to the ground as they could. The spotlight was working its way over to them. It swung right over top of them on its first pass, illuminating the hillside across the creek in the area of the spring in its white light and moved on around to their left, heading for the oak tree.

The spotlight ran up the oak and down again. It worked the right side, the left side, and all around the tree, then it jerked back right where the boys were hiding. They held their breath as the operator focused the beam into a intense spot and kept it trained right at the mound of dirt the boys were hiding behind. The spotlight then expanded to a wide angle beam with less intensity but illuminated a larger field and stayed that way for another minute or so. The boys didn't even move an eyelash.

Evidently finding nothing, the spotlight reluctantly moved on around to the smoke bank in the middle of the road. There remained only wisps of smoke now drifting in the still, night air. The spotlight snapped off but the car remained idling there in the middle of the road. Its headlights appeared to be only a soft, yellow glow after the intense brightness of the spotlight. The driver pulled the car into gear, slowly eased through what wisps of smoke remained, and headed on up the road and out of sight around the upper turn.

As soon as the car was gone, Maynard and Chip got up from their hiding place. Chip switched on the flashlight and the two boys walked over to the creek to look for Junior.

Junior was already picking his way back down the creek. Chip shined the light Junior's way to help him better see where he was stepping. "No use bothering with that now," Junior said, as he slopped his way up to his companions. "Done got my feet wet clear up to my knees." They walked together back towards the beer can.

"I don't think hiding behind the oak tree is too good a place," Maynard said.

"Sure, it'll be fine," answered Junior, "How many times are we gonna stop a car that has a spotlight on it? Jus' bad luck that time. I figured I might get spotted that time. That's why I took off ,but we'll make this one better than ever."

Junior again filled the bottom of the beer can with powder only this time he worked at it. He tamped and poured and shaped and packed until he had a pretty impressive heap of powder in the can. There was powder residue everywhere; on the sides of the can, on the ground, and on Juniors hands. He was just starting to tidy up when they heard a car coming.

Maynard was already on the run to his hiding place while Junior was fumbling around with the matches. The car was coming through the bottom turn now. To save time, Junior struck a match in the direction of the powder, but because there was so much powder residue present, the whole staging area, including Junior's Maxwell House supply can, ignited in a spectacular explosion of light and sound.

Chip and Junior remained frozen for an instant in the flash of light. The concussion knocked Junior backwards to the ground. Stunned by the force of the blast, he instinctively jumped to his feet and started heading toward his hiding place behind the oak tree but blinded by the explosion of light, he ran right smack dab into the tree. He staggered three or four steps off to the left and collapsed face down into the grass; out cold.

The car was now coming out the lower turn and heading up the straight. There wasn't much Chip could do for Junior right at that instant so he became unfrozen and made a hasty retreat over to where Maynard was. They would watch developments unfold through the grass from behind the little mound of dirt.

They hadn't realized just what a humongous and seemingly impenetrable cloud of smoke had been produced from the accident until the approaching car slowed to a stop in front of it. The cloud was so thick it splashed the car's reflected headlights off to both sides and right back at the source. Chip had never even seen the fog on Elk River that heavy before.

The driver opened his door and got out. The dome light came on and the boys could see another person sitting in the front seat. The driver anchored one foot on the road and one on the floorboard of his car. He looked over the roof of his car. The headlights reflected onto one side of his face; the other side remained in the shadow. Neither Maynard nor Chip recognized him.

He yelled over the top of his car. "Junior Dodrill, you little snot. I know you're over there, you little bastard. I'm gonna stop and tell your dad what you're doin' down here. I hope he whips the hide ofen your tail, and if I catch up with you, your little butt is mine." Fortunately, Junior was too indisposed to offer any response.

The driver bent down and said something to the passenger. There was some fumbling around in the car, then the passenger opened his door and stepped out. He flipped on a flashlight and began directing it around on the ground between the car and the boys. Two or three times the light passed right over Junior but he was plastered to the ground and remained undetected. The boys prayed that he wouldn't come around and start moaning or moving around while their antagonists were still present.

The two men at the car remained vigilant. Hoping to spot one of the culprits before the smoke cleared away, they waited there in the middle of the road, engine running, both doors open, headlights on. Chip and Maynard weren't about to give their position away. Who would break first; Junior or the two men?

A noise off to the boys' right caught their attention. A vehicle was coming down the road. The two men heard it too but they didn't move. The car came around the upper turn and slowed as it neared the other car which was stopped in the middle of the road. The headlight beams from both vehicles revealed very little remained of the smoke cloud. The vehicle coming down the road was a pickup. It eased to within twenty feet of the still stopped car and sat there for a moment. The driver of the pickup was very patient. He rolled down his window. "Hey, you guys need some help?" he asked.

"No!" came the adamant reply. "We're movin. We're movin". The two men got back in the car, slammed the doors shut, and jerked the car out of the road so the two vehicles could pass.

The truck went on its way but the car sat there for a few more minutes, half on half off of the road. Finally, it pulled back onto the hardroad and eased on up the road.

As soon as the car was gone, Chip and Maynard ran over to Junior. He was still out. Maynard took the flashlight and went over to the creek to soak his bandanna in the cold water. Chip rolled Junior over and sat him up, propping his upper body against his own. Maynard came back from the creek and trained the light on Junior's face. There was a pumpknot about the size of a good hen egg poking out of his forehead. Maynard gently pressed the bandanna against the knot and wrapped it around Junior's head. Junior groaned, then his eyes fluttered open and he slowly focused in on Maynard and Chip. "Wha......wha.....happen?" he asked.

"Nothin'", answered Maynard. "The guy didn't even stop. Jus' drove right through the smoke and went on."

Junior struggled to stand up. Maynard and Chip helped him. Once up, he staggered a moment but seemed to regain his balance. "Well, let,s try it one more time."

"Can't", said Chip, "used up all of the powder."

"Just as well. I don't feel so hot, anyway." He felt the knot on his head. "Give me my light. Find my matches. I'm goin' home. We'll do this some other time." He stuffed the matches in his jacket pocket and without so much as a "See you later", started off towards home. Every few steps he'd sway off stride.

"Well, bull's connection", remarked Maynard. "He's got my good bandanna!"

That was the life of the smoke screen trick; two episodes. Two weeks later Chip heard rumors that Junior had to be taken to the emergency room at Seneca to be treated for first degree flash burns on his arm, neck, and chest as the result of some accident in the cellar top behind his house. No one seemed to know any more about the cause of or the extent of his injuries.

IV

"The Hubcap Trick" was an innocent enough ploy. Because of its simplicity, it was probably the most popular road game. It could be played anywhere, at any time, with as many or as few players as you had with you at the time. All you needed was an old hubcap.

The trick was to stand by the road and when a car went by you'd throw the hubcap down on the road so it would make a lot of racket. Then you'd yell at the driver something like, "Hey mister, I got your hubcap." That was it. The object of the trick was to get the driver to chase after you so he could get his hubcap back. That didn't happen too often but it didn't discourage the players. Chip was never involved with the hubcap trick unless there were other Jive Five members present, and he never remembered anyone talking about playing the hubcap trick that at least one of the Jive Five wasn't there.

A few times a driver would stop his car and get out and chase after one of the kids until he realized that (1) all of this hubcaps were still on his vehicle (2) no kid had a hubcap in his possession (3)he spotted the perpetrators' hubcap and recognized it as not his (4)his vehicle had no hubcaps on it (5)so many kids were running away he didn't know which one to chase after. There were other times when a driver would chase the kids long enough to drive them away from the area and there were times when a driver would send one or two of his passengers to chase after the kids. It didn't matter to the kids, the thrill of the trick was not to get caught.

The hubcap trick could be played in the daytime. It was easier to see where you were going in the daylight but nighttime was best by far. At night, it was harder for the drivers to tell how many were involved, harder to tell if they had really lost a hubcap or not, and harder to tell if someone had really taken it; excluding #4 just mentioned. Above everything else though, the primary reason for playing the hubcap trick at night was to make it harder for the driver to tell WHO was involved.

To be any fun, the hubcap trick had to be played with at least two people. The more kids you could get to stand around and then run, the more exciting it was. The hubcap trick was the only road game that included girls. They were always fun to run and hide with in the dark. Like other road games, the hubcap trick could only be played once or twice a year or it would lose it lure and seduction to the traveling public.

Of all the hubcap tricks that Chip was involved in, there were two that really stood out. Both of them took place around at the Company Store in Sugar Tree because that was the best place to play the hubcap trick. There were vehicles coming out and going up Painter's Fork and there were vehicles coming and going along Rt.11. From a good position in front of the Company store, one could "hubcap" cars from three different directions. There was also enough light from the clock in Jobe's store window to help those on the run find their escape routes in the dark.

One warm, early spring evening during a rousing game of "kick the can" at the station, Benji found a hubcap while he was hiding over the creek bank in front of the station. As soon as the "kick the can" enthusiasm died down, he suggested they go over to the Company Store and play the hubcap trick for a little while before going home. Some of the "kick the can" crowd thought it a little too late for them to be out on a school night, so they went on home, but a crowd of from six to eight kids followed Benji, Maynard, and Chip over to the Company Store to join in the fun.

They didn't even have time to select their escape routes before the first car, coming from the direction of the station, came cruising by. It turned right at the Company Store and started up the Sugar Tree straight. Benji could have waited for another car before throwing the hubcap, thus giving everybody a chance to coordinate escape routes and delegate responsibilities, but being caught up in the excitement of the moment and without much thought to a planned approach to the matter, he tossed the hubcap after the car as it passed by and then yelled, "Hey, dummy, I got your hubcap."

The trick was played out without any warning or notice at all and the kids standing around in the store lot were caught off guard.

The driver of the car slammed on the brakes and the car slid to a screeching stop right in the middle of the road. Frozen in place by the frenzied pace of the unfolding events, the kids all looked in the direction of the stopped car. The driver's door flew open and the driver sprang out onto the hardroad. It was Leo Taylor.

Leo was twenty-five years old. He was the kind of person who seemed to live to tease, bully, threaten, and torture younger kids.

He had two younger brothers at home and Chip figured their life must have been made miserable by Leo. When he was in the presence of other adults, Leo completely ignored any kids who happen to be present, but if he caught any of them out by themselves, he'd find a way to terrorize their existence if only for a moment or two.

One summer Grandma Gates hired Leo to paint the outside of her house and she asked Chip to help him. Chip never let his guard down around Leo, knowing his penchant for preying on those smaller than himself, but for a whole week Leo treated Chip as an equal co-worker. He joked with Chip, shared bits of lunch from his dinner pail, and never once took advantage of his physical stature, but it wasn't two days later that Lewis Keener ran Leo out of the station for threatening to take Chip's pants off and throw them in creek.

Leo worked in the mines at Red Dog and from time to time, did odd jobs for folks around Sugar Tree. He lived at home and that luxury enabled him to buy and maintain his '56 Ford Crown Victoria. When he wasn't working, he was drinking, carousing, and chasing women. He chased women but didn't seem to catch any and Chip figured that was the main reason Leo was so mean and nasty. He was worse when he was drinking or when he had his two flunkies with him; Buddy Young and Nobe Legg. As fate would have it, on this particular night not only was Leo already one fourth of his way into a case of beer when he stopped there in the middle of the road, but Buddy and Nobe both piled out of the other side of the car.

When Leo hit the road, the kids scattered hither and yon like leaves before a hurricane, their screams of terror cutting through the silent, spring night. Leo stood up and yelled with an ominous note to his voice, "Well, now kiddies. Guess what? Uncle Leo is here to kick your little skinny asses right up between your shoulder blades!"

Chip's first thought was that it was every kid for himself and he broke into a run heading away from Leo and towards Painter's Fork. As he ran he could hear kids tearing through the underbrush and the woods as they climbed the hill behind the Company Store. Off to his left were the sounds of kids splashing through the creek

302

on the dead run. He didn't know where Maynard or Benji were and didn't care at that moment.

He slowed down when he neared the top of the creek bank and then slid down stopping short of the creek. He hunched down to remain in the shadows as much as possible and waddled his way down along the creek bank. At the junction of Painter's Fork and Sugar Tree Run he had to climb over the lower end of the three tubes that carried Sugar Tree Run under Rt.11 and continued on down stream.

When he reached the cinder block incinerator that sat on the creek bank above him, he knew he was directly across from the Esso station. Lewis and Bucky had closed up the station about thirty minutes earlier, right after the kids had quit playing kick the can. One solitary light bulb above the front door gave off a dim glow.

Chip sneaked up to the incinerator and peered over the edge. He searched the area over at the Company Store and noticed that Leo had moved the Ford out of the road and had parked it, with park lights on, in the Company Store parking lot.

The incinerator was the perfect hiding place. They would never look in there and from that vantage point he could keep a watchful eye on all the goings on. This is great, he thought. This is what the hubcap trick is all about. A person could play the hubcap trick for ten years and never experience this. A challenge like this might never, ever come along again. This is what hubcap players dream of. Chip was so excited he was trembling.

He slipped around to the upper side of the incinerator where the side wasn't as high and flung one leg over, then drew the other leg over, and squatted down inside the incinerator. Immediately Chip's imposition into the incinerator stirred up the smoldering embers from the trash Bucky and Lewis had dumped there and set afire when they closed the station. Chip tried to brush away the smoke rising into his face with a wave of his hand but it wasn't working very well.

He raised up to get some fresh air and to see what Leo and the boys were up to. He could see Leo leaning on the front fender of the car but he couldn't see Nobe or Buddy. Suddenly he heard a commotion coming from the upper side of the parking lot. It was

303

too dark in the shadows there to see anything but Chip could hear the shuffling sound of feet in the gravel. It was obvious there was a struggle going on. "Come on Leo," Chip heard Nobe yell. "Come on man, I got one of the little bastards."

Chip heard some more wrangling going on then he heard the slapping of leather on the hardroad as a potential victim broke free and high tailed it out of harm's way.

"Buddy, you stupid jackass," Leo said, shaking his head as he moved in to help. "Can't even hold on to one of them little punks for ten seconds."

"Well, the little prick kicked me in the shins and bit me," whined Buddy.

A movement in the dim glow of Jobe Frame's window clock caught Chip's attention. It was Nobe and he was walking down the road towards the station and the incinerator. Chip tried to decide what to do. Had he been spotted? Should he make a run for it and give himself away? Nobe was coming closer. Chip could easily outrun Nobe but could he get out of the incinerator before Nobe could grab him? Chip scrunched back down in the smoking trash and waited.

Chip could hear Nobe take a few steps and then stop. There would be a moment of silence like Nobe was checking everything out, then he would move on a few more steps. Not only was the acrid smoke from smoldering cardboard and plastic beginning to burn Chip's eyes and nose, the soles of his tennis shoes were starting to heat up considerably. Still Nobe came closer.

It was then that Chip heard Benji's unmistakable cackle of laughter coming from across the road in the alley between Keener's Store and the station. Chip couldn't see what was going on but he could hear. It sounded like Benji had deliberately stayed hidden somewhere in the shadows of the station until Nobe was almost upon him, then he jumped out in front of Nobe and taunted him into chasing after him. From the sound of things, Benji must have led Nobe around behind the station and then disappeared again into the shadows.

"Hey, guys," yelled Nobe, "Come on, I think I got one of 'em cornered." Buddy broke into a gallop down the road to help Nobe.

304

Leo remained by the car where he could patrol both roads past the Company Store.

Chip didn't care if Leo or any of his boys saw him or not, he couldn't stand the heat and stink in the incinerator any longer so he climbed back out and eased back down to the creek. Nobe and Buddy were concentrating on finding Benji and had their backs turned to Chip. Leo was too far away and too high on beer to see Chip. Chip was heartened to know that Benji had decided to hang around and apparently was enjoying avoiding capture as much as Chip. He'd bet anything that Maynard was still lurking about somewhere close too.

Chip retraced his earlier path back to the juncture of Painter's Creek and Sugar Tree Run only this time he turned right, and headed up Sugar Tree Run. He entered the middle of the three corrugated steel tubes that fed Sugar Tree Run under the road. He picked the middle one because there wasn't as much water running through it as the other two. He knew his way around these tubes because he and Benji had spent many a summer day playing in and around them. The tubes were four feet in diameter. By placing his feet on either side of the tube just above the level of the water and ducking down to fit inside the tube, he could shuffle his way along the length of the tube and stay out of the water. When he got to the upper side of the tube he swung around to the outside tube and climbed over it to the creek bank. He was now directly across the road in front of the Company Store. He carefully parted some sage brush at the top of the creek bank and peered over to the parking lot. Leo was still there leaning on his car, a cigarette in one hand and a bottle of Stroh's beer in the other.

Leo and Nobe were engaged in a very animated argument. Even though Chip was only thirty or forty feet away, the noise of the creek kept him from hearing all but the loudest words. "I ain't...........if he don't.............stupid..........No! Not now...........I said..........what the.............all night."

Chip watched as Leo suddenly raised up and made a throwing motion in his direction. He heard a beer bottle whistle over his head and smash to pieces on a rock in the creek. Although it was too late, Chip instinctively ducked down behind the creek bank. Chip figured Leo had spotted him for sure but when he and Nobe just kept on talking, Chip raised back up just a hair to look across the road. Leo ducked inside the Ford, plucked another Stroh's from his cache, and popped the cap off. Relieved that Leo hadn't seen him, Chip looked around for Buddy but never did see him. He finally gave up and slipped back down near the water's edge.

He worked his way up stream under the protection of the creek bank. He reached the footbridge that ran from Wyatt Keener's mailbox, over Sugar Tree Run, and into Wyatt's front yard. He climbed up the creek bank and walked boldly, if not softly, across the bridge. He didn't care if Leo or his boys saw him this time either. He knew he could easily outrun any of them.

Chip started up the walk that led to the front porch of Wyatt's house when he thought he heard someone coming around the right hand side of the house, so he ducked behind a Lilac bush at the edge of the walk and waited. Sure enough, in a moment Buddy came skulking around the corner of the house. He was moving very slowly and searching very carefully for orphaned hubcap participants. Chip didn't know how he heard Buddy coming, but he was thankful he had. He remained motionless for the few minutes it took Buddy to make his way around to the front of the house, move down the walk, and cross over the footbridge to rejoin Leo and Nobe at the Company Store. Buddy passed within two feet of Chip but never suspected his presence.

Once Buddy was across the bridge, Chip broke cover and headed around the left hand side of Wyatt's house. His plan was to check out the cellar behind Wyatt's to see if Benji was hiding back there. When he ran by the corner of the porch, he heard a hissing noise that made him stop in his tracks. "Pssssst. Chip.", a voice whispered. Chip looked all around but he couldn't see anyone. "Chip. We're under here." A head popped out from under Wyatt's front porch. It was Benji. "Come on man, "he said, "hurry up and get in here." The head disappeared.

Chip stooped down and peered under the porch but he couldn't see anything, it was too dark. ":Come on. Come on," Benji urged him. Chip dropped down on all fours and crawled under the porch.

Wyatt's front porch was at least thirty feet wide and ten feet deep. It had no underpinning around it so it was open on three sides. As dark as it was under the porch, Chip could still see Benji's form against the lighter backdrop of the yard outside. The porch was less than three feet high so the boys had to crawl around on the ground. Benji led Chip over to the side of the porch next to the house and there they could sit on the ground with their backs leaning against the inside wall of the house. There still wasn't much headroom under there so they had to sit with their heads tilted a little to the side. It was an uncomfortable position to stay in for very long so before long, they were slouching down far enough so they could hold their heads up straight. The ground was dry but dusty under the porch and they settled in quickly.

"My God you stink," whispered Maynard, "you smell like you been in the trash dump or somethin'". Chip didn't even know Maynard was under there with them. He was on the other side of Benji and had been obscured by Benji and secluded in the dark.

"It's a long story," Chip whispered.

"Well, here. Get yuh a rub of snuff," offered Maynard as he passed the can of Copenhagen to Benji who in turn passed it to Chip. Chip took the can and felt for the lid in the dark. He opened it very carefully and the unique, twangy aroma of the snuff seeped into his nostrils. Chip didn't particularly like to rub snuff. To him it was more like having a toothache, but he took a little pinch and inserted it between his lower lip and gum. He passed the can back to Maynard via Benji.

"Hold it," cautioned Benji, "someone's comin'". They couldn't see out much beyond the confines of the porch but they heard the clatter of leather soles on the wooden footbridge. There was more than one person but they couldn't tell if there was two or three. Looking out from under the porch, they could only see a person from the knees down and that's about all they saw for the next hour; a pair of legs running here, a pair of legs running there. There was no talking or yelling, just pairs of legs swishing by.

"Must be old Nobe," whispered Benji. "Look. He don't know whether to fart or ride a bicycle."

A pair of legs would sometimes meet and shuffle around beside the porch for a minute or two before moving on. One time, one of the prowlers stopped and hunkered down and peered in under the porch. The boys held their breath. It must have been too dark to see anything because the dark ball uncoiled itself into a pair of legs again and walked off.

The boys were starting to get stiff and cramped under the porch and it was obvious that Leo and the boys were not going to go home until they were ready. As long as they still had some beer left, they'd keep on searching.

Benji finally crawled out from under the porch and went to scout around. Chip and Maynard waited where they were. Benji came back shortly to report that all three of their pursuers were over at the car and this was their best chance to slip away.

Maynard crawled out and then Chip. It took Chip a minute or two just to be able to stand up. His legs were going to sleep and his back had a crick in it. If Leo and the boys discovered them now, they'd just have to give up. Chip could barely walk let alone run.

They did manage to walk off the cramps and kinks as they made their way around behind Wyatt's house. The house was dark inside. The boys didn't know if it was very late now or if Wyatt went to bed early. That was why Buddy and Nobe didn't make much noise when they were searching around the house. Probably didn't want to wake up Wyatt and incur a tongue lashing from him.

Benji wanted to stay and aggravate Leo and his cohorts some more but Maynard still had to walk home and even though Chip was staying all night with Benji, he still stunk and would have to take a shower before he went to bed. Besides, if Leo and the boys hung around there until the evening shift from Red Dog came by and any of those guys stopped, they could be there all night. So they decided with some reluctance, to call it a night.

They slipped around behind Wyatt's and climbed the hillside. They made their way along the edge of the woods past the station before coming down off the bank to the hardroad. They parted there; Maynard hotfooting it around the road towards home while Benji and Chip crossed Sugar Tree Run and cut in behind Jobe's store. They paused there long enough to peek around the corner of the store to see if they could catch a glimpse of Leo and the boys over at the Company Store. Yeah. They were still there alright. Leo was still leaning against the front fender of the Ford upending another bottle of Stroh's. The driver's side door was open and Buddy's feet were sticking out. They guessed he was either tired out or passed out and was taking a nap. Nobe was standing at the top of the creek bank across the road, staring out into the darkness at something. The two boys moved on around the hillside to Benji's.

It was 11:30 when they slipped in the house quietly so's not to wake the elder Lewises. Benji went right to bed. The school bus picked them up the next morning at 6:45. As the bus passed by the Company Store they both craned their necks to see if there were any lingering signs of Leo, Buddy, or Nobe. The parking lot was empty.

The second infamous hubcap trick began inauspiciously on a lazy, summer evening on the front porch of Benji's house. The Jive Five had somehow just congregated there that evening with nothing much on their minds. There were no neighborhood parties going on anywhere and since it was a week day, none of the guys had dates that night. They were just lounging around on the porch when Maynard made an off hand remark. "You know," he said, "we haven't played the hubcap trick since last spring. Tonight would be a great time to do it and we could go over to the Company Store and play it"

Benji was quick to answer, "Naw. I know something better. Let's go over and climb up on the roof of the Company Store."

"What would we want to do that for?" asked Chip.

"So you won't follow us up there, yuh big chicken!" Benji teased.

"There's no way," Link piped up from his reclining lawn chair. "You can't get up there. It must be fifty feet off the ground."

"Yeah. Sure. You're always right," Benji retorted, "but the radio really picks up good, too."

"So your sayin' you been up there before?" Maynard asked.

"Not more than four or five times. Whatda say?"

Maynard got up out of the porch swing, "What if we played the hubcap trick from up on top of the Company Store? It's never been done before. No one would ever think to look up there for us."

Interest began to pick up a little. "I think there's an old hubcap out in the woodshed that we've used before," Benji remarked. "Link, why don't you go out there and take a look around for it."

Link was comfortable where he was. He didn't want to leave his tranquil position just to go shifting through a dusty old woodshed for a hubcap. But after a few minutes, he got up and sauntered off across the yard to the woodshed.

While Link was clanking around in the woodshed, Benji went inside and got his Westinghouse transistor radio. It was as big as most table radios but it had a solid plastic handle across the top of the case for ease in carrying. Benji checked the four regular flashlight batteries in the back to make sure they had a good charge in them. He came back out on the porch about the same time Link came back with the hubcap. "Is this it?" he held it up.

"No, that's not it. I never saw that one before. Don't even know where it came from but looks good enough for me. Whatda think?"

Link handed it to Maynard and Chip and they looked it over. It was fifteen inches in diameter and made of heavy metal, chromed over. There was a hole in the middle of the hubcap where the center piece was missing. Maynard turned it over in his hands examining it like a professional dealer in precious gems. "Looks like it's off a Hudson", he said. "It'll work just fine."

About 8:00 that evening the four headed over to the Company Store with radio and hubcap in hand. No one had thought this through very much. If they were hid on the Company Store roof and there was no one standing around by the road, how could anyone yell that they had a hubcap and how could anyone run off with it? Apparently, these questions didn't enter in to the evening's plans.

Benji led them around to the front steps of the store. They hung out there for a little while so as not raise any suspicion, after all, they hung out there from time to time anyway so that was not unusual.

One by one they drifted around to the alley at the rear of the store. The alley was between the store's loading dock and a small storage building. The alley dead ended into the side of the hill. The store's delivery truck was parked in the alley behind the store. It was a '47 Chevy, ton-and-a half truck with short, solid sideboards and a canvas top stretched over the bows of the bed.

Benji handed the radio to Chip. "Pay close attention," he said, "I don't wanna have to do this more than once". He climbed up on the running board of the truck, stepped over on to the front fender, and then up on to the hood. From the hood he pulled himself up on to the roof of the cab. Then it was just a little stretch from the roof of the cab over to the gentle, sloped roof covering the loading dock. He beckoned the rest to follow. Link leaned the hubcap against the front tire of the delivery truck and started climbing up the same route with Maynard right behind. Chip stayed behind on the ground holding the radio.

The roof of the loading dock ran the entire width of the rear of the store and was attached to the main building between the first and second floors. Horizontal metal bars had been attached to the second floor windows to discourage burglars. Benji used the bars as ladder rungs to climb up far enough onto the second story, to sprawl over the edge of the roof, and wiggle his way on to the very top of the store.

The roof on top of the store was gabled. The outside next to Painter Fork sloped down to an edge that was probably close to what Link had said; fifty feet off the ground. At one time the other side of the roof sloped to a drop-off of the same height on the upper side but sometime later the Company had added a one story wing to that upper side, so now the roof sloped down to within four feet of a flat roof that covered the newer addition. That's where Benji headed. He slid down the roof and gingerly dropped down on to the flat roof section.

The flat roof part was spacious. There were two brick chimneys that poked up through the roof and a three and a half foot wall that ran along the front part of the roof. It made that part of the store look taller than it really was. It was also a good place to duck down behind, to keep out of sight. That's where the boys set up shop for the evening.

Chip climbed up on the roof of the delivery truck and handed the radio to Maynard. "I think I'll just stay down here," he said.

"Well, go get the hubcap for us while you're stayin' down there," Maynard said.

While Chip was climbing down off the truck to get the hubcap, Link was climbing up the window bars to the second story. Maynard reached the radio up to him and Link eased himself down to where Benji was standing on the flat roof and passed the radio to

311

him. Chip got the hubcap and climbed back up on the truck roof and gave it Maynard. The hubcap made its way to Benji by the same route as the radio. Maynard climbed up to join Link on the top of the roof. They both stood up. "Man, O man," Maynard yelled back down to Chip, "You can see all over Sugar Tree from up here. This is great." They lingered awhile at the very top of the Company Store taking in a vista never before experienced.

This is good, thought Chip. We've spent the whole evening trying not to be noticed. Now it stands to reason that if those two idiots can see all over Sugar Tree, Sugar Tree can certainly see all over them and not only that, yelling through a bull horn probably wouldn't carry all over Sugar Tree as well as their voices do from up there this evening.

Chip had to yell up at the two to get their attention and then he put his finger to his lips in the universal sign to hush up. Maynard immediately understood the gesture and knelt down on the roof, pulling Link down beside him. The two then waddled their way silently over to the edge of the top roof and dropped down to where Benji was.

From where he was in the rear alley, Chip could no longer see or hear the other three. He wanted to stay out of sight so he walked up the alley to the rear corner of the store. The one story addition that the boys were on extended right up against the hillside forming a V shaped chasm between the store and the hillside. At the bottom of the V the store was right up against the hillside but at the roof of the store, there was about a twelve foot gap over to the hillside.

Chip slipped his way through the V, along the upper side of the store until he came to the front corner. He stuck his head around the corner of the store and surveyed the front parking lot and the rest of the area in front of the store. It was empty.

He stepped around to the front of the store and began walking backwards away from it towards the road until he could see his three compadres on the roof. They were fooling around with the radio and didn't see him. Chip finally got their attention by calling out Link's name a little louder each time until one of them turned around and noticed him standing in the parking lot. Link motioned for him to come over closer to the store where they could talk without having to yell at each other and where Chip would be less conspicuous.

Conversation between the ground and roof was easier except that Chip had to look straight up towards the roof and since the sun was low in the sky, all he could see were three round, faceless heads peering over the edge of the little wall. Every once in a while the crackling, tinny sounds of Benji's radio would drift down to Chip.

"Listen, Chip,", said Link, "this will work out great. We can see when a car is coming from up here better than you can. You just hide around beside the store and when the car is right in front of the store, we'll throw the hubcap. You yell to the guy that you got his hubcap. He'll go crazy trying to figure out what's goin' on and where everybody is. We'll tell you when we're ready. After it's over, you get the hubcap and bring it around back and reach it up to us or maybe you can just throw it up to us. Now trust me boys. This'll work!" Chip thought Link seemed awfully excited for a person who didn't think much of this idea in the beginning.

Just then Benji broke in. "Hey. Hey. A car's comin'," he yelled. "Let's do it." The three heads ducked down behind the wall and Chip dashed for the corner of the store. He waited in the shadows listening for the car and the sound of the hubcap being thrown. He heard the car coming but it never did appear and then the sound of it faded away too.Chip thought it might have stopped in front of the store so he sneaked a quick look around the corner. There was nothing there. "Hey," he yelled up to the roof, "what's goin' on?"

A head appeared over the wall. "Aw, the guy turned off and went up Painter's Fork." It was Maynard.

Chip ambled around in the parking lot waiting for the next car to come. Up on the roof, one was keeping watch for cars while the other two were amusing themselves playing with the radio. Daylight was beginning to fade. Chip noticed that the darker it got, the better the radio seemed to play.

"Car! Car! Car!" the lookout yelled down. Chip slipped back around the corner of the store and waited. He poked his head around the corner to watch the action out of one eye. The light was dim enough now so that the only chance he could be seen from a vehicle passing by would be if the driver was looking for someone hidden beside the store. A pickup was coming along Rt.11 from the direction of the station. The driver had turned on the truck's park lights. When he got to the intersection, he made the right hand turn and started up the Sugar Tree Straight. Whoever had the hubcap up on the roof let her fly just at the right moment, but the toss was too high and too strong and the hubcap sailed beautifully, three or four feet right over the top of the pickup truck, and landed in Wyatt Keener's garden clear on the other side of Sugar Tree Run. The truck went on up the straight without even a clue to what had happened. Chip was chuckling to himself. Up on the roof, the two nonparticipants in the fiasco were laughing so hard Chip could easily hear them. Benji was the one who tossed the hubcap. He was yelling at the other two. "Shut up, yuh snots. I showed you how to get up here. It was not my idea to play this stupid trick."

Link stopped laughing long enough to try to smooth Benji's ruffled feathers. He put his arms around Benji. "It's ok, ole buddy. Don't cry. We'll take care of it. It'll be alright. I'll do the honors the next time. You just watch closely. I don't want to have to show you this twice."

When Maynard got his breath back from laughing so hard, he yelled down to Chip. "Hey, go on over to Wyatt's and get that hubcap."

The little humor Chip saw in this trick diminished quickly as he made his way over to Wyatt's garden. He had to search around for the hubcap but finally found it in the young corn plants. Its flight and subsequent crash had caused no apparent damage to any of the crops. He half expected to see Wyatt or Sarah come out on the porch and inquire as to why he was pilfering around in their garden, but they never did. He noticed that while he was searching for the hubcap, he could clearly hear the radio playing from across the way.

After Chip got back to the store, it took three tosses to get the hubcap back on the roof. It was just in time too, because another car was coming. It was coming down Painter's Fork Road. They had to wait to see which way it would turn at the intersection. It stopped and made the left hand turn up the Sugar Tree Straight. This time Maynard gave the hubcap a fling off the roof. He tried to give it a lower trajectory but aimed it too low. The hubcap shot

314

down at a steep angle, hit in the gravel parking lot, skipped out toward the hardroad, and made a glancing blow off the rear bumper of the passing car. The hubcap then rolled off behind the car and finally settled into the grassy berm on the other side of the road.

The driver jammed on his brakes and stopped. Chip wasn't about to reveal his presence. The guys on the roof settled down behind the wall. "Junior Dodrill, you little hellion. I know it's you," the driver yelled. "Wait till I tell your dad. He'll beat the livin' crap outa you. You better pray I don't catch you, you little sorry ass bastard." There was no response, only a radio playing somewhere off in the distance. He never did get out of his car, and after another minute or so, gunned the engine, and ripped on up the straight.

Chip waited in the shadows until he was sure the car had left Sugar Tree before he went out in search of the hubcap. He didn't have very far to go this time to get the hubcap and it only took one toss to get it back on the roof. He could hear Benji chastening Maynard for his errant throw. "Man, you couldn't hit a bull in the ass with a bass fiddle."

"Or the side of a barn with a handful of peas," Link added.

It was getting dusky dark now and the radio was blaring louder than ever from the roof of the store. In fact, Benji had the radio turned up so loud that the sound was actually distorted. Almost twenty minutes passed before the next car came by. It too came from the station and turned up the straight.

Link did the honors this time. He tried to avoid hitting the car like Maynard did and even though his toss skipped the hubcap right off the parking lot and along the berm of the hardroad, it was so late and so far behind the car that the driver never even heard it. Chip waited until the car was out of sight up the straight before he went out to get the hubcap. He had already made up his mind that this was the last hubcap he was going to retrieve tonight.

When Chip got to the edge of the hardroad where the hubcap lay, he glanced up the straight to make sure there were no cars coming. Not more than ninety feet away he spied a car in the middle of the road with its park lights on. As he reached down to pick up the hubcap, he subtly glanced back under his arm at the car. It was coasting along very slowly down the straight with the

315

engine off. That's when he recognized the car as belonging to constable Argil "Chester" Woods.

Chip retrieved the hubcap as casually as he could, not wanting to rouse suspicion by making any quick or hasty movements. He walked slowly back toward his hideout between the store and the hillside, fighting the urge to break into a dashing getaway.

His buddies on the roof hadn't spotted Chester yet because he hadn't drifted far enough down the straight to come into their view and even if he had, they probably were too busy horsing around to be paying any attention. Chip knew he had to warn them before they were caught dead on the roof.

As soon as he reached the front corner of the store he threw down the hubcap and made a panic retreat down the side of the store to the rear alley; all the while the list of their criminal acts were whirling around in his head; trespassing, attempted breaking and entering (they might be able to beat that rap, but what reason could they plead for being on the roof of the store?), destruction of property, disturbing the peace, and creating a traffic hazard. The trespassing alone was big time criminal behavior. Chip wondered how Chester had come to slip up on them? Had the irate driver turned them in? Had Wyatt turned them in? Had someone seen them on the roof and called the law? Whoever it was, it didn't matter now. There was only one motive; escape the clutches of the law.

Once Chip got to the alley, he cut around the front-end of the delivery truck, swung up on the running board, and climbed up on to the roof of the cab by way of the front fender and hood. He cupped his hands around his mouth and yelled in his loudest whisper trying to get someone up on the roof to look his way. He had to get their attention soon or it would be too dark for them to even see him. He tried the whispered yell again but still no head appeared at the roof's edge.

He thought he might as well try a one word loud yell directed at the boys. Maybe they would be the only ones to hear it. "HEY", he yelled as loud as he could. He waited a moment and heard the radio die down. It became very quiet. In another moment a head peeked over the edge of the roof. Chip waved his arms in a crisscrossing motion to get the head's attention. It worked because the head stretched far out over the edge of the roof to get an even better look. Chip knew it was too dark for whoever it was to see him mouth any words, so he continued to make gestures. He pointed with both hands in a big arc towards the front of the store and then pulled at the left side of his shirt symbolizing the constable's badge.

Chip figured the guy on the roof was Benji because as soon as Chip made those gestures, the figure on the roof held up both hands indicating he understood, then the figure made some gestures of his own. He first pointed to himself and then pointed towards the hillside beside the store. Then he made some jumping motions with his hands then the body slowly sank out of sight, down below the edge of the roof, all the while waving bye-bye to Chip. Chip took it to mean that they were going to jump off the roof over to the hillside.

Chip slid quietly down to the running board of the truck and carefully checked the entrance to the alley for any sign of Argil before hitting the ground. He waited in silence a moment and then stepped down to the ground.

He hurried over to the hillside at the alley's dead end and scrambled up the twenty foot embankment to the edge of the woods. He turned and looked back down the alley. Still no Argil. He more or less felt his way through the trees and brush along the top of the bank until he came to a little mossy clearing opposite the roof of the store. From that little clearing he could see the entire flat part of the roof where Benji, Maynard, and Link were crouched down behind the little, front wall facade. No one knew where Argil was but if they couldn't see him....he couldn't see them. Then just like that, a flashlight beam splashed its spot against the upper story of the store building and began working its way around the roof, poking into every nook and cranny.

The culprits on the roof waited until the spotlight shifted around towards the opposite side of the store before duck-walking their way behind the facade at the front of the store's roof over to the side where there was no wall.

The leap from the roof to the top of the embankment was across a twelve foot wide chasm. The roof was a little higher than the little clearing so at least they would be jumping at a down angle. Benji motioned for Chip to back out of the way but just as he

317

started to make his running start, Argil's flashlight beam began bouncing around in the back alley. Chip motioned for Benji to hold up and get back out of sight, then he stepped quietly back out of the clearing and in behind a neighboring poplar tree. There was no reason for Argil to be shining his light up in the woods and Chip didn't want to give him one.

From his vantage point, Chip watched Argil work his way silently down the alley and around the delivery truck. He would stop every few feet and train the flashlight on a certain spot. He shined it in every store window, under the truck, in the back of the truck, and in the cab. He searched the loading dock and even climbed up on the running board of the truck to better train his light beam across the roof of the store.

Argil knew those boys were still there somewhere on the grounds of the Company Store and he was determined to catch them. He switched the flashlight off and faded into the dark shadows of the alley. Chip couldn't see him anymore. Nobody moved for two or three minutes and then finally Argil switched the flashlight back on. He was still standing where Chip had last seen him. He turned and walked back out of the alley onto Painters Fork Rpad and disappeared around the corner of the store.

Chip knew it was now or never. He stepped back into the clearing and motioned for Benji to come over. "Come on," he whispered as loud as he dared, "Chester's goin' around to the front again."

Benji had not been lying about being up on the roof of the Company Store before, that much was obvious from the expert way he made the jump. Cradling his radio close to his chest with both hands, he made three running steps from a crouching position and sailed off the edge of the roof. He landed gracefully, right beside Chip and never wavered a bit, the radio still clasped in his arms. If roof jumping had been an Olympic event, Benji would have gotten a "10" for the way he stuck his landing. Now he and Chip urged Maynard and Link to jump.

"I'll go," said Maynard, waddling his way around Link. He didn't even wait to see if Link would argue or not. Maynard wasn't taking any chances. He stood up and ran as hard, and as quiet as he could to the edge of the roof. He planted his right foot at the edge of the roof and launched himself out into the dark. Adrenaline, fear, and the unfamiliar are factors that sometimes are not compensated for in a hasty situation, and thus was such in Maynard's case. The jump over to the hillside was much easier than Maynard had anticipated, but never having made that jump before, he wanted to be sure he didn't come up short.

Maynard cleared the gap, cleared the edge of the bank by four feet, and smacked right into Chip, hitting him chest high with his knees. The collision drove Chip backwards to the ground with Maynard landing on top of him. Chip saw Maynard coming but didn't realize where he was heading until it was too late to get out of the way. He did manage to throw his arms up to protect his face just before Maynard landed on him. Benji was rolling around on the ground laughing, while at the same time trying to keep Argil from hearing him.

Fortunately, neither of the crash victims were hurt or injured seriously. Chip only had the breath knocked out of him momentarily, and Maynard's landing was softened by landing on Chip. As soon as Benji's hysterics had subsided, the three beckoned Link to join them.

Link shook his head in the negative and waved the boys off. His reluctance to jump surprised his comrades. It didn't seem to come from the fear of being caught nor the fear of jumping itself. Link's cool and calm manner belied those factors.

"Come on you dip head," Maynard urged, still whispering. "Chester's gonna be back here in a minute. What's the matter with you anyhow?"

"I'm not jumping over into that muck and dirt and brush with my brand new Bass Weejin's on!" Link whispered back. He held one foot up to show off his new loafers. "I just got these babies and I'm not gonna take a chance on tearin' 'em up by jumpin' off this roof or clompin' around in the woods in the dark. You guys get on outa here. I'll figure a way out. Chester ain't smart enough or quick enough to catch me!"

"That's the stupidest thing I ever heard of," remarked Benji. "And you're the stupidest person who ever said it! Well, fine. We ain't got time to baby you. It's every man for himself, and you, big boy, are on your own!" With that, Benji turned and started back into the woods. Maynard and Chip followed.

They worked their way around the hillside up along the Sugar Tree Straight, away from the store. When they got far enough away from the store so that they figured Chester couldn't see or hear them, they slid down the hillside and crossed the hardroad. They discussed the possibility of sneaking down along the Sugar Tree Run creek bank past the store and through the three metal culverts, but decided there was too great a chance that Chester might discover them. Instead, they gave the store and Chester a wide berth by crossing the creek and sneaking around behind Wyatt Keener's place.

They quietly slipped down to the station, crossed the road, crossed the creek, and carefully worked their way around behind Jobe Frame's. From there, they skulked in and out of the shadows of Jobe's front yard, being mindful to keep out of the light of the store's neon light, until they gathered behind some rhododendron bushes at the edge of Painter's Fork. They were now directly across the creek and road on the lower side of the Company Store. From this vantage point they could see the front area of the store, the lower side of the store along Painter's Fork Road, and the entrance to the back alley where the delivery truck was parked. It was too dark in the alley to see anything.

Chester must have been convinced that the perpetrators were still present because he came back around the front corner of the store and limped along the lower side to the rear alley, all the while keeping the beam of his flashlight whipping hither and yon in hopes of catching one of them trying to make his escape.

The neon glow from Jobe's store window clock, plus the little bit of light emanating from the overhanging Kelvinator sign on the Company Store, provided enough illumination for Benji, Maynard, and Chip to enjoy the cat and mouse game between Link and Chester from their front row seat behind the rhododendron bushes.

Chester had just made his third trip back around to the front of the store, when the boys across the creek spied Billy Reed walking down Painter's Fork Road. Evidently Billy was heading home after a date with his girlfriend, Charlotte. They knew it was Billy even before he came into the light of the neon clock, by the glow of the cigarette sticking out of his mouth and the click of his shoe taps on the hardroad.

When Billy walked past the corner of the Company Store and into Chester's view, Chester whipped his flashlight around, right into Billy's face. "Well, good evening Constable Woods," greeted Billy. Chester returned a grumbled greeting but didn't move from his spot and Billy just kept on clicking down the road.

From his still hidden sanctuary on the roof, Link witnessed the complete exchange between Chester and Billy and since nothing came of it, Link began to conjure up his full proof escape plan.

Maynard, Benji, and Chip had witnessed the same uneventful meeting but thought nothing of it.

When Billy went clicking his way on back home, Chester went back to probing the heights of the store front with his flashlight. Benji's eye caught Link emerging from the shadows of the back alley. Link had made sure Chester was in the front area of the store and had climbed down from the roof the same way he'd climbed up.

Benji nudged Chip and nodded in Link's direction. Chip was surprised to see Link on the ground. Maynard was watching Chester but turned his attention to Link when Chip began jerking on his shirt sleeve.

Link must have also been able to watch his buddies creep in and out of the light and shadows as they made their way around to their present position because as soon as he stepped out into the road, he waved to them across the creek.

"Ok, baby," whispered Benji, "you're outa there." He stood up, still remaining mostly in the shadows, and motioned for Link to walk back up Painter's Fork Road away from Chester and the Company Store. But Link didn't do that. Instead, he held up his hands in such a way as to tell the boys he had his own plan and was rejecting theirs.

"What's he doin'?" asked Maynard, "Why is he just standing there?" Maynard stood up and gestured in the same direction Benji had.

Link waved them off again. He brushed off his clothes and straightened his shirt and began walking nonchalantly down Painter's

Fork Road toward the intersection. At just about the same time, Chester decided to make another search at the rear of the store and he and Link met face to face at the corner of the store. Chester shined the flashlight beam right into Link's face.

"Good evening Constable Woods. You gave me a quite start there for a minute," greeted Link.

Chester didn't exchange pleasantries with Link. Instead he stepped closer to Link, put his free hand on Link's shoulder, and keeping the flashlight trained in his face, began to talk to Link. The boys couldn't hear what Chester was saying because the two were so close together but whatever it was, he looked earnest in saying it. Link wasn't talking. He wasn't moving either. He just stood there with Chester's hand on his shoulder and nodded once in awhile.

After a few minutes, Chester and Link moved off towards the constable's car. Link got in the front the seat and Chester slid in under the wheel. He started the car, switched on the headlights, backed out into the road, pulled down to the intersection, and turned up Painter's Fork Road.

The boys behind the rhododendron bushes had to duck down out of sight as the headlights from Chester's car swung directly across them when he turned the corner at the intersection.

When the car passed out of sight, the three stood up. "My Lord. Chester's taking him to jail!" "No. If he was takin' him to jail, he'd go around by Hob," explained Maynard. "He's just going to take him home."

"Maybe not," countered Chip, "He could be going up to Link's first to tell his folks and let him get some clothes and stuff and then he could head on over to Seneca by the Painter Mountain shortcut."

"Surely to the Lord he wouldn't arrest Link for just climbing around on the store roof."

"Hey, the Company takes that stuff seriously and that's what they hired Chester for in the first place."

"Yeah but Link's old man is one of WYGARB's big shots, isn't he? Naw, he might be in a little trouble but they won't take him to jail. Will they?"

Chip tried to calm things down a little. "Let's do this. Let's go up to Benji's and call Link. We'll act like we don't know nothin' and see what we can find out."

"We won't have to act," stated Maynard as they started off, "cause we don't know nothin'".

They made their way hastily down to the bridge at Jobe's, crossed over to Painter's Fork Rd, and began jogging up the road to Benji's house. They were in a hurry to get off of the road. If Chester happened to come back down the road and see three boys walking along the road carrying a transistor radio, he might put three and one together and cart them all off to jail. Only after they reached Benji's front porch could they relax a little.

Benji opened the front door to go in the house but halted in mid stride. "Hey. You don't think Link would squeal on us do you?" he asked.

"Are you kiddin'?" answered Chip. "Link is eatin' this stuff up. You know him. He's probably pretending the Nazis have captured him and taken him to their headquarters where they will interrogate him and try to break him. He'll never squeal."

"Yeah but what if Chester takes him home and delivers him to his parents? Reckon they could make him talk?"

"Nah. I'm tellin' yuh, sometimes Link drifts off into these little fantasies and forgets to come back. He might rat on himself but he'd never betray his comrades."

Across the creek, a car was making its way slowly down Painter's Fork Road. The boys clamored through the door, pushing and shoving and falling over each other to get inside. They slammed the door shut just as Benji's mom came into the front room from somewhere next to the kitchen.

"My stars," she said, "what's all the hubbub about?"

"Nothin' ma," said Benji, "we're just horsin' around."

She watched the boys for a second or two but nothing in their behavior seemed to strike her as unusual. "How about some milk and sandwiches?" she said.

"Yeah ma, that'd be great," Benji answered in a tone that he hoped would move her along out of the front room and back to the kitchen. As soon as she left, Benji parted the curtains in a front window and peered out. "Yeah it's Chester alright". He tried to sound calm and collected but there was a hint of apprehension in his voice.

The other two boys quickly joined Benji at the window and all three tried to see out at the same time. "Turn off the front room lights," Maynard added. "It's easier for us to see out and harder for Chester to see in." Benji slipped over and flipped the ceiling light off.

Chester was moving awfully slowly down the road. The boys held their breath as Chester began slowing even more when he got to the bridge that crossed over to Benji's house.

He slowed, but didn't turn in. Just kept creeping on down the road. The boys pulled back from the window just in case Chester was looking that way. Once he was past Benji's, the boys flocked to the window again to see what he was going to do.

Chester coasted to a dead stop at the intersection and sat there for a minute or two. The boys could see in the back glass of Chester's car and the back light from the headlights clearly showed the silhouette of only one lone figure; the driver.

"He must have taken Link home," Maynard said. "He didn't have time to go all the way to Seneca and back and there's no sign of Link in the car."

"Maybe he's got him handcuffed and stashed down on the floor so nobody will see him."

"Shut up, dufuss. Why would he do that? He'd WANT people to see him if he was taking him to jail; especially us. Hey, look he's movin' again."

Chester turned left at the Company Store and disappeared around the corner. The boys waited another five minutes or so watching out the window but Chester never came back. Shortly, Benji's mom called from the kitchen that the sandwiches were ready.

The boys sat at the kitchen table washing down peanut butter and jelly sandwiches with ice cold milk. "We got to call up to Link's and see if we can find out what's goin' on," Maynard said. "Go call him Benji."

"Not me. Let Chip do it. Link's old man might answer the phone. I don't think he likes me as well as he does Chip. He'd probably talk

324

to Chip before he would me."

"Ok.!. Ok!" agreed Chip. "I'll just play it cool."

The phone was on the wall between the kitchen and dining room. Benji and Maynard watched from the kitchen table as Chip dialed Link's number. It rang twice and Mr. Parks answered.

"Park's residence."

"Mr. Parks, this is Chip Gates. I need to ask Lincoln something. Is he in?" Chip wanted to slap himself. Benji and Maynard wanted to slap him too. Chip pounded the top of his head with his fist. "Stupid. Stupid", he mouthed to the other two.

"Well, Chip," Mr. Parks went on, "You should know if Lincoln is in or not, seeing as how you've been with him all evening."

"Gee, Mr. Parks. I been with Maynard Samples all evening. We....I mean I, just called to ask him a question about a problem I'm having with my bicycle." Chip never was a very good liar.

"Well, I'm sorry but Link can't come to the phone right now and he won't be coming to the phone for about a month, so there would be no reason for you to call him in the meantime. In fact, I don't think he'll be doing much of anything outside of this house for the next month. I trust you can fix your bicycle on your own or with the help of your other two buddies. Goodnight." The phone clicked dead.

"Well?" Maynard and Benji chimed together.

"I don't know," answered Chip."Sounded like Link's been grounded for a month. Sounded like Mr. Parks might have known more than he was tellin' or maybe he was just tryin' to get me to slip up somewhere. Hard to tell. Anyhow, I'm going home. You comin' Maynard?"

"What about Link?" Benji asked.

"We can't do nothin' tonight," Maynard answered, getting up from the table. "Give things a couple of days to die down and we'll get the lowdown from Link then."

The guys let the weekend pass before trying to contact Link. Early Monday afternoon, Benji and Chip rode their bicycles up the road past Link's house. They tried to make it appear to be just an aimless, leisurely bicycle trek through the community, when there really was purpose to their ride. They were hoping that Link would spot them riding by and be able to either invite them in or at the least come out to the road and talk to them over the hedge that separated the front yard and the road. They also chose that particular time because they knew Mr. Parks would be at work in Red Dog. Mrs. Parks, being the typical mother, was more likely than her husband to somewhat relax, if just for a little bit, whatever restrictions had been imposed upon their son. Benji and Chip were counting on at least one, if not both, of these possibilities playing out.

As it turned out, Link was sitting on the front porch reading a Mad magazine and hailed his two buddies as they peddled by. Benji and Chip stopped out at the mailbox at the end of the front walk and Link quickly left the porch and walked out to meet them. "What's happenin' Hollywood?" Link was addressing Benji. He was the one wearing the sunglasses.

"Nothin' on this end," Benji grinned. "What's up with you?"

"Well," Link started but was interrupted by his mom who was standing on the front porch.

"Lincoln, why don't you boys come on in on the porch and talk. You're liable to be hit by a car or something out there. Come on in here and I'll bring out some lemonade."

"Here," Chip laughed, turning his back and holding his arm out behind him, "twist my other arm too!"

The boys moved in under the cool shade of the porch and in a short while Mrs. Parks brought out a glass of lemonade for each boy.

"Now you boys enjoy this," she said, "but I'm afraid you better not stay more than thirty minutes, OK? Wait another day or so and I'll see if I can't soften Ed up enough to let you boys come for longer visits. Maybe he'll lift Lincoln's punishment sooner than he first said." She went back into the house.

Link's tale was much like the escapees had witnessed. Nobody knew why Chester paid Billy no mind when he walked by, but nabbed Link without hesitating. "Chester acquired that skill after years of in-depth law enforcement experience," Chip said. "Besides that, you ninny, you could have walked out of there free as a bird and Chester would never have been the wiser."

"Couldn't do it," Link said. "No challenge, no chicanery.

Couldn't pass it up. Man, I still don't know how he knew it was me on that roof and not Billy."

"Well, you can ask him the next time you see him," Benji said. "Now tell us everything."

Link began to unfold his story in his own masterful and descriptive way but was more succinct than usual due to the thirty minute time limit.

Chester said he knew Link wasn't by himself and if he'd help nab the others that were involved, it would go a lot easier on everybody, especially Link. Link didn't crack and let Chester take him home to confront his parents. Link thought about making a break for it a couple of times and knew he could get away, but Chester already knew who he was and that would only make it tougher when he finally did get home.

Link's mom didn't say much while Chester was there but Mr. Parks did. He praised Chester up and down for the quick and professional way he performed the duty that WYGARB had hired him to do. Told Chester he was glad to know that the constable didn't play favorites and was man enough to bring Lincoln home where his parents would deal with him without involving any outside interests. Told Chester he'd see what he could do about making the constable's position a little more prestigious. Chester gave a complete report to Mr. Parks and then said he'd leave it in Mr. Parks' hands for now because he wanted to check out a couple of other leads. If there was anything else he could do or if Mr. Parks learned any new information from Lincoln, he'd be grateful if Mr. Parks would contact him. Then he left.

Link's dad grilled him for an hour or two but Link stuck to his story. He was by himself on the Company Store roof and had just gone up there because he had never been up there before and thought it was a good time to go. He didn't know anything about harassing passing cars or any of that. Maybe there were some boys somewhere else causing a disturbance and Chester just got his story confused or something.

Link's dad grounded him for one month. He couldn't use the phone. Couldn't go out of the yard except to go to church or if he was with his mom or dad. Whether by design or forgetfulness, Mr. Parks said nothing about having visitors.

Mrs. Parks finally came out and shooed the boys away, but after that initial visit, the boys felt they owed Link for not ratting them out and so they made it a point to visit him everyday he was grounded. They didn't visit on Sunday because they got to visit at church and they didn't visit when Mr. Parks was home. Sometimes all three of them went, sometimes two, and sometimes only one. Though Benji, and Maynard and Chip were free, they made a pact not to do anything or go anywhere together until Link was free to join them.

That was the last time Chip ever remembered playing the hubcap trick.

One warm, lazy, Friday evening in July, just around dusk, Skinny Walker ambled from the Esso station up to the Company Store and sat down on the front steps. He sat his half-finished bottle of Upper 10 down on the steps beside him, reclined back on his elbows, and settled in to watch the world go by. After the world had gone by for fifteen minutes or so, a '59 Mercury cruised passed the station, turned up the Sugar Tree Straight, and when it went by the Company Store, it slowed to a stop right there in the middle of the road. The driver's door opened and a man in his early thirties got out and walked over to Skinny. Skinny, figuring the guy in the Mercury might be lost, stood up, jumped down off the steps, and strolled over to meet him to see if could be of assistance.

The guy met Skinny in the parking lot and without a word, made a big round house right swing that hit Skinny right up side his jaw and sent him sprawling onto the red dog and gravel.

The guy looked down at Skinny and shook his finger at him, "Listen Junior, you little snot, I've had all of the little tricks and smart aleckness from you I'm gonna take, and since your parents don't seem to care what you do, maybe that'll teach you a little lesson you won't soon forget!"

The guy walked back over to the Mercury, got in, and drove away.

Skinny just sat there on the ground, in the gravel probing the side

328

of his head with his fingers to see if anything was broken. He was too stunned to do anything else.

Road games were not confined to the seasonal window from spring through fall. Winter just meant shifting gears to a different kind of road entertainment. Sled riding was taken seriously by the young Sugar Tree teens. Chip thought it was because they never really knew how long the sledding season might last and never knew when a particular sled ride might be the last one of the season.

Looking back, it seemed to Chip that the seasons were more defined then, than they are now. Winter was cold, snowy, and dark. The first significant snow always came before, or right around, Thanksgiving. Snowfalls came quickly and heavily and might last for up to a day. A week or two might pass before the next good snowfall came, but usually the weather would stay cold and the snow would stay on for weeks at a time. The last snows of winter might come in March but even if those snows were heavy, they just wouldn't last very long in the warming spring sun. Sledding opportunites were cherished and treasured and were utilized to the maximum.

The most popular sleds were commercially made steel runners like, Radio Flyers, Champions, and Flexible Flyers. The Gates brothers all had Radio Flyers. Their Aunt Eleanor had a Flexible Flyer that was six feet long. She got the sled when she was a little girl so it was at least thirty years old. Aunt Eleanor didn't sleigh ride anymore but she treasured that sled and forbid anybody to ride it, so when the Gates boys slipped it off of its special peg on the manger wall of the barn, it was always at night. Aunt Eleanor kept an eye on the boys when they went sleigh riding in the daytime to make sure they didn't have her special sled.

Clint's sled was just like everybody elses, but Clint took extra good care of his. Where most guys would lean their sled up against the side of the house or stick it under the porch when done for the day, Clint always took his to the barn and hung it up inside on the wall and he always wiped it down and dried it off before putting it up.

Clint painted his sled every fall. Painted the thing two tone. The wooden bed would be one color and the steel frame would be another.

He used a color scheme he'd seen on some of the more flashy cars around Sugar Tree; red and black, blue and white, black and green, etc. He'd check and tighten every rivet and sand the runners till they were shiny.

Now every good sledder knows to sand the runners down before going out for the first sled run of the season or else on that first runnin' flop start, you are apt to realize your sled won't slide. Instead, you do the sliding, right off the sled and into the snow face first. Not only did Clint painstakingly sand off his runners before the first run of the year, before he put the sled up for the season he always rubbed the runners down with an oily rag to keep them rust free and shiny until next season. Even the tow rope was replaced every year. Clint Gates had the sharpest sled in the country.

There were a number of homemade sleds around Sugar Tree as well. Maynard built a sled out of wood. He used two by fours turned up on their edge as runners. Chip helped him from time to time and claimed partial ownership of it when it was finished. The sled was at least six feet long and must have weighed seventy or eighty pounds. They called it "The Bus" since it was so big and heavy and could carry four or five kids sitting up easily. Maynard did an excellent job of curving up the front ends of the wooden runners and because the runners were so wide, the sled was perfect for coasting down through a field or meadow where the snow was deep. Even though it was heavy, the runners kept it from running very deep in the snow. The Bus was always made the first run on open hillsides to plow and pack down the snow and establish a sledding course that the steel runner sleds could run on.

There were two big drawbacks to the Bus. One of them was that you couldn't steer it. It was so heavy, even if everyone on board leaned the same way, it had absolutely no effect on the direction the sled was traveling. There were no moving parts on the sled either. The Bus was only used where the sled run was on a straight line, like down through a meadow or field.

The second drawback to the Bus was its weight. Even though it coasted over the snow and ice with little effort, dragging it up a hill to the top of a sled run would tax a youngster's strength. It was easier when two kids would run the lead rope around them and pull in tandem but it was still a lot of work and the more runs they made, the heavier it seemed to get.

One of Benji's sleds was a homemade job. One day while he was waiting to get a haircut in Bill's Barber Shop in Hob, Benji ran across an article in some magazine like Popular Science that showed how to build a sled using a piece of plywood and two, foldup aluminum lawn chairs. Benji promised if Bill would let him have the magazine, he'd bring him two or three from home to replace it. Bill said Benji could take the magazine anyway, but if he wanted to bring in some new ones that would be fine.

The plywood was no problem, there were some scraps of it out in the toolshed. He found one that could be cut to specifications. He went down to Jobe Frame's and scrounged around out behind the store in the junk pile for lawn chairs but even with Jobe helping him, they only found one that was all intact. Since it didn't have any webbing in it, Jobe sold it to Benji for $2.00.

Benji went home and rooted around in the toolshed and in the basement looking for another lawn chair; he knew there were some around the house somewhere. He finally found three under the front porch. They were in pretty good shape too, except the webbing was starting to fray on one of the chairs. The three chairs under the porch looked amazingly like the one he bought at Jobe's. Maybe that's where they bought them in the first place. In order for the sled design to work best, it was suggested that the two lawn chairs be of the same size and construction. Benji decided to use the one with the frayed webbing.

It was the week before Thanksgiving when Benji found the article and by the time he'd collected all the necessary hardware, screws, nuts, bolts, hacksaw, drill, etc, it was the week of Thanksgiving before he could actually start work on the sled. He figured his timing was perfect. Sledding season was a little late this year and hadn't started yet and he was hoping to finish the sled by the first snow. And maybe by spring time when the Lewis family got out their summer yard supplies, they will have forgotten how many aluminum folding lawn chairs they really owned.

After school every evening during the week of Thanksgiving, Benji went down to the basement and worked on the sled. Benji's dad was working the evening shift in Red Dog so Benji didn't have to worry about being interrupted or even worse, stopped by his dad. Every evening when he was finished, he put the sled's workings in the far corner of the basement and covered it up with some burlap sacks. His dad either didn't see the sawed up pieces of the lawn chair or didn't recognize them if he did. Or maybe he did both, but if he did, he never mentioned it to Benji or anyone else. Benji's mom came down to the basement a few times to get this and that while Benji was working on the sled. She always seemed interested in what he was doing and asked about his project and she always remarked about how well everything seemed to be going before she left. She didn't recognize the parts of her lawn chair either.

Benji didn't finish his project until after Thanksgiving but the snow didn't come for another two weeks. It was then he brought the sled out for its maiden voyage.

It was an ungainly looking thing. It had four independent runners; one on each side up front and one on each side at the rear. The arms of the two lawn chairs turned upside down became the runners. The plywood bed of the sled on which the rider was situated (it was a one man sled) rested on the four runners and was suspended from four bridgework, pyramid structures that rose about six inches above the bed. The sled was steerable to a small degree by pulling or pushing the little bar that ran perpendicular to the sled body; much like the guider bar on a regular sled.

The first runs were short; very short. Benlji went out in the back yard, laid down on the sled, and used his gloved hands to pull himself along through the snow. He carefully checked the undercarriage, the runners, the supports, all the while gliding through the snow. After everything seemed to be working fine on the flat. He moved up to the gentle slope behind the house and coasted down a few feet, each time going a little further up the slope. The coasting got longer and faster and Benji was pleased to find everything still holding together. By dark that evening he had decided to go find the sledding crowd the next evening and do some serious sled riding.

Still a little apprehensive the next day, Benji tied a rope to the front of the sled and dragged it up to the Sugar Tree School house and joined a crowd of kids sledding off the hill behind the school. The sled's appearance certainly raised some eyebrows. Some scoffed, some laughed, and some were actually enthralled with the sled. The scoffers and laughers were soon quieted after Benji made his first solid run down the hill. Even Benji was surprised at the ease and speed of the sled down the short but steep hill. After that initial evening of sledding, it became the show sled of Sugar Tree. Benji christened it the "Silver Ghost" because of its color and the way it slipped along through the snow. He thought of it as the Rolls Royce of sleds.

Of course the more Benji rode the sled, the more he learned of its characteristic. The Silver Ghost was best suited for light snows of less than five inches. If the snow was deeper, she was just too light to be able to plow through it and trying to steer her was useless. She didn't run well on the hard packed snow and ice of the hardroad either. Benji couldn't do anything with her. It was like she went every direction except where Benji was trying to go. However, with just a little skiff of snow on a hard surface, the Silver Ghost became a joy to ride.

Benji always carried a screw driver and pliers with him when he went sledding. The screws and bolts and nuts that held the Silver Ghost togther had a tendency to work their way loose from time to time and Benji was always tightening something here and something there. It was just good maintenance on his part.

Link's sled was a Champion. It was the second most revered sled in Sugar Tree, after the Silver Ghost. Link's dad had taken the sled over to the mine shop in Red Dog and at each of the four corners of the sled he had welded little coil springs to the frame and then fastened them to the wooden bed. Nobody knew where Mr. Parks had found the springs. Maybe he had them made there at the shop. They were of a heavy gauged, tempered steel about the size of a pencil. The springs themselves were about two and a half inches high and as round as a silver dollar. It was the only sled anyone had ever heard of with coil spring suspension.

Some of the sled runs in Sugar Tree were rougher than a washboard. They could knock the breath out of you or jar your fillings loose but on Link's baby, you just glided right over them like nothin'. The one problem Link had with his sled was when it got to bouncing too much on the springs, he inevitably would lose control of it. It had even been known to bounce him right off into the snow a couple of times.

There were three good places to sleigh ride in Sugar Tree. The Gates brothers always made a sledding course down through the orchard behind their house. The course itself was only about one hundred yards from top to bottom and it was just steep enough to make a fairly fast run but its main attraction was that it was close to home.

Opportunities for sled riding might not present themselves that often. Most of the time they only came in the evening after school or on Saturdays and Sundays. A really good sledding season would be one that included a good snow during the week of Christmas vacation. A day off from school to go sled riding would have been great but Chip could never remember getting off a day of school because of snow. At Lick Run and Red Dog there were no buses, so school was never called off because the buses couldn't run. In the four years Chip attended Elk River High, there was only one instance when the bus couldn't run and that was because a tree had fallen across the road on Renzee White Hill and the bus couldn't get through. Two other times the heater froze up on the bus and Alfred, the bus driver, told the kids at every stop on his route that they didn't have to go if they didn't want to and they would not be counted absent. On both those days there were only four kids on the bus; Chip, Judy, Rhonda Facemire, and Alfred. Chip went because he either had basketball practice or a game and couldn't miss. Judy and Rhonda went because up to that day, neither one of them had ever missed a single day in their entire public school life.

Alfred could throw a set of tire chains on the bus in seconds and with chains on, that bus could go anywhere. If the snow was very deep, the hour and a half ride to Seneca on the school bus turned into two hours because Alfred drove slower and was more cautious, but

335

the ride was smoother. If there was just enough snow to make the road slick and force Alfred to put on chains, then not only was the ride long, the vibrations from the tire chains were so bad it made the fillings in Chip's teeth hurt and his ears roar. He couldn't even carry on a conversation with Judy riding beside him in the same seat. By the time the kids got to Elk River High, they all had headaches and talked in loud voices. There were times when Alfred probably shouldn't have been on the road but he always made it through and there never were any accidents.

Sled riding after school could be done right there at the house. They didn't have to walk very far and they were able on some evenings, to sleigh ride up until 7:00 or 8:00 if there was a moon or Grandma would turn on the back porch light. It was great for Clint and Riley who had to be in bed by 8:00. Friends liked staying all night with the Gates' during the week when they could go sled riding in the orchard. Even Mr. & Mrs Gates were known to have taken a ride once in a while. "The Bus" was sometimes left at the Gates' for days at a time because the orchard was a good place to ride it.

Another good place for sled riding was on the Sugar Tree side of Renzee White Hill. There were a number of factors that made Renzee White Hill a good place for sled riding. The first was the fact that it was on the hardroad, which meant a smooth, unencumbered, and very fast, run. The lower portion of the hill below the two hairpin turns was used for sledding because it was at least a quarter of a mile long, and it ran straight down the hill before leveling out on another little stretch of straight road. This was important because sledders could see well down the road in front of them and for a distance behind them. Because it was straight, the boys could ride "The Bus" there too.

The second appealing factor for the Gates and for those kids who lived around that way, was the close proximity of the hill. It wasn't so far away that the boys couldn't walk up the road in the evening after school and sled ride a little before it got dark.. They could always find two or three others in the neighborhood to join them.

On Friday and Saturday nights, the sledding crowd often built a bonfire at a wide spot near the bottom of the hill and would sleigh ride until 10:00 or 11:00 at night. The fire could be seen from the beginning of the run and proved to be a beacon to help keep sledders on course coming down the hill in the dark. If they were real fortunate, perhaps a half or full moon would cycle through a clear or partly cloudy night sky during the sledding season on Renzee White Hill and provide light for some excellent late night sledding.

Bonfires also proved useful in other ways too. Day or night it was the place where the sledders gathered in between runs. They could take a break, warm up, or dry off, or engage in serious dialog with fellow sledders. One of the unspoken responsibilities of a sled rider was to bring to the sled course something that would burn. If there were no bonfire that particular day or night, it was ok. They could leave the fuel there for when it would be needed and that meant the next time they came they wouldn't have to bring any bonfire material with them.

He/She could carry it on their sled. It could be some pieces of fire wood or kindling. It might be a piece of log or branch that was found lying along the road and picked up on the way to the sled run. It could be coal. Some brought coal in boxes (good for burning) some brought it in burlap sacks and some just brought big lumps. It might be an old tire. Tires were great for sledding bonfires. They burned hot and long and could be used to start other tender like wet wood. The problem with burning tires was all of the black soot and ashes it created. Many a kid came home with greasy, blackened face, hands, and clothes after standing around a tire fire for two or three hours. They had to undress on the porch, leave their clothes outside, and march straight to the bathtub without touching anything in the house.

The third appealing factor of Renee White Hill was the fact that the State Road sometimes didn't get around to plowing and cindering the hill for four or five days after a good snowfall. In the meantime, the traffic would pack the snow down hard until it became ice. Once the snowplow went through, sledding was finished until the next snowfall.

Unfortunately there were a couple of negative factors that kept Renzee White Hill from being the ideal sled course and the biggest one of those was the fact that it was on Rt.11, the main route in and

337

out of Sugar Tree. That meant vehicle traffic. After any significant snowfall, the traffic of course, became infrequent. The heavier the storm, the lighter the traffic. Traffic was heaviest during the day but on weekdays, kids were all in school and there was no sled riding. Saturday mornings were about the only good times for daytime sled riding on Renzee White Hill because traffic was usually the lightest then.

Sled riding was the safest and best at night though. Once again, the traffic was lightest at night. The worse the weather, the better the sledding, and less the traffic. There was always a kid or two at the bottom of the hill by the bonfire to warn approaching drivers that sled riding was in progress. They did that by just standing there. For untold decades, the people who lived in the Sugar Tree community knew anytime there was a bonfire at the bottom of Renzee White Hill, there were kids sleigh riding on the hill and they moved ahead with caution. The kids sledding down the hill could see clear to the bottom and could spot approaching headlights in plenty of time to coast off to the side of the road out of harm's way. As far as Chip knew, no kid had ever challenged a vehicle into pulling off the road out of the way of a careening sled. Kids were left at the bonfire at the bottom of the hill to warn folks who maybe weren't from that part of the county and weren't aware of that particular sled riding tradition.

Vehicles that came down the hill behind the sledders were the real danger. Usually if the hill was in such condition to make sledding good, it meant driving down the hill in a vehicle was not so good and had to be approached very slowly. All riders sledding on Renzee White Hill developed this kind of quick, glance back twitch to check for headlights that might be gaining on them. If there were ten sleds all in a row coming down the hill, from the front sled to the rear, there would be ten riders twitching glances behind them every few seconds. Of course the one who was virtually responsible for all the rest was the one who came down last. His main job was to yell "CAR!" the moment he spotted headlights from anywhere behind him. At that word every sled, no matter where they were on the hill would veer off to the side of the road out of the way. Vehicles coming down the hill moved very cautiously and slowly and even the slowest sled could out run one, but anything could happen. The vehicle could go out of control. The sled could wreck in the middle of the road. A vehicle could be coming up the hill. The motto for Renzee White Hill was; "Get out of the way and sleigh ride another day."

The second drawback to sledding on Renzee White Hill was that the road came down the south side of the hill. That meant that when the sun came out, what little force it had was directed right at the side of the hill for most of the day. Once a little patch of hardroad was exposed, it would absorb the sun's warmth and begin to spread, melting the snow and ice as it went. One of the first hillsides to lose its winter covering was Renzee White Hill; good for cars, bad for sleds.

Once the sun came out, the snow and ice began to turn to slush and sledding would bog down. There were short patches of snow and ice where the sun didn't shine directly on the road but they were not long enough or numerous enough to sleigh ride down successfully. Many a night it would get cold enough to refreeze the slush on the hardroad and sledding would make a short comeback. The kids liked to sleigh ride on those nights just to get to watch the spectacular display of sparks the sleds would throw off when they would shoot from the ice and snow across bare patches of hardroad. Unfortunately, many a sledder wound up with facial contusions when their sled would come to an abrupt halt on a bare patch of road that had been a little too long to traverse when first attempted.

Only the lower third of Renzee White Hill was used for sledding even though it was a little more than a mile from the top of the hill to the bottom. The upper third of the hill ran from the top down to the first hairpin turn. The middle third ran from the upper hairpin turn to the bottom hairpin turn and the lower third ran from the bottom hairpin turn, to the bottom of the hill. The reason the top two thirds of the hill wasn't used for sled riding was because no one could make it around either one of the two turns without coming to an almost complete stop. The hill was too steep and the turns were too sharp. There were actual stories of guys who started at the top and made it around the first turn on a sled and although sworn to be true, most discounted those feats because the riders dragged their feet to keep their speed down or didn't start clear at the top, etc. And there were never any tales, real or made up, of anyone ever making it successfully from the top turn, down the hill, and around the bottom turn on a sled. It had just never been done, period. Boys being boys however, the Jive Five had to make the effort, and did so, unsuccessfully, a number of times.

If the State Road didn't come and plow and cinder Renzee White Hill for a week or so after a heavy snowfall and if that snow cover stayed on for three or four days, the traffic negotiating around the upper turn would eventually build up a nice bank of snow to the outside of the turn. The development of that snow bank would be the only time when a sledder had any real chance of making the turn. The outside of the upper turn dropped straight down the hillside through the woods for two hundred feet before hitting Rt.11 again as the road doubled back down the hill from the bottom turn. The snow bank was all that kept a sled from careening over the hillside.

Chip was there the day Benji made his fateful attempt to run the upper turn on the Silver Ghost. In fact he and Link were posted just at the upper end of the snow bank to snatch Benji and the sled in case they slid out of the turn and headed over the edge.

Chip's first glimpse of Benji coming down the hill on the Silver Ghost instinctively told him Benji was going way too fast for that little banked snow pile to throw him back into the road. Chip was right. Instead of swinging wide to the outside of the turn and letting the sled come around the banking, Benji dove the Ghost to the inside of the turn hoping that the quick cut to the inside would slow the Ghost down some and would make more room for maneuvering once he was through the curve. The sled didn't slow down and when Benji came out of the turn he was going too fast to get the sled to turn at all. It headed straight across the road and hit the snowbank straight on. Chip and Link couldn't get to him in time, but Benji bailed off just as the Ghost hit the snowbank.

The Silver Ghost sailed gracefully out over the drop off, then entangled herself in the limbs of a tall, red oak tree. She hung there precariously rocking back and forth in the cradle of the branches for a few seconds, and then it was like the tree just let her go. She plummeted sixty feet straight down and smashed herself to pieces on the rocks at the base of the tree.

Benji sat on the snowbank stunned . There was nothing he could do. Things had happened too fast. Chip and Link came over to check on him to make sure he wasn't hurt and to consol him as best they could.

"You want us to go down and get her?" ask Chip.

Benji just sat there in the snow for a few seconds before he answered. "Nah, it wouldn't do no good. Let's just leave her there, restin' in peace. We had a good run while it lasted but it's time to move on." Chip and Link looked at each other, shrugged, and helped Benji to his feet.

If you go down over the hillside just below the upper hairpin turn on Renzee White Hill today and dig around in the leaves and rocks, you can probably find all of the pieces of the Silver Ghost except for the plywood bed. But if you didn't know what you'd found, you would just think it to be an old TV antenna or something.

Chip also made a number of attempts at running the upper turn on a sled. His most memorable attempt happened to be his last one. This time Maynard, Benji, Link, Junior, Clint and Riley were all present.

Chip had the perfect set up. A two day snow storm had dumped eighteen inches on Seneca County almost a week ago and the State Road hadn't been over Rt.11 yet. The road itself was hard packed and smooth and the snowbank on the outside of the upper turn was as high as anyone could remember. There would never be a better time.

Chip laid down on the sled at the top of Renzee White Hill and just made a coasting start. You were allowed to do that. The sled picked up speed pretty quickly but Chip wasn't alarmed. He'd gone faster than this on previous attempts.

Halfway down to the turn, the sled was going as fast as it would go, but for Chip, it was already faster than he'd ever remembered going anywhere before. The turn drew closer, sooner than Chip had anticipated, and he had to decide now how best to approach it.

He steered the sled towards the middle of the high side of the turn; not way to the outside, but   a little more to the middle of the road. The sled began to slide sideways as he entered the turn so he swung

341

his legs to the inside, almost perpendicular to the sled trying to equalize the centrifugal   force that was pushing the sled to the outside of the turn. She kicked up a lot of snow as Chip laid hard to the inside trying to make a sliding turn into the snowbank.

The sled slowly came around and rode up high across the snowbank. Chip thought for sure she was gonna catapult right over the top and he prepared to bail off. But the snowbank kept the sled turned to the inside and she shot back down onto the road. "I made it", thought Chip but the thought was short lived.

The sled came down off of the snowbank and shot straight across the road, heading for the sheer roadbank on the left. Chip was trying all he could to steer her back to the middle of the road. He swung his legs back to the other side of the sled, shifting all of his weight to the right. He was pulling on the guider bar so hard to the right he knew she'd break any minute. He managed to redirect the sled's course enough to avoid a head on collision with the hillside, but the sled, now completely out of control, crashed into the ditchline on the upper side of the road. The left end of the guider bar hit the hillside and gouged out a big rut along the side of the hill. Chip's left hand was gripping the guider bar when it hit the hillside, it hit with such force that it knocked his hand off and whipped his arm back along his side. For a moment it felt as if his wrist was in the jaws of a vise and somebody was cranking it tighter and tighter. Then just as quickly, the sensation went away.

The sled banged from one side of the ditch to the other, plowing up rocks and dirt and snow and ice as she did. Finally, she came to rest thirty feet down the hill from the turn, still in the ditch. The left end of the guider bar had snapped off but everything else seemed to be intact. Chip, still aboard the sled, was almost buried from sight underneath the snow and debris.

All of the guys ran down the hill to Chip and began digging out him and his sled. "I thought for sure you were dead", Benji said.

"Man. Oh man. I thought for sure you had made it", Maynard said in a more encouraging tone. "What happened? Are you alright?"

Chip was ok for the most part, just a little banged up, but still in one piece. He tried to raise up off the sled but he couldn't put any weight on his left arm. It didn't hurt, but it just didn't seem to have any strength in it. He swung around to a sitting position on the sled and grabbed his left coat sleeve with his right hand and lifted it up in front of him so he could look at it. There was no blood; that was good. He tried to wiggle his fingers inside his glove but they wouldn't move. He pulled the coat sleeve up so he could look at his arm. The arm looked ok but his hand was at a weird angle, hanging limply to the outside of his arm.

Link was mesmerized at the sight. "Now that son-of-a-bitch is definitely screwed up," he remarked.

Maynard took charge. "Well, come on we better get you outa there and home so you can get fixed up."

They helped Chip out of the ditch and onto the road and then pulled the sled out. The sled looked none the worse for wear except for the broken end of the guider. They unbuttoned the middle buttons on Chip's coat and gingerly helped stow his injured arm in there. It not only worked like a sling but kept his arm warm too. They sat Chip down on his sled then Maynard and Link untied the pull rope on Maynard's sled and tied it to the pull rope on Chip's sled. That allowed the rope on Chip's sled to reach over him to the back of his sled so that Maynard and Link could walk behind the sled holding on to the pull rope and let the sled drop on down the hill at a speed they could control. Benji had Maynard's and Link's sleds piled on top of his and he walked down the hill with them and Chip. The rest of the guys walked their sleds down to the lower turn and then rode them the rest of the way off the hill. They waited at the bottom of the hill for the crash victim and the emergency services team.

Chip kept insisting that he was ok and that he could walk and pull his own sled but the other guys would have nothing of it. They wanted to be sure Chip wouldn't make his injuries any worse. They pulled Chip all the way back to his house and stayed long enough to help put up his and Riley's sleds. Clint took care of his own. They made sure Chip got into the house ok, then they headed off for their own homes. Chip's wreck had put a damper on sledding for that day.

Riley didn't wait to help put the sleds up. He raced into the house yelling about Chip wrecking his sled and hurting his arm.

343

Mr. Gates didn't pay any attention to Riley other than to lower the daily paper enough to tell him to stop shouting in the house. Mrs. Gates, however, took in every word and when Chip finally got into the house she began to dote on his condition. She helped him remove his gloves, coat, and boots and then she rolled his arm and wrist back and forth examining them closely. If she sensed anything amiss, she kept it to herself. She directed him to the bathroom where he was to remove the rest of his clothes, take a hot, steamy bath, and put on his pajamas. Chip was reluctant because it was only four o'clock in the afternoon, but did her biding nonetheless.

He felt much better after the hot bath and clean clothes but he still couldn't move his fingers and hand. He wasn't hungry but he did feel very tired so he went into the living room and laid down on the couch in front of the TV.

His mom came in and spoke to his dad. "Did you look at Chip's arm? I think there's something wrong with it."

Mr. Gates didn't look away from the TV. "He probably just sprained it or something. He'll be ok. Give him a couple of aspirin to help the pain and let him rest a little."

She brought Chip some aspirin and a warm glass of milk and he downed them both then curled back up on the couch. He woke up amidst the whole family sitting around in the living room watching TV. He must have been more tired than he thought because he had slept right through supper and The Lone Ranger and the Evening News. His mom was the only one not watching TV. She had been sitting across the room watching Chip. "Ted," she said, "that boy has not moved his arm even a little bit for almost three hours. Now are you going to take a look at it or not?"

"Oh, alright," he said. He got up and walked over to Chip. "Let me see your arm."

Chip held the injured arm up with his right hand and slid the pajama sleeve back a little. Mr. Gates looked at it for a second or two then in an even voice, almost offhanded, he said, "Well, son. Tell you what. How about we run over to Seneca to the hospital and let them take a look at your arm just to be on the safe side."

Later, on their way over to Seneca, Chip curled up on the front seat of the Merc with his head right next to his dad. The temperature outside had dropped into the teens but it was warm and cozy inside the Merc. The wind made a little whistling sound through the barely opened wing glass. The whistle changed in pitch as if searching for a melody as the Merc sped up or slowed down or as the wind outside whipped up or died down.

Chip's dad expertly guided the Merc through the snow and ice towards Seneca and after a few miles had passed in silence, he asked Chip to find something good on the radio. Chip sat up and turned on the radio. It took a little while to warm up but when it did come on, it was already tuned to WRVA out of Richmond, so Chip just left it there. He curled back up on the seat and his dad laid his a hand on his shoulder and left it there as if shielding Chip from any more potential harm.

It was a magical time for Chip. He and his dad were able to share their love of music, something they couldn't do often enough. Chip felt safe and protected. His dad wasn't a feely-touchy person but demonstrated his love and care for his family in other ways. So this was a special moment and Chip tucked it away in his treasure chest of memories and as the years would rush by, he would draw it out many times later. Whatever ordeal awaited him and his arm at the Seneca Hospital really didn't seem to be that big of a concern just now. He just wanted these moments to go on and on.

Too soon, they arrived at the hospital. They x-rayed Chip's arm and confirmed that his wrist was broken. They put him to sleep, set his wrist, put a cast on it, and sent him home.

On the ride back home, Chip tried and tried to recaptured those special moments and that close bond with his dad that he had experienced on his ride over to the hospital, but he kept falling asleep. When he did wake up for a few seconds from time to time, he'd see his dad glance down at him and kind of chuckle to himself. Then he'd pat Chip on the head a couple of times before Chip drifted back to sleep.

Chip didn't get to sleigh ride anymore that winter. By the time he got his cast taken off, spring had come.

The best place in Sugar Tree for sled riding was on the Sugar Tree side of the Panther Mountain short cut. If there was enough snow for sled riding it meant the short cut was virtually impassable for any type of motorized vehicle except for jeeps equipped with chains. Unlike Renzee White Hill, vehicle traffic was not a hazard for sled riders on Panther Mountain.

The short cut was a dirt road and since there were no homes or cemeteries located along its length, the whole winter would pass without it ever even being plowed by a road grader or dozer. The road came down the north side of Panther Mountain which meant the winter sun had no depreciating influence on the snow that fell there between November and March. The sled run would turn from snow to ice and as long as the air stayed cold, the snow would hold on for months at a time. No bare spots appeared, but when the air finally got warm enough to melt the snow, it immediately sent a small, stream of water down the sled course, exposing the mud and dirt of the bare ground underneath.

It was a little over a mile and half from the top of Panther Mountain to the bottom but for the most part, sled riding was confined to the bottom third of the mountain. Once in a while riders would make the trek up the mountain to ride all the way down from the top but it took so long to walk up to the top that most felt like it was using up time that could be best used for sledding. Sledding from the top didn't gain a rider any more thrills than the lower portion could provide either. The first half mile from the top was steep and only had one hard bend in the road which was about two hundred yards down from the top. The road straightened out after that and dropped steeply to the middle section of the mountain. If there was a light covering of snow, sled riders could make excellent speed down that first half mile but if the snow was more than six inches deep, it would take two or three sled runs to plow out an unencumbered track down the mountain.

Riding from the top of Panther Mountain was attempted mostly in the daylight unless there was a clear, moonlit night because there was no bonfire to guide the riders and there was no defined course to follow. Without some light there was no way to tell where to guide the sled. However, no matter how much speed could be gained through the top section, the middle third of the mountain was fairly level. It did have a little incline to it but it was just enough to keep a sled moving along. A rider could easily speed up his sled through the middle part by using his hands to paddling through the snow. The middle section did allow one to slow down and enjoy the vista and the passing scenery.

Where the middle section ended was where the steepest part of the mountain began. This was the normal starting place for the last half mile of the mountain. Riders who entered the last section by coming clear from the top, wouldn't be going any faster than a good running flop starter could go; maybe even slower.

The last half mile started straight down the mountain but near the bottom, the road curved to the right; slowly and smoothly back in towards the mountain. Then the road disappeared into a narrow cut in the side of the mountain before making a hard, ninety degree sweep to the left and emerging again onto flat, valley floor where sleds coasted to a gentle stop. In no time at all, the continuous sled runs down this portion of the mountain created a very fast sled course.

Daytime sledding was great on Panther Mountain but daytime sledding was confined to Saturdays and school holidays. Nighttime sledding was just as good but again, confined to only two opportunities; Friday and Saturday nights. Because these were the only times available, it was not unusual to find twenty or thirty kids sled riding on Panther Mountain at any one time. Benji said he'd seen so many kids sleigh riding on Panther Mountain that you couldn't swing a dead cat without hitting one of 'em.

The bonfire for nighttime sledding was always located on the left side of the road, going down the hill. It was in the area where most sleds coasted to a stop. A rider could see the light from the fire all the way down the lower section, thus keeping their bearings all the way down the hill. The only time one lost sight of the bonfire was when they went through the cut at the bottom of the hill. You really didn't need any light to guide you through the cut anyway. It was so narrow and the sides were so steep, a sled couldn't help but shoot right on around it.

All the way up the mountain on the outside of the sled course there were little cleared off spots called "jumping off places." They were there for two reasons. One, so those pulling a sled up the hill would have a place to get over out of the way to keep from getting hit by a sledder coming down the hill. Two; it provided different starting points for different skilled sledders. Smaller kids might not want to start clear up at the highest jumping off place so they could start wherever they were more comfortable. The older kids started at or near the upper jumping off place.

There were two unwritten safety rules for sledding on Panther Mountain; never, never start a sled run out in front of anyone who is already on the course, coming down the mountain and never, never start a sled run if there is already someone on the course in front of you no matter how far down the mountain they may be. Those were very simple rules; practical as well as courteous. Maybe that was why everybody did their best to follow them. It just made it better for everyone. Chip could not remember any major incidents on the lower section of the mountain caused by someone not obeying one of those two rules.

One evening Junior Dodrill got it in his head that'd he would be the coolest guy on a sled if he just swung in close enough to scare the bejeebees out of a bunch of kids standing in one of the lower jumping off places. Junior always started at the top jumping off place and this evening his speed was faster than usual. There were three or four kids standing off to the left of the road with their backs turned to Junior as he flew down the hill. Unsuspecting victims would be the easiest to scare.

The unsuspecting victims were Elihu, Riley, and Dog Groves. As he neared the group, Junior swung his sled off the course and into the soft snow along the edge. Junior made his sweep past the group a little too close and his sled clipped Riley's right leg out from under him. As Riley buckled backwards toward the ground, he grabbed hold of Elihu's shoulder to steady himself. All he succeeded in doing was to pull Elihu backwards too. Elihu grabbed Dog's arm in an attempt to keep from falling backwards, but jerked him down also. Riley fell backwards onto his sled that was lying there. His left arm fell across the open space between the guider bar and the front steel frame. Elihu fell on top of Riley. Dog tried to check his balance by stepping backwards, but he stepped back right on top of Riley's arm and the arm snapped like a piece of dried driftwood.

Riley's scream of pain cut through the winter evening like a razor sharp dagger. Everything and everybody stopped in their tracks and went silent. Everybody that is except Junior, who just kept on gettin' it down the hill. When he reached the bottom of the hill he didn't even wait for his sled to stop moving. He jumped off and grabbed it on the dead run and fled for home.

Chip and Maynard were up where Junior had started his run and they ran along side the sled course down the hill to where Riley lay injured.

He was holding his arm tight against his body and the tears rolled with every sob he made. Chip got him to calm down a little, until his sobs finally turned into little body jerks. Everybody on the mountain came to help. They wrapped two big coats around Riley and someone donated a belt with which Chip was able to pull Riley's arm up tightly against his chest. They sat Riley on his sled and Maynard sat behind him on the sled to cradle him and hold him immobile.

Two or three of the guys helped Chip get Riley off the hill and then helped pull the sled down to Benji's house. Chip called Grandma Gates and told her what had happened and asked her to tell his dad, so he could come around and get them.

Chip's dad wasn't home. He had gone to Lewisburg to play for a dance that night but when Benji's dad heard what had happened, he called Grandma back and told her to tell Chip's mom that he was bringing Riley around and for her to get ready. He'd take them over to the hospital in Seneca.

Uncle Fred took Riley and Chip around the road and let them out at the house to pick up Chip's mom. Edna Gates had already taken Clint over to Grandma's to stay and Chip was told to stay there also and help take care of Clint.

As it turned out, Riley's arm was broken and it was in a cast for six weeks. When he finally got the cast off, there were still a few sled riding days left in the season, but Riley was forbidden to do any more sleigh riding for the rest of that year.

If Chip and the rest of the crowd on Panther Mountain had gotten hold of Junior the day of the accident, he too, no doubt, would have had to go to the hospital. But he was able to get away. Nobody saw Junior away from his house for the next month except when he rode the school bus to Seneca and he knew there was no way anybody would risk suspension from school just to get back at him and he was right. But every one of those days, he cowered under numerous threats of retaliation and retribution from many different sources. Eventually, the desperate need to avenge Riley's accident faded away until it seemed Junior's pathetic existence just wasn't worth the effort.

Chip had the fastest sled in Sugar Tree. It wasn't the sled itself that was so fast, it was the speed Chip could generate from a running start. Chip could beat a guy with his Western Flyer, trade sleds with the guy, and beat him with his own sled. Nobody was as quick and as fast as Chip in a running "flop start". "Flop Start"; that's where you run down the hill holding the sled with both hands and when your speed is where you want it to be, you throw the sled down on the snow, still holding on to it, and flop onto it in one motion. Some kids hold the sled off to the side and then swing themselves on to it as it hits the ground. Others hold it straight up in front of them and only take a few steps before flopping down on it. Some kids swing the sled back and forth like a pendulum as they run, thinking it gives them more momentum.

The landing is really the crucial movement of the flop start. If you land after the sled is down on the snow, all of your momentum goes straight down onto the sled. There is no forward motion and the sled will lose speed. Late landings can cause sleds to buckle, beds to break, frames to bend, ribs to crack, and breaths to be knocked out.

Landing too early is just as bad. You go on down the hill on your face while your sled comes up from behind you and runs over you.

The smoothest flop start artist in Sugar Tree was Maynard. He wasn't the fastest guy around but his running starts were so smooth and effortless, that rider and sled appeared to be as one. Maynard held his sled low on his hip. The inside hand held the side of the sled just behind the guider and the outside hand held on about amidships. Maynard held the sled steady and level as he moved forward. He really didn't run. He made four or five long smooth gaits and slipped onto the sled and onto the snow on one graceful motion. He did it every time, exactly the same. If you watched closely you would swear the sled and rider actually glided through the air the first four or five feet before settling down onto the snow.

The two best riders in Sugar Tree were completely opposite in style, yet both were successful. Maynard and Chip only raced each other in fun. There was never any real competition between them. If they would have raced seriously, say, one hundred races, They both probably would have won fifty each.

Flop starts were for the serious sledders, but there were other starts too and none of them were looked down upon. The choice was up to the individual rider. Some laid the sled down on the snow then laid down on the sled and used either their hands to paddle the snow to give themselves a little speed at take off or, just let go and let gravity provide the momentum. Some sat up on the sled and used their feet on the guider bar to steer the sled. It was easier riding double if the riders sat up on the sled and with two on the sled, it would be heavier than a single rider and would gain more speed coasting down the hill. Better still, if the two riders had a buddy or two that would give them a running push in the back for the first few feet of the run. Chip didn't particularly like sitting up on the sled, single or double. There was too much wind resistence and the sled was harder to keep on a straight course.

The ultimate speed in riding double came when the riders laid down on the sled, one on top of the other. It cut down on the wind resistence and the sled was easier to hold its course. The bottom rider was responsible for steering.

For the guys, riding double was reserved exclusively for the female species and sitting up seemed to be the preferred position of the fairer sex. She could chose whether to ride in the front or in the back. Fortunately, neither rider found either position distasteful because cuddling and snuggling was an inevitable factor for any safe and enjoyable ride.

Most girls would only ride double with a boy in the prone position if they were with their boyfriend. There were rare exceptions of course but even then, the girl rode on top.

One cold and snowy Friday night, Maynard talked Link, Skinny Walker, and Chip into making a nighttime run with him starting from the top of Panther Mountain. Maynard had taped a flashlight to the front of his sled to serve as a headlight. When the convoy of sleds left from the top of the mountain, he'd go first and lead the way. Link was the only one who was never really sold on the adventure but he reluctantly agreed to go along just for the company.

They decided to walk two abreast up the mountain road and drag their sleds behind, that way they could cut at least some kind of rudimentary trail through the snow that would be easy to follow when they came back down. It was a heavy, overcast night with small snow squalls blowing in and out with irregularity and even after their eyes became adjusted to the dark, it was hard to see more than a few feet ahead. Maynard kept the flashlight off to save the batteries for the trip back down. Besides, he would have had to carry his sled on his hip since the flashlight was taped to it.

The higher they ascended the mountain, the warmer the air temperature seemed to get and the stronger the wind seemed to pick up. Soon the light of the bonfire was left behind and the yelling and chatter of young sledders faded into the deep silence of the mountain's solitude. It took them almost an hour to hike up through the snow to the top of the mountain. The night had become even darker and the weather more harsh as they prepared to set off. The four boys were now bantering among themselves constantly in an effort to keep the thoughts of their sheer isolation and remoteness at bay. They spent no more time at the top of the mountain than was necessary.

Maynard clicked on his headlight, laid his sled down in the snow, laid himself down on board, and shoved off. Each rider fell in fifteen to twenty feet behind. Skinny was second, Link came third and Chip brought up the rear.

By the time Maynard had made it through the big turn at the top, he was having trouble seeing where he was going. The snow was billowing up in front of his sled and spilling back into his face and eyes while burying the flashlight beam in its depth.

Maynard's sled began picking up a fairly good head of steam as he headed down the first long straight but since he couldn't tell where he was going, he dragged the toes of his boots and held his arms out to the side to slow the sled to a stop. He'd wait on the others and try to figure a better way to see. Maybe he could sit up and hold the flashlight up high in one hand.

Skinny had pushed off behind Maynard and because Maynard had cleared a good path through the snow, Skinny's sled was running real smooth and he was rapidly closing the gap between Maynard and him. At first it was easy for Skinny to keep sight of Maynard because he could see the light from Maynard's sled and he was pulling closer all the time, but he lost sight of Maynard when Maynard went around the turn up ahead of him. When Skinny came out of the turn himself, he saw no sign of Maynard or his light.

Skinny didn't know what to do so he continued on. He never did see Maynard stopped dead in the road ahead and his sled smashed full speed into the back of Maynard's. The impact threw Skinny forward on his belly and drove his face into Maynard's boots that were hanging over the back of the sled.

Meanwhile, Link was coming down the hill even faster. His vision was less obstructed by the flying snow and when he came out of the big turn and turned down the mountain, he glimpsed enough of the obstacles in the path before him to start an evasive move. Unfortunately he didn't start it soon enough. He cut his sled to the right as sharply as he could and missed hitting Skinny a direct blow, but the left end of his guider bar struck Skinny's sled and rode up the right side of the sled until it struck Skinny's boots. Link was still moving pretty fast and the sideswipe was strong enough to knock Skinny forward again. This time his head slipped between Maynard's boots and hit the rear of Maynard's sled. The longest wooden slat on the bed of Maynard's sled drove right into Skinny's face, hitting him between his chin and his lower lip and laying his lip open.

353

Chip had actually been enjoying a brief moment of deep revere there in the depths of the forest on the mountain top after everyone else had left, and so his own departure came somewhat later. Wanting to enjoy as much of night's adventure as he could, he kept his sled at a moderate pace down the hill. When he slipped around the upper turn and entered the straight, he was going slow enough to recognize two dark forms in the road ahead and slow enough to pull over safely to the right hand side of the sled course.

The first thing Chip noticed at the scene was Link, who was only five feet away. He was dancing around in a circle in the snow like an Indian. His body was bent over, his left arm was dangling low, and all the while he was violently shaking his left hand and mumbling curse words Chip had never heard before.

Figuring Link would be ok, Chip went over to attend to the other two. Maynard had his sled standing up and was ripping and tearing at the tape that was holding the flashlight, its beam now shining straight up through the twirling snowflakes to the heavens. There was an urgency to Maynard's actions. "See if you can help Skinny while I try to get this stupid ass flashlight off here," he said. "I think he's hurt."

Skinny was sitting in the snow off to the side of the sleds. He heard Maynard and Chip talking.

"Ah ont nah hoay ah caint uuve ii hees vehi neeah," he slurred. "Cahrnah haw no?"

Chip went over to him. "Hold on partner. Don't try to talk. We'll get you fixed up as soon as Maynard gets the light over here."

"Ah daw ow wuh... wuh....hahun. Ah caahn taw tuh guh don, " Skinny mumbled, shaking his head.

"Don't worry now," Chip soothed. "Just rest a minute."

Maynard finally made it over with the flashlight. He shined it right in Skinny's face. The first glimpse of an injury or wound is always worse than expected, but it is usually not as bad as it appears. Not so in this case. Chip's first glimpse of Skinny's face caused the blood to drain from his own. Blood was streaming from Skinny's nose. A hunk of his lip was hanging down below his chin, exposing the bottom row of his shattered and broken front teeth. Skinny probably would have been in excruciating pain, if he hadn't been knocked half silly.

Maynard and Chip quickly recovered from their first reaction and summoning their Boy Scout training, went right work, wordlessly, to help Skinny.

Chip kept Skinny sitting up while Maynard made two soft snowballs. He gave them to Chip and went off to find the tape he'd used to tape the flashlight to the sled. Chip put one snowball down the back of Skinny's coat collar to rest against the back of his neck. He gently applied the other snowball to Skinny's nose. In no time at all, the nose stopped bleeding.

Link had made it over to the group by now and he started checking Skinny over for further injuries. Whatever injury Link had suffered he seemed to have put it behind him for now as he attended to Skinny.

Maynard came back with some remnants of the black friction tape he'd used to tape the flashlight to the sled. He pushed Skinny's dangling lip back into place and held it in place by wrapping the tape over the wound, all the way around the jaw and the back of the head, and back to the chin. He had enough tape to wrap it three times.

Skinny was still in a daze but he was looking better. Maynard shined the flashlight around in the snow where they sat. There were splotches and streaks of crimson everywhere.

"Come on," said Maynard, "let's get Skinny down the mountain and home. I'll go first and sit up so I can hold the flashlight up high to see."

"Yeah," Chip said, "we'll tie my sled right to the back of Maynard's and I'll put Skinny sitting up in front of me so I can hold on to him and keep him from going to sleep. Link, you come behind me and bring Skinny's sled."

"You'll have to tie me to your sled, Chip," Link replied, "I can't use my left hand so I'll have to hold on to Skinny's sled with my right. I won't have any way to slow down."

"Can you lead three sleds down this mountain without killing us?," Chip joked.

"Well, I don't know what else we can do," Maynard answered. "The middle part won't be so hard and after we get to the bottom part, they'll be a bunch of kids to help us. So I say lets get the heck outa here."

The hardest part was coming down the remainder of the upper section. The farther they went though, the better Maynard learned to keep the sleds in the middle of the road. Chip helped control the speed from time to time by dragging his hands alongside the sled and found that that also helped with steering. The convoy flew through the upper section safely and glided on through the middle section. When they reached the bottom section, Maynard had grown enough confidence in the boys' ability to keep things in control that they flew right on past everyone on the lower course and sailed on towards home.

Skinny's nose turned out to be broken and he had three teeth knocked out and one tooth broken. It took sixteen stitches to sew his lip back together but the doctor did an excellent job considering the damage. Skinny had no speech impairment but had one long scar as a testament to his injury.

When Link sideswiped Skinny's sled, all four fingers on his left hand were mashed between his guider bar and steel frame of Skinny's sled. None of the fingers were broken. At the time of the accident, Link had filled his glove with snow, stuck it back on his hand, and just left his hand in there until he got back home. Despite those efforts, all of the fingernails on Link's left hand turned black and fell off.

One winter evening Benji and Chip were hanging out at the station shooting the breeze with Bucky and the conversation eventually turned to sled riding. Bucky told the boys he used to have a car hood that he turned upside down and used it for sled riding. He thought it was from a '52 Pontiac but wasn't real sure about that. He said it took him a whole month of sledding on the thing to learn how to control its direction. He had to learn by riding it down an open field where he had plenty of room for maneuvering and where his mistakes didn't turn into injurious mishaps. Finally, after numerous wild rides, hair raising spills, and last minute bail outs, he discovered the secret involved in controlling the hood.

The first thing he realized was that the hood was so heavy and bulky one person couldn't control it. Neither could two or three, but four good size riders could, if they all worked together. If he couldn't find four large riders, five smaller ones would do.

The second thing was to distribute the weight on the hood as evenly as possible. If he started out with too much weight on one side, the hood had a tendency to drift in that direction and sometimes the speed and the duration of the run would make any course correction unattainable. In most of those cases, bail-offs were in order.

Even with the weight problem solved, all of the riders had to work in unison. Bucky said he always rode up front with his feet braced against the turned up front of the hood and held on to the tow rope for balance. He told the crew riding behind him to do what ever he did at the same time he did it. If he leaned a little left, everybody behind him was suppose to lean a little left. If he leaned way over right, everybody behind him leaned way over right. Same if he sat straight up. Thus was achieved a modicum of control.

Thirdly, snow conditions had to be considered as well. The difference between a heavy wet snow and a light, dry snow made a world of difference in the ground effects that leaning had on the hood. Bucky said that was something he just had a feel for. He could sense the snow conditions as soon as he climbed aboard the hood by just the way she lay in the snow. Getting his riding crew attuned to riding the hood was the hardest part and usually it took two or three disastrous run with the same crew before everyone was in unison and if one of the crew left during an evening of riding, he had to start all over again. Bucky said he took training a crew of riders very seriously. The car hood was big and heavy and made of steel, if everyone had to bail off, it left the hood unmanned and completely out of control. It could go anywhere, hit anything and cause major damage or injury to humans, animals, structures or vehicles. It was also hard to get off the thing when it was moving. Bucky and his crew had learned how to roll over the side of the hood and continue to roll away from it. Bucky had enough trouble training a new rider how to steer the hood, so he just showed the new ones how to roll off if he gave the command. He said he was still worried about someone getting cut on a sharp metal edge or getting caught under the hood when trying to get off, or worse yet, not being able to get off before crashing into a stationary object of some kind.

Bucky said three of his buddies and his brother Lewis made up the best veteran team that could constantly run the hood with skill. The five liked riding together because the hood was the fastest ride anywhere, anytime, and they all got to ride. The only time Bucky let smaller or younger kids ride the hood was if he had his regular crew with him.

Benji and Chip forgot all about Bucky's tale of the car hood until the Saturday morning Bucky showed up at a Panther Mountain sled riding party driving his jeep and pulling that very same '52 Pontiac car hood on a rope behind the jeep.

Benji and Chip were the first ones to gather around Bucky and start asking questions about the hood. They learned that Bucky had intentionally gone looking for the hood, had found it, and was now loaning it to Benji and Chip so they could learn to ride it if they so desired. Of course they did. Bucky said he was too old to ride the thing anymore, but he'd be glad to show Benji and Chip what he could about riding it.

Bucky stayed awhile that Saturday morning helping Benji and Chip with the hood. Bucky had removed the hood ornament from the front of the hood and drilled the holes big enough to slip a tow rope through them. The lower third of the Panther Mountain shortcut skirted a hillside meadow that fell off to the left. It was a good two hundred yards down through the meadow to the bottom of the mountain. The road ran along the top edge of the meadow then swung back around to the left to eventually border the meadow again along the valley floor. The meadow was where Benji and Chip learned to ride the hood.

Just the two boys rode at first. Bucky thought they could learn the feel of the hood better. They made very short rides at first; no more than twenty to thirty feet down the slope. The more they rode, the better they got. Johnny Ward and Roger McGee were added to the crew because they were the only boys that hung around to help Benji and Chip with the hood. Bucky had to get back to the station, so once he saw that the boys seemed to be getting the hang of things, he departed.

The four made at least three good runs from the top of the meadow to the bottom without any mishaps. Bucky was right about the speed of the hood. It gained momentum very quickly and just zipped down through the meadow. On one run the hood was going so fast and riding so smooth, it seemed as if it was actually airborne.

The boys now had the confidence to ride the hood down Panther Mountain. It took all four of them working in tandem to pull the hood up to the farthest jumping off spot. While they were positioning the hood for their take off, Clint wandered by. He begged Benji and Chip to let him ride with them. Chip tried to dissuade him for now, telling him he could ride the next time but Clint was persistent. He said he was going home in a few minutes and this probably would be his only chance ever to get to ride the hood. Chip conferred with Benji. "He's your brother," was all Benji had to say. Chip finally relented.

The hood now had five riders. While two or three other kids held on to the hood to keep it from taking off on its own, Chip positioned each rider for even weight distribution. Clint only weighed about seven pounds soaking wet, so as far as weight was concerned, it didn't matter where he sat, so for safety, Chip sat him in the middle directly behind him. Benji sat directly behind Clint but near the back edge of the hood. Johnny and Roger sat on either side of Clint.

It was getting difficult to hold the hood back with all the weight onboard. "Now you guys be careful," warned Benji. "That ice's slicker than snot on an oilcloth tablecloth." It was like she was a good horse eager to be let loose; she wanted to get going. Chip took one more look around behind him. "Let her go", he said, and the boys turned her loose.

The hood held a straight course down the sled run. They were only halfway down the straight and already Chip knew he had never gone this fast on a sled before. The sled course down the road was rougher than gliding through the soft snow in the meadow and the hood began to bump and jerk violently as it picked up even more speed.

When they reached the place where the road begins to swing to the right, Chip began to lean a little to the right----so did the rest of the

crew. The hood's bearing didn't change. Chip leaned a little more----
nothing. They were quickly running out of curve. Chip leaned as far
over to the right as he could and everybody else followed suit but the
hood barreled on, straight ahead. The only thought that ran through
Chip's mind right then was, "she's trying to get back to where the
ride was smoother".

The hood crossed the road and plowed right through a six foot
high snow bank, catapulting Benji right off the back end of the hood
and depositing him on his head in the deep snow at the edge of the
road. The hood then sailed right over the top of the road bank,
skimmed the top rail of a four foot high chestnut rail fence, and
landed with a jolt at the top of the meadow. Now in fear for his life,
Roger who was riding on the left side of the hood, jumped
overboard. When he bailed off all the weight shifted to the right half
of the hood and it tipped that way enough to slide Clint right over
against Johnny.

Chip was trying to gain some control of the hood but she was
listing badly to starboard and her course began to drift off to the right.
Chip quickly calculated her destination up ahead and it appeared that
the hood's wide, curve to the right was going to terminate at or near
the rear of Lucy Ward's mobile home or her chicken house/granary.
There was no way Chip was going to abandon the hood with Clint in
it. Johnny had decided to ride it out with the two brothers.

Since the hood's natural inclination was to drift right, Chip figured
maybe they could exaggerate the direction by leaning in that direction
thus making the turn sharp enough to bypass Miss Ward's home
place. All three passengers leaned hard to the right. The hood was just
going too fast for Chip's strategy to be effective enough to avert the
mobile home altogether but it worked just enough to avoid a complete
disaster.

The hood sideswiped the right rear corner of Miss Ward's trailer.
That impact knocked the hood even more to the right and it skimmed
across the open alley between the trailer and the chicken house before
crashing into the side of the granary. The front part of the granary was
where the field corn, still on the cob, was stored for the winter. That
part of the corn crib was made mostly of chicken wire to allow the

flow of air to keep the corn dry. The hood crashed right through the chicken wire which slowed it down considerably, and the avalanche of ears of corn did their part in softening the impact. The three survivalists sat dazed but unhurt among the corn cobs and chicken wire.

The wreck of the hood stirred up enough commotion to arouse Miss Ward's concern. She opened the back door of the trailer and using her cane to test the surface condition of the little stoop, stepped outside the door. She had thrown her winter coat over her housecoat and had a scarf wrapped around her head, but she was still in her bedroom shoes. Her breath formed clouds of vapor in the late afternoon air. "My stars," she exclaimed, "are you boys alright?" That was about the zenith of Miss Ward's emotions.

Miss Lucy Ward was a retired school teacher with forty some years of teaching experience. Some of those years were at Lick Run School and some were at Sugar Tree Elementary. She had taught at least three generations of families living in Sugar Tree and she never forgot a student's name no matter how old they got. She had never married and lived alone in her little trailer there at the foot of Panther Mountain. She did have two or three sisters and a brother or two who were still living and they looked in on her from time to time but everybody in Sugar Tree took an interest in Miss Ward, so she was never truly alone. Nobody ever called Miss Ward by her first name. She was always Mrs. Ward and to call her anything else would just have been so out of place for someone of her character and class. If she had been married, even her husband would have called her Miss Ward.

"We're ok," Chip yelled over to her. "Please, Miss Ward, you need to get back inside. It's too cold out her for you. We'll come over as soon as we get this mess fixed up some."

"Land sakes, sonny, this isn't anything to what I've seen in my years." She pointed her cane at the boys. "Now I'm going back inside but you boys come over here and get warmed up first, before you do anything else. I'll fix you some hot cocoa."

The boys untangled themselves from the wreckage and with some effort dragged the hood back out into the yard. They decided to take

Miss Ward up on her offer of hot cocoa so the three headed for the back stoop. Something caught Johnny's eye though because he stopped in mid stride right by the corner of the trailer where the hood had hit. "Hey, Chip," he said, kneeling down in the snow, "take a look at this."

Chip stopped and retraced his steps over to Johnny. He knelt down beside him. "What?"

Johnny nodded toward the base of the trailer. "Take a close look at that trailer and tell me if it doesn't look like it's been knocked out of line."

Chip looked closely down the length of the trailer to where it met the back stoop. There was a three or four inch wide strip of bare ground that paralleled the base of the trailer. "I just think that's where we hit the underpinning and knocked it out a little," Chip explained, not really sure himself.

"Maybe," answered Johnny, "but take a look at where the trailer and the stoop come together."

Chip got up and walked over for a closer look. There was a three inch gap between the stoop and the trailer. Chip walked on around to the other side of the stoop. The same bare strip of ground was visible along the edge of the trailer only not quite as wide. In fact, it narrowed in width until it finally disappeared altogether at the left rear corner of the trailer. The boys hadn't seemed to notice it but the hood sideswiped the trailer with enough impact to knock one end of the forty foot mobile home at least three inches off its foundation.

Chip was concerned. "Hey Johnny, why don't you take Clint and go on in and I'll take a quick look under the trailer to make sure we didn't break any water lines or gas lines or anything."

Johnny and Clint knocked on the back door and waited for Miss Ward's invitation to come on in. Chip didn't hear it but apparently Miss Ward gave it, because the two boys opened the door, stepped inside, and began taking their boots off as the door closed.

Chip found the opening for the crawlspace in the underpinning and unfastened the latches that held the door. He removed the door and peered inside. It was too dark under there to see anything so he waited a moment to see if his eyes would adjust to the dark, but they didn't.

362

The only way he was going to be able to see anything under there would be with a flashlight. If he couldn't see, maybe he could hear. The space under the trailer was so low he had to lay down on his stomach to enter. He crawled in under the trailer until his feet were just even with the entranceway. He held his breath and listened intently for any telltale sounds, especially hissing water or gas leaks. He heard nothing. He waited another couple of minutes to see if he could smell any gas. He didn't, so he crawled back out, fastened the door back on, and brushed himself off.

Chip didn't feel there was any real need to tell Miss Ward about the trailer. There didn't appear to be any real damage. No need to worry her unduly. When they come back to fix the granary, he'd bring a flashlight and check everything out real good. He went inside and had a cup or two of hot cocoa. He told Miss Ward unless she thought it was an emergency, they would temporarily patch up the granary as best they could for now, then as soon as the weather got better they would come back and fix it up right. She said that would be fine. She was just glad no one got hurt.

Johnny and Chip mended the chicken wire back together as best they could with some help from Clint. It was minus a few wooden slats and had a couple of oversize gaps in the chicken wire but the boys tossed as many of the scattered ears of corn as they could find hidden in the snow, back into the granary and strategically place them so they wouldn't fall out.

As it turned out, the weather cleared that very next week and so on the following Saturday, Chip headed to Miss Ward's for repair duties. He didn't feel Clint needed to come and Clint was satisfied to stay home and watch cartoons. Johnny couldn't come because he had a dentist appointment that morning so Chip had talked Benji into helping him. He said if he hadn't been thrown off the hood in the first place maybe the wreck wouldn't have happened or if it had happened anyway, at least he would have been there to help, sure enough.

The boys didn't tell Miss Ward when they would be coming back because they really didn't know for sure at the time. They just figured they'd show up and repair everything to its original state before she even knew they were there. When they got to Miss Wards and walked around to the chicken house/granary, they found everything neatly repaired. New wood had been applied and new chicken wire strung and the crib was more full of corn than even before the accident.

The boys were perplexed but none-the-less grateful. Chip still wanted to check under the trailer so he and Benji went around to the rear of the trailer and removed the door to the crawlspace. Benji looked at the gap between the stoop and the trailer. "That crack's so big you could throw a house cat through there," he said. Chip switched on the flashlight and crawled in on his stomach. He traced every waterline and the gas line from one end to the other with the beam but detected no leaks.

Benji knelt down by the crawlspace entrance, "How's it look?" he asked.

"Everything looks good so far", Chip answered from somewhere back in the dark. He was having to squirm around foundation pillars to be able to see every line clearly.

Miss Ward came out on the back stoop and looked over at the granary. She didn't see anybody there, but as she turned to go back inside the trailer she saw Benji kneeling on the ground and the underpinning removed.

"Well, I thought I heard voices out here. Is everything alright, Mr.Lewis?"

"Yes ma'am, "Benji said, as he stood up. "Chip's under your house checking for a gas leak. He thought he smelled gas a little bit ago when we came in."

"Well bless his heart. You tell him when you all get finished to come on in for some hot cocoa."

"Yes, ma'am, we sure will."

Miss Ward went back into the house and a few minutes later Chip crawled out from under the trailer. His coveralls were draped in spider webs and insulation and covered with dust and dirt. Everything looked okay under the trailer. He could find no misalignment of any vital service utilities, but a couple of foundation blocks had been knocked a few inches askew near that right rear corner, attesting to the violent impact the hood had made. The blocks were in no danger of collapsing.

Chip put the underpinning back, took off his coveralls, and shook the dirt and debris off of them as best he could and dropped them in a pile by the back door. Benji reminded him that they needed to remove their boots before going in.

Over a cup of cocoa, Miss Ward explained that her brother Carl had come over on Monday and not only repaired the corn crib, but had brought enough corn from his own farm to replenish her depleted stock. There was really no need for the boys to come back. Chip told her that while they were already there they would be glad to take care of any unfinished or needed chores that might need completion. Miss Ward assured them that indeed there was nothing pressing at that moment. She did express her gratitude to Chip for thinking enough of her to crawl under her tailer and check for a gas leak. That made Chip feel about as low as an old hound dog caught in a chicken house. He just couldn't bring himself to tell Miss Ward about her out-of-kilter home because he wanted to spare her any unnecessary worry, yet keeping it from her was eating him inside out.

Before they left, the boys checked the gap between the back stoop and the back door that had been widened because of the wreck. It was a wider gap than before but it was back under the door's bottom threshold and was virtually unnoticeable.

Chip never did tell Miss Ward about the damage the hood had done to her trailer and nothing ever came of it, but his omission haunted him until he had grown to be a young man. When Chip was in high school, Miss Ward moved away to live with one of her brothers where she could be with someone who could take care of her. He didn't see her again until a Sugar Tree Baptist Church homecoming brought her home and back into Chip's life. By then Miss Ward was in the twilight of her years. Chip finally took the opportunity to unburden his guilt by confessing to her the real and complete details of that incident, now, many years gone by.

Miss Ward listened patiently and intently to Chip's story. She may have been frail and weak in body but her mind was still sharp as ever. "Can you ever forgive me?" Chip said when he ended his confession.

Miss Ward paused for a moment and then in a gentle smile she said, "Mr. Gates, that is indeed the most astounding apology I have ever received, especially in light of the fact that it took nigh on fifteen years to be delivered, and also because I never even knew I was due one. I would be less than gracious if I did not accept it fully. It's obvious your parents and this community raised you well. The Bible says if you train up a child in the way he should go, when he is old, he will not depart from it, so may it be with you. I always wondered what you and Mr.Lewis were really up to that day you came to repair the granary but I never questioned anything you were doing because I knew whatever it was, it was because you boys had a good heart and I left it at that. Now come over here so your old softie of a teacher can give you hug."

Chip stooped down and gave her a long hug. "You were many things to us Miss Ward," he said, "but old softie certainly wasn't one of them."

Bucky left the car hood at Panther Mountain the rest of that winter for riding purposes but it was never ridden on the road again. The smaller kids rode it once in a while in the meadow that ran off to the left of Miss Ward's. The hood was too heavy for them to pull very far up the hill so their rides remained short, slow, and safe. Chip wondered whatever became of the hood?

Bucky was always showing off the rugged capabilities of his jeep so a couple of times a winter he'd put chains on the front wheels and spend the day hauling sled riders to the top of Panther Mountain. He could only get six riders at a time in his jeep and that was quite remarkable in itself. The riders would tie their sleds to the back of the jeep and let Bucky transport them all to the top of the mountain. Sometimes he could take an extra rider or two if they were willing to ride on their sled towed behind the jeep.

He'd always wait a few minutes after the last rider had shoved off before heading back down the mountain himself. He'd keep the jeep in first gear, low range and let her ease herself down the mountain. That way he didn't have to worry about catching up to the riders.

Maynard's most serious sledding mishap occurred on Panther Mountain. It started out as a normal, lying down sled run from the upper jumping off spot, and it wasn't all Maynard's fault. While Maynard was making his way down the sled run, the Crites brothers were pulling up to the bottom of the mountain in their two ton, Reo log truck. Earl and Jesse Crites had decided to take that Saturday off instead of hauling logs to the mill at Bumtown. Not only had they decided to take the day off, they had already started celebrating their weekend vacation by nipping on some Thunderbird wine.

The crowd standing at the bonfire at the bottom of the mountain saw the Crites boys coming but figured they would pull up and stop to chat and that may have indeed been the case, but Earl was driving and not only was he too polluted for his reflexes to work fast enough to stop, he hit the gas instead of the brake and drove the truck on past the bonfire and into the cut at the bottom of the hill. He finally got the Reo stopped when she kicked up spinning just at the entrance to the bottom turn. It was then that Earl and Jesse thought to stay and chat for awhile. Most of the gang from the bonfire ran up to the truck urging and pleading with Earl to back the truck back down the hill to the flat. The brothers, still trying to organize their speech into something intelligible, thought everyone had come running just to see them so they were just trying to be sociable. They never did comprehend what all of the hubbub was about.

All of this was unbeknownst to Maynard as he made his usual speedy flight down the mountain. He was feeling pretty cocky too, as he made the smooth swing to the right and entered the upper end of the cut. He and the Radio Flyer were working as one. He swung her hard back to the left and rounded the sharp turn. Suddenly, there before him in the middle of the road sat the Reo log truck. Its huge front wheels were almost wedged tight against each side of the steep walls of the cut. There was nowhere for Maynard to go. The truck was coming up on him too fast and there was no way he could stop. He ducked his head down as low to the sled as he could, steered straight for the middle of the truck, and closed his eyes tight..

He shot through under the front steel bumper with a good two inches of clearance room. His cap and coat collar brushed along the entire length of the engine's oil pan wiping off dark oil and grease as the sled rocketed on beneath the underbelly of the truck. He cleared the transmission and middle frame with ease and would have made it home free but at the very rear of the truck, he raised up a hair to see where he was and his head struck the bottom of the rear axle punkin and knocked him out cold.

The sled continued on and flew out from under the rear of the truck with the unconscious rider still on board. The sled veered off to the right, slowed to a crawl in the soft snow beside the road, and nosed gently into a snow bank where it stopped.

The crowd at the truck had shifted attention to Maynard as he slipped underneath the truck and reappeared at the rear. They now ran to his aid. Maynard was coming around but still on queer street. The top of his forehead had an ugly looking red knot sticking out about the size of a grade A hen egg. Behind the knot, along the top of his scalp, there was a small stream of blood overflowing down the right side of his head. His cap was nowhere to be seen.

They sat Maynard up and applied snow to his wounds and to the back of his neck. They kept him awake as they pulled him home on his sled; all the while constantly ministering to his injuries. Maynard kept mumbling to himself all the way home "Could have made it......... Could have made it.........."

Maynard had a mild concussion and it required eight stitches to close the wound to his scalp. He had to stay inside and rest for the next two days but was back on the mountain in another week.

Evidently the Crites brothers never did catch on to what all the hubbub was about. When everybody left the truck to go help Maynard, they must have figured they had overstayed their welcome, so they backed the truck out, turned around, and went home.

One might think that sled riding in Sugar Tree was a dangerous and unsafe form of recreation when in fact, accidents like those just depicted were only the worst and they were the ones Chip recalled most vividly. For the shear number of kids sledding every day that weather and time permitted, the pure joy of sledding far outdistanced the pain and injuries suffered. Chip's most memorable and pleasurable sled ride is a case in point. It happened just around dark one Saturday evening at Panther Mountain.

Chip and the rest of the Jive Five had been sled riding for a couple of hours along with about fifteen other kids from here and there. Chip was standing by the bonfire at the bottom of the hill taking a break and trying to warm up. Standing with his back to the fire, he noticed a lone figure walking up the road toward the fire. As the figure drew closer, Chip recognized her as one Cricket Hill. Cricket was a senior at Elk River High but she could pass for a senior at WVU. She was eighteen going on twenty-six. The good Lord must have put in a couple of extra hour's work in finishing such a perfect creation. Cricket was dressed heavily for the occasion. She had on two pairs of pants, a heavy sweater, topped off with a fur lined hooded parka. All together, the clothes could do nothing to conceal those perfect proportions. You could put Cricket in a deep sea diving suit and could still tell it was Cricket. She had the parka's hood thrown back so that her long, shiny brown hair cascaded over her shoulders.

Cricket never dated any of the local guys, older or younger. She was always dating college guys or other young single men, always from who-knows-where. She was always riding off with someone in a Corvette, Jaguar, Triumph, or once in a while, a luxury car like a Lincoln or a Buick. She had never been seen in a pickup or a family sedan.

Cricket was anything but stuck-up. She was as gregarious and sociable, and in some cases even more so, as any of the eligible girls in Sugar Tree. Her demeanor was always happy-go-lucky and carefree. She didn't flirt with every boy she came in contact with, but her friendliness just convinced the boys she did. She seemed to be admired and somewhat of a mentor to the younger girls. She would often be found in the center of a group of girls talking in whispers as if she were imparting to the girls some mystic, female revelation learned from her wealth of worldly experiences and maturity.

Cricket just had romantic inclinations that evidently involved opportunities that could usher her out of the environs of Sugar Tree and into a more upward social experience. No one faulted her for her ambitions; "Good for her", they'd say. "She'll make it just fine. She couldn't have gotten a better upbringing than here in Sugar Tree, but now it's time to move on." It was more than surprising then, when

Cricket walked right past the crowd standing at the bonfire and stopped in front of Chip.

"Chip, would you be a dearest and take me for a ride?" she cooed. Her breath was sweet as maple syrup and the words seemed to flow like the same. Chip was trying to be cool but those full, pouty lips and those big, brown, bedroom eyes were melting the ligaments in his knees. His mouth was too dry to speak, so he didn't say anything. Didn't have to. Cricket softly took his hand and started off toward the mountain.

Chip gathered himself together enough to follow along, dragging his sled behind. He became aware that all activity had ceased, and that everybody else on the mountain was staring in disbelief at this most unlikely couple. He mustered enough self confidence as was needed to play the role of dominant party before the still incredulous throng, but he didn't want to ruin whatever relationship Cricket was establishing at that moment, so he decided to let Cricket take the lead and he would follow where ever it led.

Chip's stride pulled him even with Cricket as they ascended the sled run. He knew the easiest path to take up the hill and was better able to help her and guide her along the slick and steep parts if he was by her side. She talked to Chip all the while they walked up the hill together. She asked Chip about his family and how basketball was going and other topics, and it wasn't just chatter either, because every so often she would solicit an opinion or a response from him.

When they reached the upper jumping off spot, Cricket kept on going. "Let's go a little further on," she urged. So they walked hand-in-hand farther away from the revelers below. It was getting dark and they had walked beyond sight of the flickering bonfire before Cricket decided they had gone far enough.

"Let's go from here," she said. "You know the way down so you'll have to guide us." She was still in control and Chip was the willing respondent. "Now I'll get on first," and she laid down on the sled. "Now you get on. I'll show you how." Chip followed her every instruction.

Cricket directed him to kneel on the sled with his knees between her legs, then to stretch his body forward and lay down against her.

370

That shifted most of his body weight back along his legs so that he wasn't smothering Cricket. His body then just seemed to mold itself to hers. Next, she showed him how to slip his arms under hers so he could reach the guider bar. She certainly knows what she's doing, he thought.

The sled began to drift slowly forward. They were still on the level spot just above the lower section of the mountain. As the sled began to pick up speed, Cricket secured her position better by wrapping her arms around Chip's and intertwining their legs together. Her actions allowed Chip to nestle his face in that billow of silky, fresh scented, brown hair, right at the nape of her neck.. She made no attempt to shift her position. They were locked together.

The sled coasted faster and faster. Chip became oblivious to the cold, stinging night air. In fact, he had become oblivious to the rest of the outside world in general. He didn't know where he was and didn't care. Wanted only that this ecstasy continue forever. Chip's sled, that always before jolted and jerked its way over the hard, rough dips and bumps of the sled run, now floated along---undulating slowly and softly down the silky smooth run.

The sled reached the lower end of the hill and flew by the envious, and the jealous, and the resentful, and the admirers, all standing silently in the snow. Chip didn't notice them though. He had become lost in this whirlwind world with Cricket.

But the ride always has to end, and so the sled slowed to a snail's pace as it passed the bonfire and drifted a few yards off into the fading light before coming to a complete stop. Chip was drifting back into reality at about the same pace. As he did so, he discovered that the ride down the hill must have been more physically challenging than he realized. Why else would he be breathing so hard and his heart be pounding like he'd just run a half a mile? Cricket seemed to be a little breathless herself. They both remained glued together for a few more moments, neither one wanting to disengage.

"You ok?" ask Chip.

"Sure," whispered Cricket. Her voice was kind of husky sounding and seemed to come from far away. "That was great fun." She didn't move.

Reluctantly, Chip raised himself back up on his knees and then stood up, off to the side of the sled. He reached down to help Cricket up. She took his hand again and let him help her to her feet. Chip was standing with his back to the fire but the glow from the firelight was flickering and dancing about Cricket's face as she looked into his eyes. To Chip's surprise, she put her arms around his neck. "I've got to get on home, Chip," she said in a sultry whisper. "Thanks for taking me down the mountain. I've never, ever, had a sled ride with anyone like I had with you."

She pulled Chip close and reaching up on tiptoe, kissed him. It wasn't just a little peck of a kiss, it was a real kiss; soft, wet, long, close your eyes, suck your breath away, curl your toes, kiss. She finally pulled away but slipped her hand into his. "Thanks sweetie," she whispered, "I'd love to do it again with you sometime."

Chip was regaining his composure and it seemed to be coming back tenfold. "Anytime you want, Cricket," he said, looking deep into her eyes. "You just let me know."

"I will," she said, "and that's a promise." She gave him a wink, squeezed his hand, turned, and started for home. Chip thought about going after her to walk her home, but then he would no longer be letting Cricket take the lead. He didn't want to spoil the moment or their relationship, imagined or not. He stood his sled up and knocked the snow off of it, then he hung his arm over the guider to rest his head there as he watched her walk away into the cold night.

Almost every night for the next two years, Chip drifted contentedly off to sleep with warm and blissful visions of those moments together with Cricket. There were even more blissful visions of some moments he WISHED they'd had together.

Panther Mountain gained some notoriety in the late fifties and early sixties as the place to be for sledding parties. Older teens and young adults from Red Dog, Hob, Devil's Backbone, and Seneca often made their way over. There was even a group of skiers from Seneca who came over more than a few times to make the mile and a half run down the mountain.

SERIOUS ROAD GAMES?

Once a person reached the driving age, you'd think their new approach to road games would take on a more sophisticated and mature nature. It didn't. The real noticeable difference, in most road games which involved vehicles, was the competitive factor. Where before most road games were played for the mere enjoyment and thrill of the game, now the challenge of being the best or of accomplishing the task seemed to be the paramount motivating factors.

There were two vehicle road games that came into existence in Sugar Tree because of a mistake made by the Rose County State Road Commission. In 1962, the Rose County State Road decided to pave the road from Mill's Bottom to the Seneca County line which was at the top of Red Dog Hill, and upgrade it into a two lane. Nobody knew why the county had decided to pave an absolutely crooked road that ran twenty-five miles through the woods to nowhere but it turned out to be a godsend for many people in Sugar Tree.

Whoever was in charge of the paving crew thought the Rose County/Seneca County line was at the forks of the road in Sugar Tree, at the Company Store. So they paved right on past the real county line at the top of Red Dog Hill, on down Sugar Tree Hill, and finished up at Painter's Creek Fork there at the Company Store. When the paving crew radioed back to headquarters in Mill's Bottom to tell them they had finished paving to the county line in Sugar Tree, headquarters had a conniption fit. But what was done was done. They couldn't undo it. What were they gonna do, take it back up? Because of the mistake, Sugar Tree got its first real development into the modern era of transportation; a two lane, hardtop road.

Although the two lane ran all the way from Sugar Tree to Mill's Bottom, the only real significant portion of that road for the people of Sugar Tree was in that three mile stretch from the Company Store to the top of Red Dog Hill. The miners and the mantrips running the road daily from Sugar Tree to Red Dog probably appreciated it the most. When it was first paved, there were those who loaded up the family in the car or the truck and drove back and forth over that little stretch just for the convenience and experience of not having to drive off on the berm to share half the road with an approaching vehicle. The novelty of the two lane wore off after a month or two but at the time, it was the biggest development in Sugar Tree since regular telephone service.

Lewis and Bucky Keener now had the ideal track for racing their hot rods. Never again would they thunder past the Gates' home. It was a major disappointment for everyone except Riley. The advent of the Keener brother's hot rods on the new pavement turned the Sugar Tree Straight into a gathering place for the local wannabe drag racing crowd.

Serious drag racing took place over on Rt. 19, at the Moonlite Straight. There, guys raced for money and pink slips. The middle portion of the straight was marked off in the quarter mile with a start and finish line painted across both of the wide lanes. There, cheater slicks were mounted and headers uncapped. Challenges and challengers came from all over the tri-county area and from as far away as Ohio.

Even after the Sugar Tree Straight was paved into a two lane, it was not really wide enough to accommodate full blown, high horsepower drag racing. Side-by-side burn out starts and high speed, side-by-side racing put those cars in too close proximity to each other and too susceptible to a collision with one another. However, the straight was an ideal track in which to make solo trial runs for purposes of seeing what your buggy could do, tuning the engine, practicing speed shifts, finding the best combination of rpms and tire pressure for quick, hole shots, and for just showing off.

The folks who lived in Sugar Tree often had their Friday and Saturday night's sleep disrupted by the howling of tires and the roar of exhaust as some lone hot rodder announced his arrival back home by making an all out run up the straight. Everybody in the neighborhood knew when Junior Windon was back in town. It seemed at least twice a month Junior found time to come back to Sugar Tree. He always arrived on Fridays around 1:00 in the morning and announced his presence by burning rubber halfway up the straight That was Junior's signature. Nobody ever laid down rubber like

Junior. The neighbors would be aroused at 1:00 on Friday night, "Well I see Junior's back in town."

The thing that was so annoying was that Junior had the cars that could burn rubber half the way up the straight. That's why he came home every chance he had, to show off his wheels. Making matters worse was the fact that every year he brought a different car home. Junior was a GM guy. Chip can remember him coming home in a 409 equipped, '57 Chevy convertible, with full continental kit, twin spot lights, and bubble skirts. A 67' GTO, 389, dual quads, and a '64 427, fuel injected Chevy Impala, to name a few.

The Sugar Tree Straight was seven tenths of a mile long with a slight drift to the left. The straight stretch ended in a sharp ninety degree turn to the right. Unofficial race distance started at the Company Store and ended at Vernon Adkins' mailbox. It was about one hundred yards from Vernon's mailbox to the end of the straight. That gave drivers plenty of time to slow down to make the curve at the end.

Racing was always done at night. That way racers could see the headlights of any vehicles coming from the opposite direction and it would give them time to get out of harm's way. There were two rules of racing on the Sugar Tree Straight; (1) the very second an approaching headlight was spotted, the race was aborted and declared void. It didn't matter who was where when the race was called, it didn't count as a race. (2) The winner of a coin toss before the race got to pick which lane to occupy. That was significant because the driver in the left lane was the one responsible for aborting his racing when a car was spotted coming toward them and that was because he was in the opposite traffic lane. The guy racing up the right hand side of the straight was to keep right on hummin' to make it easier for the other racer to slow down and swing in behind.

The straight was sufficient for the local, less sophisticated drag racer. Link and Benji were the only high schoolers in Sugar Tree who owned their own cars and they would frequently race them. Chip raced his Plymouth and Maynard raced his dad's Corvair a few times before it was taken away from him. Most of the racing done in Sugar

Tree was done by folks who raced the family car or truck because it was the only set of wheels they had. There was always an odd sort of vehicles drag racing; pickup trucks, station wagons, four door sedans, jeeps, etc. There were no staggered starts. No matter what you were running or who you were racing against, everybody lined up at the same starting line and started on the same signal. What you did during the race was up to the individual driver.

There were a few "smokers" hidden among those family vehicles. Jeff Rogers' dad had a plain black '58 Chevy, four door sedan with a three speed on the column and a 348 under the hood. That baby would flat out get it. If there was anybody among the locals who could beat Jeff's dad's car it may have been "Happy" Cooper's dad's '61 Chrysler Newport. It too was a four door sedan, push button automatic, and nestled under it's hood was a 383 hemi. The only time Hap and Jeff ever raced, Hap took the air cleaner off the Chrysler in hopes that more air intake would increase his horsepower. He was right, but the 383 quit six seconds off the line after it sucked up some insulation out of the hood.

Nate Gill's dad had a sneaky fast, '59 Rambler Ambassador, 327 automatic. The problem with the Rambler was two fold. It was loaded with extras; power steering, power seats, power windows, and air conditioning and it seemed as if there were eight or ten belts on that engine to keep all of those accessories running. Every time Nate would get a good run going, one or two or all of those belts would fly off. It'd take Nate half an hour to put all of those belts back on.

Nate finally got to make a complete run in the Rambler one night. He was racing against "Horse" Collins who was driving his dad's '56 Ford pick up. Nate got out ahead quickly and stayed there but he'd done that before. He was almost in disbelief when he passed Vernon's mail box and all the Rambler belts were still intact. "Horse" backed off at the mailbox but Nate figured he might not ever do this again and he wanted to see what the Rambler could really do, so he kept on cranking. The Ambassador hit eighty about a hundred yards from the turn at the end of the straight and that's where all the belts decided that they had had enough. When they came undone, Nate lost his power steering. He was braking hard and trying to muscle the

Rambler through the turn but he was still going to fast and the steering didn't respond like it should have. The Rambler slid out of the turn and slammed sideways into a monstrous pile of sawdust the State Road had dumped there for treating Sugar Tree Hill. Nate didn't get hurt and there was no damage to the Rambler except that there was sawdust everywhere; in the grill, in the engine compartment, and inside the car where Nate had left both the front and rear windows down. "Horse" used the pickup to pull Nate out of his semi-buried state.

Nate's dad had to drive the Rambler to church the next morning as it was. Nate never told anyone what kind of an explanation he gave his dad as to how all of that sawdust happen to permeate every crease and cranny of his Ambassador. No one could remember if Nate ever got to drive the Rambler again after that.

Norris Wright had moved to Ohio right out of high school and got a job in a GM plant. His selective service number came up a year or so after he moved, but he was classified 4-F and was never inducted. Norris was as skillful and talented driver as there was in Sugar Tree, when he was sober. Norris was so broken up and partially mended from his many motorcycle and car wrecks that he couldn't pass the army physical. Some of his wreck injuries were so bad they were being treated in phases and were ongoing at the time of his physical. Some of his broken bones had mended well but had been broken again in other wrecks and after the doctors had reset the same break two or three times, it didn't always come out as straight as the good Lord had first made it. Norris's mobility was hindered by the many rods, plates, and pins implanted to hold him together and he was in constant pain. Norris just wasn't smart enough to realize the vicious cycle he was sinking into. He now drank more to help cope with the pain, but he continued to drive like a speed freak, relying on his driving skills to keep him safe. His drinking was impairing and deteriorating those skills and before long he'd have another wreck which would require more hospitalization and cause more pain, so he'd drink a little more.

Norris showed up back home in Sugar Tree one weekend tooling around in a fuel injected 427 Corvette. He had made some good money racing over on the Moonlite Straight but had run out of competitors. He had come back over to Sugar Tree with a new and simple challenge. It was a very simple ploy and the Sugar Tree Straight was the perfect place to pull it off.

Norris would tape two money bills of equal domination to dashboard on the passenger side of the 'Vette. He'd put up one bill and the challenger would put up the other. He'd pull the 'Vette up to a starting position in front of the Company Store and from a dead start, he would rip off the line. From the moment Norris turned the 'Vette lose, if the passenger could snatch the two bills off of the dashboard before Norris hit third gear, he could keep them. If he couldn't get them, they were Norris'.

Probably the biggest challenge was whether or not to ride with Norris. No amount of money was worth riding with Norris if he had been drinking and it didn't take him long to realize that he couldn't get any takers if he was drinking. Nobody was that stupid. When Norris showed up sober then, more times than not, he got to keep the money.

Unfortunately, the guys who gathered over on the Moonlite Straight didn't know about Norris' drinking and driving and one night in a flat out drag race with a '64 GTO, Norris lost the Corvette when he shifted from second to third. The 'Vette fishtailed into the GTO and kocked it off onto the berm on the other side of the road where it plowed headfirst into a culvert. Norris tried to save the 'Vette but his reflexes weren't quick enough. She slid sideways down the road for fifty feet, then shot straight off of the road, sped through the Moonlite Tavern's front parking lot, hit the concrete curb that ran along the front of the Tavern, and jumped high enough to smash through the front plate glass window, before coming to rest three feet short of the bar.

Miraculously, nobody was killed. The two guys in the GTO were belted in and sustained only minor injuries. Even Norris escaped uninjured that time, but alas, the 'Vette was totaled. .

For whatever reason, Norris finally gained some practical sense in his preference of a car. He never again owned a high horsepower car but instead bought these cheap, already half junk, four door sedans.

If he was bound to wreck, he might as well be going at a reasonable rate of speed and even if the car was totaled, he wouldn't be out that much and, it would have to help make his already outrageous insurance rate a little easier to afford.

Norris bought a used '61 Dodge four door sedan and as if that car wasn't ugly enough, he and his brother Flavy decided to paint it. The only paint they could find was some yellow Kemtone, inside house paint, and using some rollers, they had just enough to cover the faded gray on the Dodge.

They drove the yellow beauty down to the station one evening and joined up with a couple of their good buddies who were heading over to the Nite-N-Gale for a couple of beers. Norris got the OK from Bucky to park the Dodge off to the side of the parking lot at the station while they would be gone. It rained pretty hard that night while they were gone. Norris and Flavy didn't get back to the station until after midnight. They hopped in the Dodge and drove on home. The next morning when Bucky arrived to open the station there was a huge yellow circle in the parking lot in the outline of a '61 Dodge. The rain had washed all of the Kemtone off of the Dodge. Norris decided to leave the Dodge a faded gray.

One night while Norris and Flavy were cruising around in the Dodge, they were pulled over on Rt.19 just out of Hob by a Seneca County Deputy Sheriff. Norris never did know why he was stopped. Maybe the deputy recognized the car as belonging to Norris and figured he was probably drunk. It was one time Norris wasn't drunk and in fact, hadn't had so much as even one drink the whole night. The deputy made Norris get out of the car and ask him to walk the yellow line in the center of the road as a field sobriety test. Norris' physical condition just wouldn't let him walk a straight line. He probably could have done better walking if he had had four or five beers.

Norris tried to walk the yellow line but the deputy had seen enough and called him back. Norris kept walking away. The deputy ordered him to stop but Norris' gait became a little faster and he kept on walking. The deputy thought Norris couldn't hear very well so he yelled one more time, but by then Norris was hobbling away into the darkness as fast as he could go.

The deputy jumped back in his car and tore off down the road looking for Norris. He searched both sides of the road for a half mile in each direction but never found him. Flavy waited in the darkness, in the Dodge, by the side of the road until the deputy finally came back. He was mad, embarrassed, and frustrated. He told Flavy to get that car home and if he ever saw either one of those boys out here on 19 after midnight, he'd haul them both to the county jail.

Flavy wasn't intimidated by the deputy's threat but he played the submissive role anyway just to keep himself out of trouble. After the deputy left, Flavy drove up and down the road for thirty minutes leaning out the driver's window yelling for Norris but in the end, went home by himself. Norris showed up the next day around noon. No questions were asked. No explanations were given.

Chip and Link came up with an interesting road game one night while coming home from Red Dog in the Falcon. Coming down Sugar Tree Hill, Link decided to see if he could coast clear off the hill without using his brakes. They were almost to Dead Man's Curve when the inspiration hit him and he drifted the rest of the way off the hill in high gear. They made it easily to the bottom but the urge to make a complete run down the hill spurred them to go back and try it from the top.

Link started from a dead stop right at the top of the hill. He shifted into high gear, pushed the clutch in, and took his foot off of the brake. The Falcon rolled slowly forward then began to speed up on the down slope. When Link felt the speed just right, he let the clutch out and the transition into high gear was so smooth, the Falcon never deviated from her progression of speed.   Most people thought that Dead Man's Curve was the hardest turn to negotiate on Sugar Tree Hill, but it wasn't. Dead Man's Curve was a quick, hard turn to the left coming down the mountain but it was banked about twenty degrees and the outside of the turn was right up against the hillside. The boys found out that the toughest curve to get around was the one right above Dead Man's Curve. It was the first curve in the road coming down from the top of the hill and it was at the lower end of a half mile long straight. At the end of that straight was where a coasting automobile would reach its peak of speed. It was a long curve to the right which put the outside of the turn overlooking a drop of a couple of hundred feet straight down over the hillside. There was no banking to the curve at all, in fact the curve may have even sloped a little toward the outside. That curve led directly into Dead Man's Curve and that involved an immediate change of direction. Once through Dead Man's Curve, there were only a couple of small, gentle turns in the road and the lower part of the hill wasn't nearly as steep as the upper portion. Link's Falcon was light and compact and in high gear, the boys had no trouble making it down the hill without using the brakes. The car actually lost some speed going around Dead Man's Curve. Link thought it was too easy so they went back up to try it with the car out of gear.

The little Falcon picked up so much speed heading down the straight that Link had to ride the brake way before he got to the upper turn. They turned around in a wide spot beside Dead Man's Curve and went back up to try it again. Link got closer to the upper turn that time before he began braking but he knew they would never make it. They tried four more times that night and the last time the Falcon made it into the curve but when she began sliding across the road, Link jammed on the brakes. She just couldn't do it out of gear.

Chip's Plymouth was heavier than Link's Falcon and it coasted a little faster, but the Plymouth was wider and had a lower body profile than the Falcon and it's running gear was so worn out that Chip could easily coast all the way off the hill in high gear without using a brake. It took three or four attempts coasting in neutral before Chip was successful and even then he scared the beegeebees out of himself.

Thus was born the Sugar Tree Hill Challenge. Link and Chip could brag that they could coast their respective vehicles from top to bottom without touching a brake. It was true if they coasted in high gear. The failed attempts made in neutral were never mentioned.

The Sugar Tree Challenge was always run at night because the only way a driver could make the upper turn and Dead Man's Curve was to use all of the road. He started on the inside of every curve and let the car drift to the outside as much as possible to keep control through the turns. That meant spending some time in the opposite lane, which could also mean a head-on collision with anyone coming up the hill. By coasting off the hill at night, drivers could see the headlights of an approaching car coming up the hill in plenty of time to slow down and gain control. Meeting a car anywhere on the hill meant that the coasting attempt was aborted.

Bragging rights to a successful coast had to be witnessed by at least two independent observers. There were many unofficial runs to be sure, and some of them were probably legitimate but a driver couldn't brag about making a successful run if there were no official witnesses. The earliest official runs were legitimized by having another car follow the coasting car down the hill and watch to see if the brake lights came on; simple enough. But then guys began doing things like unhooking their brake lights or putting the car in a lower gear or barely engaging the emergency brake. So it became a necessity that the observer or observers had to ride with the driver to make sure it was an honest run. Maynard was the first and last observer to ride with a driver trying to coast off Sugar Tree Hill. It only took one harrowing ride down the hill with some nondrivin' idiot to instill in everyone's mind that following along behind in another car would be official enough-----and much safer.

Buzzy French showed up at the station one evening when Benji and Chip happen to be there and Buzzy commandeered the two to be the official observers on his attempt to coast down Sugar Tree Hill. Buzzy had a '62 Pontiac Bonneville, two door hardtop. It was an automatic with the floor shift located in the console. It was a land yacht to be sure, but it had "wide track" and Buzzy figured she would stick to the road with ease. Benji and Chip had to deliberate for a few moments before consenting. They were trying to figure out how long it had been since Buzzy's last wreck and if the time was about due for another one. They decided they would take no chances and would follow along behind Buzzy in Benji's Chevy.

The Bonneville picked up speed quickly as Buzzy let her drop down through the upper straight in Drive. According to Benji's speedometer, the Pontiac was just passing sixty when Buzzy steered her to the inside of the first curve. Instead of swinging wide then cutting to the inside, Buzzy hugged to the inside right from the beginning. The Pontiac made it through three fourths of the turn with no problem but Buzzy had chosen a line through the curve that meant a pretty severe turn to the right to keep an angle in the road for entering Dead Man's Curve. When Buzzy made that cut, the Pontiac's tires started howling in protest as she slid through the turn. Benji and Chip could see Buzzy fighting to keep the Pontiac in the road but the brake lights never did come on.

When the Bonneville's rear end went off onto the left berm, Buzzy whipped the wheel to the left and stomped on the gas. To the boys in the Falcon it looked like five feet of the Pontiac was sticking out over the edge of the hillside. Dirt and red dog spewed up from the back of the Pontiac like a motor boat wake. She was trying to gain the hardtop again but her sideways momentum was pushing her further down the hill. Buzzy whipped the wheel back to the right just as the rear wheels grabbed the edge of the hardroad. The Pontiac catapulted itself straight across the road and smashed head-on into the solid rock hillside.

Benji and Chip saw it all. Benji had to swerve the Chevy around the Pontiac which was crossways in the road. He pulled off the road at the wide place below Dead Man's Curve and he and Chip ran back up the hill to tend to Buzzy.

When they reached the still smoking and steaming Pontiac, they found Buzzy slumped over the steering wheel---out cold. Little rivulets of blood were running down the side of his head and cheeks. There was a spider web indentation in the windshield right above the steering wheel where Buzzy's head must have hit.

The front end of the Bonneville had been accordianed right back to the windshield and the doors were jammed shut. Benji and Chip yanked on the doors trying to get them open but couldn't, so they pulled Buzzy out through the window and half carried and half dragged him over to the side of the road and laid him down in the soft grass. Chip took his shirt off and wet it with the water that was trickling off of the rocks right above the stoved-in Pontiac. The boys gently applied it to Buzzy's scalp to help stop the bleeding and the cold water slowly brought him around to consciousness.

Buzzy had faired better than the Pontiac. The bleeding stopped and he had to pick a few chunks of glass out of his head. He was sore from head to foot but nothing had been broken or damaged. The Pontiac was totaled. Coasting off of Sugar Tree Hill seemed to lose its appeal after that and just kind of faded away.

One of Chip's favorite road games was driving around the back roads at night with his headlights off. Chip had gained that particular gem from his dad who use to delight his three sons by suddenly switching the headlights off as they cruised along a country lane in the still of the night. Chip had cultivated the ploy somewhat from his dad's version.

First off, Chip never told anybody else about driving around with the lights off, not even the Jive Five. The only other person who ever knew about Chip's little diversion was Judy and that was because she was often with him when he did it. It would have been less than safe to have four or five other people driving around with their headlights off too.

Secondly, Chip knew when the conditions were best for driving without lights and so held to his own safety principles. There had to be a good moon, anywhere between a half and the full moon would do. Of course the fuller the moon, the more moonlight. Cloudy or foggy nights were out. Late fall through early spring was the best season because there was less foliage to block the moonlight and thus less numerous dark and shadowy spots. That didn't mean that Chip never drove lightless in the summer, it just meant he didn't do it quite so often.

He never drove with his lights off before 11:00 PM. There was a whole lot less traffic after 11:00, especially after the evening shift change at Red Dog.

Finally, Chip confined his lights-off driving to County Rt.11, County Rt. 1, and any of the single lane dirt roads that traversed the countryside in and around Sugar Tree. It was too dangerous to try it anywhere else, like on US 19 for instance. Not only was it dangerous, Chip would have a hard time explaining this quirky driving habit if he were pulled over by a state trooper or a county deputy. He had a hard enough time trying to explain it to himself. There certainly was less chance of coming upon a state trooper or county officer out here in the sticks in the middle of the night.

It must have been the adventure and the thrill that spurred Chip to make these nightly cruises. He would turn off the headlights, turn off the dash lights, and depending on the available light, slow to a comfortable speed. It was like moving through a dream in slow motion, a black and white dream. There were no colors, just different shades of gray and black. The moonlight not only bathed the countryside but splashed and flickered through the car's interior as well. He drifted quietly by farm houses, many of which whose windows were now completely black at such a late hour, or perhaps a lone light from an upstairs window told of someone still awake.

Chip wondered, were they sick? Were they reading in bed? Had the noise from his darkened automobile awakened them or aroused their curiosity and they turned on the light in a moment of perplexity? The whole world was asleep except for him and he was drifting in slow motion through this timeless, colorless, surreal world. He slipped on through the night, dark and silent.

Farm animals in the fields and enclosures close to the road watched the dark form as it passed by with a casualness not unlike they exhibited when he passed by in the middle of the day.

Unexpectedly, the flash of headlights from an approaching vehicle, still not in sight, alerted Chip to turn on his own headlights. Chip often wondered too, what the approaching driver thought when this car seemingly appeared where there had been no car before.

Years later, Chip would enthrall his own daughters by turning out the headlights from time to time. They would scream and giggle with anxious delight and after he'd turned the lights back on, they'd beg him to do it again. Chip had grown more cautious by then, with good reason. He was responsible for more than just himself and Judy. There was so much more traffic. The trees had grown over the road so much it was like driving through a tunnel, not much moonlight got through to light the way, and the stupid digital clock in the dash board actually got brighter when he turned the headlights off. The glare made it hard to see out the windshield. He had to hold one hand over the clock to shield the glare and drive with the other hand . It was an uncomfortable position and he couldn't hold it for very long.

OFF ROAD VEHICLES

The muscle cars of the mid to late '60's unintentionally became the first Off Road Vehicles in WV.

In the '60's there were two major factors that sucked the young life blood from the little community of Sugar Tree and surrounding neighborhoods. The first was employment, or more to the point, the lack of it. When the mines in Red Dog closed in the early 60's, the only local industry the area had ever known, disappeared, never to be revived again. Older workers retired. Some middle-aged workers stayed on in the area and found other mining jobs within an hour's drive of home. However, most middle-aged and younger workers moved to other areas to find gainful employment and a majority of those workers moved to Ohio and Kentucky. Of those who moved to Ohio, most found work in the many automobile related industries that the state had to offer.

Ohio beckoned because the pay was good and the work was steady and less hazardous than mining. The pay was not as good as the mining industry but they offered other benefits that mining did not; staple benefits like retirement, workers compensation, hospitalization and insurance. Ohio beckoned because there were so many other West Virginians relocating there, the migrants didn't feel out of place. In many instances, neighbors in Sugar Tree or Red Dog were reunited as neighbors in Canton, Lodi, Akron, Wooster, Alliance, Warren, and Ravenna. Ohio beckoned because it was only a five or six-hour drive back home. There was an old joke going around about that time that tells about St. Peter taking a new arrival on a tour through heaven. They pass by a mansion with large glass windows and the new arrival spots a number of people inside who are chained to the walls. Astounded at their situation, he asks St. Peter why those people are bound to the walls. "Aw, those are West Virginians", he explains. "They try to go home every weekend."

The second factor that depleted the younger generation was the Vietnam War, and though every little community across our great nation suffered from that malignant atrocity, West Virginians were inducted at such a high percentage of the eligible population that their absence had a most detrimental impact on the mountain society.

For which ever of those two reasons a young male adult left WV, the first thing he did was to buy a new car. Single males spent their hard earned money on the latest and fastest cars. Corvettes, Z-28's, Gran Sports, GTO's, Mustangs, Super Sports, Chevelles, Chargers, GTX's, 442's, any other vehicle powered by a 283, 289, 290, 327, 348, 350, 360, 383, 409, 413, 427, 440, 442, 454 cubic inch engine, and those with fuel injection, three duces, or dual quads.

Those cars were plentiful and at a price range to fit the average income of a single male, even on a serviceman's pay. But those cars were built to be run on interstate highways and freeways or where the roads lay flat and straight, and in the early '60's, West Virginia had none. The very first place a guy headed in his new car was back to West Virginia and back to those mountainous, crooked, and narrow roads.

Ask any fifty to seventy year old native West Virginian today, and they will tell you, "Yeah, I had a car like that once." You would be hard pressed today, to find an original '60's muscle car that had been bought or driven in WV. Where did they all go? What happened to them? Parts of them can probably still be found in junkyards, embedded in trees, telephone poles, and mud banks. Some in rivers, lakes, creeks, and ponds. Scattered over hillsides and down in ravines, gullies, and hollows.

Former West Virginia owners of said vehicles were either killed, crippled, or had a deep spiritual conversion as a result of mixing muscle cars with West Virginia back roads. If they didn't wreck while trying to gain a few extra minutes to start their home visitation, or didn't wreck in their hurry to get back to work on time after staying too long on their home visit, they wrecked while at home showing off for some friends or racing some other West Virginian who was home for a visit. Many WV servicemen who bought a high horsepower car, left the car in the hands of a friend, brother, or other family member while they were away serving their duty. Sadly, most of those cars too, met the same fate.

CREEK JUMPERS

The Rapp brothers were the first in the Sugar Tree vicinity to modify vehicles for off road use. The Rapp family lived in the third house down the "holler". Fred and Chloe Rapp had four boys and two girls before Fred was killed in the mines in 1954. Chloe raised the family herself. She received a one-time pittance of benefits from WYGARB when Fred was killed, but that just barely covered funeral expenses. She did receive some social security benefits and the family's monthly allotment of commodities from the state welfare department was beneficial. The family raised a modest, but plentiful, garden in the summer and what wasn't eaten fresh out of the garden was canned and kept for winter.

Shelby was the oldest of the kids. She graduated from Elk River High School with B+ average and with an interest in academics that probably could have carried her through college but she elected to stay home and help with the family. She helped Chloe with the domestic chores and managed all Rapp family resources.

Edsil was the oldest of the boys at twenty-four. He worked off and on as a general laborer in the mines at Red Dog. WYGARB would have liked to have him as a full time worker in a specific skilled position because Edsil had a gift of being able to see just what needed done and how best to do it, regardless of what the task involved. Edsil's problem was that he usually worked himself out in three or four days and then wouldn't show up for work for a couple of weeks. His WYGARB pay was a well received supplement for the family finances.

Edsil's brother Palace, was the next oldest. Palace wasn't suited for academics so he dropped out of school when he was sixteen, still in the eighth grade. Palace was a brute of a young man with an aptitude for mechanical devices and hard labor. Palace made a little income by hiring himself out to the local farmers who needed some extra hands at various times during the year.

Rosie was the next oldest. She was in high school. Rosie was a capable high school student but her interest was primarily boys. She was a very attractive girl and was always neat, clean, and fresh. Rosie's interest in boys was not a frivilous nor a casual kind. All of her romantic relationships seemed to be long and intense and though she had many suitors, the shortest of those engagements was a little less than a year. Her romances continued on like that for two or three years after she graduated from high school and eventually the cycle returned to a former high school sweetheart to whom she married.

Thinking back on it now, Chip realized that Rosie dated about every boy in Sugar Tree except him. He never did know know why such seemingly sincere and serious relationships with Rosie did not last or why there had been so many. Maybe Rosie called them off for one reason or another, or maybe it was always her beaus who ended them. Never having been involved with Rosie, Chip had no clue.

He remembered one night when the Jive Five had planned a late night cruise out to the fire tower. Link, Maynard, and Chip were sitting in the Falcon in front of Rosie's waiting for Benji, who was dating Rosie at the time, to conclude his date with her and join them as had been arranged. It was uncomfortably quiet in the Falcon because both Link and Maynard had been previously, and apparently, seriously involved with Rosie themselves. Chip read their melancholy stare at Rosie's house that seem to say you don't know how it hurts to know she's in there with another.

In a few minutes, Benji came out and joined the boys in the Falcon. He was welcomed with playful jabs to the ribs and snide retorts about his and Rosie's nocturnal habits. That seemed to quickly dissolve Link's and Maynard's pensive mood. There was no animosity toward Benji and certainly, there were no ill feelings towards Rosie regarding what could have been.

The youngest Rapp children were twin boys, Raymond and Waymond. They were about Riley's age and attended Lick Run School. The Rapps may not have had much but Chloe kept her house and her school-aged kids neat and clean.

When Fred was alive, his income from the mines at Red Dog was more or less a supplemental income because the Rapp family's real vocation was the making and selling of their own moonshine liquor. The family recipe for moonshine had been handed down through three generations of mountain folks. But just as important as the recipe, the family's painstaking adherence to time, materials, and instinct had been handed down as well. It took years of experience to learn the perfect Rapp brewing procedure. Fred had learned well from his dad and the older folks who had bought shine from the Rapps for all of those years, said they couldn't tell any difference in the Rapp's moonshine in the last forty years. Fred had begun the teaching process with Edsil and Palace when they were young boys but being so young, the true art and Rapp pride in brewing moonshine hadn't been instilled in them before Fred had died. The boys knew how to brew shine the Rapp way, but hadn't yet learned all the little nuances that made it special. And though it was still the best moonshine in the tri-county area, it wasn't brewed in the quantity that Fred turned out either. Edsil and Palace had other interests and they only brewed when they felt like it.

Everybody knew the Rapps sold moonshine but nothing was ever done to try and stop the illegal practice. Even a few of the past and present county and state law enforcement officers were known to stock some of the Rapps' shine in their personal liquor cabinets. Of course they were never seen personally buying 'shine from the Rapps, but it was a known fact that they were preferred customers.

Chloe was known to have lent a helping hand in the moonshine business from time to time especially in measuring portions, furnishing the Mason jars, and tending to the corn growing. She knew the money that came from the sale of the shine was making it possible to give her kids and her home some amenities they would never otherwise experience. But Chloe would never permit her daughters to be a part of any of that business and adamantly forbid the sale of moonshine from her home.

When a batch of Rapp moonshine was ready for sale, Edsil would load the bed of the family's '50 Ford pickup with the produce and drive out of the holler. The moonshine was sold in quart-sized Mason jars and for safe transport, the filled jars were packed in empty dynamite boxes filled with sawdust. Edsil brought the sawdust and the dynamite boxes home from the mines when he worked. They threw a canvas tarp over the cargo to at least be a little discreet.

They would park in the wide place where the holler road intersected Rt.11 for awhile, then they'd move on to the top of Red

Dog Hill. After a spell there, they might drive back down to the station. They didn't like to stay in one spot too long because being visible was their main form of advertising, so the more they moved around, the more people would see they were open for business. Everybody knew when they saw the Rapp's pickup parked by the road somewhere with the tarp over the bed, that they were open for business.

They always set up shop for a little while, along the back roads away from Sugar Tree and Red Dog to accomodate those clients who would rather not be seen doing business with the Rapps. After a short while, they would move to the Esso station in Sugar Tree where they did their best business.

Bucky and Lewis had an unspoken agreement with the Rapps that if they parked at the station, they would not park next to the store but would park off to the upper side of the lot so as not to interfere with the regular business at the station. It helped both parties because the Rapp's could locate in the center of the best market and the extra trade they brought in usually wound up also doing a little business at the station.

Sometimes Edsil would take some 'shine with him when he went to work in the mines just to see if there were any buyers. There always were. Sometimes he'd take orders for the next day but Edsil never sold moonshine to any miner he didn't know and never, ever, to any miner who was was not coming off his shift.

Edsil and Palace devoted their recreational time to building and driving "creek jumpers". Creek jumpers were cars modified so they could be run up and down the three and half miles of the holler road. Even though Palace was the one with the mechanical aptitude, Edsil was no slouch himself when it came to working on cars and what the boys lacked in real mechanic tools and equipment, they improvised from what materials they did have.

They never paid more than a hundred dollars for a car that was potential creek jumper material and in most cases, paid much less. These were cars that had been wrecked or had the engine blown or were just worn out, hence the cheap price. If the Rapps thought they could make an abandon or forsaken car run again as a creek jumper, they would try to deal for it. Sometimes a local might get in contact with the brothers and make an offer on a car they were trying to get rid of.

The Rapp's garage was the shaded, bare ground area under a big sycamore tree in their backyard. They were the original shade tree mechanics. Their engine hoist was a come-along fastened to a low slung limb and it seemed there was always an engine hanging from the come-along, a few feet off the ground. There were car parts and parts of cars scattered throughout the back yard, the front yard, and across the road in front of their house. The carcasses of a few use-to-be creek jumpers were scattered along the holler road; abandoned where they had expired. .

The most dramatic and basic modification the Rapp's used to transform a vehicle into a creek jumper was to remove part of the chasse from the frame. They left the front end, the front fenders, the hood, and the windshield in tact. The fenders, hood, and front were left to help protect the engine from water, mud, brush, branches, and debris. The windshield was left to protect the driver and front seat passengers from same. The doors, body shell, trunk, and rear fenders were removed. The brothers had no cutting torch so Palace hacked the body away with a pole ax.

For the brothers, pickup trucks made the best creek jumpers. The bed was easy to remove and if they could keep the cab fully intact, it would provide optimum protection. The one drawback to the pickup was that it could only carry three people safely. There was no way to add extra seating room in the rear without some effort and that was too much work for a leisure activity. The Rapps kept the modified pickups for their own personal use.

Sedans presented more work than pickups but when completed, they offered twice as much room for passengers. Holler runs were always more fun with a group. They built a wooden box into which they could carry tools, extra parts, and various necessities. The boys made the equipment box interchangeable with the pickup or the sedan. It was fastened to the pickup right behind the cab and on the sedan it went right behind the rear seat where the trunk would normally have been. It made for easy access. Whether pickup or sedan, the boys tried to keep at least one working headlight for nighttime driving and they always left the front and rear bumpers attached for purposes of pulling or pushing.

One day Chip's dad decided to sell the family Mercury. It was ten years old and even though it still ran like a Singer sewing machine, the paint was faded, the body and frame were beginning to rust from those ten winters of driving through calcium chloride the State Road used to treat the ice and snow on the roads, and she was starting to show the wear and tear she suffered from one hundred and twenty thousand miles of the three Gates brothers' abuse. Mr. Gates had his eye on a '51 Mercury that was actually in better condition than their own '50, and the owner was willing to make Mr. Gates a good deal. By word of mouth, Mr. Gates made it known that he'd take four hundred dollars for the Merc.

The Rapp brothers broke their own principle and showed up at the Gates, with four hundred dollars in hand to buy the Merc. Much to the relief of the rest of the family, Mr. Gates refused to sell the car to the Rapps. They negotiated for about an hour out on the front porch but Mr. Gates wouldn't give in. The Rapp brothers left, mumbling to themselves; they never understood.

Mr. Gates told the family that it was hard enough having to part with a beloved member of their family and there was no way he was going to let the Rapps desecrate such a wonderful old automobile right there in sight of her home. With the blessing of the family, he decided to keep the old Merc in the family and keep her running as long as he could and if he did get rid of her, he'd trade her in on another car.

The holler road stretched three and a half miles from its beginning off the hard road to its end at the Pino Butcher Hole. The first two miles of the holler road offered the best driving and that's where the Rapps roamed the most. There were no hills because the road ran almost at the same level as Sugar Tree Run, and in some instances, was below the level of the creek. The road was wider on the upper end of the holler and the base was mostly sand and gravel which made for a smooth and unencumbered ride. The holler valley was very wide here; one to two hundred yards wide in some places. The long hours of sunlight kept the road bed dry and firm. The only road obstacles in those first few miles were the six creek crossings that had to be forded. Hence the derivative of the name, "creek jumper". The Rapps liked to run those upper two miles because they could make good speed, the road was not too abusive, and there wasn't so much brush and limbs hanging over in the road to wack at them when they sped by.

Another reason the upper two miles of the holler road stayed in such good condition was because there was more traffic than just creek jumpers. Regular sedans and pickups traversed the road hauling kids to the Big Rock and the Redfin Hole for swimming, fishing, and picnics. There were six families that lived along those two miles and they traveled the road in and out of the holler not to mention those who came to visit. There were two hayfields and a number of gardens that were attended by folks who didn't live down the holler and finally, there were numerous sand and gravel bars located along the creek that were easily accessible from the road, providing the locals with an abundant and cheap source of materials for mixing cement, mortar, and other fill material.

There were times when that section of the road was inaccessible to most vehicles. Sometimes the water was too high to ford the creek crossings safely or the high water flooded the road itself. Winter snows sometimes were too deep to drive through and it was common in the winter for the creek to freeze over, making it too dangerous to attempt a creek crossing. Four of the families that lived down the holler kept horses for work and transportation but sometimes conditions were too treacherous for even horses. During those times, walking was the safest way in and out of the holler.

The two mile upper section of the holler road ended just below the Big Rock. From there on down to the Pino Butcher Hole, the road and the driving conditions deteriorated quickly. The road crossed the creek at least three more times but the holler narrowed down there, until there was only room on the valley floor for the road and the creek and in two places, it was so narrow the road and the creek merged into one. In one of those places the road ran right down the middle of the creek for a hundred yards and in the second, the road followed the creek for only a hundred feet. The going was slow and very rough and in both places one had to watch the opposite side of the creek closely to know where the road turned up out of the creek.

The trees and brush were so crowded together in that narrow part of the holler that they formed a canopy over the road that was virtually impenetrable to the rays of the sun. Not only did it stay relatively dark down in there, it was swampy and muddy because the ground just never got enough sun to dry completely out.

Just before the road reached the Pino Butcher Hole, it dipped down into the creek and emerged into the sunlight once again. The road ended on a sand bar at the upper end of the Butcher Hole. Actually, the road disappeared into the creek and never appeared again. The Butcher Hole was the large end of the funnel that fed Sugar Tree Run into a narrow, rocky ravine. The hole of water itself was fifty to sixty feet long and drafted down to a depth of six or seven feet before spilling out in swift rapids at the lower end. The water hole was too deep and the creek was too rocky and swift below that to drive a vehicle any further down the holler. The hillsides were too steep and high to drive around the creek and even though it was only another mile from the Butcher Hole to Elk River and the mouth of Sugar Tree Run, the only way a person could get there would be to wade down the creek.

Chip wasn't that familiar with the Rapps, except for Rosie, because all the rest were either older or younger than he was and they never had an occasion to fraternize much. Maynard was more familiar with the older boys because he lived closer to them than Chip did. It was Maynard's round about acquaintance with the Rapp brothers that led to Chip's one and only creek jumper joy ride.

Maynard and Chip had spent the better part of a summer day swimming and fishing at the Redfin Hole. When they heard the 3:00 whistle blow, they started hoofing it up the holler road for home. They hadn't gotten very far when they heard the roar and clatter of an approaching vehicle. The noise from the vehicle was echoing around in the valley so loud they couldn't tell from which direction it was coming, but in the next instant, it appeared around a little bend in the road up ahead of them. Chip couldn't tell what the car was because the entire grill, parklight assembly, and headlights were missing. Maynard said he thought it was a '49 or '50 Oldsmobile, going by the hood ornament that was still in place.

The boys stepped back off the road into a rhododendron thicket as the Olds sped on by. Edsil was driving and when he saw the two boys, he shoved the clutch in and locked up the Olds. The only brake working was the left rear so the Olds didn't stop until that left rear wheel had dragged fifty feet though the sand. Edsil threw her up into reverse and spun fifty feet backwards to jerk to a stop beside Maynard and Chip.

"Hey Samples," he yelled above the noise of the idling but unmufflered engine, "you boys wanna take a ride? We're goin' down to the Butcher Hole. Ain't been down there for awhile. Won't be gone long. Just down and back. Come on. Whatayuh say?" Maynard looked at Chip. Chip shrugged.

Edsil looked at the boys, "Well. Goin' or not?" He revved the engine.

"Come on," said Maynard, "what the heck."

Edsil waited while the boys hid their fishing poles and backpacks in the rhododendron thicket they were standing in. As they were climbing into the back seat, Edsil jerked the Olds down into first gear and stomped the gas. The rocket take-off dumped Chip, shoulder first, into the back of the seat. Maynard actually stumbled against the bottom of the seat and flipped right over the back and into the wooden tool box. Fortunately he didn't get hurt but he was holding on with all he could to keep from falling off the back of the car. Chip had to help him climb back over the seat to settle in.

The two boys learned quickly that by pressing their feet against the bottom of the front seat they were able to wedge themselves against the back of their seat and that kept them from becoming airborne when the Olds went over any significant dips or humps in the road. Holding on to the bottom of their seat also kept them from being flung out of the car sideways when Edsil made any quick turns of the steering wheel. By the time they had figured out the best way to stay in the seat they were at a creek crossing.

Edsil jammed the Olds up into second gear and hit the creek wide open. Just before the Olds nosed down into the creek, Edsil and Palace ducked down low in their seats. Maynard and Chip saw what they were doing but by the time they figured out why, they were soaked by the spray of water that was kicked up by the Olds.

The Olds sputtered and backfired and then jerked her way back up into the road on the other side of the creek as Edsil fought to keep the engine running. He stopped in the road and let the water drain out and off of her. The engine was missing badly but was still running. He just let it run that way for a moment or two hoping the hot engine would dry itself off, but she had taken on too much water. He and Palace would have to dry her out themselves.

Edsil shut the engine off. "Give me a swig," he said to Palace. The boys hadn't noticed the half empty mason jar of moonshine riding secure between Palace's legs. Palace pulled the jar out and unscrewed the lid. He took a little sip himself before passing it over to Edsil.

"Smooooooooth," said Edsil after taking a long sip. He passed the jar over his shoulder to the boys in the back seat. "You boys want some?"

"I can't," Maynard lied. "Got a heart condition. Doctor said one drink of liquor could kill me dead."

Chip was trying to keep from laughing. "Me neither," he said. "I got to keep in condition for basketball."

Those answers must have seemed plausible to Edsil because he made no comment. He took another sip from the jar before passing it back to Palace.

"I'll go dry out the engine if you'll let me drive," Palace offered.

"Aw go ahead. No need us both gettin' out. You can drive some I reckon."

Palace carefully set the mason jar down on the floor, swung out of his seat, trotted around to the front of the Olds, and popped the hood latch. He retrieved a sawed off broom handle from under there somewhere and propped the hood open. He fiddled around under the hood for awhile then leaned back and looked around the open hood at Edsil. "Try her now," he said. The Olds ground over and over but wouldn't hit a lick.

"Hold it a minute," Palace said. He grabbed the bare end of a plug wire with his fingers. "Try it again". Edsil turned her over again. "Nothin'," Palace declared. He ducked back under the hood and banged around a few more minutes. "Now try her"

Edsil hit the starter and Palace jumped three feet off the ground, banging his head on the side of the upraised hood. "By god she's firin' now," he said, rubbing his head. "Try her again."

The Olds hit as soon as Edsil turned the starter. "Smooth as the day I was born," Palace said, admiring his work.

"Come on, dufus. Let's get goin'," Edsil said, as he slid across to the passenger side of the seat.

Palace stuck the broom handle back from wherever he kept it, closed the hood, and slid in under the wheel. "I bet I could give A.J. Foyt a run for his money, anytime."

Edsil reached down and got the mason jar and unscrewed the lid. "Well, A.J. ain't here now. It's just us. So see if you can git us to the Butcher Hole and back". He tipped the jar up to his mouth to take a swig.

Palace was looking down the road. "Right chief," he said, and he shifted into first and stomped the gas to the floor. The Olds kicked sideways, spinning up the sand and gravel as she tried to get some traction. The moonshine sloshed out of the jar and Edsil took a face full. He was choking and sputtering and gagging. Moonshine was running out his nose. It must have set his whole head on fire.

"You stupid hillbilly," he gurgled. "What kind of fool are you anyway? Igrant hick.."

Palace jammed on the brake. Edsil pitched forward almost into the floor but he managed to keep from spilling anymore 'shine.

Palace's face was an angry red. He pointed his finger at Edsil. "Don't call me a fool. Don't never call me a fool. You call me a fool again and I swear I'll......... "

"I didn't call you a fool, you idiot. I said you act like one." He slapped Palace's finger away. "Don't act like one and I won't have to say anything. Here have another drink."

Palace looked at Edsil for a second then grabbed the jar and took

399

a good healthy drink. He passed the jar back to Edsil.

Palace eased the Olds back into motion again. Maynard and Chip didn't know how much the Rapp boys had to drink before they were picked up, but the moonshine was beginning to mellow them out. Palace made the next two creek crossings at a slower pace and they made it across without incident. Maynard and Chip had learned to duck down behind the back of the front seat whenever they saw Edsil and Palace duck and thus they were able to stay fairly dry and avoid the tree limbs and brush that whipped by.

The joyriders cruised deeper and deeper into the holler. They reached the first spot where the road actually ran down the creek. This was the long stretch of creek road and the ride was rough. Palace tried to go slow but the creek bed was awfully rocky and the Olds jumped and bucked so hard, the boys thought they were going to be bounced right off their seat into the creek. Edsil stood up and looked over the windshield searching for the shallowest part to drive through. He kept giving Palace directions and Palace nursed the Olds along until they finally made it back up onto the semi-dry road.

They didn't go but a little ways before they had to drive back into the creek for a hundred feet. The going was a bit easier because the creek bed wasn't as rocky and it wasn't as deep as the last stretch had been. Palace eased the Olds right on down the creek and turned up the incline to drive out on the other side. The incline wasn't very high, but it was steep and muddy. The front wheels of the Olds reached the top of the bank but when the rear wheels came out of the water they could get no traction in the mud and kicked up spinning. Palace was still in first gear so the first thing he did was shoot the gas to her. The rear wheels slung mud and water clear over the back seat, over the front seat, and all over the dash and the inside of the windshield. The backs of the seats protected the riders from the shoulders down but the mud sprayed all over the backs of their heads and neck. Amid the anguished cussing from Edsil, Palace finally realize what he was doing and let off. He pushed the clutch in and let the Olds drift back down off the incline and into the creek.

Edsil was giving him instructions laced with more profanity. "Ok. Ok. Ease her back into the creek and get a little run at it. It ain't

Pike's Peak you know."

"Well, that's just what I was gonna do Mr. Numbnuts, before you started mouthin' off. So just shut up and let me handle this!" Palace was afraid to make too fast a run out of the creek for fear of drowning the engine out but on the third try, he finally got the Olds up onto the flat road.

They slipped and spun their way through the mud and slop for two hundred yards before pulling up short in front of a twenty foot long mud hole. The mud hole covered the entire width of the road. There was too much brush and too many trees growing on both side of the road to find a way to skirt around the mud hole and even if they could find a path around it, the ground on both sides didn't look much better than the mud hole. To find a place to turn around and go back, they would have to back up the Olds clear to the last creek crossing.

Edsil got out and found a nice size stick with which he proceeded to poke around in the mud hole, checking its water and mud depth as he walked around the edges. He came back to the Olds and laid the stick in between the backseat and the tool box like he knew he'd need it later. . "You'll be alright," he directed Palace, "if you'll hang to the left hand side of the mud hole. It's not as deep over there and the bottom is more solid."

Palace nodded in the affirmative, shifted the Olds into first, revved the engine a couple of times, and headed for the lefthand side of the mud hole. The Olds leapt into the mud hole and went about five feet before she buried up in the mud; her frame resting on the mud in the bottom of the hole. The riders watched in fascination as the Olds pushed a three foot high wave of muddy water out in front of her. The wave rolled clear to the other end of the mud hole, hit the bank on the far side, and began its return trip toward the Olds. Now they watched in dread as the wave hit the front end of the sunken Olds just above the front bumper. What part of the wave that didn't swirl in through the open grill and drown the engine, split in two then rolled along the sides of the car before coming together again covering the floorboards and rear deck of the Olds. The boys stood up on the back seat to keep their feet dry.

"Good job, A.J. Jerkoff!" Edsil announced.

"I went right where you told me to, scum head. You shoulda checked it out better."

Edsil shook his head. "I knew I should never have let you drive. Guess I'll have to get us out of this mess." He got up clutching the jar of moonshine to his chest and stood up on the seat. He stepped from the seat over to the edge of the mud hole and his feet flew right out from under him. He did a fast little Fred Astaire shuffle with his feet while his arms went windmilling wildly in the air. Unfortunately, the first windmill flung the jar of moonshine over his right shoulder. It soared through the air in slow motion, somehow missing all those tree trunks and tree limbs, before smashing to pieces on the only rock in the whole swampy part of the holler. All that Edsil did was for naught. He slipped and slid knee deep into the mud hole. The guys in the car were falling down laughing at Edsil's antics until the jar of moonshine went flying, then Palace's demeanor went from jovial, to anger, and then he looked like he was going to cry. "You dumbass hillbilly," he yelled. "Look what you done!"

"Look what I done? Look who got us into this fix to begin with, you butthead."

"Well what we gonna do? We ain't got no more liquor and we're stuck in this friggin' mud hole!"

Edsil grabbed an overhanging tree branch and pulled himself out of the mud hole. His pants were slick with mud and water clear up to his crotch. "Don't cry, little boy. I'll take care of it."

He sloshed his way around the mud hole to the rear of the Olds and made a leap onto the rear deck. "First, lets see if this extra jar of 'shine is as good as the last one," he grinned. He rummaged around in the tool box for a moment. "Son of a bitch," he said, holding up a broken mason jar. The only part of the jar still intact was the lid and the mouth of the jar. He hurled the top of the jar at a nearby tree but missed. "Well, that's all of that", he said in finality. He dove back into the tool box and finally wrestled a come-along out of all the jumble of stuff in there.

He tossed the come-along over to the edge of the mud hole. Palace didn't say a word. He just got up and jumped from the Olds over to the bank. He looked from the come-along to the Olds and back.

"Somebody's got to go in there and hook that come-along up," he said.

"Yeah. Somebody," Edsil agreed.

"Well you're already muddy. Won't hurt you none."

"Yeah, I'll hook it up but I ain't cranking on it any. You boys can figure that out."

Palace let the rachet out on the come-along and Edsil wadded back into the mud hole dragging the cable with him. In the deepest part, the muddy water came up midway on Edsil's shin. While he hooked the cable under the front bumper of the Olds, Palace was letting the cable unwind and looking for a tree to secure the other end. He finally found a good size tree off to the right hand side of the mud hole where he could hook it to, but there was only twenty feet of cable on the come-along which meant they could only winch the Olds about halfway through the mud hole. They would have to unhook the come-along, string out more cable and find another tree on down the road with which to hook up to.

Palace wound a piece of chain around the tree and fastened it together with a nut and bolt and slipped the hooked end of the come-along onto the chain. He pumped the handle on the come-along a couple of times and pulled what little slack there was out of the cable. The first few pulls on the rachet were easy but as soon as the cable tightened up, the pulling got harder. In fact, as big and strong a man as Palace was, he was having trouble cranking any of the cable up. The Olds was moving inch by inch but it was slow, hard work. After he had moved the Olds a foot or so, he sat down by the tree, exhausted. "That baby is really stuck", he said in between breaths. "Must be hung up on the frame or somethin'. I ain't never seen anything that stuck since Frank Adkins' mule fell into Frank's old outhouse hole when he was movin' it over to his new hole. You boys will have to come over here and give me a hand."

Maynard and Chip were more than happy to lend a helping hand. All along they felt like they ought to be doing something to earn their passage on this particular jaunt but they didn't know what to do or whether or not they should even offer to do anything. Maynard reminded Chip that they were asked to go on this ride. It wasn't like they had stopped the brothers and asked for a ride. He suggested they just wait and see what happened. So when Palace ask them to help, they jumped at the chance.

Palace was right about one thing. The Olds was stuck fast. With both boys pulling on the handle with all they had, the Olds moved only inches forward. Edsil had been watching the boys and the car from his spot across the mud hole. He got slowly to his feet, waved his arms, and yelled, "HOLD IT! HOLD IT!. Hold it just a minute." The boys relaxed. Edsil jumped over the into Olds' front seat and knocked the gear shift from first, where Palace had left it, into neutral. The cable immediately went slack. "Now try it yuh bunch of jackasses. Jackasses! Got a jackass brother and two jackass passengers."

Maynard and Chip began racheting up the cable on the come-along and the Olds slipped right along through the mud hole. It was so easy the boys took turns on the handle. They winched the Olds as close to the tree as they could without pulling her sideways and turned things back over to Palace. The Olds was more than halfway through the mud hole.

Palace let the slack out of the cable, unhooked the come-along from the tree, and unfastened the chain. He let the cable unwind all the way out as he walked down past the end of the mud hole looking for another tree. When he found one to suit him, he reattached the chain, hooked the come-along up, and started pulling the Olds on through the mud hole. After ten minutes of pumping the rachet handle, Palace quit. Maynard and Chip went right over to help but Palace didn't quit because he was tired. He quit because from where the come-along was presently anchored, they were only going to be able to get half of the Olds out of the mud hole. He was going to have to move the come-along one more time so he figured now was as good a time as ever. The whole relocation process was started over but this time Maynard and Chip jumped right in and helped and it didn't take but a few minutes.

All of this time, Edsil was resting in one of the few sunny spots to be found under that heavy canopy of trees and he had either passed out or was just taking a nap. Palace and the boys soon had the Olds back on semi-solid road.

While the boys put the come-along and chain up, Palace went to work under the hood of the Olds. "Now listen," he told the boys, "don't wake Edsil up just yet. If he wakes up before I get this thing runnin', he won't let me drive no more. If I can get her runnin' before he wakes up, we'll all jump in and then wake him up. He can't do nothin' but ride along. Serves him right, too, lazy dip."

Palace worked some more on the engine. He wanted to be sure she'd start on the first crack or Edsil would wake up for sure. After a few minutes he jumped in the driver's seat and hit the starter. She turned over and over but wouldn't start. Edsil woke up just as she decided to fire up. Palace and the boys were already in their seats ready to go but the hood was still up. "Hey," Edsil yelled jumping up and running up to the car. "Go put the hood down."

"Can't," answered Palace, "got to keep her runnin' ". He gunned the engine a couple of times.

Edsil continued on around to the front of the Olds mumbling more obscenities under his breath and slammed the hood shut. Palace turned and grinned to the boys in the back seat. When he turned back around there was Edsil still standing in the road in front of the car. He was giving Palace the finger with both hands and for emphasis, was pumping them wildly up and down. Palace gave a big horse laugh and gunned the engine a couple more times. Edsil jumped quickly out of the way and swung around to the passenger side of the Olds. He slid in the front seat. "Ok AJ Jerkhead", lets go man, go!"

Palace spun out and shifted into second but they only managed to go about fifty yards before they encountered another mud hole. This one wasn't nearly as long as the one they had just traversed. Edsil got out and retrieved his poking stick. This time he walked all around the mud hole poking and prodding very carefully with his stick and the riders all watched his every step. He came back to the car and got in. "Now listen to me this time, mule head."

"Yeah, I listened to you the last time for all the good it done."

Edsil paused for a moment, "Just shut up............ If you'll hold her to your side, you can get the left up along that sand bank. That side's not very deep anyway but you gotta keep her movin' but not so fast that she'll drown out. Want me to take her through?"

"That's a laugh," Palace replied. "Watch this."

Palace jerked the Olds down in first and jumped on the gas. She kicked sideways a bit and the front end jumped down into the mud hole but then climbed right up on top of the bank on the left side. Palace wasn't about to lose that trajectory so he gunned the Olds a little more. Edsil was standing up on the front seat leaning over the windshield. He was yelling at Palace, "Slow down. Slow down, dumbass. You're gonna drown her out!"

The Olds was pushing a two foot wave of muddy water ahead of her but she kept right on gaining ground. She was sideways in the mud. Palace had the wheel cut as far to the right as it would go. The front wheels were running straight along the edge of the mud hole but the body was at a right angle with the front wheels. Palace and Edsil were looking straight ahead through the windshield at the tree limbs and brush sliding by while both rear wheels were now buried under the water but apparently still getting enough traction to push the Olds along the side of the mud hole.

The Olds came out of the mud hole on the other end right behind the two foot wave of muddy water. She looked like a prehistoric dragon lizard of some kind. There were little rivulets of mud and water running off her and columns of steam and smoke escaping from numerous unknown cracks and crevices.

Palace was pounding the steering wheel in glee. "I told yuh. I told yuh. AJ Foyt ain't got nothin' on me."

"No. Ifin you got me to navigate. See what you can do when you listen to me."

"Well, I reckon it'll take both of us to get us outa here. So don't get so cocky, bubby ."

Edsil was just as relieved as Palace to make it through. "Right, bubby," he answered.

They made the last half mile down to the Butcher Hole without incident. Edsil and Palace's animosity towards each other had seemed to mellow as long as things went well. Maynard and Chip were just happy to be at the half way point of this journey.

Edsil got out and directed Palace in getting the Olds turned around on the sand bar in front of the Butcher Hole. When the Olds was finally facing back out of the holler, Palace turned the engine off and he and the boys got out.

Edsil slipped along the edge of the water hole to see if he could sneak a look at some of the fish in the hole before they were frightened out of sight. Palace picked up a rock the size of a basketball and held it over his head as he sneaked up on the hole. He looked around in the hole for a moment then heaved the big stone right toward the middle of the hole. It hit with enough force to splash water on his unsuspecting brother. "Whatayuh doin', yuh stupid jackass?" Edsil yelled at Palace.

"I's tryin' to kill that big ole bass I seen in nair," Palace explained.

Edsil looked at him. There was water dripping off his nose and chin. "You're about the stupidest..........no, you ARE the stupidest assed hillybilly I ever seen. No use hangin' around here anymore. Come on lets get outa here."

Palace was closest to the Olds so he made a dash for the car and jumped in the driver's seat.   Edsil tried to shove Palace over to the passenger seat. "Come on, AJ Jerkoff, it's time I did the drivin' ".

Palace held on to the wheel with both hands. "No, you said I could drive and by god I'm drivin' ".

Edsil wasn't strong enough to move Palace out of there. "Ok," he said, "but if you screw up one more time. I'm drivin'. No excuses, no question. You got that?"

"Yeah. Sure. I got it."

After everybody got settled, Palace hit the starter. The Olds turned over awful slowly but after a moment of indecision, the engine roared to life. Edsil checked the amp gauge. "She's dischargin'," he announced. "Must be the battery goin' bad. No use unhookin' her now. We'll have to turn her off at the long mud hole anyway, we'll fix her then." He waved Palace on ahead. "Come on. Let's go. Time's a wastin' ".

Palace drove up the road to the first mud hole and stopped just a few feet short of it. He shifted into neutral and kept revving the engine to keep it running. Edsil surveyed the mud hole from his standing position looking over the top the windshield. Chip thought

407

of the captain of a ship as he stood at the helm looking out over the narrow inlet he had to navigate through.

"Let's see. We run this baby over to the right here, didn't we?" he asked, motioning to the upper side of the mud hole.

"Yeah we did," confirmed Palace.

"Well try and make it back through there, mule brains, so we don't have to get out and winch through there. You can do that much, can't you?"

"You hide and watch," answered Palace.

He shifted into first and revved the engine again. The bank on the right side was just about a tire's width wide and Palace eased the Olds right along on top of that bank until the rear wheel gained a purchase there too. The left side of the Olds dropped down into the mud hole but Palace kept her at an even speed and with a tight grip on the steering wheel, he babied her right through the mud hole without a bit of trouble.

Once through that one, Palace sped up and covered the fifty yards to the next mud hole in a rush. He slid the Olds to a stop and turned off the engine. There wasn't much else they could do. So everybody hopped out and went to work. Edsil hooked the cable end of the come-along under the Olds and passed the other end to Palace who let the cable string out as far as it would go before deciding which tree to hook to. Maynard and Chip fastened the chain around the tree and Palace hooked the come-along up. They took turns winching the Olds through the mud hole until they used up all of the cable. They only had to move the cable twice to make it all the way across to the dry road on the other side but working together, they made short work of the process.

When the boys got everything unhooked and stowed away, they settled in their seats for the ride back. Palace turned the key on and hit the starter. The Olds clicked a few times but that was it. The battery was dead. "You unhook the battery and take it out," Edsil directed. "I'll get the extra battery in the tool box and we'll hook it up."

They switched batteries. Edsil stood by the open hood. "Ok. Try her,." he said.

Palace turned the starter switch but the Olds didn't even click. The

408

extra battery was deader than the one they had in it. Edsil started cussing to himself as he switched the batteries back around again. "Now try her". Palace hit the starter but the Olds only clicked a few times. "Ok. Ok. Fine! If that's how you want to act, you piece of junk, we'll fix your hind end. Make sure the key's off." Palace turned the key off and Edsil removed both batteries and piled them in the wooden tool box on top of everything else. He slammed the hood shut and walked back around to the boys. "Come on," he motioned for the boys to get out. "We'll push her up the road and jump start her. Palace, put her in second gear and when I tell yuh, you let the clutch out. Not before.....but right when I tell yuh. Got it?"

"Yeah, yeah, I got it!"

The road had a slight up grade to it here so they were going to have to push uphill, but that was all they could do because the mud hole was just behind them. Edsil, Maynard and Chip got behind the Olds and got her rolling frontwards. The car was lighter than the boys had expected because of all the body parts that had been removed. It was still an exhausting job but the three did get the Olds moving with enough speed for Edsil to yell, "Now, hit it!" to Palace.

Palace popped the clutch and the Olds jerked a couple of times but stopped dead in its tracks. "Son-of-a-bitch. Thought for sure we had enough speed to start her. I know she'll run 'cause I jus' put a rebuilt generator on her." The three sat down to rest a minute.

Palace glanced down at the ignition switch. He had forgotten to turn it on. He couldn't tell Edsil why the Olds didn't start because Edsil wouldn't let him drive anymore and probably worse. He switched on the key. "Hey, I bet if you pushed her backwards it would be easier to start."

"Easy for you to say, ridin' up there without a care. Won't you get back here and push some and I'll start her."

"Naw. You guys are doin' fine. It's even a little downhill. Pushin' will be easier".

The three got up and went to the front of the Olds. Not only did going downhill make it easier, because there was a full front end on the Olds, the three could find more comfortable places in which to apply rearward force. They got the car rolling at a good speed backwards before Edsil gave the signal. Palace popped the clutch and the engine jerked to life again. Palace kept her revved up while the rest climbed in and then they took off.

Palace kept the Olds running as he eased her along the road and through the creek until they neared the rhododendron patch where Maynard and Chip had first gotten on. Edsil informed the boys that they were afraid to stop the Olds to let them off but they would slow down as best they could and the boys could jump off. Since they couldn't stop the car, they couldn't wait around to pick up the boys again so they would have to walk the rest of the way out of the holler.

Maynard and Chip alighted from the Olds at the rhododendron thicket where they had left their fishing gear. They heard Edsil say "Come on baby. Lets MO-TO-VATE." Neither of the brothers looked back as they sputtered on up the holler road but they did give the boys a little wave before disappearing around a bend in the road.

The boys gathered up their stuff and resumed their walk out of the holler. It would take them another forty-five minutes of steady walking just to get back to the hardroad. Maynard looked at the shadows on the ground and checked the position of the sun. "Must be after 6:00," he said.

"All I know is that it's way past supper time and I'm starvin'," Chip added. The boys walked on.

After thirty minutes walking, they reached the Rapp place. The Olds was parked around back but there was no hint, nor hair of anybody stirring. The boys thought at first to stop for a rest and a cool drink of water before going on, but since they didn't see anyone about, whether there was or not, they sensed that it was a kind of unwelcome signal and continued walking on up the road.

They reached the hardroad and Maynard departed right, Chip to the left. It was 7:30 when Chip walked into the front room of the house.

Chip had no more experiences with the Rapps and their creek jumpers but Clint and Riley did. Clint and Riley went to school at Lick Run with Raymond and Waymond and were good after-school chums. Mr. & Mrs. Gates let Clint and Riley go often down to the twin's to play but they didn't know that the boys were riding in the creek jumpers with Palace and Edsil.

Chip knew because Clint and Riley would come home and spin tales of their adventures with the Rapps. How they were always arguing and getting mad at each other. One time Edsil tried to run over Palace. Chased Palace all around one of the big fields down the holler. Palace got tired of Edsil's whining one evening and started peppering him with rocks. Rocks bounced and banged off the creek jumper and smashed the windshield while Edsil was trying to get turned around. He was finally able to drive away and leave Palace to walk home alone.

One time they ran out of gas and poured moonshine in the tank. The creek jumper ran enough to limp home. Another time they had two creek jumpers running at the same time. Edsil drove one and Palace drove the other. They raced up and down the holler half the night. They even started racing around the perimeter of one of the open fields until they got mad at each other and began using the cars like a demolition derby. It was times like those when the twins and Clint and Riley would slip off and walk home. It seemed they did that quite often.

Of all of Chip's involvement with the road, one of the most endearing, one of the most memorable, and certainly the most lasting was "laying in the road".

Laying in the road came about quite innocently. One warm, spring night in early April, Maynard and Chip were walking home from a boy scout outing. They had managed to catch a ride from Sugar Tree over to Red Dog to attend the cookout but they had to hike with the rest of the troop two miles up to the Sportman's Club Park, spend two hours there, hike back to Red Dog, and make it back to Sugar Tree as best they could. They wound up walking all of the way out of Red Dog, out Red Dog Ridge, and halfway down Sugar Tree Hill before Chip suggested they stop and rest for a couple of minutes.

When they got to Dead Man's Curve, Chip took off his knapsack and laid it down on the ground just off the edge of the road. He looked around for someplace to sit down but the ground was still damp and cold from the long, recent winter so he decided to sit down along the edge of the road. The road was dry and still warm from the day's sun. Maynard unloaded his own burden and sat down beside Chip on the road. After a few moments Chip thought it would be more of a break if he could just stretch out there on the road.

Dead Man's Curve was banked a good deal and by moving down near the bottom of the inside of the curve, Chip found he could stretch out on his back with his head higher than his feet. Immediately Chip's feet and legs began to relax and his whole body seemed to slowly start rejuvenating. "Ah, this is great," he told Maynard. He clasped his hands behind his head using them as a pillow. "Come on, try it."

Maynard moved down and stretched out beside Chip. He laid there for a minute or two then sat up suddenly. "What if a car comes?" he asked.

"Not to worry," assured Chip. "We can hear any cars coming up the hill long before they get here and we can see the headlights of any car coming down the hill in plenty of time to get out of the road. Probably can see the headlights from any car coming up the hill too.

412

Besides we haven't seen a car anywhere on this road in the last hour. What makes you think one's gonna come along now?"

Maynard still couldn't seem to relax like Chip. He just couldn't seem to shake the fear of being run over. Every once in awhile he'd bolt up to a sitting position. "Shhhhh. Listen," he'd say. "I think I hear a car comin' ". No car came. Or he would roll over so he could look up the hill and watch for approaching headlights.

"Tell you what," Chip said to ease Maynard's fear. "You watch for cars coming down the hill and I'll watch for them coming up the hill. That way you won't have to keep getting up." That seemed to work for Maynard.

Chip lay looking up through the break in the trees to the night sky. There was no moon that night and the stars were brilliantly lit points against the black reaches of space. There were so many the sky seemed to be about to burst open and rain them down upon the earth. The blurred white streak of the Milky Way split the sky from horizon to horizon. A high flying jet blinked its way from one star to another as it drifted silently across the sky. It was nearly out of sight before the whispered roar of its engines reached the boys. The noise lagged behind the direction of the plane long after its source disappeared behind a mountain.

This is great, thought Chip. Don't know why I never did this before.

"Car! Car!" yelled Maynard, shattering Chip's tranquillity. Maynard jumped to his feet. Chip glanced over in Maynard's direction. No hint of a car coming down the hill. He shifted his gaze to Maynard. Maynard was looking down the hill past Chip. Chip jerked his head backed to his right and sure enough there were headlights bouncing up and down as a car made its way up Sugar Tree Hill. Chip got to his feet and he and Maynard stepped back off of the road out of the way as the car motored around Dead Man's Curve and then slipped out of sight around the turn just above them. The dark night quickly enveloped them once again. "Come on, let's go now," Maynard said.

"Not just yet," Chip replied. "Let's rest just a little more, then we'll go." He laid back down on the road. What little warmth the road

413

had retained from the spring day began to seep through Chip's clothes. It seemed to have a magical, medicinal effect and the next he knew, Maynard was shaking him awake. "Come on Chip, get up. Let's get going."

Chip stretched then got to his feet. Surprisingly refreshed, he pulled on his knapsack and with Maynard leading the way, trekked on down Sugar Tree Hill and home. But those few stolen moments of respite, gathered on a quiet spring evening in the middle of the road, would become almost as addictive to Chip as "going on the hill".

Laying in the road was always done at night and the later, the better. There was less traffic and nature seemed to be at its quietest in the early hours of morning. In the long history of layin' in the road there were only a couple of preferred locations. The best place ever was always the spot where weariness from walking made laying down in the road a necessity. But aside from those moments of necessity, Dead Man's Curve was probably the best place. Unfortunately Chip never laid in the road there but for that one time. It was too far to go just to lay in the road.

When the Jive Five didn't have anything special going on, they would often congregate on the steps of the Company Store just to hang out for awhile. Not only was the Company Store centrally located for the Jive Five, the Store's portico provided shelter from the weather as well.

Chip tried layin' in the road at the Company Store because the road was banked a little in front of the store, but there was just too much traffic and it came from so many diverse directions, Chip figured he would have to have five other people layin' in the road with him to watch for traffic in all of the directions from which it could come.

The ideal place for laying in the road was the midpoint of the Lick Run straight stretch that ran by the Gates' home. One person could lay in the road there and hear or see a vehicle approaching from either end of the straight in plenty of time to get up and get out of the road. The trouble with only one person laying in the road meant that too much time was spent watching for cars rather than enjoying the vista the night sky provided. Laying in the road was always more enjoyable and safer with at least two people. One could watch up the road and the other could watch down the road. Both directions would be covered and one could devote more attention to gazing at the heavens.

Laying in the road at the Gates' was convenient. Chip could go there anytime at night when the weather permitted. "Going on the hill" remained his primary escape from the busyness of the world and, except for Judy, he kept it the solitary experience he had come to relish. Layin' in the road seemed to somehow augment that escape. Laying in the road was just a different kind of experience.

Visiting members of the Jive Five, whether it be one, two, or all, always found time to lay in the road. Other relatives and friends who stayed with Chip often found Chip's request to join him laying in the road, a bit off-the-wall at first, but would come to find their own escape in the experience. Clint and Riley often joined Chip.

No matter where the "laying in the road" experience would take you spiritually, emotionally, or mentally, there was really only one physical feat that was essential and that was watching. Talking was often an attribute to laying in the road but it wasn't a requirement. It depended on the mood of the layees, and though conversations were vastly improved by the more people involved, Chip mostly left it up to the others with him whether or not conversation would be a mainstay or not. Clint and Riley and he would often spend hours laying in the road talking about this and that. There was never any history of a female having laid in the road, not even Judy.

Mr. and Mrs. Gates never said much about Chip's practice of laying in the road until they found out Clint and Riley had been doing it. Chip's dad laid the law down then. No more laying in the road. But, boys will be boys, especially rebellious teens and preteens, so the boys slipped out to lay in the road every chance they got. It became the ultimate, clandestine, act of defiance for the Gates brothers.

Thinking back on it now, Chip suspected that his parents really knew the boys were laying in the road but they never seriously confronted the boys about it. As the boys grew older, laying in the road became an even more important part of their bond as brothers. No matter what sibling conflicts arose during those years, they never lasted longer than the interval between the times they could lay in the

415

road together.

If Mr. Gates was present anytime the boys left the house at night, his last words to them were always the same, "Remember, boys. No layin' in the road!" Their answer was always the same.

"Right, dad."

By the time the boys were in high school, Mr. Gates had abandoned the direct approach and had gone to a more subtle and psychological ploy. He'd always find newspaper articles to read to the boys. "Hey, listen to this," he'd call to their attention. "A thirty-five year old man was killed on Rt. 20 just outside of Quinnwood, Saturday, when he was run over by a car. The driver of the car said he did not see the man in time to swerve out of the way. Police did not know why the man was lying in the road."

"Rookie," Clint stated.

"Drunk and passed out," Riley offered.

If he couldn't find a newspaper article, Mr. Gates would just relate a news item he'd heard on the TV or radio. "Hey, I see where a guy was run over by a train yesterday in Gassaway. Investigators could not determine why the man was lying on the railroad tracks, unless he'd gone to sleep there."

"Must have been drunk and passed out," Clint said.

"Or already dead," Chip interjected. "The noise and racket from a train is usually loud enough to wake the dead!"

Mrs. Gates looked up at the boys from her ironing. "Don't you boys go to sleep out there on the road and get run over!".

"You heard what your mother said," Mr. Gates confirmed.

"Don't worry mom. At all times, one of us is always awake."

Those warnings, subliminal or direct, were casually, if not respectively, dismissed by the boys on their way out to lay in the road.

Even today as grown adults with families of their own, no visit to the home place is complete unless they can go out and lay in the road even if just for a little while. Chip has had calls from his college buddies who might be passing through and want to stop for a visit, or who call just wanting to come to visit for a day or so and invariably Chip always asks the question, "What do you want to do while you're

416

here?" Whatever itinerary is suggested, it will include laying in the road.

"Well, let's just shoot some pool, visit the New River Gorge Bridge, and lay in the road."

Local friends often call on the phone, "Hey, Chip, if you're not doing anything Friday night, lets lay in the road."

Laying in the road might not seem noteworthy enough to be included in this tribute to the road, but of all the road games, of all the road experiences, through all of the years, laying in the road has endured. Those road events that are now considered childish, immature, and sophomoric have been experienced and honored in their own right of passage, in their own time, and are but rekindled memories. But laying in the road has become the one, youthful constant maintained through all of those years. It is a part of Chip's past that still lives on today and each "laying in the road" event is as fresh and as exciting and as rejuvenating as it was that first time, fifty years ago. The most common topic of conversation with the Gates brothers while laying in the road these days? What else but reliving those very same road exploits which inspired this writing.

BASKETBALL

Chip walked out with the team into the entrance of the field house floor. As they stood there waiting to take the floor for pregame warmups, Chip turned and looked up at the crowd in the stands. The players were near the student section so he recognized the frenzied faces screaming down at them, but he couldn't distinguish anything they were yelling. It was like a scene from the movie "Hoosiers". Only this was the field house at West Virginia University, and this was 1962, and this was the West Virginia State High School Boys Championship Game.

When the team took the floor for their warmups, Chip could feel this would be their night. This would be his night. He could feel it, sense it. It was in the bounce of the ball, the lightness in his feet, the quickness in his hands, and the smooth confidence in his mind. No clutter there, just the focus on the game before him.

He couldn't remember the introductions, the National Anthem, or the coach's last minute instructions. Before he knew it, they were jumping the ball up at mid-court.

The tip came to Chip. He broke around two defenders on the run, drove down the lane, and laid the ball over the front of the rim. From then on, he knew he was in control. He could do nothing wrong. He threw perfect passes. He could work his way open for a shot anytime he wanted. He never once looked at the scoreboard, but he knew they were ahead and they just kept pouring it on. It was as though Chip's confidence and skill had become contagious and had infected everybody else on his team.

On a three on two fast break, Chip passed the ball to the fat kid in the corner. The fat kid starts a drive along the base line but is cut off by two defenders. He bounces the pass between them both, right back to Chip coming down the lane. Chip soars through the air, head high with the rim, and makes a two handed slam. Everything is clicking.

With only a few seconds left in the game, Chip comes down the sideline in front of his own bench, dribbles out of bounds and comes straight towards the couch his team is sitting on. He steps up on to the arm of the couch, then on to the back, and launches a shot from there at half court. The ball sails up through the rafters of the field house and comes straight down through the net just as the buzzer goes off.

But the buzzer keeps on buzzing and buzzing and buzzing and then begins to fade into a more familiar sound before Chip, still half asleep, reaches over to the night stand and fumbles around in the dark to snap off the alarm on the clock radio. The clock reads 5:30 AM.

He laid there quietly, slowly awakening from the night's sleep. He sat up and switched on the bed lamp. He was still high from the dream he'd had. He figured this particular dream must have been triggered by the reality that tonight, Chip's youngest daughter was playing in the WV State Girl's Basketball Tournament in Charleston. That's all his family had been talking about and preparing for since the girls won their regional qualifying tournament a week ago.

Judy got up, put on her robe, and went out to the kitchen to start breakfast. Chip got some clean clothes out of the dresser and went barefoot down the hall to the bathroom to shave and shower. He would go to work this morning, come home early, and pick up Judy. Then the two of them would drive the two hours to Charleston to the game at the Civic Center which was scheduled for 7:45.

Chip's daughter Lea, was a senior and the point guard for Elk River High School. This little high school girl's basketball team had given Seneca County more excitement than they had seen in a coon's age. This was only the second basketball team in the history of Elk River High School to ever make their way to the state finals. Until now, the first and only other team to do that was Chip's senior year at Elk River, thirty-seven years ago.

This morning his thoughts drifted back to that time. He remembered it as if it had been yesterday.

II

Basketball had no place whatsoever in Chip's world until he was in the sixth grade. He never even knew it existed until then. His dad took him to his first high school game that year and he was at once captured by it. What was it that so fascinated him about the game? It would seep into his consciousness in later years but right then, he had a consuming desire to learn the game.

One of Chip's best friend in the 6th grade at Red Dog was Robbie "Casey" Jones. Casey was already an accomplished athlete in Chip's eyes, being a pitcher on a little league team. One day Casey brought a real basketball to school and during noon hour he showed Chip how to dribble and pass the ball. They worked together on passing and dribbling for a whole week. It was like learning to ride a bicycle. Once Chip got the hang of it, it came naturally. He could run and stop and maintain a dribble and not walk or carry the ball or double dribble and he didn't even know what those violations were.

Three weeks after Casey's introduction to basketball, he talked Chip into trying out for the 6th-grade team. Casey made the team easily but Chip was cut that first day. However that experience of putting on shorts, shoes, and tee shirt and playing inside a building on wooden floors with real backboards and real nets was so exhilarating, Chip was hooked forever.

He began to watch the few college and NBA games that the Gateses could get on the three TV channels they got. After the games, he'd go outside and emulate the players and their moves on makeshift baskets he would create.

Chip put up anything he could find that would suffice for a rim. Old rusted buckets or water pails with the bottom cut out worked best but you couldn't shoot with a regulation size ball because it was too big to go through and too heavy for the flimsy basket, so he used an inflated rubber ball that Riley had gotten for his birthday. It was a little larger than a softball but just perfect for Chip's purposes. He nailed the buckets to every thing on the farm. The first place he tried was the side of the barn but the ground beside it was too steep and the ball kept rolling down into the creek. He tried the upper side of the barn which had a level surface to play on, but he could only get the bucket up to six feet high and still stay a safe distance beneath the edge of the tin roof.

Putting the bucket on or near either one of the two houses would draw the ire of the inhabitants therein so that was out of the question. He finally put it above Paw Paw's garage door across the road. The ground was flat and hard and there was ample room over the door to use for a backboard, but it could only be mounted between seven and eight feet high. Best of all, when the doors were opened and the car was out, you could make driving lay ups and run under the basket just like in a real gym. Unfortunately, ball playing over at the garage only lasted three days because Chip left the ball outside one evening and one of the dogs bit a hole in it.

Next, he cut the bottom out of a two pound coffee can and tacked it to the back wall inside grandma's wash house. There was an old two burner, open gas stove in the wash house that was used to heat tubs of water on wash days but during nights, Chip would fire up the old stove and spend hours playing basketball games against imaginary teams while the rain and snow and wind would assault the little wooden building to no avail. Once the tin covered walls on the inside began to sweat, Chip knew it was warm enough to turn the heat down. A little carbon monoxide didn't seem to bother him too much, only made the eyes burn a little.

The hardest thing about playing in the wash house was to find a ball that would work. He used ping pong balls at first but they were too hard to hold on to. A sock stuffed with rags worked ok but he couldn't dribble it and it wouldn't bounce back to you off of the wall, which was your teammate. He found a sponge ball about the size of a baseball which was the right size to use in the wash house but to get it to bounce you had to throw it too hard and then it made too much noise banging off the tin walls. A tennis ball, it turned out, was just perfect. Chip got three old balls from his dad's friend who had about twenty of them he carried around in the trunk of his car because his girl friend liked to play tennis and she had a dog that liked to chase them and gnaw on them. Chip treasured his tennis balls and kept them hid in the wash house for basketball games only.

For Christmas that year, Chip got an official size steel basketball rim with a cotton net and a used, genuine, leather basketball that his dad had somehow procured. He went right out and built his own square backboard, attached the rim to it, and put it up on a wooden pole on the flat behind the chicken house.

Chip never did learn to shoot the jump shot until years after high school. None of his high school or junior high coaches ever stressed or taught the fundamental mechanics of a good jump shot. They all just let players develop their own style and shooting skill. This was Chip's weakness. The flaw in his game. It's hard to learn to shoot a twelve-foot jump shot using a ping pong ball and a coffee can, or a tennis ball and a lamp shade. Even the basket he put up on the little flat across the creek wasn't much help. On dry, sunny, calm days it was fine for practicing shooting but those days were too uncommon in the winter. More often, it was so cold he had to wear gloves because the mud and water and ice made the ball too cold and slippery to control. Other times the wind blew in gusts that tended to deviate the planned trajectory of the ball. Sometimes the old leather ball got so wet it felt like shooting a five pound sack of sugar. Many times he had to wear so many clothes he moved around like Robbie the Robot.

Chip never did develop that picture perfect jump shot. He never felt confident shooting it. If it was on line, it was too short or long. If the distance was right, it was off left or right or didn't have enough arch. Benji once told him he couldn't hit the broad side of a barn with a handful of peas. However, because of his improvised practice routine, Chip did become very proficient in two areas of the game .

He could handle the ball with ease. Hours of dribbling a sponge ball, tennis ball, and ping pong ball had made his hands quick and soft. After dribbling the old leather ball for hours around the farm yard over rock piles, sand bars, and cow piles, dribbling a real ball on a flat smooth surface was nothing. The ball became an extension of his own hand. He could make the quick first step and be by an opponent in a flash. He could also keep the ball away from defenders while watching the entire play on the court around him at the same time.

The second phase of Chip's game was a natural sense or awareness of where everybody was on the floor. Not only could he see the entire floor in play, he seemed to know where players were at any one time even if he couldn't see them. This didn't happen all the time but when Chip sensed it, he knew when and where to whip a pass. Some players have extra ordinary peripheral vision. Chip had peripheral radar. Passing and ball handling became the ultimate high for Chip's game just like scoring thirty points might be for someone else.

Chip made the Junior High team at Red Dog both his seventh and eighth grade years and became the starting point guard both years. Casey was the shooting guard and leading scorer. The Jr. High season was only twelve to fifteen games long which included a ten team, 7th and 8th grade county tournament at the end of the season. Red Dog finished third when Chip was in the 7th grade and second when he was in the 8th grade. Chip spent the rest of the winter playing basketball in the wash house and out behind the chicken house by himself.

At the end of his eighth grade year, Chip had decided he would transfer to Elk River High School in Seneca, instead of remaining at Red Dog. There were a number of factors in his decision to transfer and his parents' approval was one of them. Elk River High was located in Chip's home county and the bus to the high school ran right by the house. There were also rumors that WYGARB was going to sell all of its holdings and operations in Rose and Seneca Counties which, if true, would hold uncertain fate for the town of Red Dog and all of its entities. Elk River had an enrollment of close to a thousand compared to Red Dog's one hundred, which meant not necessarily better instruction, but a broader scope of curriculum.

The one big drawback to attending Elk River was the fact that it was thirty-two miles away, as compared to five to Red Dog. It was eight miles from Chip's home to Hob, on County Rt.11. US Rt.19, running north and south through WV, flashed right through the center of Hob. The town of Seneca lay twenty-four miles to the south of Hob on Rt. 19. There were no communities or villages between Hob and Seneca, just some houses and farms scattered here and there. Freshman basketball was practiced after school at Elk River and there was no way Chip's parents were going to let him stay after school to practice that late and worry about him getting home, let alone the problems that would arise about getting home after ball games. It would also be hard to survive a cut with twenty to forty prospects who would come out for basketball at Elk River High. Anyway, those were problems that Chip wouldn't have to concern himself about, since there didn't seem to be any way he could go out for basketball at Elk River.

III

It was late in the summer, between Chip's eighth and ninth grade years, that Chip discovered the Community Building in Sugar Tree. Why he had just now become aware of it was a mystery to him because he remembered attending movies there with Benji, Saturday afternoons years ago. At one time the building had been a mule barn belonging to Hayman Monroe. Hayman owned and operated his own little private punch mine in Sugar Tree where he mined coal and delivered it to the homes and businesses in the area for heating purposes. The mules were used to pull the cars in and out of the mines.

Hayman loved children and young people and was always doing things in the community to further their enjoyment. He donated the land where the school was located in Sugar Tree and excavated the playground and ball field himself with his own equipment. Every summer he'd use his equipment to dam up Painter's Creek so the kids would have a place to splash around in and the church could hold baptisms. He built a new mule barn closer to the mines and renovated the old barn into a recreation building.

Mr. Monroe extended the old building twelve more feet and laid down a floor of tongue and groove oak. As a barn it had had a hayloft, so when he removed the lower floor of the loft, it raised the inside ceiling height to sixteen feet. Actually, there was no ceiling just the rafters supporting the roof. There were no windows and only one door. The floor and the walls were all of rough cut lumber. It was one big room, sixty feet long and forty feet wide. Electricity had been strung to the building when it was still a barn.

Initially, Mr. Monroe used the community building to show old black and white B westerns and Tarzan movies along with two or three part serials like Lash Laroo or The Copperhead. Movies were shown on Saturday afternoons and Monday nights during the summer only because there was no heat in the building. Mr. Monroe also would have candy bars, gum, peanuts, and cold pop for sale for the movies. It cost twenty five cents to see a movie but if you didn't have it, Mr. Monroe would say he'd credit it to you. You did have to have a nickel for the refreshments though.

The rest of time Mr. Monroe would open the Community Building so kids could roller skate in there. He didn't charge anything for roller skating but you could only roller skate in the daytime because there was only one little light bulb for light in the building.

Mr. Monroe usually just left the door open during the day and locked the building up at night. Because of failing health, he was in his late 80's, Mr. Monroe could no longer look after the community building so he cut off the electric and boarded the place up. It had stood in disrepair for five years.

The summer Chip discovered the Community Building, he had run into Paul and Jacky Boggs at the Esso station in Sugar Tree. They were in the process of refurbishing the community building so you could play basketball in it. Paul was the oldest brother at twenty three. He worked the day shift in the mines at Red Dog. Paul had graduated from Red Dog and had played baseball and basketball for the school. He probably could have been a better athlete if he would have developed his skills more seriously. He just enjoyed playing and was satisfied with his performance however it might be. Jacky was only nineteen. He, too, had graduated from Red Dog High and was a better athlete than Paul but after high school, his interests had switched from basketball to women and honky tonking. Paul explained to Chip what they were doing at the Community Building and asked him if he would like to come and take a look and possibly lend them a hand from time to time.

As it turned out, Chip worked in the evenings at least twice a week and some on Saturday afternoons with Paul and five or six other men about Paul's age, fixing up the Community Building. Once in a while Jacky would show up to help.

First, they got rid of all the junk that had been piled up inside. There was everything from old appliances and car parts to lumber and rats. Next, they cut out two windows on each side of the building, then nailed the cut-out portion of the window together to make a shutter. The windows were six feet tall and four feet wide. There was no glass in the openings but they could close the shutters when it was cold outside, or swing them open to let in the light or provide for ventilation. For those who weren't playing basketball, it was also a good place to sit and watch and a good place for those who chewed or rubbed snuff to spit as they ran by while playing, though the latter discouraged the former.

One of the men had fashioned or had someone to fashion, two heavy wooden fan shaped backboards. These were painted white and were mounted on braces on each end of the building. The braces allowed the backboards to stick out a foot from the wall instead of being flat against it. Someone else in the bunch came up with two brand new heavy gauge rims and bolted them to the backboards.

One of the men, who was an electrician in the mines at Red Dog, reconnected the old power line from the transformer on the power pole outside the building to the fuse box outside the building. Then he helped wire the inside for lighting. The entire wiring system inside the Community Building consisted of stringing two lead wires, with light sockets on the end, from the fuse box, up over the rafters. They then hung two 500 watt light bulbs two feet or so from the rafters above the middle of the floor and spaced them apart for the best lighting effect for the whole court. Chip didn't think the power company was aware of the hook up. There was never a power bill to pay and nothing was ever said about it. In fact, there were several things Chip wondered about, but never asked about. Like for instance, where did all the material come from? None of it had WYGARB stamped on it but, it sure had the look of supplemental mining supplies. There weren't too many places around that sold 500 watt light bulbs.

Somebody even dragged in an old coal stove and set it up alongside the wall close to the halfway point between baskets. By September of that year they were playing basketball in the Community Building.

There were some problems with the upkeep of the Community Building. Replacing the light bulbs that were constantly being struck by flying basketballs was one of them. The guys that played there a lot tried to make everybody aware of the problem. Full court passes were frowned upon because sooner or later, one pass would result in a broken light bulb. The problem always came from visitors or those who didn't play there much. With them you invariably wound up playing half court on the end where the one remaining light was still functioning.. They also had to stop the game to sweep the broken glass off the floor. With the windows open in the daytime, they could see well even with no lights turned on.

Actual replacement of light bulbs was left to a twelve year old kid named Potty Grimes. Potty just lived up the road about a quarter of a mile from the Community Building. Potty was the only one brave enough or stupid enough to do the job. Besides, he only weighed about forty pounds soakin' wet so he was not putting any undo stress on the building. When someone showed up with a replacement bulb, they'd have to go and get Potty to put it in.

Potty would stand on the shoulders of the tallest guy there and could usually reach one of the lower brackets that held the backboard to the wall. Once he grabbed on to that, he could swing his legs up to the opposite bracket and then stand and climb up between the backboard and the wall until he was on top of the backboard. He could then stand up on the top of the backboard leaning against the wall and reach the cross beams of the rafters.

Once he pulled himself up into the rafters, he could step from one cross member to the next and balance himself by holding on to the upright beams in the rafters. Finally he'd lay down across a couple of cross members and pull the light cord up, unscrew the broken end of the old light bulb, and screw in the new one. He carried the new one with him by holding it in his mouth between clenched teeth.

The first time he attempted to install a new bulb he put the small end down in his front pocket but as careful as he was in climbing up, the bulb got broken. Holding it in his mouth worked best but made breathing a chore. No one else was fearless enough to climb out on those rafters. It made Chip nervous even watching Potty do it. Everyone always chipped in with their loose change to pay Potty for replacing the bulb. He usually went home with from fifty cents to a dollar for his labors.

The 100 and 150 watt bulbs were tougher and could withstand some harsher treatment than the bigger bulbs but the lighting was dimmer. The lower watt bulbs were much easier to come by also. They could be bought at the Company Store or Keener's. The 200 watt and higher bulbs were better, though they were more fragile. Where those big watt bulbs came from was still a mystery to Chip.

He himself had looked in the stores at Mill's Bottom, Seneca, and Hob and he couldn't find them. It was always somebody that worked for WYGARB who brought in the big watt bulbs.

Another aspect of the Community Building that proved a problem was the coal stove. Even though it was almost right up against the wall, it was out on the floor and was a hazard. Because the building was so small there were no side lines or end lines to mark out-of-bounds. The walls themselves were the out-of-bounds. There was no way that little coal stove could heat up that large an area, but its benefits were utilized to the fullest. When the temperature dropped to less than thirty-five degrees, everyone would just forego any ball playing in there till it warmed up.

Everyone who came to play ball in the Community Building when the air got cold carried some coal or wood with them to burn in the stove. Sometimes one of the older guys would drive up in a vehicle with some wood or coal in the back and they would unload it and store it around back under the building. Other times guys just brought in pieces of wood or coal they had scoured up from various places as they walked around the road.

The stove was really only good for a couple of things. Once it was fired up and generating some good heat, they would stop playing every fifteen or twenty minutes and just gather around it to warm their hands and body. It was also used to warm up the ball so it would bounce better. The few really good leather or rubber coated basketballs were only brought out in the summer or when the temperature was above fifty degrees. Heating them up over the stove didn't keep them lively long enough. However, a five dollar rubber basketball from the Ben Franklin Store was just perfect for cold weather playing. It was official size and weight and the coldness didn't effect its grip much. It only needed to be held over the stove for a short time before it would become lively enough to use for the next half hour. They had to be careful not to hold it over the stove too long because it would expand to about the size of a beach ball. It would bounce true enough but would hardly go through the hoop.

There were always a couple of game delays involving the stove. Once in a while somebody would run into the stove and injure themselves or knock the stove over. The fire   always stayed contained inside the stove and there was never any danger of the building catching on fire. There were two specially carved pieces of wood kept close at hand for setting the stove back up and it took four people to do it.

Anytime the stove pipe got knocked down when the stove was lit meant a delay. They had to wait till the pipe cooled down until it could be handled to be put back together and in the meantime, smoke filled the place up so badly that they all had to go outside until it cleared.

From autumn to spring, basketball in the Community Building was played in jeans and sweatshirts. Some winter nights would require two or more layers of clothing or a jacket. When it got cold enough that they had to wear gloves, they went home.

Warm nights afforded T-shirts, but nobody with any sense played in shorts or without a shirt. Tennis shoes were best but guys also played in street shoes, army boots, five buckle arctics, or whatever they had. Warm days and nights also put away hazards of the stove and brought out the good basketballs.

Long before the three point goal became an established feature of basketball, Community Building house rules awarded three points for any shot made that was launched over at least one rafter.

Chip's old leather basketball had long since worn out and he had no ball of his own to take to the community building. He always felt that there would be others there who would have a basketball or two but just in case, he would stop at a friend's house along the way, who did have a basketball, and invite them to come along. Usually he could find someone willing to go, but if they couldn't go for some reason, they would loan Chip a ball and he would return it on his way home that night. If no one showed up to play ball at the Community Building, at least Chip could shoot around for a while.

Maynard liked to go around to the community building to play ball but Maynard didn't have a basketball. Benji had a basketball, but he never loaned it to anyone. If Benji couldn't go along with his ball, they would both stay home.

One year Benji got a brand new rubber-coated official, regulation Wilson basketball for his birthday. It was probably a twenty dollar plus basketball. Big money for a basketball then. It was a beautiful dark orange color with All American Cotton Nash's signature on it.

Now all the other guys in Sugar Tree who had basketballs used them outdoors as well as in the Community Building even though there weren't that many backyard baskets in Sugar Tree and every basketball owner dribbled their basketball on the road when walking to and from the community building. Not Benji. He vowed his basketball would never touch the ground. He carried it to and from the Community Building under his arm. He would dribble it in the house and in the basement, but never outside. That's why he never loaned it to anyone, he never knew what kind of abuse it might suffer at the hands of strangers. It was the best basketball ever to be used in the Community Building.

Unfortunately, its life in the Community Building was short lived. During its second game at the community building, somebody attempted a three point shot over two rafters and the ball impaled itself on a spike nail that was sticking out of a rafter and there it stayed. Benji, upset and disheartened, went home. The ball remained secure on that spike nail and became a permanent fixture of the Community Building. Benji lost interest in playing basketball after that.

Chip learned to dunk the ball in the Community Building. Not just dunk, but rammin', slammin', turn around, two handed stuffs. What he learned to do was run and jump on the wall with one foot and spring up in the air in front of the rim. The higher up on the wall he could plant that right foot, the higher he could spring in the air. Chip developed his off-the-wall dunk slowly, becoming more creative as his confidence and skill level increased. Eventually, he could dunk off the wall by making just one running step. On a good, on-the-run dunk, he could get his chin above the rim. He became so adept at the off-the-wall plays that he could time his leaps to rebound a shot that bounced two feet above the rim or swat an opponent's shot away from the basket. It was goal tending but it still looked good.

Maynard also learned to dunk off the wall at the Community Building. He was a little heavier than Chip and his agility wasn't quite as good, but he could still sky, and his slams were more forceful than Chip's. During pick-up games Chip and Maynard

431

would do their over-the-head and windmill dunks as part of their warmup. If there were some visiting players on hand, Maynard and Chip would use this ploy to try to psyche them out.

Off-the-wall plays didn't count in a game because the wall was out of bounds. If they did it in a pick up game with their own Sugar Tree guys, everybody would get mad because it was old hat to them. They said it destroyed the integrity of the game. Maynard and Chip would always try it early in a pick up game against first time visitors though, just to see if they could get away with it. They couldn't. There was always someone well schooled in basketball rules and regs and immediate protests would issue forth. Sometimes one of them would pull an off-the wall play anyway, if the game was lopsided or not taken seriously.

There were two things to be careful about when flyin' around the basket. One was not to land on anybody. One could hurt himself or somebody else. Maynard and Chip learned to grab hold of the brace below the rim and then hang there for a moment to check the floor underneath before dropping. Never did either one, at any time, swing or hang from the rim.

The other thing to watch out for was slick shoes or a damp wall. One slip could lead to a face full of splinters, floor burns upon one's shoulders and arms, or a twisted ankle.

Maynard's claim to fame wasn't in his off-the-wall dunk. It was his ability to spin the ball on his finger tip. He could spin it forever and then give it a little flick with the other hand to keep it going. Chip tried and tried to learn how to do that but he never could keep it going for more than two or three seconds. The only other guy with a basketball gimmick was Hobert Bradley.

Hobert was about five feet ten and weighed about one hundred and twenty pounds but he had fingers that belonged to someone seven feet tall. He could easily palm a basketball in either hand. Sugar Tree's pregame warmup went like this; Hobert would grab a basketball and do some Harlem Globetrotter's stuff, like pretending to shove the ball at you with one hand, then pull it back. He'd do that a couple of times then flip it over to Maynard who would spin it on his fingers, hold it high over his head, then bring it down low. Then he'd slap it off his finger right to Chip who took it to the wall for a three-sixty two handed jam. Still didn't impress anybody, but it was their routine and it was fun.

As that first summer drew to a close, Chip was playing basketball in the Community Building at least two nights a week from 6:00 until 11:00, sometimes on Saturday, and almost every Sunday afternoon. Once in a while, basketball would have to wait if there was some other activity like roller skating already in progress. Whoever got to the community building first had possession rights until they quit or relinquished the court. Sometimes there would be a basketball game in progress on one end, while some kids might be roller skating on the other. The Community Building was also a favorite arena for fist fights. Somebody would say something about someone's sister or girlfriend and to defend her honor they would schedule to fight in the Community Building at say, three o'clock Sunday afternoon.

Fighting in the Community Building made sense. Combatants would not be out in the weather. There would be no mud or dirt or rocks to wallow in. The lighting was good. There was plenty of open space so they didn't have to worry about trees, windows, or other obstacles to fall on or over, and the floor was not as hard as concrete or asphalt. There were always a few people around to act as seconds or make sure nobody got an unfair advantage. Many a basketball game was interrupted by a scheduled fight. Players would just mill around and watch until the fight was over and then go back to playing ball. Fights took precedence over any other activity in the Community Building.

Pickup basketball games were not always very competitive. Some nights only four or five guys would show up but usually they would be the best four or five players in the community. There were a couple of boys younger than Chip who were developing into pretty fair basketball players. Most of the serious players were guys like Paul Boggs.

Paul always brought at least four other guys with him when he came to the community building to insure there would be enough players for a game. Sometimes his brother Jacky would be with him and sometimes, not. It seemed like Paul could always scrounge up enough players.

If there were other players already there like Chip, Maynard, or Benji then all the better. Paul would take charge, even up the teams, and play ball. He even scheduled games with other small community based teams in the area when they were able to pick up four or five young men to play. Chip had watched them play a few times and their brand of basketball was surprisingly well organized and deliberate.

One evening Chip and Maynard and a couple of others were playing in the Community Building when Paul and Jacky stopped by to shoot some baskets. Paul asked Chip if he and Maynard would like to play for Sugar Tree in an upcoming game.

Chip was apprehensive about playing with and against these older men. Their games were smooth and well coordinated, not the herky-jerky pace he'd been used to. Their games were also very physical and intimidating. He wasn't sure how they would accept a punk kid tryin' to play with the big boys. But Paul reassured him.

"Listen," he explained, "these teams we play are all made up of people I know and we have a mutual respect and understanding about these games. They are all good friends of mine. We're all too old and have moved beyond that rah rah stuff. We like to play because it's fun, and we can still get around pretty well. Because we can pick and choose who we play and where we play, we can play the style that best suits us and that's at a nice, easy going pace. There is no dominate player or team around here, we're all about the same. Heck, sometimes we can't even find enough players to make a whole team. We're just a bunch of old ball players who still think there's a little ball playin' left in us. We just can't go at it every night like we were sixteen years old."

Then he smiled, "Now you've played here with us for a couple of months now and I'm tellin' you, if you and Maynard play for us, it'll give us a little advantage 'cause there is no one around here who can handle the ball like you Chip, and Maynard will be able to play enough to give us old guys some rest during a game."

Chip decided to go along for the ride for awhile to see what it was like. Maynard said he'd play when he could, but he wasn't makin' it a priority at this stage of his life. Paul said that was fine.

Chip's presence gave Sugar Tree three dependable players. There was of course Paul, who was the unofficial player/coach/manager and Pee Wee Holcomb. Pee Wee Holcomb could always be counted on. Pee Wee was about six-five and weighed around two hundred fifteen pounds. Thus the name Pee Wee. Six-five was really big in this league. Pee Wee reminded Chip of Hoss Cartwright in both size and temperament.

Pee Wee was a senior at Elk River High and had earned conference honors as a football player. He also had an undiscovered talent as a basketball player. He was not quick or clever but he was dependable. He rarely screwed up. Rarely threw a bad pass or took a bad shot. He was never emotional. He was Mr. Steady. Pee Wee could always keep things in perspective and on an even keel, usually by a good humored threat or a subtle word of caution.

The fourth member of the team was sometimes Paul's brother Jacky, but they never knew if Jacky would show up from one game to the next. Rocky Miller sometimes showed up to fill a spot. Rocky could play basketball alright, but his claim to fame was his exploits as a brawler. Rocky was two years out of high school and worked off and on for Hayman Monroe doing little piece work at the mines, or he'd work for the Keener boys at the Esso station from time to time. When Rocky got tired of work or earned enough money to go drinkin' for a couple of days, he'd just quit. When he ran out of money, he would head back to Hayman or the station for a couple of weeks.

Nobody messed with Rocky. If he was your friend, or even if he liked you a little bit, he would never instigate any trouble with you. He did like to carry on with the younger guys like Chip, doing stuff like punching around on them or coercing them to box with him in his back yard.

Rocky was also prone to bedevilment; knocking down a mail box, shoplifting cigarettes from the Keener's, sneaking his uncle's jeep out for a joy ride, piling fodder shocks up in the road and setting them on fire, little things like that. But the thing Rocky liked best was visiting the neighborhood beer joints in pursuit of a good fight. He had scars on his knuckles, face, and chest. His nose had been broken three or four times and his front teeth had all been knocked out. At this stage of Rocky's fighting career, he had learned to take his teeth out before he fought. As beat up as he was, no one could ever remember him losing a fight.

Rocky had been on the basketball team when he attended Red Dog High School. Rocky's role, as assigned by Coach Mullins, was to get into the game and specifically start a fight with their opponent's best player. Rocky was so good at it, sometimes they would throw the other player out and not him, but most of the time both players would be tossed. Coach Mullins figured he'd always come out on the better end no matter what happened. It usually didn't matter. Red Dog would lose anyway. Chip remembered in a four year stretch, Red Dog won only one basketball game, and that was against an alumni team. They lost the other three times they played the alumni.

Sometimes Maynard played on the Sugar Tree team and sometimes Paul would bring a couple of other fair players with him like Eugene Morris or Buster Mollohan. On rare occasions, Sugar Tree had five starters and even a substitute or two, but most of the time their fourth and fifth players would be someone they borrowed from the other team or talk some bystander into playing for them.

Opponents would always lend you a quality player! Some nights Sugar Tree had to use kids nine or ten years old, girls, drunks, or old men. Other times they just played with the three or four they had. This happened at away games as well as home games.

They usually traveled in Paul's car to the various places they played. Paul would set the games up a day or so in advance and sometimes they wouldn't know where they were going until Paul told them in the car on their way. Paul liked to arrive at a game a little late so he could check out the cars in the parking area. It was his way of scouting who might be playing against them that night. He'd name off whose car he recognized or whose car was not there and then proceed to tell them what kind of a game they could expect.

Chip learned quickly that most of these games were played in a good natured, competitive way. They were clean, but hard fought. There were no stakes involved except the acknowledgment from their opponents for a game well played and they expected the same from Sugar Tree. Paul did not like to schedule more than three games a year with any one team. That way, no revenge, contempt, arrogance, or pride could turn friendly rivalries into heated and volatile confrontations.

Sugar Tree traveled to junior high or high school gyms to play most of their games. These gyms were adequate and some even quite impressive. The gym at Red Dog was a great facility. Usually the team had to come up with five or ten dollars to help pay for the gym time, but sometimes they were just the guests of their opponents and didn't have to pay anything to play. Some facilities were quite interesting.

The building they played in at Jillpoke had one post in the middle of the floor that helped hold the roof up. Someone had wrapped a wrestling mat around the post and tied it there to help cushion the blow if you ran into the post.

As the story goes, Jillpoke got its name as a result of the first settlers in that region. It seems the settlers, traveling by wagon, got stuck in some heavy clay mud and got their wagons "jillpoked", "saddle bagged", or "cattywamped". They decided they had traveled far enough into the mountains and for convenience sake, this is where they would settle.

The building at Marie's Store had the foul lanes painted on the floor but the building was so small that the top of the opposing foul lanes intersected and formed an elliptical circle that designated the mid court.

The gym at Mill Creek had a coal stove too, but it was right in the middle of the floor. It was protected by a steel cage that completely surrounded it.

Wakefield High School's basketball court was up on the stage of their auditorium. They were always losing players and retrieving balls that fell off the stage.

One Sunday afternoon about half-way through a hotly contested game against a team from Rock Camp at the Community Building, Rocky Miller and his brother Abe strolled in. Rocky was not there to play ball. He was there to keep an appointment to fight a guy from Red Springs. Seems this guy, Cecil, and his brother Gary had gotten into a pool game with Rocky and Abe the night before at the Moonlite Tavern and before long, the pool game had turned into a heated exchange of words and verbal taunting. Fortunately, a

Seneca County Sheriff's Deputy happened to stop in and calm the situation.

He made the two sides leave and go home, but before they left, they set the time and place to settle their disagreement; two o'clock Sunday afternoon at the Community Building.

Cecil and Gary showed up about fifteen minutes later. Honor among these brawlers demanded that they come alone and not involve anyone else. Play was stopped and the basketball players all took up their accustomed seating arrangements for the fight. Rocky took off his shirt and with a smile and an air of swagger, stepped out into the middle of the court. He kicked off his penny loafers. He could get better traction on the wood floor in his socks than he could with those leather soled loafers. Cecil took off his leather jacket, but kept his white tee shirt on. He kept his green suede shoes on, too. They had spongy soles good for quick movements. Cecil quick-stepped unto the floor, but before the two could even start circling, Abe yanked his sweat shirt off and jumped in the middle of the two.

"Wait a minute," he demanded, talking to Rocky. "This fight is between me and this little prick. You'll have to wait till we're done then you and that other pansy can have at it".

"You cool it," replied Rocky, "who do you think set this whole thing up? Besides that son-of-a-bitch's been asking for it all along."

"Yeah. Well, you're right there! But I'm the one who's gonna teach him not to fool with these Millers."

"No way, man. Now get out of the way before I take you out."

"Well, that's the only way your going to get to him."

"Fine, you little bastard, if that's the way you want it."

So Rocky and Abe went at it. Chip supposed it was to see which one would get to fight Cecil. It was kind of funny, though nobody dared laugh out loud. They just mostly wrestled around on the floor but you could tell they were really mad. They never swung or tried to hit each other with their fists.

After watching this for about five minutes, Cecil got fed up, walked back over and put his jacket back on, and he and Gary left.

Rocky and Abe wore each other out and then just laid there on the floor for a little bit, trying to get their breath back.

"Now look what you did, dumbass. Let those two punk jamisons just walk on out of here for nothin'," Rocky wheezed between breaths.

"Come on, get up you pussy. Maybe we can still catch them," replied Abe.

They got up, put their clothes back on, and still breathing hard, staggered out the building and on down the road stalking after their quarry.

The basketball game resumed.

IV

Sugar Tree's basketball games were played for fun and the enjoyment of the game and within an atmosphere of respect. Everyone was glad to see each other and expressed much gratitude for the fact that they had someone to play and someplace to play. Most of the time after a game, someone would break out an ice chest full of beer and cokes and everyone would sit around together outside in the cars, or mill around in the parking lot and shoot the bull for half an hour or so.

There were no referees for these games so a mutual code of procedure was always agreed upon by the two teams before the game started and usually the code was adhered to fairly consistently to keep the flow of the game from being interrupted too much.

Fouls were called by the defensive player or by consent of the defensive team. There were no foul shots awarded for fouls, the offended player's team just got the ball out of bounds. Out of bounds violations were on the honor system usually confirmed by a consensus of those close to the play, but if there was some uncertainty or downright disagreement with an out of bounds violation, there were several options for settlement.

Usually the ball was given to the team on whose end of the floor the violation occurred so everyone wouldn't have to go clear down to the other end to resume play. Another solution was to have a jump ball with a mutually agreed upon player to toss the ball up or whoever called "ours" first or loudest, got the ball.

There was no clock or scoreboard so the teams would sometimes play to twenty-five baskets, not points, and change ends of the floor as a half-time. The first team to score fifty baskets won. One player from each team would be designated to keep a running score and shout out the score after each goal. Some nights nobody kept score. They just played until everybody got tired or started to horse around too much and then quit. Some nights they might play an hour and half before anyone would even get to twenty-five baskets, so everyone would just quit and go home.

One night Sugar Tree piled all five players into Paul's Chevy and rode down to Bumtown to play them at their community building in a game that Paul had scheduled with some of the men he worked with in the mines at Red Dog.

The Bumtown community building had a full size court with large square wooden backboards and one set of permanent bleachers about four rows deep along one side of the building.

Bumtown's basketball strategy was, "the bigger the better". That was fine for their style of basketball, which was actually closer to football than basketball. They were big.

One of Bumtown's players played in jeans with no shirt. The belt that held up his jeans was made from four motorcycle chains soldered together side by side so that it was about three inches wide. Chip wondered how the guy would even be able to jump. As it turned out he couldn't, but that didn't effect his style of play either. Halfway through the first half, as the guy was running up the court, he tripped over someone's feet. He fell onto his stomach and slid about fifteen feet out of bounds. His motorcycle chain belt left three or four huge gouges, five to six feet long in the floor of the gym. His team then persuaded him to take off the belt for the rest of the game. Chip guessed they were afraid of any more damage to the floor.

The wife of one of Bumtown's players kept the score and she would shout it out from where she sat in the bleachers. The score was easy to keep up with in the early part of the game, but after they got into the 40's, and 50's, it got confusing.

Paul's brother Jacky had made this trip and he kept coming up to Paul and tellin' him and the rest of the Sugar Tree players that Bumtown was cheatin' them out of points. Finally, every time the girl in the bleachers would call out the score, Jacky would correct her. The more she called the score, the more forceful Jacky yelled and that drew baleful glances from Bumtown's players. Paul finally had to call time out and draw the team over in a far away corner and huddle up with them.

"Listen Jacky," he pleaded, "if you don't shut up about the score, the husband of the scorekeeper, along with his buddies here, which are probably all her brothers, are gonna be scoring points for bouncin' our heads off this floor. Who gives a dip about the score anyway. Lets just finish playin' and go home!"

"Tell you what Jacky," it was Pee Wee with that fatherly expression in his voice. "Why don't you just keep the score mentally in your own head as we go along, and in the car going home, you can tell us what the real score finally was. Let them believe whatever they want about the game, but we'll really know who won and you'll be happy too."

That settled Jacky down and the rest of the game was fun and enjoyable. In the car going home, Jacky was ecstatic.

"Ha, we beat them dudes straight up, baby," he laughed. "No sweat."

"What was the real final score?" asked Paul.

"Fifty-six, fifty, us," revealed Jacky, pounding the dash for emphasis.

"No it wasn't," came the gentle voice from Pee Wee in the back seat. "I kept the score too, for the whole game. You dote, we lost by two. Fifty to forty-eight." Jacky's face was red but he didn't say anything. After about five seconds of silence, everybody broke up into hysterics.

Sugar Tree only ran into trouble once that fall. One Friday night a bunch of guys from Hob showed up at the Community Building for a game. Even though it went against Paul's better judgment, Sugar Tree had already played Hob three or four times this year. A couple of those games were played over at Hob, on the outdoor concrete court behind the grade school but the players from Hob really liked coming over to play inside in the community building. Truthfully, none of the Sugar Tree players had a problem with the guys from Hob. Paul worked in the mines with a couple of them, and two of their players went to school at Elk River with Chip and Maynard, though they were seniors. The short distance between Hob and Sugar Tree made it convenient to play each other often. The games were casual, but high spirited. This Friday night would be different.

Paul had always coordinated these games with his good friend Gilley Sebert but Gilley wasn't with this bunch. Paul thought he knew who one of the guys was, but Chip didn't recognize any of them. They must have congregated at the Nite & Gale before coming to Sugar Tree because the smell of beer was strong as they banged their way in.

They went down to the other end of the floor, set their beer in the window so they could grab a sip now and then, and began to warm up. They never said a word to anybody, not even to each other. At the other end of the floor, Chip's heart began to pound a little harder and he tried not to look in their direction. Finally Paul went down to explain the format for the game and go over some ground rules.

Chip watched him talking to the guys from Hob, but not once did they even nod their head or ask for a clarification of anything. They seemed to be ignoring Paul. They just kept shootin' and drinkin'. Paul came back and shook his head.

"I don't know about this," he said. "We'll just let 'em go and see what happens. Chip, I want you to tone it down. Nothin' fancy or flashy. Just basic stuff guys, and keep it simple. I don't want anyone to talk it up or hot dog. Be courteous and easy. I don't want some trouble here over a stupid ball game and those guys act like they came here lookin' for some."

There was no one else in the community building but Paul, Chip, Pee Wee, Jacky, Maynard, and the players from Hob.

Sugar Tree played as slow and as courteous as they could but still went ahead seventeen to five and could have walked away from Hob easily. Hob didn't seem to care about anything except puttin' the ball through the hoop. They never asked for the score. They never disputed a call. They never said a word. They did knock a few people down, including their own teammates, and they fell down a lot on their own. It got awfully quiet in there. Benji would say the atmosphere in there was as tight as an eight day watch.

Paul grabbed a rebound and lobbed the ball to Chip. Chip grabbed the ball at mid-court and started to drive for the basket. He felt a hard shove from behind him, then his feet got tangled up, and he fell hard, sprawled out and slidin' on the rough wood floor. He jumped up and turned around.

"Hey man," he shouted, hurt, scared, and mad. "What the ...."
But he never finished.

One of the big goons from Hob was already on him, pushing him back against the wall. Chip's head banged hard against the wall as the goon pinned him there with a forearm smashing against his chest. His greasy face and beer stained breath smothered Chip.

"You little pimple faced weenie," he snarled, "I'm gonna beat the hell out you!"

Suddenly the pressure on Chip's chest eased off and the goon was falling backwards to the floor, helped by a gentle tug on the back of his shirt collar by Pee Wee. Pee Wee was standing over the goon with his hands outstretched and turned up like he was apologizing. He was speaking so softly Chip could barely hear what he was saying.

"Now listen Mr. Wise Acre," Pee Wee said serenely, "if you even breathe on that little fella again, I'm gonna stomp on your head so bad, you'll be able to put it in that beer bottle over there to keep the rain offen it".

Then there was a shout at the door and everybody turned that way.

"Marion, you stupid bastard, you get your junk and get outa here now. If I see you or any of these boys again tonight, I'll take a two by four and beat the daylights outa all of yuh! Now get outa here and I mean now!" It was Matthew Sebert.

"Jesus, Jesus, I'm sorry, Paul", Matthew apologized, after Marion and rest of the goons had gone. "Those guys were suppose to come with me over here tonight to play but I couldn't come until later on. I guess they didn't want to wait on me. Must have left over home around three o'clock this afternoon. Should have known Marion would have been up to no good. The rest of those guys are ok, but Marion, man when he starts drinkin' he's a real hard ass. Come to think of it, he's a real hard ass even when he's not drinkin'. I'm really sorry about all this".

"Let me tell you something, Matthew". It was Jacky. He was shakin' with anger and the words came out too loud and too strong. "Those sons-of-a bitches come in here and try that crap again, I don't care who they are, I'll kick their ass from here to Hob and back. They're lucky they got outa here with just a cussin."

444

"Whoa, whoa, hot dog," Pee Wee said gently and quietly, "everything's cool. Nothin' happened 'cept Chip here got knocked down a little and that happens in every game. Right Chip."

Basketball with the Sugar Tree crew drifted on into December and January.

During freshman science class at Elk River High one cold, February morning, Mr. Collins, the science teacher, just happen to eavesdrop on a conversation between Chip and Steven Prince. It was during science lab as Mr. Collins was circulating around the room.

Steven had been up at the Community Building the night before watching Sugar Tree and Pond Gap play a game. Steven and Chip were talking about the game as they worked together on a science experiment.

"Come on Chip," Steven was saying, "how many did you get last night?"

"I don't know." Chip was pretending to be annoyed. "I think around twenty or something like that. Will you get on with it."

"Well, I was there," stated Steven. "In fact, if you remember, I was the official scorekeeper last night and I can tell you straight out, you got thirty-two points."

Chip looked at Steven in an incredulous sort of way. "You sure, Steven? If that's true, that's the most points I ever scored."

"That's a fact, sure as I'm sittin' here," grinned Steven. "But you weren't even the highest scorer last night. Jacky also had thirty-two and that Wade guy from Pond Ridge had thirty-six."

"Thirty-six what?" interrupted Mr. Collins.

"Points," expounded Steven, "Chip scored thirty-two points last night."

"Thirty-two points at what?" asked Mr. Collins.

"At basketball, what else?"

"You scored thirty-two points in a basketball game last night? For whom and for where did all this occur?" Mr. Collins asked, as he settled down on one of the lab stools nearby.

"It was just a little pickup game over at Sugar Tree last night. Wasn't much," explained Chip.

"How come you didn't come out for freshman basketball this year?" Mr. Collins asked..

"Don't have any way to get home in the evenings after practice."

"You live over at Sugar Tree?"

"Yes I do," answered Chip, with a bit of pride in his voice.

"I tell you what," stated Mr. Collins, "I guess you know I'm the freshman basketball coach here. If you could find out if it would be ok with your folks, I'll let you come to practice tomorrow and work out with the team just to satisfy my curiosity. Just come and practice with us tomorrow and see what happens. The varsity and the JV will be playing tomorrow night, so we are able to move the freshman practice time up to fill in when the varsity usually practices."

For a few years in the late 50's, varsity practice for all sports could be held the last two hours during regular school time. At Elk Valley, varsity practice began at 1:30 in the afternoon and ended around 3:10. Players had time to shower and catch their bus home, which left at 3:30. Players did not have to stay after school hours to practice except for the freshman practices. There was only one gym, so freshman had to practice after school. According to Mr. Collins, since the varsity would be playing tomorrow night, they wouldn't be practicing at 1:30, so the freshman could be excused from their regular classes to practice in the afternoon. Chip could practice with the team and then ride home on the bus.

Mr. Collins finished up his talk with Chip. "Go home and ask your parents if it is ok with them. If it is, bring your shoes and some practice shorts and tee shirt tomorrow. Let me know first thing in the morning, so I'll know whether or not to get you excused from your afternoon classes."

Chip didn't know quite how to react to all of this. He was excited to be sure but was also a bit anxious. How would he be accepted by the other players? How would he match up against players his own age who were in tip top shape and well coached? What was the sense in practicing one time with a team he knew he couldn't become a member of because of the practice schedule? What if he made a fool of himself? What if they laughed at his beat up Red Ball Jets? Why would Coach Collins even consider such a crazy thing based on the conversation between   two pubescent teenagers? These things whirled around in Chip's mind all that day.

Chip went home that evening and asked his mom and dad about it. They were all for it. Said it would be a good experience. Nothing to lose. Give it a shot. His mom washed his Red Ball Jets in the bathroom sink and hung them in the best place in the world to dry; in the closet where the hot water heater was. The hot water tank had a little external unvented, gas fired burner in a little stove attached to the side of the tank and it could dry little bunches of stuff in no time. He dug out a pair of gym shorts he'd worn when he was at Red Dog, hoping they weren't too small. They weren't. He topped that off with his lucky Cincinnati Red's tee shirt. He had trouble going to sleep that night and just before he finally dozed off, around midnight, it dawned on him that he had entirely forgotten about playing ball around at the Community Building that evening.

Chip knew some of the guys who played on the freshman team because he had classes with them and evidently, Coach Collins must have told the team that Chip might be practicing with them today because after he saw Coach Collins that morning at school, a couple of the guys were waiting for him in the hall outside Mr.Collins' classroom. Lanty White and Marty Willis were the first to offer any help.

After finding out if Chip was going to practice with them or not, they told Chip to wait on them when he got to the gym and they would help Chip through pre-practice warm ups and such.

At first Chip wasn't convinced that the seemingly ready way the team accepted this new outsider into its fraternity was genuine. He thought they might be secretly playing him for the fool, but as practice progressed it became obvious that Lanty and Marty and the rest of the team never gave one thought to him being an intruder. They were too busy playing ball. No jealousy, envy, or resentment was apparent.

Playing ball at the Community Building so often had done Chip good and he was able to keep up with everyone during endurance drills. That even surprised Chip. Coach Collins glanced Chip's way once in a while, during drills, but his countenance never changed. During the full scrimmage aspect of practice, Chip sat on the bench. Finally, with twenty minutes or so left in practice. Coach Collins had Chip don a practice jersey and go in for the second team as a guard.

Just play under control Chip kept telling himself. Don't do anything stupid and just try to help out as best you can.

Practice went fine. It was just like playing at the Community Building. Marty and Lanty and Chip talked it up in the dressing room after practice. Chip found out that Coach Collins was a tough disciplinarian, but was fair. He really seemed genuinely interested in his boys and not just as players, but as students and young men as well. Sometimes he seemed more concerned about developing good players than he was about winning and if you could play, you would play. His players always tried to play their best for him and that's all he ask of them. He called Chip into his office after practice.

"Now here's how we can do this," he began. "If you want to finish playing the season with the team there are two things you have to do and there is one thing I have to do. You have to have a physical before you can play. No way around it. State requirement. Can you get a physical examination by Monday?"

Chip shook his head in the affirmative, "I think...I'm pretty...yeah sure."

"If you do that, you can start practice on Monday. You have to have at least fifteen days of practice before you can play. Looking at our schedule that would leave you eligible for two regular season games and our freshman conference tournament. If you think it's worth all of this to maybe play some in five games, then here's what I'll do if you are willing. I can arrange it so you can practice right along with the varsity during their scrimmage time and you won't have to stay over after school. When the varsity has their games during the week, we will be practicing during their time, just like today, and you can practice with us. In the meantime, we have five regular season games we will be playing without you. You won't be missing much except our defensive set and a few offensive plays, but you can catch up on them when we practice in the afternoon. Now the only other thing you have to figure out is what your going to do if you play in those last three or four games. Only one of those games will be here. One is over at Wattsville and the tournament is being held in Red Springs this year. So you and your parents will have to figure out how you can get home or where you can stay after those games. So what do you think?"

There was a long pause.

"Well, tell you what. Don't give me an answer right now. Go home. Think about it. Talk it over with the folks. Just let me know something by Friday. That's the day after tomorrow. Ok?" A small grin had appeared with these last few words.

Chip stood up and extended his hand to the coach. That was the first time he ever took the initiative to shake hands with an adult. "Thank you Coach." That was all he said.

All the way home Chip kept pondering the answer to the really big question in his head. Why would Coach Collins do all of this just so he could play a couple of games of freshman basketball? One thing about it, he thought. It makes an awfully convincing argument in my favor when I present it to Mom and Dad.

He really didn't need to make any convincing pleas, his parents agreed to it wholeheartedly, which seemed to surprise Chip somewhat. They figured the problem of getting home after the three or four late season games could be addressed when the time came.

Chip's dad took Chip over to Red Dog on Thursday to get his physical and he passed it ok.

On Friday before science class, Chip turned in his physical to Mr. Collins and told him he had decided to practice these last few weeks of the season.

Mr. Collins took the physical and asked Chip what size shoe he wore. Chip wasn't sure, but thought it was about an eight and a half. Mr. Collins asked Chip to come down to the gym at noon and he'd see if he couldn't dig up a decent pair of white Converse All Star high tops, the shoes of the varsity and freshman teams. Chip had to pay almost ten dollars for the shoes but they were the same as brand new and felt and looked great.

Chip reported to the main office on Monday, received his new schedule change, which was already completed, and started his new class assignments.

Alton Brown was in his second year as Elk River's head basketball coach. He had been a teacher and track coach at Elk

River for ten years. His first love was teaching American History and his second was coaching track. He had taken over the head basketball position, when the former head coach moved up to be an assistant superintendent.

Coach Brown's first year as head coach had produced a 14-8 season which was really as good a season as Elk River had enjoyed in the past ten years, so the administration had decided to keep him on for awhile, if he wanted. He was a very devout believer in conditioning, which was probably a reflection of his track coaching philosophy, but his teams were always quick and tenacious on defense, and like to run their opponents into a state of fatigue. With fatigue came mistakes and uncoordinated team play. The fourth quarter, and any subsequent extended time after that, almost always belonged to Elk River. Opposing schools may have better athletes, taller players, and better coaching strategies than Elk River, but if they didn't jump out to a big lead early and hold it, Elk River players knew they would make a game of it, late.

Coach Brown and Coach Collins thought alike when it came to understanding the fundamental skills of passing, dribbling, shooting, and defense. Of the almost two hours of practice, only about thirty to forty minutes were spent in actual game situation scrimmages. The rest of practice was devoted to conditioning and skill drills. Coach Brown only had about six different offensive sets depending on the game situation and his defense was an all out, pressing, man-to-man, trapping defense, which was deployed all the time everywhere. He felt too much strategy could only become confusing and that high school kids couldn't handle more than thirty minutes of intricate strategy preparation. Any time over that was a waste of time. Keep it simple and repetitive. So far that coaching philosophy had been successful.

Interestingly, both coaches addressed their players by their first name; Jimmy, Eddie, Marty, etc. Chip couldn't remember them even yelling at their players using their last name. It seemed to him to create a sort of father/son relationship.

Coach Brown must have been receptive to Coach Collins' plan for Chip's eligibility because he accepted Chip's presence during practice time just as if he'd been there all along. Chip participated in all the drills and conditioning workouts with the rest of the

450

players. He never got to actually take part in any scrimmages but some of the practice drills would require a team of from three to five players and Chip was always included as one of those team members. He learned a great deal from just watching the varsity scrimmage and was always picking up on little tips from Coach Brown. The juniors and seniors on the team took him under their wing and encouraged him just like he was their little brother and Chip developed a good friendship with Jimmy Butcher, a sophomore who lived in Hob, and who had been over to the Community Building a couple of times to play ball.

Chip got in at least four practices with the freshman team before his first game. It was a home game against Whetstone and a preliminary game before the junior varsity and varsity, so it started at 5:00.

Chip played a couple of minutes in the second quarter and all of the fourth. Elk River lost the game by ten points. Chip didn't score any points but he only took one shot. He did have three steals and three assists and no screw ups. His dad drove over to Seneca around 7:00 to pick up Chip. He did get to watch a little of the b-team game in which Jimmy was a starter.

Chip was still playing ball at the Community Building a couple of nights a week. Paul had only scheduled one game during this stretch of February. It had been too cold to play much in the Community Building. The lone game was played at Mill's Bottom High School gym and that was on a Sunday afternoon. Paul couldn't believe that Chip was playing with the freshman team, and even more surprised to learn he was practicing with the Elk River varsity. Chip was kind of proud that he was the first Sugar Treeian to be a member of an Elk River High School athletic team.

The last regular season game for the freshman that year was played at Wattsville which was a good hour and a half bus ride from Seneca. Marty Willis lived right on the outskirts of Seneca, and had arranged for Chip to go to his house after school and eat supper that evening. After the bus got back to town that night Chip went back to Marty's house where his dad picked up him up around 9:00.

451

Elk River beat Wattsville fairly easily. Chip made two baskets, one off an intercepted pass and the other on a driving layup down the lane right through Wattsville's defense.

The freshman tournament at Red Springs was a four team tournament. The teams were all part of the New River Valley Conference and were seeded according to their overall records. Elk River was seeded fourth and had to play number one seed, Meadow Gap, on a Thursday night. Chip was very surprised to learn that he would be starting. His mission, which he had no choice but to accept, was to defend Meadow's best player, Art Crowley, a sharp shooting guard and their leading scorer. Coach Collins' strategy was to keep Crowley from getting the ball so much when Meadow Gap was in scoring position. If Crowley wanted the ball on offense, Elk River would make him have to dribble the ball up court himself, under pressure.

Chip was never much of a factor on offense that night, but his defense on Crowley yielded only six points to the frustrated guard, and four of those were on foul shots when Chip was guarding a little too closely. Meadow Gap won the game in three overtimes on a desperation heave from half court at the buzzer.

Elk River played the consolation game against Clay on Saturday evening at 6:00. Chip was shuttled in and out at the guard spot during the game and was kept in the game mostly for his ability to get the ball up the floor and to the scorers. His defense was tenacious as always. He made a couple of steals and had five assists. He only shot one time. It was a quick turn around from the base line right, about ten feet out. He had the line but the shot was short. The rebound came right back to him which he grabbed over a much taller player. He bounced it between the defenders legs right to Lanty who was wide open standing in the lane under the basket. The pass took Lanty completely by surprise but he recovered quickly enough to put it in the basket.

Elk River beat Clay by six points to earn third place. Meadow Gap won the tournament with a convincing win over Red Springs. Art Crowley went on to be named MVP of the tournament, scoring twenty-three points in the championship game. Lanty was named all tournament from Elk River.

Meadow Gap was presented the championship trophy which was about three feet tall. Red Springs was presented the runner-up trophy which was about two feet tall. For their third place finish, Elk River was presented with a genuine official Wilson basketball with "3rd Place--NRVC Freshman Tournament--1960" handwritten with a black marker across the middle of the ball.

The team was announced to come forward to the center circle and receive their trophy. Since Lanty was the captain, he received the ball on behalf of the team. The team just stood in a little circle at mid-court for a minute and looked at the ball in Lanty's hands. Nobody said a word. Then suddenly, Babe Crouch, who was the starting guard on the team, grabbed the ball out of Lanty's hands. It was a little flat and didn't bounce very well but as if in defiance of being slighted by the tournament, right there in front of God and everybody, Babe pounded it right down the floor and made a layup. The crowd sat silent with their mouths hanging open. Chip and the rest of the guys went crazy, yelling and running after Babe to congratulate him on such an inspirational overture. Coach Collins dropped his box of popcorn and shook his head. What could he do?

Later, the team and Coach Collins all signed the ball and put it in the trophy case at school where it can be seen to this very day.

Chip went back to Marty's after the tournament. Since Chip didn't know for sure what time the tournament would be over, the plan was to call Benji's house when he got to Marty's. Benji's mom or dad would drive around the road to Chip's and tell his folks Chip had called, then Chip's mom or dad would drive over to Seneca and pick him up.

Chip loved the experience. His confidence in his basketball ability grew. He was no star to be sure, but he had played against some of the best of his own age and against junior and senior varsity players and felt he had held his own. He couldn't wait until next year. If there was anyway possible, Chip planned to try out for the varsity.

Basketball season at the high school ended just as winter began to fade and as the nights grew warmer, basketball in the Community Building peaked the last two weeks of April. Chip was playing every weeknight but Friday, and almost every Sunday afternoon.

The only incident to mar the spring season at the Community Building came during a pick-up game when a bunch of little punk kids pulled the lever down on the main fuse box outside the building, throwing the place into absolute darkness. In an effort to catch the little snots, Maynard ran to an open window on the side of the building where the fuse box was and vaulted over the window sill into the yard outside. Not being able to see very well in the dark, he landed right in a pile of scrap wood and ran a nail through his sneaker and into his foot. Fortunately, the nail missed any bone, but it did poke clear through the fleshy part between the big toe and the second toe. Maynard got a tetnus shot and limped around Sugar Tree for a week or so but he was through playing basketball for the rest of the season.

V

Chip made the cut his sophomore year at Elk River and was one of the fifteen players kept by Coach Brown. Practicing with the varsity the year before had certainly helped. Coach Brown even called Chip by name the first day of practice. Practices were still held the last two hours of the school day and Chip could ride the bus home in the evenings.

Chip and Marty always paired up together in practice. Over the weeks of varsity practice they developed their own mutual admiration for each other. Marty was six-two and weighed about twelve pounds. Had fingers as long as a no. 2 pencil. He just kind of glided along. Didn't even raise a sweat going through conditioning drills in a sweat suit. He had a weird way he held the ball when he shot it. Held it with the ends of his fingers on both sides of the ball so when he shot it, it had a sort of sideways rotation. He never missed. Well, not never, but seldom. It was such a soft shot that when it hit anywhere on the rim, it would fall in. Mostly, it never hit the rim, it just kind of tinkled the net when it went through.

Lanty was the "class" of the sophomores however, and after a couple of dominating B-team games, Coach Brown quickly moved him up to varsity. Having played with both, Chip felt Marty was a better all around player than Lanty. But at six-six, Lanty was the tallest player in uniform for the Elks and with his bulk, 210, could move inside at will. He was slow on his feet and had no deceptive moves, but he didn't need them. He was a power player and nobody could play the inside game as well as he.

Chip noticed that a few days before basketball practice was to begin, Coach Brown took down the two old nets on the main court baskets and replaced them with brand new ones. Elk River had two practice baskets on each side of the court which were pulled up into the rafters when not being used. The two main nets that were taken from the main baskets were used to replace the two worst practice nets. Chip saw those two discarded nets in one of the senior player's gym bag that evening and asked about them. He said whoever asked first, got the old worn out nets to take home.

Practice started in early November but the official season didn't begin until the first week of December with the first regular season game. The last week of pre-season practice was the last week in November. There was no school on Thanksgiving Day or the following Friday but the team would practice at the school on Friday. It was during this last week of practice that Chip came up with the idea for the "Sugar Tree Invitational Turkey Trot Basketball Tournament". He wanted to run the idea by Paul first though, to see what he thought. Chip wanted to invite three other teams to come over to the Community Building on Saturday after Thanksgiving, and play a round robin tournament in which each team would get a chance to play every other team.

Paul liked the idea especially after Chip told him who he was trying to recruit for the tournament. So during practice that Thanksgiving week, Chip asked Marty if he could round up five or six players from Seneca and come over to Sugar Tree on Saturday. He asked Jimmy Butcher if he could find enough guys in Hob to come over and play and finally he asked the same thing of Lanty White, who was from Big Cat Ridge. By Friday's practice all had said yes to the invitation and the tournament was set to begin at ten o'clock in the morning with whoever was there first.

It was an unusually warm day for November and the stove did not have to be lit. The guys played basketball all day long until they were so tired they started being silly. The two teams that weren't playing took orders for pop and snacks and went down to the Esso station to fill them. At least three of the players on each team were guys who played for Elk River except for Sugar Tree, who just had Chip. There were only two other guys as old as Paul and the rest of the teams were made up of junior high aged boys.

Kenton Young had brought the boys from Big Cat Ridge over to Sugar Tree in his dad's Buick, but when they pulled into the lot at the side of the community building, the strong smell of gasoline led them to discover a dent and a small hole in the gas tank. Must have run over something. Kenton scraped up a little money from everyone and Paul drove him down to Wyatt's Store where he bought ten or twelve pieces of bubble gum. When he got back to the Community Building, he gave everybody a piece of gum to chew. Maynard wanted five or six pieces for himself so he could really chew it up right, or so he said. After ten minutes chewing, all the gum was kneaded into a big ball to be stuck on to the gas tank

456

covering the hole. Well, not all the gum. Maynard wouldn't give his up. Anyway that gum sealed the leak in the tank and it held as far as Chip knew, till Kenton got home that evening. The First Annual Sugar Tree Invitational Turkey Trot Tournament had been a rousing success.

Chip and Marty wound up playing B-team ball that year. They started for the B-team and got to play a lot and that's what it was all about. They still got to dress for the varsity games but only saw limited playing time. That usually came in the fourth quarter when Elk River was ahead or behind by twenty points.

B-Team ball was fun. B-Teams were designed to keep the five or six other players on the team in shape and give them valuable playing experience. The offense made some futile attempt to execute the varsity plays, but Coach Brown was seldom even around to watch them.

When Chip was running the offense, it was run and gun and have some fun. The assistant coach sat on the bench and ate popcorn and flirted with the cheerleaders. No one kept records of wins or losses or point totals or individual records for the B-team and that was fine for Chip. Playing the game was Chip's high.

The plan for getting home after ball games worked like this: If the game was at Seneca, Chip would walk uptown to Bill and Marilyn Cook's house and Chip's mom or dad would drive over from Sugar Tree and pick him up around 9:00.

Chip liked staying at Marilyn's. She always would have some popcorn or potato chips and coke to snack on, and if Chip got there early enough, there would be time to play around with the kids before they had to go to bed. Bill liked attending the home games when he could. He had played both football and basketball for Elk River in the early fifty's. On nights the team played away and got back to Seneca after 10:00, Chip would stay all night at Marty's. He'd bring clothes and necessities with him to school on those days and leave them in the gym to pick up when the team got back to town.

Marty's family just adopted Chip right into their home. Marty had two brothers. One was a junior at West Virginia University studying engineering and the other was an eighth grader at Seneca Junior High. Both were pretty good basketball players themselves.

The varsity finished up with an unglamorous record of thirteen and eight that year but it seemed to Chip that Coach Brown was using basketball season to keep his boys in shape and ready for track season to which he was really devoted and to which his team would dominate the New River Valley Conference for another year. Chip couldn't remember the B-team's record. He could remember if they won or lost a game at the end of that particular game, but couldn't remember the record for the whole season. It did seem to him that they won a lot more games than they lost. He had no idea what any of his or anybody elses individual stats were. He didn't know about the rest of them but he didn't care much anyway.

In between varsity games, basketball continued as usual at the community building and for another month and half after the high school season. Big changes were about to shake things up.

VI

The first big change in Chip's junior year at Elk River came about with the hiring of a new head basketball coach. His name was Ward Perry. He had just graduated from WV Tech with a degree in Health and P.E. He had also played four years of basketball for Tech where he was co-captain and made WVIAC All Conference as a senior. Chip's first encounter with Coach Perry came when he boldly approached the coach in the gym a few days before practice to ask if he could have the any of the old nets that would be taken down. Coach Perry just wanted to know what Chip was going to do with them if he got them. Chip told him about their little gym at Sugar Tree and how they were in desperate need of nets and they just couldn't scrape up enough money to buy real good ones. Coach Perry replaced all six of the old nets and Chip got two pretty good ones out of the deal. Chip thought this seemed to be a good start for both the coach and him.

It was pretty hard to put up really good regulation nylon nets in the Community Building. First of all, there were no hooks on the rims in the Community Building so they just had to guess at the spacing of the loops. If they divided the loops up, then put up the two opposite one first, it didn't come out too lopsided. Black friction tape worked fairly well but it's durability wasn't very long. After a couple of weeks, they seemed to have to retape a loop every game. First aid adhesive tape seemed to do a good job and lasted longer than friction tape. It was harder to find and they usually had to buy it. Friction tape could be found lying around anywhere. Usually a combination of both could be spotted in the Community Building.

The second difficult task came in getting someone up to the rim to tape up the net. If there were enough guys there they could take turns standing or sitting on each other's shoulders to tape up the net. Standing didn't work very well because the tape-er had to hold on to the rim with one hand to balance himself while he tried to unroll a piece of tape and hold the net with the other. Also the tapee couldn't stay up for more than a minute or so, because it was too much strain on the bottom guy's shoulders. Sometimes they could heft someone up till he could climb onto the rim then he'd sit on the rear part of the brace of the rim with his back against the backboard and try to tape the net on.

Sometimes they would send someone up or down the road to a neighbor's house and borrow a step ladder, carry it back to the Community Building, fix the nets up, and carry the ladder back to its owner. That was the best way. However they did it, it brought a little class and a little dignity to the Community Building. It transformed it from a reconditioned barn to a basketball arena.

Changes were evident right from the first day of practice. Coach Perry knew a little bit about the boys on this team but they knew nothing of him, so the first two days of practice were crucial. Chip began to worry a little about whether he could even make the cut, so he hustled all out during conditioning and skills drills.

Chip was only five feet ten inches tall but so were about seven other guys trying out. His shooting definitely wasn't a strong point though it did go in.......sometimes. So he exhibited as little of his shooting ability as was necessary and instead, he decided to go with his strengths which were quickness, defense, and ball handling. Chip was the quickest and the fastest player on the floor and he did push himself in that area on defense as well as offense in an effort to make as good a first impression as he could. Showcase your strengths, shelter your weaknesses.

Chip made the final cut. By the third week of practice, three things about Coach Perry had become evident. One; Perry was a meticulous adherent to structured play. That was his style. Learn the plays. Run them over and over and over until they were fundamentally sound and indelibly imprinted upon your mind. Then, very slowly, add two or three options at most, until they too were automatically reinforced into everyone's play. If the play didn't work, move 'em out and start over again or go to another play. There would be no room for creativity. No room for spontaneity in this Coach's game plan. Everyone had to learn the plays and be able to execute them perfectly because there would always be reasons for substitutions and Perry hated that.

No one could run his plays like his first five. He'd ride a starter worse if he didn't play a whole game than if he'd shoot all night and never score a point. It just really screwed things up if a sub had to run a play that he might not be as familiar with as the guy he replaced. That was mostly Perry's fault. If you didn't play first string, you always played defense when the first team was on offense and when the first team was on defense, the second team had to run the opposing teams offense. Perry rarely would move anyone in or out of his starting five, unless there was an injury or an absence. This led right into revelation number two.

Coach Brown had always approached winning from a defensive standpoint. You didn't have to worry about your defense being on or off from night to night. Defense was defense, and usually any mistakes could be made up just by hustling a little more. The better your defense was, the less points you would have to score to win. Coach Perry's approach was opposite. The more you shot, the more you'd make, and the more points you'd score. Now if you could find five pure shooters, your chances of success in this realm of thinking would be greatly enhanced. Coach Perry selected and molded this team to fit his style perfectly, and they seemed to be made for each other.

The first five featured pure shooters and Perry's plays were all designed to free them up for that open, clean, picture perfect, ten to fifteen foot jump shot. A fine concept and strategy it was, but it left some players, like Chip, out.

After that third week of practice, Chip decided he needed to make another solitary trip "on the hill" to sort all of this out. Solitary, because you couldn't count Major and Specks as real people, although the way Chip talked to them you'd have thought different. He sat down on the rock, pulled a piece of sage brush out of the ground, broke off the end of it, and began to chew on it as he thought to himself:

He was only 5'10", but so were about five other guys who made the team. He knew he was the quickest and fastest of any of the twelve who had the honor of wearing a varsity uniform. He had more moves than even he knew he had, but they were not going to be utilized in the game plan of this ball team. One thing he had to face as the truth was his ignorant jump shot. The sucker just wouldn't go in. He felt smooth when he shot it. It looked fairly decent rotating slowly through the air to the hoop but it always wound up short, long, or off to the side. Apparently Perry had given up on him already as being a vital contributing factor in his scheme of things. If you couldn't hit eight out of ten from fifteen feet, you couldn't shoot.

The more he thought about it, the more he felt he could be satisfied with whatever role he was expected to play this year, if he would get to play even a little bit. He'd have to stop worrin' about being on the first team and make the best of the time he did get to play. Playing the game was his real love.

He was disappointed at the prospect of not getting to see as much varsity playing time as he had hoped, but he didn't have much control over that, and if that's the way it was going to be, he was anxious to get going. He knew how good he was even if others didn't recognized it. Was that recognition more important than getting to do something he truly loved? So he could express his talents playing B-Team ball. In the end, it was only what mattered most to Chip Gates.

Marty moved up to a starting spot that year as did Jimmy Butcher and Lanty White. Two other seniors Bob Reed and Larry Gibson rounded out the starting five. One other junior, Ruben Wainwright, became Perry's sixth man. Chip was relegated to captain of the B-team and saw limited varsity action.

Even playing B-team that year began to dampen Chip's enthusiasm as the season wore on. True, he got to play a lot of quarters, which limited his varsity playing time, but Perry now helped coach the B-team. Where else could he see that his reserve players gain valuable experience running his offensive plays. Whatever freedom Chip had before as a junior varsity player was now pretty much stifled by Perry's ever present influence.

Coach Perry called everybody by their last names. Didn't seem like such a big deal in the beginning but "Hey, Chip, try to run that play to the weak side first," made him feel a little more like trying again than, "Hey, Gates, you're suppose to run that play to the weak side first." It got worse.

Coach Perry told those remaining after the last cut that he was not their father nor their teacher. He was their coach and he was there to win ball games. Chip guessed he thought he was George Patton or somebody. "I don't care if you like me or not. You're here to play basketball for me and if you can't do that by giving one hundred percent and remaining loyal to this team, then you might as well get your shirt and shoes and hit the road. I got ten or eleven guys who didn't make this team just waitin' for another chance."

The next big change came from the WV Secondary Schools Athletic Commission. School athletic practice could take up no more than one hour of actual school instructional time. If a student participated in at least two team sports at his school, he did not have to take P.E. and would receive a required credit in P.E. toward graduation. The credit thing didn't matter to Chip. The real problem was, now he was going to have to find a way to get home every evening after practice.

Practice started at 2:30 and ended at 4:30. After showering, and dressing he had to walk about a quarter of a mile into downtown Seneca where US Rt.19 ran right through the middle of town. He rarely got there before 5:00.

US 19 headed north out of Seneca and ran 15 miles up Raven Valley before it hit Panther Mountain. Rt.19 took two miles to climb up the south side of the mountain to the summit then took another three miles or so to wind its way down the north side to the bottom. It was about three more miles from the bottom of Panther Mountain to Hob.

Other than County Rt.11 that turned off Rt.19 towards home from Hob, there was only one other paved road that intersected US 19 between Seneca and Hob and that was State Rt. 4. Rt. 4 intersected US 19 about eight miles out of Seneca, up Raven Valley. Rt.4 headed east away from Rt. 19 towards Granny's Creek.

During his four years of school at Elk River, Chip rode the bus to school. He could catch the bus in front of his house around 7:00 am and barring some unforeseen delay, would arrive at the high school in Seneca, around 8:30 am. Chip couldn't remember much about riding the bus to school those four years because he usually slept all the way to Seneca. He was thankful that he was one of the first twenty kids to get on the bus because by the time it left Hob, there were three kids on every seat and about five more who had to stand up or switch places with someone who was seated about half way there.

The bus didn't stop to pick up anyone after it left Hob. It took almost fifteen minutes for the loaded bus to pull the long, steep side of Panther Mountain. Chip only rode the bus home a handful of times after his sophomore year at Elk River because of after school athletics.

It was beneficial if Chip could get to Rt.19 in Seneca by 5:00 in the evening. Then the day shift miners would be coming through on their way home and there was a better chance of hitching a ride towards home. There were some miners heading towards Hob, but none were going clear to Sugar Tree. And although US 19 was a major north-south artery, after six o'clock in the evening, traffic would die down to mostly local folks. The later it got, the less traffic would pass heading in his direction.

Jimmy Butcher and Chip hitch-hiked together that year at least as far as Hob, where Jimmy lived. From Hob on home, Chip was on his own. It was a lot safer in tandem and having a companion made the time go by easier while you were walking.

By January of that year, Jimmy had made a deal with one of his uncles, Leonard, to pick the two of them up regularly at the Chevrolet garage in Seneca. Leonard would come by around 5:15 every evening on his way home from work. Leonard lived right in Hob, so they had a regular ride to Hob every day after practice. Jimmy and Chip both offered to pay Leonard $2.00 a week each for their ride but Leonard wouldn't hear of it. The only stipulation Leonard lay on the deal was that if Jimmy and Chip weren't at the garage by 5:15, Leonard was to go on home. There were a few evenings when Jimmy and Chip didn't make it to the garage on time but if they were no more than ten minutes late, Leonard was always there waiting on them. Family ties left some privileges.

The after-game schedule stayed the same. If very late, stay at Marty's overnight. If it was a home game or if they got back into Seneca early enough, Chip went to Bill and Marilyn's. A giant leap into twenty-first century technology by Grandma Gates of all people, proved a life safer to Chip that year. Grandma got a telephone. Now Chip didn't have to call around to Benji's and have them drive around the road to tell his folks when he was ready to come home. He could call Grandma's from Marilyn's and someone would walk over to the house and relay the message.

Coach Perry did institute a bit of class to his basketball program by providing a pre-game meal at "The City Cafe" in downtown Seneca for those players who lived out of town. The meal was set up by the athletic department at the little restaurant to feed those players who lived too far out of town and who couldn't go home and get back for the home game or to catch the bus leaving for the away game. The coaches were always there to eat and preside over the meal and sometimes the whole team would show up to eat. No player was ever turned away. Chip ate there before every game. He traveled the farthest of anyone on the team.

On practice days, Chip rarely made it home before 7:00 in the evening. If it wasn't too cold or snowy, he would fix some peanut butter and crackers, wash it down with a big jelly glass of ice cold milk for supper, and head around the road to see if anyone was playin' ball that night in the Community Building. He usually had to walk around to Sugar Tree although sometimes he'd be lucky to enough to catch a ride. Whether there was anyone playing at the Community Building or not, unless Paul was there, Chip would have to hoof it back home. If Paul was there, he would always bring Chip home. Most nights, Chip wasn't home and in bed before 11:00. That was the biggest reason he slept all the way to Seneca on the bus in the mornings.

The biggest change, and the most devastating one to Chip, came about because of an insignificant incident during the second annual Sugar Tree Turkey Trot Invitational Tournament. All the regular teams were there; Sugar Tree, Marty's bunch from Seneca, Lanty had his crew from Big Cat Ridge, and Jimmy hauled some guys over from Hob.

They played all day Saturday and had a great time. Among the players Marty brought with him from Seneca was Ruben Wainwright and a couple of football players for Elk River. One of the football players was their senior quarterback and captain, Marshall Tyson. Marshall was a very good athlete and no doubt could have played a lot of basketball for Elk River but he chose instead to wrestle for Elk River in the winter and keep in shape for track. During one of the games, Marshall turned his ankle. It hurt like heck for a little while as Marshall limped around trying to put some weight on it, and eventually he walked it off and was able to resume play. Somehow the football coach at Elk River found out about Marshall's injury.

Now football season was over at Elk River, and had been for four weeks, and Marshall's career as a quarterback at Elk River had ended then too, but that didn't keep the coach from lamblasting Marshall for putting his future prospects as a collegiate player in jeopardy and for dragging any other Elk River football players with him into that peril. But the worst thing the football coach did was tell Coach Perry.

First thing at practice Monday, he gathered all the players together in the bleachers and laid down "Perry's Law" to them. Although he addressed the whole team, there were ten guys present who had no idea what Perry was talking about.

"Let me tell you one thing," he began, "I know all about your little basketball tournament and there will be none of my players playing any kind of pick up basketball games anywhere, anytime while you're playing for me. You got that straight. None. Nowhere. No time. With nobody!" He kept a steady, glaring stare fixed on Chip. Chip and Marty were sitting together, side by side, but Perry never looked at Marty or Lanty. "If one of my players gets hurt in a stupid pick up game, I don't care who he is, he'll not play for me ever again."

"I'll tell you something else," he continued, "if you knew it or not, it doesn't make any difference, but the West Virginia Secondary Schools Athletic Commission expressly forbids a member of any WV high school basketball team to participate in any kind of organized or unorganized games of basketball outside the school's regular basketball program during the regular season. That means if someone turns one of you in to the SSAC for playing basketball with another team, any kind of team, then Elk River would be sanctioned by the Commission and forced to dismiss the player from the team, forfeit all high school games played to that point, and the school would be ineligible to participate in the state high school basketball tournament. This is serious stuff. So you better pay attention."

The ringing echo of those last words caused every player to melt under the menacing pronouncements of Coach Perry. Marty and Chip's countenance at once shriveled and the color drained from their faces. Chip's mouth was dry and his ears felt like they were burning.

Later, during lay up drills, Chip, Lanty, and Marty confided in each other while standing in line. This revelation was incredulous.

"Did you know anything about this SSAC thing?" Chip whispered.

"My Lord, no!" answered Marty through clenched teeth, "I've always been playin' ball on weekends with the guys down at the grade school."

"You! What about me. I been goin' around to other towns playing ball against other teams for three years! No one ever said a thing or asked about me or anything. But you know, I never really thought about this before, I never saw any other high school aged players on any of the teams we played. Guess now I know why."

Jimmy and Chip discussed the repercussions of Coach Perry's lecture all the way home. Chip pondered it by himself as he made his way home from Hob. Though it was a disappointing and frustrating decision to make, he really didn't have any choice. He couldn't put the high school in jeopardy or let his teammates down. He'd just have to quit playing for Sugar Tree.

He stopped off at the house and fixed a bologna and lettuce sandwich which he could eat on his way around the road to the community building. He hoped Paul would be there so he could explain his dilemma.

Paul was there and so was Maynard and Claude Freeman. They were down at one end of the floor playing h-o-r-s-e. Chip asked if he could join in.

"Yeah, you can come in," growled Paul, "but you got to come in with an "h", an "o", and an "r" and you cannot, I repeat, cannot, do any off the wall dunks."

That didn't bother Chip any because he was never allowed to do any dunks in a h-o-r-s-e game anyway. Only he and Maynard could dunk, but Paul seemed a little more agitated than usual.

"Look what jerkhead did with his dumbass dunking," spit Paul, pointing to the basket at the other end.

Chip couldn't tell much from where he was so he walked down to the other end continuing to look at the rim. When he got down under the basket, he could tell that the brace welded to the bottom of the rim was broken on both sides. Maynard hung his head and stared at the floor.

"Now I got to take that rim down and take it with me to work so the guys at the shop can weld it back. Then I got to come back over here and put the thing back up. I ought to kick your hind end all the way to Red Dog and back," Paul proclaimed.

"Aw, bull, Paul," Maynard said, trying to apologize. "I'll take the thing down and put it back up if you'll just take it over to the shop and get it welded. If it costs anything, I'll pay for it myself".

"Durn right you will," answered Paul, softening up a little.

Chip thought this was a real good time to tell Paul about Coach Perry's ultimatum so he waited a little while longer before he broke the news. Paul didn't say anything while he was concentrating on his next shot. He stood under the basket facing the right side wall and threw the ball underhand high off the wall, ricocheting it in a high arc back towards the basket where it hit the rim, but didn't go in.

"Well, listen, Chip," he said, chasing the ball down in the other corner, "I know you like playing ball with us but you better do the right thing now. You can still come around and shoot some with us. Maybe play a little three on three or such. You just can't play in any of the games we organize. After your basketball season is over, the weather will warm up some and we'll be playing more games then anyway. You can play basketball with us anytime or anywhere you want and no one can get in trouble unless, like you said, you get hurt and Coach Perry won't let you play anymore."

"Shoot, I'm not going to let that keep me from playin' with you guys," Chip answered, kind of relieved. "Doesn't look like I'm going to get to play that much for him anyway."

Chip thought maybe things wouldn't be as bleak as he first figured. Sugar Tree won't be playing that many games at the Community Building when it's cold anyway. He could still go around and play whenever he wanted, as long as there were not guys from somewhere else playing a game. He wondered too, if Paul knew all along that Chip was violating SSAC rules. He never hinted that he knew one way or the other but he seemed to know an awful lot about the ruling.

One of the highlights of this season of B-Team ball for Chip would be Elk River's game with Red Dog. The town of Red Dog was slowly dying since the WYGARB conglomerate had sold all of their holdings to a United Mine Worker's Union company. At the end of Chip's sophomore year at Elk River, the town of Red Dog began plans to close the high school and send all of those students to the other county high school at Mill's Bottom. The first year they sent the junior and senior classes to Mill's Bottom to complete their high school education there. That left only the seventh through the tenth grade at Red Dog High School. Since there weren't enough older, experienced players to make up a high school varsity team at Red Dog, they only played other high school's junior varsity teams.

The first meeting of these two schools would be in Red Dog's gym and it would be an afternoon game in front of the whole school. Except for one or two guys he didn't know because they were families who had moved into Red Dog with the new company, these were the same guys he'd played junior high ball with at Red Dog. The only sad note to this reunion would be the absence of Chip's close grade school friend and basketball mentor, Casey Jones. Casey's family had moved away when WYGARB sold their holdings to a United Mine Workers Union company. Casey's dad was laid off by the new company. Seems he wasn't much of a Union man.

Not only had Chip played junior high ball with these guys, but they also played against each other a couple of times a month in pick up games at the Community Building or over in Red Dog's gym. To add to the excitement even more, Chip knew just about everyone who attended Red Dog, not only because he went to school there himself, but because there were still some kids in Sugar Tree who were attending Red Dog High School.

One more element added to Chip's anticipation of playing Red Dog was the fact that his mom was still teaching there and would be able to attend the game. She had never seen him play.

There were two players from Chip's junior high days at Red Dog he was still close to, Bobby Nash and his older brother Tony. Tony was a sophomore and Bobby was a freshman at Red Dog. They were black kids and probably the best all around athletes to ever play for Red Dog. When they were involved in athletic

469

contests against each other, they were always taunting the other about who played the best game or who made the best play and in fact, all three players kept a running dialogue of trash talk throughout the whole contest. That was an ingredient of their relationship that was formed when they played on the same team in Junior High and had continued since. To those innocent bystanders who knew not of their relationship, they probably wondered if such animosity between them was a result of their competitiveness or was even perhaps, racially motivated.

Coach Perry himself took the B-team to Red Dog that afternoon as the head coach. Chip had a terrible game. Thinking back to that game, going over it and over it in his head as he later made another trip "on the hill", he knew he pressed too hard. He wanted so much to have a good game in front of his friends and family that he just tried to do too much.

First thing, right off the jump ball, the tip came to him and he drove around two defenders and flew down the lane for an uncontested lay up which hit the bottom of the backboard. Of course, Bobby fought his way through a whole crowd of players so he could be the first to start ridin' Chip about that shot, "Hey, white boy, I see you've been workin' on your lay ups 'cause they're gettin' much better." As frustrated as he was, Chip had to bite down on the inside of his cheeks to keep from laughing at Bobby's remarks.

About half way through the first quarter, Bobby lobs the ball into Tony who is set up in the high post just off the foul line. Tony makes a quick gesture with his eyes for Bobby to cut down the lane so he can fed it back to him. Chip was the only one in the whole building who saw the gesture and knew what it meant. So Bobby breaks off a screen and cuts to the lane for the ball. Tony pivots to the basket like he's going to shoot but Chip drops off of Tony and cuts to where Bobby is headed down the lane to steal the pass from Tony. Only Tony had no intention of giving the ball back to Bobby. Even Bobby knew that. Tony turned to the basket and with no one on him, took a dribble to the basket, and laid the ball in. They had snookered Chip but good and made sure he knew it. "Hey Gates, who you suppose to be defendin', the invisible man?"

Perry jerked Chip out of the game in the second quarter. Chip brooded awhile on the bench, but watching Bobby and Tony play lifted his spirits. After the coach chewed him out at half-time, making sure Chip knew why he was not playing varsity and was not likely to do so unless his play improved considerably, Chip settled down and blamed himself for letting the game itself become his focus. When he was reinserted into the game for the third and fourth quarters, he was playing his good and steady game. He finished up with only eight points but had seven assists and three steals. Perry's brand of basketball didn't allow for any spectacular or creative plays and though Elk River won by fifteen, it was a rather mundane evening for Chip.

Since Chip's mom was at the game, Coach Perry allowed him to remain in Red Dog after the game instead of returning with the team to Seneca. Chip visited with some of the kids who stayed around the gym after the game and then he and Bobby and Tony shot around for awhile.

Back home after the game that evening, Chip's mom made no mention of the game but his dad brought up the subject at supper. "How'd the game go today?" Chip's mom answered. Said Chip played a good game and Elk River won. Chip knew it wasn't such a stellar performance and thought his mother covered it pretty well, so he didn't add anything to the conversation. Right after supper he headed off around the road to the Community Building.

The rematch with Red Dog came in early February and it was played at Elk River in front of the student body. The Elk River student body out numbered Red Dog's by about eight to one, so the gym was packed for that afternoon treat.

Chip was leading the B-team in scoring and assists and was the controlling and influential floor leader of the team. Coach liked it when Chip took the initiative to get things rolling, to get some action going, and to get his boys to movin' and thinkin'. What Chip didn't know was that because of his undisciplined style of play, Perry would never use him for very long in a varsity game. It was too scary and too uncertain of a game plan for Perry's style. He had no control over the offense and his team's victories lived or died by his predetermined game plan, incorporated by his programmed starting five players. Chip would continue to play B-team ball and only play varsity when someone was hurt or in foul trouble or, it

471

was late in the game and Elk River was either ahead or behind by more than fifteen points.

Chip had a good, solid game against Red Dog that day and that "can do nothing wrong/light footed" feeling returned to his mindset. Elk River pulled away early and managed to stay ahead by fifteen plus points. With three seconds to go in the game, Red Dog had the ball out of bounds on the end line under Elk River's basket. Tony Nash inbounded the pass to his brother Bobby, who Chip had to pick up because Elk River was still playing a full court pressing defense even though they were ahead by fifteen points.

Bobby turned to head down the floor and Chip backed off a couple of steps and whispered, "Take it, hot dog".

Bobby did a sort of hook throw and launched the ball the length of the court. It arched high up through the glare of the lights and came down clean, cracking through the net at the other end of the floor right at the buzzer.

Chip stood mesmerized. Good thing we were ahead by so much, he thought.

On the next Saturday following the game with Red Dog, Chip rode over to Red Dog with his dad, who had to pick up some pictures he had left at Uncle Roy's. When they drove by the Red Dog playground Chip saw some guys shooting baskets so he got his dad to let him out there with a promise to pick him up on his way back out of town.

The temperature had warmed up into the low fifties and some of the dirt court had melted off. Chip hurried over to the end of the court that was not covered with snow and found Bobby and Tony and a couple other guys. First thing Bobby does is start bragging about the shot he made against Elk River. "Yeah, there have only been five shots from that distance ever made in the entire history of WV high school basketball. I looked it up. I'll be in the record books forever."

"Listen to me, 'Hollywood', cause I know all about this stuff," Chip countered. "First of all, that was a B-team game and they don't even keep records of stuff like that in B-team games."

"That's no sweat, baby. I'll just do it a couple more times when I play for Mill's Bottom next year to make sure everyone knows how good I am."

"Who do you think you are? Meadowlark Lemon or somebody?" yelled Chip. "You couldn't do that again if you dedicated the rest of your life to tryin'."

"Oh yeah," answered Bobby taking the ball and walking down to the other end of the court where the snow hasn't been shoveled off. "Watch this shot, ole pale one".

Standing in the snow that reaches almost to the top of his five-buckle arctics, Bobby whipped the ball with that hook shot movement and it sails through the low, dim February sun, with the dirt and mud and snow flying off it, and goes through the rickety bent rim at the other end so hard that it rips off the straggly, cotton net. Everybody goes crazy, hootin' and hollerin' with laughter. Bobby just prances around like nobody but Meadowlark himself.

The rest of Chip's junior season of basketball was pretty uneventful after such a bewildering start. He did get his driver's license that year but it didn't help his getting home any better because the Merc was home and he was in Seneca. He never did get to drive to school that year because Mom and Dad needed the car.

He finished up his B-team season first in scoring and first in assists. That was unofficial, but that's what Lanty said. He said he saw the B-team stats book once when Coach Perry left it lying in the gym bleachers. Chip knew he led the team in assists and was far ahead of whoever was second. He really didn't care that much about the scoring but it did seem to impress the kids on the bus and at the Community Building anytime Chip scored in double figures.

Coach Perry kept the varsity stats posted on the bulletin board in the locker room. Chip's wasn't much; played in nineteen games, scored thirty-six points for a 1.9 scoring average, had forty rebounds, was four for six from the foul line, had twenty one steals, and fifty-three assists. Chip was proud of the assist total. It was almost three assists a game. Playing in nineteen games was misleading. Chip's average playing time for the varsity was probably only three or four minutes a game, so that was almost one assist every minute he played. No starter could even boast about that average.

Elk River won both their games in the sectional part of the state tournament that year, capturing their first sectional title since 1950.

They lost in the first round of regional tournament at Elkins to Washington Irving but finished with a 17-6 record. Things looked even better for next year.

Six months later, after the first two weeks of practice, Chip found himself sitting on the rock in the middle of the field on the hill, trying to figure out what to do. Major was off in the woods barking at a red-headed woodpecker who seemed to be cackling at him from its perch high atop an old dead chestnut tree.

Chip figured for sure he would be a starter this year for Elk River. Jimmy Butcher, Bob Reed and Larry Gibson were all gone. Graduated. There were only four seniors. Marty, Lanty, Ruben, and Chip. Lanty and Marty both started last year and Ruben was sixth man. Surely he would move Chip up. After two weeks of practice it looked like six-six junior Alex Deitz would be starting, along with a new kid who had just transferred to Elk River. The new kid was Joey Fry who had been a freshman at Greenbrier High School last year.

Chip understood that it would have been pretty stupid of Coach Perry not to start Alex. He was the tallest guy on the team and had been a force on the B-team even as a sophomore last year. Last year Perry had his players set and Alex wasn't a part of that scheme then, but it was a new year now.

After two weeks of practice it was apparent that this Fry kid, who was just a sophomore, was the perfect player for Perry's style of play. He was green and played out of control some, but the potential was there. Chip could tell that the kid had a head for the game and he lived and breathed on every word Coach Perry spoke. If Perry would have told him to run through a brick wall, Chip bet the kid would try. It was hard to accept that Perry would start an unknown ahead of someone who was a senior and had played his butt off for him last year.

Chip was trying to reason with himself this gray November day, but his emotions kept getting in the way. He could only do his best. He couldn't control Coach Perry's mind. He knew he wasn't Perry's kind of player. It wasn't anything personal. He couldn't go anywhere else and play this last year. If he changed his style and attitude about the game it would no longer be any fun. Ha! That's it!. Fun!. That's the reason he played this game anyway. It was becoming clearer now. Not to impress anybody. Not to get his name in the paper. To have fun. He's got to play me some. I'll just use my time the best I can and not worry about it. I know I'm a better player right now than Joey Fry is anyway, so there!

Joey wasn't the only new Fry to show up at Elk River that year. His cousin Frankie, who was a senior, joined Elk River's basketball team at the same time. Chip couldn't remember playing B-team ball against Frankie when he was at Greenbrier and it was obvious in these first two weeks of practice that Frankie didn't play varsity at Greenbrier. Chip wondered why he transferred to Elk River and more puzzling was why Coach Perry had not cut him by now.

It was a standoff between Major and the woodpecker, so Major ambled over to where Chip was and climbed up to lay his head in Chip's lap, looking no doubt for an encouraging rub behind the ears. After Chip obliged for a minute or two, Major dropped down and commenced with one of his favorite diversions. He'd lay down, roll over on his back, and slide down the gentle slope of the meadow where they were. With a little push once in a while with his hind legs, Major could slide down the hill through the sage and undergrowth for fifty or sixty feet. Stupid dog, thought Chip, some worried life he's got. Chip pointed a finger at Major when he finally got back on his feet, yelling at him, "Yeah, you. You stupid looking thing. Caninus Stupidious. If you don't shape up I'm gonna come down there and kill your ass. You got it?" Major just stood there lookin' back with his tongue hanging out and his tail wagging back and forth. Yeahyuh. Yeahyuh. Whatever you say, oh great master. What else you want to do?

With the Fry matter and the role conflict settled, Chip felt some better. Better enough to jump up off the rock and chase after Major as they made their way back to the house.

By the time the first game rolled around, Chip and Joey Fry had developed at least a mutual respect for each other. Joey kept hanging around with Marty and Chip in practice trying to learn more about the game and Chip, as tough as it was to admit to himself, envied Joey's physical stature and future opportunities.

One of Chip's dilemmas at the beginning of the season was how to get two used nets from Coach Perry to use in the Community Building. He was afraid if he asked the coach for the nets it would bring up the matter of playing ball in the Community Building, which was absolutely forbidden. He thought about telling the coach it was just for his own use at home but he knew that wouldn't fly. He thought about telling the coach it was for the Community Building but that the Sugar Tree Grade School was practicing in there and they were the ones who would benefit. That was all true, but Chip was afraid that any mention of the Community Building would remind Coach Perry of it and Chip was hoping he had forgotten about it. No since taking any chances of that happening. He knew Coach Perry favored Marty above all his other players and that didn't interfere with his and Marty's relationship at all, so he asked Marty to ask Coach Perry for the two nets. Of course, Marty got the nets. In fact, they were the two best of the six that were replaced.

The first game of the season was at home against Red Springs. Coach Perry came into the dressing room downstairs looking very dapper in his slacks and blazer of matching school colors with the school mascot on the blazer pocket. Had his play diagrams on a clipboard in one hand and a basketball in the other.

"All right fellows". He looked stern and determined. "This is it. We can't go undefeated if we lose the first game." There's a few chuckles down the row of players.

"Let's go and do our warmup drills on this end of the floor so you'll be down by the bench on offense for the second half. Chip, you shoot fouls with the first five before the introduction of players. Now boys, I'm expecting a lot from you this year. So are those people out there, this town, and this school. I'll tell you now. This could be the best team that's come out of here, ever! You've got to think. Don't get in a hurry. Stay with basics and they'll pull you through. This is it. This is what you've worked your butts off these last months for. Don't let it go to waste. Don't let Red Springs take it away from you. OK. Let's do it."

The team moved out of the dressing room and ran together up the steps out onto the floor. There was so much noise bouncing around in that little gym you couldn't even talk to the player right next to you. The pep band was blaring and thumping the school song and there must have been at least three hundred people jammed into that den. Chip moved in behind Marty for the warmup drills.

"You ready, "O"?" he shouted. Chip called Marty "O" after Oscar Robertson of the Cincinnati Royals because he was the smoothest basketball player Chip had ever seen.

"I don't know man, I got the shakes and butterflies real bad, you know."

"Yeah, I know. We got to get movin' and loosen up. Maybe we'll be all right."

Marty started to go in for another lay up but he turned back to Chip. "OK, what you got to do on this shot is go in on this side, put it up with the right hand, bring it back down, go on under the hoop, and throw it up left handed off the glass from the other side, dig."

Marty took off for the pass, then hollered over his shoulder, "For a dollar". He looked smooth going in but his hang time is short and the ball flew back over the rim missing everything.

Chip streaked in behind him, took the pass, double pumped it on the fly, went under the basket, put a little spin on the ball and flipped it in clean off the glass. He caught up with Marty on the other side. "You ready now, "O"?

Marty just laughed with his eyes sparkling. "I'm ready, hot dog, but I don't know if Coach is or not".

Chip kind of glanced at Coach Perry out of the corner of his eye without actually turning towards him. Perry is standing on the sidelines glaring at both of them. "Don't worry 'bout it. You know you're the only guy on this team that can get away with that kind of crap without a chewin' by Coach. He won't chew me 'cause he'd have to chew you too".

The horn blew and the game gets underway. Perry's boys go to work and the machine clicks smoothly. Their defense stinks but Red Springs can't hit and by the end of the first quarter they are up by six points, 23-17. The second quarter belonged to Marty Willis. He hit five in a row in the first four minutes of the quarter including two offensive tip ins. He ends the half with seventeen points and Elk River is up by eleven. Chip was oblivious to pretty much everything that was going on except watching Marty do his thing.

The half-time talk from Perry wasn't emotional. It was technical and precise. Think and execute. Rediagram and refresh those fundamental plays. There was no mention of defense.

The third quarter wasn't so smooth. By then, the Red Springs coaches had figured out at least half of Perry's plays and were defensing them to shreds. Lanty was forcing all his shots and none of them were even close. Alex was in a complete state of confusion. He'd try to hide back inside with the crowd underneath the basket, so he wouldn't have to handle the ball. When Marty saw a play starting to fall apart, he'd go to the basket hoping to get a rebound to put back in. He tried to hold them together and scored all but five of the team's third quarter points. Still, with three minutes to go in the third, the lead had been cut to two points and Perry called time out.

He was furious. "Run the damn A, B, & C plays," he screamed. He hit his clip board with his fist with such force that it broke. He slammed it down on the floor. "Willis is the only one of you dumbasses out there that knows what to do. Run A, B, & C damn it and get him the ball". His face was red and he was still screaming.

Chip sat on the bench and stared out at the floor while all this hub-bub was going on. He looked over at Marty who was standing over the kneeling, ranting coach but Marty was looking up in the stands. Chip turned around and looked too, just out of curiosity, but he couldn't tell what Marty was looking at. He looked back at Marty who was looking at Chip now. Marty just winked at him and jogged back out onto the floor with the other players.

The time-out didn't help. As soon as the ball was in play, Red Springs threw up a full-court zone press and Joey and Ruben couldn't get the ball into the front court to even start plays A, B, & C. Somehow they held on and were still up by two at the end of the quarter.

Chip and the rest of the bench got up to let the struggling five sit down for the one minute rest between quarters but Perry made them sit back down so he could yell at them face to face.

"If your gonna sit around on your ass out there in this game, you sure as hell don't need to sit down for a rest now," he explained. "Gates, you go in for Fry. Don't do no shootin'. Jus' get the ball up the floor to Marty or Ruben and try to act like you know what you're doin".

My god, thought Chip, pulling off his warm up. I can't do this. I don't know what to do. I just can't go out there cold and jump into that mayhem. He started feeling sick.

Marty slapped him on the back. "Now we gonna have some fun, hot dog". Chip just stared blankly at him. He was so nervous he couldn't even feel the floor under his feet.

Ruben got the tip to open the quarter and hit Marty in the right corner. Marty put up that soft rainbow from twenty feet and it never even rippled the net when it went through. Chip felt like he was stood up in box and nailed to the floor at center court. Everything seemed to be a blurr around him. The noise was deafening. He was afraid to move. Afraid the box would fall over face down with him in it.

Marty grabbed ahold of him as the team ran back down the floor on defense and dragged him to his spot at the top of the lane. Chip put his hands up in defense. The guard for Red Springs brought the ball right up to Chip and stopped. He looked right in Chip's face, then hit a jump shot from right there. Now Chip had to handle the ball.

He moved quickly to his right and took the inbound pass from Ruben. The ball felt oversized, unfamiliar, and slippery to his numb brain. He turned and started up the floor but after one dribble a Red Springs guy cut over in front of him and Chip stopped. He saw Marty cut up the sideline ahead of him and tried to yell at him, but nothing came out. He threw the ball in that direction anyway but another Red Springs player came out of nowhere, picked off the pass, and went flyin' by Chip and laid it in for two more. The crowd was going crazy.

Chip got the ball out of bounds and looked for someone to throw it to. Lanty ran by across the court and Chip feebly pitched him the ball and then cut to run up the opposite side of the court. Lanty immediately threw the ball back to him but before he could securely hold it, another blur of an arm smacked down hard on his hands and knocked the ball loose. The blur made a continuous flash on by and laid in two more points.

Chip ran to get the ball to throw it in bounds again but everybody was walking off the court.

"Time out, Chip, time out," someone was yelling at him. He did hear that. It was Marty.

Chip walked off the floor seeing no one, hearing nothing. His heart was thumping violently in his chest and his mouth was so dry he couldn't even speak. He sat down on the bench in his accustomed place right next to Coach Perry. Joey went back in the game for him and the blur and noise continued on out on the court.

Chip turned the noise and the action off. He withdrew into himself. He talked to himself. He listened to himself.

I can do this, he thought. There's not one of those guys out there on either team that's that much better than I am. There's not one of them more experienced than I am, and I will not be pushed around like that. If I'm gonna feel like that all of the time I'm out there, then what am I doing this for? That wasn't me out there just now. That was some little kid who got lost from his mother in a train station or something. Big deal, this game of basketball. Win or die. Fight or be conquered. Be tough or get stepped on. I thought you came out here to have some fun. My lord, this is big time. This is for the world championship of everything. I really don't give a big doo-dah who wins this game but I sure as heck would like to play some in it. I was away for a while but now I'm back. Let's see, he looked at the clock, 4:18 to go and tied up. Well, it don't matter much anyway, I won't be playin' for this team anymore, anywhere for awhile.

Just then Coach Perry stomped his foot on the floor so hard it brought Chip back to reality. Ruben had fouled out. Perry called time out and everybody came over and stood around him leaving the bench players to squeeze in where they can to hear what's going on in the huddle.

"Gates, come here," Perry commanded. Chip got up and sauntered over to the huddle.

"You're all we got now." He pinched Chip's leg between his thumb and forefinger till Chip instinctively jerked it away. "You hear me. You better not screw up now 'cause by next game I'll find somebody who won't. You're a senior, boy. Seniors don't play like that and neither do basketball players who want to play for me.

Now, boy, if you're a basketball player, get out there and play some basketball.........." It went on and on.

Chip's was thinking. Yeah, yeah, Coach. I heard it all before. Well, this one ain't for you, baby. This one's for me. This one's for all them guys in Sugar Tree. This one's for Hopalong Cassidy and Claudine Cardinalle. For Otis Redding and Major. This one's for God and Judy.

Chip reported to the scorer's table and walked back out on to the floor with the team. He looked over at Marty. "You ready 'O' ?"

"Jeez Louise, hot dog. What the flip you think I been doin' out there the last three quarters, playin' tiddley winks?"

"Well, you better be. If you want to get twenty-five tonight you better not turn your eyes away from the ball 'cause I'll hit you right between them with it".

Red Springs was still pressing full court as Chip tried to get the ball into Joey. He did and as soon as he got back inbounds, Joey threw the ball back to him. The Red Springs' guard cut in front but Chip faked left, then went up the right side of the court to the mid court line where another Red Springs' guard stepped in his path. A little cross over dribble, a little skip with the left foot, and bam! Chip broke around the guy, scooted to the top of the lane, and went down to the foul line. He stopped. Looked left, and bounce passed right to Marty breakin' for the hoop who laid it in.

All right mama, all right. Chip pumped himself up. Let's try this one.

As the Red Springs' guard started to throw the ball in, Chip turned away and took two steps back down the court, but he turned back suddenly and picked off the pass leisurely intended for their other guard. He got the ball right under his own basket and flipped it in off the glass cleanly. Man, that's the oldest trick in the book, he grinned to himself.

Then the noise was gone. The rapid pulse of the game was gone. It seemed to him everybody else was in slow motion. There were no plays. Maybe everyone else was running them but all Chip knew to do was get the ball to whoever was open and let them make the shots.

On defense once, the same Red Springs' guard brought the ball up to the top of the key on the dribble with the same intentions of driving right up to Chip and shooting the jump shot right over him. Chip didn't wait for the guard to come to him, instead he charged toward the guy and at the same time slapped up for the ball instead of slapping down at it.

They can't call a foul on you if you reach up at the ball instead of trying to knock it away by hitting down on it, he reasoned. He knocked the ball out of bounds. He must have done that two or three times the rest of the game but he could only remember that one time.

Chip never did know what the score was at any time during those last four minutes and would never have known the game ended if the whole place hadn't erupted. He had to look up at the scoreboard to see who won.

And so it went. He was caught up in it again. Playin' this game because he got so high and getting so high because he was playin' this game. He was poised and cool on the outside but his insides were busting and screaming to cut loose. He wanted to run all night. He was wound up like an eight day watch, every muscle straining on the inside but rhythmic and smooth on the outside.

Chip began to see more playing time in the next two weeks. He still wasn't starting but now he went in when things began to drag or someone wasn't performing up to Coach's expectations. He knew he wasn't going in to score points but that didn't make any difference to him. He'd still take that stupid jump shot if the shot was there, and he'd still fill the lanes on a fast break for a lay up, but his strength was his uncanny ability to handle the basketball and get it to an open player. He was totally involved in what was going on at a particular moment on the court and his entire being seemed to be able to absorb every minute aspect of the moment, dissect it right before his eyes, and still gather in the next second without a pause. It was like a sixth sense he developed. He knew where everybody was on the floor at a precise moment and what each person was going to do in the next second.

He could actually see these lanes and avenues open up between him and the basket. No matter where he was; baseline left, baseline right, top of the key, right wing, left wing, twenty-two feet out or six feet out, he could see these alleys straight through five guys with their arms and legs all sticking out like in a brier thicket. It was just like a path through the thicket. He wondered why other people couldn't see them. He'd even yell to his teammates, "Cut through. Go through. There it is." But they evidently didn't know what he was talking about.

These lanes would only appear for a second or so, then close up, but they always reappeared again somewhere else or some way different, and Chip knew they were there long enough for him to skip through them. Most of the time though, he'd see them when he didn't have the ball. When he did have the ball and could catch an opening, he'd skip, flash, or bound right down through them. Then it seemed like he was in a tunnel. He could see nothing on either side of him but he could see the end of the tunnel and there he would find the basket or an open teammate.

This quality of "penetrating", as it would later be called, was Chip's highest of highs. On his moves to the basket he was often fouled or made an easy lay up. Neither of these results ever hyped him up much, although they seemed to stir everybody else up judging from all the noise they made. No, his greatest satisfaction came when an opponent would cut him off or try to impede his progress. Then he would have to use his sixth sense and his innate skills to dish the ball off to a teammate who was left unguarded or try to make a shot through some kind of unnatural gyration.

The one thing Chip's teammates knew for sure when he was in the game, you'd better be in the ball game with all your concentration on where the ball was and where Chip was or you might get hit in the face with one his passes. They could come from anywhere at any time and you had to be ready.

Chip and Marty usually kept a running conversation going while they were on the floor. "Help me. Help me on this side," Chip would yell on defense. "Watch out "Big O" here he comes".

"What's a matter, hot dog, he too quick for yuh," poked Marty.

"If you can't make them grade school shots I'm feedin' yuh, I'm gonna throw the ball to somebody who will appreciate it."

Actually Marty was the only player on the team who would acknowledge a scoring opportunity brought about by a Chip pass. Sometimes he'd just point his finger at Chip after a basket.

One thing Chip couldn't understand. How a team sport like basketball could have such selfish players. How many times had he come down the floor on a fast break and being one of the cutters on the wing, break to the basket wide open and then the middle man with the ball would pull up at the foul line or beyond, and shoot the ball? It didn't hurt because he didn't get to shoot or get two points. If the ball handler would pass it to someone else who might be open it would at least be an act of motivation for Chip. Even if the guy made the shot, it didn't instill any sense of confidence or unity for Chip. It just kind of took the wind out of his sails. To work hard to get open and then some clown making it a wasted effort by refusing to acknowledge anybody else's contributions. Perry loved it because it scored points. Chip hated it when they did that.

Chip could recall isolated incidents in a ball game that to him were almost magical in their beauty of conception but remained lost to others during the entire scope of the game and the incidents were always overshadowed by the ever permanent, won or lost conclusion.

He remembers once when he was on offense, out front at guard with Alex, when Alex takes this jump shot about fifteen feet out just to the right of the key. Chip goes in for a rebound, in case there is one, and Alex's shot misses. The ball suddenly bounces straight down at Chip's feet. His sixth sense unscrambles the mess of arms and legs and bodies surrounding him trying to get the basketball, and in a vision flash, he can see Alex still standing at that spot he shot from even though Chip's back is to him. It was like lookin' through the back of his head. In one motion he scooped the ball off of the floor, back between his legs and smack into Alex's stomach. Alex is so surprised he drops the ball, picks it up, looks at everybody under the basket idiotically, and pumps it back in.

Another time on a fast break, Chip flashed to the foul line with the ball. He had two defenders in front of him. One came right up to cut him off at the foul line and the other waited to see where Chip would pass the ball. Chip sensed Marty cutting to the basket to his left. He jumped to his right and the defender went right too. Fine so far. Chip pulled up as though to shoot, but intended to fire a jump pass to Marty. The other defensive player though, went left and leaped high to intercept Chip's pass to Marty.

Chip's mind clicked right along as the play developed. This guy is taller than I thought but it's too late to change my mind now. I'll just float along here, a few feet off the floor and see it I can out wait him.

As the big man reached his zenith, Chip lobbed the ball up over his outstretched hand. The ball floated up over the hand, as the hand was coming down, and fell softly into Marty's hands who was behind the defender, heading for an easy two.

Chip grinned to himself, hope that guy didn't hurt himself trying to go back up before he had come clear down to the floor.

He can also remember his greatest shot. It was the greatest shot for him, but unrecognized as a great shot by anyone else. That time Lanty had picked off a pass and as soon as Chip saw it developing, he took off down the floor ahead of everyone. Lanty lobbed the ball upcourt to him. Chip took it to the top of the key and started down the lane. Right behind him was a defender that Chip figured was about nine feet seven inches tall and was either going to slap his shot clear through the swinging doors at the exit or knock Chip clear through the swinging doors at the exit. One dribble took him to the foul line with Godzilla still breathin' on his neck. Chip stops on a dime but so does Godzella. Then Chip extended both arms straight out in front of him and with his back shielding the ball and his arms, he scooped the ball up toward the rim. Godzella doesn't jump because Chip didn't jump and he never saw the ball until it was already to the rim, too late to take a swipe at it. The ball falls over the front of the rim and Godzella stands shaking his head.

The one thing that frustrated Chip the most was not being able to fully extend his energies. It was like being grounded at 8:00 on the night of the prom after you'd worked and planned and prepared all year for it. Every time Chip got flyin' high in a game he would be substituted for. He'd spend the next fifteen or twenty minutes on the bench in a nervous and anxious state of mind and body. He never felt the ecstasy of total exhaustion and fulfillment. The game was always over too soon. He was always left with the yearning to do more; to satisfy his spirit that had given all it could and the best he had; to drain himself completely of this boiling, churning energy inside of his mind and his guts.

The fifth game of the year came against Mill's Bottom in the Elk River gym. Tony and Bobby Nash were now playing for Mill's Bottom since the Red Dog High School had been closed. Tony was a junior and Bobby was a sophomore and Mill's Bottom's basketball program had improved two hundred percent with the Nash brothers in the starting line up.

Mill's Bottom arrived and went right to their locker room. Elk River players were already in the gym but when Mill's arrived, the team broke into two groups. The junior varsity players went downstairs to dress for the preliminary game and the varsity players sat in their customary little section in the bleachers right behind the Elk River bench.

When Mill's Bottom's jv team came out onto the floor for warmups, their varsity players crossed over to the other side of the gym and sat together on the top row of the bleachers.

As soon as the B-team game started Coach Perry came over to Marty and Chip and sat down beside them. "Listen," he said, talking to Chip, "how about you and a couple guys go over there where Mill's is sitting and start talking to the boys, since you know them pretty well, and just talk about anything you want, but try to find out if everything is ok with them. You know, I mean, kind of get us a scouting report. Find out if anybody is hurt or sick, or just maybe how they plan to play us tonight. You know, see if you can find out something that might give us an edge tonight, ok, boys." He winked and slapped Marty on the leg and then left. Chip and Marty just looked at each other for a second.

"You know, I was goin' over there anyway to see Tony and Bobby," Chip said. "Come on. They're cool. I'll introduce you."

Chip and Marty stepped down on the seats of the bleachers and crossed the end of the floor and climbed up the other side to the top, back row where the Mill's Bottom coaches and players are sitting.

"What you say animal," Bobby greeted them, smiling. "We gonna smoke you cats tonight."

"Yeah. Yeah. I heard it all before," Chip answered as he sat down. He introduced Marty and they talked awhile about nothing much. Tony had been ogle eyeing one of Elk River's cheerleaders.

487

"I sure would like to buzz butter her buns," remarked Tony. It suddenly got very quiet in the little huddle on the back row.

Chip looked right at Tony. "Don't come over here to Elk River and start pitchin' your jive. Maybe you'd just be better off to stick to your own kind, if you know what I mean." Not only did it get quieter, but a couple of the Mills Bottom players got up and moved a couple of rows away.

Tony stood up. "Yeah. I know exactly what you mean." He hesitated before he went on. "But them Mill's Bottom cheerleaders are the ugliest one group of girls I ever seen."

"I don't know," quipped Marty, "I wouldn't mind meetin' that perky little red head down there on the end".

Bobby broke in, "Yeah. I know her real well, man, but I couldn't fix you up with her. She's way too fast for you. She'd probably screw up your basketball playin' for the rest of the year".

Later in the locker room as Coach Perry is pumping up the boys and going over the game plan, he asked Chip what they found out from Mill's Bottom. Chip grimaced inside and looked at Marty across the room. Marty looked up at the ceiling in a state of anxiety and then looked at Coach.

"Oh, uh, yeah, coach," Marty cleared his throat. "I almost forgot. The big Nash kid's been constipated for about three days now and can't hardly move around much. Wasn't sure how much he would get to play tonight, if any."

Chip got up and went around behind the lockers pretending to get a drink of water so he could hide his red face and keep Perry from seeing the tremors coming from his laughing so hard. He could hear Perry on the other side.

"Ok. That's good. We'll just give him token pressure and concentrate our defense on the other guys."

During varsity warmup drills, Chip and the Nash brothers yell back and forth to each other. Man, oh, man, thought Chip, this is like playin' at the Community Building. Hope we all play as good here as we do over there. It'll be a good show for the home folks.

Elk River won the game by ten, but it was close the whole game. Tony wound up with twenty-eight points, nine rebounds, two blocked shots, six assists, and was all over the place. Marty spent the whole game running up and down the far side of the court, as far away from the bench as he could get.

VII

It was the latter part of January. The days were short. The snow cover on the ground, which had fallen soft and white three weeks ago, was now hard and crusty and dirty. The only bare spots on the ground were where the road and sidewalks and driveways had been shoveled and plowed. The nights were crystal clear and cold and that little frost in the air never went away even when the sun sneaked around the hilltops in the daytime.

Basketball practice was over around 4:30 in the evening but by the time everyone had showered and dressed and spilled outside to head for home, it was getting dusky dark. By the time Chip walked off the hill from the school and the quarter mile up the street into the heart of town, his damp hair would be frozen and the daylight would be almost gone.

Jimmy Butcher had graduated and Chip was on his own, or more poignantly, he was alone. Early on in the season, Chip waited downtown for Jimmy's Uncle Leonard to come by but Chip never saw him again.

The soft lights of town and the hustle of traffic made it seem warmer than it really was. Chip buttoned up his dark plaid, waist length trench coat, donned a pair of ear muffs, and pulled on his woolen mittens. He stuck out his thumb and started hitchhiking as soon as he got to the intersection in the middle of town and would continue to thumb for a ride walking backwards with the flow of the traffic. He had to be always watchful in town because he had to walk along on the edge of the road and usually there was no where to step back off of the road without climbing over a three or four foot pile of snow that had been pushed to the side by the snowplows. If he walked up on the sidewalk that paralleled the street, motorists wouldn't know if he was hitchhiking or not.

Sometimes he'd hit it lucky and catch a ride in town. A few times he'd catch someone going clear through to Hob, but most of the time he wound up being let out somewhere between Seneca and Hob. Most times his luck consisted of catching three or four rides that might go five or six miles each along US 19. He mixed in walking two or three miles to stay warm, before he'd arrive in Hob at the turn off to Sugar Tree.

490

Funny thing about Rt.19, during the daytime, traffic was abundant; moving north and south and darting in and out of driveways and farm lanes and dirt roads, but after six o'clock in the evening it trickled down to a car here and a truck there only about every thirty minutes or so. Where did everybody go?

If he got a ride part of the way up Raven Valley towards Hob, he hoped it would at least be to, or past, the Rt.4 turn off because there would be a chance of more traffic feeding unto Rt.19 and some of it would go north towards Hob.

In some places Raven Valley was a half mile wide. US 19 skirted up the left side of the valley so as not to dissect the flat farm land. Both sides of the valley gently climbed up some low rolling hills before encountering the steeper, wooded mountainsides. When the leaves were off the trees, in some places Chip could see Rt.19 curving around the sides of the valley, peeking in and out, for up to a mile or a mile and a half ahead of him.

There were farmhouses scattered from one end of the valley to the other but none of them was closer than a half a mile of each other. Most were built close to the main highway but some sat back on top of the low rolling hills overlooking the valley. A dirt covered lane would run from Rt. 19, across the valley floor, and up to those houses. A person would have to open and close three or four gates to get from the highway to the house.

Once out of Seneca, the winter night turned blacker and seemingly, twenty degrees colder, as he walked along the lonely road. The only sounds breaking the still, black night would be the crunch of Chip's shoes on the crystallized snow and once in a while a lone dog would start barking at something unseen in the dark. Perhaps it was Chip. He moved on out near the center of the north bound lane where it was bare of snow and his steps became less intrusive upon the silence. He kept walking at a leisurely pace, not to pass the miles but to keep warm. He could see the headlights from an approaching vehicle long before it got to him and usually could hear it even before seeing it's lights. Plenty of time to get off to the side of the road by the snow bank and stick out the thumb.

If a vehicle going his way did not begin to slow down as it approached, Chip learned quickly to turn his back to the car. When a car or truck blew past you at fifty-five plus miles an hour, it whipped up a cold gust of wind that blasted right through your garments and into the bone. Tractor trailers were the worst. Chip never even attempted to thumb them. They never stopped anyway. As soon as he'd see or hear one coming, it didn't matter in which direction, he'd scramble off the road as far as he could get or maybe hide behind the lee ward side of an obstacle like a tree or a bus house until the whirlwind passed.

He didn't mind walking up Raven Valley under certain conditions. On crystal clear nights, the stars were so bountiful and so brilliant you couldn't take your eyes off them. He didn't have to worry about stepping on snakes that came to lay on the warmer-than-the-ground road because it was too cold for them. But other critters, like skunks, opossums, deer, or fox, would come to lick the remnants of salt scattered to melt the ice and snow, and they were to be avoided. No matter how dark it was, if there was any snow cover at all, it would reflect enough light so he could make out the lay of the adjacent land and easily tell where the bare roadside ended and the snow banks began.

A small moon was okay to walk along under but a large moon, like a full moon, reflected too much light and you could see too well. Things stood out in the full moonlight just enough to be unrecognizable but discernible enough to cause concern. Was that black object moving across the upper meadow towards him, still a hundred yards away, a cow, a bear, a person, a shadow from a cloud, a dog, or was it a tree stump and not moving at all? Under a dimly lit moon, he'd never see that object at all but would still be able to see well enough not to be stumbling around in complete darkness.

Some evenings when the temperature was mild, between forty-five and fifty-five degrees, the hitch-and-ride trip through Raven Valley was not unpleasant. Every so often from out of nowhere a current of surprisingly warm air would drift across Chip's path, and in the next minute, he'd walk right into a bank of cold air that seemed to be just lying around there in the road.

Chip would walk by a farm house with the yellow glow from the lights inside splashing on the snow or sometimes reflecting clear out to the road and wonder what the folks inside were doing now. Were they watching TV? Eating supper? Out feeding the livestock? Was there anyone home or had they gone to church and left the light on so people would think they were home? Sometimes he could see into a room from the road and he'd stop and wait to see if anybody passed by the window or if there was any activity at all framed in the window. He'd wait a minute, then move on.

The Moonlite Tavern was located in Raven Valley just about halfway between Seneca and the bottom of Panther Mountain. The Moonlite had a loud speaker hung on the wall right over the front door that was tapped into the juke box inside. On a good quiet night Chip could hear the tinny sound of country music squealing out of that speaker for almost a mile in either direction of the place. To help pass the time, he'd try to figure out what song was playing. He listened intently to the music as he got within range and continued to do so until it finally faded away into the darkness as he passed by, trudging on down the road.

He was never really sure if he wanted anybody coming out of the Moonlite to give him a lift toward Hob or not. Though it was early in the evening, there were those who began their beer drinking early in the afternoon and might just now be running out of money or just ready to quit. Chip always checked the cars parked out front to see if he recognized anyone's. Most nights during the week there would only be one or two and some nights there would be none. Problem was, if he went inside to see who was there, he might miss a car passing by outside going his way. January nights like this, he'd forsake safety for a warm ride and a soft place to sit.

A few times Chip would make it as far as the Moonlite and just wait in the parking lot out front for a ride to come along. At least he could stand outside the front door, under the gable of the roof and watch for cars if it was bad out, or step inside and warm up a little even if he did take a chance on missing a ride.

One evening during a light snow storm, Chip was standing in the Moonlite parking lot out by the road. As he did often, he would stand with his feet inside his gym bag to keep them warm and dry. One of the patrons from the Moonlite stumbled his way out to his car, got it started, and pulled out to head for home. He saw Chip standing by the road so he stopped and backed up and reached over and rolled down the passenger side window. Chip bent down and peered in the window.

"Hey, young feller," he slurred, "what you doin' out here on the road on a night like this?"

"I'm trying to get home over to Sugar Tree," Chip responded.

"Hell, boy you'll never make it tonight. Nobody's out here but me and I'm headin' for the house. Say, why don't you get in and I'll take you over to the house with me and you can call your folks and tell them where you are and that you're staying with me tonight."

"Aw gee, I'd really like to mister, but I've got school tomorrow and I've got to get home and get stuff for tomorrow," Chip could feel the warmth from the car heater flowing out the open window.

"Boy, I'm tellin' you things are mighty bad out here tonight. Sure you don't want to come on home with me?" The car started drifting siowly down the road as the guy was talking but he didn't seem to notice until he could no longer see Chip in the window.

Chip had to almost yell back at the open window, "No, I'm sure but thanks again." The red taillights faded away into the dark.

Chip waited in his gym bag out by the road for twenty more minutes and was just getting ready to head for the inside of the Moonlite when Duffy, the owner, turned off the lights inside the beer joint but left the "GOOD FOOD/COLD BEER" sign on at the front of the building. Chip was left in the cold and dark. Well now I am stuck, he thought.

Just then he could see the headlights of a car coming up the road through the swirling snowfall but it was going the wrong way. The car slowed as it passed Chip and then turned into the Moonlite parking lot where it swung around and pulled up beside Chip. The passenger side window rolled down and Chip bent down and peered in the window. It was the same guy as before.

"Hey boy," he said, but he sounded sober this time, "I got to worryin' 'bout yuh out here and I come back to see if I can git yuh to come on home with me. The wife says it would be the Christian thing to do."

Chip was ready at least to get in the car and discuss it with the man and reached for the door handle but then a car heading Chip's way and driving slowly because of the snow, approached the two from behind. The approaching car had to maneuver around the parked car but when it swung into the other lane to go around, it stopped and the passenger window went down.

"Hey, Chip, that you?" Chip couldn't tell who it was.

"Yeah, it's me".

"Come on over here, man. Let's go to Red Dog."

"Close enough," answered Chip.

"Sorry mister," Chip turned back to the guy in the car, "I sure do thank you for trying to help me though. You be careful going back home now and tell your wife I thank her too".

"I'm just glad you'll be okay now. Anytime you need anything you just let me know. I'll be happy to do what I can". The man waved good-bye, rolled up the window, and drove off. Chip never did know who he was.

The worst conditions for hitchhiking were snow and rain. When it was snowing, Chip could not see his hand in front of his face. He had to walk with his head down to keep the cold snow out of his face. He couldn't hear vehicles coming or see them until they were right on him and most times they couldn't stop if they wanted to. Other times they were afraid to stop. Afraid they couldn't get going again. It was hard walking because his leather soled penny loafers were slicker than snot on the fresh snow and the snow easily spilled over into them, wetting his socks and feet. Boots weren't cool. He'd rather look cool and take a chance on catching the flu than looking square and keeping warm and dry. Another sacrifice in the name of coolness.

If it was raining steadily when he came out of the gym, he'd walk up to Marilyn's and call home to see if somebody could come and get him. If it was a sporadic evening of showers, he'd take a chance and hitchhike home. The times he got caught out on the road in a sudden rain storm were miserable. His trusty old trench coat with the zip-in lining did a fairly good job keeping the heat in and the wet out, but he'd have to carry his gym bag on his head to help keep the rain off while he would seek shelter in a bus house or an old barn or shed close to the road. A few times he just stepped up on somebody's porch to get out of the rain. If there was no shelter close by he would just keep on walking till he could get to one. There wasn't much else he could do.

At the north end of Raven Valley, Rt.19 climbed two miles up Panther Mountain, then turned down the other side, winding three crooked, steep miles to the bottom. Usually when the roads in this part of the state reached the top of a ridge or mountain they ran along the ridge for a couple of miles before dropping down into the next valley but not Rt.19. When it got to the top of Panther Mountain, it topped right over and started down the other side. There was a wide place at the top of the mountain where cars and trucks could pull over to check brakes, let the engine cool down, or let traffic pass by. Directly opposite the wide place across the road was the Panther Mountain Shortcut. It was the dirt road that turned off to Sugar Tree. It left US 19 at the top of Panther Mountain, followed the ridge atop the mountain for three miles, then dropped off another mile and a half down the mountain before leveling out in the valley at the upper end of Sugar Tree. It was only four and a half miles from the top of Panther Mountain to Sugar Tree if one took the shortcut. If one continued to travel on 19 from the top of Panther Mountain down to Hob, then turn off to Sugar Tree on State Rt.11, it was at least thirteen miles to Sugar Tree. Chip never ventured over the Panther Mountain Shortcut even if it meant less than half the distance. There were no houses, no dwellings, no human contact anywhere along the short cut and because the State Road Commission never cleared the little dirt road this time of year, it became almost impassable except for jeeps and other four-wheel-drive vehicles. In fact, there were no houses, no dwellings, no human contact anywhere on Panther Mountain. Only the wind and the woods and the woodland creatures shared occupancy with US 19 and the short cut.

Chip never had to walk the complete distance over Panther Mountain in one trip. He had, however, walked every step of that mountain from the bottom on the Seneca side to the bottom on the Hob side. All the times he had walked the mountain he had caught a ride somewhere on that route.

Only one time did he walk from the top clear down to Hob. That evening he had caught a ride with a guy driving a flat bed truck loaded with bales of hay. The guy was supposed to have delivered the hay to a farm back in Raven Valley but he was unfamiliar with the territory. By the time he got to the top of

Panther Mountain he had realized he had come too far. With some difficulty, he managed to turn around in the wide place at the top of the mountain and head back down to Raven Valley. Chip did not want to retrace his journey, so he got out and started walking down the mountain towards Hob. He met not another vehicle coming up or going down the mountain until he was a mile or so past the bottom of the mountain.

One frigid evening, Chip had caught a ride in Seneca that took him to within a half mile of the bottom of Panther Mountain. When he got out of the car the icy cold wind nearly took his breath. He immediately set out at a brisk walk up Rt. 19 towards Panther Mountain. The pace he set was not only to keep his circulation going in an attempt to stave off the cold, but to keep his mind from worrying about what night critters might be awaiting him on that desolate stretch of highway.

Not one car passed him in either direction. He kept his head scrunched down in the turned up collar of his varsity jacket. The road was dry but the normally dark asphalt was now a light gray color, turned so from the remnants of the salt used to treat the road. Chip looked neither to the right nor the left but followed the dull gray ribbon of highway that stretched before him.

As he ascended the short side of Panther Mountain, the air actually began to warm the further up the mountain he went. In fact, the air temperature at the summit was quite tolerable and the gentle climb up the mountain had helped warm him up. He was, however, in too big of a hurry to get off the mountain to be able to stop and rest. As soon as he started down the other side, he began to sink deeper and deeper into the frigid, damp air settling in the valley below.

When he was half way down Panther Mountain, Chip could see a solitary car, the only one he'd seen since he started walking, slowly creeping up around the mountain. It was still more than a mile away but Chip could see its headlights flickering in and out of sight as the car climbed around the mountain side road below him.

From that distance, the car seemed to be going rather slow but it actually was moving at a good clip. In another moment, its high beam headlights were blinding Chip's vision. He couldn't tell where he was on the road so he turned his head away from the headlights and stepped off to the side of the road and stopped in his tracks. He'd have to wait till the car passed and his eyes regained their night vision before he could attempt to go on.

The driver certainly wasn't expecting to see anyone walking down Panther Mountain on a night like this but he finally realized his lights were blinding Chip and he quickly dimmed them.

The car seemed to slow for a second and Chip got a quick look at it, but then it sped up again. It was a white '61 Chevy Impala. Chip waited a minute for his eyes to become accustomed to the dark before he stepped back out on the road.

He hadn't walked but a few steps when he heard a car coming down the hill from behind him. Well, he thought, maybe my luck's changing.

He stepped back off on to the berm between the road and guard posts as the car neared. It was the Chevy that had just passed him. The car slowed and stopped and the passenger door opened. When the door opened, the dome light came on and Chip could see inside the car. The driver was Jimmy Butcher, and his lone companion, sitting on a personalized, handmade pillow laid over the center seat console, was his girlfriend, Linda.

Jimmy leaned over Linda and motioned for Chip to get in. "What in the world are you doin' out here on a night like this?" he said, as Chip slid in beside Linda. "No wait, lemme guess. Perry the fairy's got you practicing basketball."

"You got it!" said Chip, thankful for the warm air blowing out of the Chevy's heater. "Hi, Linda"

"Hi Chip".

"Man o' man I wish I was back in high school playin' for ole Perry. I swear, I'd drive him nutso. I thought that was you when we came up the hill. I was taking Linda back home and I said I gotta go back and get Chip. Can't leave him out here by himself on a night like this the boy might freeze to death. Lemme run you down to Gaylord's and you can warm up and see if there's anybody going over to Sugar Tree."

That was the closest Chip ever came to walking the entire distance over Panther Mountain in one trip.

The thought in the back of Chip's mind that helped him hurry along the crossing of the mountain was why this was called Panther Mountain in the first place. He knew also this was prime hunting territory for bear, fox, wildcat, and bobcat. All these were motivational thoughts. The best conditions for walking across Panther Mountain would be an air temperature between forty and fifty, no rain, and just enough light to see where you were walking. A good ten to fifteen mile an hour wind was nice to cover up the little rustlings and trampings in the woods and the patter of pads and claws on the road ahead or behind him.

The one thing that would cause indecision and mild panic would be to see the outline of a critter caught in the headlights of an approaching vehicle, scurrying or loping across the road a hundred yards ahead of him. He knew for a fact that there was something up ahead. He'd seen it. Did he stop and wait where he was? How long should he wait? Should he make a bunch of noise like yelling and stomping his feet? One habit Chip learned early. As soon as you started walking on Panther Mountain, wherever you started from, you always walked over to the upper side of the road where the ditch was and find two or three nice hand size rocks for throwing. He carried them with him in his hand or in his gym bag until he got a ride or made it off of the mountain.

On more than one occasion, a woodland creature of some sort had trailed behind Chip as he made his way across Panther Mountain. On those quiet nights when there was no breeze or rain or traffic noise to cover up the rustling through the woods of these creatures, Chip could definitely hear one following behind him. Usually they kept to the woods above the road and would slink along keeping a short distance behind. When Chip would stop, the creature would stop.

Sometimes Chip would stop and just stand silently for a few minutes to see if the creature moved on. It wouldn't make any noise. When Chip would start walking again, the creature would resume its stalking. A few times, something followed Chip right down the middle of the road behind him. It would stay at a distance far enough behind that Chip couldn't see it, but could hear it's pads making contact with the road. When he stopped, it stopped. Chip's grandfather had said a fox would do that.

Once he made it to Hob, if he could catch a ride at the turn off to Sugar Tree, it usually meant at least half of the eight miles would be traveled in the warmth and comfort of a vehicle. There was not much traffic on Rt.11 to Sugar Tree at that time of the evening. Catching any kind of ride on the Sugar Tree road was a godsend.

If it was raining or snowing very hard when Chip got to Hob, he would walk on past the turn off and go down to the Gulf station to see who was hanging out there. Maybe somebody from over Sugar Tree way would be there. He could also get out of the cold or wet and warm up in there. He knew the owner, Gaylord Hall, and Gaylord was always glad to see Chip.

Gaylord always kept up on Elk River athletics and was always looking for someone who would listen to and appreciate his slant on the coaching or the playing of any one of Elk River's teams and games.

Chip got his first ride in a Volkswagen one snowy evening from the Gulf station to the top of Renzee White Hill. He had made it to Hob late that evening because of the snow and walked on down to the station to see if his dad had driven over from Sugar Tree to drive him home. It was 8:30. His dad wasn't there. The thought of having to walk eight more miles in this snow storm to get home left him disappointed and angry. After he warmed up a bit, he walked out in the snow and cold and started home. He hadn't gotten out of the Gulf station parking lot when he heard Claude (pronounced Clod-dee) Miller fire up his Volkswagen. Claude had been in the Gulf station with a bunch of other guys playing the bally-hole pinball machine when Chip was there. When Claude heard about Chip having to walk home, he ran outside, started up the Volkswagen, and pulled up alongside Chip.

Chip knew Claude. Knew he was a carefree single guy who was prone to boast a little about himself or his accomplishments, but was quite amicable.

He rolled down the window. "Hey, Chip. Come on man, get in. I'll take you home. Let me show you how this little baby can go in the snow as good as any jeep."

Chip got in and away they flew. It was like flying in a way. The snow was already six to eight inches deep and on the Renzee White

Hill it had drifted two or three feet deep. The Volkswagen lurched and jerked and bucked as it plowed through the snow as deep as its running boards and bumper. It looked more like a boat plowing through the water with snow flying by the windows like the spray from the bow. There were no tracks to follow along the one lane road, but Claude kept her headed down the middle as best as he could. Only a couple of times did they drop off on to the berm, then Claude would down shift and speed up to eventually climb back on the road. Chip held on as best he could to the handle on the dash in front of him. Claude was afraid if he slowed down the snow would bog him down. He had to make a run at Renzee White Hill. He down shifted and slowly began to gain some speed but he never shifted back up.

"The secret," he said, sawing the steering wheel back and forth with one hand while the other was resting on the gear shift ready for action, "is to keep up a good and steady speed. Don't shift up or down. Don't slow down or speed up and never stop unless there is no where to go." He shot around the lower side of a Ford pickup that was crossways by the side of the road with its front end in the ditch. A man was putting a set of chains on the rear of the truck.

They made it to the top of the hill and only fishtailed a couple of times. Along the ridge, Claude had to build up speed a couple of times to burst through a snow drift. When he got right to the place where Renzee White Hill turned over to Chip's place he stopped the Volkswagen right in the middle of the road.

"Well, this is it Chip. I ain't goin' no farther. This baby is good but I'm afraid if I go down this side of the hill I'll never get back up. Too steep and too crooked. It's only what, a mile or so down to your place. You can make that easy. It's all down hill from here. One thing. Stick around and help me turn this baby around if I need it."

"I sure do thank you Claude," said Chip as he got out. "You're right. This little thing did a good job. Take care of her, and be careful."

Claude didn't need any help turning around as he shifted and spun and steered the little humpback right around in the road and headed back towards Hob. He'll be alright, thought Chip, it's all down hill from here. He turned and started walking off the hill towards home.

One other evening Chip made it to Hob in good time and in fine weather but just as he started walking towards Sugar Tree, without a hint or a warning, there commenced a torrential rain storm. Chip was already a mile from Hob so there was no use heading back there for shelter. He carried his gym bag on his head and kept on walking. The skating rink was located about three miles out of Hob and was the only commercial building located on the road between Hob and Sugar Tree. Chip figured if he didn't catch a ride by then, he could at least get out of the rain under the short front porch at the rink. He thought this was the same night that his dad went bowling over at Seneca and if it was, he would surely see Chip walking in the rain and pick him up. Even if his dad took him back to Seneca until he finished bowling, at least he'd be warm and dry and could take a little nap in the car.

As it turned out, the rain never let up and Chip hadn't caught a ride by the time he got to the skating rink. The rink was closed during weeknights but the awning over the front steps provided some shelter.

Just as Chip got under the awning and began to take stock of his situation, his dad went by in the Merc headed for Seneca. He never slowed down. Never glanced in the direction of the skating rink. Chip guessed he was too busy concentrating on the road that he was trying to navigate through this heavy, pouring rain to notice his own son standing under this meager shelter needing a ride to somewhere. He wondered if his dad even thought about or knew that his son was somewhere out on the road on a night like this and might be in need of help, or was he more concerned about rolling a good game to help his league bowling team?

There was no traffic that night and it didn't look like the rain was going to slow up even a little bit, so after a bit of a rest, Chip broke camp and started walking towards Sugar Tree. He walked all the way up Renzee White Hill, clear out the ridge, and had just turned over the top, heading down the last mile and a half for home, when his mom, driving the Chevy station wagon, came up the hill and stopped to pick up Chip. Chip just stood there beside the road.

His mom rolled down the driver side window. "I got worried about you, son. I'm glad I found you. I was afraid I'd pass you in a car somewhere and not know it and I'd wind up driving clear to Seneca looking for you. Come on and get in. I'll take you home."

"Thanks anyway mom," Chip said exasperated, "I've already walked this far. Might as well walk the rest of the way!"

"Ok," was all she said. She rolled up the window, drove on up to the top of the hill where she turned around, and drove back down the hill to the house, passing Chip walking along in the rain. It turned out that Chip's dad had been looking for him that night as he drove to Seneca and would have taken him back home if he would have seen him but he never did spot him. At least that's what he said.

VIII

The first week in February things started going sour for Chip. On Wednesday night of that week Chip had to walk almost two miles on Rt. 19 to the Sugar Tree turn off in Hob, and then the whole eight miles home. He got home around 10:00, ate supper and went to bed, but his legs and feet continued walking along all by themselves, all night long.

Chip was listless in practice Thursday evening. He gave it all he could but his mind and his legs weren't working very well together.

Perry yelled at him all through the early drills. "What the hell's a matter with you Gates? Come on pick it up will yuh!"

"I'm sorry coach but I didn't get home 'till ten last night." He started to tell Coach about the ten miles he'd walked last night but Perry cut him off.

"Well, we'll just give you the rest of the day off to recuperate," derided Perry. "Johnson, go in for Gates."

Chip sat in the bleachers the rest of the evening with a little five foot seven inch, pimply faced sophomore, who was the son of a Board of Education member, while the other thirteen teammates went through scrimmage. He was still going to be there until 4:30 and have to hitch hike home in the dark.

While practice was going on that evening, it snowed five or six inches and by the time Chip and Marty started downtown after practice, the temperature had dropped to eight above.

"I'm afraid to try to get home in this stuff," Chip confided to Marty as they walked along together.

"Why don't you just stay with me tonight?" Marty asked.

"I can't. We got a game tomorrow night and my uniform and game stuff are all at the house. How am I goin' to get it? Besides that, I can't wear these clothes again tomorrow they'll stink too bad."

"Come on home with me and we'll call over to Sugar Tree. Just tell your mom to pack your uniform in a poke or something and get it to somebody who rides your bus. They can bring it to school with them in the morning and we'll meet the bus when it gets to school. You can put on a pair of my pajamas at the house tonight and mom

504

will wash and dry your clothes so they will be fresh in the morning. Whada yuh think?"

"Let's do it." There was no hesitation in Chip's response.

They went to Marty's and called Grandma and waited for someone from the house to come over and take the call. It was Chip's mom.

The first thing he told her was that he was staying with Marty tonight and what he was doing for clean clothes the next day. Next, he told her to collect everything she could find in his room that even looked like it was part of a basketball uniform. He told her if she wasn't sure about something to check with his dad and then put everything in a bag. If they didn't want to go around to Sugar Tree and give the stuff to Judy or Benji, to bring to school, they could just wait out by the road in the morning and put it on the bus when it stopped to pick up Chip.

Everything worked out perfectly except when Chip checked in the bag for his uniform the next morning. His mom had packed both his home uniform and his away uniform but his home uniform knee socks were missing. Elk River was the only high school that Chip knew that wore knee socks which matched their uniform. In fact, the only other basketball team he could think of that wore knee socks were the Los Angeles Lakers. This would have to be a home game. Chip wasn't mad at his mom and didn't blame her. She did the best she could do and that was all Chip asked her to do. There wasn't much else Chip could have done under the circumstances. The problem was going to be how to tell Coach Perry he didn't have all of his uniform.

He figured if he waited until they were in the locker room dressing before the game and pretended he just then realized he didn't have the knee socks, there wouldn't be much Coach Perry could do.

So while everyone was getting dressed for the game, Chip searched through his gym bag looking for the nonexistent pair of socks. Finally, he padded across the locker room dressed in his home uniform, minus the socks and shoes, and poked his head around the door of the Coach's office. "Coach," he cringed.

Coach looked up from whatever he was reading on his desk, "What is it Gates?"

"Well, Coach, I can't find my knee socks. They're not in my bag."

"Maybe some of the guys took them to play a joke or something."

"I don't think so, Coach. I already checked with everyone. No one seems to know anything about them. I think maybe I forgot them at home."

Coach Perry's demeanor began to change from a casual indifference to an irate indulgence. He rose slowly out of the chair like he was levitating and he levitated right over in Chip's face. "What do you mean you forgot them at home? That is the stupidest thing I ever heard." His voice was getting louder and louder and by now the locker room had become deftly silent.

Perry's words bounced all around the brick room. "So because you forgot your damn socks, this whole team has to go out there tonight in front of a home crowd, and play without knee socks. Lookin' jus' like the same bunch of hillbillies we play against all the time. I try to give this team a little class, a little team spirit, and you screw the whole thing up because you forgot your socks!" He had backed Chip right on out the door into the locker room and down to the end of the bench. The rest of the team sat looking at the floor or the ceiling, anywhere but at Coach Perry, and Chip was afraid to look anywhere else but right into his eyes.

"Now what the hell am I suppose to do? I've a great mind to make you go out there and be the only one without knee socks. Or better yet, not let you go out there at all." He stopped for a moment as if weighing his options. He didn't want to be too rash and then not have a way to back out if it didn't work.

"Ok," he finally said, "Ok, everybody take off them damn socks. We'll all go out there and look like a bunch of redneck hillbillies and if you play like a bunch of redneck hillbillies I'll run your redneck hillbilly asses till you drop on Monday. You got that? Gates you better find a nice soft, comfortable spot to sit cause that's where your gonna be all night tonight!"

Chip and Marty talked it all over during warmups. It would probably be the last time they would be this close together to talk the rest of the night. Both agreed they weren't sure if they had ever

506

seen Coach Perry this upset before. Then they both agreed they had. Marty thought the whole incident was kind of humorous but Chip was afraid to laugh or smile. Coach Perry kept glaring at him from the sidelines all during warmups. His face was so red Chip was afraid he was going to pop a blood vessel.

Chip never knew if it was the fear of Coach Perry, the absence of knee socks, or a weak opponent, but Elk River never played such a flawless game before or after that night. Everything worked. Even Perry's diagrammed offense. Marty got thirty-six and didn't even play the fourth quarter. Elk River won by twenty-three. Everybody played. Even Chip got in the last two minutes. Everybody scored except Chip.

Chip wondered if Coach Perry would let his players play the next game without knee socks. It never happened.

Coach Perry seemed to be in a more mellow mood Monday evening during practice. He even took part in the scrimmage against the first team, playing the big man in the middle for the b-team. He chided and taunted Marty and Alex in a friendly kind of way. He even encouraged Chip, his teammate that evening, to look to shoot the ball more from outside. Chip did shoot way more than he would have ordinarily done, but he knew the real reason Perry wanted him to shoot more was so he could teach Marty and Alex some fundamentals in rebounding and blocking out. Nonetheless, Chip felt the tension between Coach Perry and him seem to ease a bit and Chip did have fun beating the first team in the game situation scrimmage. The Elk River team was loose and ready to take on Mount Carver tomorrow night.

Chip's dad decided to drive over to the game that night and he piled Clint and Riley in with him to take them along too. He said he wanted to see Chip play but Chip figured he mostly wanted to make sure Chip would get home for at least two nights that week.

During the game, Chip could sense his dad's presence in the gym and though he knew his dad was there, it was as if the other two hundred or so folks had all gone home and his dad was the only one left. He wasn't going to press things tonight to gain his dad's approval and in fact, had to contain his enthusiasm somewhat to fit into the game smoothly, and surprisingly, the game came right to him. Combine that with the good feeling he had about the practice the night before, and it produced an almost faultless game for Chip.

It was nothing spectacular, but for Chip himself, it was the best game he'd ever played. He scored eleven points even though he saw limited action. It wasn't the points, though ten of them came on driving, floating, spinning moves to the basket, it was the total contribution he made. Sky high rebounds with one hand at only five-ten; deftly accurate passes that sneaked and whipped and bounced out of nowhere right to an open teammate.

Unfortunately, the only mar in his whole game that night may have been the straw that broke the camel's back.

It was in the fourth quarter with about three minutes left in the game. Elk River was up by thirteen points. Chip took the ball down the court on a three-on-two fast break. He took the ball to the foul line in the middle with Marty on his right and Ruben on his left. He looked right; leaned right; and both defenders went right; one to cover Marty and the other to cut off Chip's move or pass to the right. Ruben cut to the basket on the left wing, wide open.

Chip started to whip the ball behind his back to the left, but just as he started to release it, he felt a wet spot on the ball and it began to slip out of his fingers. He tried to correct for the slip when he released the ball to compensate for the loss of control, but it never slipped at all. If Ruben had been ready for the pass, even if his hand-eye coordination was a bit on the slow side, he could have caught the pass. It was within reach, but instead it sailed over his head and hit the wall, out-of-bounds.

Chip stood perplexed at the foul line. Marty ran by and slapped him on the butt. "That's alright baby, you still looked good," he said. Chip just stood there.

Ruben yelled to him on his way back up the floor, "My fault man, I shoulda been lookin' for it. What a sweet pass. I wouldn't have known what to do with it if I hada caught it."

Chip stood there and Perry screamed at him. "What the hell kind of pass was that? Who do you think you are, Bob Cousy? Get your ass out of there now."

Chip walked over to the bench and sat down. Perry kept on yelling at him but he didn't hear. He wasn't embarrassed. He wasn't anxious. He wasn't angry. He was completely perplexed. He tried

508

to reason it out in his head and all the while Perry kept on yelling at him. The pass felt so good, he thought, it came so naturally. It was just the right thing to do and the right way to do it. How did I screw it up? I bet I could do that a thousand times perfectly. Chip mauled these thoughts over and over the rest of the night. His spirits weren't dampened because to him, it was only a small fracture in an almost perfect game.

Riding home in the car after the game, Chip joked and rough housed with Clint and Rilley until his dad made them stop, but even he was in good enough spirits to stop at the Moonlite and get them each a hot dog and a coke at the curb service.

There was no school Thursday because of some kind of teacher's convention or something, but Perry scheduled practice that day at nine o'clock in the morning. Elk River was to play Mill Creek, Friday night and Mill Creek was undefeated.

Thursday morning Chip got up at 6:00, his regular getting up time, ate, dressed, and was out looking for a ride by 7:00. His dad had taken the Merc to work at 6:00 and his mom left in the Chevy around 7:30. It had snowed about three inches during the night and the little one lane road only showed three tracks from vehicles passing over its surface. Chip stood by the road in the snow stomping his feet and waiting for someone to come by headed towards Hob.

By 8:00 he was soaked through with the cold, so he went over and stood on Grandma's porch out of the snow and watched for a ride coming up the road from Sugar Tree. By 8:30 he realized that even if he caught a ride right now that went all the way to Seneca, he still couldn't make the nine o'clock practice. He convinced himself that it would be stupid to stand out here and freeze for another thirty minutes just so he could practice maybe for half an hour and then freeze for two more hours trying to get home. It wasn't worth it. He picked up his gym bag and went back into the house. He climbed back into bed and as soon as he warmed up, he went back to sleep.

The school was buzzing all day Friday anticipating the big game that night. They even had a pep rally in the gym that afternoon; unheard of at Elk River for a basketball game. The team members

509

and coaches were all introduced to the student body and everyone was in high spirits.

In the locker room before the game the guys were all loose and giddy trying to cover up their jitters. Even Coach Perry had seemed to lighten up a bit. Everyone finally got dressed, began to settle down, and to fill up the bench in front of the blackboard. One by one, each began to quiet down, alone, thinking his own thoughts. Just before they went up to warm up, Perry went over the last details of his plays and game plan, and then told Monty Russell to shoot foul shots with the starting five instead of Chip. That didn't bother Chip because Perry often did that. What did begin to bother Chip was the realization that as the game ticked away, Monty was doing a whole lot more that just shootin' fouls and was beginning to use up Chip's playing time.

Elk River was smokin'. They were running on all cylinders. Mill Creek couldn't get untracked. At the half, Elk River was up by nine and it could have easily been nine more. Chip hadn't even taken his warm up off. The half-time talk from Coach Perry was straight and unemotional. Perry knew Elk River was at its peak and he didn't want to screw it up by making things too complex. Just let it happen.

The third quarter was a blowout. Elk River jumped out early and outscored Mill Creek twenty-six to eight. Early in the fourth quarter Perry could sense it was going to be a rout so little by little, one at a time, he began to replace his starting five. Everyone got to play some. Everyone but Chip. He just sat on the bench with his warm up zipped up, staring out at nothing in particular on the floor while the game flashed back and forth in front of him.

Chip was hurt. He was confused. He was afraid to look at Perry because Perry might look back at him, but Perry never seem to notice he was there. It was like he was invisible.

Perry was feeling good. He patted his players on the back when they came near, yelled directions out on the floor, and even conversed with the referees in a buddy-buddy fashion.

Chip became self conscious. He knew everyone in the gym was looking at the bench trying to see who it was down there that was so bad, he couldn't even be allowed to play in a game such as this. He was sure everyone was watching him instead of the game.

Every one of Mill Creek's players got some playing time too. Chip squished himself right into the back of the bench trying to make himself as inconspicuous as he could.

As Marty and the other regulars were substituted for, they returned to the bench and put on their warmups. Chip noticed that they began to crowd in around him until they were all bunched up together on his end of the bench. There was a big vacant space between the bunch and Coach Perry. None of the players on the bench spoke to anyone. Not even each other. There was no emotion in their spirit nor did any show in their faces. It seemed to Chip as though they were either sort of protecting him like a mother bear would shelter her cubs, or they were taking sides against Perry and openly showing their contempt for the Coach's action. That was how Chip felt.

Actually, they were just angry at Perry for not allowing Chip to share in this total team victory.

Chip sat on the bench in front of his locker after the game, quietly changing from his uniform into his street clothes. He decided not to take a shower since he hadn't even raised a sweat. The jv and the substitutes who had played most of the fourth quarter were yelling and venting their high spirits in a rowdy manner. The regular players had already showered, dressed, and gone quietly. They had not said a word to Chip in the dressing room but had left him alone with his thoughts. It gradually quieted down as the last stragglers went outside. Chip looked down the row of lockers and saw Coach Perry walking towards him. They were alone now in the little room.

"You know why I couldn't let you play tonight, don't you?" asked Perry.

"No, I don't," answered Chip matter-of-factly, looking right into Perry's eyes.

"You didn't come to practice yesterday and I didn't feel it was fair to the other players since they all managed to get here. You know my conditions for skipping practice."

Truthfully, Chip didn't know his conditions for skipping practice until that very minute. Perry certainly hadn't mentioned it at anytime in Chip's presence since he had become Elk River's coach, and Chip had been to every team meeting, every practice,

511

every tryout Perry had ever held except for yesterday. Maybe he announced it yesterday, thought Chip. Wait a minute. Had there been other players who had missed practice before? Yes, there was. Had they ever had to sit out a whole game? No, they hadn't.

Perry went on. "We have a real team here this year, son, that...............and   tradition........one   hundred percent..............dedication..........." Chip's own thoughts began to crowd out whatever garbage the coach was spewing. Even though he kept looking right into Perry's eyes without flinching, he wasn't hearing a word. He was talking to himself.

Tell him, Chip said to himself. Tell him how many times a starter has missed a practice during school time and not only got to play, but in some cases kept his starting position. Tell him that you travel farther than any other player on his team just so you can play basketball here. Tell him about the snow, and the cold, and the rain, and the nights you don't even get to go home. Tell him about the 10:00 suppers. Tell him he could of at least demanded or asked for a reason for missing practice. Tell him he could of at least told you in the team meeting before the game that you weren't going to play tonight and why. Tell him he could have made some sacrifices on his own like letting you go early on bad days so you could have a chance to get home at a reasonable hour. Tell him. Tell him what playing basketball means to you to. Tell him about dedication. Tell him...tell him......tell him nothing! Ask him nothing!

Chip eyes were burning and watering. He couldn't swallow. He knew if he opened his mouth it would all come out in a whining blubber. All he was conscious of now was Perry's last words as he turned away to go back to his office. "You understand, Gates", he said, "I have to have some discipline on my team." Then he finished with a quick phrase thrown over his shoulder as he walked away, "See yuh at practice Monday."

Was that suppose to make up for everything? Chip asked himself. He didn't even give me the opportunity to say anything. Was that an apology? An apology for what? Is that suppose to make me feel better? To do better for God and my country, to obey the Scout law at all times, to keep myself physically strong, mentally awake, and morally straight? For some reason Chip felt a little easier inside.

512

IX

Chip spent the whole weekend moping around the house. He didn't go around the road to play ball on Saturday or Sunday. He was depressed. He was anxious. He was restless. He was subdued and quiet. Sunday afternoon he sat with his dad in the living room watching an NBA game on TV.

"I was glad you brought the boys over to the game the other night," he said. "It's the first time I have ever been aware of people watching us play. I never really thought of it before, but it seems everyone thinks we play these games to entertain them. I know some players project the image that their soul is dedicated to the task at hand. That they need to be in the spotlight. They need to be the best there is." Chip paused for a moment. "I guess I'm not like that."

It was very hard for Chip to talk to his dad about personal things like this, but he had to talk to somebody. "I like playing basketball because I enjoy the challenge of the physical aspects each game sets before me. I enjoy it because it is something I can do well. No one will remember what happened in a game from one week to the next, but I remember what I did or what I learned from a certain experience. I don't really care if we win or lose because that doesn't mean as much to me as just being able to participate and contribute something to the game. I guess I'm not competitive enough or something. I can't really explain it. You know what I mean?"

His dad sat quietly for a moment watching the game and then he said, "You know you are not a bad basketball player. I really wanted to come to the game the other night to watch you play and I could tell you have accomplished much in these last few years. No matter what you did or didn't do well in the game, at least you were enjoying what you were doing. I could tell that just by watching you play."

He turned to Chip and then said, "I know too, by watching you this weekend, that something happened that has upset you an awful lot. Something that you didn't enjoy." He paused for a moment then added, "I think maybe that 'just playing basketball' means more to you than you will admit, and maybe it means more to you than it should. It's not life or death you know. It's not the only thing you know how to do."

Chip sat watching the game. He wondered if his dad knew about him not getting to play Friday night and maybe, his dad had said just what Chip had wanted someone to say to him for two days. He continued watching the game with disinterest but he was beginning to feel better inside. He tried to think of something to say to his dad in the way of gratitude but he was afraid it would sound too mushy or something, so they sat together the rest of the afternoon, enjoying the game together in a silent camaraderie that both of them understood and accepted as a natural father/son relationship.

After the game, Chip walked up through the orchard where Clint and Riley and a couple of other neighbor kids were sled riding. Major and Specks were romping in the snow with the kids, tugging on their clothes, and chasing off after them down the hill as they glided by. Chip stopped for a while to watch and give advice on the best route to take down through the orchard, but the kids would find their own best way just to spite Chip.

He continued on up through the orchard and headed on the hill. Near the top, Major and Specks caught up with him and almost knocked him over as they jostled around him. They were vying with each other to be the leader. Chip didn't stop at the rock but passed on by and started out the ridge.

When he couldn't find the dogs anywhere up ahead of him, he turned and looked back out the ridge. There they both were, sitting at the base of the rock. They were looking in Chip's direction as if to say, "Hey, I think you forgot to stop here like you're suppose to". Chip's quick word and pat on his pants leg was all they needed to be motivated enough to get up and trot over and pass Chip, and once again battle for the lead. They forgot about the rock and went to scout ahead.

Chip didn't need to sit on the rock and contemplate his dilemma. He had already decided what he was going to do. He just needed some time alone to walk and mull over the consequences of his decision. It was getting late and cold that February evening as Chip made his way along the ridge in the snow. When he decided he had gone far enough, he turned and started back home. He stopped and looked out towards the horizon where the sun had just set. The mountains, now purple and dark gray, and barren of their covering, lay in repose, as if they were trying to cuddle up close against the warm glow of the sunset in an effort to savor the last bit of the day's warmth before the cold February night set in.

Monday evening at 2:30, Chip went down to the locker room in the gym, cleaned out his locker, packed his two uniforms neatly in his official Elk River High School gym bag, and knocked on the coach's door.

He had thought of the speech he was going to make to Perry. He had worked it and rearranged it all night in his head. All the things he thought of last Friday night and some of the things he and his dad had talked about were in the speech, but when Coach Perry asked him to come in and asked him what he wanted, he just set the gym bag down softly on the floor and said, "Coach, it's just too hard for me to play ball here because I have so far to go and everything, so I am going to have to quit."

Coach Perry looked at him for a moment and then said, "Gates you are a good basketball player. I hope your quitting doesn't have anything to do with the other night."

"No it doesn't," Chip lied. "It's like I said. It's just been too hard for me."

Without even getting up and extending a hand, Perry responded from behind his desk, "Well, good luck son. I'll see that you get your schedule rearranged for this period."

Chip turned and walked out. There were only two thoughts that entered his mind in the short distance he walked from Coach Perry's office to the basement door that led outside, behind the gym.   One of them was reoccurring, Perry didn't even seem surprised. He didn't ask Chip to think it over. Didn't offer any encouragement at all. In fact, it didn't seem to effect the coach at all. The other thought was of getting out of there before Marty or anybody else knew what he was doing.

Once outside, he felt like he had just been set free from a two year sentence in solitary confinement. He rode the bus home that evening, much to the surprise of the driver and the regular riders. He didn't get to sit by Judy though until the bus discharged its passengers at the Hob grade school and turned for home. Nobody

515

knew Chip was going to ride the bus home that evening, not even Judy, so she hadn't saved a seat for him.

Chip's mom was surprised to see him getting off the bus at the house that evening. She asked him the reason why, and he told her cf his decision to quit basketball. Her only comment was, "Does this mean you'll be coming home every evening on the bus in time for supper?".

"Only until track practice starts in a month," laughed Chip. The conversation at the dinner table was lively and spontaneous that evening but the subject of Chip's decision to quit basketball never entered in. Chip figured his parents felt that it was his decision and he would accept the responsibility for it. So they left it alone.

After supper that evening, Chip headed around the road to the Community Building to play ball. He stopped at Maynard's house on the way and after helping Maynard walk up to the barn and feed the cow and horses, they walked on around the road to Sugar Tree.

Chip was hoping Paul would be at the Community Building but when they arrived, no one was there. They turned on the lights and did a little shooting around and eventually Benji, Pee Wee, and a couple of grade school kids showed up, so they chose up sides and started playing. Sure enough, Paul and Jacky showed up about 7:00.

They had a real good go at it for about an hour. Paul was hot and he shot the ball from all over the place. He never passed off. As soon as he got the ball he fired away. If he got a rebound on the other end, he'd bring the ball up the floor and let her fly. If you passed the ball to him, you didn't get it back.

"Come on Paul," Jacky would yell at him. They were on the same team this night. "Pass the ball or I'm going home."

"I don't care what you do," said Paul in between dribbles, "I ain't never been this hot anywhere, anytime in my entire life. This will never happen again so I'm not going to quit until I start missin'. So, shut up!"

Another ten minutes went by and it became obvious that Paul's streak had ended. They horsed around for another fifteen minutes or so and then just quit. They turned the lights out, piled in Paul's car, and headed home. Paul dropped everyone off as he cruised around to Chip's. Maynard was the last one before Chip, so only Paul and he were left in the car.

Paul said, "I stopped at the station and some of the guys said you had quit basketball. I knew where you probably would be so I drove on up to the Community Building to see for myself."

"Well, it's true," answered Chip. "I didn't feel like I was appreciated and besides that, Coach Perry and I had different philosophies about basketball. I wanted to play..... and he didn't want to play me."

"So you want to play some more for Sugar Tree since you are no longer under SSAC sanctions?"

Chip couldn't hardly contain himself. "You're the first person I went lookin' for this evening to see if you were still playin' ball".

"We've been playin' at the Community Building some but I've not taken any of the guys and gone anywhere to play. We couldn't ever find enough guys to play. But that's no problem if you want to play. I can find us some games anytime."

It wouldn't matter to Chip. He was loose and free. He was back to playing basketball his style. The excitement and the enthusiasm was back. He was flying again and doing all the things with a basketball he had always wanted to do without any imposed restrictions and limitations. The inspiration had returned.

Three weeks later Paul loaded the guys up and drove over beyond Seneca to a little grade school multipurpose room at a place called Bent Creek. After going at each other for a couple of hours both teams just quit and sat around on the folding metal cafeteria chairs shooting the breeze and drinking ice cold pop from the ice chest while they cooled off.

One of the players from Bent Creek came over and introduced himself to Chip. "Hey, don't you play basketball for Elk River?" he asked.

"Used to, but had to quit."

"I thought I knew you from somewhere". He and Chip shook hands. "I'm Bill Stover. I'm the assistant basketball coach at Greenbrier."

"Oh yeah," recalled Chip. "I remember you."

517

"You know your coach stole Joey Fry from us." He said it in an offhand way with a little smile but Chip wasn't too sure where this was going to go.

"No. I don't know what you mean, exactly," replied Chip.

Stover sat down and beckoned Chip to the seat next to him. Chip could sense a more relaxed atmosphere. "Well, Joey has always been a Greenbrier County boy. Grew up here. Played grade school basketball here. Played jr. high basketball for Greenbrier. Then just like that, he transferred to Elk River. Joey lives over where Seneca and Greenbrier Counties come together. Seneca County school buses travel into Greenbrier County and Greenbrier County buses travel into Seneca County. We got Greenbrier County kids going to Elk River High and we got Seneca County kids goin' to Greenbrier High. Kind of give and take and nothin' much has ever been said about it. Only we found out the real story behind Joey's transfer to Elk River High. Here's the deal and we found out about this from a very reliable source in the Seneca County Board of Education's central office."

"Seems Coach Perry promised Joey that he would start all three years at Elk River. We would have given him the same deal at Greenbrier. Perry also offered to pay Joey's family so much per mile, round trip from Joey's house to Elk River and back, every evening after practice, and after every game, if they would let him come to Elk River and play. I guess he paid them out of the athletic fund or paid them himself because evidently, the Board doesn't know or doesn't care about what's going on."

Chip thought about all this for a moment. It made sense the way Joey was always hanging on every word and every direction the coach gave. Joey's parents were always there after practice and at every game, home or away. But what did Frankie have to do with all this? Did he live with Joey?

"What's the story with Frankie?" Chip asked.

"Story is, that Joey finally agreed to transfer to Elk River High only if Coach Perry would find a place for Frankie too. Joey said he wouldn't transfer unless Frankie could go too. We would not have cut Frankie at Greenbrier if he'd come here, but he never would have been a major player for us. Probably play about like he does for you guys now, but Joey.......Joey is all-state material.

518

Course he made his own choice about where to go to play ball, but he was always our 'favorite son' and we all thought for sure this is where he would play his high school ball. It was just natural. Perry is not well thought of in this neck of the woods. I can tell you that."

Son-of-a-gun, thought Chip. All that stuff I went through to play ball for him, and it didn't mean one thing to him. He sure didn't offer me any incentives to keep playing.

As painful as it was when he thought about those two years with Coach Perry, it hurt even more because that last year, Chip's senior year, the year he quit, was the only time in the history of Elk River High School that a basketball team ever made it to the quarter finals of the WV State Boys Basketball Championships. The winners of each of the state's eight regionals met in Morgantown at the WVU Fieldhouse for the state championship tournament. Elk River lost by seventeen points in the opening round of the tournament to Logan, who went on to win the class AA state championship that year.

Chip sat alone in his bedroom back in Sugar Tree and listened to the game on his transistor radio. Chip had always been, and would always be, true blue and loyal to his beloved Elk River, and he hoped that Marty would score thirty points and be the tournament MVP, but secretly, and with much chagrin, he rooted for the Logan Wildcats that night.

Marty did win all-tournament honors that year and was named to the AA all-state second team. He went on to attend WVU after high school and became a well respected attorney in the county of Seneca.

Joey Fry lived up to his reputation and became a two-time All State player in WV. He went on to become a standout player for Fairmont State College in the WVIAC, making all-conference three years, and was named to the NAIA All American second team his senior year. He was drafted by the Virginia Squires of the ABA and played three seasons with them.

In the late 1970's, though over thirty years old, Chip was still playing pickup games of basketball around the county. One Sunday afternoon during a game in the gym at Red Dog, a WV State Police cruiser with two State Troopers in it pulled up beside the gym and the two got out and came into the gym. Of course play stopped immediately. The biggest trooper was about six-five and had a rolled up bundle under one arm and a pair of basketball shoes in his hand. He spoke first.

"Hey, you guys mind if I play some with you a little while?"

Everybody kind of mumbled and shuffled around some, "Nah, we don't care. You can play with that bunch from Red Dog. They need all the help they can get." Snickers slipped out from all around.

The other state trooper went back out and sat in the car, monitoring the radio while his partner played a little basketball inside.

He was good. Very good. Too good to be playin' with a bunch of over-the-hill, bald guys. Chip could tell he was just playing around with them. He could do anything he wanted, anytime he wanted, but he just slipped right in with the flow of the game and made everybody a little better.

Chip took a break after awhile and sat down in the bleachers and watched the state trooper play. There was something familiar about him. Newman Acree came over and sat down beside Chip. "I swear Chip, that guy looks like a guy that used to play for the Virginia Squires," he said.

"Holy moly, " thought Chip, "it is him. It's Joey Fry!"

Just then the other trooper came back in the gym. "Hey, Joey," he said. "We gotta get going. You 'bout done?"

"Yeah, just gotta get dressed. Be right out. Hey, you guys play over here often?" he asked as he came off the floor.

"Yeah," somebody said, "there's always somebody here playin' on Sunday afternoons."

"Great," said Joey. "If you guys don't care, I can slip over every once and awhile and play for a couple of hours."

Chip had slipped down the bleachers where Joey was changing back into his trooper's uniform.

"Hey, you probably don't remember me, but I'm Chip Gates. We played basketball together a Elk River High School a few years ago." Chip stuck out his hand.

Joey looked at Chip and grabbed his hand and shook it, "Yeah, sure man. I remember you. How yuh doin'?"

Chip could tell by the forced compliment and that kind of cover-all cliché, that Joey really had no idea who Chip was, so Chip didn't press it anymore. "Are you stationed somewhere close around here?" he asked.

"Yeah, I've just been transferred to Mill's Bottom so I'm not that far away. You'll be seeing me more often. Nice to see you again, Chet." He picked up his stuff and headed out the door.

They never saw Joey again. Must have gotten transferred somewhere else.

EPILOGUE

In 1963, WYGARB associates sold all of their holdings in Red Dog, including the town itself, to a coal industry magnate from Pennsylvania. The new company was also a stalwart UMWA affiliate. All of those employed by WYGARB at the time of the buyout were discharged. Some of those who were known union supporters from previous years were rehired by the new company and stayed on at Red Dog but the majority were let go. Those WYGARB employees who lived in Red Dog lived in WYGARB houses, but since they no longer worked for WYGARB and since WYGARB was no longer their landlord, they had to move. Union workers that the new company brought in with them took over the vacated houses.

The new company's first and foremost focus was on producing coal as fast and as cheaply as possible. There would be no interest in running a town or seeing to the social or civic needs of its workers. Their workers would have to meet those needs on their own. The new company basically shut the town down. The Town Hall was closed. No more movies, no bowling, no pool playing, no hamburgers, french fries, or fountain drinks. No barber shop or beauty salon. It didn't matter a whole lot though because there were no teenagers to fill the booths and seats. They closed the high school and the Rose County Board of Education transported those students twenty-four miles through the woods to Mill's Bottom. The company kept the high school building and used it as a grade school.

Both of the WYGARB Company stores were closed, including Store #2 in Sugar Tree, and all of their merchandise shipped out. A congregation of Holy Rollers moved into the Sugar Tree Company Store and held services there. A couple of times Chip and some of the guys met at the store on nights when services were conducted. They stood out in the road in front of the store and watched the goings on through the open front doors. One thing was for sure, Holy Roller services were spirit filled and they definitely had a good time. Word was that the Holy Rollers had kind of taken over the store on their own without anyone's approval so they were ask to vacate shortly after they moved in. The store in Sugar Tree stood vacant for five or six years before someone bought it for the lumber and tore it down. Wyatt Keener's store in Sugar Tree returned to its prominence as the only general store between Mill's Bottom and Hob and remained so for three more years. Wyatt, then in his eighties, retired and closed the store. Bucky and Lewis moved what merchandise they could handle over to the station.

The Bank of Red Dog was closed and the new company was ordered to return all of their clients' money, dollar for dollar with US currency. The bank building was later torn down and hauled away but the bank's massive steel vault could not be moved or dismantled. The vault had been transported to Red Dog by train, unloaded by railroad crane, and set in concrete. The bank building itself was then built around the vault.

Medical Center closed. Grill, closed. Rooming house, Club House, Gulf garage and service station, closed. Sportsman Club Lodge closed. Sportsman's Park swimming pool, tennis courts, and fish pond excavated. The Rose County Board of Education leased the gymnasium from the new company, paid the insurance on the building, and kept it open for ten more years.

The new company also closed all of the deep mines. Mine equipment that was relatively new and in good working order was shipped out by train. The rest, including motors, loaders, cutting machines, cars, and track were shoved back into the now abandon mines and entombed there as the mine portals and drift mouths were sealed closed by dynamite.

Coal was now abstracted from the mountains by cutting high walls all along the mountain side to expose the coal seam. Three foot diameter augers were drilled hundreds of feet into the coal seam. The coal was corkscrewed out along the auger bit onto a conveyor belt that dumped the coal into a Euclid truck. The truck hauled the coal back along the high wall bench and eventually to the tipple where the coal was dumped into railway cars. The company kept the tipple and the railroad intact to ship its coal out but they had to renovate both to suit their needs.

The tipple was converted to nothing more than a loading facility. The coal was no longer washed and it was no longer crushed to different sizes; one size fit all. A loading ramp and dumping pit were built so the Euc's could dump their load directly into the tipple.

While the company was waiting for four of its diesel locomotives to be transported to Red Dog from other operations, they used the four remaining MC & E steam engines for transporting the coal to the B & O line at Mill's Bottom.

WYGARB's property also included the town of Bumtown and the lumber mill located there. The new company temporarily closed the mill until they could figure out what to do with it. In the process, they not only laid off the hundred or so workers who worked the mill, but also evicted them and their families from the old WYGARB houses in Bumtown.

Eventually the new company sold their timber rights to Georgia Pacific who came in and reopened the mill. Georgia Pacific brought their own men with them and housed them in the old WYGARB houses in Bumtown. Georgia Pacific also used the MC &E line to transport their lumber to market. When the coal operations in Red Dog ceased, Georgia Pacific worked the lumber mill for two more years, shipping their lumber to market by truck.

The MC & E established its niche in American history by being the last commercially steam operated railroad in the US. After the diesels arrived, the company sold all of the MC & E rolling stock. Most of it went to various tourist railroads up and down the east coast, but the MC & E's honorable distinction can never be taken from her.

The new company's strip mining process produced twice as much coal with half as many workers as WYGARB's deep mining did but the strip mining process just abstracted the easily accessible part of a coal seam and left much buried deep in the mountain, untouched. Strip mining also ripped mammoth benches around the sides of the mountains with high walls sometimes as high as fifty and sixty feet. Strip mining also produced millions and millions of cubic yards of earth that was dumped into the valleys and hollows at the bottom of those stripped mountains. In less than three years of strip mining, the new company had extracted all of the coal it could attain by staying within its proposed operating budget, so it packed up all of its workers and equipment and moved on; perhaps to Pennsylvania, perhaps to another struggling WV coal town. Their departure left the once, pristine, beautiful hills of this central part of the state with monstrous gouges ripped out of their sides and those stripped benches sometimes ran for miles and miles.

Chip had been flown over this area a few times and the devastation was easily recognizable from very lofty heights. It reminded Chip of some type of ancient ruin, like the Inca or the Maya.

Old timers still say there is twenty or thirty years of coal mining left in those abandoned hills and the new company did retain all of its mineral rights purchased from WYGARB. Maybe they plan to return one day to mine the coal once again. Though many of those old timers were laid to rest, with a glimmer of that very hope still buried within their heart, it hasn't come to pass and to those, it makes no difference now.

Some of the old patriarchs who had lived in Red Dog all of their lives and had no other place to go, were allowed to live on in the old WYGARB company houses. The new company wouldn't sell those lots or those houses but did lease them to tenants for as little as a dollar a month. Whatever dwellings and buildings the company did sell to private parties had to be torn down and hauled off the company's property. Those buildings were sold at rock bottom prices and many locals took advantage of the bargains. They would carefully dismantle the buildings, salvaging what lumber they could, and use the material to build additions to their present homes or add garages and other outbuildings. One individual bought all of the steam pipe in Red Dog, cut it up and installed his own home water and irrigation system. Bucky and Lewis bought all of the contents of the Gulf garage to refurbish their own station. The tipple was torn down and sold for scrap metal.

A few years after the new company had pulled out and abandoned Red Dog, there was some talk of making Red Dog a tourist attraction. The idea was to allow tourists to experience the life and culture of a

1930's era coal town. The rail line was still intact from the B&O to Red Dog so the tourists would be transported to Red Dog on a steam operated railroad. Most of the important buildings in Red Dog were still standing and could still be made usable without much expense. The boarding house, rooming house and club house would be available for lodging and meals. Entertainment could be found at the town hall where '30's movies would be showing and dancing to live bands, plays and vaudeville acts would be available. The residents of the town would be employees of the tourist company, dressing in 30's attire and running the various attractions. That plan would have been feasible at the time of its conception but for some reason it died in its infancy. Twenty years later the idea surfaced again but by then there was nothing left of the town except for the few residents who still lived there.

Eventually all the company related buildings were torn down and hauled away. The Sportsman's Club Lodge stayed intact for more than ten years and was used as a camp by hunters until some drunken vandals caught it on fire one night and it burned down. In the mid '70's the Rose County Board of Education closed the elementary school and transported those kids to school in Sugar Tree. A local church bought the gymnasium, dismantled it, and moved it over near Marie's Store. They used the materials to build a new church with a beautiful sanctuary of yellow popular. The post office in Red Dog is still operational and the Baptist Church keeps its doors open for the sixty some residents who still live there.

There was another movement afoot in the '80's to organize a Red Dog Day Reunion. It was to be held in the center of town on the vacant lot where the Town Hall use to stand. Only a handful of people gathered for that first reunion and the majority of them were folks who lived in the local area. Some of the families that lived and worked and raised their kids in Red Dog either didn't know about the reunion or knew about it, but didn't care to attend. So many years had passed before the reunion was organized that sadly, most of those folks had passed away. That one Red Dog Reunion was the first and the last.

In the early 1980's, the US Department of Mining and Reclamation ordered the state of WV to recontour all of the abandoned mountainsides in WV that had been strip mined before 1977. They were also ordered to reclaim all abandon gob and slag piles by layering the gob with earth and contouring it with the surrounding mountains and valleys. Federal monies were applied to these projects. Although the WYGARB gob piles were reclaimed, the strip benches left by the Pennsylvania company remain to this day, not only a memorial to mankind's greed, but to his callous and indifferent relationship with his environment.

But mother nature is a force that cannot be denied nor contended with. It took some time and work but eventually she somewhat rejuvenated the mountain sides and the valley where the town of Red Dog and the mining operation thrived for sixty years. Mossy Creek once again runs clear and pure. Grass, wild flowers, and sage brush are growing on vacant lots, and the forest has moved its boundaries down from the tops of the mountains, over the abandon mine and railroad tracks, right to the edge of the county road that passes through the valley. If a person unfamiliar with the locale drove through Red Dog today, they would see it as no different from the thousands of other WV mountain valleys. They would have no inkling of the town and the operation that once flourished there, except for the one monument that remains. In the middle of a well manicured, grassy lot, surrounded by a scraggly woods, stands a very visible, mammoth, steel, box-like structure. Above its doorless entrance read the words; BANK OF RED DOG.

In 1965, the Seneca Board of Education closed the Lick Run School. Those students could walk to school in Sugar Tree or catch the Elk River High School bus and be dropped off at the elementary school in Hob.

Chip, Riley, and Clint were not present to witness the realization of their most hoped for, dreamed of, and highly anticipated event. While Chip and Riley were away at college and Clint was doing a stint in the army, the Seneca State Road Commission made Rt.11 a two lane highway from Hob to Sugar Tree. It didn't have painted center lines and it didn't have guard posts but it was finally moving towards becoming a modern era highway.

Even though Rt. 11 from Sugar Tree to the top of Red Dog Hill had been a two lane for more than nine years before the rest of it was paved, it had no center line either. It was about this same time that the Rose County State Road painted the first center line on the road from Mill's Bottom to Sugar Tree. The first week after the painting there were six wrecks on that stretch of road. Driver's had driven that road for ten years with less total mishaps than had occurred in that one week following painting the road. The problem stemmed from the fact that even as a two lane blacktop, the road was just barely wide enough for two vehicles to pass. Everybody that drove the road knew that and learned to drive accordingly. Now all of a sudden the State Road comes along and paints a center line and takes a foot and a half out of the middle of the road. The road is the same width as it always was but now drivers try to stay over on their side of the line and there wasn't enough room. They kept running off the road. It was probably fortunate that the State Road didn't paint those little white lines along the edge of the road.

In December of Chip's freshman year at Marshall College he received a letter from Benji. Receiving a letter from Benji quite unnerved Chip because Benji just never wrote letters. He opened it and read:

Dear Chip,

Last night we had a heavy snowstorm in Sugar Tree and sometime during the night, the Community Building fell in. I thought it would be better if you heard about it from me first, instead of some stranger.

Your cousin,
Benji

Chip got the letter a day or two before Christmas break was to begin and on the following Friday he headed for Sugar Tree. He didn't get in until late Friday night, but early Saturday morning, Benji came around, picked him up, and then drove them back around the road to take a look at the Community Building.

The snow still lay deep on the ground and it crunched under the tires of the Chevy as they slowed to a stop in the middle of the road beside where the Community Building used to stand. Chip got out and surveyed the disaster area. The morning air was cold and damp and his breath drifted away in misty clouds of vapor when he exhaled. The whole building had collapsed into a pile of jumbled wood. There were a few boards sticking out or standing up at weird angles, but the snow had completely covered the pile of rubble and to the unknowledgeable, it would appear to be just a big pile of snow.

"Good thing no one was in there playin' ball," Chip remarked.

Benji walked around the car and stood beside Chip. "Nobody plays ball in there anymore since you left." He paused before going on. "It's like the old building didn't have any purpose for being anymore and just gave up." There was nothing more to say. The two boys stood on the edge of the road and stared silently at the shattered pile of memories.

A pickup truck eased it's way down Painter Fork Road and stopped. Benji and Chip got back in their car and pulled over to the edge of the road to let the pickup pass. The driver waved at the two boys as he passed. Chip gave the scene one more hard look and then turned away. "Let's go," he said.

In 1978, the WV Department of Natural Resources announced that maintaining fire towers during fire season was no longer cost effective. Fire spotting could be done better and cheaper by aerial reconnaissance, so they tore down the Horse Ridge Fire Tower and sold it for scrap. The little house was bought by six local residents who dismantled the house and rebuilt it as a hunting cabin on a remote ridge off of Panther Mountain.

In 1980, the Seneca County Board of Education closed the elementary school in Sugar Tree citing its remote location and distance from the Board of Education's Central Office in Seneca as the cost effective factors. Elementary students in Sugar Tree had the choice of either riding the bus to the school in Hob or take the one hour bus ride to the elementary school in Mill's Bottom.

The closing of the elementary school in Sugar Tree had a devastating effect on the little village's social and cultural climate. First, the school building itself was used for all kinds of civic and social functions outside of the normal school-community activities. It served as a meeting place for the Community Action Committee, the Boy Scouts, Weight Watchers, and 4-H Club. With nowhere to meet, all of those community organizations disbanded.

The school had served as the local voting precinct since the early 1900's. Now voters had to drive to the elementary school in Hob in order to vote. Residents in Sugar Tree had always felt like the foster child of Seneca County; neglected by those officials because of their isolation. They had no economical or industrial value to the county, and had no distinguished or politically important citizens among its populace. Many of those in Sugar Tree even doubted if there were any county officials who actually knew Sugar Tree existed let alone knew it was located in Seneca County. The moving of their precinct to another community some ten miles away only served to confirmed their suspicions. Needless to say, Sugar Tree's voting turnout dwindled to a handful.

When the school was open, trucks delivered groceries and produce once and sometimes twice a week. A bakery truck came every Wednesday and a dairy truck made its rounds every Monday and Friday. Because those companies had to come to Sugar Tree to supply the school, they were able to supply the service station at the same time. With their business savvy and a just plain likeable nature, Bucky and Lewis were able to convince those drivers to fuel up at the service station when they made their deliveries to Sugar Tree. The dairy truck actually stopped at various residents along its route into Sugar Tree to deliver products directly to the home. When the school closed, there just wasn't enough business from the station alone to warrant running a truck clear to Sugar Tree.

At first those deliveries were cut to a once a week, then Bucky and Lewis were informed that Hob would be the nearest drop off point of their orders and that they would have to make arrangements on their

530

own to get the merchandise from there to their business. The brothers had to cut back on their stock of produce and grocery. For another year, they would drive over to Hob four times a week to load up on bread, milk, snacks, and pop.

Gasoline was costing the brothers big bucks but they bit the bullet on that one because they didn't want to see the locals having to drive to Hob or Mill's Bottom for gasoline. That lasted until the EPA in WV required all gas stations to post a one million dollar insurance bond to cover their old, in-ground, metal tanks, or convert their tanks to above-ground, or invest in some kind of new in-ground tank formulated to never leak. Bucky and Lewis could no longer survive under those conditions and sadly closed the doors of the Esso station.

Probably as a compensatory gesture for closing Sugar Tree Elementary, later that very same year, the Seneca County State Road tarred and chipped one lane of the entire length of the Panther Mountain Short Cut. It cut twenty minutes or more off the drive from Sugar Tree to Seneca. Residents could now shop and buy in a variety of name brand establishments. The new paved short cut squeezed Jobe Frame out of business. He couldn't compete with the large hardware and building supply businesses in Seneca, either in price or inventory, so he sold all of his inventory, along with the building and his house, at an estate auction and retired to Florida. The only original buildings left intact in Sugar Tree, other than residential homes, are the Baptist Church, the Nazarene Church and the Post Office.

The "Hubcap" trick is but a memory and can't be resurrected because they no longer make hubcaps. Besides, they are now called "wheel covers" and they're made of plastic; no good for flinging in the road. One rarely sees hitchhikers anymore. People are afraid to hitchhike, and drivers are afraid to pick up hitchhikers.

Junior Dodrill joined the Army right out of high school and became an MP. When his hitch in the army was over, he used his MP experience to gain a position with the Maryland Highway Patrol. There he lived out his two greatest loves; driving fast cars and carrying firearms.

Buzzy French and Norris Wright were killed in separate car wrecks in Ohio. Palace Rapp was killed at home when a tree he was cutting down split at the butt and kicked back into him.

When the WYGARB mines closed, Paul Boggs moved to Mingo County and became a night shift foreman in a deep mines there. He was caught in a rock fall two years later and had to have his crushed leg amputated just above the knee. A few years later, he showed up at an independent basketball tournament down at Mill's Bottom that Chip was helping to officiate. To Chip's amazement, Paul was still playing basketball and although he had lost much of his mobility, he was still a darn good player. Chip was the only one there that night who really knew how much of Paul's basketball prowess had been lost. Chip noticed Paul didn't play in shorts but wore a pair of sweat pants while on the floor. After the game, in which Paul's team won, the two former teammates and friends had time to fill in the gap between their separation and this surprise reunion.

Rocky Miller served two terms in Vietnam as a Green Beret doing the thing he did best; fighting. Near the end of his second tour of duty he was wounded in the leg and spent a year in the VA Hospital undergoing a number of operations to save the leg and then extensive rehabilitation. He was discharged with a forty percent disability. Though he was physically able to hunt and fish and work on his cars and keep his house and ten acres in good repair, apparently he wasn't able to perform any kind of gainful employment. His veteran's disability check and his social security disability kept Rocky supplied with enough booze and pot, so that it was hard for anybody to remember when they had last seen him sober.

Uncle Roy and Uncle Fred were fortunate enough to be rehired by the new union company when it took over WYGARB's operation in Red Dog. When the new company petered out, both men were given an option to stay with them but they would have to move to their operation in Reston, Virginia. Instead, Uncle Roy and Uncle Fred, along with four other men from Sugar Tree, found work in a union mining operation in Webster County. It was an hour's drive from Sugar Tree to the mines but the men went together and purchased a small van. Each one took a turn a week buying gas and driving the others to work. Those men all were able to work the Webster County mine until they retired. Uncle Roy bought his house and lot in Red Dog and lives there still. Uncle Fred still lives in Sugar Tree.

Benji graduated from Elk River High School a year behind Chip and rather than wait for the draft, enlisted in the Air Force. High blood pressure kept him from passing his physical and he was classified 4-F, however, he was required to take a new physical the next year. He failed that physical for the same reason and was permanently classified 4-F. He enrolled at Marshall University and earned a degree in business administration. He went on to earn a masters degree in Safety Administration.

He got married during his graduate year at Marshall. Chip was the best man and Link and Maynard served as ushers. The Jive Five began celebrating Benji's Bachelor's Night over at the Nite-N-Gale playing the pinball machine and shooting pool until they were finally run off at closing time. They finished up the night laying in the road at Chip's, telling lies about each other and laughing and joking as they recounted the exploits of the Jive Five.

As the morning hour drew closer, it became increasingly more difficult to break off the revelry. Chip had felt a gnawing pang deep within that at first was only an annoyance. It was something that was present which he couldn't identify, but it kept intruding into his subconscious enough to dim his spirits and put a twinge in his heart. Over the course of those few hours, the specter slowly transformed itself into a realization that Chip was trying hard not to accept. This would be the last time the Jive Five would ever be together again. It kept nagging at his heart and he knew it was true, but didn't want it be. He wondered if the others felt the same way. If they did, they were remaining as silent on the matter as he was. They all were hanging on to these last moments together as long as they could , savoring every second.

But life must go on and Benji had to get married, so they broke up at dawn. There were no labored words of parting or long drawn out embraces. A couple of high fives and a "See yuh in a little while" would suffice. They parted company as they always had; as if they were meeting tomorrow for a bicycle trip out to the Horse Ridge Fire Tower. The Jive Five would never be together again, in this world.

Benji's master's degree earned him a position with a well recognized airline company in Washington, DC. He and his family live in Arlington and they still come home often to visit Benji's parents and they usually spend part of their annual vacation in Sugar Tree. Benji and Chip remain close.

Lincoln Parks' dad moved the family to Charleston when WYGARB closed the mines and found a position as an engineer for the state of WV. Link finished high school at Stonewall Jackson and went on to Morris Harvey College. His draft number came up after his sophomore year at Morris Harvey. He opted to enlist in the Marines where he qualified for and successfully completed jet flight training.

On a ten day leave, before being sent to Vietnam, he passed through Sugar tree on his way to Charleston and spent the night visiting with Maynard and Chip. The three called Benji and were able to share some quality time together on the telephone. Later that night, they went out and laid in the road.

There was no talk of what they were doing now or what they might be doing in the future. Their talk mostly consisted of getting up-to-date on former and current acquaintances of Sugar Tree. It was obvious in Maynard's demeanor that Link's presence had put him in an exceptionally good mood. He was so obliging to Link and Chip he was almost unbearable. But they tolerated his doting, perhaps to a degree of abuse, and no one seemed the worse for it.

The next day, Link said his goodbyes and promised to stop by on his way back to base if just for an hour or two. A week later, Link called Maynard to say his orders had been changed and he was being assigned to another base and wouldn't be able to come by. He'd see them when his tour of duty was over. That was the last they heard from Link. He was killed when his plane was shot down over North Vietnam on just his third mission.

Maynard's family stayed with the farm when Mr. Samples was laid off at Red Dog. Mr. Samples made it public knowledge that he and his family would rely on the Lord to show them which direction they should move. The Lord certainly seem to test Mr. Samples' faith because the family was barely making it. They were eligible for state and federal commodities but Mr. Samples wouldn't accept any. He said they could give his share to those who really could use it.

He applied for work at the mines in Webster County and in Seneca County but was turned down. The family spent all their extra time working in their little garden, nurturing a few fruit trees, tending their cow, chickens, and pigs, and canning vegetables and fruit. What little savings they had put away was being used up for gas, electric, and store bought supplies. Mr. Samples went to work doing carpentry and household repairs for folks in Sugar Tree, and Mrs. Samples sold eggs and milk. The income from those two endeavors, though meager, kept the household finances just above water. Maynard joined the army out of high school and three of the older girls got married and moved away. The fourth oldest daughter got married but lived in Sugar Tree. Elihu and his younger sisters were all living at home.

The Lord rewarded Mr. Samples' faith by eventually providing an opportunity for him to accept a pastor calling at a little Baptist Church near Hob. Mr. Samples didn't accept the position for the money. He felt the Lord had directed him to this little church for a reason and considered it a privilege to be able to serve the Lord and minister to the people in such a capacity. Gradually the membership of the little church grew until they were able to give Mr. Samples a respectable salary for pastoring. Through contact with his congregation, Mr. Samples contracted enough carpentry and repair work to develop a full time business in which he was able to hire an extra helper and provide Maynard summer employment.

Maynard returned home after his stink in the army and went to

535

work helping his dad with his little home repair business. Link's death seemed to be a turning point in Maynard's life. For months after receiving the tragic news, he'd seem distant and preoccupied and unresponsive for awhile then, in the next moment he'd lash out at a friend or a family member in an angry outburst over something trivial. He kept to himself a lot. Once in a while Chip could talk him into going for a cruise or going fishing down the holler but even then, Maynard remained solemn and disinterested. It was as if much of the laughter Maynard had found in the world had been taken away with Link's death. Chip tried to keep Maynard's spirits up by spending time with him but Maynard's melancholy mood was beginning to affect Chip the same way.

Chip felt like he was abandoning Maynard when he left for Marshall College the following autumn but he had his own life to live. He wrote Maynard every week and always made it a point to spend time with him whenever he came home. Chip began to worry less and less about Maynard that year and even though it seemed Maynard wasn't his old self, Chip felt he would be okay.

Chip didn't get to see much of Maynard since he was working at the Esso station everyday. When Chip went back to Marshall that fall, Maynard enrolled at Glenville State College. For the next three years the two saw each other only during Thanksgiving and during semester break at Christmas. They tried to make the most of their visits and spent some time together. They went deer hunting a couple of times, not expecting to even see a deer but just to get out in the woods together. A few times they got to go to an Elk River High basketball game and one other time they spent the evening at the Moonlite with some other high school and college buddies. Every time Chip looked at Maynard, he thought of Link. They never talked about Link, never talked about the old times, and Chip didn't want to press the matter, he figured when Maynard was ready he'd bring it up.

Maynard graduated from Glenville and took a job teaching in Parkersburg. He married a girl he'd met at Glenville. At first Chip was surprised when he heard Maynard had received a calling to preach the gospel but after he thought about it awhile, it seemed right.

Another three years would passed before Chip and Maynard were reunited. It was at a Sugar Tree Baptist Church Homecoming. The two men slipped off from their families and walked down by Painter's Creek. They sat in the shade of the sycamore trees and tossed pebbles into the creek. The first thing Chip noticed about Maynard was his rejuvenated spirit. That mischievous sparkle had returned to his eyes and his smile was so intense it wrinkled his whole face. "You know Chip," he said, "after Link was killed, I never thought I'd be able to laugh or enjoy myself ever again. I know you tried to help me through my grief but I was too caught up in my own self pity to let you help. I'm sorry for all of that. We can't change things that have already happened but we certainly can repair the damage done, ask for forgiveness, and try to make tomorrow a little better."

He turned to Chip. "Would you forgive your old buddy after all of these years?"

"Listen to me you lunkhead, there is nothing to forgive. I was just worried about you, that's all. I felt stupid because I didn't know what to do. I actually think my trying to help you kept me from dwelling so much on Link's death."

Maynard slapped Chip on the back. "Well. Will you forgive me anyway? I need to hear it from you."

"Ok. Done." said Chip. "I forgive you. Now tell me, that's pretty deep stuff you're layin' on me. What happened to you anyhow?"

"It was my dad. He watched me struggle with Lincoln's death for months. He tried to help too but I wouldn't let him. He never tried to force anything on me. One day he just said, 'Son I'll not bring this up again but I've got to say this to you and I hope you've got enough respect for me to listen.' I thought about getting up in his face but the part about respect made me hold back. I figured I might as well let him have his say and get it over with. Maybe he'd lay one of his sermons on me. I didn't say anything so he went on. 'Lincoln's gone. I know that's what's bothering you. Nothing you can do can bring him back but you've got a decision to make. Either you let this go and rebuild your own life or let this tragedy, and I know it's ripped your heart out, destroy what life you have left. It's your decision and only you can make it but remember this; ask yourself what Lincoln would do if he saw you like this. Remember too, you can't bring Lincoln back, but like David in the scriptures, you can go to him. Your answer can be found in the Word but you've got to search for it there. I don't have the answer, but prayer can bring it to you. I just wanted you to know that, and to tell you that your mother and I have been praying for you all along.' "

"Well, I listened and I was more miserable than ever. I believe the Lord was convicting my heart all along but like the rest of you all, I wouldn't listen to him either. I couldn't sleep at night I was restless. Couldn't focus on anything, my grades were falling and I wasn't eating. One Sunday night, just like a hundred other Sunday nights, dad asked me if I wanted to go to church with him but this night, I went. I was miserable that night too and I don't even remember what dad preached but I remember I couldn't go on like this so in the middle of the invitation, I got up to leave. Only when I got to the isle, something told me it was just as far to the alter as it was to the door. If I went to the door, I'd have to suffer through all of this again, if I went to the alter, I could unload all my burden and I could be free. So that's about what happened.

The Lord let me enjoy my renewed relationship with him until I had grown some, spiritually, and then he began troubling my heart about preaching his word. I didn't want to go through that again so I submitted to his calling. I've not regretted one moment but like everybody else who is saved, I always have regretted not coming to the Lord sooner.

But the one thing that has been troubling in my life has been the missed opportunity to explain to you where I was and where I was coming from when Link died, and to ask your forgiveness. I could have called you on the phone or written a letter to you but that just wouldn't suffice for true friends, ay."

He paused for a moment before he went on, "I wanted to wait until I could spend some time with you and talk face to face. Man, this is harder than preaching a sermon to a dead church. You know me, I'm not much for words."

"Yeah, right!" Chip answered sarcastically. "I'm happy for you, Maynard. Rest assured you've never done anything to me that would need my forgiveness. I love yuh even though you are an old grouch."

Maynard gave Chip a punch on the arm, "Old! Who you calling old?"

The two friends sat in the shade beside the still waters of Painter's creek, sharing stories of the Jive Five and trying to make up for the lost years of separation until the sun began to settle behind the mountains. Their reunion was finally broken up by the chattering and frolicking of their children as they finally located their respective daddies.

Maynard eventually was called as a full time pastor to a large Baptist church in Parkersburg. He is very involved with his sons activities and still finds time to serve a number of community and civic organizations and projects.

Maynard came often to Sugar Tree to visit with his parents and he and Chip never failed to spend some time together. When Maynard's dad passed away, Maynard held his services at the Sugar Tree Baptist Church. Maynard's message that day turned a funeral into a celebration of life and instilled within each one who attended, the hope of another homecoming in which all of those who have chosen the correct path will be reunited again.

Maynard continued to visit his mom in Sugar Tree after Mr. Samples died but when her health began to fail, he moved her to Parkersburg where he could take care of her. Now, he and Chip only see each other once every couple of years but they do talk now and then on the phone.

Riley Gates served in Vietnam as a mechanic in the motor pool. When he returned home he enrolled in a prestigious automotive school in Wyoming and graduated with certifications in engine and body repair and a Bachlor's degree in Business. He returned to Sugar Tree and opened up his own service station and repair service in Seneca.

By 1985, Riley had dropped the gas and oil selling department and went exclusively with repair service. He now owns two separate repair services, one in Seneca, and one in Kanawha City and only oversees the work done in his service centers. He and his wife handle the book work end of the business. He lives in Seneca with his wife and their two sons and two daughters.

Clint Gates attended West Virginia University and graduated with a degree in broadcast journalism. He became a producer and part time DJ for WV Public Radio. He has his own independent DJ service. He lives in Beckley and does play-by-play broadcast of football and basketball games on a local radio station for high schools and college teams in the Beckley area. He also finds time to play bass for a little jazz quartet out of Bluefield, VA. Clint is not married.

Chip's dad was laid off at the mines in Red Dog when WYGARB sold out but with a degree in education and a background in music, he was hired as teacher and band director at Mill's Bottom High School. Chip's mom also felt the ax because the Red Dog High School was closed soon after that. She was placed at the high school at Mill's Bottom as well, and the two of them worked together at that school until their respective retirements.

Chip earned his undergraduate degree in Elementary Education from Marshall and went right to work, teaching at Sugar Tree Elementary. Chip's draft lottery number was very high and he was never called to military duty. He was able to finish his college education without interruption.

Chip lived at home the first two years of teaching at Sugar Tree. During that time Judy worked as a telephone operator in Charleston. They got married then and lived in a little rented, one bedroom cottage out on Devil's Backbone while Chip, his dad, Judy's dad and her brothers all helped build a house for them on Gates' property just across the road from the old home place. It would take a year and a half to complete. They raised three daughters in that home and Chip and Judy live there today.

With the whole Gates family living together on the old home place, both Chip's mom and dad were able to teach their granddaughters to read music and play the piano. From those roots, the girls all became accomplished musicians.

The old, dilapidated swimming pool in the front yard of the Gates' laid dormant until the late 1970's. Chip's dad was the one who decided to resurrect the pool so his granddaughters could use it. He commandeered Chip to help. Chip was thirty years old, had his own job, had a wife and family, had his own house. For two summers, his dad would come over to the house and bang on Chip's bedroom window at 6:00 in the morning. "Come on boy, time's a wastin' and we got things to do." Chip had to get up and go to work. Sometimes Clint and Riley would come by to help.

The upper wall on the shallow end of the pool and the wall that ran along the right side of the pool were still standing. The left side wall was still intact although it had fallen over to the outside and was lying against the bank. They left it lying just where it was.

The lower wall on the deep end had completely fallen in so they removed all of the old blocks and debris from that end and built a new wall using sixteen inch cinder blocks instead of eight inch blocks. They built the new wall about four feet closer in so it wouldn't have to be so high. It made the pool a little shorter than before but still big enough.

They filled the pool with water from the creek and kept it filtered and chlorinated with a new filter and pump. The pool has been used every summer since its final completion. All of Chip's girls along with a number of their cousin's and neighborhood friends have learned to swim there. Two or three birthday parties, 4th of July, Memorial Day, anniversaries, and other family celebrations are centered around the pool during the summer months.

Chip's daughters learned to sled ride by riding down the meadow and through the orchard at home. Eventually the time came when Chip felt they had mastered the art enough to be able to handle the thrill and experience of sled riding down Panther Mountain. So on one snowy Saturday evening, he loaded the girls and their sleds in his '50 Willys Jeep truck (the girls dubbed it "The Beat-Up Truck") and hauled them "around the road".

To Chip's amazement, there was nobody there; no bonfire, no discarded sleds, no sled tracks, no remnants of any activity that might have taken place there days or even weeks before.

Undaunted, he put the truck in four wheel drive and headed right on up to the top of the mountain, thinking they might as well go all out since they were here.

When they got to the top and unloaded, Chip instructed the girls, as best as he could remember, about the mountain and its tendencies. He let them go in whatever order they chose, making sure they kept plenty of distance between each rider. Chip would follow them down the mountain in the truck. He waited until the last girl had disappeared around the upper turn, then he started down the hill in the truck.

As Chip came out of the upper turn, he caught sight of the last sledder but she was already a good hundred yards or more down the mountain. He sought to catch up to her so he sped up accordingly but she was still pulling away. He glanced down at the speedometer. It was bouncing around between thirty-five and forty. He was still in four wheel drive but at that speed, on the down grade, the old truck was a handful to keep in the road. Chip was afraid he was going to lose control so he backed off. He finally caught up with Dawn on the middle section and stayed just behind her until she dropped down the last section. Chip again let the truck pick up to thirty-five in an effort to keep up with Dawn, but she was soon out of sight.

The girls must have made five trips that evening before finally relenting to their dad's pleas to call it a day. They never did know what their top speed was that day but at thirty-five miles an hour, the beat-up truck couldn't keep up with them.

The song, "Three Steps From the Altar", by Shep and Limelights is about two sweethearts who are about to be married. There is a poignant and profound line in that song that says "last night was our last date". To Chip that always seemed like a sad commentary about marriage, so for the first twenty-five years of their marriage, they celebrated each anniversary by going out on a date.

Sometimes they went to the Granny's Creek Drive-Inn, sometimes they went out to eat, and sometimes they just cruised around in the car. But the date wasn't complete until they drove up to their sacred

542

parking place at the Morris Cemetery and parked.

To embellish the moment, Chip would play his Cruisin' series tapes on the car's 8-track player. Later he played those Cruisin' tapes on the cassette player in their car and by then, he was able to add some of his and Judy's favorites including their own "Our Day Will Come". On those evenings they were transported back to that special time and special place in their lives.

When his daughters were young, Chip always tried at least once a month to take them and Judy on the hill and cookout for supper. They never went to the same area twice and they managed to go in every season and in every type of weather except rain.

Chip would pile up some rocks and build a little fire and they'd eat hot dogs and soup or something simple, and then sit around roasting marshmallows for dessert.

A few times the family got real ambitious and even camped out over night on the hill. The girls always complained about going and about smelling like Smokey-The-Bear, but as grown young ladies now, they still like to have a cookout on the hill once-in-a-while.

Chip teaches at the Elementary school in Hob and Judy is the postmistress in Sugar Tree.

Grandma Gates died in 1982. Aunt Eleanor still lives by herself in the original home surrounded by Theodore and Edna and Chip and his family.

The Greek philosopher Heraclitus, said no man can step into the same river twice. Because the waters flow by, the river is constantly changing and it is not the same river in the same place from moment to moment. Thomas Wolfe wrote, "You Can't Go Home Again". In the song "Down Home" Little Eva sings about how things use to be "down home" but she ends the song with these words, "but there's no way to get back home, 'cause down home's just a memory."

Now, those may be considered truisms in our modern culture and from the point of view of someone who returns to a place they knew before, it probably is true. Both the place and the person have changed. But Chip's philosophy was simple. You see, if you never leave a place, you don't have to return to it. If you never leave home, you don't have to go back there again. If you never get out of the river, it is always the same to you and you're not aware of any changes.

Existence is just an extension of previous experiences. Doesn't matter if that experience was yesterday or twenty-five years ago. It's all the same, and in Chip's mind's eye, there is no difference.

The November evening breeze drifts in over the hilltops and seems to carry with it the fading wail of a steam whistle from somewhere off in the distance. The chill in the breeze jolts Chip back to the present and back to reality. The sun has once again settled in behind these beloved mountains and the time has come to head off of the hill to the house.

Reluctantly, he gets up off the old familiar rock and turns his feet down the hill through the meadow towards home. His steps aren't as lively as they were fifty years ago but he is in no hurry to leave. He knows that something of a great wonder will occur here and he won't be there to experience it.